Until recently, gardeners have paid little attention to the ecological requirements of perennials when planting them in parks and gardens. This book describes a new way of using perennials in parks and gardens based on ecological rather then purely aesthetic principles. It demonstrates how attention to ecological needs of herbaceous perennials can result in low-maintenance plantings in parks and other public spaces. It will be an indispensable reference work for all those involved in planting herbaceous perennials.

Perennials and their garden habitats

Richard Hansen
and Friedrich Stahl

Translated by Richard Ward

Fourth edition

TIMBER PRESS
Portland, Oregon

Published in North America in 1993 by Timber Press, Inc, 9999 SW Wilshire, Suite 124, Portland, Oregon 97225

ISBN 0 88192 222 6 hardback

First published in German as *Die Stauden und ihre Lebensbereiche in Gärten und Grünanlagen* by Eugen Ulmer, Stuttgart, and © 1981, 1990 Eugen Ulmer GmbH & Co., Stuttgart, Germany.

English translation © Cambridge University Press, 1993

First published in English in North America by Timber Press, Inc 1993 as *Perennials and their garden habitats*

First published in English outside North America by Cambridge University Press 1993

Printed in Great Britain by Butler & Tanner Ltd, Frome and London

Contents

Preface to the German edition   xi
Preface to the fourth edition   xii
Introduction   1

Perennials in cultivation   2

Forms of growth   4
Propagation   16
Longevity   20
Long-term performance   22
The influence of the environment   26
The influence of the gardener   27

The right place for the right perennial   29

Wild perennials and border perennials: their needs and differences   29
The use of perennials in public parks   31
The place for perennials in the garden   32
Garden habitats for perennials   33
Perennials that die down after flowering   35
The dangers of mass-planting   37

The design of perennial plantings   38

Trees and shrubs: the framework of a planting   38
Structure and rhythm in a planting   38
Grouping (sociability) within a planting   39
Planting distances   40
Colour   46
The right place for spring-flowering perennials   47
Perennials that flower in early summer   48
Autumn-flowering perennials   48
Bulbs, corms and tubers: the finishing touch to a planting   48
Laying out a border planting   53
Laying out an ecological planting   56
The use of annuals in border plantings   57
Rock gardens   58
Water gardens and marshy areas   65

Planting perennials   72

Preparation of the planting area   72
The proper time to plant   74
How to plant perennials   75
Planting lilies   78

Examples of plantings   80
Introducing perennials into existing vegetation   87

The maintenance of perennial plantings   88

Nutrient supply and care of the soil   88
'Weeds' and the long-term development of a planting   90
Cutting back perennials   94
Protection in winter   96
Pests and diseases   97
Maintenance calendar for the herbaceous border   98

Perennials in their garden habitats   104

The different garden habitats   104
Explanation of the lists   105

1   Woodland   109

1.1.   **Shade and light shade in a garden setting (including newly landscaped areas)**   110
1.1.1.   Low, shade-tolerant perennials (also suitable for extensive groundcover)   111
1.1.2.   Tall-growing shade-tolerant perennials   114
1.1.3.   Hostas   115
1.1.4.   Shade-tolerant grasses and sedges   118
1.2.   **Shade and light shade within the mature woodland of an established park or garden**   119
1.2.1.   Predominantly low-growing, temperate European woodland perennials   120
1.2.2.   Predominantly low-growing, Mediterranean or non-European woodland
         perennials (for plantings requiring a little garden-type maintenance)   123
1.2.3.   Woodland sedges, grasses and rushes   126
1.2.4.   Ferns   127
1.2.5.   Perennials for rhododendron plantings   132
1.3.   **Special sites in shade and semi-shade**   133
1.3.1.   Cool, partly shaded, mostly damp and humid sites   133
1.3.2.   Perennials for enthusiasts   137
1.3.3.   Special conditions for more difficult perennials   139
1.3.4.   Perennials for summer drought under deciduous trees (park-type maintenance)   143
1.3.5.   Needle litter under mature conifers   144
1.3.6.   Mor soils under mature broadleaves and conifers   144
1.4.   **Bulbs, corms and tubers for woodland areas**   145

2   Woodland edge   146

2.1.   **Perennials confined to the woodland edge**   148
2.1.1.   Groundcover perennials for shady woodland edge conditions   149
2.1.2.   Widely spreading (and creeping) groundcover plants for sun and semi-shade on
         the woodland edge   149
2.1.3.   Groundcover plants that tolerate mowing
2.1.4.   Low, undemanding groundcover plants for garden-type maintenance in shade
         and bright shade on the woodland edge   152
2.1.5.   Climbing and sprawling perennials (without spreading rhizomes)   153
2.1.6.   Perennials for shade and bright shade on moist, nutrient-rich soils   154
2.1.7.   Perennials for sun or bright shade on an open woodland edge (moderately dry,
         loamy, alkaline soils)   157

2.1.8.   Perennials for an open woodland edge on dry to moist, sandy, silica-rich soils
           in sun and bright shade   160
2.2.   **Perennials more loosely bound to the woodland edge**   163
2.2.1.   Perennials with border character, for garden-type maintenance   163
2.2.2.   Further perennials loosely bound to the woodland edge   167
2.2.3.   Invasive perennials loosely bound to the woodland edge   169
2.2.4.   Tall perennials with border character for moist to damp soils   170
2.3.   **Perennials for special conditions on or near the woodland edge**   171
2.3.1.   Perennials for cool, damp, sunny or lightly shaded sites   171
2.3.2.   Perennials for warm, sunny (or bright shady) corners, particularly on the
           woodland edge   174
2.3.3.   Perennials for moderate summer drought in bright to shady conditions, also
           under trees and shrubs   176
2.3.4.   Perennials for summer drought on a sunny woodland edge   179
2.3.5.   Tall, highly invasive perennials for large parks and gardens   181
2.4.   **Spring-flowering bulbs and their allies**   183
2.4.1.   Spring-flowering bulbs, corms and tubers for warm, sunny positions   184
2.4.2.   Spring bulbs, corms and tubers for bright but cool positions   187
2.4.3.   Daffodils and other narcissi   189

3   Open ground   191

3.1.   **Perennials as a lawn substitute**   191
3.1.1.   Perennials and dwarf shrubs for extensive, lawn-like areas   191
3.1.2.   Species for small lawn-like areas   193
3.1.3.   Species for full sun on specially prepared soil   196
3.2.   **Flowering meadows and other types of grassland**   197
3.2.1.   Species for a wildflower meadow on moist to moderately dry soil   199
3.2.2.   Species for dry calcareous grassland and meadow steppe (prairie)   201
3.2.3.   Heaths and heathers, *Erica* and *Calluna*   204
3.2.4.   Heathland perennials for sandy soils   208
3.3.   **Plants from hot, dry, stony steppes (prairie)**   210
3.3.1.   Drought-resistant dwarf and sub-shrubs   211
3.3.2.   Dominant, eyecatching perennials for stony steppe plantings   213
3.3.3.   Further perennials for stony steppe plantings (and rock gardens)   217
3.3.4.   Grasses for stony steppe plantings and similar sites   222
3.3.5.   Slightly tender perennials and dwarf shrubs for rocky, steppe-like plantings   225
3.3.6.   Somewhat tender bulbs, corms and tubers   227
3.4.   **Perennials for warm, sunny sites with moderately dry to moist soils**   228
3.4.1.   Wild perennials for well-spaced planting   229
3.4.2.   Short-lived species for warm, sunny positions   233
3.4.3.   Short-lived species for special uses   234
3.4.4.   Plants for well-spaced or dense planting   235
3.4.5.   Wild perennials with border character for sunny sites   237
3.4.6.   North American wild perennials with border character   240
3.4.7.   Grasses   243
3.4.8.   Tall, specimen perennials   244
3.5.   **Perennials for sun or bright shade on moist to damp soils**   245
3.5.1.   Species that flower in spring and early summer (meadow perennials)   245
3.5.2.   Species that flower in late spring and summer   247
3.5.3.   Tall grasses for more or less damp, sunny places   249
3.5.4.   Species that flower in high summer and autumn (tall herbs and grasses with
           border character)   250

3.6.	**Large ornamental herbs and grasses for sunny sites on damp soils**	253
3.6.1.	Hardy species	253
3.6.2.	More or less tender species	254

4	**Rock gardens**	256
4.1.	**The decorative, formal rock garden**	257
4.1.1.	Vigorous, colourful cushion- and carpet-forming perennials for sun or bright shade among rocks	257
4.1.2.	Short-lived species	265
4.1.3.	Vigorous cushion- and carpet-forming perennials for bright shade and semi-shade	266
4.1.4.	Bulbs and corms	271

Rock garden perennials with special requirements: species that are more or less dependent on rock

4.2.	**Plants for gritty soil in dry, sunny positions among rocks**	273
4.2.1.	Commonly available, mostly vigorous species	273
4.2.2.	Houseleeks, *Sempervivum* and *Jovibarba*	282
4.2.3.	Plants recommended for enthusiasts	285
4.2.4.	Bulbous species	292
4.3.	**Species for moist, gritty soil in sun or bright shade among rocks**	295
4.3.1.	Common, vigorous species	295
4.3.2.	More demanding species, for enthusiasts	301
4.4.	**Plants that are not closely dependent on rock**	310
4.4.1.	Species for sunny positions on moderately moist soils that dry out in summer	310
4.4.2.	Bulbs, corms and tubers	313
4.4.3.	Species for sun (or bright shade) on moist soils	316
4.4.4.	Bulbs, corms and tubers for sun and bright shade on soil that stays moist in summer	319
4.5.	**Shade, semi-shade and bright shade on the rock garden**	320
4.5.1.	Perennials for bright to full shade on moist to damp soil among rocks	320
4.5.2.	Plants for the enthusiast (mostly tender species)	322
4.5.3.	Perennials for shady and semi-shady woodland conditions on the rock garden	326
4.5.4.	Species for moist soils that are moderately dry in summer, particularly in woodland edge conditions on the rock garden	328
4.5.5.	Bulbs, corms and tubers for woodland edge conditions with intermittently dry to moist soils in summer	331
4.6.	**Special planting positions for species that are not dependent on rock**	333
4.6.1.	Sub-alpine tall herbs for large rock gardens	333
4.6.2.	Enthusiasts' plants for sites enriched with peat and moory soil	335
4.6.3.	Autumn gentians, *Gentiana*	336
4.6.4.	Plants for damp (to wet) sites on the rock garden	337
4.6.5.	Plants for damp, gravelly places and wet scree, particularly at the edge of a pond or stream	339
4.6.6.	Bulbs for periodically damp sites on the rock garden	340

5	**Border perennials**	341
5.1.	**Border perennials derived from woodland species**	342
5.2.	**Border perennials derived from woodland edge species**	345
5.2.1.	Cool, sunny or bright shady places with moist to damp soil in summer	345
5.2.2.	Lilies for cool positions in sun and bright shade	351
5.2.3.	Warm, sunny places with moist to dry soil in summer	353
5.2.4.	Lilies for sunny positions	356

5.3.	**Border perennials derived from open ground species**	357
5.3.1.	Warm, sunny sites with soil that is mostly dry in summer	358
5.3.2.	Warm, sunny sites with moderately dry to moist soil	363
5.3.3.	Lilies for sunny and bright shady sites with moderately dry to moist, well-drained soil	364
5.3.4.	North American border perennials for sunny sites with moderately moist to moderately damp soil	367
5.3.5.	Sunny (or bright shady) sites with moist to moderately damp, nutrient-rich soil	377
5.3.6.	American hybrid lilies for moist to damp soils in sun or bright shade	383
5.4.	**Tulips and hyacinths**	384
5.5.	**Short-lived border perennials**	392
5.6.	**Tender border perennials**	397
5.6.1.	Plants for the enthusiast	397
5.6.2.	Red hot poker, *Kniphofia* hybrids	399
5.7.	**The rural herb garden and its perennials**	400
5.7.1.	Herbaceous perennials and sub-shrubs	403
5.7.2.	Annuals and biennials	405
5.7.3.	Variegated grasses	408
5.7.4.	Native and naturalised medicinal plants	408
6	**Water's edge and marsh**	410
6.1.	**Perennials for planting in the vicinity of artificial ponds without wet margins**	410
6.2.	**Perennials for wet pond margins and shallow water**	411
6.2.1.	Vigorous and invasive species for wet soil and shallow water	411
6.2.2.	Non-invasive perennials for wet soil and shallow water	413
6.2.3.	Tender species for damp or wet soil, and very shallow water	414
6.3.	**Perennials for mostly sunny, wet or marshy sites (not only at the edge of a pond)**	415
6.4.	**Perennials for special conditions**	418
6.4.1.	Sites that are wet in spring and early summer but dry in winter	418
6.4.2.	Variably damp or wet, predominantly moory conditions	418
6.4.3.	Acidic, moory, damp or wet conditions	420
6.5.	**Plants for water-filled depressions and shallow ponds**	420
7	**Water**	422
7.1.	**Perennials with floating leaves for still water**	422
7.1.1.	Waterlilies (*Nymphaea* species and hybrids)	422
7.1.2.	Further perennials with floating leaves for still, sunny conditions	425
7.1.3.	Perennials for special conditions in still water	426
7.1.4.	Small floating ferns and duckweed	427
7.2.	**Perennials for springs, streams and ditches**	427
7.2.1.	Perennials for running water	428
7.3.	**Hardy submerged aquatics**	428
Source material		429
Species index		431
Picture credits		450

Preface to the German edition

After several decades' work, sorting herbaceous perennials with respect to their ecological requirements, we believe it is now possible for professional and amateur alike to make rational use of these sometimes highly sensitive plants. Most perennials will tolerate a certain amount of mishandling, but the creation of successful long term plantings is only possible when growing conditions are properly taken into account. Our aim is to introduce people to this close relationship between plants and the environment, and to foster an appreciation of gardens as a place of encounter with the living world.

Some of the lists reproduced in this book have been published previously but now appear in a revised and expanded form. We have tried to include all the different herbaceous species that are currently available from German nurseries. In addition, the detailed classification of garden habitats has sometimes made it necessary to list species that are almost unobtainable in the trade but could nevertheless play a useful role in colonising difficult areas of a garden.

The lists are intended as an aid to creating viable plant communities. For some readers, this may provide the inspiration to try out new and unfamiliar species, using the lists to determine appropriate planting positions. However, those who are involved professionally in the design of stable and effective plantings must have a thorough knowledge of the plants they use, and they are advised not to rely exclusively on the very short descriptions that are given here. Fortunately, there are now a number of perennial trial gardens where the necessary knowledge may be gathered at first hand. Such places often provide an attractive demonstration of the way in which an enduring mantle of freely flowering vegetation can be spread right across the garden, provided only that sufficient respect is paid to the laws of nature.

Intensive maintenance makes it possible to grow herbaceous perennials in almost any combination we choose, and the large garden festivals often contain extreme examples of a purely decorative and artificial approach. Sadly, these plantings are mostly so expensive to maintain that they have to be scrapped as soon as the exhibition is over and never have a chance to reach maturity. The lack of absolute rules can lead even accomplished designers into making mistakes, and this has tended to bring perennials into disrepute. As a consequence, herebaceous plantings are seldom seen in public parks. Instead, we are most often confronted with a standard package of groundcover plants, serving only to remind us of the many opportunities that have been lost. People are increasingly seeking renewed contact with the complex world of nature that has all but disappeared from our towns and cities. With the aid of our recommendations for an ecologically sensitive use of perennials we hope to promote a 'hands off' approach to gardening and point the way to an attractive and richly differentiated but natural type of garden in which colourful ornamentals, botanical rarities and a variety of wild creatures can all find a home.

The work of ordering perennials according to their garden habitats would not have been possible without the nursery-men and women who make so many of these plants available. The following have kindly advised us in the choice of outstanding cultivars from among the larger assortments: C. Feldmaier (lilies), Dr H. Simon (new introductions and bamboos) and Frau H. von Stein-Zeppelin (irises and day-lilies). In addition, Prof. Dr J. Sieber provided us with records of perennial trials. Much has been gained from the exchange of ideas with Dipl. Ing. H. Müssel, Superintendent at the trials garden in Weihenstephan. He also kindly read through the lists for us. U. Walser gave his support with a contribution of valuable plant photographs. All of these people deserve our sincere thanks.

Our special thanks go to Frau G. Stölzle who generously allowed us to use her photographs of perennials, taken for the most part in her unique garden in Kempten.

Finally, we should like to thank our publisher R. Ulmer and his colleagues for their very patient and helpful advice on the structure and layout of this book.

Preface to the fourth edition

Whatever its teaching,
any doctrine
that forbids discussion
is best forgotten.
Martin Buber

We are always grateful for any contribution to the theme of garden plant ecology. Our sincere thanks go to all those specialists, and in particular to Prof. Dr Hans Becker of Berlin, who have pointed out errors and inconsistencies in the first edition.

The Authors

Weihenstephan and Nürnberg

Introduction

It is extraordinary, almost shocking, to see the indifference with which perennials are often planted in our parks and gardens, massed together without regard for their individual character and the interplay of different forms. Perennials develop slowly, sometimes needing years to attain their full beauty. They cannot be planted like annuals that come and go in a single season.

The dynamic nature of a perennial planting only becomes apparent when the plants' ecological requirements are sufficiently taken into account. Given the proper garden habitat (to which the various species are here assigned), and in combination with a suitable choice of neighbours, each plant can develop and unfold to display its full potential for beauty.

In selecting perennials for a particular spot it is worth considering that in nature there are two broad strategies by means of which the various plant species manage to survive and find their ecological niche. These may be characterised as specialisation on the one hand and adaptability on the other. Both sorts of plant, the fussy and the tolerant, are to be encountered in our gardens, and the better we are in assigning them a planting position appropriate to their nature and ecological needs, the less maintenance they will ask of us and the more sense there will be in growing them.

Perennials grown together under the correct ecological conditions can be the source of fascinating observations. One notes, for example, that the habit and appearance of the different species are not superficial, chance characters, but rather an expression of the particular conditions to which the plants are adapted, giving their combined appearance an integrity of quite another order to that of species chosen and set together according to some other criterion. The significance of mutual competition or tolerance becomes obvious, in such a planting, and one learns that it is not just the showy plants but also the more modest ones whose contribution is important to the whole.

The treatment of perennials contained in this book reminds us how very varied the conditions in a garden can be, and how greatly this can influence the choice of plants and type of planting. Once the main structural and architectural elements of the garden are established it remains the task of the gardener – preferably in conjunction with a garden designer – to make use of the rich variety of perennials in bringing these features to life. Those seeking fulfilment in their gardens will discover that nature has an endless supply of forms and patterns whose inspiration can greatly enrich our lives.

All of this has naturally to do with garden maintenance: not a blinkered and unimaginative tidying-up, but the recognition of inadequate and labour-intensive plantings and the subsequent correction of their faults. In public parks, on the other hand, maintenance means for the most part preservation and enhancement of the natural groundcover, a practical contribution to the much-discussed conservation of our threatened landscape.

The essence of a garden is life in progress and our first duty is therefore to let things grow. Development, fruition, seeding and spread are all part of the experience that awaits us in a garden that is kept close to nature.

Perennials in cultivation

In all the thousands of years during which mankind has made gardens, the range of cultivated perennials has never been greater than in recent times. These modest, soft-stemmed plants, which return each year after dying down in winter, are available today in an almost unimaginable variety for the furnishing and decoration of our parks and gardens, a true reflection of our delight in the natural beauty to be found within their colourful ranks. The wealth of shapes and forms, of different flowers and leaves, of scents and colours, is inexhaustible; and to perennials belong the special joys and disappointments of seasonal change and annual return.

Can it be that our love for these plants springs from a half-conscious appreciation of the role that they play as living groundcover under trees and shrubs, and home for many wild creatures, wherever the natural landscape has not been altered or destroyed? From dense woodland they spread out across heathland, meadows and pasture. On field headlands and in hedges they seek refuge from the plough, or make their homes by streams, ponds and marshes. Their variety is greatest on the edge of a thicket or wood. On intensively farmed land and in forest plantations, wherever the human influence is strongest, perennials are on the retreat. Only on wasteland and among rocks, along riverbanks and in streams, lakes and ponds can a few characteristic species retain their foothold. The most beautiful among them have been collected from far and wide to provide pleasure in our gardens. Today they are bred and raised in specialist nurseries, and assessed in trial gardens for their reliability and possibilities of use.

A garden without these plants has now become inconceivable. Of course, perennials have always had their place in the garden, but it is only in this century that the real breakthrough has been made. With the influential championship of people like William Robinson, Georg Arends, Gertrude Jekyll and Karl Foerster, herbaceous perennials have conquered our gardens, filling them over and over with their flowers.

Perennials, whether native or foreign, lend themselves readily to combination with trees and shrubs, forming pleasing and completely natural associations which are particularly telling in conjunction with buildings and other structural features. Their seldom-appreciated ability to grow and thrive in the most extraordinary conditions gives them a special versatility in this respect. Whether it be poor soil and burning heat or deep shade and standing water, there is hardly a place in the garden where a permanent use of perennials is not possible. The many plant associations described in this book bear witness to this.

A further development in the way we use these plants has now started to appear. Prompted by the current devastation of the natural environment, garden designers are increasingly giving thought to the ideas of Karl Foerster who, like William Robinson, promoted the concept of a wild garden with its many different habitats for plants and animals. Today's parks and gardens need perennials that can grow outside the framework of a traditional herbaceous border, in plantings that deck the ground with a living and largely self-maintaining mantle of green.

In a long involvement with gardens and perennials, one comes to know these plantings, their characteristic ageing and regeneration, their shifting patterns of growth and constant struggles for dominance and survival. With their coming and going, flowering and decay, they bring so much life to the garden that even the gardener has a hard time keeping track of it all.

Proponents of a purely natural garden see no overcoming the contradictions between art and nature, and therefore favour a completely spontaneous development of garden vegetation. With our soils and climate, some sort of vegetation will appear on even the barest ground without any need for human intervention. In some cases – one need only imagine a field full of poppies, an embankment strewn with mullein or else foxgloves in a woodland clearing – the results of this first colonisation can be so disturbingly impressive and beautiful that it is no wonder when voices are raised proposing that our plantings should everywhere be left to nature. It is seldom appreciated that these eye-catching pioneers soon disappear entirely, to be replaced by a mostly commonplace mixture of herbs and grasses.

These weeds are present in every garden. In a poorly conceived planting they can become such a problem that many of today's gardeners will have nothing more to do with a natural form of gardening. They plant their perennials like flower arrangements in a bed, or set them between rocks on a slope so that nothing else has a chance to grow. In a garden left entirely to nature it takes years for a colourful grassland flora to beome established, or until sweet woodruff and wood anemones can grow as they do in the wild. Only with the correct choice of plants and with appropriate improvements to the soil is it possible to jump the stages of this slow development.

In the special case of an old, mature garden or park, it can be relatively easy to reintroduce the species of a natural ground flora under trees and shrubs; but a fine appreciation of the plants and their environment is necessary even here, and any planting must still be protected from unwanted competition until it is well established.

A far greater range of beautiful perennials is available for our private gardens than would be suitable for use in public open spaces. In specialist nurseries all these different species stand alongside one another, responding equally well to the uniform treatment and making it irritatingly difficult to see where and under what sort of conditions they will thrive and develop to their full beauty in a garden. The choice of perennials according only to height, colour and time of flowering leads inevitably to disappointment. To help against this, many German nurseries have now introduced numbered keys into their catalogues, giving information on the preferred garden habitat, together with any special characteristics and requirements that are relevant to their use. These keys, though developed by the present authors in conjunction with H. Müssel in the trials garden at Weihenstephan, are not to be found in this book. They are based on a rather more detailed division of the various garden habitats than is dealt with in these pages.

Faced with the whole range of currently available herbaceous perennials one feels a sense of obligation to encourage their spread and proper use. The place for perennials is not in botanically

Blue Gromwell (*Buglossoides purpurocaerulea*)
The character and use of each species of herbaceous perennial is determined by its habit and form of growth.

ordered plant collections, but in plantings that bind together the various elements of a garden, bringing expression to timeless harmonies, and giving each of us, in our gardening, the opportunity for a deep personal fulfilment.

Forms of growth

A better understanding of perennials and their means of propagation can be acquired by close observation of their different habits and forms of growth. Tall and low-growing, dainty and coarse, the great variety of bulbs, corms and tubers, cushion and rosette plants, sub-shrubs and succulents, with their often strangely shaped roots and storage organs, bear witness to the enormous range of habitats in which perennials have made their home and the correspondingly diverse conditions required for their growth.

Herbaceous perennials are plants with soft, as opposed to woody, stems, dying down at the end of each vegetation period but then sprouting again, in contrast to annuals such as cornflowers or *Zinnia*. It is often said that perennials overwinter beneath the earth, but this is only partly true. A great many species have overwintering buds that are either level with or directly below the soil surface. Others, particularly among the low-growing perennials, do not die back at all but remain green throughout the winter. These mostly creeping or else tussock- and cushion-forming plants can be particularly useful to us as groundcover.

This very robust golden-leaved thyme (*Thymus citriodorus* 'Golden Dwarf') turns golden-brown in winter.

Acaena microphylla turns reddish-brown in winter.

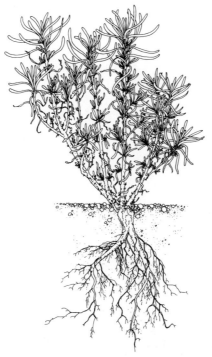

Lavender (*Lavandula angustifolia*) is a sub-shrub.

Perennials that do not die down in winter and whose overwintering buds are situated above ground

The stems and leaves of these plants can give us pleasure right through the winter, provided they are grown in the right company. To be effective they should be set together in groups where their own kind dominates and not, as so often seen, scattered singly among plants that die down in winter.

Sub-shrubs have their overwintering buds above ground and belong botanically to the woody plants, but for gardening purposes are more conveniently grouped with herbaceous perennials. Evergreen species such as spring heath (*Erica carnea*), periwinkle (*Vinca*) and lavender cotton (*Santolina*) are particularly beautiful. Some, like candytuft (*Iberis sempervirens*), lavender (*Lavandula*) and the rockroses (*Helianthemum*), lose most of their leaves at the end of winter.

Vegetative propagation is from cuttings, just as for the larger trees and shrubs, though a few, such as *Hypericum calycinum* and *Vinca*, make life easier by forming ready-made roots on their long, creeping stems. These need only be torn apart and can immediately be planted again. Many sub-shrubs appreciate the insulating effect of snow in a cold winter and can suffer in areas where snow does not lie. Sufficiently protected, they can live for many years, provided they are occasionally cut back to promote new growth.

Mat-forming plants, whose overwintering buds lie close to the ground and whose horizontal growth can cover quite large areas, may be conveniently divided into two groups: those that make roots as they grow along, and those that do not. Plants of the first group, including catsfoot (*Antennaria*), pearlwort (*Sagina*), creeping Jenny (*Lysimachia nummularia*) and many *Sedum* species, are easily propagated. Other familiar garden plants, such as rock-cress (*Aubrieta*) and the dwarf phloxes (*Phlox subulata*), belong to the second group, whose propagation requires the cutting-frame and a greater or lesser degree of gardening expertise.

These three perennials retain their decorative green and bluish foliage in winter.

Sedum hybridum 'Immergrünchen'

Cheddar pink
(*Dianthus gratianopolitanus*)

Euphorbia myrsinites

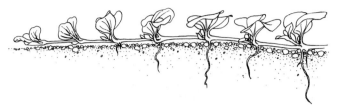

Creeping Jenny
(*Lysimachia nummularia*)

Cushion plants, such as thrift (*Armeria*), some of the gentians (e.g. *G. acaulis*) and many of the pinks (*Dianthus*), are similar to this last group in possessing a single rootstock. With luck a few may be propagated by division but many will only grow from cuttings. **Rosette plants** are a particularly mixed lot. Some, such as the houseleeks (*Sempervivum*) and rock-jasmines (*Androsace*), can be divided without difficulty, whereas others, including some saxifrages and primulas (especially older plants), are difficult to get established after division.

Succulents will put up with a lot of mistreatment. The broken-off leaves of several species (e.g. forms of *Sedum album*) can be planted (or even just scattered about) outside, and develop roots in no time to form strong, healthy plants. Other succulents are more difficult to propagate: *Euphorbia myrsinites* and *Asphodeline* spp., for instance, are best grown from seed, although the latter may also be divided.

Many alpine plants overwinter as a cushion. Easily divided cushion plants are *Androsace* spp. and *Jovibarba* spp., which fall apart by themselves. Mossy saxifrages and alpine thrifts are more difficult to propagate.

Cushion phlox
(*Phlox subulata*)

Rock jasmine
(*Androsace sarmentosa*)

Hen and chickens
(*Jovibarba sobolifera*)

Mossy saxifrage
(*Saxifraga caespitosa* hybrid)

Dwarf thrift
(*Armeria cespitosa*)

Trumpet gentians (*Gentiana acaulis*) overwinter as a
cushion of broad, green leaves.

Garden primroses (*Primula × polyantha*
'Grandiflora') form evergreen rosettes in a sheltered
position.

Alpine asters (*Aster alpinus*) usually grow up out of the ground and disappear within three years of planting. Their young rosettes need an accumulation of scree and rock rubble in order to form roots.

Veronica incana

Catsfoot
(*Antennaria*)

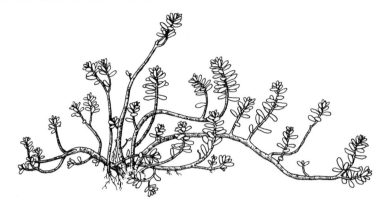

A red-leaved stonecrop
(*Sedum album* 'Murale')

Sedum lydium 'Glaucum'
is bluish in summer
and reddish in winter.

Sedum sexangulare retains
its fresh green foliage right
through the winter.

Many grasses and sedges are **evergreen tussock-formers;** examples are blue fescue (*Festuca glauca*) and Japanese sedge (*Carex morrowii*). These plants should only be divided in spring. Indeed, grasses generally, even those that die down in winter, should never be taken up and divided in autumn. *Hepatica, Asarum* and some of the ferns are among a whole series of woodland perennials that stay green in winter. Their foliage is mostly protected by dry leaves from the winter sun. Hellebores are also worth mentioning here, though these can suffocate among too many fallen leaves.

Finally, there are the unique root-stems of yuccas and a few euphorbias. However, it is not often that we can provide the right growing conditions for these plants and they are correspondingly seldom to be encountered in our gardens.

Perennials that die down and overwinter at ground level

Many perennials have overwintering buds that sit on or near the soil surface. If these buds are set too deep in the ground then the whole plant suffers. Irises, peonies and bleeding heart (*Dicentra spectabilis*) are particularly sensitive in this respect; planted too deep they refuse to flower and will tend to rot instead.

Perennials belonging to this group are very varied. Anyone who has dug up and replanted a herbaceous border will know that several species become quite woody in time and can only be divided with a knife or spade and a certain amount of brute force. Among these are important wild and border perennials such as:

Achillea filipendulina 'Parker'	*Astilbe* spp.
Aster amellus	*Chrysanthemum* × *hortorum*
Aster novae-angliae	*Delphinium* spp.

Erigeron hybrids
Heliopsis scabra
Hemerocallis spp.

Paeonia spp.
Phlox paniculata

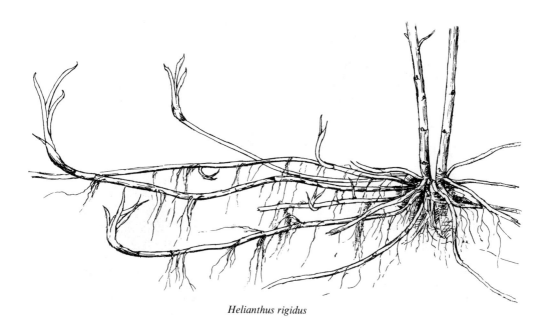

Helianthus rigidus

Michaelmas daisies (*Aster novi-belgii*) have shallow rhizomes that spread out so strongly over the years that the plants must be divided.

Hemicryptophytes with tap roots are difficult to propagate.

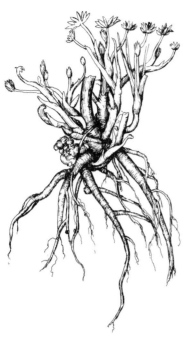

The individual shoots of garden lupins (*Lupinus hybrids*) have no roots of their own.

The shoots of scabious (*Scabiosa caucasica*) have very few roots of their own, making them difficult to propagate.

Columbines (*Aquilegia*) can only be propagated from seed.

Eryngium planum may be propagated from root-cuttings but not by division.

The following are particularly hard to divide:

Eremurus spp.
Lupinus hybrids
Lychnis chalcedonica
Scabiosa caucasica

Plants with deep-reaching tap-roots are similarly difficult:

Adonis vernalis
Pulsatilla vulgaris
Aquilegia hybrids
Gypsophila paniculata
Incarvillea spp.
Oenothera missouriensis
Phytolacca spp.

These, by contrast, tend to fall apart upon lifting and are thus easily divided:

Aconitum spp.
Convallaria majalis
Helianthus atrorubens
Physalis franchetii

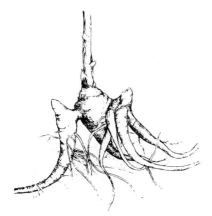  

The rootstock of a monkshood (*Aconitum*) falls apart in autumn as the newly formed crowns break away from the mother plant.

Purple coneflowers (*Echinacea purpurea*) often grow up out of the soil.

The very long-lived day-lilies (*Hemerocallis*) form root tubers on mature plants.

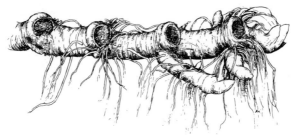

Solomon's seal (*Polygonatum multiflorum*) has powerful, finger-thick rhizomes.

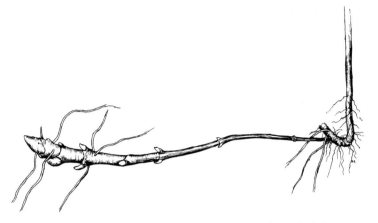

The shoots of *Helianthus rigidus* dry up in autumn, together with their roots.
Only the newly formed rhizomes perennate to make fresh plants in spring.

Lily of the valley (*Convallaria majalis*)
is easily divided after lifting.

The following plants can also be torn or cut up, especially when young, into ready-rooted divisions
which grow on well:

Achillea millefolium
Aster novi-belgii
Aster tongolensis
Chrysanthemum maximum
Doronicum spp.
Helenium hybrids
Iris germanica
Lamium spp.

Much could be written about the strange root-systems of plants such as wood anemones whose roots grow in woodland humus. Extraordinary too are the starfish-shaped roots of some foxtail lilies (*Eremurus*), which tend to rot in heavy, undrained soil. However, these belong to the next group of plants, whose dormant buds lie deep beneath the soil surface.

Perennials with deep-lying overwintering buds

The overwintering buds of many bulbs, corms and tubers lie well beneath the ground. In many cases it would be pointless to dig these up in order to propagate them. In the right spot they will multiply quickly without our aid, and when they refuse to flourish they should be transplanted to a more suitable site. Many warmth- and sun-loving species, for example, will languish where the ground is too damp, and do better among the dense roots of a lilac, thuja, sycamore or birch.

The overwintering buds of some perennials lie deep in the ground
(e.g. *Eremurus, Lilium regale, Fritillaria imperialis*).

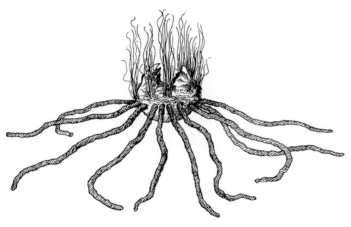

The starfish-like rootstock of *Eremurus bungei* grows immediately below the surface in damp, clayey soil, but in dry soil it pulls itself deep underground.

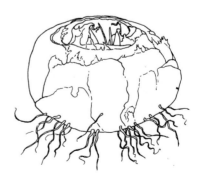

Lilium regale. Lilies gradually pull themselves deep into the soil as they grow older. For this reason they need to be planted in loose earth.

Crown imperials (*Fritillaria imperialis*) should be planted 25 cm deep in loose soil to avoid frost damage in winter.

Here their seeds can germinate undisturbed and the young plants grow on without competition (see spring bulbs, list 2.4).

Water-plants

Many perennials grow not on dry land but in or on the water, adapted to the different conditions by specialised forms of growth. The leaves of many are grassy and reedlike, emerging from an often strong and extensive rootstock to grow up above the water surface, where some are flattened out into spoon- or arrow-shaped blades. Alongside these grow plants such as waterlilies whose floating leaves are anchored to a thick rhizome in the mud. Their division and replanting in spring, as soon as the water is warm, usually presents no difficulties.

Propagation

Division, already mentioned in the last chapter, is the gardener's most important means of propagating perennials. Generally speaking, plants should be lifted in autumn or in early spring, before growth has set in, and cut into sections with a knife or sharp spade. However, a few genera such as *Iris* and *Pyrethrum* are better divided during the growing season, immediately after flowering.

It is worth emphasising that one should *never* transplant a strong, well-rooted herbaceous plant in the garden without, where possible, dividing it. An undivided transplant never recovers its strength again and cannot compare in vigour and beauty to the product of a fist-sized or even smaller division. When dividing perennials, one should take care to remove any weeds that have

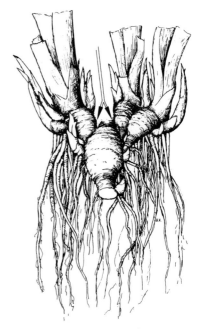

Chinese peonies (*Paeonia lactiflora*) can be divided with a knife (see arrow). Old plants must be hacked apart with a spade, preferably in September.

This iris (*Iris germanica* hybrid) may be divided into three young plants (see arrows). Irises are best divided in July, directly after flowering.

 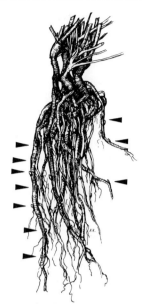

The very woody rootstocks of bugbane (*Cimicifuga*) are difficult to divide, even with a knife.

The roots of a Japanese anemone (*Anemone japonica*) bear tiny buds, which the gardener encourages to shoot by taking root-cuttings.

crept into the rootstock. If the new plants are not immediately required they can be heeled-in as reserve stock or kept as potential gifts.

Not all species are so readily increased and the propagation of more difficult subjects from cuttings and unrooted fragments is a specialised area of gardening technique. In the past it was almost always necessary to propagate named cultivars by vegetative means. Nowadays, however, an increasing number of these plants have been bred to come true from seed. A great many wild species may also be raised from seed, making this an important means of propagation.

For the average gardener the most important time to sow is in spring, though some seed is better sown immediately upon ripening or in early winter. The best sowing medium is a light and humus-rich compost, lightly shaded from the wind to prevent drying out. The use of seed-trays or shallow pots rather than a seed-bed has the advantage that the growing seedlings can be more gradually introduced to the sun. A cold-frame too can sometimes be useful. Compost should be gently compressed before sowing and the seed lightly covered using a sieve. Thinly sown, the young plants can grow on without choking one another and are ready to plant out at the end of May.

Autumn and early winter sowings are best done in seed-trays. These can then be set outside for a couple of months in the frost and snow before being brought indoors to germinate in warmth. The seedlings are then pricked out into pots, which can be put into a cold-frame to grow on in spring. The correct moment for pricking out varies with the species. Delphiniums, for instance, must be pricked out quickly, while most gentians can remain for five or six months in the original seed-tray. Cyclamen are pricked out once and then remain for two years in the same pot. Slow-growing alpines should be set as densely as possible so that the compost is quickly covered. Often there are individual peculiarities to be taken into account and a lifetime is not long enough to find out all there is to learn.

The following table gives conditions and time of sowing for some perennial species.

KEY

1   Spring sowing in Feb./March–May.
2   Early winter sowing; cold treatment.
3   Sowing immediately the seed is ripe.

×   Best sowing position.
+   Other possible sowing positions.

I   Seed-tray or shallow pot.
II   Raised bed or cold-frame.
III   Seed-bed outside.

	Species	I	II	III
2	*Aconitum* spp.	×	+	
2	*Allium* spp.	×		
1	*Althaea ficifolia*		+	×
1	*Alyssum argenteum*		+	+
1	*Alyssum saxatile*	×	+	
3	*Anemone pulsatilla*	×		
1	*Aquilegia* spp.	+	×	+
1	*Arabis caucasica*	×	+	
2	*Aruncus silvester*	×	+	
1	*Aster alpinus*	+	×	
1	*Astrantia major*	+	×	
2	*Bergenia* spp.	×		
1	*Buphthalmum salicifolium*	+	×	+
1	*Campanula carpatica*	×	+	
1	*Campanula persicifolia*	+	×	+
2	*Campanula*, alpine spp.	×		
1	*Centaurea macrocephala*		×	+
1	*Centranthus ruber*		×	+
1	*Chelone barbata (Penstemon barbatus)*		×	+
1	*Chrysanthemum coccineum*	+	×	
2	*Cimicifuga cordifolia*	×	+	
1	*Crucianella stylosa*	+	×	
3	*Delphinium* × *cultorum*		×	
1	*Dianthus deltoides*		×	+
1	*Dianthus caesius (D. gratianopolitanus)*	+	×	
1	*Dianthus zonatus*	+	×	
3	*Dicentra spectabilis*		×	
3	*Dictamnus albus*	×	+	
1	*Digitalis purpurea*		×	+
1	*Dodecatheon* spp.	×		
2	*Draba* spp.	×		
1	*Echinops ritro*		×	
1	*Eryngium giganteum*	×	+	
1	*Eryngium planum*	+	×	
1	*Gaillardia* spp.		×	+
1	*Galega bicolor*		+	×
3	*Gentiana acaulis*	×		
2	*Gentiana* spp.	×		
2	*Globularia* spp.	×		
1	*Gypsophila paniculata*	+	×	

	Species	I	II	III
3	*Helleborus* spp.	×		
3	*Hepatica nobilis*	×		
1	*Heracleum* spp.		+	×
2	*Heuchera sanguinea*	×		
2	*Hosta* spp.	+	×	
2	*Hypericum*	×		
1	*Incarvillea grandiflora* (*I. mairei*)	+	×	
1	*Inula ensifolia*	+	×	
2	*Iris* spp.	×	+	
1	*Kniphofia* hybrids	+	×	
1	*Lathyrus latifolius*	+	×	
1	*Lavatera thuringiaca*		+	×
1	*Leontopodium alpinum*	×	+	
1	*Lilium regale*	+	×	
1	*Lilium*, all other spp.	×	+	
2	*Linum flavum*	×	+	
1	*Linum perenne*	+	×	
1	*Lupinus* hybrids		+	×
1	*Lychnis chalcedonica*	+	×	+
1	*Malva moschata*		×	+
2	*Meconopsis* spp.	×		
2	*Morina* spp.	×		
1	*Oenothera missouriensis*	+	×	
1	*Oenothera fruticosa*		×	+
1	*Papaver nudicaule*	+	×	
2	*Platycodon grandiflorum* 'Mariesii'	+	×	
1	*Potentilla aurea*	×	+	
1	*Potentilla nepalensis*	+	×	
2	*Primula vulgaris* 'Grandiflora'	×	+	
2	*Primula elatior* 'Grandiflora'	×	+	
1	*Primula auricula*	×		
2	*Primula bullesiana* and relatives	×		
2	*Primula denticulata, japonica* and relatives	×		
2	*Primula rosea*	×		
2	*Rodgersia* spp.	×		
1	*Salvia* spp.	+	×	
1	*Saponaria ocymoides*	+	×	
1	*Satureja montana*	+	×	
2	*Saxifraga* spp.	×		
2	*Scabiosa caucasica*	×	+	
2	*Silene* spp.	×		
1	*Statice* spp. (*Limonium*)	+	×	
1	*Thalictrum aquilegifolium*	+	×	
1	*Thalictrum dipterocarpum*	×	+	
2	*Trollius cultorum*	×	+	
1	*Verbascum* spp.	+	×	
1	*Veronica spicata*	+	×	
2	*Veronica*, alpine spp.	×		
1	*Viola* spp.	+	×	

In order to fill our gardens with a diverse selection of suitable perennials it may often be necessary to raise a few ourselves from seed, particularly some of the wild perennials, which can be difficult to find in nurseries. To spare the work of pricking out, seed may be sown in ready-segmented trays of compressed peat or another material, using a mixture of equal parts sand and loam, or a commercially available seed-compost. The trays are set out in a sheltered spot in the garden, preferably within reach of a tap, and kept moist and shaded from the sun. In the absence of more precise information, it is safest to sow directly after harvesting, for some seeds quickly lose their potency. The time required for germination is variable. When seedlings appear they should be thinned so that not more than 2–4 are left in each segment. After growing on, young plants can be put out into prepared planting positions where, after one or two years of careful weeding, many wild perennials will be strong enough to survive and spread without further assistance.

Longevity

The lifespan of different perennial species and cultivars varies considerably, just as it does for other living creatures. As we grow old with our plants, we frequently marvel at the tenacity of some delicate-looking individual that reappears year after year in the same spot, while lamenting the fate of others, often acquired at great trouble and expense, that vanish quickly after a short burst of glory.

There is a clear distinction to be made between long- and short-lived perennials, though this does not imply that the latter always disappear quickly from a planting. Often it is precisely these perennials that seed themselves most strongly, so bringing a measure of true spontaneity into the garden. Others, such as pyrethrum and ox-eye daisies, have such valuable flowers for cutting that they are worth a little trouble to propagate or buy in regularly from nurseries. Short-lived perennials are included in many of the lists that follow, and for some garden habitats they have been given a list of their own (see lists 3.4.2, 3.4.3, 4.1.2 and 5.5).

Without knowing the year of planting it is almost impossible to determine the age of a particular perennial. Plants are surprisingly unpredictable, changing from year to year with no fixed pattern, sending out runners and rhizomes of indeterminate length, or forming a variety of different rosettes, mats and cushions. With increasing age they often go patchy or bare in the middle, offering ideal gaps for the germination of all sorts of seeds. In the course of our trials we have often noted how these seedlings can grow up and displace an ageing plant. Some species, particularly among the sub-shrubs, fall prey to moss in their centres, falling apart and eventually going to ground.

If we consider the stable vegetation of a species-rich meadow or dry grassland in this connection, it becomes apparent how dependent such a plant community must be on the patchwork of tiny niches that results from the life and death of its short- and long-lived constituents. In a well-conceived and largely self-regulating ecological planting the situation can be similar.

One might think that under the controlled conditions of a formal border planting the age of individual plants would be easier to determine. However, this is not the case. For many perennials that creep or seed themselves about, it is often difficult to say if a certain individual is the same one that was originally planted. The bulbs of tulips and daffodils die upon flowering, though many varieties will continue flowering in the same place year after year, one or more new bulbs forming each time to replace the old. Other varieties tend to disappear quickly, without apparent cause.

Exotic perennials are frequently less vigorous and shorter-lived in our gardens than they are in the wild, and many modern cultivars have a weaker constitution than their wild ancestors. This is the case, for example, with red-flowered forms of *Arabis, Aubrieta*, hybrid pinks and asters, along with several breeds of *Delphinium, Astilbe* and *Phlox*. Many hybrid lilies must be replanted every two or three years. By contrast, *Lilium martagon* 'Cattaniae' has been growing now for more than twenty years on the same woodland edge in the trials garden at Weihenstephan, in a planting shared with *Corydalis solida, Eranthis* hybrids and *Dryopteris robertiana*. Only in the last few years has its flowering slightly decreased, not least because encroaching branches have changed conditions with their shade.

It is tempting to try to grade perennials according to their expected life-span and endurance. However, the practical impossibility of this task is well illustrated by the following table (compiled by H. Müssel and L. Römer), summarising many years of experience growing perennials on different soils and in different climates, within the region of Bavaria alone.

Variation in the longevity of several herbaceous perennial species recorded in Bavaria
(Key: I, short-lived; V, very long-lived.)

	Weihenstephan (Freising)	Starnberg (Socking)	Triesdorf (nr. Ansbach)
Soil	loam (Tertiary)	loam (morainic)	sand (Keuper)
Average annual rainfall (mm)	814	1101	679
Average annual rainfall April to September (mm)	527	702	405
Border perennials			
Anemone japonica	IV	V	I–II
Aster amellus	II	II	IV
Astilbe arendsii	V	V	I
Helenium spp.	III	II	I–II
Heliopsis spp.	V	(IV)	III
Paeonia lactiflora vars.	V	V	III
Trollius europaeus	IV	V	I
Wild perennials			
Anaphalis triplinervis	IV	(IV)	II
Asphodeline lutea	IV	IV	II
Gentiana lagodechiana and relatives	IV	V	III
Linum narbonense	II	II	IV–V
Primula acaulis and *P. elatior* vars.	III–IV	IV	I

The life expectancy of any plant is dependent upon factors such as the environmental conditions and degree of competition under which it is grown. If *Iberis sempervirens* is planted, as so often recommended, between roses in a bed, then it will not live as long as in the undisturbed conditions of a rock garden. In the trials garden at Weihenstephan there are many different varieties, all growing in their proper garden habitat among rocks. The plants are now more than thirty years old, hanging far down the face of a dry-stone wall and providing an unforgettable sight each year when they bloom.

The manner of planting is also very important. Perennials mostly live longer if they are widely spaced rather than set into dense groups. The extent to which competition can influence life expectancy has been forcefully demonstrated to us by the example of border phlox (*Phlox Paniculata* hybrids) in the garden at Weihenstephan. Wherever the various cultivars are planted alongside one another for purposes of comparison they must regularly be lifted and replanted after a maximum of eight years. Even when the initial planting distances are generous, competition gradually increases and the plants go steadily downhill. Elsewhere, where small groups of phlox are set between annuals in a bed, the plants are still going strong after thirty years without lifting.

Every garden plant needs some sort of maintenance. If we forget to prune encroaching trees and shrubs, fail to feed our borders, ignore the threat of certain pests (e.g. root-aphid on *Lychnis chalcedonica*) and neglect the weeding, then this is bound to have a negative effect on the life expectancy of our plants. However, correct maintenance can also mean leaving some plants in peace. Woodland perennials, for instance, cannot thrive wherever the ground is too intensively cultivated, and wild perennials of every description should be left largely to themselves to avoid damage through ill-advised feeding and watering.

Long-term performance

In considering this important topic it is useful to distinguish between long-lived, structural plants, effective throughout the growing season, and their less imposing, perhaps short-lived and at certain times unsightly or else insignificant companion plants. Sadly, there is no body of comparable information from the various trials gardens, and the following results stem largely from our own experience in Weihenstephan. However, it may be assumed that they have some general relevance.

It is at once clear that the proper garden habitat has a marked positive influence on long-term performance. The true potential of a species can only be assessed in plantings where growing conditions are suitable and competition not too intense. Observations from the trials garden in Weihenstephan (founded 1947) are based on mostly species-rich plantings of various ages, in which perennials are grouped naturally among suitable neighbours, without lifting or renewal of any kind.

The species and cultivars listed for each planting below can be expected to remain effective for several years to come. Apart from the border perennials, they have hardly received any maintenance beyond that required for their initial establishment.

The long-term performance of various perennials in the trials garden at Weihenstephan

On the heavy loam soil of Weihenstephan, with an average yearly precipitation of 814 mm, the following perennials have remained healthy and effective for many years without replanting and (with exception of the border perennials) without any sort of maintenance apart from the occasional removal of stray weeds. Numbers refer to the lists further on in this book, where plants are ordered according to their proper garden habitat.

20–25 year old plantings in woodland

Planted in patches covering 2–3 m²

1.2.1   *Asarum europaeum* – very dense; no intruders; seeds itself.
1.1.2   *Astilbe taquetii* 'Superba' and *A. chinensis* – spread themselves.
1.1.1   *Symphytum grandiflorum* – dense; no intruders.
1.1.1   *Vinca minor* – very dense; no intruders.
1.1.1   *Waldsteinia geoides* – dense; no intruders.
1.1.1   *Galeobdolon luteum* 'Florentinum' – spreads strongly.

Planted in small clusters

1.3.1   *Aruncus sylvester* – seeds itself prolifically.
1.2.1   *Galium odoratum* – tends to invade neighbouring plants.

2.1.4 *Astilbe chinensis* 'Pumila' – dense; no intruders.
1.2.4 *Dryopteris filix-mas* – along with many other ferns.
1.1.1 *Epimedium alpinum, E. pinnatum* 'Elegans', *E. × rubrum, Epimedium × versicolor* 'Sulphureum' – all spread themselves; no intruders.
1.2.2 *Hepatica angulosa* – spreads to form dense carpets.
1.1.3 *Hosta* species – especially in bright places.
1.2.4 *Matteuccia struthiopteris* – spreads strongly.
1.2.2 *Polygonatum × hybridum* – spreads itself loosely about.

More or less long-lived companion plants that have all increased notably by vegetative means or seeding

1.2.1 and
1.2.2 *Anemone nemorosa, A. blanda, A. ranunculoides* – particularly under hazels.
1.2.1 *Hepatica nobilis* – in deep summer shade.
5.2.2 *Lilium martagon* – even seeds itself among *Vinca minor*.
2.1.6 *Primula elatior* – in bright places.
1.1.1 *Scutellaria altissima* – sometimes troublesome self-seeding.

20–25 year old plantings in woodland edge conditions

Planted in patches covering 2–3 m²

2.1.1 *Geranium endressii, G. macrorrhizum, G. magnificum*
2.1.2 *Hypericum calycinum* – spreads itself; no intruders.
2.1.4 *Omphalodes verna* – dense; almost no intruders.

Planted in small clusters

2.3.3 *Helleborus atrorubens*
2.3.3 *Helleborus × hybridus* – seeds itself freely.
2.3.1 *Hemerocallis* spp.
2.2.4 *Ligularia* spp.
2.2.3 *Lysimachia punctata* – spreads strongly.
2.1.2 *Polygonum compactum* 'Roseum' – spreads strongly.
2.3.5 *Polygonum polystachyum* etc. – spreads strongly.
2.1.6 *Pulmonaria angustifolia* – leaves wilt a little in summer.

Long-lived companion plants that have increased notably by seeding

2.2.2 *Brunnera macrophylla* – in semi-shade.
2.1.2 *Geranium sanguineum* – in bright places.
2.1.6 *Lamium orvala* – in shady places.

20–25 year old plantings on open ground

Planted in patches covering 2–3 m²

3.3.3 *Acaena buchananii* – occasional intruders after 10 years.
3.2.3 *Erica herbacea* – mossing-up in interior after 15 years.
3.3.3 *Phlomis samia* – spreads strongly.

3.1.1   *Sedum floriferum* 'Weihenstephaner Gold' – partly invaded by grasses after 25 years.
3.1.1   *Sedum middendorffianum* 'Diffusum' – partly invaded by grasses after 25 years.

Planted in small clusters

3.4.8   *Acanthus longifolius* – spreads strongly.
3.3.3   *Asphodeline lutea* – spreads itself.
3.4.8   *Echinops exultatus* and relatives – spread themselves.
3.4.8   *Inula magnifica* – makes an imposing specimen plant.
3.4.8   *Macleaya cordata* and *M. microcarpa* – spread themselves.
3.6.1   *Petasites japonicus* – spreads itself.
3.4.4   *Paeonia tenuifolia* – rather insignificant after flowering.
3.5.1   *Polygonum bistorta* 'Superba' – spreads itself.
3.6.1   *Miscanthus* spp. – spread themselves.

The following wild perennials with border character (lists 3.4.5 and 3.5.4) can remain in the same spot for well over 15 years if they are not planted too densely. (Older plantings could not be observed because of replanting.)

Achillea filipendulina 'Parker'
Chelone obliqua
Coreopsis tripteris
Eupatorium cannabinum 'Plenum' and *E. purpureum*
Filipendula rubra 'Venusta' and *F. kamtschatica*
Leptandra virginica
Polygonum amplexicaule
Rudbeckia laciniata

Long-lived companion plants that have spread themselves by seeding

3.2.2   *Adonis vernalis* – limited self-seeding.
3.2.2   *Pulsatilla vulgaris* – prolific self-seeding.
3.2.2   *Inula hirta* – limited self-seeding.
3.5.1   *Polemonium caeruleum* – prolific self-seeding.

20–25 year old plantings in border conditions

Planted singly and in small groups

5.2.1   *Dicentra spectabilis* – not very attractive in summer and autumn.
5.3.2   *Helianthus rigidus* – spreads very strongly.
5.2.1   *Hemerocallis* hybrids – many cultivars; red- and pink-toned cultivars appear to be shorter-lived.
5.3.1   *Iris* Barbata Elatior hybrids – especially diploid cultivars.
5.3.5   *Iris sibirica* – beautiful in autumn too.
5.3.6   *Lilium harrisianum* and hybrids – spread themselves.
5.2.3   *Paeonia lactiflora* – all cultivars.
5.3.4   *Phlox paniculata* – some cultivars.
5.3.4   *Rudbeckia nitida* – spreads itself.

Some cultivars of the following plants could certainly remain for well over 10 years in the same spot without replanting. In Weihenstephan, it is customary to replant them every 7–10 years in the course of the herbaceous trials, partly because some of them tend to go bare in the middle.

5.2.1 *Aconitum* spp.
5.1   *Anemone japonica* and relatives
5.1   *Astilbe arendsii* and *A. thunbergii*
5.2.1 *Delphinium × cultorum*
5.3.4 *Aster novae-angliae, A. novi-belgii* and small-flowered asters.
5.3.4 *Helenium × hybridum*
5.3.4 *Helianthus decapetalus*
5.3.4 *Heliopsis scabra*
5.3.4 *Solidago* hybrids

20–25 year old plantings on the rock garden

Planted in small groups (mostly without competition) among rocks

4.2.1 *Acantholimon glumaceum* and relatives – in the rock.
4.1.1 *Aubrieta × cultorum*
4.1.1 *Cerastium bibersteinii* and relatives.
4.1.1 *Iberis sempervirens* cvs.
4.2.1 *Ptilotrichum spinosum*
4.1.1 *Stachys lanata*

The following have only been observed over the past 10–15 years but could certainly live for 20 years

2.3.3 *Bergenia cordata* and relatives.
4.1.3 *Bergenia* hybrids – numerous cultivars.
4.1.1 *Campanula portenschlagiana, C. poscharskyana* – spread strongly.
4.1.1 *Ceratostigma plumbaginoides* – spreads itself.
4.1.1 *Geranium dalmaticum* – spreads itself.
4.3.1 *Globularia cordifolia*
4.2.1 *Minuartia graminifolia* and relatives.
4.1.1 *Phlox subulata* 'G. F. Wilson' i.a. – spread themselves.
4.1.1 *Phuopsis stylosa* – spreads itself.
4.1.3 *Polygonum affine* 'Superbum' – spreads itself.
4.1.3 *Saxifraga arendsii* 'Schneeteppich', 'Purpurteppich'
4.2.1 *S. paniculata* and relatives
4.1.3 *S. umbrosa* and relatives
4.1.1 *Thymus citriodorus* 'Golden Dwarf'
4.2.1 *Sedum middendorffianum*
4.1.1 *Sedum spurium* and *S. stoloniferum*
4.2.2 *Sempervivum* spp.

More or less long-lived species that have spread themselves by seeding

4.1.3 *Corydalis lutea*
3.3.3 *Euphorbia myrsinites*
4.2.1 *Sedum sexangulare* and relatives

The influence of the environment

Ecological factors are of decisive importance for the well-being of any perennial planting. Careful planning and loving maintenance are no guarantee of success if basic ecological requirements are not taken into account. Differing combinations of soil, drainage, nutrient supply, climate and microclimate, light and shade, slope and surrounding topography subtly determine the great variety of growing conditions to be found in a single garden. The range of possibilities can readily be appreciated when one considers that a given soil can be sandy or clayey, organic or stony, limy or acidic, and either dry, moist or decidedly wet.

The influence of soil moisture has been especially important in putting together plant associations for this book. Perennials react very differently with respect to moisture. A few, for example, do particularly well in soil that is alternately very wet and then dry.

Furthermore, a site with (say) dry soil can be either sloping or flat, exposed to the sun, or else shaded by trees or a house wall. The climate may be mild, with cool winters and little snow, or else hot in summer with cold and snowy winters; all subject to the further influence of a particular microclimate. Continuous biting winds can impair growth, so that many plants do best in a quiet and sheltered corner. The trees, shrubs and buildings that give a garden its structure create a variety of different niches for the plants that grow near them. A planting under trees has its character determined by the patterns of light and shade in summer. Soil moisture and the change in light intensity as trees break into leaf can also be important factors. For shade-tolerant perennials such as wood anemones and lily-of-the-valley, adequate moisture is much more important than strong light. Perennials from poor, dry soils, on the other hand, tend to require a lot of light.

An important consideration when choosing plants is that the conditions in a newly laid-out plot are different from those in an old, mature garden or park. Lists 1.2.1–1.2.4 contain perennials that will only thrive in a mature woodland setting. Given the right conditions, and grown in association with ecologically related species, native plants are mostly more persistent than non-natives. On the other hand, plants that are rare in the wild tend to need special culture and maintenance.

All of these factors must be taken into account when planting perennials. Many plantings fail because the chosen perennials are unsuitable for the site in question. Either the conditions have been misjudged and the wrong species selected, or else plants are put in without sufficient regard for their requirements. The results of such efforts have prompted more than one gardener to give up in despair.

On the other hand, it is often possible to adapt an initially unsuitable site in order to give a particularly desired planting, such as woodland, streamside or ornamental border, a proper chance. In most such cases it will be necessary to improve the soil or to change its composition and structure. A heavy, clay soil, for example, can be made lighter and more porous by the addition of sand and fine gravel, or warmer and organically richer by incorporating peat and compost. In the same way, sandy soils retain water and nutrients better when mixed with either loam or chalky clay. In extreme cases, such as a heath or moor garden, it may be necessary to replace the original soil in its entirety.

Drainage is another factor to be considered in the light of an intended planting. It could be, for instance, that a layer of sand or gravel is needed to improve drainage on a wet site, or that water must be held back to create a damp area on dry ground. Artificial irrigation and the provision of shelter in the form of a fence or hedge are other ways in which the devoted gardener can bring an influence to bear.

Finally, there are the regular maintenance operations that deliberately introduce a new factor into the garden environment. The use of fertilisers and the protection of plants against cold and damp in winter or premature emergence in spring, are all good examples, having a significant influence on the well-being of certain plants.

The success of a perennial planting invariably depends on a proper appreciation of the given ecological conditions and the chosen plants' ecological requirements. The wealth of perennial subjects is so great that a suitable selection can be found for even the most unpromising site. Dogs, hens and a gardener's folly are the only enemies against which no perennial can prevail.

The influence of the gardener

The gardener is an inextricable part of the life and environment in a garden. Humankind prefers to live in structured space and our gardens bear the stamp of this preference. Without us they would become an undifferentiated wilderness, and home for a more limited variety of our fellow creatures.

For all the constrictions that climate and soil place upon us, there is hardly another area of our lives where we can so freely indulge our creativity as in a garden. Today it means more to us than ever before to be able to devote ourselves to plants we have grown ourselves, to get acquainted with the feel and smell of the soil and the fruitful cycle of earth, plant and compost. The rewards of this involvement go far beyond the pleasures of relaxation and recreation in a public park. Within the small world of our own garden we have a freedom and responsibility that is seldom granted to us in working life. The patient pursuit of our own ends, and the opportunity to correct and learn from our own mistakes, can give us a personal fulfilment that is often lacking within the confines of a nine-to-five job.

Even where a garden's basic structure has been determined by an architect, the perennial plantings remain very much a concern for the gardener. When it comes to selecting the type of planting and style of maintenance, even those architects whose knowledge extends to plants and the art of gardening will be obliged to consult with those who must later tend their work.

There is no getting away from nature in the garden. It may be simpler to look after a collection of urns, boulders and cartwheels, or to use concrete instead of stone, but the absence of nature robs a garden of everything that can make it worthwhile. It is a common enough experience to come across sad, neglected gardens, the victims perhaps of insufficient time or money, whose owners hope one day to develop and improve. Not surprisingly, the perennials in these gardens have mostly been scattered about indiscriminately, though if properly chosen and sited they could have brought life and gaiety to the odd corner without requiring any special maintenance.

Perhaps it is exaggerating to say that the most interesting bits of a garden are the patches of bare soil between the plants: but how great are the possibilities here, particularly when perennials are growing nearby! It is by no means always weeds that come up in these gaps. However, an overdeveloped sense of tidiness compels many people to remove every scrap of vegetation that has not been planted, and so it is that some gardens are composed only of clean-cut evergreens in a well-kept lawn with perhaps a little bed of roses or summer annuals in between.

There are two main types of garden: the ornamental type, which is built and planted to a finished plan, and the more natural type in which patterns of growth are determined by ecological conditions and maintenance is purely extensive, allowing, for example, all those seedlings to grow which are not directly disruptive of the planting as a whole.

In an ornamental garden the plantings are denied all possibility of dynamic development and change by a constant process of digging, dividing, cutting-back and transplanting so the original picture can always be retained. In such a garden it is often the showier perennials that are most important, selected according to height, colour and seaon of flower, and set together in herbaceous borders (see border perennials, list 5.1) or ornamental rockeries (list 4.1.1) with sporadic use of the more eye-catching steppe plants (list 3.3.2) and ornamental tall herbs and grasses (list 3.6). In the more natural type of garden, on the other hand, one of the main principles is to 'let things grow' and here it is wild perennials that are most important. Set in the appropriate garden habitat and allowed to develop largely undisturbed, these plants can grow together to form a harmonious whole whose value is far greater than the sum of its parts. Depending on the situation, such plantings may be species-rich or species-poor. The important thing is that they are largely self-regulating and do not require the intensive maintenance of a traditional herbaceous border. Of course, they may change considerably as time goes by, and the necessity for occasional measures to protect slow-growing species from their more aggressive neighbours is not here excluded.

Most near-natural gardens have a few ornamental elements and an ornamental garden is bound to contain its share of wild perennials, though these are often planted in the wrong conditions and thus require as much maintenance as a border perennial. Experienced garden designers and enthusiasts are able to combine both approaches successfully on a single site. There are other types of garden, too, which do not fit into either of our two categories. One need only think of the plant collector's garden or of those especially lovely gardens where fruit and vegetables are carefully tended, and flowering annuals and perennials fill the gaps between.

Much has been written about gardeners who have made something unique out of their gardens, and about others who found the key to a profound experience of the natural world. Living with plants enables us to share in the apparent peace of nature, that great and silent force, so mysteriously and wonderfully indifferent to our aims. A thorough acquaintance with gardens brings us a new perception of colour, light and shade, heightening our appreciation for the interplay of different forms and the unity of plants with their environment. We become more sensitive to the needs of plants and this in turn affects our approach to their maintenance. 'The true gardener would rather see a stone lying peacefully on the path than two plants quarrelling in the border' (K. Foerster). Again and again we step in to end the argument and seek out a better arrangement.

The joys of a garden are not confined only to its creator, for the gardener too is part of a wider world of family and friends. Children, especially, should not be confined to the paths and driveways but allowed free roam in at least a part of the garden for their games and discoveries. Although unconscious of its meaning at the time, they will grow to thank their parents and as adults seek out the garden experience, with its rich store of memories, once again.

In addition to all of this, there are the admittedly not always undivided joys of the animal and insect life that finds its way unaided into our gardens. According to the weather and time of year, there is always something new to discover: birds and their nests, a hedgehog that has given birth within a thicket of leaves, lizards sunning themselves on the dwarf shrubs of a rock garden, young slow-worms in a shady, rotten tree-stump, and, above all, the varied life on the margins of a pond.

In time we learn to recognise hoverflies, dependent on nectar from our flowering perennials, and discover that their larvae feed on aphids, as do ladybirds, lacewings and earwigs. We learn to value these helpers and would never dream of harming them with chemical sprays. Together with bees, spiders and butterflies, they are a self-renewing and inseparable part of the garden. A particularly important role is played by those mostly hidden creatures like earthworms and the various different beetle larvae, springtails, millipedes and woodlice that feed on rotting wood and leaves, so helping to bring nutrients back into the soil. Ants, too, should be left in peace wherever they are not directly troublesome. Not only are they food for many birds, they also help in the distribution of certain seeds, so contributing, for instance, to the spread of our spring bulbs.

This rich web of life can only develop where the human element remains in harmony with the whole. Of course, when pests and diseases threaten to take the upper hand then drastic measures are sometimes called for (see p. 97). However, it is always better to remove a sickly plant than to keep it going with repeated applications of various chemicals.

The right place for the right perennial

Wild perennials and border perennials: their needs and differences

In order to cope with the countless different perennials that are offered in nursery catalogues, it is first necessary to classify them with respect to their mode of use, dividing them between the two basic groups of 'wild perennials' and 'border perennials', each with its various subdivisions.

This choice of classification reflects the source and lineage of the plants as well as their maintenance requirements and possibilities of use. To the **border perennials** belong all those plants that are the result of many years' breeding and selection by gardeners, including peonies, irises, delphiniums and many of the showier flowers of summer. To these may be added a number of wild species, both native and exotic (e.g. lists 5.2.1 and 5.2.2), that share the same requirements. All need the open, well-cultivated soil of a flower-bed, with a free root-run and mostly sunny conditions. They tend to look well planted in rather formal borders, combined with architectural features such as a house, or a hedge, fence or wall. However, their use in an informal setting among trees and shrubs is by no means excluded, wherever their growing requirements can be met.

In view of the intensive maintenance that these perennials demand, it is perhaps as well to grow them in clearly structured plantings. The constraints of design will not often allow that plants, as in some cottage gardens, are easily accessible from all sides, and it is therefore worth thinking twice before planting a wide border. A narrow border is rather easier to maintain.

Plantings composed of border perennials (henceforth 'border plantings') often suffer from lack of maintenance, losing all semblance of harmony in an uncontrolled chaos dominated by a few robust species. Worst of all is when wild perennials have inadvertently been planted with the rest. Border perennials require an open soil. Particularly in the first few years of a planting, the ground must be kept open with a hoe or grubber, just as in a vegetable garden. Wild perennials, on the other hand, tend to cover the ground completely in a short space of time, causing border perennials to suffocate in their dense mats. It *is* possible to grow wild perennials in a border planting, but plants must be carefully kept apart and the more vigorous spreaders avoided.

Wild perennials with border character form a transition to the wild perennials proper. The majority are selections that have preserved their wild character and associate well with either wild or border perennials.

Exotic wild perennials are best grown informally, perhaps in conjunction with some small feature such as a bird-bath, garden seat or pond. Generally speaking, wild perennials are easiest to grow and maintain in conditions that correspond closely to those of their natural habitat. Once plants are established, any sort of digging or cultivation is deleterious, only interfering with the process of natural spread. Such 'near-natural' or 'ecological' plantings are particularly beautiful given a framework of shrubs, semi-shrubs and grasses, or set among trees. Wild perennials are distinguished less by any dazzling show at flowering time than by a year-round character and beauty of form. For this reason, ecological plantings remain attractive right through the winter, when frost and snow pick out the shapes of various shrubs and the persistent stems and leaves of some herbs and grasses. At this time of year, border perennials have already been cut down and the earth between is dug-over and empty.

In contrast to border perennials, which regularly require dividing and moving apart, wild perennials must be given abundant peace to develop their full beauty. Nevertheless, an ecological planting of exotic wild perennials needs constant observation and adjustment. A spade and grubber are hardly necessary for this work, but a certain amount of weeding is inevitable, particularly in the early stages, and some slow-growing species may have to be helped along by cutting back their more vigorous neighbours. If a planting is not too large, then the work can be stimulating. One gets to know the plants intimately, delighting at the discovery of rare seedlings and always on the look-out for possible additions that could harmonise with the whole. Moreover, there are always new surprises in store, especially when a planting has been left undisturbed for several weeks at a time.

Native wild perennials are much too little used in our public parks and gardens, where they could readily contribute to a more varied and interesting groundcover. Of course, any species used must be adapted to the conditions on site. Kingcups (*Caltha palustris*) can be found growing wild on damp, calcareous soils throughout much of Europe and North America. Grown in a garden on dry, sandy soil it may still be native, but is in no way suited to the prevailing conditions, and is unlikely to do well.

There are many different areas in a park or garden where native wild perennials can find a use: dry, sunny slopes, damp hollows, ponds, meadows, and wherever the grass no longer grows under trees and shrubs. Plants should be distributed according to their natural patterns of growth (see p. 39) and then allowed to spread unchecked. Planted over a sufficiently large area, their different forms will gradually harmonise to make a picture of balanced natural beauty.

One more small division remains to be described: that of the **specimen perennials**. These belong to various garden habitats and are grouped together in lists 2.3.5, 3.4.8, 3.5.3, 3.6.1 and 3.6.2. Sometimes they are given a structural role in the garden, more fitting to a tree or shrub. This runs against their character, and they are better planted like exotic wild perennials, in association with some permanent garden feature. Since suitable companions are hard to find, it is best to put them in a spot where they are effective as individuals or in small groups on their own.

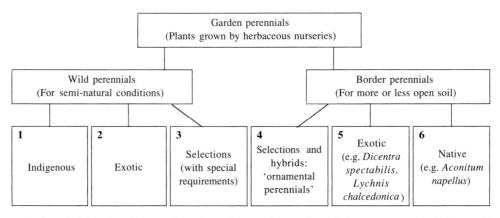

A thoughtful and artistic combination of perennials set into their proper garden habitat will develop, with very few exceptions, into a beautiful and harmonious planting. With regard to maintenance, the different groups of perennials, as displayed in the table above, (grown in the right conditions) may be characterised as follows:

undemanding: groups 1 and 6
moderately demanding: groups 2 and 5
very demanding: groups 3 and 4.

Wild perennials with border character mostly occupy an intermediate position between the last two categories. It should perhaps be added that, in our experience at Weihenstephan, the maintenance of group 4 plants requires only unskilled labour, apart from the occasional tasks of dividing and transplanting.

The use of perennials in public parks

Before we consider perennials in their role as garden plants, it would be as well to look briefly at their use in parks and other public open spaces. The time is ripe to start thinking about ways in which the threatened natural groundcover that can still be found in some of the less frequented areas of our parks can be protected from a further loss of species, or perhaps even enhanced by means of suitable plantings and sowings. Of course, the intensity of public use can severely limit the scope of any such measures, but parks are a varied lot and each case should be considered on its own merits.

A park must serve its public, and this includes not just those who are content to amuse themselves on the grass, or the dogs and children who tear about beneath the trees. There are people, too, who may not have a garden of their own, but who would like to see flowers as they stroll around or sit on the benches, perhaps enjoying memories of a previous, more rural way of life, when they were able to experience nature in quite a different way. There is no need here for the highly-coloured ornamentals of a garden festival: 'A walk in the woods is an opportunity to look at things that do not grab for our attention. Observation without clamour. Some people want silence.' (S. Lenz.) Our appreciation of nature and the feelings it arouses in us are personal matters, but this does not mean they can be ignored in the public sphere. The least that can be done in this respect is to see that there is more on offer in our parks than a mishandled and species-poor scattering of vegetation.

Perennials make it easy for us to infuse life into a park. Wildflower meadows and patches of planting on the water's edge can be planned into all but the most intensively used recreation ground or playing field. The soil must be kept free for a while under newly planted trees and shrubs, but once these are established, perennials should be brought in wherever possible. In intensively maintained areas there are even opportunities to create border plantings, perhaps in conjunction with summer annuals (see list 5.7.2).

In an old, mature park many run-down areas can be brought to life with perennials, particularly if they can be protected from trampling. Special features such as gullies, slopes and streams can be given extra prominence by a carefully considered planting of strong-growing native or even exotic plants. The better the chosen species fit to their surroundings the less likely they are to attract vandals.

Flowering bulbs can bring pleasure in many places. A suitable choice for woodland and woodland edge conditions is given in lists 2.4.1 and 2.4.2. Woodland grasses and ferns from lists 1.2.3 and 1.2.4 can also be used to good effect. In more open areas the meadow species from lists 3.2.1 and 3.5.1 will be important. Even if much of the grass is kept short, it may still be possible to allow a rich woodland-edge flora to develop at chosen points along paths. This can be achieved quite simply by keeping the mower well clear of certain groups of trees and shrubs, and perhaps sowing a few appropriate species to help things along. Aquatic and marshy habitats can be planted up with perennials from lists 6.2.1, 6.2.2 or 6.3.

Such plantings, and the measures taken to protect them, have additional importance in a city, providing home and refuge for several sorts of wild creature, especially if the surrounding countryside has been spoiled by pollution, fertilisers and chemical sprays. The success of this type of project requires the cooperation of ecologically minded botanists and knowledgeable gardeners in the planning, execution and subsequent maintenance. The following table indicates the maintenance requirements for various types of planting:

The maintenance demands of mature perennial plantings in public parks

The planting itself should only be carried out by experienced personnel; every planting needs intensive maintenance in its first year.

	Border perennials and wild perennials with border character	Exotic wild perennials, including some with border character	Native wild perennials
Garden habitat	Border	Woodland Woodland edge Rock garden Water's edge, marsh Water	Woodland Woodland edge Open ground Water's edge, marsh Water
Maintenance during growing season	More or less regular	Occasional	Minimal
Labour	Unskilled	Skilled	Skilled and enthusiastic
Plant knowledge	Unnecessary	Beneficial	Necessary
Main types of work	Weeding, soil cultivation, occasional fertiliser application, watering, cutting down, transplanting	Weeding, occasional adjustments, individual maintenance for some species, promotion of self-regulation	Removal of disruptive species to promote self-regulation

The place for perennials in the garden

Many perennials are only effective during the growing season and are thus best planted in association with permanent architectural features or with structure-giving trees and shrubs. One sometimes sees border perennials arranged in beds cut in the grass but these sorely lack the anchoring and support that a building or tree would give them. Given the appropriate conditions to develop free and undisturbed, perennials are able to link the individual features of a garden and give emphasis to its architectural forms. They should not be used as solitary specimens in place of trees and shrubs, and it is wrong to plant them in masses as if they were summer bedding. Such plantings often flower for a relatively short time and then degenerate to an untidy mess, completely out of context with their surroundings. It is very difficult to make a large perennial planting the focal point of a garden. Such features can only be effective when trees, shrubs and tall grasses are included to divide and give shape to the whole.

The best places for perennials are to be found adjacent to architectural features such as the house and its patio, or alongside garden steps and walls. Although sites near the house are often very convenient for maintaining a border planting, they are just as well suited to plantings of wild perennials, especially when conditions are somewhat extreme (e.g. a very hot south wall or a shady north one). Rock gardens are frequently built adjoining the house or patio and thus become themselves a part of the architecture. Bird-baths, pools and sculpture help give character to a garden and often require the emphasis of an appropriate perennial planting, particularly in the case of a pond. Benches, too, need perennials, to underline their position beneath a tree or overhanging shrub.

Border perennials can look well planted in rhythmic sequence along the line of a fence, wall or formal hedge. Robust plants can even be used in gaps between bushes to make an informal boundary planting. Hot, sunny corners on thin, stony soil, wet hollows, woodland, and the dense shade beneath the crown of a large specimen tree – all those places where the lawn no longer flourishes and it seems that more than just trees and shrubs are required – are reserved for the planting of wild perennials. Even a dense mat of tree roots can form an ideal (though seldom recognised) planting position for some species, including a variety of smaller bulbs.

Garden habitats for perennials

In order to simplify the selection of plants for every position in the garden, we have sorted perennial species into lists reflecting their ecological requirements and proper garden habitat. A summary of these different habitats is given on page 104. With few exceptions, the lists contain only those species and cultivars that are currently obtainable from nurseries. Among the cultivars, only those with already proven worth have been listed, together with a few promising newcomers. Some rather modest but occasionally indispensable species are included that can only be obtained as seed for propagation at home (e.g. several species for the wildflower meadow). A bit of do-it-yourself is a necessary part of all gardening.

Those who have seen the effect of a particular perennial growing wild in its characteristic environment, and compared it with the same plant's sad destiny in some of our gardens, planted here and there according to some arbitrary conceit, will surely understand this attempt to place perennials in their correct garden habitat. Only here can they truly complement their surroundings, combining with their carefully chosen neighbours to form a properly integrated whole.

Conditions can vary tremendously within a garden. The correct choice of plants for any given spot requires detailed investigation of the planting position and careful consideration of all possible candidates. If this is done well, then a stable and long-lasting plant community can develop, often requiring just a bare minimum of maintenance, yet forming a convincing feature in the garden design.

We have named the main garden habitats according to garden elements that correspond to the natural habitats of perennials in the wild, as follows.

Woodland
Woodland edge
Open ground
Rock garden
Border
Water's edge and marsh
Water

Within the various subdivisions of these garden habitats the right spot can be found for every one of our perennials. Here they will grow with a minimum of maintenance in the conditions that best suit their constitution. Combined with a few ecologically related species, their powers of evocation, and their ever-changing relationship to the animate and inanimate parts of the environment, make them a constant source of delight. Even just one or two species, set together according to the lists, can produce a fascinating appearance of harmony, similar to that almost indescribable and deeply moving impression of order that we sometimes encounter in nature.

In a balanced and well thought-out planting, the development of these harmonies through time and space can be an absorbing object of study at almost any time of year, particularly if the plants are left to grow without human interference. The indeterminacy of this process, the unbelievable tenacity of some species and the spreading power of others, the many different stages of growth and ageing, all contribute to the continuous wealth of experience provided by a garden that can never be called finished or complete.

Given sufficient maintenance (e.g. on the systematic beds of a botanic garden) perennials can be grown under almost any conditions, and in a garden intended chiefly for recreation and outdoor activities it might at first seem pointless to plant up the few tiny beds with perennials selected according to the garden habitat. However, this is largely a question of quality. Border perennials are more effective subjects for an intensively maintained flower-bed than any of the wild perennials that are often planted and perhaps even flourish there. Similarly, in places where the soil is not kept open, border perennials cannot attain their full beauty, and here it is the appropriate wild perennials that are more effective. A well-conceived grouping of plants grown in their proper garden habitat has dimensions that other plantings do not possess. The interplay between the different species, and between the plants and their inanimate surroundings such as water, stone or brickwork, produces an effect that is more than simply ornamental. Moreover, if we can meet a plant's natural requirements, it will reward us with longevity and a low demand for maintenance. Even groundcover plantings can become quite labour-intensive in time. In Weihenstephan, however, given their proper garden habitats rather than a row of demonstration beds, several such plantings have needed little maintenance now throughout several decades.

It can sometimes be difficult to establish clear boundaries between the various garden habitats. Conditions can vary on even a small site and may not always remain constant in time, particularly in a newly laid-out garden. In an older garden there are often transitional areas where habitats meet and overlap. Such difficulties are all part of the fascinating complexity attached to gardening. As can be seen from the lists, many perennials have a wide tolerance and it may be possible to use species from two or more different habitats together in a single planting (e.g. woodland and woodland edge or woodland edge and open ground). A complete mixture lacks character, however, and the trick is to arrange small groups of associated species within a unified background planting.

A detailed investigation of the site and prevailing conditions is a necessary first step in planning a perennial planting. It is important that any structural and spatial elements are not thrown out of balance, and this applies as much to private gardens as to public parks, where the overall impression of peace and harmony depends on a sympathetic ordering of space and appropriate treatment of the vegetation, whether rough meadow and woodland or carefully tended shrubbery and lawn. Any perennial planting must be fitted into a general scheme that determines, among other things, the possibilities for its maintenance. In a private garden it is especially important to decide which parts are to be used by the family, the children and pets. Mature gardens mostly have a greater variety of strongly differentiated habitats than new ones. It is worth bearing in mind that a fragmentary planting, composed of just a few or even a single species, can often be more effective than a great mixture of plants.

The immense variety of possible planting positions is reflected in the many subdivisions of each garden habitat. Of course, species from any given list will vary in their value and significance, depending on the peculiarities of a particular planting. The individual character of each species, its capacity for spread, its naturally preferred grouping, its form, texture and colour are all factors that should influence our choice. An effective use of perennials requires a creative imagination and aesthetic sensitivity, as well as some experience of design.

It is worth remembering that there are perennial plants for *every* set of conditions, able to fulfil their natural needs without the assistance of a gardener. Changes in growing conditions, caused by encroaching trees and shrubs, or the seeding and spread of some herbaceous plants, and the effects of digging, cutting back and weeding are often unpredictable, and inevitably result in the loss of some species as a planting gradually matures. Other species will spread out, and it is one of the gardener's privileges to be able to steer this development and maintain its balance, or let things go on in their own way, bringing surprise after surprise in a way that monotonous groundcover plantings can never emulate. It should perhaps be added that every planting of wild perennials needs careful maintenance in its first year, and occasional weeding and watering until it is fully established.

Plant communities

It is always dangerous to give recipes for successful planting. The recommendations embodied by the lists in this book are not based on any personal preference but rather on the results of many trials and long experience. Each perennial has been assigned to a particular garden habitat by virtue of its ecological requirements and most effective mode of use. The cultivars that sometimes appear in the lists of wild perennials are thus selections that experience has shown to have retained their wild character. Similarly, those few wild species, such as bleeding heart (*Dicentra spectabilis*) and the nutrient-hungry wolfsbane (*Aconitum napellus*), which are assigned to the border perennials, have been found unsuitable for cultivation in all but the open soil of a well-maintained border.

The question of whether native or exotic species are to be preferred is best solved pragmatically. Plant communities in a garden are not the natural plant communities of botanical science, though the aim of planting in an established park might be to encourage the development of a more or less natural groundcover. Demand for native plants is getting stronger, but most of the species currently on offer are really only suitable for use in mature gardens. Elsewhere, exotic species have an important role to play.

The proper garden habitat for some exotic species is not the same as their habitat in the wild. Some plants that occur naturally on wet ground do better in our gardens on soil that is merely moist or even intermittently dry (e.g. *Boltonia latisquama* and *Iris sibirica*). Others, such as masterwort (*Astrantia major*) and the Turk's cap lily (*Lilium martagon*) can be found growing wild on mountain slopes in full sun but require rather more shade in a lowland garden. Many mountain plants, including edelweiss and gentians, must be grown among rocks or in open soil in the garden, although their natural habitat is a grassy alpine sward.

Here and there in the lists it becomes apparent that certain species and groups of cultivars are limited geographically in their use to areas whose precise boundaries are not yet sufficiently known. Thus, astilbes can only be recommended for fairly mild areas. British varieties of delphinium are only satisfactory in maritime (north-western) parts of Germany. *Phlomis samia* spreads strongly in (continental) south Germany on nutrient-rich soils but does miserably in north Germany. In south Germany *Acaena buchananii* does far better than *A. microphylla* though in north and central Germany the reverse is true. Our conclusions are the result of careful trials, but the possibility remains that some gardener's experience may turn out to be different, perhaps owing to some particular combination of climatic conditions.

The same holds for different types of soil. Many perennials behave differently on loamy and sandy soils. Peonies, pyrethrums, globeflowers and hepaticas need a heavy loam in order to flourish, while *Aster amellus* and *Gypsophila* 'Rosenschleier' ('Rosy Veil') prefer a well-drained, sandy soil. Rhizomatous perennials such as the powerful *Macleaya cordata*, the semi-shrubby *Perowskia abrotanoides* or the delicate *Campanula rotundifolia* need relatively little space on heavy ground but become such troublesome spreaders in sandy soil that they can only be recommended with caution.

Perennials that die down after flowering

It cannot be said often enough that all perennials present a continually neat and tidy appearance before they start to flower. Many remain effective even after flowering, but some species have the unfortunate property, even under the best possible conditions, of becoming unsightly or even dying down altogether after their flowers are gone. Most of them are bulbous, tuberous or rhizomatous plants, which can store their reserves underground.

These species should not be planted in large patches, but spread about singly or in small groups, combined with plants that cover the ground throughout the year or else flower in late summer and autumn, expanding late to hide any empty spaces with their foliage. In this way the appearance

Colour plates

plate

1   Above: *Symphytum grandiflorum* 1.1.1 (20-year-old planting in the perennial trials garden at Weihenstephan); *Polygonum weyrichii* 2.3.5 in the background.

Below: *Campanula latifolia* var. *macrantha* 'Alba' 1.1.2; *Epimedium* × *versicolor* 'Sulphureum' 1.1.1, with *Tiarella cordifolia* 1.1.1.

2   Above: Solomon's Seal (*Polygonatum* × *hybridum* 'Weihenstephan') 1.2.2 with asarabacca (*Asarum europaeum*) 1.2.1 and *Digitalis ferruginea* 1.1.2 under oaks in the perennial trials garden at Weihenstephan.

Below: Flowers of cuckoo-pint (*Arum maculatum*) 1.2.2.

3   Above: Wood anemone (*Anemone nemorosa*) 1.2.1.

Below: Solomon's seal (*Polygonatum* × *hybridum* 'Weihenstephan') 1.2.2; *Hepatica nobilis* 1.2.2.

4   Above: Bugbane (*Cimicifuga racemosa*) 1.3.1, with *Peltiphyllum peltatum* 1.3.1; *Rodgersia podophylla* 1.3.1.

Below: Goatsbeard (*Aruncus sylvester*) 1.3.1 and *Luzula nivea* 1.2.3.

5   Above: *Geranium* × *magnificum* 2.1.2.

Below: Two pictures of the same planting in Frau Stölzle's garden: Left, in June: *Stachys grandiflora* 'Robusta', opposite the white spires of *Campanula grandis* 'Alba'. Right, at the end of July: *Centranthus ruber* at the front, opposite *Lythrum virgatum* 'Rose Queen', behind these *Erigeron* 'Sommerneuschnee'. At the back *Hemerocallis, Lythrum salicaria* and *Rosa* 'New Dawn'.

6   Above: *Geranium renardii* 2.1.1.

Below: Oxlips and sweet violets (*Primula elatior* and *Viola odorata*) 2.1.6.

7   Above: St. Bernard's lily and bloody cranesbill (*Anthericum liliago* and *Geranium sanguineum*) 2.1.7.

Below: St. Bruno's lily (*Paradisea liliastrum*) 3.4.1; *Chrysanthemum corymbosum* 2.1.7.

8   Above: *Dicentra eximia* 2.2.1.

Below: Columbine (*Aquilegia vulgaris*) 2.2.1; *Primula sieboldii* 2.2.1.

9   Above: Planting position in bright shade and semi-shade, *Geranium grandiflorum* 'Johnson's Blue' 2.1.6 and *Luzula nivea* 1.2.3 in the foreground, *Meconopsis betonicifolia* 1.1.3 on the left.

Below: *Polygonum amplexicaule* 'Atropurpureum' 3.5.4 and *Artemisia lactiflora* 2.2.4.

10   Above: *Lavatera olbia* 'Rosea' 5.5.

Below: *Ornithogalum umbellatum* 2.4.1; *Lychnis* × *walkeri* 'Abbotswood Rose' 3.4.2.

11   Above: *Acaena microphylla* 3.3.3, very maintenance-intensive when used for extensive groundcover; *Liatris spicata* 3.4.6 in the foreground

Below: *Veronica filiformis* 3.2; Flowering meadow with ox-eye daisies (*Chrysanthemum leucanthemum*) and red clover (*Trifolium pratense*) 3.2.1.

12   Above: *Iris pumila* and *Sedum album* 'Murale' 3.3.3.

Below: *Marrubium supinum* 3.3.3 with *Sempervivum* hybrids 4.2.2; *Oenothera missouriensis* 3.3.3.

13   Above: *Asphodeline lutea* 3.3.3.

Below: *Opuntia phaeacantha* and *Yucca filamentosa* 3.3.2 with the tender, silvery grey *Calocephalus brownii* and *Delosperma cooperi* 3.3.5.

14   Above: *Eryngium* × *zabelii* 3.4.1.

Below: *Eryngium giganteum* 3.4.2; *Carlina acanthifolia* 3.4.1.

15   Above: *Aster* × *frikartii* 'Wunder von Stäfa' 5.3.2.

Below: *Achillea filipendulina* 'Coronation Gold', *Salvia* 'Mainacht' 3.4.5, *Festuca mairei* 3.4.1 and *Salvia sclarea* 3.4.2.

16   Above: *Molinia arundinacea* 3.5.3; *Chrysopogon nutans* 3.4.7.

Below: *Pennisetum compressum* 3.4.1.

19

29

17   Above: Dry-stone wall with pinks (*Dianthus petraeus* and *D. gratianopolitanus*), *Aster alpinus*, *Saxifraga paniculata* and *Aethionema grandiflorum* 4.1.1 and 4.2.1.

        Below: *Sempervivum arachnoideum* 'Tomentosum' and *S. tectorum* 'Othello' with *Dianthus plumarius* (cushion) and *Sedum album* 4.2.1 and 4.2.2.

18   Above: *Saponaria* × *lempergii* 4.1.1; *Campanula carpatica* 'Weisse Clips' 4.1.1.

        Below: *Iberis sempervirens* 'Zwergschneeflocke' 4.1.1; *Aster alpinus* 4.1.2.

19   Above: Shady rock face with *Saxifraga* × *urbium* 4.1.3.

        Below: *Polygonum affine* 'Superbum' 4.1.3.

20   Above: *Geranium subcaulescens* 'Splendens' 4.2.1; *Stachys lavandulifolia* 4.2.1.

        Below: *Nepeta* × *faassenii* 3.3.3 and *Hypericum polyphyllum* 4.2.1.

21   Above: *Helichrysum milfordiae* 4.2.3.

        Below: *Onosma alborosea* 4.2.3; *Lewisia* hybrid 4.3.2.

22   Above: *Androsace sarmentosa* 4.3.1.

        Below: *Omphalodes cappadocica* 4.5.4 with *Primula veris* 2.1.7; *Scutellaria baicalensis* 4.5.4.

23   Above: *Chiastophyllum oppositifolium* 4.1.3.

        Below: *Corydalis cheilanthifolia* 4.5.1; *Gentiana acaulis* and *Potentilla chrysocraspeda* 4.4.3.

24   Above: *Anemone hupehensis* 'September Charm' 5.1; *Astilbe thunbergii* 'Prof. van der Wielen' 5.1.

        Below: *Fritillaria imperialis* 'Rubra Maxima' 5.2.3; *Paeonia lactiflora* 'Angelika Kauffmann' 5.2.3.

25   Above: *Dicentra spectabilis* with Mendel tulips 5.2.1.

        Below: *Lilium* 'Flammenspiel' 5.3.3; *Lilium* 'Golden Clarion' 5.2.4, *L. davidii* 'Willmottiae' 5.3.3. *Delphinium* 'Piccolo' 5.2.1 and *Miscanthus sinensis* 'Gracillimus' 3.6.1.

26   Above: *Iris germanica* (Barbata Elatior hybrid) 5.3.1; *Sedum* × *telephium* 'Herbstfreude' 5.3.1.

        Below: *Aster amellus* 'Blütendecke' 5.3.2 with *Stipa pennata* 3.3.4; *Aster pyrenaeus* 'Lutetia' 5.3.2 with annual *Calceolaria scabiosifolia*.

27   Above: Sensitively laid out enthusiasts' garden (H. and M. Hald) with perennials from various garden habitats. Border perennials such as the bearded iris are situated in open soil.

        Below: *Aster dumosus* 5.3.4 with *Panicum virgatum* 'Rehbraun' 3.4.7 in the perennial trials garden at Weihenstephan.

28   Above: *Helianthus atrorubens* 5.5 and *Delphinium* × *cultorum* 5.2.1 with *Verbena bonariensis* 5.6.1 and *Pennisetum caudatum* (annual grass).

        Below: *Helianthus salicifolius* 3.6.1 with *Coreopsis lanceolata* 5.5, *Solidago* 5.3.4 and *Ageratum houstonianum* 'Schnittwunder' (annual).

29   Above: Border perennials and annual flowers in the Schloßgarten Stuttgart. Grasses as theme perennials: *Calamagrostis* × *acutiflora* and *Panicum virgatum* 'Rehbraun' 3.4.7. Border perennials: *Rudbeckia deamii* and *Helianthus microcephalus* 5.3.4. Annual: *Verbena bonariensis* 5.6.1.

        Below: *Helenium* cultivars 5.3.4 with *Cosmos sulphureus* 'Sunset' and other annuals in the perennial trials garden at Weihenstephan.

30   Above: *Phygelius capensis* 5.6.1 between *Cortaderia selloana* 3.6.2 and *Miscanthus floridulus* 3.6.1; *Phlox paniculata* cvs. 5.3.4

        Below: *Lysimachia clethroides* 3.5.4; *Filipendula rubra* 'Venusta' 3.5.4.

31   Above: *Trollius* × *cultorum* 5.3.5 in the Schloßgarten, Stuttgart.

        Below: *Iris sibirica* 'Caesar' 5.3.3; *Polygonum campanulatum* 3.5.4.

32   Above: *Primula rosea* 4.6.4 with *Caltha palustris* 'Alba' 6.3 and *Lysichiton americanum* 6.4.2 in the background.

        Below: *Nymphea alba* 7.1.1; *Pontederia cordata* 6.2.3 with *Butomus umbellatus* 6.2.2.

of large bare patches is avoided. The disappearance of one plant coincides unobtrusively with the growth of its neighbours and the overall impression of the planting retains its balance.

Small, early-flowering bulbs, corms and tubers from lists 2.4.1–2.4.3 are suitable for naturalising under specimen trees and shrubs, especially on the edge of a lawn. Here they flower and fade in the springtime sun, dying down as other plants break into leaf and soon disappearing entirely below ground. Some of them may also be set in loose, irregular drifts among late-emerging perennials. In Weihenstephan, for instance, purple fumitories (*Corydalis cava*) cover the ground thickly in spring between slowly emerging hostas. By the time the leaves of the hostas have unfurled, these delicate plants have already finished flowering and are starting to wither away.

Many springtime woodland flowers disappear quite early in the year, among them the afore-mentioned fumitory (*Corydalis cava*), various anemones (*A. apennina, A. blanda, A. nemorosa* and *A. ranunculoides*) and sometimes also *Trillum* spp., and *Hylomecon japonicum*.

The same property is shared by many perennials that flower in early summer, among them:

Aquilegia spp.
Chrysanthemum coccineum
Chrysanthemum leucanthemum
Dicentra spectabilis
Doronicum spp.
Lilium spp.
Paeonia tenuifolia
Papaver orientale
Primula sieboldii
Thalictrum aquilegifolium

The late emergence of certain perennials, such as hostas and *Eupatorium* spp., presents fewer difficulties.

Late-developing grasses that are unsightly in spring

Grasses that first start growing in May but later strongly influence the character of a planting can be a disturbing factor early in the year. The following should not be planted in beds for year-round display without careful consideration:

Arundo donax
Chrysopogon nutans
Cortaderia selloana
Miscanthus spp.
Panicum spp.
Pennisetum spp.

The same applies to the following sedges:

Carex grayi
Carex ornithopoda
Carex pendula

The evergreen *Carex morrowii* is unsightly for just a brief period in May when its old leaves are dying back.

Massed plantings of any of the above-mentioned species inevitably appear empty or disorderly for long stretches of the growing season. Some gardeners try to fill the gaps with annual plants, but solutions of this sort are seldom satisfactory. All those perennials whose growth, flowering and decay occupy only a short part of the growing season should be set together with plants whose habit, growth and flowering are complementary. Border perennials that flower in spring and early summer should be placed away from the front of a planting, particularly when they can be associated with trees and shrubs growing at the back. The only exceptions are tulips and hyacinths, which disappear without trace shortly after flowering.

The dangers of mass-planting

People commonly attempt to imitate the perennial displays of a flower-show or garden festival within their own small gardens. The peculiar circumstances of such plantings, often designed to produce a unique but short-lived decorative effect, are thereby mostly ignored. The result tends to be a massing together of just a few species, incapable of any effective and long-lasting contribution to the garden. The same applies to both wild and border perennials. Wherever conditions allow, plantings should be richly diverse, containing a wide range of different species and cultivars set together in varied association. Of course, the number of different species must not be too great. Limits are set by the size of the planting and the necessity for a rhythmical repetition of various themes within the overall design.

A massed display of just a few species can be monotonous and tends to need a lot of maintenance. Large groups of spring- and early summer-flowering perennials often leave ugly or bare patches later in the year, and a great mass of autumn-flowering plants can be dull until its late climax. A varied but orderly association of ecologically related species and cultivars is crucial for the healthy development and harmonious appearance of a perennial planting. Other plants, such as shrubs, sub-shrubs and grasses can contribute greatly to the overall effect.

The natural grouping of any particular species is closely allied to its form of growth. Strongly spreading rhizomatous plants such as lily-of-the-valley produce a different effect from that of clump-forming species such as hepatica. These different degrees of sociability must be taken into account in the design of planting (see p. 39).

The design of perennial plantings

How does one lay out a perennial planting? Which species should come at the front and which behind? Should plants be used singly or in groups? Is it right that autumn-flowering perennials are best set at the back of a planting, spring flowers at the front and the rest somewhere in the middle? Where do bulbs, corms and tubers belong?

Before giving our attention to these questions, there is another important consideration to be dealt with.

Trees and shrubs: the framework of a planting

Perennials need the support of structural and architectural garden elements in order to be fully effective. It is therefore important to consider any appropriate trees and shrubs before laying out a perennial planting. Trees and shrubs provide the permanent framework of a garden, remaining effective in winter when other plants are dormant underground. Moreover, they can often provide shelter from the wind and improvement of the microclimate in front of a draughty wall or hedge.

This complementary use of herbaceous and woody plants often reflects their characteristic occurrence in the wild, particularly in a planting of wild perennials. Of course, a flowering border can be a beautiful sight with or without trees and shrubs. In winter, however, when the yellowing stems of perennials have been tidied away and snow lies on the ground, it is the woody species, together with some equally persistent grasses, that come into their own, freed from the competition of their more colourful companions and periodically transformed by the countless tiny crystals of a hoar frost.

A constantly flowering border is almost unthinkable without shrubs. One possibility is to set a planting of summer- and autumn-flowering perennials in front of a free-growing hedge of spring-flowering shrubs, with perhaps a few bulbs to add to the early display. Alternatively, it may be perennials that dominate in spring, followed by roses and other late shrubs in summer. Even those plants that serve primarily as structural elements should also be considered in the light of their possible contribution to the flowering sequence.

A well laid-out garden does not flower a little bit everywhere and all the time, but is composed of thoughtfully arranged plant groupings with a harmonious and complementary succession of flowering highlights. Trees and shrubs form the persistent framework for these groupings. It is therefore natural that they should be the first plants to be selected and put into position.

Structure and rhythm in a planting

Just as most perennial plantings require a persistent framework of trees and shrubs, they also need a secondary structure of dominant herbaceous plants to give them life and impact. These can be characterised as 'theme plants'. Among border perennials they are distinguished by their striking habit, exceptional flower colour and abundance of bloom. These help them to stand out from among a mass of other perennials, and they do much to determine the flowering climax of a whole border.

The principle is just as applicable to a planting of wild perennials. Here, too, one should first place the dominant, character-giving perennials before ordering the spaces between with plants of a quieter nature.

Theme plants form the basis of any herbaceous planting, particularly where border perennials are concerned. Arranged rhythmically throughout a planting, they are the ordering principle that binds everything into a unified whole. Their repetition should not be allowed to become a rigid pattern of equally sized groups and intervals. Powerful species can be set in an irregular sequence of one to three individuals, weaker ones in groups of three to five. Different cultivars may be used to bring variety to the theme plants. Delphiniums can be planted in a range of different blues and purples; border phloxes in various tones between white and red. The assortment is large enough to give plenty of room for experiment.

Deliberate ordering is essential to the creation of a well-balanced border planting. The arbitrary arrangement of a great many randomly chosen perennials can never lead to satisfactory results. It produces only a disordered and expressionless jumble of forms, colours and flowers, mostly lacking in any sort of harmony. Of course, we are all free to plant whatever takes our fancy. However, our collector's instinct and pride of possession, love of flowers and passion for novelty and change, often result in plantings composed of a large number of single specimens and small groups, not unlike the systematic beds of a botanic garden. Such an overloaded and densely planted arrangement promotes excessive competition between plants and a high demand for maintenance, exhausting to both soil and gardener.

As the result of many years' breeding and selection, border perennials have become so imbued with our culture that we are now constrained to use them in a clearly-structured, rhythmic and controlled style that reflects a human rather than a natural order, and so complements their artificiality.

How should one proceed? In spite of the limitations imposed by the conditions on any particular site, there are all sorts of possibilities in the design of a border planting, and it is important that there should be a clearly defined intention in laying out the plants. Perennial plantings do not belong to the primary structure-giving features of a garden but must be harmoniously worked into the existing spatial framework. One of the first considerations is therefore the shape of the planting, including the height of its various constituents.

We can rightly reject the popular method of assigning the front third of the border to low plants, the middle to middle-sized and the back to tall ones. If this scheme is carried out evenly along the entire length of the border then the effect is boring and seldom beautiful. It only becomes interesting when the individual zones vary in their width; when the low plants are sometimes extended towards the back of the planting and sometimes confined to a narrow strip at the front, allowing the medium and tall plants to move backwards and forwards in corresponding fashion and so preparing the way for surprising details and different visual effects.

Another possibility is to place taller perennials either singly or in small groups among a carpet of lower plants. The effect of such a planting relies heavily on the contrast between the tall and low-growing plants, and this can be accentuated by a careful choice of colours and flowering season. It should be noted that the selection of plants, particularly among the tall species, must be severely limited to avoid spoiling the effect with a chaotic mixture of different forms and colours. Coordinating themes, whether of flowering season, flower colour or habit of growth, must be especially well conceived and clearly brought to expression.

Grouping (sociability) within a planting

As we have seen, the unified appearance of a border planting depends on the repetition of differently sized groups of various perennials. On the whole, these will include a few tall species, rather more middle-sized and many low ones. A planting of wild perennials, on the other hand, has its composition determined by the texture and shape of the individual plants and not by any formal consideration of height. Nevertheless, it remains important to group the various species according to their inherent sociability, always taking nature as a guide. An arbitrary distribution can severely limit the long-term viability of a planting.

The sociability of any particular perennial depends largely on its form of growth (see p. 4). However, this is not the only factor to be taken into account. The carpet-forming *Ajuga reptans* and *Thymus serpyllum,* for instance, should not be planted in extensive patches, although they are both strong spreaders. Their maintenance requirement becomes too great when used over large areas. *Waldsteinia geoides,* a clump-forming species normally suitable for planting singly or in small clusters, retains its tidy and attractive foliage throughout the growing season and can therefore be used additionally as extensive groundcover. Peonies, on the other hand, are best used singly because grouped together their large clumps would take up too much precious space on a herbaceous border. Perennials that become unsightly or die down after flowering should never be set in large groups, though some (e.g. *Aquilegia*) may be dotted around singly over a sizeable area. Habit is another factor that determines sociability: big-leaved hostas lose much of their unique appeal when they are massed together without regard for their solitary, clump-forming nature.

In collaboration with H. Müssel we have attempted to grade the sociability of various perennials according to their natural disposition and our experience in growing them. Expressed in terms of the proper mode of use, the scale reaches from I (singly or in small clusters) to V (extensive, for large areas). Grade I has been assigned primarily to non-invasive, clump-forming perennials that are at their best planted singly or in small, close-set clusters. Their distribution within a planting should not be too regular, and a careful choice of neighbours should allow them to develop properly without losing their solitary character. They are not to be equated with the powerful and mostly very tall-growing 'specimen perennials' (see p. 30), which are also planted singly but often without neighbours of any kind.

Perennials grouped according to these grades of sociability can make a telling contribution to a planting. It may be possible to set plants with a grading of IV or V in rather smaller groups than normal, particularly where space is limited. However, the attempt to use species from grades I–III in the manner appropriate to a higher grading produces unstable plantings with a high demand for maintenance. Large numbers of these species may only be used if they are scattered in groups of an appropriate size.

A good planting contains a balanced mixture of different sized groups and single plants. The shape of a grouping may be varied at will, and the few small diagrams on page 42 cannot convey the great diversity of possible forms. Long, narrow drifts, for example, can be very effective for the sprawling woodland edge perennials from list 2.1.2.

Planting distances

All perennials wander and spread about, changing constantly and growing towards one another until they form a dense groundcover. Our desire for long-lived and well-balanced plantings can only be fulfilled if we refrain from planting too densely. Each plant must be given enough space to develop into a strong individual, able to withstand competition and survive for many years as the planting matures. The spreading power of different perennials is very varied. It is a good idea to set short-lived species around plants such as peonies and delphiniums which spread slowly and need a long time for their development. After a few years the short-lived plants disappear without a struggle, leaving the others space for further expansion. Ox-eye daisies and the other perennials from list 5.5 can all be used like this in a border planting. Short-lived species for ecological plantings are contained in lists 2.3.2 and 3.4.2; those for the rock garden are in list 4.1.2.

The correct planting distance depends on several factors, including the size and strength of the original plants. Figures given in the following table are based on standard nursery sizes. It is difficult to give absolute values because conditions vary with the particular planting position. Important considerations are the spreading power of the different species and the length of time needed for their optimal development. Plants of the same species can often be set closer to one another than to plants of another kind, though some may lose their impact when planted too closely. This is particularly so for species from list 3.4, and for plants such as *Carex morrowii*, whose graceful habit is lost in a planting denser than seven individuals to the square metre.

Broadly speaking, the best planting distance for most border perennials is 5–6 to the square metre, or 2–3 for very bushy species. Low-growing border perennials can be set at 6–8 to the square metre, rock garden plants at 8–10. Carpet-forming species can be planted much more densely (15–20/m²) though the plants themselves may be very small. *Vinca* and some *Sedum* species are best torn into fragments and planted at intervals of 10–15 cm, but not all carpet-forming plants can be treated in this way (see p. 5).

In collaboration with H. Müssel and R. Weisse, we have determined suitable planting densities for some of the more commonly grown perennials, including the increased density required for short-term displays that must rapidly grow together but need not remain effective for long. Our figures are reproduced, together with gradings for sociability, in the following table.

Planting distances for some border perennials (in cm)

Name	In groups of the same plant	To short-lived neighbours	To long-lived neighbours
Rudbeckia nitida	90	50	90
Aster novae-angliae	90	50	90
Helenium × hybridum	60	60	70
Paeonia lactiflora	60	40	50
Delphinium × cultorum	50–60	40	60
Phlox paniculata	50	40	60
Erigeron × hybridus	30–40	30	30–40
Chrysanthemum maximum	30	30	40
Chrysanthemum coccineum	25	25	25–30
Chrysanthemum leucanthemum	25	25	30

Planting density and sociability of some commonly available perennials

First column: Plants per square metre for a long-lived planting. Ground almost completely covered or shaded within two growing seasons.

Second column: Plants per square metre for rapid groundcover, particularly in the context of a garden festival. Thinning out may be necessary after a few years.

Third column: Recommended sociability for general planting. The Roman numerals refer to the sketches reproduced below:

I singly or in small clusters.
II small groups of 3–10 plants.
III larger groups of 10–20 plants.
IV extensive planting in patches.
V extensive planting over large areas.

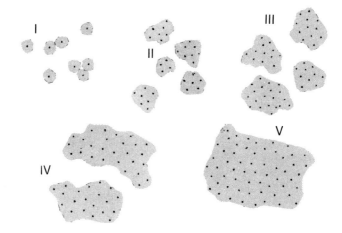

	Long-lived planting	Rapidly effective planting	Sociability
Acaena buchananii	6–7	12	IV
Acaena microphylla	7–8	12	IV
Achillea clypeolata	5–6	9	II
Achillea filipendulina 'Coronation Gold'	4–5	7	II, III
Achillea tomentosa	7–8	12	III
Achnatherum calamagrostis	2–3	3	I
Aconitum spp.	5–6	7	II
Adiantum pedatum	7–8	9	II
Ajuga reptans cvs.	8–9	16	III
Alchemilla mollis	4	5	II
Alisma spp.	4	7	II
Anaphalis triplinervis	4	9	II, III
Anemone sylvestris	7–8	12	III
Antennaria dioica	10	20	III, IV
Anthemis biebersteiniana	7–8	16	II
Anthemis tinctoria	4–5	9	II
Arabis procurrens	6–7	20	IV
Aruncus sylvester	1–3	3	I, II
Asarum europaeum	10–12	16	III, IV
Asphodeline lutea	5	7	I, II
Aster amellus cvs.	3–5	7	II, III
Aster dumosus cvs.	4–5	9	III
Aster laevis	2–3	5	II
Aster linosyris	4–5	9	I, II
Aster novae-angliae cvs.	2–3	3	II
Aster novi-belgii cvs.	3	5	II
Aster tongolensis cvs.	7–8	16	II
Astilbe × arendsii cvs.	4	7	III, IV
Astilbe chinensis 'Pumila'	6	12	V
Astilbe japonica cvs.	4–5	9	IV

	Long-lived planting	Rapidly effective planting	Sociability
Astilbe simplicifolia cvs.	5	9	II
Astilbe thunbergii cvs.	3	5	II
Astrantia major	5	9	III
Azorella trifurcata	8–10	20	IV
Bergenia cordifolia i.a.	4–5	7	III
Blechnum spicant	5–6	9	II
Brunnera macrophylla	4	7	III
Calamagrostis × *acutiflora*	2–3	3	I
Caltha spp.	4	9	II
Campanula lactiflora	3	5	I
Campanula latifolia macrantha	5–6	9	II
Cardamine trifolia	9–10	16	II
Carex buchananii	4	9	I
Carex montana	8	12	II
Carex morrowii	4	7	III
Carex pendula	2	3	II
Centaurea bella	4	12	III
Centaurea pulcherrima	4	12	II
Centranthus ruber	4–5	9	II, III
Cerastium tomentosum	6–7	12	III
Chelone obliqua	3	5	II
Chrysanthemum arcticum	6	12	III
Chrysanthemum coccineum	4–5	7	II
Cimicifuga acerina	5	7	III
Coreopsis verticillata	4–5	9	II, IV
Corydalis lutea	6	25	III
Deschampsia cespitosa	3	5	I
Dianthus caesius 'Nordstjernen'	6–7	12	III
Dicentra eximia	4–5	12	III
Digitalis × *mertonensis*	5–6	9	II
Digitalis purpurea	5–6	12	III
Doronicum caucasicum	5	12	II
Dryas × *suendermannii*	8–9	10	III
Echinops spp.	3	3–5	II
Epimedium pinnatum i.a.	5–6	12	IV
Epimedium × *youngianum*	7–8	16	III
Eryngium spp.	4	5	I
Eupatorium purpureum	1	3	I
Euphorbia amygdaloides	4	5	I
Euphorbia polychroma	4	7	I
Festuca amethystina	4	7	I, II
Festuca glauca	5–6	12	I–III
Festuca ovina forms	5–6	12	I–III
Festuca punctoria	10	16	I
Festuca scoparia	4	12	IV
Festuca tenuifolia	8	16	I, II
Filipendula hexapetala	4–5	16	II
Filipendula palmata and *F. rubra*	3	5	II

	Long-lived planting	Rapidly effective planting	Sociability
Filipendula ulmaria	3–4	7	III
Galeobdolon l. 'Florentinum'	8	9	V
Geranium endressii	5–6	12	V
Geranium macrorrhizum	4	8–10	V
Geranium platypetalum hort.	3–5	8–10	II–IV
Geranium sanguineum	5	10–12	IV
Geum coccineum	7–8	16	IV
Gypsophila paniculata cvs.	1	3	
Gypsophila 'Rosenschleier'	4	7	II
Helianthemum × hybridum	5	12	II
Helictotrichon sempervirens	1–2	3	I
Hemerocallis spp. and hybrids	3–4	3–5	II
Herniaria glabra	8	20	IV
Heuchera × brizoides	6	12	III
Hosta moderately vigorous	5–6	9	III
Hypericum calycinum	5	9	V
Iberis sempervirens	4–6	12	II
Inula ensifolia	6–7	16	II
Inula magnifica	2	3	II
Iris Barbata-Elatior	7	7	II–IV
Iris Barbata-Nana	6–8	12	II, III
Iris ochroleuca	3–4	5	II
Iris pumila	10	20	II
Iris sibirica	5	7	II, III
Iris spuria	3–4	5	II
Kniphofia spp. and cvs.	3–4	5	II
Lamium maculatum	8	12	II
Lathyrus vernus	5	7	I
Lavandula angustifolia	4–6	12	III
Liatris spicata	5–6	12	II
Ligularia spp.	1	3	I, III
Linum flavum	8	12	II
Linum narbonense	6–8	12	II
Linum perenne	6	16	II
Lotus corniculatus 'Plenus'	6	16	III
Luzula nivea	6–7	12	II
Luzula silvatica cvs.	3	5	III
Lysimachia punctata	4–5	12	V
Macleaya cordata	3	5	I
Miscanthus floridulus	1	3	I
Miscanthus sinensis forms	1	3	I
Molinia arundinacca	1	3	I
Molinia coerulea	6	9	II
Monarda × hybrida	4	7	II
Nepeta × faassenii	5–6	12	III
Oenothera missouriensis	3	7	II
Oenothera tetragona	6	12	II
Omphalodes cappadocica	8–10	25	II

	Long-lived planting	Rapidly effective planting	Sociability
Omphalodes verna	7–8	16	III, V
Onoclea sensibilis	8	16	V
Origanum vulgare 'Compactum'	5	16	III
Pachysandra terminalis	8	12	V
Paeonia tenuifolia	4	5	I
Panicum virgatum	1	3	I
Pennisetum compressum	1	3	II
Phyllitis scolopendrium	6–8	12	II
Physostegia virginiana	6	9	II
Platycodon grandiflorus	10	12	II
Polemonium spp.	5–6	7	I
Polygonum affine 'Superbum'	6	12	V
Polygonum compactum 'Roseum'	4	9	V
Polygonum weyrichii	1	3	I
Polystichum setiferum	5	7	II
Primula denticulata	8–10	12	II
Primula rosea	8–10	16	II
Prunella × webbiana	8	16	III
Pulmonaria angustifolia	7	16	II
Pulmonaria saccharata	6	12	II, III
Pulsatilla vulgaris	6–7	9	I
Ranunculus aconitifolius	4	5	II
Rodgersia spp.	1	3	II
Rudbeckia sullivantii	4	9	III
Salvia haematodes	4	7	I
Salvia nemorosa 'Ostfriesland'	5	9	III
Saxifraga umbrosa 'Elliot's Var.'	8–10	12	III
Scabiosa caucasica	5	9	II
Sedum cauticolum	9	16	II
Sedum floriferum	8	12	II–V
Sedum middendorffianum 'Diffusum'	8	16	II–V
Sedum spathylifolium	10	25	II
Sedum spurium 'Album Superbum'	8–9	16	V
Sedum telephium 'Herbstfreude'	5	5	I
Sesleria varia	5–6	9	II
Sesleria heuffeliana	4	12	II
Solidago caesia	4	7	I
Stachys grandiflora	4–5	9	II
Stachys byzantina	6–7	12	V
Symphytum grandiflorum	5	9	V
Teucrium chamaedrys 'Nanum'	8–10	16	IV
Thymus pseudolanuginosus	8	16	III
Thymus serpyllum	8	16	III
Tiarella cordifolia	7	16	V
Tiarella wherryi	8	16	II
Tradescantia × andersoniana	5	7	II
Trollius × cultorum cvs.	6	9	II
Uniola latifolia	4	5	II

	Long-lived planting	Rapidly effective planting	Sociability
Verbascum bombyciferum	3	3	I
Verbascum olympicum	2	3	I
Verbascum pannosum	3	3	I
Vernonia crinita	2	3	I
Veronica incana	8–10	16	II
Veronica longifolia	4	9	II
Veronica teucrium	7–8	16	II
Veronica virginica	3–4	5	II
Vinca minor	7–8	16	V
Waldsteinia geoides	7	16	II–V
Yucca spp.	3	3	I

Colour

What would a garden be without the colour and splendour of its flowers! The contemplation of colour, in all its different tones and combinations, is an integral part of gardening, and one of the great joys of life. Of course, it is quite possible to create beautiful colour associations without any theoretical knowledge. However, just like the schooling of a musician or composer, the study of colour instructs our senses, inspiring us again and again to make improvements in the composition of our plantings. The special appeal of colour in the garden is its intrinsic relationship to the structure of plants and, more closely observed, to the different shapes of flowers and inflorescences. We all appreciate the importance of structure and colour harmony in a flower arrangement. A perennial planting is ordered on a different scale, with much more concentration of form and colour. Here it is the mosaic of different flat and sculptural elements that most strongly influences the play of colours, and this should be borne in mind when determining the size of any groups within a planting.

Of course, colour is more important in a free-flowering border planting than in an ecological planting, with its richer contrasts of form and texture. Border perennials lend themselves to a purely decorative use, combining readily with brightly coloured, long-flowering annuals (see p. 57). A complex border needs a lot of space, but even the simplest of colour harmonies can make a valuable contribution to a small garden.

Colours must be carefully coordinated at the planting stage of any border planting. Descriptions in a nursery catalogue seldom convey an exact flower colour, especially when it comes to fine gradations of hue and tone. Coloured illustrations can also be misleading, depending on the quality of print. A thorough acquaintance with living plants is therefore a necessary condition for the creation of any worthwhile colour composition.

In general, one can distinguish between powerful, luminous colours, effective at a distance, and more delicate colours for close range. The former (e.g. white- and red-flowered border phlox) are best planted at some distance from points of observation such as a bench or patio. The latter (e.g. day-lilies and some irises) should be kept closer to hand, where their softer tones can be better appreciated. In many cases, it is better not to plant perennials with distance and close-range effect together. Powerful colours can dominate the attention, leaving the more modest but no less beautiful quieter tones in obscurity.

It is always a disappointment when intended flowering partners fail to bloom at the same time. Some associations are not produced every year because flowering times sometimes vary by several days without apparent cause. Intended partners should therefore be chosen to flower as simultaneously as possible. This is particularly important for plantings based on contrasting complementary colours such as blue and yellow, or purple and orange, and for those based on three-colour harmonies such as blue–yellow–red, white–orange–blue, or grey–blue–scarlet. One-colour plantings (e.g. the 'blue garden') are only of interest to the specialist and have no general relevance here.

It would be a fine thing to be able to give rules for arranging perennials according to their flower colour. Nevertheless, the variety of possible planting sites and many fine gradations of colour make it dangerous to generalise. Colours that normally fit well together can produce a lesser impact if inappropriate tones or intensities are used, or a nearby contrast might serve to heighten their effect. One can safely say that red, pink and blue tones harmonise well, or yellow, brown and orange, but a careful addition of other colours to such well-tried schemes should not be excluded.

A few general indications might here serve a useful purpose. Among the various grades of yellow, a coarse golden-yellow is very much harder to incorporate into a planting than a pale lemon-yellow, particularly where red is a further component. Large concentrations of pale yellow are normally required in order to create an impact among other colours. An exception is the combination with different shades of purple, so that a few pale yellow roses are enough to provide contrast in a carpet of lavender. Blue always has a restful and distant effect, and can exert a moderating influence in many plantings. The blue of a delphinium is hardly ever out of place. Nevertheless, too much blue can be rather cold and uninviting. A few splashes of coppery red (e.g. *Cosmos sulphureus*) or warm pink can bring the picture to life. An overabundance of yellow and red has a restless impact that can be softened by the addition of blue. Red tends to call for green and green for red.

White plays a special role. As a background it brings out the colours better than green, and acts as a moderator between tones that might otherwise clash. As a consequence, white can be used to good effect scattered in modest amounts between the more colourful elements of a whole planting.

A word of warning about the glaring 'brick-red' and 'salmon' colours of some recent cultivars (and a few wild species). These dangerous colours can destroy the harmony of even the most beautiful planting. They are best used against rocks and walls, or in rocky steppe-like plantings, combined with brownish or blue-green species.

The colour of surrounding features, such as house-walls, rocks and woodwork, is a significant factor to be taken into account. The same applies to any nearby trees and shrubs, whose flowering can be coordinated with that of the perennials. Anyone who has seen a planting of iris or tulips against the sun will appreciate the importance of light, too, in modifying colour.

Colour associations seldom succeed at the first attempt, particularly in the proportion of their various elements. Corrections are always necessary, but the simple harmonies and complex symphonies of colour that may result can sometimes be unforgettable.

The right place for spring-flowering perennials

Our joy at the first heralds of spring, announcing a return to life after long months of winter, is probably the main reason why spring-flowering perennials always get put at the front of a planting. There, close to the path, we can watch them emerging and observe their flowering from close range.

However, this time-honoured arrangement does not stand up to investigation. Apart from typical alpine species, nearly all spring-flowering perennials grow wild under the protection of trees and shrubs; in woods, on the woodland edge, in hedges or among scrub. Here are the natural habitats for snowdrops, wood anemones, lungworts, violets, hepaticas, hellebores, primroses and lily-of-the-valley. They all flower at a time when sunshine still penetrates the bare branches of trees and shrubs to warm the ground and its covering of vegetation. As leaves break and the shade becomes denser, they die away and remain more or less invisible until the next spring.

In the garden, these plants should therefore be used in direct association with trees and shrubs. It is especially beautiful when they are arranged to awaken the impression of spreading out from under a tangle of protecting branches. Perennial plantings often back onto a free-growing hedge or shrubbery, and this makes it easy to produce the right effect. Similar opportunities are provided by specimen shrubs set within the planting itself.

If spring-flowering perennials are kept to the back of a planting then the foreground is kept free for summer- and autumn-flowering plants. In spring these are only just emerging and so allow a clear view of the flowers behind. Later, they can be relied upon not to leave unsightly gaps until well into autumn. Contrary to popular belief, there are many very beautiful cultivars of summer- and autumn-flowering border perennials that do not grow very tall and are therefore well suited to the front of a border.

Perennials that flower in early summer

Border perennials that flower in early summer present difficulties similar to those of spring-flowering perennials. Most of them remain attractive and orderly until they bloom in May or June but, soon after, their leaves begin to yellow and die down. It is therefore inadvisable to set them at the front of a planting or in large masses that are going to leave ugly gaps later on in the season. All such disadvantages can be overcome by setting the plants singly or in small groups behind summer- and autumn-flowering perennials. Any gaps are then hidden behind a mass of later growth. The same applies to larger groups, if they can be cleverly concealed.

Fortunately, this sparing use towards the back of a planting well suits the character of early summer-flowering perennials, enabling them to make a positive contribution to the garden as a whole.

Autumn-flowering perennials

Autumn-flowering perennials retain their attractive and orderly appearance right through the growing season, giving a special importance to their role in a garden. In a conventional border, these mostly rather tall perennials are commonly planted towards the back. By the time they come to flower, most of the spring- and summer-flowering perennials in front of them are already over and often present an unsightly appearance. The effect of such a planting is therefore far from satisfactory.

It is much better to use autumn-flowering perennials in the middle or at the front of a border, where they remain attractive throughout the year without obstructing our view of the spring and summer flowers, yet helping to conceal their later disarray. There are many beautiful, low-growing cultivars of perennials such as *Aster, Rudbeckia, Helenium* and *Solidago* that are suitable for this purpose.

The principle remains valid even for tall-growing plants. The full beauty of their soaring habit can only be appreciated towards the front of a border, and here they invariably make a positive contribution to the planting as a whole.

Bulbs, corms and tubers: the finishing touch to a planting

The wealth of these extraordinary plants and their adaptability for garden use are still much too little appreciated. In spite of their minimal demands on space and maintenance they manage to conjure up garden delights year after year with ever-increasing intensity. Using them, we can lengthen the flowering season by several weeks. From the first sunny days at the end of winter till the late autumn frosts, they are constantly popping up to provide a finishing touch to our plantings.

Snowdrop
(*Galanthus nivalis*)

Galanthus elwesii

Spring snowflake
(*Leucojum vernum*)

Dog's-tooth violet
(*Erythronium dens-canis*)

Anemone blanda

Winter aconite
(*Eranthis hyemalis*)

Snakeshead fritillary
(*Fritillaria meleagris*)

Grape hyacinth
(*Muscari botryoides*)

Spanish bluebell
(*Hyacinthoides hispanica*)

Scilla siberica

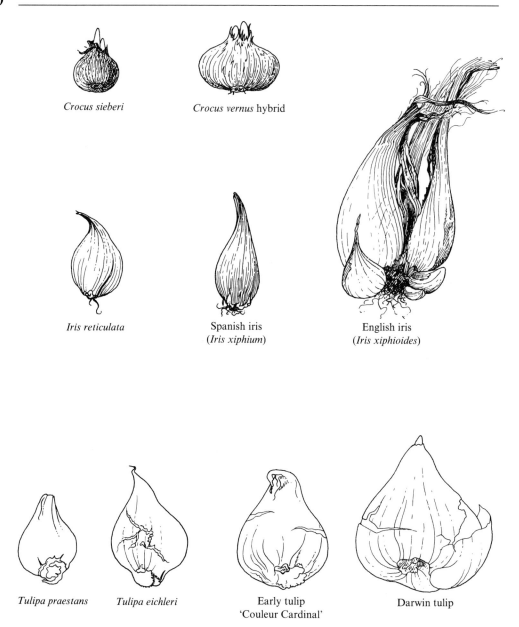

Crocus sieberi

Crocus vernus hybrid

Iris reticulata

Spanish iris
(Iris xiphium)

English iris
(Iris xiphioides)

Tulipa praestans   Tulipa eichleri   Early tulip
'Couleur Cardinal'   Darwin tulip

As with other perennial plants, it is first necessary to distinguish between highly selected cultivars and original wild species in order to do justice to their individual character and growing requirements (see p. 29). Dainty spring bulbs such as snowdrops, scillas, winter aconites and wild crocus cannot be successfully combined with border perennials because their shallow planting depth makes them liable to be disturbed or even destroyed by the division, transplanting and soil-cultivation necessary on a herbaceous border. In an appropriate planting of wild perennials (e.g. woodland or rock garden), where the soil is left uncultivated and bulbs are not disturbed, these same species can do so well that they will spread about in masses. A highly bred tulip cultivar, on the other hand, does not flourish for very long among the closed vegetation of an ecological

Garden hyacinth
(*Hyacinthus orientalis*)

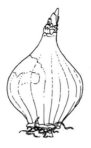

Narcissus × *poetaz*

Narcissus minor

Narcissus poeticus

Narcissus × *incomparabilis*

Narcissus pseudonarcissus

Tender bulbs:
Oxalis adenophylla

Ranunculus asiaticus

planting, where nutrient supply and other growing conditions do not meet its more stringent requirements.

Bulbs, corms and tubers must be combined with perennials whose growing requirements they share. With this in mind, there is hardly a place in the garden whose effect cannot be heightened by addition of these plants.

Although many smaller bulbs look well in self-sown carpets, larger species and their distinguished cultivars should not be reduced to cheap articles of mass-production by an unjustified use of enormous numbers. The great battalions of tulips that are commonly encountered in public parks and exhibitions mostly have a distinct decorative purpose which can serve no example for a harmoniously composed planting of perennials. The secret of these plants' most effective use lies in the recognition of their value as the true gemstones of a garden, distinguished not only by their glow and brilliance, but also by an almost limitless endurance. It is always a special thrill when plants reappear unexpectedly again and again, like the small group of *Tulipa kaufmanniana* 'The First' planted twenty years ago on a warm woodland fringe in the trials garden at Weihenstephan, returning year after year as an ever more delightful incident. An expensively planted crocus lawn whose massed cultivars are liable to disappear completely within a few years is not to be compared with the century-old stands of *Crocus vernus* var. *neapolitanus* in the grounds of Schloss Husum, which every year bring visitors from far and wide to marvel at their springtime display.

The varied uses of bulbs, corms and tubers are best elucidated with reference to their garden habitats. Snowdrops, *Leucojum vernum* and the other species from lists 1.4 and 2.4 should preferably be encountered under the protection of trees and shrubs, especially at the woodland edge. They are sociable species, and look well planted in irregular and variously sized groups and drifts. Where several species are used, they should not form a homogeneous mixture but a series of discrete concentrations spaced widely enough to take account of their later spread. Daffodils will flower shortly afterwards in the same areas, spreading out gradually from under trees into adjacent beds and borders. Some varieties may even colonise stretches of grass. With a little maintenance, various species of lily (lists 5.2.2 and 5.2.4) can also be induced to grow in woodland or at the woodland edge. Their impressive and often strongly perfumed flowers contribute novel forms and colours from early summer until the beginning of autumn. Sadly, these treasures are seldom seen in our gardens. Their bulbs are much too precious to be planted in masses, but a few individuals set in a well-chosen spot can bring a secretive magic to the dappled light and shade of a woodland planting. The full beauty of their flowers is best appreciated in front of a simple background. Taller species in particular are very effective singly or in small groups set amongst trees and shrubs. Autumn crocuses (*Colchicum* spp.) and the autumn-flowering true crocuses (lists 2.3.4 and 4.4.2) complete the cycle, appearing as leaves begin to colour and flowering everywhere comes to an end.

A planting of border perennials on well-cultivated, nutrient-rich soil makes an especially suitable home for the wealth of very popular but somewhat demanding garden tulips (list 5.4), whose rainbow-coloured display can transform a garden for weeks at a time in spring. In a planting of summer- and autumn-flowering perennials it is not difficult to create a springtime display based entirely on tulips. Their cycle begins with the low, mostly single-flowered Dwarf and Early tulips, followed by Mendels, Triumphs and Darwin hybrids, and reaching a climax when Rembrandt, Breeder and Darwin tulips flower together, to be succeeded by late-flowering Cottage cultivars. In the midst of these others, the strangely shredded blooms of Parrot tulips and the elegantly formed Lily-flowered tulips bring new and interesting shapes into the assortment. The latter especially are increasingly popular at present.

A good combination of colours is just as important as the coordination of flowering times, not least because other spring-flowering perennials must also be taken into account. It is particularly effective when three or four main colours are distributed throughout a planting, interrupted by small patches of contrasting hue. White tulips should not be planted in masses. Where space is limited it is better to be sparing in the use of different forms and colours. Too much variety can destroy the impact of individual plants and creates a restless impression. Bulbs should not be tightly packed into shapeless blotches, but laid out in loose, irregular, star-shaped drifts that dwindle out in various directions, and in a large planting can have several distinct centres of concentration (see also list 5.4).

The use of tulips as an accompaniment to roses can also be mentioned here. It is commonly attempted to improve the early appearance of an ornamental rose bed by planting tulips in gaps between the bushes. However, the maintenance demands of roses and tulips cannot easily be reconciled. Bulbs are often damaged by the intensive soil cultivation that roses require, and it takes skill and effort to lift bulbs after flowering and store them successfully for planting out again in autumn.

Hyacinths (list 5.4) are very difficult to work into a planting because their compact flowering spikes do not blend well with other perennial forms. Double-flowered cultivars easily get knocked over by rain so it is best to choose single varieties and set them in small groups near the house, where the bulbs will not be disturbed in summer. The general shortage of blue flowers in spring can make blue hyacinths useful as a complement to tulips.

Flowering at the same time as hyacinths and early tulips, the crown imperial (list 5.2.3) is a most unusual bulbous perennial with extraordinary habit and flowers. It too can be set among the perennials of a border planting, where a few scattered specimens or small groups make a good effect in the neighbourhood of trees and shrubs.

No border should be without lilies in the summer months (see list 5.3.3). Beautiful white regal and Madonna lilies, and glowing red fire and tiger lilies are among the most appropriate species. Some lilies almost have the character of wild perennials, and these must be given special conditions within a border planting (see lists 5.2.2, 5.2.4 and 5.3.6). Generally speaking, lilies should be planted singly or in small groups in the choice positions warranted by their special worth.

A rock garden contains many suitable sites where little nests of the smaller bulbs can spread their dainty flowers from spring till autumn, particularly wild *Narcissus* species and the various hardy cyclamen (list 4.2.4). The flowers of vigorous cushion plants such as aubrieta, alyssum and candytuft are so well complemented by wild tulips (list 4.1.4) that the resulting blaze of colour can hardly be matched at any other time of year. Ornamental alliums (lists 3.3.2 and 4.4.2) are equally at home among the wild perennials of a rock garden or steppe planting. Given the right conditions they spread rapidly so it is enough to plant just a few bulbs in any one place. Autumn-flowering crocuses (list 4.4.2) are among the last rock garden bulbs to flower, bringing a final gay note to the varied display.

Bulbous perennials play an important role within the plant associations for warm, sunny places on open ground or among rocks (see lists 4.4.2, 4.4.4 and 4.5.5). First to flower are the dwarf irises (list 4.2.4), wild crocuses and grape hyacinths, which can all be scattered in large drifts across a whole planting. These are followed by wild tulips, whose distribution should be more concentrated at various points. Alliums do especially well in these conditions, drawing attention by the strange and beautiful form of their inflorescences rather than their colour.

Fritillaria meleagris, Leucojum spp. and *Gladiolus palustris* all belong in the wetter parts of a rock garden (list 4.6.6) or at the side of a pond (list 6.3). They are most effective spread generously into large patches and colonies, which reflects their natural distribution in the wild. Where conditions allow, enthusiasts may wish to grow the giant lily (*Cardiocrinum giganteum*, list 1.3.2) or panther lily (*Lilium harrisianum*, list 5.3.6), both of which thrive in damp soil.

Lawns form an additional habitat for a variety of bulbs, corms and tubers, some of which can transform whole areas into a carpet of flowers. The topic is dealt with in more detail in list 2.4.

Laying out a border planting

Before going any further, the reader is advised to study the following sequence of drawings. They represent an area in front of a house wall (thick, dark line), bounded by a paved path. Similar conditions could also be found in front of a formal hedge or informal shrubbery. The drawings illustrate a practical method for planning and laying out a planting of border perennials.

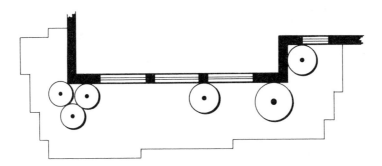

First to be planted are the woody species (circles with central dot). Together with the wall they form a persistent framework. Trees and shrubs give structure to a planting and serve to improve the microclimate, which can be particularly draughty at the corner of a house.

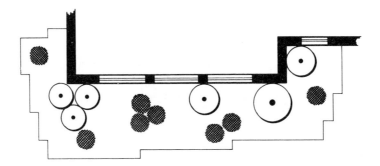

Theme perennials (shaded circles) come next, arranged rhythmically to dominate the planting. The planner must decide whether a single cultivar (e.g. red phlox) or several different cultivars (e.g. red, pink and white phlox) should be used.

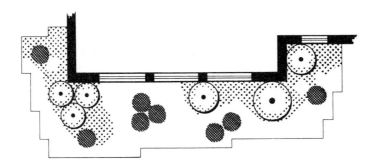

Spring-flowering perennials (dots) are set towards the back of the planting, spreading out from under trees and shrubs. Their final extent can only be decided when the other plants are all in position. Not all of them should be hidden behind summer- and autumn-flowering perennials. In spite of their modest appearance later in the year, they can still contribute significantly to a planting's structure, helping to prevent the formation of a dense herbaceous thicket.

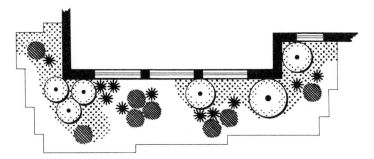

Early summer perennials (stars) belong at the back of a planting, where they are well hidden after flowering. Many, such as oriental poppies, die down completely later in the year. The more vigorous among them (peonies, lupins) can be planted singly. Others, such as globe flowers and ox-eye daisies, should be set in threes at the most so that they do not take up space that is better reserved for summer- and autumn-flowering perennials.

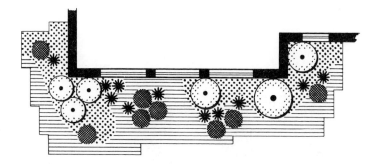

The remaining area (horizontal shading) can be devoted to summer- and autumn-flowering perennials, which always remain attractive until late in the year. Proper coordination with the theme perennials and an effective colour-scheme are both factors to be borne in mind. Plants should be well varied in height to avoid the appearance of a dense thicket. No species should appear just once in a border. Autumn-flowering perennials should be kept in the foreground as much as possible.

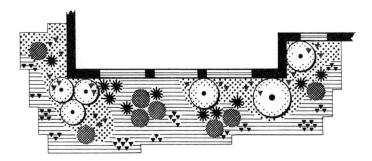

Flowering bulbs (triangles), especially tulips and hyacinths, can be set in drifts at the front of the planting to give colour early in the year. Other species associate well with the spring flowers under trees and shrubs.

Laying out an ecological planting

The great variety of different garden habitats makes it difficult to give a general planting scheme for wild perennials. From the following illustrations it should be possible to gain some idea of the character of an ecological planting and the natural way in which different species are set together.

Plantings of this sort were designed by I. Kaiser and U. Walser for the national garden festival in Stuttgart in 1977, and carried out on a large scale under an alley of old plane trees. The detail from one of their planting plans demonstrates clearly that the design of a small section is enough to allow the planting of large areas, provided that conditions are everywhere constant. Tall, dominant plants should be laid out first. Fill-in plants are used right at the end to close any gaps.

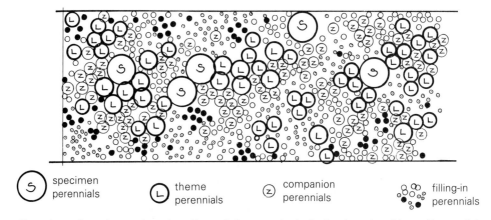

(S) specimen perennials	(L) theme perennials
(z) companion perennials	filling-in perennials

Experience has shown that the effect of these ecological plantings is seldom disrupted by spontaneously occurring weeds. Furthermore, their maintenance requirements are generally much lower than those of conventional plantings with their rigorous and artificial blocks of colour (see sketch below).

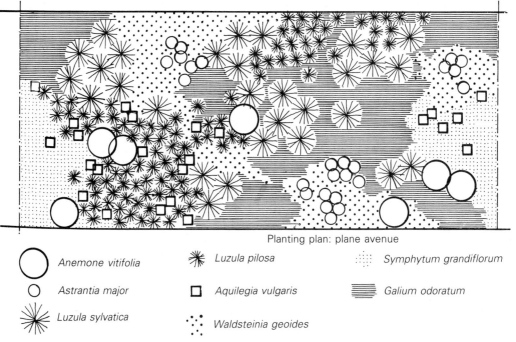

Planting plan: plane avenue

◯ Anemone vitifolia	✳ Luzula pilosa
○ Astrantia major	☐ Aquilegia vulgaris
✳ Luzula sylvatica	⋰ Waldsteinia geoides
▦ Symphytum grandiflorum	▤ Galium odoratum

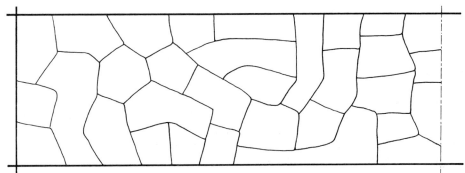

Widely used, artificial planting scheme.

The use of annuals in border plantings

Even the most splendid of border perennials does not flower for so long as most of our annual and bedding plants. Wherever a long flowering display is required, it is worth considering the possibility of uniting perennial and annual species in an expressly ornamental planting. The perennials benefit thereby from the protective shade cast on the open soil between them, and the planting of annuals can be adapted each year to fit the changing pattern of their spread.

Not all those bedding plants that are generally available in the trade are suitable for this sort of planting. Popular dwarf selections are of more limited value than taller plants (themselves often tender perennials) whose habit corresponds better to that of most border perennials. Such plants contribute more than just their flower colour. In association with perennials, their individual character acquires a significance that is often lost in a purely decorative bedding display. A few well-sited groups can lend a special atmosphere to the whole garden. Even when the last perennials have finished flowering and their leaves and seed heads start turning to shades of brown and red, their combination with annual plants is in no way unsightly. Such scenes signal the end of the growing season, powerfully evoking the richness and bounty of autumn.

No combination of annual and perennial species can succeed without well chosen colour harmonies and a balanced proportion of annual to perennial plants. Over the years, much experience has been gathered in the trials garden at Weihenstephan where, especially in high summer and autumn, several plantings of this sort exert a powerful attraction on visitors. Even though their flowering is concentrated in summer and autumn, these plantings are appealing and full of promise from early on in the year, particularly if the spent tulips between clumps of perennials are planted over with annuals in late spring.

In a very colourful border it is often better to restrict the use of annuals to a single species. A varied collection of *Aster novi-belgii* cultivars planted only with the pink Natal grass (*Rhynchelytrum repens*) can be an unforgettable sight at flowering time. Of course, when one colour or a few related colours are dominant, as with *Helenium* cultivars, then the reverse applies and a colourful mixture of annuals may be used to advantage (see p. 370). These same annual plants associate well with other mainly yellow-flowered assortments such as *Solidago* and *Rudbeckia*, though in each case we have noted only those species which in our experience are particularly effective (see lists 5.1–5.3). Many of our results stem from trial beds planted with a single perennial assortment (e.g. *Phlox* cultivars) but they can nevertheless serve as inspiration for more varied plantings.

Sadly, some of these annual and half-hardy perennial species are hardly obtainable from nurseries, making it necessary to raise plants from seed. This should provide no great difficulties for a town parks department. Those responsible should appreciate that these ornamental features combining annual and perennial plants are cheaper and need substantially less maintenance than a conventional bedding display.

The life expectancy of a border planting can be considerably lengthened by giving the plants enough space to spread unconfined, and filling the bare soil around them with annuals and half-hardy perennials. A newly planted border is particularly suitable for this sort of treatment, especially if the perennials are not expected to grow much in the first year.

Once the annuals have been tidied away at the end of the season, it is crucial for the border's future development that all nutrient losses are made good and the original soil conditions restored. This also applies to plantings where frost-sensitive perennial species such as dahlias are employed. With a little skill, the low, single or semi-double flowered cultivars, and especially the Mignon dahlias, can be fitted well into a border planting, and these are to be preferred to the giant flowered cultivars.

Gladioli are to be used with caution. Their stiff habit and luxuriant flowers make them difficult to combine with hardy perennials. In Weihenstephan they associate exceptionally well with tall annual grasses such as *Pennisetum caudatum, P. ruepellii* and *P. villosum. Anemone coronaria* and *Ranunculus asiaticus* can be set in small groups among spring-flowering perennials. These tender species can be planned into a border right from the beginning, provided that proper facilities are available for their overwintering.

Short-lived and tender species for plantings of border perennials are dealt with in lists 5.5 and 5.6.

Rock gardens

Different sorts of rock garden

A 'formal' or 'architectural' rock garden has stone retaining walls and steps that form geometrically shaped terraces for planting. A 'natural' rock garden, on the other hand, consists of unworked rocks set together so as to awake a natural impression. A lay-out of this sort, planted with an enthusiast's collection of difficult alpine plants, might be termed an 'alpine' rock garden. Various transitional forms are also possible, arising mostly from the peculiarities of a particular site.

Examples for the construction of a rock garden on a natural slope (dashed line) with optimal use of available soil. Planting omitted for ease of illustration.

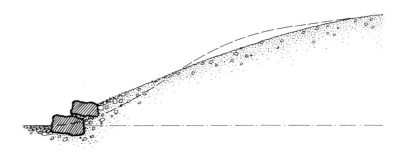

The simplest sort of rock garden: a natural stone facing to a sunken path, with minimal alteration to the slope. Path composed of gravel. Planting in immediate vicinity of the stones, with lawn behind.

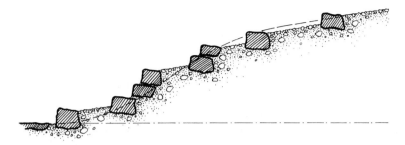

A natural rock garden, closely following the original contours of the slope. Path composed of irregular stone slabs. Planting across the entire slope, in small, somewhat sloping patches of soil, and in cracks between the rocks. Transition on top of slope to low-growing wild perennials or lawn.

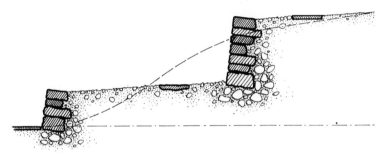

Formal rock garden or terrace garden with slope interrupted by two dry-stone walls (batter 10–20%). Paths composed of irregular stone slabs or artificial paving. Stepping stones on the terrace to act as maintenance path. Planting on the gently sloping ground between the walls, above the upper wall and in cracks between the stones. Lawn beyond the slabs.

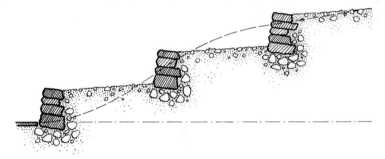

Terrace garden with slope interrupted by three dry-stone walls (batter 10–20%) of equal height. Path composed of stone slabs or artificial paving. Planting on the gently sloping terraces. Planting or lawn above the upper wall.

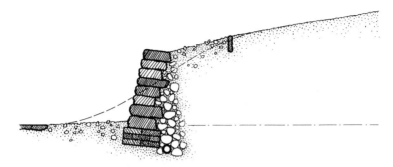

Stone retaining wall (dry or mortared, batter 20–30%) with brick foundation forming a marked interruption in the slope. Loose stone filling behind wall to carry off seepage from slope. Path composed of stone slabs or artificial paving. Planting between path and wall and in cracks between stones (dry-stone wall). Planting above wall divided from lawn by sunken kerbstones.

The plants

The arrangement of plants in a rock garden is determined largely by their individual growing requirements (see lists 4.1–4.6). It is worth remembering that alpine plants are adapted to very different conditions from those that occur in lowland areas. In the mountains, abundant rainfall and high humidity are combined with strong, persistent winds, extreme variations in temperature, intense ultra-violet radiation, a short growing season and a thick, protective covering of snow in winter. Soils are strongly influenced by these climatic conditions as well as the underlying rocks. Other factors, such as drought in summer or winter, may also play a role, and the frost-sensitivity of some species from distant mountain ranges can make them difficult to grow in temperate gardens.

In spite of all this, an astonishing number of different species will survive on our rock gardens, flourishing with a minimum of maintenance wherever conditions are right for them. Great care must be exercised in the choice of planting positions. In the end, it is small variations in light and shade or in the lie of the land that can play a decisive role.

The more robust species that have been assigned to the decorative, formal rock garden (see lists 4.1.1–4.1.4) do not require any special protection from frost, damp or drought. Some of them can be grown in normal garden soil, associated with colourful cultivars from other garden habitats.

The material

The most suitable materials for natural rockwork are various sorts of stratified sedimentary and metamorphic rocks, such as limestone, sandstone, quartzite and slate. These can easily be laid as single blocks, fitted together to form natural-looking outcrops. Porous tufa cannot always be recommended, in spite of its several advantages. It weathers rapidly, encourages the spread of undesirable weeds and is quickly covered in moss.

Wherever possible, the building material for a rock garden should come from the immediately surrounding area. Each rock should be laid more or less horizontally, according to its natural lie. It is better to use a few large pieces than a heap of smaller ones, and these should be concentrated into groups rather than scattered evenly about the slope. The natural impression can be heightened by setting any strata at a constant, slight angle. Only one sort of stone should be used, and any steps or paving must be made of the same material. A well laid-out rock garden is a rare sight, in contrast to those boring and unnatural features where bits of stone are scattered randomly across a mound. A tasteless arrangement of rocks cannot be rescued by any amount of future planting.

Alpine plants may still be grown in places where the local topography is unsuitable for building a natural rock garden. In a garden without slopes of any kind, enthusiast's plants can be grown

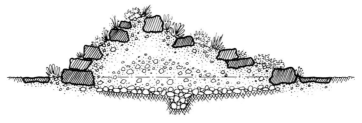

Section through a rock garden bed (width *ca.* 3.50 m, height *ca.* 80 cm). Rocks sloping downwards and inwards. Drainage layer of rubble or coarse gravel with soak-away on impervious soils. Rocks laid in planting mixture on a free-draining soil core containing stones or rubble. Boundary of natural stone paving.

Cross-section and elevation of a dry-stone wall made of slate or similar stratified stone (width below *ca.* 70 cm, height *ca.* 45 cm. batter 30%). Filling of free-draining planting mixture with coarse stones underneath for drainage. Corners reinforced with large rocks. Soil for cushion plants between and under the paving stones.

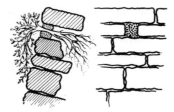

Section of dry-stone wall with cushion plant. Large gap between stones plugged with clayey soil after planting.

in a so-called rock garden bed. This is an oblong, more or less formally shaped feature, two or three metres across and several metres long, which must be sensitively worked into the design of the garden. Where possible, the bed should run in a north–south or northwest–southeast direction, with a steep face to the west or southwest and a gentler slope to the east or northeast. The height should not exceed 80 cm. This manner of construction provides all the necessary sunny and shady positions for the most delicate of perennials. Slopes directed away from the sun are important for alpine plants because they remain bright while the low angle of incidence of the sun's rays prevents overheating, and guarantees higher soil moisture and humidity.

A dry-stone wall requires even less space than a rock garden bed. It is a narrow, free-standing feature with sides constructed of loose stone walling, 100–120 cm wide at the base, 50–70 cm high and a few metres long. Its formal shape allows it to be placed near the house or terrace, where it is conveniently situated for intensive maintenance and observation. The building material should be a slate-like stone with individual pieces not more than 10–20 cm thick, arranged with a batter (upward and backward slope) of 20–30%. The resulting fine structure gives a greater number of planting opportunities than could ever be provided by coarser stone. The most suitable filling is a loose, free-draining soil, with provision to ensure the escape of excess water.

Section through a solid stone trough garden. Layer of coarse stones over drainage hole and soak-away. Free-draining planting mixture with rock fragments. Transitional zone of stones or coarse gravel planted with suitable perennials around the base.

Trough gardens are miniature rock gardens, suitable for the smallest of sites on or near a terrace or sitting area. Their construction in an old stone water-trough or hollowed-out boulder requires much skill and devotion. The trough should have a drainage hole at the bottom and is filled with the usual planting compost for alpines over a layer of coarse gravel.

A further opportunity for using rock garden plants can be created by building a sunken path or driveway with a retaining strip of fairly large rocks on each side. The difference in height should not exceed 40–50 cm, so that two or three irregular layers of rock are normally sufficient. Good drainage is important. Vigorous cushion plants are especially suitable for this sort of feature.

A flight of steps offers further possibilities. However, unless the steps are intended purely as a decorative feature, the cracks between treadstones are not as suitable for planting as those on the risers or side walls. Constant trampling is unwelcome to any plant.

Large, decorative boulders may also be set together to make a sort of rock garden, effectively lending emphasis to certain types of ecological planting such as heathland, moor and woodland gardens. Such boulders are mostly composed of igneous rock (granite, syenite, porphyry, basalt or quartz), though sometimes also of sandstone, quartzite or dolomite. They should always be laid on their 'lazy' side, and not set up artificially like a monument. Any lichens, mosses and other plant growth should be carefully preserved, and the boulder placed to lie in the same direction as when it was found. In this way the living patina of the stone is retained and can go on developing undisturbed.

Log-terraces of unstripped wood are mostly seen in association with some sort of peat bed. However, they may also sometimes be appropriate in place of a rock garden on a very shallow, shady, north-facing slope. Wood is in some respects more attractive for combining with perennials than cold, bare rock. Oak and false acacia have both proved very suitable. Their wood is hard

The proper use of rocks in a natural rock garden.

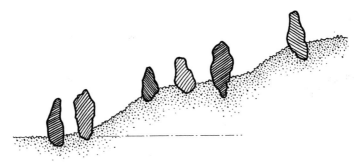

Wrong: Rocks sticking up on end from level parts of the slope. In time they will fall over, crushing any nearby plants. Steep planting slopes are threatened by soil-slip and erosion. Rooting conditions are unsuitable for alpine perennials. Shade from the rocks is an additional handicap.

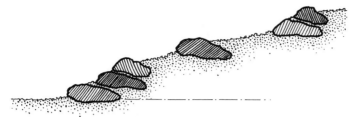

Correct: The same rocks built horizontally into steeper parts of the slope. Here they help keep the soil in place and provide an optimal root-run for alpine perennials. Planting areas are much less steeply inclined and the overall effect is more natural.

Garden detail with large boulders laid naturally on their lazy sides. Woody plants and perennials give this little feature its life.

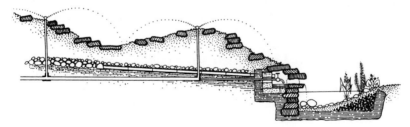

Section through an alpine rock garden with sprinkler system and pond. Chamber for spring built of bricks faced with natural stone. Puddled clay at base of pond. Substrate for water plants covered with sand and gravel. Water supply to pond regulated independently with a tap. Free-draining planting mixture over an impermeable core. Drainage pipe laid in coarse gravel leading to spring. Pond overflow (not illustrated) leading to soak-away, or lower-lying part of the garden.

and durable, and their coarse, twisting branches with deeply fissured bark make them highly attractive. Where rhododendrons are grown it is better to use logs from coniferous species, which do not carry the potentially damaging *Phytophthora* fungus. Logs must have a diameter of at least 12–15 cm if they are to retain their impact when up to half their thickness is set below ground. Gaps between logs are somewhat difficult to manage, but plugged with moss or clay they can be planted most effectively with small ferns, periwinkle, asarabacca, woodrush and other evergreen perennials. The particular species chosen must be selected with regard to the character of the lay-out as a whole.

The combination of rocks with water is particularly exciting. A secretive spring, the quiet, reflecting eye of a garden pond, an exuberantly splashing stream, graceful fountain or formal pool, all contribute substantially to the success of a garden. In a spot that is protected from wind, water evaporation cools and humidifies the hot, dry air of summer and moderates extremes of temperature, creating a microclimate that is especially beneficial to alpine plants. All such water features should be fitted naturally and believably into the rockwork, avoiding where possible the twin mistakes of tweeness and artificiality.

Soil preparation and planting

Woody plants are a necessary constituent of any rock garden. Small shrubs, sub-shrubs and dwarf conifers form a living architecture that helps determine the overall shape of the design. In winter their diverse forms maintain the interest when herbaceous plants are invisible beneath the snow. Even a dry-stone wall or trough garden can be given an extra dash of character with a few carefully selected dwarf shrubs.

The choice of rock garden perennials is determined by the conditions available for their growth (see lists 4.1–4.6). A long-lived and healthy community of these plants can only develop to its full and characteristic beauty if individual species are chosen with sufficient regard to their nature and requirements for growth.

All of the more delicate alpine perennials thrive in soils that have been modified with finely crushed stone or gravel. The type of stone is normally of little significance, since soil structure is mostly more important than pH. Soils should be loose, airy and well-drained, but water-retentive and well supplied with humus, without being too rich in nutrients. Any definite preferences for either acidic or alkaline soils are specifically referred to in the lists. True rock crevice plants do well in a soil mixture composed of equal parts light, unfertilised garden soil, clean, coarse sand, heavy loam or marl, and moistened peat. Plants that need more humus prefer a mixture of:

1 part coarse, gravelly sand
1 part heavy loam or marl
1 part leaf compost or a commercial, peat-based compost
2 parts moistened, coarse peat.

It is advisable to add a certain amount of coarser material (stones, coarse gravel) to help bring air into the mixture and guard against extreme variations in temperature. The further addition of crushed chalk or limestone (*ca.* 1 kg/m^3) is necessary for chalk-loving alpines.

Typical calcifuge plants are less adaptable than most chalk-loving species. In the garden, just as in the wild, they are completely dependent on acid soil. It is not enough to put a little extra peat or acid sand into each planting hole. The soil must be correctly prepared over the entire planting area, and factors such as the neutralising effect of hard water (from run-off or irrigation) must also be taken into account. A suitable mixture would be:

2 parts light, sandy garden soil
1 part coarse quartz sand
4 parts coarse peat (well moistened)
2 parts needle litter or heathland/moorland soil.

It is not advisable to add any sort of fertiliser to these soil mixtures, especially in the case of nitrate fertilisers and artificially enriched compost. Excessive nutrients lead to accelerated growth, insufficient ripening, reduced flowering, susceptibility to disease, and distortion in the characteristically dainty growth of many alpine plants.

Planting of cracks and crevices must be undertaken with care. New plants should not be set too deep or shallow, otherwise they may become buried or else lifted by frost. Rosette-forming perennials are particularly sensitive in this respect. The chosen crevice must be large enough to provide space for any roots, and contain sufficient nutrients to feed the plant until it has reached the soil behind the stones. To prevent soil washing out of the opening, a collar of heavy loam may be set around the top of the roots. After planting, the area must be very gently sprayed over to wet the soil without washing it away.

Rock garden plants need at least 30–40 cm of soil for their roots. The low, compact appearance of most alpines above ground should not deceive us about their roots, which are often much more extensive, penetrating far below the surface to colonise the cool, moist soil beneath rocks. Many plants prefer 'a hot head and cold feet', so any rockwork should be embedded with a half to two thirds of its bulk under the soil to avoid excessive heating. The use of large and heavy stones is to be preferred for more than just aesthetic reasons. Small fragments of rock lying on the soil surface heat up quickly under a hot sun and can damage any sensitive roots growing beneath them. Neither are they substantial enough to hold up a heavy bank of earth.

In their natural habitat alpine plants are exposed to very high rainfall, heavy dews and spring meltwater. In spite of this, they are very sensitive to standing water above or below ground. Any water they receive must immediately flow away or soak down into deeper layers. This means that the foundations of a rock garden should be made of freely draining materials such as unwashed gravel, quarry waste or building rubble. If the subsoil is impermeable then some sort of drainage system will also be necessary to carry off excess soak-water. According to the size of lay-out and the particular soil conditions, this may consist of stone-filled trenches, clay drainage pipes or a layer of coarse gravel. Ideally, any water should be lead into a cleverly designed garden pond, but house drains are an acceptable alternative when no such feature is available.

Irrigation must also be provided, particularly if the local climate is dry and the rock garden is not planted exclusively with drought-resistant perennials (see list 4.2). The best irrigation is provided by a built-in sprinkler system. Spray-heads should be situated as invisibly as possible close to the ground. Sunken spray-heads are especially good but an ordinary lawn sprinkler may also be used. It is important to keep the spray as fine as possible to avoid compaction of the soil surface.

Water gardens and marshy areas

The diverse perennials which live in and around water and in marshy areas are dealt with in lists 6 and 7.

In most gardens it is necessary to create a special water feature in order to grow these plants. The impermeable mud and silt at the bottom of a natural pond or stream is replaced in the garden by an artificial layer of puddled clay, plastic liner, concrete, fibreglass or bitumen. Planting positions must be provided in the form of containers or else built into the overall design (see illustrations, p. 68).

A good deal of careful attention is required in the design and construction of such planting areas. The importance of depth is apparent from the illustration on p. 67. The possible danger to small animals is another point to be borne in mind. A shallow zone at one end acts as an escape route for any creatures that accidentally find their way into the water. A wooden ramp is a useful substitute in an already existing pond.

Planting

The unique character of a water garden lies in its strongly contrasting forms of growth, whose reflections pattern the water against a picturesque and ever-changing background of sky and clouds. For the planting to be effective, the many different reed-like species with their narrow, ascending leaves must be placed in correct relation to the broad-leaved plants growing on or near the water surface. Too much variety creates a restless impression, so a few well-chosen plants are preferable to a mass of different species.

If the intention is merely to liven up a bare expanse of water then the plants should be arranged in small concentrations extending inwards from the water's edge. This ensures that the water surface remains substantially intact and preserves its structural relationship to the garden as a whole. A proper water-plant feature contains large areas of closed vegetation, but here too water is the determining element and should therefore remain clearly in evidence.

Restraint is advisable in the choice of different species. One should not forget that many water plants grow naturally in large stands without much variation.

No plant can withstand the constant spray of a fountain. Plantings should be kept far enough away from this sort of feature to avoid any disturbance.

Water and marsh plants in the rock garden

A water feature can be particularly attractive within the context of a rock garden. In this sort of situation, a small container let into the ground can be just as effective as something larger and more complicated. It is important that the type of feature should reflect the character of the layout as a whole. In a formal rock garden a fairly solid, geometrically shaped basin may be appropriate, but a natural rock garden demands a much freer style of construction. Artificial springs, water-courses and streamlets are all variations worthy of consideration. Such features must be sensibly fitted into the overall design, taking care to avoid any tweeness or over complication.

Water gardens

The enthusiast may wish to grow a variety of different marsh and water plants in a special water-garden made up of several pools of different size and depth, each tailored to the needs of a particular plant community.

Wherever possible, the pools should be set in terrace-like sequence on a gentle slope, connected to one another by little cascades and waterfalls. Imaginative construction and planting can create an intimate but arresting garden picture that might easily become the focal point of an entire garden landscape.

The presence of water brings new riches to the life in a garden. Nimble pond-skaters, glittering dragonflies, and the little frogs that so delight our children, all start to appear by themselves. Fish must be introduced by the gardener but these too belong to the magic of a living garden and have a practical use in keeping the water clear and free from mosquito larvae.

One garden treasure deserves special mention here: the Japanese iris (*Iris kaempferi*, list 6.4.1). Recent selections and advances in technique now enable us to make far more extensive use of these noble perennials, which formerly had to be imported from Japan. The Japanese material had the disadvantage that it was exceptionally sensitive to even the smallest amounts of lime in the soil or water. Meanwhile, however, extensive breeding in the USA and elsewhere has produced cultivars that appear to flourish in any normal garden soil. With the aid of plastic sheeting we can now easily provide the appropriate living conditions for these plants. *Iris kaempferi* lives naturally in areas that are subject to flooding. In order to grow well it needs a wet or moist soil in spring and early summer, and can even stand in a few centimetres of water until it flowers. Thereafter, in late summer, autumn and winter, the soil must be kept dry. If no suitable pond is available then the soil should be excavated to about 40 cm in a sunny part of the garden and the resulting hole lined with plastic sheeting to within 5–10 cm of the surface. The lined hole is then filled with a nutrient-rich mixture of soil and humus, and the irises planted with their leaf-bases buried about 5 cm under the surface. The soil should then be kept fairly moist throughout the year, though drainage must be provided to guard against excessive waterlogging after heavy rain.

If a pond is available, the Japanese iris plants can be kept in baskets and removed after flowering to be plunged in a normal bed. Simpler still is to lower the water level in the pond so that the iris can dry off after flowering. However, the plants should never be allowed to dry out completely. Experience with the more recent cultivars has shown that they will even develop and flower well in a normal bed of loamy soil enriched with peat, provided only that they are kept well watered.

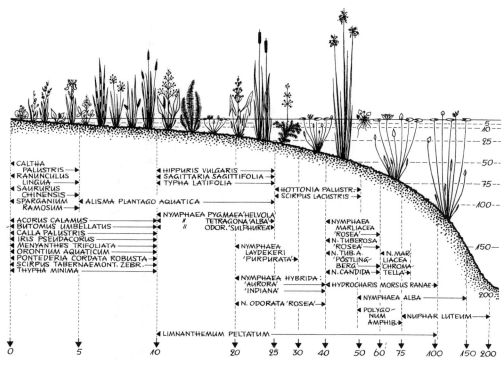

Optimal water depths for the most common aquatic perennials.

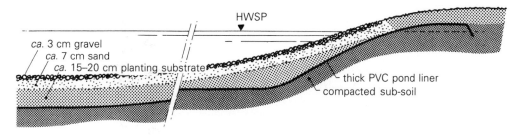

Use of a pond-liner to create planting positions at the bottom (left) and at the edge (right) of an artificial pond. HWSP, highest water level.

The best planting time for water and marsh plants is in mid-spring, from the middle of April to the middle of May. At this time of year the water is already getting warmer and growth is beginning, allowing the plants to root quickly and start to make new leaves. This is also the right time for lifting and replanting already established plants. Aquatic perennials require a loose and humus-rich garden soil. The addition of peat, coarse sand, and a coarse hornmeal fertiliser is invariably beneficial. Care should be taken to ensure that the emerging shoots are situated slightly above the soil surface, not forgetting any subsequent covering of sand or gravel. The dangers of planting too deep are just as severe in water as on dry land!

On the banks of a pond or stream, small carpet-forming perennials such as *Ajuga reptans* and *Lysimachia nummularia* (see list 2.1.3) should be considered, along with the species from list 6. The ability of these plants to form a dense groundcover which is tolerant of mowing makes them especially useful in creating a smooth transition from plant-bed to lawn. In the same way, they can form the link between a pond and the surrounding grass wherever a clean cut is not possible right to the water's edge. In wet areas these plants are vigorous enough to stifle the growth of lawn grasses, but they rarely pose any kind of threat to other moisture-loving species. If they become a nuisance then they are easily cut back or removed.

Planting areas for marsh and water plants

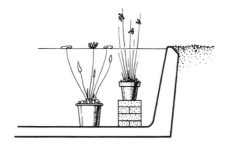

Sketch of a concrete-lined pond. Water-plants are set in various containers at different depths.

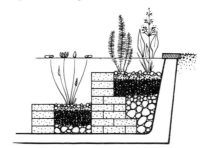

Concrete-lined pond with additional plant-beds made from bricks.

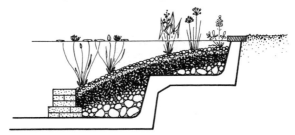

Concrete-lined pond with sloping plant-bed. Stones and coarse gravel to help circulation at base. Substrate covered in sand or fine gravel.

Concrete-lined pond with adjoining bed for marsh or water-plants in a preformed basin filled with layers of coarse gravel, planting substrate and sand.

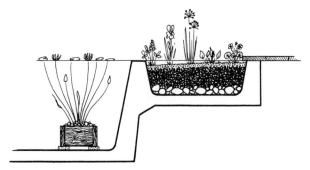

Concrete-lined pond with built-in marsh bed filled with layers of coarse gravel, planting substrate and sand. The planting area could have its own overflow into a drain or soakaway (not illustrated).

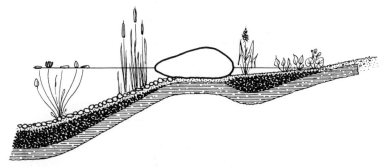

Garden pond with special section for low-growing or moorland plants. Partitioning by means of boulders which also serve as stepping-stones. Puddled clay construction. Substrate covered with sand and gravel.

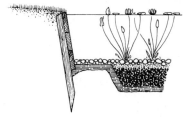

The edge of a pond constructed with wooden planks and stakes. Bottom of pond sealed with puddled clay. Sunken planting area covered with sand and gravel.

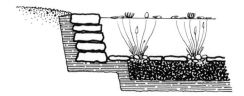

Edge of a pond suitable for paddling with sunken planting area for scattered water plants. Puddled clay construction. Sides and bottom lined with stone. Sand and gravel between stones and around plants.

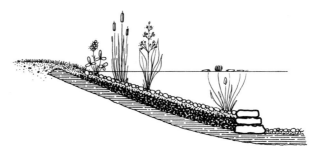

Garden pond with built-in sloping planting area supported by stones. Puddled clay construction. Directly adjacent to lawn.

Garden pond with planting area separated by hardwood stakes that also serve as stepping-stones. Puddled clay construction.

Wooden wash-tub for water-plants, set within a lawn or plant-bed. Adjoining marsh area made with puddled clay.

Planting position for streamside plants on a small watercourse made from puddled clay covered with coarse gravel.

Soil preparation and maintenance

Whatever the form of pond or basin, the substrate provided for water plants must be a nutrient-rich, sandy loam, preferably enriched with a slow acting hoof and horn fertiliser. Even better is to use the substrate from an existing pond, though this method involves the potential hazard of introducing various fish diseases. The use of artificial fertilisers is not to be recommended since even the smallest amounts may cause burning and root-damage, or upset the ecological balance by promoting excessive algal growth.

The planting substrate must be evenly mixed and placed in the pond before any water is let in. Depending on the size and variety of the plants, a substrate depth of 15–25 cm is necessary to ensure a good long-term development. A 5 cm layer of sand and gravel can be put on top of the soil to prevent it washing away and clouding the water.

Most water plants are not fussy about pH. Only a few species (lists 6.4.3 and 6.5) such as water primrose (*Hottonia*) and bladderwort (*Utricularia*, list 7.1.3) are dependent on soft, acidic water.

Planting perennials

Preparation of the planting area

The soil in a flower-bed may be sandy, stony, loamy or even clayey, and the area may be dry, moist or wet. The aim of any improvements must be to create a friable, well-aerated soil containing just the right amount of moisture and nutrients for the chosen plants. Only thus will they stay vigorous and healthy, and so develop to their full beauty.

In a vegetable garden the soil need only remain at its best for the lifetime of the particular crop it is carrying. By contrast, the soil of a perennial planting must remain in good condition over a period of many years.

As far as plants are concerned, soil is the underground environment for roots, rhizomes, bulbs, corms and tubers, as well as protection during the dormant season when nutrients are being stored and new growth is in preparation. Soil is the main source of a plant's water and nutrients, an essential resource shared with neighbouring trees and shrubs, soil-borne fungi and a myriad of other tiny organisms.

For **border perennials** the soil should be deep and easy to work, well drained and aerated with a fine, crumbly structure, high organic content and a vigorous community of soil organisms. The preparation must therefore be thorough. At least 50 cm depth of soil is required for deep rooted, delicate or specimen perennials. Low-growing and shallow-rooted perennials may make do with 30 cm.

If the available soil is unusable or full of persistent weeds then it must be removed and replaced. On heavy ground the subsoil should be broken up as deeply as possible with a fork and spade. New topsoil is then added to a depth of 10–15 cm and mixed with the loosened subsoil to create a transition zone. The rest of the topsoil is then piled on top. If a sufficiently mature and weed-free compost is available then this too can be worked into the topmost layer. Should all of this prove too expensive or time-consuming then it may be possible to combat the weeds by growing a soil crop such as potatoes (applying a lime-based fertiliser) or sowing out green manure in the form of clover or nasturtiums. Radical herbicides such as Terebol are too dangerous for all but professional use, and should be avoided wherever possible.

The soil for an intended border planting seldom contains sufficient humus and nutrients. Improvement is therefore necessary in the form of bulky organic fertilisers, especially those which are based on peat. Additional nutrients can be provided with hoof and horn, bonemeal, dried blood or an artificial fertiliser. The incorporation of coarse peat is invariably beneficial and can be combined with the application of any sort of fertiliser. Three or four bales of thoroughly moistened peat should be spread over an area of about 100 m² and fertiliser scattered evenly on top. The whole is then lightly worked into the soil surface and is immediately available to the young plants when they are set out.

An unbalanced soil may need additional treatment. Light, sandy soils are improved by mixing with a heavier loam (not pure clay). Alternatively, the water- and nutrient-holding capacity can be increased by incorporating vermiculite, perlite or bentonite. A heavy, wet soil becomes easier to work with the addition of ash, coarse sand or peat, and can be made crumblier, warmer and better aerated by application of algal derivatives. A soil that is poor in humus should be enriched with well-rotted compost or peat, which help stimulate soil microorganisms to greater activity.

Manure from cows, sheep, goats, poultry and pigeons is always beneficial, provided it is composted before use. The manure is spread in autumn and worked lightly into the top few centimetres of soil. The treated area should then be left to freeze and thaw in winter before being planted up in spring.

All of the commoner border perennials flourish on a normal garden soil though a few, such as lupins, are thankful for lime-free conditions. Experience at Weihenstephan indicates that most border perennials grow especially well in slightly acidic soil. Care should therefore be taken when applying lime to ornamental cherries, roses and other woody species growing among perennials. Except on almost lime-free soils, the amount of lime present in commercially available fertilisers is enough to hold the lime concentration at a suitable level.

Alterations and improvements to the soil of an **ecological planting** are only required for features such as heathland, steppe, marsh, streamside and moorland, which seldom occur naturally in a garden. The addition of nutrients is rarely necessary and should be confined to plantings where wild perennials with border character dominate or where the soil is excessively poor.

Planting sites for heathland and steppe perennials must be adapted by adding large amounts of sand and fine gravel, even to the extent of completely replacing the original soil. Slope and aspect of the site may also be altered to expose the plants more fully to the sun. Species from lists 2.1.7 and 3.2.2 appreciate the addition of lime to the soil. Those from lists 2.1.8 and 3.2.4 prefer acidic conditions.

Woodland perennials (see list 1) need a soil enriched with leafmould and compost or peat. If the original soil has a good humus content then improvement may be unnecessary, especially when native wild perennials are planted. A constant supply of humus is provided by the annual fall of leaves, which should on no account be removed from such plantings.

In order to create the special conditions required for a moorland planting (lists 4.6.2, 6.4.2, and 6.4.3) the soil must be enriched to a depth of at least 40 cm with moist peat, leaf mould or a naturally occurring acid earth. An annual top-dressing of an acidic fertiliser such as super-phosphate (50 g/m^2), ammonium sulphate (40 g/m^2) or saltpetre (25 g/m^2) can be applied in spring but other fertilisers are not to be recommended. Simplest to use are the products specially developed for heathers and rhododendrons, including the peat-based planting substrates.

Rock garden perennials have very diverse requirements. It is important to remember that these plants live in the mountains on scree and in fissures, or in alpine swards, closely associated with the rock. Though many species are tolerant and appear to do well in ordinary garden soil, it is nevertheless better to grow them in a special, nutrient-rich, moisture-retentive but well-drained, gravelly mixture to ensure their long-term success.

Any dry-stone walling which is to be used for growing cushion plants must be back-filled with humus-rich loam or soil enriched with compost. The rubble produced in building the wall may also be incorporated but any large pieces should be discarded or else placed well away from the planting crevices. The best way of dealing with the plants is to set them carefully into position as the wall is built up. However, this is only possible if the wall is being constructed at planting time.

Cushion plants growing in the joints between slabs on a path or terrace also need sufficient soil if they are to thrive and spread in these somewhat harsh conditions. The paving should therefore be laid on at least 10 cm of a suitable planting medium and not on the usual sand or mortar bed. In this way, a smooth transition can easily be established from intensively used, hard-jointed paving, through loosely scattered cushion plants, to a fully planted bed.

The passage of heavy machinery and the constant treading involved in building a house and garden make it difficult to avoid compaction of the soil. The resulting damage to pore-structure and drainage retards root growth, causing stunting and general lack of vigour. Even the most obliging of perennials will only thrive when such a soil has been radically improved.

The proper time to plant

There is a widespread belief that perennials, like trees and shrubs, are best planted in autumn or spring. However, perennials are a varied lot and a more appropriate rule is that planting should take place directly after flowering. Spring-flowering perennials should thus be planted in late spring or early summer, and summer- and autumn-flowering perennials in autumn or early spring.

Generally speaking, border perennials can be planted from the beginning of March to the middle of May and from the middle of August to the middle of November. Alpines, cushion-plants and wild perennials have a slightly longer planting season, especially if they are grown in pots. None the less, a rock garden is best left completely undisturbed in autumn. The best planting time for water and marsh plants is in the spring (see p. 67).

The length of season can be influenced by various external factors. A warm and well-drained, sandy soil prolongs the planting season but creates problems in late spring when a persistent drought or heatwave can prevent roots becoming established, thus damaging the entire plant. Constant watering is often of no help in such a case. On the other hand, a cold, damp, clayey soil does not allow planting either too early or too late in the year. A late autumn planting should be avoided at all costs on heavy soils.

Certain species do not respond well to planting in autumn, especially on a clayey soil. Ferns and grasses are particularly bad in this respect and should therefore only be planted in spring. The same applies to:

Bugloss	*Anchusa* spp.
Japanese anemone	*Anemone japonica*
Chamomile	*Anthemis* spp.
Michaelmas daisy	*Aster amellus*
Garden chrysanthemum	*Chrysanthemum × hortorum* (Koreanum and Rubellum groups)
Shasta daisy	*Chrysanthemum maximum*
Iris	*Iris spuria*
Red-hot poker	*Kniphofia* spp.
Lupin	*Lupinus* hybrids
Catmint	*Nepeta* spp.
Scabious	*Scabiosa* spp.
Mullein	*Verbascum* spp.

Spring-flowering bulbs, corms and tubers should be set in the ground as early as possible from the middle of August to the middle of November, though never when the earth is frozen. Autumn-flowering species are best planted in July, directly their leaves have died down. Spring planting is also possible for plants that have a root-ball or are grown in pots.

Depending on the species, lilies must be set out in autumn or spring, though potted bulbs may be planted at any time. Lilies suffer serious damage if their bulbs are disturbed as new rootlets are developing. This is especially true for *Lilium candidum*, which must therefore be planted in August while its bulbs are still dormant.

In a new planting the differing individual requirements of the various species cannot all be respected. However, an experienced gardener can take many peculiarities into account when transplanting single specimens. Irises, for instance, are best moved in July; peonies in September. Crown imperials and fox-tail lilies can be most safely transplanted after flowering in June and July. If weather conditions are right then snowdrops can even be moved in full bloom.

How to plant perennials

Perennials have sensitive roots, adapted to the stable, well-protected conditions of life underground. Exposed to the wind or sun they soon dry out and can easily be damaged or killed. Fortunately, many species have developed robust storage organs, which quickly produce new roots when the old ones have died.

Nevertheless, planting should take place whenever possible in dull weather, especially if large areas must be laid out before the plants are finally set in the soil. If plants must be left exposed for more than half an hour (fifteen minutes in full sun) then they should be lightly sprinkled with water from time to time, taking care not to wash soil away from the roots or saturate the planting area. Plants that have been grown in pots are a little less sensitive.

Protecting the soil is just as important as protecting roots. The laboriously prepared, loose and crumbly planting soil should not be trodden on more than is absolutely necessary. The compaction caused by heavy feet during laying out and planting is not easily removed, especially on a clayey soil. Wherever possible, plants should be put in position without leaving the path or lawn. Planks may be laid to help reach difficult areas. Wide beds should be made accessible with a system of maintenance paths. In principle one should be able to reach every plant in a planting without damaging the soil.

Any new planting should be laid out and adjusted where necessary before finally committing any plants to the ground. Groups of perennials should not be lined out in rigid formations but ordered informally, keeping the planting distances approximately equal. The same applies even for low groundcover plants.

Delphinium plants (*D.* 'Berghimmel') in various qualities.

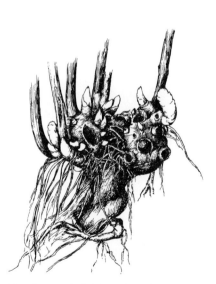

Very good nursery plant.

Poorly rooted division of an old plant.

Good nursery plant.

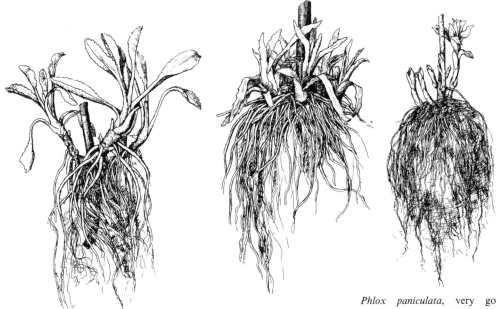

Chrysanthemum maximum, the dried remains of last year's flowering stem visible in the centre.

Helenium hybrid; the five or more shoots develop in the course of the season to strong flowering stems.

Phlox paniculata, very good nursery plant. Each shoot develops into a powerful flowering stem.

Chrysanthemum leucanthemum, very good nursery plant.

Geum hybrid; the good crowns produce healthy flowering shoots.

 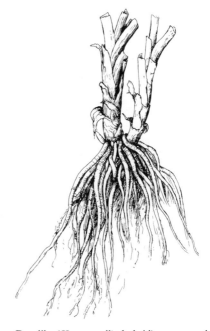

Globeflower (*Trollius* hybrid). It is important that the plants are well rooted.

Day-lily (*Hemerocallis* hybrid); nursery plants of some precious novelties only have a single shoot.

Care should be taken while planting that the roots are arranged in their natural position in the earth. Long, hanging roots can be shortened to about a hand's width with a knife. Plants should not be set too deep or too shallow but at a depth corresponding to their previous stand and specific form of growth. Peonies, and perennials such as *Iris* and *Polygonatum*, whose rhizomes grow just under the soil surface, should never be set deep in the ground.

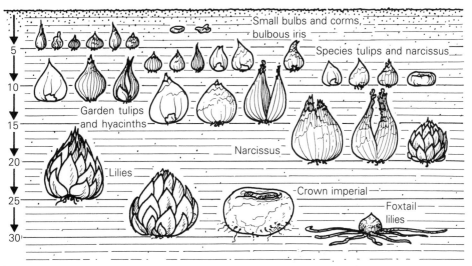

Sketch illustrating the planting depth for various bulbs and corms. The given depths are only valid for mature plants. Flower stems are less liable to be knocked over if the bulbs are set somewhat deeper in light, sandy soils. In heavy clay soils they should be planted less deeply.

Initially, plants should be set a little higher than their final depth so that when the soil is firmed and watered they can sink to their proper level. Soil is filled in around the roots, and any hollows removed by shaking. The plant is then firmed in evenly with the hands, taking care that pressure is applied away from the roots. On sandy soil, sturdy perennials may be lightly trodden in. Large, old rootstocks should be divided before replanting, but old specimens of *Aster amellus, Gypsophila* and all legumes such as lupins and *Galega* do not transplant well.

After planting, each perennial should first be thoroughly watered with a can. The stream should not fall directly onto the plant but in a circle tight around its base. The process can be repeated two or three times where necessary. Finally, the whole plant must be quickly sprayed over to wash off any clinging soil particles without flattening its leaves to the ground.

Bulbs and tubers form a category to themselves. They are often planted too shallow and are pushed up to the surface by frost in winter or cannot support the weight of their shoots in spring. As a general rule they should be set at three times their own depth in the soil. On a light soil they may be set deeper, on a heavy one somewhat shallower though never less than 5 cm. Crown imperials and some of the lilies require a planting depth of 25 cm.

On poorly drained, clayey soils it is advisable to guard against rotting by setting the larger bulbs of tulips, daffodils, hyacinths, lilies and crown imperials in a bed of coarse sand. The planting hole is dug a little deeper than normal and first filled with 4–5 cm of sand or fine gravel. When the bulb is in position, it can be surrounded with more of the same material before the soil is returned and lightly pressed into place.

Established iris rhizomes lie very close to the soil surface.

When everything has dried off after watering, the soil between the newly planted perennials should be carefully worked over with a suitable tool to remove footprints and even out irregularities. In dry weather or where the ground is very permeable, a second watering may be necessary. However, too much water may cause rotting because new plants are unable to use much moisture before they are rooted in. A slightly dry soil promotes deep rooting, especially in young plants.

Planting lilies

Lilies are usually offered for sale in spring and autumn. However, the best time to plant them is in autumn, particularly early autumn. Madonna lilies (list 5.3.2) form an exception and should be planted in August if they are to bloom the next year. The American wild species must also be planted as early as possible. By contrast, *Lilium speciosum, L. auratum* and their hybrids (list 5.2.2), and the trumpet lilies (list 5.2.4) may all be planted in spring.

If roots are present they should be carefully protected and on no account removed. With a few exceptions (see *Lilium candidum* and *Cardiocrinum giganteum*) the bulbs should be planted with two to three times their own depth of soil (7–20 cm) above their tips. In a light, sandy soil they may be set even deeper, in a heavy soil somewhat shallower. Remarkably enough, the bulbs of many species are gradually pulled to the right depth by their roots as they dry out and contract in the autumn.

Many lilies form a dense, annual network of roots from the underground part of their stem. In view of this, the soil above a lily bulb should be loose, rich in nutrients and full of humus. On the other hand, the roots that grow from the base of the bulb need a porous, well-drained, inorganic soil and the bulb itself should never come into contact with organic matter.

Lily roots have a very high oxygen demand. The planting area must therefore be thoroughly dug over and the subsoil mixed with sand and gravel, or vermiculite and expanded clay. The saying goes that you can plunge your arm right up to the elbow in soil that is fit for growing lilies.

On a heavy clay soil the bulbs may be protected from getting too wet by planting them in a raised bed of loose soil over a permeable layer of stones or rubble. An annual mulch of peat, pine needles or leafmould late in the year protects the bulbs from the cold and damp of winter and helps keep the ground warm in autumn when the roots are starting to grow. If the plants start to lose in vigour after a few years then it may be necessary to feed them, using a high-potassium fertiliser applied towards the start of the growing season.

Lilies have a variable lifespan. The cultivated species come from very different regions of the world and it is not always possible to meet their requirements in the garden. Some species tolerate lime; others do not. All are grateful for soil that is not too wet in winter, though a few American lilies, in particular *Lilium pardalinum* and its derivatives, thrive in moisture and appreciate a heavy soil.

Most lilies love the sun, but some of them flourish in half shade too. The pure species are often more difficult than the many cultivars, which have been developed in the last few decades. Several Markham and Bellingham hybrids have survived now for more than 20 years on the heavy loam at Weihenstephan. Martagon hybrids are just as successful but oriental hybrids must be lifted every two or three years to be replanted in carefully prepared earth. *Lilium lancifolium* (*L. tigrinum*) and *L. pumilum* are also short-lived in Weihenstephan.

Sadly, some lilies prove very sensitive to various fungal diseases. Even in the best of conditions the plants remain susceptible and these diseases are the bane of every lily enthusiast. The use of chemical fungicides seems amply justified when precious plants are threatened. Should the scales of a valuable bulb become spotted with a grey-blue mould (penicillin rot) then immersion in a 0.1% suspension of Ronilan should put a stop to the damage. The same product can be used to combat grey mould (*Botrytis elliptica*) on stems and leaves. Even stem rots (*Phytophthora*) can be controlled by watering with Previcur solution before the fungus attacks the bulb. Equivalent fungicides are available in America from the North American Lily Society.

The disease resistance, properties and uses of the various different species of lily are covered in lists 5.2.2, 5.2.4, 5.3.3 and 5.3.6.

Examples of plantings

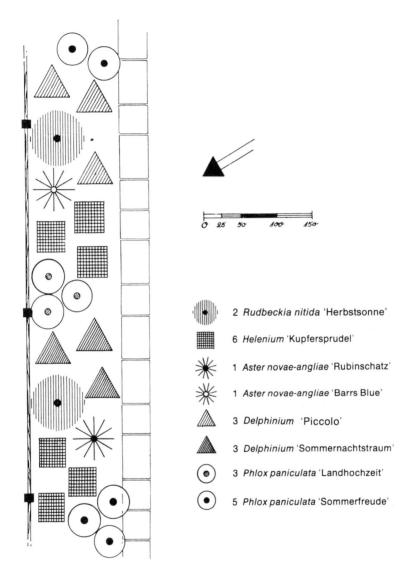

0 25 50   100   150

	2	*Rudbeckia nitida* 'Herbstsonne'
	6	*Helenium* 'Kupfersprudel'
	1	*Aster novae-angliae* 'Rubinschatz'
	1	*Aster novae-angliae* 'Barrs Blue'
	3	*Delphinium* 'Piccolo'
	3	*Delphinium* 'Sommernachtstraum'
	3	*Phlox paniculata* 'Landhochzeit'
	5	*Phlox paniculata* 'Sommerfreude'

Section of a narrow border along a garden fence. The front is bounded by a maintenance path made up of concrete paving slabs (40 × 40 cm and 40 × 60 cm). The planting is rhythmically structured with the same perennials repeated in different varieties and differently sized groups. The places for spring-flowering tulips and hyacinths are not illustrated. Pansies, myositis, wallflowers and daisies may all be set between the perennials but should be cleared away in early summer when they have finished flowering.

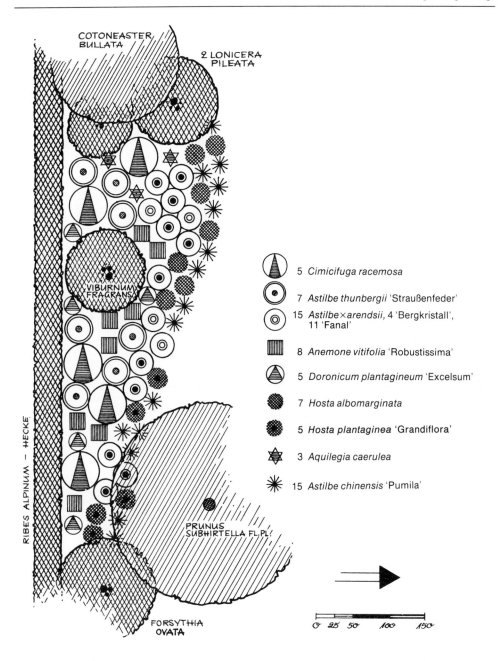

COTONEASTER BULLATA

2 LONICERA PILEATA

VIBURNUM FRAGRANS

RIBES ALPINUM – HECKE

PRUNUS SUBHIRTELLA FL.PL.

FORSYTHIA OVATA

5 *Cimicifuga racemosa*

7 *Astilbe thunbergii* 'Straußenfeder'

15 *Astilbe×arendsii*, 4 'Bergkristall', 11 'Fanal'

8 *Anemone vitifolia* 'Robustissima'

5 *Doronicum plantagineum* 'Excelsum'

7 *Hosta albomarginata*

5 *Hosta plantaginea* 'Grandiflora'

3 *Aquilegia caerulea*

15 *Astilbe chinensis* 'Pumila'

0 25 50   100   150

Border in front of a narrow hedge of medium height. Shade and semi-shade with moist, nutrient-rich soil, well supplied with humus. The chosen plants provide flowers from spring until autumn. Places for primroses, scillas and daffodils around the trees and shrubs are not illustrated.

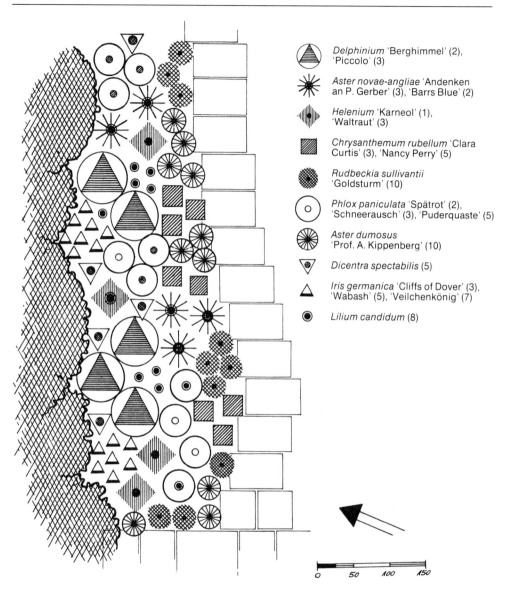

Delphinium 'Berghimmel' (2), 'Piccolo' (3)

Aster novae-angliae 'Andenken an P. Gerber' (3), 'Barrs Blue' (2)

Helenium 'Karneol' (1), 'Waltraut' (3)

Chrysanthemum rubellum 'Clara Curtis' (3), 'Nancy Perry' (5)

Rudbeckia sullivantii 'Goldsturm' (10)

Phlox paniculata 'Spätrot' (2), 'Schneerausch' (3), 'Puderquaste' (5)

Aster dumosus 'Prof. A. Kippenberg' (10)

Dicentra spectabilis (5)

Iris germanica 'Cliffs of Dover' (3), 'Wabash' (5), 'Veilchenkönig' (7)

Lilium candidum (8)

0   50   100   150

Planting of border perennials set in front of a shrubbery and bounded by concrete paving slabs (50 × 70 cm). The plants are all so placed that they dominate the border at flowering time. Autumn-flowering perennials have been set towards the front. Places for mid- and late-flowering garden tulips that liven up the planting in spring are not illustrated.

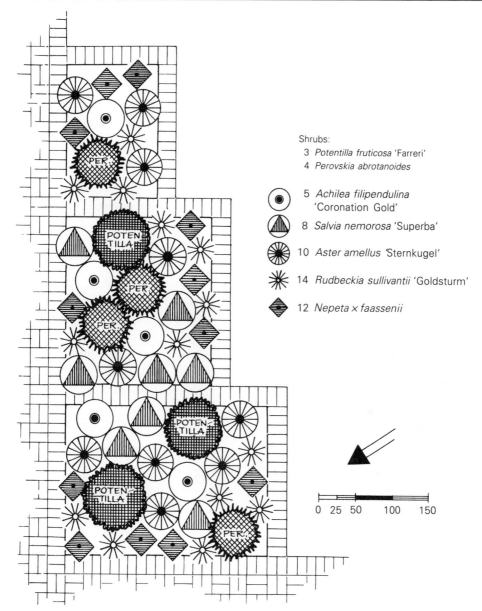

Shrubs:
  3 *Potentilla fruticosa* 'Farreri'
  4 *Perovskia abrotanoides*

  5 *Achilea filipendulina*
    'Coronation Gold'

  8 *Salvia nemorosa* 'Superba'

  10 *Aster amellus* 'Sternkugel'

  14 *Rudbeckia sullivantii* 'Goldsturm'

  12 *Nepeta × faassenii*

0 25 50   100   150

Planting on a hot, dry site, surrounded by brick paving (25 × 12 × 6.5 cm). The sub-shrubs give structure to the beds and are dominant in winter. Catmint (*Nepeta*) should be cut down after flowering to encourage an abundant second crop in autumn. Garden tulips, or some of the stately species hybrids, provide colour in spring.

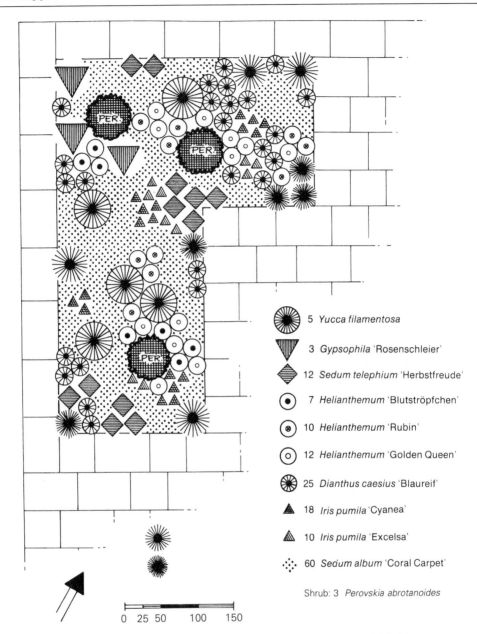

5 *Yucca filamentosa*

3 *Gypsophila* 'Rosenschleier'

12 *Sedum telephium* 'Herbstfreude'

7 *Helianthemum* 'Blutströpfchen'

10 *Helianthemum* 'Rubin'

12 *Helianthemum* 'Golden Queen'

25 *Dianthus caesius* 'Blaureif'

18 *Iris pumila* 'Cyanea'

10 *Iris pumila* 'Excelsa'

60 *Sedum album* 'Coral Carpet'

Shrub: 3 *Perovskia abrotanoides*

0   25 50   100   150

Planting in a sunny position on a concrete paved terrace (50 × 50 cm and 50 × 57 cm slabs). The yuccas, grasses and sub-shrubs (*Perowskia*), together with the red-brown stonecrop (*Sedum album*) give the planting a special character right through the year. Spring- and autumn-flowering wild crocus should be scattered in the *Sedum* carpet.

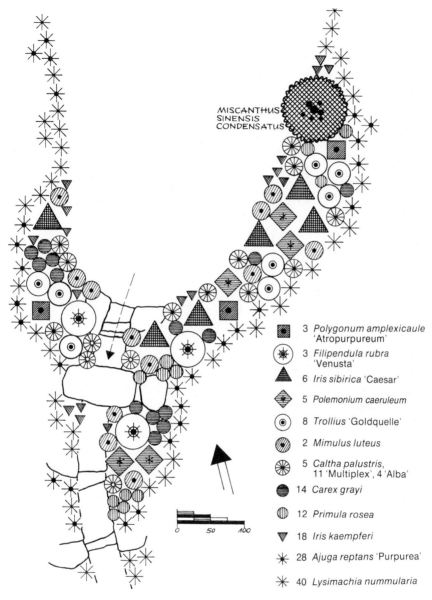

MISCANTHUS
SINENSIS
CONDENSATUS

	3	*Polygonum amplexicaule* 'Atropurpureum'
	3	*Filipendula rubra* 'Venusta'
	6	*Iris sibirica* 'Caesar'
	5	*Polemonium caeruleum*
	8	*Trollius* 'Goldquelle'
	2	*Mimulus luteus*
	5	*Caltha palustris*, 11 'Multiplex', 4 'Alba'
	14	*Carex grayi*
	12	*Primula rosea*
	18	*Iris kaempferi*
	28	*Ajuga reptans* 'Purpurea'
	40	*Lysimachia nummularia*

0   50   100

Streamside perennial planting on the banks of a garden pond and stream. Open, sunny position on permanently moist, retentive soil. Pond of puddled clay covered with sand and gravel. Water level flush with base of surrounding beds. Planting area dominated by specimen *Miscanthus*, and structure-giving tall perennials (*Iris sibirica*). Outer edges with bugle (*Ajuga reptans*) and pennywort (*Lysimachia*), which both tolerate mowing. Snowflakes (*Leucojum vernum* and *L. aestivum*) and snakeshead fritillaries (*Fritillaria meleagris*) would be suitable bulbs.

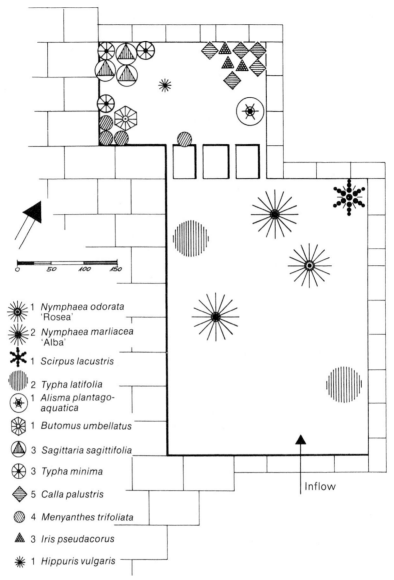

1 Nymphaea odorata 'Rosea'

2 Nymphaea marliacea 'Alba'

1 Scirpus lacustris

2 Typha latifolia

1 Alisma plantago-aquatica

1 Butomus umbellatus

3 Sagittaria sagittifolia

3 Typha minima

5 Calla palustris

4 Menyanthes trifoliata

3 Iris pseudacorus

1 Hippuris vulgaris

Inflow

Marsh- and water-plants in a sunny pool. The smaller basin (1.50 × 2.50 m) has a depth of 5–10 cm, suitable for marsh-plants. The large basin (3 × 4 m) has 30–50 cm of water intended for waterlilies. Reedmace (*Typha latifolia*), rushes (*Scirpus*) and other shallow-water plants can also be accommodated in containers. Fresh water enters via a pipe or small sculpture on the lower edge of the pool. The overflow into the small basin provides the marsh plants with water of an even temperature. The pool should remain full in winter.

Introducing perennials into existing vegetation

A simple way of introducing new perennials into an already established planting is to sow seed of species that are compatible with the existing vegetation. Wild-collected seed is very good for this purpose, provided it is not gathered indiscriminately. The coarse, easily handled seed of plants such as primroses and foxgloves is simpler to collect and sow than very fine seed, which must be rubbed from the spent flowers and is easily blown away by the wind. Sowing should take place as soon as possible after harvest, directly into the desired position within a planting or sparse area of lawn. No soil preparation is necessary. If the seed cannot be used at once then it should be stored in a cool place until the autumn.

The introduction of small flowering bulbs into gaps in the existing vegetation can also be recommended, especially in the neighbourhood of trees and shrubs (see list 2.4). Colonies of the desired plants may already be present in the garden and these can be lifted shortly before they die down in June. Bulbs must be stored in a warm, dry place as low temperatures can cause premature sprouting. They should be planted out again in autumn, preferably before leaf-fall.

The herbaceous layer in a park woodland deserves much more attention. Why shouldn't ferns, grasses and woodland flowers find a place here? Once these plants are established they need no maintenance other than some protection from animals and park visitors. All that is required is careful planning and a conscientious gardener, capable of dealing with the peculiarities of each site and the difficulties to be encountered in getting the plants established.

It certainly seems most sensible to start planting in places where there is no vegetation at all. There are few species that thrive under conditions of intense root competition, low light intensity and summer drought. In such places it is best to plant spring-flowering bulbs. Where the growing conditions are a little more friendly and the ground supports at least a sparse scattering of vegetation, small groups of perennials may be introduced. Digging brings many disadvantages in this context so the soil is merely loosened, taking care not to damage existing plants. Afterwards, the planting can be mulched with leaves and carefully tended until it is established.

Small perennials such as anemones, sweet woodruff, lungwort and primroses can be grown on in thin wooden boxes or fruit trays and planted out as a complete unit in a wooded area. In this way the new plants are not immediately subject to any competition and can gradually grow through the rotting wood to establish themselves in the surrounding soil. These units are easier to look after than scattered individual plants. A large planting of this sort needs much careful planning. The choice and propagation of species, together with the preparation of the boxes and choice of planting positions, all require careful deliberation.

The existing vegetation must always be taken into consideration. Wherever ground-elder (*Aegopodium podagraria*) is established, the ground is best left undisturbed and should on no account be dug over. Sometimes it is possible to plant the Florentine nettle (*Lamiastrum galeobdolon* 'Florentinum') to combat ground-elder. Experience at Weihenstephan has shown that the dense shoots of the nettle can smother the dreaded ground-elder and replace it in the course of time.

Garden enthusiasts will always discover new ways of enriching an old planting. Nevertheless, one should bear in mind that some plantings are more effective left just as they are.

The maintenance of perennial plantings

If we are to consider the garden as a living organism, with the gardener as one small part of the whole, then garden maintenance can no longer be regarded in the same light as tidying up the sitting room or polishing the new car. Nevertheless, prejudices abound: who will risk planting a tree which may gradually start to shade a neighbour's garden? And who dares to let their lawn develop into a flowering meadow, or to plant wild perennials, when their seed may start coming up next door? A whole arsenal of chemicals and equipment is now available to ensure that our gardens are kept tidy and all weeds are destroyed.

It should be clearly understood that a garden which is left entirely to itself will never develop an attractive and varied plant population, however well planned and constructed it may be. A garden requires maintenance. Even those plantings which, once established, hardly require attention cannot be excepted.

The maintenance of a public park mostly consists of protecting the vegetation from trampling, vandalism, theft and other environmental influences. In a garden, where the planting is more varied and ambitious, it is only by a process of continual observation and careful modification that a rational system of maintenance can be developed, often decreasing gradually as the years go by.

Of course, the maintenance of a perennial planting is largely dependent on the choice of species and the manner in which they are combined. We have therefore tried to arrange the perennials into lists of ecologically related species, which can be used in the creation of viable plant communities. As far as possible we have taken competitive ability into account and set particularly strong- or weak-growing species into lists on their own.

The maintenance of border perennials is clearly different from that of wild perennials. However, it should be borne in mind that an ecological planting requires as much attention as a formal border until the plants have grown together. A thoughtless combination of wild and border perennials demands a high and often unrealistic level of maintenance. Only the least invasive wild perennials, such as the wild perennials with border character or the clump-forming wild grasses, may be incorporated into a border planting.

Nutrient supply and care of the soil

Border plantings

The highly bred border perennials are adapted to grow in well-cultivated garden soil and demand an intensive soil maintenance if they are to do their best. The soil crusting that comes from long periods of drought, and the compaction resulting from heavy rainfall or inexpert watering must both be prevented by repeated loosening of the soil surface between plants. The bed itself should not be trodden, for this brings the danger of gradually increasing compaction at deeper levels. In view of this it is advisable to plan a maintenance path or system of stepping stones into the border right from the start. These should be made as inconspicuous as possible and so constructed that every part of the border is easily brought within reach.

Care should be taken when loosening the soil to prevent damage to plant roots. Digging should be avoided wherever possible, and can only be recommended between large and robust perennials.

Especial care is needed wherever bulbs and tubers are present in the ground. Digging is the cause of much unnecessary damage in late autumn and spring when tender shoots are still invisible underground. Nevertheless, a shallow going-over with a fork or grubber during the dormant season when the plants are cut down can be good for the soil and produces an attractive finish to the bed.

A convenient way of keeping the soil open and combatting weeds at the same time is mulching. The ground must be loose and well weeded before any mulch is applied. A compost formed from the woody parts of plants is very suitable for the purpose and may be brought out in autumn or spring. Coarse, fibrous peat is another useful material. It retains its elasticity in spite of heavy rain, thus remaining light and porous over a long period. A mulch decays slowly, helping to improve soil structure and providing valuable humus to the ground. Under its protective mantle weeds are kept down and the earth stays moist. Soil temperature and the exchange of air and water are all well regulated, allowing beneficial soil organisms to thrive in the uppermost layers.

Fresh lawn clippings often contain seed of such weeds as daisies and annual poa, making them unsuitable as a mulch for border perennials. It is far better to let dry clippings decay on the compost heap before use. Unfortunately, even compost is often full of viable seed. Where space allows it is therefore advisable to maintain a separate heap of seed-free material for use as a mulch and fertiliser. The remaining compost can be of valuable service mixed into the soil in preparation for a new planting.

The level of nutrients available to perennials in a border planting depends largely on the condition of the soil. A loose, well-cultivated soil is the best source of nutrients and helps to promote vigorous growth. Nevertheless, the overall reserves must occasionally be topped up with the aid of a suitable fertiliser. Different species have different requirements in this respect. Some perennials respond well to an application of fertiliser, whereas others may be damaged or else react with uncharacteristic patterns of growth. All such cases have been dealt with in the lists.

In a garden with good loamy soil, where dead and cut down material is all composted and returned to the beds, it should hardly be necessary to use a fertiliser. Compost works wonders in a planting of perennials. The careless use of some fertilisers can cause drastic fluctuations in soil chemistry, but compost cannot do damage in this way. Plants do not grow unnaturally lush or tall but develop a strong and sturdy habit, increased resistance to disease and an exceptional abundance and beauty of flower.

None the less, some of the more highly selected and demanding border perennials occasionally require an additional fertiliser, especially where the soil is poor. Organic, or mixed organic and artificial fertilisers are best for this purpose. Great care is required in the use of purely artificial fertilisers, especially on light, sandy soils where bulky, peat-based products are more suitable and safer to use.

The chosen fertiliser should be scattered evenly on the open soil between plants. The amount can easily be calculated from the manufacturer's recommendations. Peat-based fertilisers also provide a mulch for the soil and should be spread out to a depth of two or three centimetres. Other recommended organic fertilisers are hoof and horn, bonemeal and dried blood. All decompose relatively slowly, giving an even and lasting effect. An approximate application rate is 80–100 g/m².

If a purely artificial fertiliser is the only product available, it should be spread carefully between plants, with due regard for its corrosive properties and easy solubility. The normal rate is 50 g/m². A single application in rainy weather at the start of the growing season is usually sufficient for the whole year. With a bit of extra effort a quick-acting liquid fertiliser may also be made up for use as a top-dressing through the season.

Animal fertilisers, sewage and liquid manure should never be used in their fresh form. All should first be made into compost combined with earth and peat. With increasing experience, one begins to appreciate that fertilisers can have negative as well as positive effects. This applies particularly to their use in ecological plantings.

Ecological plantings

Wild perennials require a different sort of maintenance. In contrast to border perennials, they mostly form a closed groundcover within a few years. An ecological planting can only develop satisfactorily if the ground is free of perennial weeds. Annual weed species must be removed during the first year after planting. By the second year, when the ground is well covered, they will no longer be a problem, reappearing only if the soil is broken with a hoe or spade. Thereafter, maintenance consists largely in the removal of unwanted perennial seedlings and control of weeds under the motto: 'a weed is a plant growing in the wrong place'. Total neglect can lead to a reduction in the variety of species, as vigorous seedlings gradually crowd out their less robust neighbours. Nevertheless, a true ecological planting changes its appearance from year to year, and it is precisely this uncontrolled and spontaneous element that constitutes its special charm.

The particular maintenance requirements of wild perennials for different habitats are dealt with in the lists. The success of many woodland and some woodland edge plants, for example, is dependent on the carpet of leaves spread annually over the ground in autumn, rotting gradually to form a loose and humus-rich soil. Many woodland perennials thrive in leafmould and compost. Others prefer compost mixed with the acidic needle litter from coniferous woodland. Mulching with coarse peat can have a harmful effect in an ecological planting because it interferes with the desired germination and development of self-sown seedlings.

Some cultivars of woodland plants may need an annual application of fertiliser. Organic products are to be preferred but where these are not available an artificial fertiliser may be used at about two thirds the rate of application normally used. Astilbes do not tolerate cow manure and should be given well-rotted horse manure instead.

Depending on the situation and type of planting, wild perennials for open habitats also require occasional applications of compost and other nutrients. The maintenance of flowering meadows and perennial groundcover is covered under lists 3.1.1. and 3.2.1.

Rock garden perennials hardly need fertilisers if the initial planting soil is good. Wherever growth is unsatisfactory it is better to replace the soil than to add nutrients. The great variety and beauty of alpine plants is at least partly due to the many different types of poor, stony or peaty soil where they are found. It is more important to keep the soil around young plants open and free of weeds than to give potentially damaging applications of fertiliser. The cultivars in list 4.1 may be encouraged by an occasional top-dressing of soil mixed with compost in spring or autumn. Wild species too can sometimes benefit from the same treatment.

With the exception of some of the more delicate enthusiasts' plants, marsh and water perennials require very little in the way of either maintenance or fertilisers. If the initial planting soil is well prepared then additional nutrients are usually unnecessary. Fertilisers should at any rate be avoided in garden ponds, where they are the cause of undesirable algal growth.

Care of the soil and the application of nutrients are both means by which we can help to give perennials a healthy and balanced environment in which their optimal growth is assured. Our purpose has been achieved when the individual plants of a community no longer just appear to be attractively combined, but start to grow together into a living unit. Such units are never completely stable, however, and a certain amount of further maintenance is required in order to retain the balance.

'Weeds' and the long-term development of a planting

The steady and unending process of development in the plant life of a garden is a phenomenon that never ceases to amaze. In nature, a few mostly rather short-lived species appear in masses wherever the ground is disturbed, making way later for perennial plants via the different stages of botanical succession. Our plantings could benefit greatly from the use of such pioneer species in preparing the way for a mature plant community. However, on the whole, we must be content to lay out the desired perennials right from the start in a species-rich planting, arranged as naturally as possible to improve the long-term chances of success.

In a purely decorative garden the aim is to prevent all change and development by means of intensive maintenance. Plants are kept in well-defined beds to confine their spread; shrubs are regularly pruned and perennials are continually divided and renewed. Nevertheless, the balance subtly changes. Some plants succeed in spreading while other grow old and weak, or even disappear entirely. In a more natural garden the purpose of any maintenance is to ensure that the plantings remain attractive and more or less self-regulating. This strategy can only succeed if the initial steps are well thought out and the right perennials chosen for each planting position.

Experience shows that wherever an ecological planting is well adapted to its garden habitat, the spontaneously occuring weeds often fit so well into the existing plant community that they do not detract from its appearance in any way. Such plants need only be removed if they threaten to squeeze out their neighbours.

In Weihenstephan we take delight in several such intruders, which could not be tolerated in an ornamental border planting. Here and there herb Robert (*Geranium robertianum*), and the long flowering wood forget-me-not peep out from between the woodland edge perennials. Lesser celandines with lush green leaves flower in bright yellow splashes under the trees; by July they have disappeared again without trace. In April the little white-flowered crucifer *Cardamine hirsuta* blooms in the rock-garden and vanishes again by the end of May. Like the dainty, brown-leaved, yellow sorrel (*Oxalis corniculata*), which flowers in summer, it cannot be said to cause much harm. Ground-ivy, bugle and some of the speedwells are similar: where necessary they can all be removed before becoming a nuisance. If the soil around plants is kept open then seedlings from some garden perennials may also start to appear. However, this is a (for the most part) welcome exception rather than the rule.

Unfortunately, there are a few very troublesome weed species such as dandelions, thistles, docks and bindweed, whose roots go deep and must be dug out in their entirety. Removal of the aerial parts is of no use here because the severed roots grow on and produce a new crop of leaves. The most dangerous weeds of all are without a doubt couch grass, ground-elder and creeping yellow-cress (*Rorippa sylvestris*). Introduced with other plants or invading from the edge of a bed, their long rhizomes quickly penetrate through the entire planting, infiltrating the rootstocks of ornamental plants and becoming irretrievably entangled. Once established, these weeds are particularly difficult to control. If they are not detected and dealt with at their first appearance, they eventually form a dense mat of weed in which all other perennials are condemned to perish. Once things have got to this stage the only remedy is drastic action. Every plant must be lifted and divided to remove entangled roots. The soil must then be thoroughly cleared of all remains or, better still, replaced in its entirety.

Occasionally, various rhizomatous grasses can become troublesome when they start to get established inside the crown of a plant. The first signs of any such 'grassing-up' should be taken seriously. Later on the plants become impossible to separate without lifting.

The invasion of rhizomatous weed species from the edge of a planting can be effectively prevented by an underground barrier of doubled roofing-felt or concrete slabs 40 cm deep. The boundary to a lawn is best secured by laying concrete or stone paving along the edge of the bed.

A completely neglected planting changes more or less rapidly into a wilderness of nettles, ground-elder or couch grass. Invaders such as these should be removed from plantings as a matter of course. However, we should not destroy every weed that spontaneously occurs in an unused part of the garden. Stinging nettles, for instance, are the unique food plant for the caterpillars of several beautiful butterflies, including peacocks, red admirals and the small tortoiseshell. These species depend on stinging nettles for their survival. Some gardeners might even consider helping them by cutting back the old plants in June to promote a flush of growth suitable for egg-laying.

It is high time for some of the more beautiful native wildflowers to be given a place in our gardens. Many of them can give that special character to our plantings which has been lost from the ruined landscape around towns and cities. Native plants are indispensable to many insects

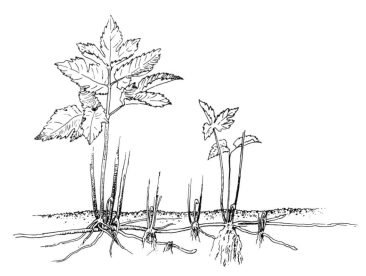

Ground elder (*Aegopodium podagraria*). This woodland umbellifer first appears under shrubs if it has not been introduced with other plants. Infested perennials should be removed at once.

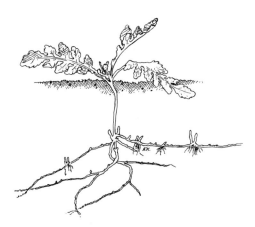

Creeping yellow cress (*Rorippa sylvestris*). Care must be exercised wherever these plants start to appear. Tiny fragments of root can develop into dangerous weeds, especially on damp, loamy soils. Even very small plants must be dug out with a large root ball.

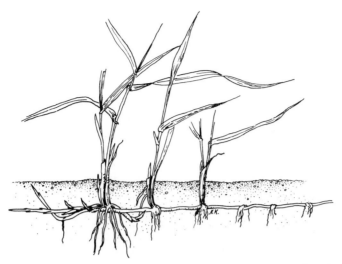

Couch grass (*Agropyron repens*). The long rhizomes of this grass must be dug out with a fork wherever they appear. Every piece of root should be carefully removed.

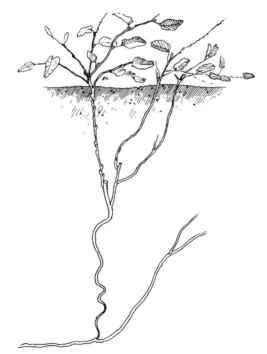

Bindweed (*Convolvulus arvensis*). A deep-rooted perennial weed that is hard to eradicate completely. Plants can be weakened by continual cutting back and removal of the tap roots. They thrive in full sun and are discouraged by a dense, shady groundcover. If they are strongly established, the only remedy may be to convert the area to lawn.

such as flies, beetles, wasps and bees, and these in turn provide food for many birds. The use and maintenance of native species requires considerable knowledge and understanding. Their special attraction is often not immediately obvious but first makes itself felt in a well-established garden.

Cutting back perennials

Cutting back has an important function in the life-cycle of many perennials. We can distinguish between a purely cosmetic cut, designed to preserve the orderly appearance of a bed, and a regenerative cut. The latter leads to an increase in vigour and life-expectancy, repetition or intensification of flowering and improved resistance to disease and the weather. It is particularly well demonstrated in the case of dwarf shrubs, for which the secateurs can sometimes do more good than any fertiliser.

A cosmetic cut is required by all those perennials (particularly border plants) which become unsightly after flowering. In addition, many of them, like tulips, daffodils, hyacinths and lilies, benefit from not having to set seed. Highly selected border perennials must be cut back after the main flowering to prevent them seeding into their own crowns, where new plants may slowly get established. Such seedlings are seldom true to type but often more vigorous than the mother plant. In time, they grow up and displace the original cultivar. Border phlox (*Phlox paniculata*), spiderwort (*Tradescantia × andersoniana*) and other long-lived perennials are particularly prone to this sequence of events. Trials have established that some old delphinium cultivars have already been replaced by their seedlings in this way.

In other cases, self-sown seedlings can greatly enrich a garden. One need only think of the colourful progeny of *Aquilegia*, *Thalictrum* and *Polemonium* species, or the varied hybrids that grow up between different *Ligularias*. In our experience, the late summer- and autumn-flowering border perennials remain uncommonly beautiful long after they have finished flowering. The combination of their brown tones with the blooms of late-flowering annual plants makes a colourful and evocative display, powerfully expressing the mood of autumn. No-one would think of cutting down such a planting until the first hard frosts have arrived.

Perennials may be divided into those that may be cut right down to the ground after flowering and those for which dead-heading may prolong the period of bloom. Several important spring- and summer-flowering perennials belong to the first group. Delphiniums, for instance, should be cut down after flowering to within a hand's breadth of the soil to ensure a good second crop of flowers in late summer. The same applies to the following species:

Mountain cornflower	*Centaurea montana* 'Grandiflora'
Pyrethrum	*Chrysanthemum coccineum*
Fleabane	*Erigeron* hybrids
Lupin	*Lupinus* hybrids (leaves should remain)
Catmint	*Nepeta × faassenii* etc
Salvia	*Salvia nemorosa*

By contrast, the following plants benefit especially from dead-heading:

Achillea filipendulina 'Parker's Variety'
Removal of the large central flower head promotes the development of secondary flower heads.

Heliopsis spp.
Dead-heading prolongs the flowering period to an extraordinary degree.

Scabiosa caucasica
The removal of spent flowering stems can produce a flowering season from June to November.

Stachys byzantina
The mat of silvery leaves degenerates if flower heads are not removed.

Chrysanthemum maximum
Stronger and more numerous shoots are produced for the next season if the old stems are cut down early.

The lifespan of a whole range of short-lived, normally biennial species can be prolonged by several years if they are cut down after flowering. Unlimited seed production saps their strength and leads to death. If the flower heads are removed before seed starts to set, the plants are frustrated in their life's purpose, thus stimulating them to renewed shoot production and a further year of flowering. This having been said, it is often much more exciting to let the plants seed themselves after all! The following species belong to this type:

Hollyhock	*Alcea rosea*
Golden marguerite	*Anthemis tinctoria*
Sweet rocket	*Hesperis matronalis*
Dusty miller	*Lychnis coronaria*
Iceland poppy	*Papaver nudicaule*
	Anchusa italica (Cut back right to the roots, 1–2 cm under the soil surface.)

A similar situation occurs with perennials that flower themselves to exhaustion and are consequently unable to form buds for the following year's shoots. To prevent this happening, the whole plant should be cut back in early autumn to stimulate vegetative growth. Such prolifically flowering perennials include:

Coreopsis	*Coreopsis grandiflora* 'Badengold'
	Coreopsis lanceolata
Blanket flower	*Gaillardia aristata*
Red valerian	*Centranthus ruber*
Shasta daisy	*Chrysanthemum maximum*

Where required, the flowering time of some summer and autumn perennials can be delayed by cutting at the appropriate season. The stems are shortened by 10–15 cm when the flower buds start to form. In this way, the flowering of border phlox, *Helenium* and asters can be put off for several weeks. If just a few stems are so treated then the flowering is prolonged at the cost of its usual abundance.

Perennials with woody stems, correctly known as dwarf and sub-shrubs, must be cut back to about a hand's width whenever they start to die back or grow leggy. Examples are:

Ling (*Calluna vulgaris* cvs.).
Every year in spring by intensive maintenance; otherwise every 3–5 years.

Spring heath (*Erica herbacea*).
Very occasionally, after flowering.

Rock rose (*Helianthemum* spp. and cvs.).
Every 2–3 years, after flowering.

Rose of Sharon (*Hypericum calycinum*).
Annually in spring.

*Lavender (*Lavandula* spp. and cvs.)
Every 2–3 years, in spring (inflorescences annually).

*Perovskia (*Perovskia* spp.).
Annually in spring.

Cotton lavender (*Santolina* spp.).
Every 2–3 years.

*Germander (*Teucrium* spp.).
Annually in spring.

Thyme (*Thymus* spp.).
Every 3 years in spring.

Those species marked with an asterisk tolerate regular cutting so well that they can even be used in low, formal hedging. Such features are especially beautiful at flowering time.

Border perennials are finally cut down to the ground in late autumn so that the soil between can be broken up or lightly dug over. Wild perennials are better left standing until the spring. The more one comes to know these plants the more pleasure one discovers in observing them, even when their flowering is finished. The fruiting heads of *Eryngium, Anaphalis* and *Limonium* species are especially beautiful when placed in the right setting. Many grasses bear attractive fruits and stems. These are best removed in late winter, before they start to clash with the arrival of spring.

Protection in winter

The care and maintenance of a perennial planting includes its protection against the inclemencies of winter. If a species is described as hardy, then it is primarily frost-hardiness which is implied. This means that, under normal conditions of growth, the plants can put up with the usual winter cold of our climate without being damaged. It does not follow that they are immune to other climatic evils such as a mild, wet autumn and early winter, harsh frosts with bright sunshine in the absence of snow, or persistent drying winds. The unpredictability of our weather makes it advisable to protect certain perennials in winter, particularly those whose frost-hardiness is in question. These species are referred to in the lists of enthusiasts' plants or have sometimes been given a separate list on their own (e.g. lists 3.3.5 and 5.6).

Perennials with dense tufts of foliage, such as *Kniphofia, Yucca* and the larger clump-forming grasses, can be loosely bound together and mounded up with leaves. Other plants that respond well to a deep, loose covering of leaves are:

Japanese anemone	*Anemone* Japonica hybrids
Perennial sunflower	*Helianthus atrorubens*
Giant reed	*Arundo donax*

In addition, various evergreen and semi-evergreen perennials sometimes need protection for their exposed shoots, leaves and rosettes. This is particularly so for rock garden plants, which often miss the persistent snow cover of an alpine winter. The best protection for all perennials in winter is an even, 10–20 cm layer of dry snow over a lightly frozen soil. For frost-hardy evergreen perennials and alpine plants it is sufficient when they are thinly covered with overlapping branches of Norway spruce. These should be fastened down at the edge to prevent the whole lot flying away in a storm.

All new plantings appreciate some degree of protection in their first winter. A loose covering of conifer branches is normally sufficient. The same applies to freshly planted bulbs and tubers, particularly if they are set out late in the year and do not have time to make proper roots. In Europe protection of this kind helps curb the activities of blackbirds whose industrious search for food disturbs the soil and muddies the path around a bed. Conifer branches should not be brought out too early in the year, but after the frosts have set in around Christmas. Norway spruce (*Picea abies*) is to be preferred to fir (*Abies alba*). Spruce needles tend to drop off towards the end of winter, so allowing the plants to adapt again slowly to full daylight and an unprotected existence. The premature emergence of frost-sensitive shoots is thus avoided.

The winter protection of perennials should not be overdone. When cushion plants are buried under a great mound of twigs, they will grow soft and start to rot. All coverings must be removed in spring. A few sprays should nevertheless be kept on one side for use against late frosts. The following species have shoots that are particularly sensitive to late frosts:

Bleeding hearts	*Dicentra spectabilis*
Fox-tail lily	*Eremurus* spp.
Regal lily	*Lilium regale*
Rodgersia	*Rodgersia* spp.
Plume poppy	*Macleaya* spp.

and, to a lesser extent:

Astilbe	*Astilbe* spp.
Japanese anemone	*Anemone* Japonica hybrids
Siberian bugloss	*Brunnera macrophylla*
Bugbane	*Cimicifuga* spp.
Delphinium	*Delphinium* spp.
Hosta, plantain lily	*Hosta* spp.

An early frost at the end of September or beginning of October can also be an unpleasant surprise, causing damage to the following perennials:

Japanese anemone	*Anemone* Japonica hybrids
Hardy plumbago	*Ceratostigma plumbaginoides*
Arctic daisy	*Chrysanthemum arcticum*
Garden chrysanthemum	*Chrysanthemum × hortorum*
Bugbane	*Cimicifuga simplex*

If the first frosts come early in the year, it is worth preparing a few cardboard boxes, sacks or plastic covers to protect autumn-flowering plants from the worst of the cold. By careful attention to the weather forecast their flowering can be prolonged by several weeks with a minimum of effort.

Of course, local peculiarities of climate, soil and topography can lead to very different opinions concerning hardiness. The surest conclusions can be thrown into doubt when damage occurs unexpectedly after years of successful culture and careful observation. Such surprises are often the result of several factors coming together in a single growing season. Perennials are living creatures, reacting sensitively to every influence from their environment. We should not think less of them just because they are subject to the normal ups and downs of life.

Pests and diseases

In common with other plants, perennials (especially border perennials) are occasionally subject to pests and diseases. Particularly feared are the fungal wilts and mildews that affect Michaelmas daisies (*Aster novi-belgii*), and the eelworms that attack the stems of border phlox (*Phlox paniculata*). Similar problems turn up among fleabanes (*Erigeron* spp.), *Aster amellus* and *Sedum* species. Now and then peonies exhibit distinctive yellow blotches on their leaves, a tell-tale sign of virus infection. A different virus leads to crippling of the flower stalks in lupins. Plants affected by any of these pests and diseases should be removed immediately, together with as much of their roots as possible. The variety of garden perennials is so great that we can well do without such poorly individuals. Often there are very similar species or cultivars which we can use instead. *Aster novi-belgii*, for instance, can be replaced by the invariably healthy *A. novæ-angliae*. The especially recommended phlox cultivars in list 5.3.4 have all proved fairly resistant to eelworm, and the delphiniums selected by Karl Foerster (list 5.2.1) are immune to mildew.

Suitable growing conditions are the most important factor contributing to a plant's good health. If Christmas roses and hepaticas are planted in an acid soil, they will soon become diseased. The same goes for lupins growing in strongly alkaline conditions. On the other hand, it may sometimes be difficult to do completely without chemical assistance. The lily enthusiast is unlikely to forsake the use of fungicides when it comes to protecting a stock of precious bulbs.

The worst animal pests are mice and voles, whose natural enemies such as weasels and hedgehogs are often missing from a garden. They may be controlled with special traps or poison baits. Canisters with smoke or poison gas are also available in the trade and if these are placed in as many holes as possible then they too effect a temporary end to the problem.

In a wet year considerable damage can be inflicted by slugs and snails. The use of slug bait should be avoided where possible because their natural predators such as toads and hedgehogs can also be poisoned in this way. Either the pests must be picked off individually or the plants must be changed. Slug-prone hostas, for example, can often be replaced by *Peltiphyllum peltatum* or *Rodgersia* species.

The rich animal and bird life in a near-natural garden can be of advantage in some respects. However, rabbits, hares and occasionally even deer can all cause considerable damage and it is advisable to screen off endangered areas with wire netting in autumn. European blackbirds can be very troublesome when they start picking around in the beds. Sparrows sometimes tear up crocus flowers, and pigeons do the same to tulips.

All such problems are not to be compared with the epidemics that sometimes break out in nurseries. The chemical sprays and powders which are then employed in order to rescue valuable crops do not belong in a private garden. Exceptions ought perhaps to be made for the treatment of stem aphids on *Aconitum* species and ox-eye daisies, or for dealing with an attack of the lily beetle. However, it should be borne in mind that the use of any insecticide is likely to kill off the natural predators (e.g. ladybirds) of the pests concerned. It is always worth considering whether the same ends cannot be achieved by purely mechanical means, such as manual removal of the troublemakers or cutting back infected plants, before upsetting the ecological balance of a garden with chemical sprays that destroy many useful insects and contribute to the emergence of resistant strains of pest.

Maintenance calendar for the herbaceous border

In contrast to wild perennials, the highly selected border perennials require regular intensive maintenance throughout their lifetime in order to remain healthy and develop to their full beauty. The drawings on the following pages are designed to illustrate the more substantial maintenance operations on a herbaceous border in the course of a year. At the same time, they are intended to give some impression of the growth, flowering and decay that constitutes the annual cycle of development in a perennial planting.

The plants have been so arranged that the bed remains tidy and presentable throughout the growing season. At the front of the planting are midsummer- and autumn-flowering species, including the theme perennials, and a scattering of plants for early summer. Behind them, between the maintenance path and the hedge, are the spring-flowering species. Tulips, together with the other bulbs, corms and tubers, are distributed throughout the border, forming the main attraction early in the year and contributing also to the summer and autumn display. Crocuses extend the early spring flowering into the adjoining lawn.

The total width of the border, including maintenance path, is 3.7 m. The hedge at the back is regularly cut and gives the planting its structural anchor. For reasons of clarity the roots of perennial plants have been omitted. Bulbs, corms and tubers, on the other hand, have been included to illustrate their seasonal growth.

The cross-section has been simplified by ignoring the staggered and overlapping arrangement of plant groups in a real border. Only the most significant maintenance tools have been illustrated. Hose, watering can and secateurs are all taken for granted.

Occasional measures for the control of pests and diseases have been omitted from the text.

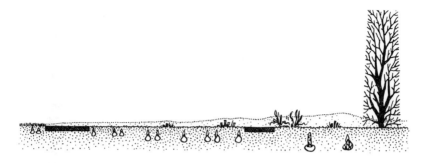

February

Late winter: the ground is cold or frozen. From time to time, snow covers the border, melting slowly as the sun gains strength. Everything appears dormant but beneath the ground the bulbs and tubers of the earliest spring flowers are beginning to put out shoots. As yet there is nothing to do.

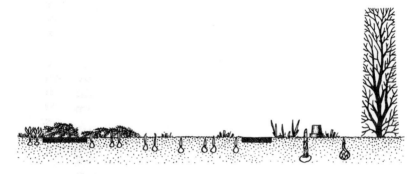

March–April

The first spring flowers begin to appear. If the border has been covered for the winter with leaves or conifer branches, these should now be removed. A few branches can be kept for use on cold nights to protect the sensitive shoots of early plants such as bleeding hearts. Sackcloth, plastic sheeting and (especially for lilies) flower pots also make suitable covers. Any ornamental grasses should now be combed out or cut back, and all dead and dying foliage (e.g. *Iris*) removed. Weeds must be pulled out and the soil loosened, taking care not to disturb any bulbs.

April–May

The earliest flowers are fading and the main spring bloom is getting underway. All covering materials may now be discarded. Weeds must be removed and the soil carefully loosened without damaging the bulbs. A mulch of coarse peat or compost-based fertiliser may be applied. The nutrient supply must be replenished using a suitable fertiliser. During long dry periods the border should be thoroughly watered.

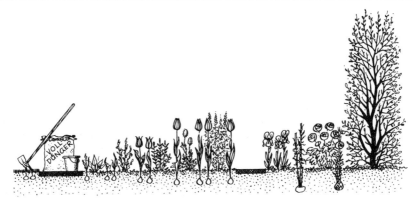

May–June

Spring flowers still dominate the planting as the early summer perennials start to bloom. The old leaves and seed-heads of spent flowers (early tulip, crown imperials) should be cut away to prevent seeding except where this is desired (e.g. winter aconites, snowdrops and scillas in front of the hedge). The soil must be kept open and free of weeds. Any mulch that has been applied, may need thickening up in places. Water and fertilisers should be applied as necessary.

June–July

The spring flowers are over and the interval between these and the main summer display is covered by the early summer perennials. The yellowed leaves and seed-heads of spent spring flowers should be removed. Bulbs, corms and tubers should not be cut down too early but allowed to die back properly. The main stems of plants liable to wind damage (delphiniums, hollyhocks) should be individually staked (not bundled together!) with proper regard for their natural habit. Running maintenance consists of weeding, loosening the soil and periodic fertilising. Irrigation is necessary during dry weather and plants should be quickly sprayed over in the early morning or late afternoon (never at midday) when it is hot.

They are seldom of great importance and are not normally confined to the treatment of perennial plants. The local influences of site and climate make it impossible to give a precise illustration for each month of the year. A seasonal range, applicable to western Europe but adaptable for most north temperate regions, is therefore given for each stage in the sequence. Annual variations in the weather can have a particularly strong influence on the length of flowering in autumn.

Finally, a piece of good advice: as can be seen from the illustrations, border perennials require especially intensive maintenance in the summer months. Those who go on holiday during this period should not forget to leave their borders in skilled and loving hands! Wild perennials need hardly any attention at this time of year.

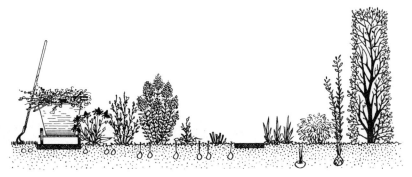

July–August

The summer-flowering perennials reach their climax. The foliage of early summer perennials dies down quickly, and should now be cut away, along with what remains of the spring plants. Dead flowers must be continually removed to prevent seed setting. Plants that bloom a second time in autumn (fleabane, delphinium, globeflower) should be cut down immediately after their main flowering, to within a hand's breadth of the ground. This promotes the formation of new shoots. Staking continues. The soil must be kept open and free of weeds. Irrigation and spraying should not be forgotten when necessary. No more fertilisers should be applied, allowing the plants to harden off for winter.

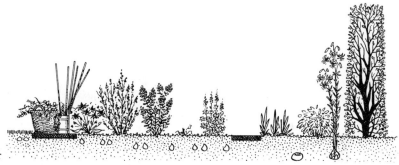

August–September

At the height of the late summer bloom, the first autumn perennials begin to flower. The yellowing foliage and spent flowers of summer perennials must be cut back to prevent seed setting. Staking continues (sunflowers, tall coneflowers). Regular soil cultivation, weeding and irrigation all remain necessary. No fertilisers.

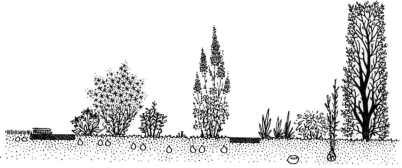

September–October

The late summer display passes seamlessly into that of autumn. Some of the early summer perennials (see July) are now flowering for a second time. Plants should be staked where necessary. The summer perennials are cut back as they die down, and spent autumn blooms are removed to promote flowering on side stems. Occasional weeds are no longer a menace. Irrigation is only necessary in a very dry autumn. Protective covers (sacking, towels, plastic sheeting, packing paper) should now be prepared to guard the autumn display against early frosts, and it is important to pay attention to the weather forecast.

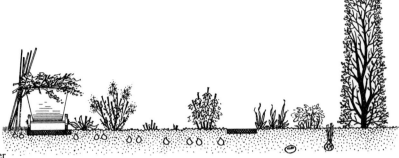

October–November

A few late blooms prolong the display during mild weather. The rest of the late summer and autumn perennials die back slowly and should be cut down to ground level. Protection of the last few flowers against frost can greatly prolong the display with a minimum of effort.

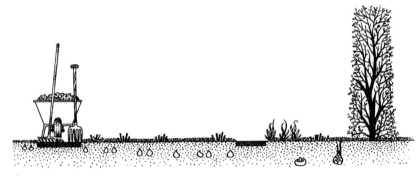

November–December

All growth and flowering has come to an end and the border now enters its dormant phase. Plants gather strength for the next season. Now is the time to replenish the supply of humus and make long-term improvements to the soil. First, old stems must be cut off at ground level and removed. Only grasses and evergreen rosette- and tussock-forming perennials (e.g. red-hot pokers) remain uncut. All weeds are removed and the soil between plants is carefully loosened with a fork or spade (avoiding all roots and bulbs). The soil should be left in coarse lumps; if raked down it will puddle and compact over winter. Without covering the plants themselves, a 4–5 cm layer of coarse compost, leaves, peat or a mixture of these should then be spread across the border to provide humus for the soil. Improvements to a sandy or clayey soil can be undertaken in the same way. If the ground is dry then it is advisable to water deeply one more time, especially among the roots of trees and shrubs, or along a house wall. Frost-sensitive perennials receive their winter protection of leaves or peat held down with conifer branches. Grasses and other perennials with grassy tussocks can be bound together and packed around with insulating materials. It is not necessary to cover the entire planting in winter, though it may be advisable where birds constantly tear up the soil and muddy the paths. Winter protection should only be put out once the cold weather has set in. Finally, do not forget to turn off the water and drain all outside pipes and hoses.

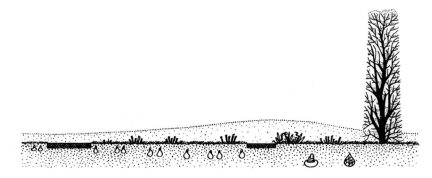

January

The cycle of seasons comes to an end. Snow sometimes covers the border, giving plants the best possible protection against the cold. Woody plants and grasses still reveal the framework of the planting. Everything appears dead, but hidden away beneath the ground early spring-flowering bulbs, corms and tubers are already forming shoots whenever the weather is mild.

Work on the border is finished. Now is the time to clean and mend garden tools, ordering them neatly so that everything is ready to hand when spring returns.

Perennials in their garden habitats

Perennials will thrive under many different conditions, provided only that they are kept free from competition. Apart from alpine and wetland plants, and a few other species with particularly specialised growing requirements, the perennials that are listed here under the various garden habitats will all grow perfectly well on an intensively maintained bed in full sun. These unnatural, growth-promoting conditions are essential when it comes to raising plants commercially. However, with the exception of the border perennials and wild perennials with border character, all of these plants can contribute far more to our parks and gardens when they are set within a community of ecologically similar species in conditions that are appropriate to their wild nature. Only so can they fulfil their purpose without the need for intensive maintenance.

All the herbaceous perennials currently available in the trade can be assigned to one (or sometimes two) of the many subdivisions within the main garden habitats: woodland, woodland edge, open ground, rock garden, border, marsh and water's edge, and water. The three stages in planning a herbaceous planting are as follows:

(1) Recognition of the garden habitat represented at the planting site.
(2) Choice of correct species list for the precise conditions.
(3) Selection of perennials from the list to create an attractive and viable plant community.

It can sometimes be just as difficult to evaluate a planting site as it is to set limits on the garden habitat for some perennial species. Transitional areas are especially problematic in a small garden.

Possible companions for the different plant communities are mentioned in the text at the head of each list. Some perennials have a wide range of tolerance, and if particular species are suitable for more than one set of conditions then this too is recorded.

The following short description of the various garden habitats may help in selecting the right lists for a planting.

The different garden habitats

The first of the garden habitats to be dealt with is not the popular and widespread perennial border (lists 5.1–5.7) but **woodland**, which forms an important structural element and is the natural end-point of the vegetational development in wild parts of the garden. The term 'woodland' is used here in a broad sense, including even the small area dominated by a single tree or shrub. The first few lists deal with shade-tolerant species for use in a newly laid out garden. These are followed by plants requiring mature woodland conditions. The remaining lists contain perennials for special situations.

The **woodland edge** is intimately connected with woodland proper. Plants that thrive under the protection of overhanging branches, or that are otherwise confined to the woodland edge, are covered first. After these come lists of perennials that are more loosely associated with woodland, together with species for special situations, and flowering bulbs.

Open ground is land away from the influence of trees, though in certain situations shrubs may still be present. Plants suitable for low groundcover, flowering meadows and dry grassland are followed here by lists for more or less extreme situations and damp areas.

The **rock garden** has some features in common with open ground but nevertheless forms a special habitat of its own. The most widespread and well known species of the formal, decorative rock garden are listed first, followed by plants for general use, enthusiasts' plants, and species for shade and other special conditions.

Border plants include all the popular ornamental perennials and large bulbs that require an open, cultivated soil for their growth. They have been loosely classified according to their ecological character, or that of their original wild ancestors. However, many of them can be used decoratively in a wide range of different garden situations. The traditional and often symbolic culinary herbs and medicinal plants of the old rural herb gardens are treated in a section of their own.

Perennials that belong to **marshland and water's edge** and those that grow in **water** are all listed according to their special requirements and tendency to spread. A separate list deals with plants for normal soil in the vicinity of a pond.

Plants selected from a single list (or in some cases from several) and cleverly arranged within their proper garden habitat develop harmoniously together, complementing one another's beauty and the beauty of the whole. There are always at least a few suitable perennials for even the most unusual garden situation.

This classification of herbaceous perennials is the result of many years' experience in German gardens. The variations in behaviour under different climatic conditions are most worthy of attention. The author would be grateful for any relevant observations.

Explanation of the lists

The Latin plant names in the left-hand column are based for the most part on Zander's *Handwörterbuch der Pflanzennamen*. A cross (×) before or after the generic name signifies a hybrid. The average (as opposed to maximum) height in metres, and a rough guide to flower colour, are given in the middle column. Where necessary, the height of the foliage and flower stems are given separately (e.g. *Tiarella cordifolia* 0.10/0.20). The flowering season in western Europe is indicated in Roman numerals. Where several months are given, this does not purely represent the length of bloom but also the regional variation in flowering time. The right-hand column contains aids to identification, special properties and requirements, useful cultivars and closely related species. Plants that are listed without further characterisation can be employed in association with the other species of that list but their most appropriate use will be found together with the plants from another list.

Key to page headings

The ± sign means 'more or less'.
'Demanding' and 'undemanding' refer to tolerance with respect to planting position and ecological conditions.

Longevity

Short- and long-lived perennials (see p. 20)

Annuals	Plants that complete their life-cycle from germination to seed-set in twelve months or less. Germination is in spring (summer annuals) or in autumn (winter annuals). See p. 57.
Biennials	Plants that need two summers and one or two winters from germination to seed-set. These are mostly sown in summer, overwintering as rosettes before flowering in the following year.

Temperature

Warmth-demanding   Species that cannot tolerate low winter temperatures, or are damaged by untimely frosts in spring or autumn.

Cool-demanding   Species that require shade in warm areas, and elsewhere prefer a planting position with low temperature fluctuation, out of direct sun.

Mild areas   Areas with a temperate, humid climate characterised by mild winters, e.g. those parts of NW Europe whose climate is strongly influenced by the Atlantic Ocean, and the Pacific Northwest and East coast areas such as Martha's Vineyard and much of Long Island in North America.

Light

Full sun   Sun from dawn till dusk, or a sunny area where heat builds up (e.g. in front of a reflecting wall).

Sun   Sun for most of the day, including all of the warmest part of the day.

Bright shade   Bright, but shaded for most of the day, including all of the warmest part of the day. North-facing slopes of 1 in 3 (30%) or steeper.

Semi-shade   Shaded by trees or buildings to the east or west, or lightly shaded by trees for most of the day, including the warmest part of the day.

Shade   Permanent shade from trees or buildings.

Soil moisture

Moisture present directly around the roots and not, for example, at deeper levels. (Partly after Ellenberg.)

Dry   Generally dry to the touch. Species prefer or at least tolerate occasional drought.

Moist   Generally a little moist to the touch. Species do not tolerate long periods of drought or a damp soil.

Damp   Moist to the touch for two thirds of the year. Species do not tolerate even occasional drought.

Wet   Commonly more water present than the soil can take up. Trenches fill with water. Species normally tolerate damp soil.

As can be seen from the lists, some species require an open-structured, airy soil with a marked drought in either summer or winter. Water retention and the amount of moisture available to plant roots are both dependent on the structure of the soil. Improvements can often be made by the addition of peat, compost or sand. If an ecological planting needs regular watering then it is a sign that the wrong species have been chosen.

Nutrient supply

Nutrient-rich	Deep, well mineralised, loam and clay soils. If there are no specific shortages among the trace elements (soil test), no fertiliser is required for wild perennials. However, the nitrogen contained in the yellowed foliage and old flowering stems which are removed in autumn should be replaced by an application of compost or leafmould.
Nutrient-poor	Open-structured, light sandy soils, rich in silica and quartz. These do not need fertilising if the appropriate plant communities (e.g. heath, dry grassland) are exploited. For more demanding perennials, conditions can be improved by the addition of vermiculite, perlite and bentonite in combination with a moderate application of lime and fertiliser (potassium and phosphorus).

Types of humus (after Kubiena)

Mull	In moist, alkaline soil organic material decomposes quickly and is mixed with mineral components, especially through the activity of earthworms, to produce mull. Typical mull plants are many of the woodland perennials, such as *Primula elatior* and *Pulmonaria*.
Mor	Where the soil is acidic or dry, organic material is divided up by soil organisms and partially decomposed by fungi. The organic and mineral components are only loosely mixed and humus formation is inhibited. The end product is called mor. Typical mor plants are *Linnaea, Maianthemum, Trientalis* and *Vaccinium*.
Raw humus	Where conditions are unsuitable (extreme acidity, cold climate, resistant organic material), decomposition occurs very slowly and there is no mixing of organic and mineral soil components. Raw humus builds up on the soil surface. Typical plants are *Rhododendron, Calluna, Erica* etc.

Country of origin

This refers to the natural range of the wild species. Information on natural distribution can sometimes be useful in putting together plant communities.

Abbreviations

Afgh.	Afghanistan		Am.	America
Afr.	Africa		Anat.	Anatolia
Alban.	Albania		Apenn.	Apennines
Alger.	Algeria		Arg.	Argentina

Ariz.	Arizona		Med.	Mediterranean area
Arm.	Armenia		Mex.	Mexico
Austral.	Australia		Mongol.	Mongolia
Balk.	Balkan peninsular		Mts	Mountains
Braz.	Brazil		N	North
Bulg.	Bulgaria		NZ	New Zealand
C.	Central		Norw.	Norway
Calif.	California		Nr East	Near East
Can.	Canada		Port.	Portugal
Canar.	Canary islands		Pyren.	Pyrenees
Carp.	Carpathians		Rum.	Rumania
Cauc.	Caucasus		Russ.	Russia
Cors.	Corsica		S	South
Cosmopol.	Cosmopolitan		Scand.	Scandinavia
Czech.	Czechoslovakia		Serb.	Serbia
Dalm.	Dalmatia		Sib.	Siberia
E	East		Subtrop.	Subtropics
Engl.	England		Swed.	Sweden
Eur.	Europe		Switz.	Switzerland
Fr.	France		Taiw.	Taiwan (Formosa)
Germ.	Germany		Temp.	Temperate
Him.	Himalayas		Tex.	Texas
Hung.	Hungary		Tib.	Tibet
Ind.	India		Transc.	Transcaucasia
Indoch.	Indochina		Trop.	Tropics
It.	Italy		Turk.	Turkey
Jap.	Japan		Turkest.	Turkestan
Kamch.	Kamchatka		Ukr.	Ukraine
Kashm.	Kashmir		Venez.	Venezuela
Leb.	Lebanon		W	West
Maced.	Macedonia		Yugo.	Yugoslavia
Manch.	Manchuria		Yunn.	Yunnan

1 Woodland

The woodland habitat is not strongly represented in the majority of house gardens. Often it is just a small group of trees or a single specimen, perhaps in combination with the shade of a house wall, which provide the only viable planting positions for woodland perennials. Suitable species can be found for every set of conditions and intensity of maintenance. However, it should be borne in mind that all woodland plants, including ferns, need a reasonable amount of light in order to flourish.

Woodland: areas of shade and light shade among established trees and shrubs. Except for the spring-flowering geophytes, all herbaceous perennials need plenty of indirect light in summer.

In compiling the lists, a broad division has been made between species that can grow in newly laid out plantings (list 1.1) and those that need the mature conditions of an established woodland garden (lists 1.2 and 1.3). Within these two categories plants have been grouped according to their individual properties and suitability for specific growing conditions. The possibility is not excluded that some species may also find a use in a different part of the garden among the perennials of another list. Many of the more widely available herbaceous plants are very obliging and will put up with a lot of mistreatment. However, perennials that are placed merely according to whim are generally short-lived, require excessive maintenance and tend to detract from the planting they are meant to serve.

There are no adequate replacements for the perennials that are listed here for the mature woodland of a large garden or park. On a smaller scale, the different garden habitats are often poorly defined and there may be no clear distinction between woodland and woodland edge. It is therefore worth noting that woodland plants will mostly do quite well on the edge of woodland, but woodland edge plants cannot survive in woodland proper except under special circumstances (e.g. a bright glade).

Many native perennials find their way unaided into the mature woodland of an established park or garden, and these should always be allowed to develop undisturbed. Nevertheless, it is often possible to enrich this naturally occurring vegetation by means of well-considered plantings that do not require any long-term maintenance. In spring, the sun still penetrates the branches, and warmth, light and moisture abound; windflowers, woodruff and lungwort can flower together, to be followed by Solomon's seal, stretching up into the already fading light. Elsewhere it may be the shapely forms of ferns and grasses which dominate the picture. This sort of harmonious, species-rich planting can bring delight under the trees of a small garden too. It is here that the exotic woodland species from list 1.2.2 make their contribution.

The large-scale use of herbaceous perennials under newly planted trees and shrubs, where the shade is still sparse and the ground not yet converted to mull and mor, can only be recommended in special cases, such as a public garden festival. Normally speaking, the soil should be kept open for the first few years to encourage the development of the woody species. In a garden setting it is possible to protect the freshly planted trees and shrubs from too much competition by appropriate maintenance, including the use of fertilisers and irrigation. Where this is so, the planting of shade-tolerant woodland edge perennials or even border perennials can be undertaken right from the start. Only when the woody plants are well established can the true woodland perennials for mature conditions begin to find a home.

From time to time, planners may attempt to conjure up the peace and harmony of natural woodland by an extensive use of low groundcover plants such as *Pachysandra* and *Vinca*, ignoring thereby their long-term maintenance requirement in comparison with indigenous woodland perennials. This sort of groundcover is best suited to small-scale public areas where the visitor pressure is high and a mature ground vegetation cannot develop properly. Extensive groundcover can also be useful in private gardens under trees and shrubs, but there are many beautiful perennials species that will thrive in just the same conditions and bring life and variety into the garden at a cost of very little maintenance (preparation of the planting areas, see p. 72).

Of course, the woodland habitat also has its share of the more demanding, enthusiasts' plants. However, these must always be fitted into the planting as a whole, in places determined by the possibilities for their special maintenance.

1.1. Shade and light shade in a garden setting (including newly landscaped areas)

There are many shade-tolerant perennials for bright but rarely sunny places in the garden. The following (with the exception of some *Hosta* species) are all thoroughly robust perennials, which can be recommended for newly landscaped gardens. Although they are more effective and flourish better in mature woodland conditions, these plants will all grow in places where the shade is still sparse, humidity and soil moisture fluctuate strongly and the soil is not yet rich in woodland humus.

Species that require special conditions have been listed separately. Shade-tolerant perennials from other garden habitats (e.g. border and woodland edge) may also find a use under newly planted trees, especially where the soil is moist and fertile. However, such plants must give way to proper woodland species as conditions mature. All these perennials require intensive maintenance until they cover the ground completely, or until the trees have created a dense shade.

1.1.1. Low, shade-tolerant perennials (also suitable for extensive groundcover)

These reliable species form the backbone of plantings in the shade in a newly landscaped garden. Given sufficient light, they also flourish in established woodland, wherever the soil is not too poor and dry (species for dry shade, see list 1.3.4).

Other shade-tolerant perennials for extensive groundcover can be found in the section covering woodland edge. These species (e.g. *Dicentra*, *Omphalodes*) will grow well under newly planted trees or in the shade of a wall, but prefer the woodland edge to mature woodland conditions.

The barrenworts (*Epimedium*)

The long-lived, undemanding, shade-tolerant epimediums are for the most part attractive throughout the year. The foliage of semi-evergreen species dies off and becomes unsightly in early spring, when it should be removed. The dainty flowers are like tiny columbines, appearing in loose panicles as the leaves unfurl. Epimediums love a moist, open-structured soil. They are tolerant neighbours even though some of them spread at the roots and eventually cover wide areas. They all flower in early spring. The following are species currently available from nurseries. The smaller ones among them are also effective in shady parts of a rock garden, together with the perennials from lists 4.1.3 and 4.5.3.

Epimedium alpinum E & S Alp., Balk.	0.30 red	Small flowered, leafy; very undemanding, also suitable for dry and partially sunny sites; spreads and covers the ground well; foliage dies in winter.
E. × *cantabrigiense* (*E. alpinum* × *E. pubigerum*)	0.30 pale red and yellow	Flowers held high over the foliage; clump-forming.
E. × *rubrum* (*E. alpinum* × *E. grandiflorum*)	0.35 red	Large flowers with cream-coloured interior and white spur; undemanding clump-former; young foliage sometimes veined reddish purple and green.
E. × *warleyense* (*E. alpinum* × *E. pinnatum* ssp. *colchicum*)	0.30 orange	Strongly spreading, closed groundcover; semi-evergreen foliage with colourful tints in winter. Available in some catalogues as *E.* 'Ellen Willmot'.
E. pinnatum 'Elegans' W Transc.	0.40 yellow	Large, spurless flowers; broad, leathery, semi-evergreen leaves; strongly spreading rhizomes. *E. pubigerum* (0.30), daintier and with hairy stems; small, cream flowers held high over fresh green foliage; semi-evergreen.
E. × *versicolor* (*E. grandiflorum* × *E. pinnatum* ssp. *colchicum*) 'Sulphureum'	0.35 sulphur yellow	Large flowers, small leaves; foliage reddish when young, bronze in winter; spreads weakly. 'Cupreum' has abundant, coppery flowers.
E. grandiflorum (*E. macranthum*) Jap.	0.20 white	Large orchid-like flowers and attractively divided small leaves; does not spread; somewhat difficult (lists 4.1.3 and 4.5.3) but fully hardy. 'Rose Queen' (0.20), dainty, narrow, pink flowers. 'Flavescens' (0.25), yellowish white. 'Normale' (0.25), reddish violet. 'Violaceum' (0.20), violet.

E. × youngianum (*E. diphyllum* × *E.* *grandiflorum*) 'Niveum'	0.20 white	Small, very dainty leaves; does not spread. 'Roseum', (0.20), pink. 'Lilacinum', (0.20), pale violet.
E. perralderianum Alger.	0.30 yellow	Large, shiny leaves with spiny margins; semi-ever-green; spreading rhizomes; undemanding but sensitive to extreme cold. Attractive cultivar: 'Fronleiten', stays green far into winter (zone 7); somewhat taller and stronger than the type. (*E. × perralchicum* (0.35), large, yellow flowers; semi-evergreen; drought-resistant.

Further low-growing, shade-tolerant perennials, also suitable for groundcover

Yellow archangel *Galeobdolon luteum* (*Lamiastrum gale-* *obdolon*) 'Florentinum' Eur., Near E. See list 1.2.1.	0.20/0.30 yellow	V–VI, variegated, semi-evergreen, nettle-like leaves; few flowers; overwhelms and suppresses its neigh-bours; also suitable for semi-shade and woodland edge. See list 1.2.1.
Hypericum calycinum		List 2.1.2.
Spotted dead-nettle *Lamium maculatum* 'Argenteum' Eur., Near E., N Iran	0.20/0.25 red	V, nettle-like leaf, spotted with silver; tidy ground-cover for small areas. 'Roseum', pink. 'Beacon Silver' ('Silbergroschen'), lilac flowers and silvery leaves. 'White Nancy', white flowers and silvery leaves. 'Chequers', lavender-pink.
Luzula sylvatica		List 1.1.4.
Pachysandra terminalis Jap., China	0.25 white	IV, dwarf shrub, invaluable as groundcover; small spikes of white flowers; rhizomes must be planted horizontally; acidic, humus-rich soils; slow-growing but reliable. 'Variegata', leaves splashed white; weakly growing. 'Green Carpet', shorter (0.15) and daintier than the species; only reliable in shade. *P. procumbens* (0.20), pale pink flowers; long rhi-zomes; bronze-coloured young foliage.
Red (Carpathian) lung- wort *Pulmonaria rubra* Balk.	0.15/0.30 brick-red	III–IV, pale green, softly hairy, unspotted leaves; vig-orous and undemanding; soil moist or somewhat dry. 'Bowles' Red', red, very strong-growing.
Bethlehem sage *Pulmonaria saccharata*	0.15/0.30 red, then blue	IV–V, sturdy leaves splashed with silver; larger and more intensively coloured flowers than *P. officinalis*;

'Mrs. Moon' S Eur.		undemanding; seeds itself abundantly. 'Argentea', very pale green leaves. 'Pink Dawn', (0.30), pink flowers; decorative, silver-spotted foliage. 'High Dawn', dark blue. 'Frühlingshimmel', (0.25), sky blue. 'Sissinghurst White', (0.25), white.
Pulmonaria angustifolia		List 2.1.6.
Pulmonaria officinalis		List 1.2.1.
Skull-cap *Scutellaria altissima* SE Eur., Cauc.	0.25/0.35 lilac and white	VI–VII, upright tuft of leaves with spike-like inflorescence, which remains attractive after flowering; uncommon but reliable groundcover for moist, rich soils; abundant self-seeding may be a problem in gardens.
Symphytum grandi-florum Cauc.	0.10/0.25 creamy yellow	V, coarse, ovate–lanceolate leaves; rhizomatous spread; dense, robust groundcover; proof against lawn grasses; not for poor soils; drought-resistant. 'Wisley Blue', silvery blue.
Foam flower *Tiarella cordifolia* Mts of E N Am.	0.10/0.20 white	V–VI, daintily lobed, matt green leaves; airy inflorescence; indispensable groundcover with coppery autumn and winter colours; particularly long-lived in moist, slightly acidic, woodland humus. 'Harry Elkins', prettily marked leaves. 'Lilacina', pinkish flowers. 'Major', salmon to wine-red flowers; sturdy plants. 'Marmorata', foliage bronze, becoming dark green, marbled purple. 'Purpurea', purple flowers. *T. wherryi* (0.35), V–VII, prettily marked, emerald-green leaves; does not spread; very long-flowering.

Periwinkles (*Vinca*)

Greater periwinkle, Blue buttons *Vinca major* W & C Med.	0.50 blue	V–VI, large flowered, large leaved and very vigorous; thrives in a warm, shady position. 'Variegata' ('Elegantissima'), yellow and green variegation. 'Reticulata', green leaves netted yellow. The species and its cultivars are all evergreen in mild districts; good for the woodland edge.
Lesser periwinkle *Vinca minor* S & C Eur., Cauc., As. Minor	0.15 blue	IV–VI, reliable, evergreen groundcover; suitable also for dry, shady positions. Vigorous cultivars: White flowers: 'Gertrude Jekyll' and 'Alba', both vigorous, densely growing, narrow-leaved plants; the former is especially beautiful, with flowers that stand clear of the leaves. Red flowers: 'Atropurpurea' ('Rubra'?). Double-flowered red and blue cultivars are also available in the trade.

| | | Green foliage: 'Green Carpet', very dense; broad, rounded leaves; few, pale blue flowers.
White variegated foliage: 'Argenteo-Variegata', broad, rounded leaves; few flowers.
Yellow variegated foliage: 'Aureo-Variegata', pointed, elliptic leaves, often entirely yellow when young; blue flowers. |
| *Vinca minor*
'Bowles' Variety' | 0.15
deep blue | IV–V, ('La Grave'), large flowered; compact and vigorous, hardly spreading; tolerant companion for other woodland perennials.
'Sabinca', (0.05), densely growing; small leaves and flowers. |

Waldsteinias

Waldsteinia geoides SE Eur., W Ukr.	0.20/0.25 yellow	IV–V, clump-forming; hairy, 3–5-lobed leaves; good groundcover.
Waldsteinia ternata (*W. sibirica, W. trifolia*) SE Eur., Sib., Jap.	0.10 yellow	IV–V, spreads by means of stolons; shiny, semi-evergreen, trifoliate leaves; suitable for grave planting; tolerates summer drought in warm, dull or shady positions.

1.1.2.   Tall-growing shade-tolerant perennials

The following species thrive with a little garden-type maintenance in the shade and semi-shade of a newly landscaped area, together with the plants from list 1.1.1. Shade-tolerant border perennials, such as astilbes and Japanese anemones (List 5.1), and the woodland edge plants from lists 2.2.1 and 2.2.2 may also be used successfully under these conditions but will need replacing when the trees become established. The same goes for species such as *Artemisia lactiflora* and *Telekia speciosa* (List 2.2.4), which are more loosely associated with the woodland edge.

Panicled monkshood *Aconitum paniculatum* Alp., Carp.	1.00 blue	VII–VIII, branched inflorescences, flowers in short lateral racemes; thrives in light shade. 'Nanum', dwarf form.
Yellow Monkshood *Aconitum pyrenaicum* (*A. lamarckii*) S Eur.	1.00 pale yellow	VI–VII, sturdier and more solidly built than the otherwise similar *A. lycoctonum* (*A. vulparia*).
Aconitum variegatum M & S Eur.	up to 1.50 violet, often marked white	VII–IX, open inflorescences; flowers with high-domed hoods; moist or damp, nutrient-rich soils; rare in the trade. (Other *Aconitum* species: see lists 2.2.4 and 5.2.1.)
Artemisia lactiflora		List 2.2.4; in clearings.
Aruncus dioicus		List 1.3.1
Astilbe chinensis N China	0.25/0.50 mauve-pink	VIII–IX, slender, pyramidal panicles of flowers; dense foliage; spreads strongly, only suitable for large areas; undemanding; seldom available from nurseries (see also list 2.1.4).

Astilbe tacquetii (*A. chinensis* var. *tacquetii*) 'Superba' E China	0.40/1.00 mauve-pink	VIII–IX, dark green foliage; narrow, upright panicles; spreads at the roots; robust and undemanding; moist soils. Selection: 'Purpurkerze', carmine red.
Giant bellflower *Campanula latifolia* 'Macrantha' Eur., As.	1.00 violet	VI–VII, clump-forming; large bells on powerful, rigid, smooth stems; leaves down to base. 'Alba', white-flowered; brightens up areas of shade and semi-shade. 'Gloaming', pale blue.
Cimicifuga spp.		List 1.3.1.
Gillenia trifoliata		List 1.2.2

In glades and clearings

Perennial foxglove *Digitalis* × *mertonensis* (*D. grandiflora* × *D. purpurea*)	0.80 pink	VI–VII, powerful, compact flowering stems; leafy; short-lived.
Rusty foxglove *Digitalis ferruginea* 'Gigantea' S & SE Eur., Asia Minor	1.80 yellow-brown	VII–VIII, pointed lanceolate leaves in a very decorative rosette; biennial.
Common foxglove *Digitalis purpurea* W Eur., N Afr.	up to 1.20 red	VI–VII, powerful flowering stem over semi-evergreen rosette; short-lived (biennial species). Excelsior strains, large-flowered and colourful. 'Gelbe Lanze', pure yellow (list 5.1).
Digitalis lutea Eur., NW Afr.	0.70 lemon yellow	VI–VII, small, tube-shaped flowers on stiff stems; long, serrated, shining, dark green leaves; long-lived, especially on limy soils; rare in the trade.
Senecio nemorensis (*S. fuchsii*) C & S Eur.	up to 1.50 yellow	VII–VIII, loose, low-branched inflorescence on stiff, red-brown stems with finely serrate to coarsely dentate, ovate to lanceolate leaves. Selection: 'Sternspiegel', rare in the trade.

1.1.3. Hostas

In spite of their tough and undemanding character the attractively leaved hostas need a moist and fertile soil in order to develop their full beauty in the shade. Wherever the chosen site is suitable, particularly in association with the trees and buildings of an established garden, their mostly tall stems of bell-shaped flowers in shades of violet-blue and white can have a breathtaking effect for a few weeks at flowering time. Hostas start to emerge comparatively late in the season and it is a good idea to combine them with early-flowering species such as fumitories (*Corydalis cava* and *C. solida*), which die down before the hosta leaves unfurl.

The variety of these old culture plants from China and Japan is very great, and includes hundreds of recent cultivars, particularly from N. America. Unfortunately the nomenclature is somewhat confused. The following lists contain only a sample of the species and cultivars available.

Huge, large-leaved plants

Hosta crispula	0.50/0.90 lavender	VII, large leaves with narrow white margins which are slightly wavy; old plants form very large, dense clumps. 'Viridis', green leaves; a seedling of *H. crispula*, or mutation from another species.
Hosta elata (*H. montana*)	0.70/1.30 pale violet	VII, broad, green, elongate cordate leaves; forms large clumps; pale yellowish-green bracts conspicuous on flower stems.
Hosta fortunei 'Viridis'	0.60/0.80 lilac	VII, large, mid-green leaves; massive habit. 'Hyacinthina', (0.40/0.70), VII, dark violet; broad, grey-green leaves. 'Glauca', VIII, blue-green leaves. 'Obscura', VIII, very large, dark green leaves. 'Rugosa', VIII, very large, dark green, wrinkled leaves; old plants form huge clumps. 'Stenantha', VIII, reddish violet; matt, dark green leaves.
Hosta fortunei 'Marginato-Alba' ('Albo-Marginata')	0.60/0.80 lilac	VII, large, glaucous leaves with white margins; massive and very vigorous.
Hosta fortunei 'Aureomarginata'	0.60/0.80 lilac	VII, large, glossy leaves with yellow margins. 'Aureopicta' ('Aureomaculata'), creamy white leaves with a narrow green border. 'Sharmon', yellowish-green leaves in spring and summer. 'Aurea', young foliage golden yellow, turning green in summer.
Hosta plantaginea 'Grandiflora'	0.60/0.80 white	VIII–IX, broad, conspicuous, pale green, glossy leaves; large, fragrant, trumpet-shaped flowers; for warm, bright and even sunny positions (in regions with a cool summer). Hybrids: 'Honeybells', IX, pale lilac; sensitive to sun. 'Royal Standard', VIII–IX, white.
Hosta sieboldiana 'Elegans'	0.80/0.90 bleached violet	VII, gigantic, blue-green leaves; sturdy flower spikes standing just above the foliage. Less immense: *H. sieboldiana*, (0.80), VII, large, sea-green leaves. Selection: 'Lilac Giant'. 'Frances Williams' ('Aureomarginata', 'Gold Edge'), blue-green leaves with yellow margins. 'Semperaurea', (0.50), young foliage yellowish green, yellow in summer.
Hosta undulata 'Erromena'	0.60/1.00 lilac	VIII, wavy, green leaves extending up the stems; dense clumps; very vigorous.
Hosta ventricosa	0.60/1.00 dark violet	VIII, very dark green, broad, glossy, heart-shaped leaves; pretty inflorescences with bell-shaped flowers in long racemes.

'Minor' (0.40/0.60), smaller than the type.
'Aureomaculata', dark green leaves with yellowish white blotches.
'Aureomarginata', leaves with pale yellow margins into autumn.
'Variegata', dark green leaves with yellow margins.

Middle-sized plants

Hosta sieboldii (*H. albomarginata*)	0.30/0.50 violet	VIII, narrow green leaves with a narrow white margin. 'Alba', white flowers. 'Louisa', VII, violet; narrow, white-edged leaves. Selection: 'Weihenstephan', flowers very prolifically. 'Slim Polly', VIII, green leaves. 'Lavender Lady', VIII, abundant lavender-blue flowers; green leaves; valuable plant. 'Kapitän', VIII, yellow leaves with a green margin. 'Snowflakes', VIII, white; green leaves. 'Spatulata', VIII, very narrow, green leaves. 'Williams', VI–VIII, white; white-edged leaves.
Hosta decorata	0.30/0.40 violet	VII, smaller, oval leaves with white margins. 'Normalis', green leaves.
Hosta fluctuans	0.50/0.80 pale lilac	VII, broad, green leaves; rare in the trade.
Hosta lancifolia	0.30/0.50 violet	VIII, arched, glossy leaves with long petioles like narrow, dark green spears; forms large clumps. 'Betsy King', somewhat broader-leaved. 'Sentinals', VIII, pale violet.
Hosta longissima (*H. japonica* var. *longifolia*)	0.30/0.50 violet	VIII, very long, narrow, upright, dark green leaves; long, erect flowering stems with nodding, campanula-like flowers.
Hosta montana 'Praeflorens'	0.10/0.30 pale lilac	VI–VII, broad, green, wavy leaves that tend to lie on the ground.
Hosta rectifolia	0.40/0.70 violet	VIII, fresh green, ovate-lanceolate leaves. *H. longipes,* (0.30/0.70), VII, early flowering; laxer flower stems. Hybrid: 'Chionea', narrow white margins to the leaves. *H. helenioides,* (0.20/0.60), similar to the above; violet flowers on tall stems; upright, wavy, dark green, lanceolate leaves.
Hosta rupifraga	0.20/0.30 lilac	VIII, short, dark green, pointed, spoon-shaped leaves.
Hosta tokudama	0.30/0.40 whitish	VII, short, bluish, rounded, spoon-shaped leaves; dense flower heads; many new cultivars and hybrids. 'Variegata', leaves patterned yellowish green.

Hosta undulata 'Univittata'	0.30/0.50 pale violet	VIII, leaves wavy with feathery white marking. *H. undulata* 'Mediovariegata', (0.20), shorter, with smaller leaves and stronger markings; very common in nurseries.
Hosta undulata 'Albomarginata' ('Thomas Hogg')	0.30/0.50 pale violet	VII, long, slightly wavy, pale green leaves with a narrow white margin. Hybrids: 'Blue Diamond', (0.40/0.70), VIII, pale lilac; blue-green leaves. 'Butter Rim', (0.25/0.50), VII, lilac; white-striped leaves. 'Dorothy', (0.40/0.50), VIII, green leaves; intense lilac-blue flowers. 'Freising', (0.30/0.50), VII, white; abundantly flowering; green, oval leaves. 'Helen Field Fisher', (0.30/0.40), VIII, lilac; broad, blue-green leaves. 'Purple Profusion', (0.40/0.60), VIII, large, violet-blue flowers; light green leaves. 'Sweet Susan', (0.30/0.50), VIII, large, violet-blue flowers; broad, pointed, green leaves. 'Tall Boy', (0.50/1.20), VIII, violet; fresh green leaves. 'Wayside Perfection', (0.50/0.70), VIII, large, white, fragrant flowers.

Dwarf plants (also suitable for shade in the rock-garden: see list 4.5.1)

Hosta minima	0.10/0.30 violet	VII, small, green, slightly wavy leaves in dense clumps.
Hosta nakaiana	0.20/0.40 violet	VIII, dark green, heart-shaped leaves; compact inflorescence on a dark, leafy stem.
Hosta × tardiana	0.20/0.40 lilac	VIII, broad, blue-green, spreading leaves; flowers prolifically.
Hosta tardiflora	0.15/0.20 pale lilac	IX–X, small, dark green, lanceolate leaves; pale, waxy blooms; valuable late flowerer.
Hosta venusta	0.05/0.10 lilac	VII, very small, dark green, heart-shaped leaves; one of the tiniest species.

1.1.4.   Shade-tolerant grasses and sedges

The following evergreen grasses and sedges provide a structural element in association with perennials from lists 1.1.1–1.1.3 and lists 5.1–5.2.

Japanese sedge *Carex morrowii* 'Variegata' Jap.	0.40	IV–V, clump-forming evergreen for moist or damp soils; leaves with pale margins; best planted singly or in small groups; somewhat unsightly in May. *C. hachyoensis* 'Ingwersen' ('Evergold'), dainty tufts; arching leaves with yellowish centres; 'Variegata Aurea', leaves with yellow stripes and margins. *C. elata* 'Old Gold', (0.50), yellow variegated leaves; vigorous.

Pendulous sedge *Carex pendula* (*C. maxima*) Eur., Cauc., C Asia	0.60/1.50	V–VI, arched culms up to 2 m long; evergreen leaves; frost-damaged plants should be cut down in spring; for use singly or in small groups; damp soils (see also list 6.3).
Tufted hair-grass *Deschampsia cespitosa* Eur., Asia, N Am., NZ.	0.30/1.00	VI–VIII, beautiful woodland and meadow grass; dark green, hemispherical clumps; for damp, bright spots; tolerates sun; can be used singly or *en masse*; stalks turn yellow in VIII, seeds itself prolifically. Many garden cultivars, including: 'Bronzeschleier' ('Bronze Veil'), brownish flowers; early. 'Goldschleier' ('Gold Veil'), yellowish flowers; early. 'Schottland' ('Scotland'), (up to 2.00). 'Tardiflora', stalks remain green in VIII and IX; late. 'Tautträger', airy inflorescences on rigid stalks; late.
Greater woodrush *Luzula sylvatica* Eur., W Cauc.	0.25/0.40	IV–V, shiny, evergreen leaves; can be used to cover large areas; soil may be dry and acidic but preferably rich in humus. 'Tauernpaß', particularly broad leaves. 'Marginata', leaves with yellow margins. 'Hohe Tatra', stronger and taller than the type. 'Schattenkind', 'Farnfreund', good clump-formers. *L.s. sieberi*, (0.30), stiff habit; narrower leaves than the type.
Hakonechloa macra Jap.	0.30/0.60	Spreading, rhizomatous grass; leaves linear, bluish on upper surface; loose panicles of flowers; for sheltered, cool, damp positions in mild districts. *H. m.* 'Aureola', striped with shades of bronze and yellow; available as a pot-plant.

1.2. Shade and light shade within the mature woodland of an established park or garden

The following, mostly delicate-leaved perennials, are often characterised simply as 'plants for shade' but cannot be recommended for use in newly landscaped areas, where they tend to demand a great deal of maintenance. For the most part, they are woodland plants whose requirements include not just reduced light intensity but also the compost formed from an accumulation of fallen leaves. Of course, peat can be used to a certain extent as a substitute for leafmould, but the equally important woodland microclimate with its stable temperatures and high humidity cannot be simulated in this way. As a result, the special charm and beauty of these modest and graceful perennials first becomes apparent beneath the shade-giving trees of an old, established park or garden. Here they form a closed groundcover, developing and spreading without any need for maintenance. Given a well-prepared, peaty and weed-free planting position, they may also be used in a garden setting to accompany the plants from list 1.1.1.

Cultivated varieties (included in the right-hand column) and the species from list 1.2.2 do better under a garden- rather than park-type maintenance regime. In a garden, the plantings can be kept under constant supervision, and the protecting hand (or very rarely spade) of the gardener is always ready to remove whatever starts to threaten the more precious and slow-growing species.

It may be no more than a few seedlings growing in the wrong place or a branch that is hanging too low. Adjustments such as these do not stifle change. In the long run, some species will be unable to compete with their neighbours, and disappear, while others thrive, becoming ever more beautiful as they spread. A woodland planting is particularly dynamic in this way.

This sort of detailed attention is only required for the first few years of a planting intended for park-type maintenance. Once the predominantly native perennials are rooted and established they are capable of looking after themselves. Subsequent maintenance is restricted to the removal of tree seedings together with any particularly aggressive invaders. Such plantings are largely self-regulating and many of the spontaneously appearing 'weeds' make thoroughly welcome additions to the overall picture.

The perennials for planting in woodland areas in established gardens have been ordered as follows:

Temperate European woodland perennials
Non-European (or Mediterranean) woodland perennials
Woodland grasses
Ferns
Perennials for use with rhododendrons.

The species from these different lists can often be successfully combined in plantings that require only a very little garden-type maintenance.

1.2.1.   Predominantly low-growing, temperate European woodland perennials

Plantings for park-type maintenance

These enchanting European native species thrive in moist or moderately damp, more or less nutrient-rich soils under trees and shrubs, where ornamental flowering perennials could not possibly flourish. Once they are established they need hardly any attention. Digging should be avoided and the leaves left to lie in autumn. In a park setting they may be combined with woodland grasses and ferns or with the fairly undemanding species from list 1.1.1. All grow best in bright shade.

Actaea spicata		List 1.2.2
Wood anemone	0.15	IV, widespread spring flower in deciduous woods in
Anemone nemorosa	white	Europe; insignificant in summer; uncommon in the
Eur., E & NE Asia		trade; needs leafmould, and as much light as possible at flowering time. Cultivars:
		'Alba Plena', V, double white; spreads well.
		'Allenii', light blue.
		'Blue Beauty', light blue.
		'Blue Bonnet', pale blue.
		'Frühlingsfee', reddish.
		'Robinsoniana', lavender blue.
		'Rosea', pink and white.
		'Royal Blue', dark blue.
Yellow windflower	0.20	V, foliage similar to that of *A. nemorosa*; damp, limy,
Anemone ranunculoides	yellow	nutrient-rich soils; uncommon in the trade; spreads
Eur., Cauc., W Sib.		surprisingly fast as the plants get older.
		'Superba', brownish-green leaves.
Lords-and-ladies		List 1.2.2;
Arum maculatum		rare in the trade.

Asarabacca, European wild ginger *Asarum europeum* Eur., W Sib.	0.08 brown	IV, flowers hidden at ground level; glossy, evergreen to semi-evergreen, kidney-shaped leaves; covers the ground well on moist, loamy soils.
Sweet woodruff *Galium odoratum* (*Asperula odorata*) Eur., Sib.	0.15 white	V, whorls of narrow, pointed leaves; pleasantly scented; spreads without threatening neighbours; nutrient-rich, loamy soils; tolerates a fairly dry position.
Masterwort *Astrantia major* Eur., Cauc.	0.80 whitish	VII–VIII, button-shaped flowers on stiff, upright stems; flourishes on damp, alkaline soils; seeds itself prolifically. Selection: 'Rosea', pink; does not seed itself.
Nettle-leaved bell-flower *Campanula trachelium* Eur., Sib.	up to 0.80 violet-blue	VII–VIII, funnel-shaped flowers on rigid, angled, hairy stems; rough, nettle-shaped leaves at base; does not spread; rather short-lived, but seeds itself in moist shade. Selection: 'Steigerwald'. 'Alba', white.
Carex sylvatica		List 1.2.3
Lily-of-the-valley *Convallaria majalis* Eur., W Asia, Cauc., E Asia	0.20 white	V, thrives in soil that is alternately moist and dry (see also list 2.1.4). *C. m.* 'Grandiflora', thicker stems; larger and more abundant flowers; old garden variety.
Purple fumitory *Corydalis cava* (*C. bulbosa*) Eur.	0.25 pink, lilac, white	III–IV, pretty raceme over delicate foliage; tuberous; dies down soon after flowering; for moist or damp, nutrient-rich soils. *C. intermedia.* IV–V, not so vigorous; scale-like leaf immediately above the tuber; rare in the trade.
Corydalis solida Eur., Asia Min.	0.15 murky red	III–IV, dainty, tuberous perennial; flower bracts deeply lobed; for light, woodland soils; prolific self-seeder; uncommon in the trade. 'Transsylvanica', pink. *C. angustifolia* (o.15), white; vigorous; carrot-shaped roots.
Helleborus foetidus		List 2.3.3
Hepatica nobilis (*H. triloba*) Eur., E Asia	0.07 blue (pink, white)	IV, three-lobed leaves; for alkaline but not for sandy soils; for double-flowered varieties, see list 1.3.2.
Yellow archangel *Galeobdolon luteum* (*Lamiastrum galeobdolon*) Eur., Near East	0.30 yellow	IV–VI, dense, dark green foliage; less aggressive than the much used *G.l.* 'Florentinum' (list 1.1.1). 'Silberteppich', silvery, green-veined leaves; weak-growing; bare in winter. 'Variegatum', rounded, heart-shaped leaves with silver patterning. 'Typ Ronsdorf', (0.10), low growing. *Lamium maculatum*, see list 1.1.1.

Spring pea *Lathyrus vernus* (*Orobus vernus*) Eur., W Sib., Cauc.	0.30 red-violet	V, forms dense little clumps; best planted singly on nutrient-rich soil. 'Alboroseus', red and white flowers. 'Albiflorus', white. 'Roseus', pink.
Lilium martagon		List 5.2.2
Perennial honesty *Lunaria rediviva* Eur.	up to 1.00 pale lilac to white	V–VI, open habit; triangular heart-shaped leaves; silvery-white seed pods; prefers a humid position; not for dry soils. *L. annua* (Honesty), biennial.
Maianthemum bifolium		List 1.3.6
Melittis melissophyllum		List 2.1.6
Dog's mercury *Mercurialis perennis* Eur., Near East	0.30 greenish	IV–V, elongate-oval leaves appear early; insignificant flowers; covers the ground well on nutrient-rich soils in deepest shade; rare in nurseries.
Oxalis acetosella		List 1.3.6
Solomon's seal *Polygonatum multi-florum* Eur., Med., Near East, Him., Sib., E Asia, N Am.	0.60 white	V–VI, tall, decorative, lightly arched stems with oval leaves and nodding flowers. Other species, see list 1.2.2.
Primula elatior		List 2.1.6
Primula vulgaris		List 2.1.6
Pulmonaria angustifolia		List 2.1.6
Lungwort *Pulmonaria officinalis* Eur.	0.20 reddish violet	III–IV, unassuming plant with rough, hairy, faintly patterned leaves. *P. saccharata* and *P. rubra* (list 1.1.1) are more imposing.
Sanicle *Sanicula europaea* Eur., C & E Asia	0.05 white	V–VI, small capitate umbels over lobed, glossy, dark green leaves; for the enthusiast.
Scutellaria altissima		List 1.1.1
Vinca minor		List 1.1.1

For use only after careful consideration

Ramsons *Allium ursinum* Eur., Asia Min., Cauc., Sib.	up to 0.30 white	V, rounded heads of flowers; ovate–lanceolate leaves, which die back in summer; unpleasant smell; rapid coloniser, especially on moist or damp, nutrient-rich soils; rare in the trade.
Enchanter's nightshade *Circaea lutetiana* Eur., Asia	0.40 white	VI–VII, graceful habit with small flowers and hairy, heart-shaped leaves; spreads rampantly; dangerous weed in most plantings; occasionally useful for damp

sites under trees; hardly ever available from nurseries.
C. × intermedia, list 4.5.3).

Temperate European woodland grasses (seldom available in the trade)

These beautiful but invasive woodland grasses are often troublesome in a small planting but can
sometimes find a use in park-like situations. (Grasses for a garden setting: see lists 1.1.4 and 1.2.3).

False brome *Brachypodium syl-* *vaticum* Eur., Near East, Jap.	0.30/0.60	VII–VIII, fresh green clumps with arched leaves and narrow, overhanging racemes of flowers; very prolific seeder; good in light woodland or on shady slopes.
Calamagrostis arun- *dinacea*	0.30/1.00	VI, awned florets; clumps of shiny, grey-blue leaves, dark green beneath. Selection: 'Purpurea', rare in the trade.
White-flowered sedge *Carex alba* Eur., Cauc., Sib.	0.20/0.30	IV, delicate, narrow, light green leaves; far-spreading rhizomes can become invasive on rich soils; forms an attractive, lawn-like groundcover on moist or dry soil under trees.
Giant fescue *Festuca gigantea* Eur., W Asia	1.00	VII–VIII, shiny green leaves; graceful stems; does not form a proper clump; no spreading roots but intolerable self-seeder on damp, rich soils.
Wood millet *Milium effusum* Eur., Sib., Him., N Am.	1.00	V–VII, medium–tall woodland grass, effective in flower; short rhizomes; does not form proper clumps; rare in the trade. 'Aureum', (list 1.2.3), bright young foliage.
Poa chaixii Eur., Asia Min., Cauc.	0.30/0.90	VI–VII, strongly flattened stems; broad, rigid, deep green leaves with strongly hooded tips; good in large groups; valuable clump-former for a bright position on loamy, humus-rich, acid soil; fairly drought-tolerant.

**1.2.2.   Predominantly low-growing, Mediterranean or non-European woodland perennials (for
plantings requiring a little garden-type maintenance)**

The following perennials belong in selected woodland areas of the garden, wherever there is
opportunity for their occasional maintenance. Here they may be combined with plants from the
previous list, or with woodland ferns and grasses, *Corydalis* species, spring-flowering bulbs and
woodland shrubs such as witch hazel and *Daphne mezereum*.

White baneberry *Actaea alba* (*A. pachypoda*) N Am.	0.70 whitish	V–VI, leaves pinnate with 5 leaflets; large white berry-like fruits on red stalks (VIII–IX). *A. rubra*, (0.40), *A. spicata* 'Rubra', (0.30), red fruits; rare in the trade. *A. spicata*, (0.60), black fruits; native European species. *A. s.* 'Alba', (0.30), white fruits. *A. neglecta*, (0.60), orange-red fruits.
Anemone apennina S Eur.	0.20 blue	IV, makes a dense, leafy mound covered wth flowers; tuberous rootstock.

Anemone blanda SE Eur.	0.15 blue	III–IV, flowers long before *A. apennina*; loose habit; fragile rhizomes; seeds itself; red, white and pink forms available.
Arum italicum S Eur.	0.30 pale green and reddish	V, arrow-shaped leaves with pale veins; coral-red berries; semi-evergreen; new shoots appear in autumn. *A. i.* 'Pictum', showy, pale yellow veining. *A. maculatum*, native species with dark green leaves and red berries; more robust.
Asarum canadense N Am.	up to 0.10 red-brown	IV–V, insignificant flowers; large, matt green leaves with fine hairs; very vigorous groundcover, like a deciduous ivy; for rich soils; rare in the trade. *A. caudatum* (Mouse plant, N Am.), matt, evergreen leaves; good groundcover for brief summer drought and shade on acid soils; rare in the trade.
Astilbe chinensis 'Pumila'	List 2.1.4.	
Astilbe glaberrima	List 4.5.3.	
Cardamine trifolia C Eur., Carp., C It.	0.10/0.20 white	VI, dark green, trifoliate leaves; groundcover for moist or damp shade; uncommon in the trade.
Dentaria penta-phyllos (*Cardamine pen-taphyllos*) Alp., Pyren.	0.30 lilac	V–VI, racemes of small flowers over dense foliage; old plants form dense, dome-shaped clumps. *D. enneaphyllos*, (0.25), IV, cream flowers. *D. heptaphylla*, (0.40), IV–V, white; undemanding but unfortunately difficult to obtain.
Bowman's root *Gillenia trifoliata* N Am.	0.80 white	VI–VII, dainty, much-branched panicles; reddish calyces; for a bright spot.
Hacquetia epipactis E Alp., Carp.	0.10/0.15 yellow	IV, heads of tiny yellow flowers surrounded by greenish-yellow bracts; rounded, 3–5 lobed basal leaves; warm, humus-rich soils; difficult to propagate.
H. transsylvanica (*Hepatica angulosa*) Trans.	0.10 blue	III–IV, similar to *H. nobilis* but with larger, coarsely lobed leaves; spreads to form a dense carpet; not for sandy soils. 'Buis', large, light blue flowers; yellowish anthers. *H. acutiloba*, (Liverleaf, USA), light blue; leafier than *H. nobilis*; leaves with pointed lobes.
Hylomecon japonica E Asia	0.20/0.30 yellow	IV–V, roots run through leafmould like a wood anemone; crowded, pinnate leaves; large, striking, luminous yellow blooms; dies down in summer; intolerant of limy soils.
Isopyrum thalictroides SE Eur.	0.10/0.20 white	IV, bowl-shaped flowers over elegantly divided leaves; forms large stands; dies down completely at the end of June.
Welsh poppy *Meconopsis cambrica* W Eur.	0.30 yellow	VI–X, long-stemmed, poppy-like flowers; pinnately cut, hairy leaves; short-lived but seeds itself readily. 'Aurantiaca', orange-yellow; also thrives on the woodland edge.

Virginia cowslip *Mertensia virginica* E USA	up to 0.50 light blue	IV–V, dainty, arching stems; dies down after flowering; for planting singly. *M. v.* var. *alba*, pristine white flowers.
Bishop's hat *Mitella caulescens* N Am.	0.15 pale yellow	V, insignificant flowers; basal rosettes form flat carpets on soil that is not too dry. *M. diphylla, M. nuda, M. ovalis,* somewhat taller.
Omphalodes verna		List 2.1.4
Primula vulgaris var. *sibthorpii*		List 2.1.6
Solomon's seal *Polygonatum com- mutatum* N Am.	1.50 white	VI, oval leaves on powerful, arching stems, angled at the base; up to 6 flowers in the leaf-axils. *P. × hybridum* (*P. multiflorum × P. odoratum*) 'Weihenstephan', (0.90), V, more imposing than *P. multiflorum*; similar to *P. commutatum* but flowers earlier and is considerably more vigorous. *P. latifolium*, (0.60), densely leaved; spreads strongly; rare in the trade.
Whorled Solomon's seal *Polygonatum verti- cillatum* Eur.	0.70 white	V–VI, narrow, whorled leaves; grows in mountain woods; needs cool, damp conditions to prevent premature yellowing; rarely available from nurseries. *P. roseum*, small, pink flowers and red fruits.
Saxifraga × geum		List 4.1.3
False spikenard *Smilacina racemosa* N Am.	0.70 whitish	V–VI, similar to Solomon's seal but with striking panicles up to 15 cm long; forms a clump; very free flowering.
Smilacina stellata N Am.	0.60 white	V–VI, narrower leaves than the former species; spreads like lily-of-the-valley.
Symphytum cordatum Hung, to Rus.	0.30 yellow-white	V–VI, rounded, heart-shaped leaves; very long-lived but not invasive; rare in the trade.
Wake robin *Trillium grandiflorum* N Am.	0.30 white	IV–V, particularly beautiful representative of this N American woodland genus; all prefer a damp soil in spring and die down in summer. 'Roseum', pink; rare in the trade. *T. nivale* (0.10), white. *T. sessile* (0.40), reddish. *T. s.* 'Rubrum', red; very large flowers. *T. s.* var. *californicum* (0.40), white. *T. erectum*, red-brown. *T. chloropetalum* 'Snow Queen', white; large-flowered.
Uvularia grandiflora N Am.	0.30 pale yellow	V–VI, arching stems with narrow, pendent flowers, up to 4 cm long; increases gradually; impressive at flowering time.

		U. perfoliata, shorter and with paler flowers; for acid soils.
Vancouveria hexandra W USA	0.35 white	VI, similar to *Epimedium*; leaves biternate, deciduous; valuable, rhizomatous groundcover; not for harsh climates.
Early blue violet *Viola palmata* N Am.	up to 0.20 reddish violet	IV–V, long-stemmed flowers; lobed, irregularly toothed leaves; rare in the trade.

1.2.3. Woodland sedges, grasses and rushes

These mostly clump-forming European native species combine well with the dainty woodland plants of lists 1.2.1 and 1.2.2.

Carex digitata Eur., Cauc., Urals	0.10/0.30	III–V, thin, fingery spikes of flowers; narrow, dark green, evergreen leaves; forms a lawn-like groundcover under deciduous trees; fairly drought tolerant; rare in the trade.
Bird's-foot sedge *Carex ornithopoda* 'Variegata' Eur.	0.20	IV–V, very decorative, green and white tufts; unspectacular flowers. 'The Beatles', attractive, dark green mops of foliage.
Carex plantaginea N Am.	0.15/0.30	IV–V, wide, bright green, evergreen leaves; effective in small groups; for acid, humus-rich soils; invasive where summers are warm.
Wood sedge *Carex sylvatica* Eur., Asia Minor, Cauc.	0.20/0.40	IV–V, evergreen; nodding inflorescences on arched stems; thrives along woodland paths.
Luzula luzuloides (*L. albida*) Eur.	0.30 (0.50)	VI–VII, puffy, creamy-white inflorescences; loose habit; for moderately moist, loamy, lime-free soils; rare in the trade.
Luzula nivea Alp., Pyren., Apenn.	0.50	VI–VII, long, narrow, evergreen leaves with whiskered edges; dainty, white flowers and fruits on tall stems; best in small groups; moist, loamy soils; intolerant of summer heat. Selections: 'Silberhäschen' ('Silver Bunny'), 'Silberhaar'.
Luzula pilosa Eur., Cauc., W Sib.	0.15/0.25	V–VI, pretty, evergreen tufts; undemanding; also on acid, humus-rich soils.
Luzula sylvatica		List 1.1.4
Mountain melick *Melica nutans* Eur., Asia	0.30/0.40	V–VI, nodding flowers in narrow panicles; forms a sparse, light green groundcover; rarely available.
Wood melick *Melica uniflora* Eur., SW Asia	0.30/0.40	V–VI, fresh green leaves; spreading rhizomes; forms an attractive, lawn-like groundcover under trees; moist, humus-rich, preferably lime-free soils; rare in the trade.

Golden wood millet	1.00	V–VII, very beautiful bright yellow new foliage in
Milium effusum		spring; seeds itself; see also list 1.2.1.
'Aureum'		

1.2.4. Ferns

Most ferns do especially well in the cool, but bright, shade of a well established, high crowned tree. Since ferns do not flower it is especially important to make good use of their attractive foliage and habits of growth. The right choice of neighbours is therefore critical. Tall, imposing perennials should mostly be avoided, though in damp places goatsbeard (*Aruncus dioicus*) and drooping sedge (*Carex pendula*) can be used to good effect. Tolerant and appropriately modest neighbours include may-lily (*Maianthemum bifolium*), wood-sorrel (*Oxalis acetosella*), various anemones (*A. nemorosa, A. blanda, A. apennina*, etc.) and the woodland perennials from lists 1.2.1 and 1.2.2. Among the grasses and their relatives, the woodrushes (particularly *Luzula pilosa* and *L. sylvatica*) are especially important.

In a large planting, sufficient space should be left for the low, rhizomatous species, such as oak and beech ferns. Newly planted, they may seem insignificant, but given the right conditions they spread out over the years to take in an impressive area and so bear witness to the passing of time.

The soil for ferns should be moist or damp and not too poor in nutrients. If no natural leafmould is present then plenty of peat must be worked into the planting site. Fallen leaves are vitally important for a woodland fern's well-being and should on no account be removed. In other respects they are undemanding, though all do poorly wherever the precipitation is less than 60 cm per year. Special requirements are mentioned for the individual species.

The following selection includes all those ferns that are normally available in the trade, apart from a few low-growing species that have been assigned to the rock garden (lists 4.5.2 and 4.5.3).

A particularly good spot for most of these plants can be found among the perennials from list 1.3.1.

Ferns with spreading roots

Extremely invasive ferns that need a lot of space

Hay-scented fern	Tall, rhizomatous species (0.50–0.90) with elegantly
Dennstaedtia punctiloba	divided fronds up to 20 cm wide; bright, dry, and even
N Am.	stony places; somewhat tender in damp conditions.
Shuttlecock fern	Grows in large groups on streamsides and in shady,
Matteuccia struthiopteris	wooded gorges; 1.30 tall in damp places, otherwise
Eur., Cauc., N Asia	0.80; the 'shuttlecocks' enclose rigid fertile fronds;
	yellows early in a dry position.
	M. pennsylvanica, (2.20), larger in all its parts; long-stemmed fronds; spreads little or not at all.
	M. orientalis, (0.60), coarser fronds; fertile fronds grow outside the rosette; up to 1.50 wide but does not spread; rarely available from nurseries.
Sensitive fern	Grows (up to 0.90) in damp, wooded hollows and
Onoclea sensibilis	wet meadows; long-stemmed, triangular, fresh green
N Am., E Asia	fronds appear early in the year; fertile fronds shaped like strings of pearls; spreads rapidly in a damp spot under trees to form luxuriant carpets (see list 6.4.2).
	O. s. 'Rotstiel', reddish stipes.

Bracken
Pteridium aquilinum
Cosmopol.

Tall (2.00), deciduous fern; widespread in open wood-land on acid, humus-rich soils; not available in the trade; uncontrollable once established; not to be rec-ommended.

Shorter-growing ferns, which can nevertheless spread to cover large areas in the course of time

Oak fern
Currania dryopteris
(*Dryopteris linnaeana*)
(*Gymnocarpium dryopteris*)
Eur., Asia, N Am.

Native to deciduous woodland on humus-rich soil; delicate, triangular fronds borne horizontally on long, wiry stipes.

Limestone polypody
Currania robertiana
(*Gymnocarpium robertianum*)
Eur., Asia, N Am

Rough, dull green, upright fronds; from rocky, moun-tain woods and limestone screes; tolerates sun.

Polypody
Polypodium vulgare
Eur., Asia

Narrow, leathery, coarsely pinnate, evergreen fronds (0.30); shady slopes in humid districts; also for sandy soils, especially in maritime climates; best suited to the rock garden, list 4.5.3.
P. interjectum 'Cornubiense', (0.40), *P. cambricum* 'Barrowii', (0.45), taller and with unusually cut fronds.

Beech fern
Thelypteris phegopteris
Eur., Asia, N Am.

Grows in shady, mixed-deciduous woodland; light green, triangular fronds; basal pinnae point down-wards; best in groups.

Marsh fern
Thelypteris palustris
(*Dryopteris thelypteris*)
(*Thelypteris thelypteroides*)
Eur., Jap., N Am.

Grows in stagnant hollows (0.50), often in association with alders; unassuming plant for the bog-garden enthusiast; see also list 6.3.
T. noveboracensis, similar.

Clump-forming ferns

Tall, stately species

Athyrium distentifolium
(*A. alpestre*)
Eur., Cauc., Sib., E Asia, N Am.

Mountain woods and shady alpine pastures (up to 1.50); dark green fronds with straw-yellow stipes; rare in the trade.
'Kupferstiel', reddish stipe and rachis.

Lady fern
Athyrium felix-femina
Eur., Asia, N Am., S Am.

Widespread in damp, shady woods (over 1.50); large, feathery fronds, which turn brown and disintegrate in late autumn. Many garden forms, including:
'Corymbiferum', hanging, tassel-like pinnae.
'Cristatum', fronds with forked pinnae.
'Fieldiae', narrow, erect fronds with crossed pinnae.
'Frizelliae', very narrow (1 cm), bow-shaped, ruffled fronds.

'Minor', (0.30).

'Multifidum', (0.50), grotesqely twisted fronds.

'Rotstiel', red-brown stipes; more popular in Germany than the type.

'Victoriae', (up to 0.40), pinnae form a regular checked pattern.

'Bornholmiense', (up to 0.40), 'Congestum', (0.30), 'Minutissimum', (up to 0.40), all dwarf forms.

Dryopteris atrata (*D. hirtipes*) S. China, Ind., Ceylon, Polyn.	Broad, dark green fronds (0.80) with tips rolled like an elephant's trunk; tender, enthusiasts' plant for mild areas.
Golden-scaled male fern *Dryopteris affinis* (*D. borreri*) (*D. paleacea*) (*D. pseudo-mas*) Eur., Cauc.	From humid mountain woods (0.80); broad funnels of erect, leathery, shining, semi-evergreen fronds with golden-brown scales on stipe and rachis; robust and worthwhile fern for damp, shady places; nursery plants are seldom true. 'Pinderi', (0.90), attractive form with narrow fronds; late to emerge. 'Cristata', (0.90), regular cresting. 'Crispa', (0.50), dwarf form with ruffled fronds.
Dryopteris × *tavelii* (*D. filix-mas* × *D. affinis*) Eur.	Distinguished male-fern hybrid with characters from both parents; semi-evergreen; rare in the trade but can be propagated from spores.
Broad buckler-fern *D. dilatata* (*Dryopteris austriaca*) Eur. W Sib., Asia Min., Cauc., E Asia, N Am.	Often grows together with *D. filix-mas*; broad, arching, much divided, semi-evergreen fronds (0.60–1.50). *D. carthusiana* (*D. spinulosa*), (0.40–0.90), narrower, upright fronds; undemanding; prefers damper conditions.
Male-fern *Dryopteris filix-mas* Eur., Asia, N Am.	Widespread and common woodland fern (up to 1.20); robust and undemanding; fronds brown as they unfurl. 'Barnesii', (1.00), long, narrow, upright fronds. 'Furcans', (0.60), forked pinnae. 'Grandiceps', (0.70), hanging, tasselled pinnae at the tip of each frond. 'Linearis Polydactylon', (0.70), hanging, fingery extensions to the pinnae.
Dryopteris goldiana N Am.	Moist, humus-rich woods in the USA; broad, long-stemmed, light green fronds (1.30); for damp, sheltered positions; not very hardy (needs protection in winter).
Royal fern *Osmunda regalis* Eur., Asia, Am., Afr.	Damp moorland, marshes and bogs in shade or sun; brown fertile fronds; planting site should be deeply enriched with peat. 'Purpurascens', reddish on emergence; tolerates lime. 'Gracilis', (0.70), coppery on emergence; rare in the trade.

Osmunda cinnamomea
E. N Am., E Asia

Cinnamon-brown, fertile fronds (1.30) appear in the middle of the plant before the dark green, pinnate, sterile fronds.

Osmunda claytoniana
E. N Am., Korea, Taiw.,
SW China

Light green fronds with 3–5 pairs of brownish, fertile pinnae in the centre of each frond.

Shorter-growing species

Adiantum pedatum
N Am., China, Jap., E Sib.

From damp woods on humus-rich soils; delicate, pale green, horseshoe-shaped fronds (0.40) on wiry stipes. *A. japonicum*, similar; light reddish-brown new growth.

Japanese painted fern
Athyrium nipponicum
(*A. goeringianum* 'Pictum')
Jap.

Unique and beautiful, long-stemmed fern with bipinnate fronds (0.60) lightly toned with bronze.
A. N. 'Metallicum' (0.40), reddish and silvery-grey tinted foliage.
A. vidalii (0.50) (E Asia), dainty, elegant fern.

Hard fern
Blechnum spicant
Eur., Jap., Pacif. N Am.

Flat, spreading rosettes of semi-evergreen, sterile fronds; stiffly erect, dark brown fertile fronds (0.30); acid soils; difficult to get established.
B. penna-marina, see list 4.5.3

Cystopteris bulbifera
N Am.

Damp, shady and often rocky places in the eastern part of the USA; slender, evenly-divided fronds (0.40) carrying small bulbils; rhizomatous; stronger and more resistant than *C. fragilis* (see list 4.5.2).

Japanese holly fern
Cyrtomium fortunei
Jap., China

Upright, glossy, dark green fronds (0.60); half-hardy; for damp, shady places in soil or among rocks.

Crested buckler fern
Dryopteris cristata
Eur., W Sib., N Am.

Slender, pale green, fertile fronds (up to 0.70) with broad basal pinnae and grooved stipes, surrounded by low, sterile fronds; forms a loose clump; wet, moory, fairly acid soils; rare in the trade; see also list 6.4.2.

Copper fern
Dryopteris erythrosora
Jap., China, Nepal

Damp, mountain woods in Japan; broad, flat, evergreen fronds (0.40) with scarlet spore-capsules; reddish young growth.
D. oreades (*D. abbreviata*), (0.30), hardy, upright, dark green fern; rare; for a sunless spot in the rock garden (list 4.5.3).
D. wallichiana (0.50–0.70), semi-evergreen fronds with black rachis and blackish-brown basal hairs; beautiful new growth; mountain woods in SE Asia.

Hart's-tongue fern
Phyllitis scolopendrium
(*Scolopendrium vulgare*)
Eur., Jap., N Am.

From cool, shady, mountain woods on alkaline soils; glossy, dark green, undivided fronds (0.30); semi-evergreen. Many garden forms, including:
'Angustifolia' (0.30), narrow, leathery fronds.
'Marginata' (0.20), very narrow, horny-edged fronds.
'Capitata' (0.20), ruffled fronds widened at the tip.

'Crispa' (0.35), prettily waved fronds; mostly sterile; available often (but falsely) as 'Undulata'.
'Digitata-Cristata' (0.25), finger-like extensions of the frond tips.

Christmas fern
Polystichum acrostichoides
N Am.

Mountain species (0.40) from E and S N America; narrow, leathery, pinnate fronds; evergreen; for lime-free, humus-rich soils.
P. munitum (0.50), similar but more tender.
P. rigens (0.30), difficult, weak-growing, Japanese fern with rigid, dark green fronds.

Hard shield-fern
Polystichum aculeatum
(*P. lobatum*)
Eur., E Asia

Grows wild in shady, wooded gorges; leathery, bipinnate fronds (0.30–0.80) with a shiny upper surface; semi-evergreen.
P. × bicknellii, (1.00).
P. a. 'Acutilobum', particularly fine form.

Polystichum braunii
Eur., N Am.

Soft, upright, sparsely hairy fronds (up to 0.70); sensitive to late frosts; rare in the trade.

Polystichum lonchitis

List 4.5.3

Polystichum polyblepharum
'Bornim'
Jap.

Striking, glossy, dark green fern (0.40–0.60) with wide-spreading, semi-evergreen fronds; somewhat tender and sensitive to late frosts.

Soft shield-fern
Polystichum setiferum
Eur., Med., Asia

Stately, semi-evergreen fern (0.80–1.00) with finely divided, brown-ribbed, matt green fronds; from damp, shady, deciduous woodland in highland areas.
'Iveryanum', (0.30), moss-green fronds, forked at the tip.

Polystichum setiferum
'Dahlem'

Vigorous cultivar (0.60–0.80) with broad, arching, dark green fronds; similar to *P. aculeatum*.

Polystichum setiferum
'Proliferum'

Very finely divided, narrow fronds (0.40); young plants grow from bulbils that form along the rachis; spreading habit; can be used as groundcover.
'Proliferum-Herrenhausen', (0.40), broad, dark green fronds; plants *ca.* 1.30 m across.
'Proliferum-Wollastonii', (0.50–0.70), very elegant habit and foliage; seldom true in nurseries.

Polystichum setiferum
'Plumosum Densum'

Soft, almost mossy fronds (0.50) with crowded pinnae; scaly stipe and rachis; bulbils; spreading habit.

Millipede fern
Thelypteris decursive-pinnata
E Asia

Grows (up to 0.40), in damp, rocky, mountain woods; densely crowded fronds with short stipe and long, narrow pinnae.

Thelypteris limbosperma
Eur., Asia, N Am.

Grows (0.80), in mixed, mountain woodland and along streams (list 4.6.1); dark green fronds with pale stipe and rachis; fruity fragrance; for lime-free soils.

1.2.5.   Perennials for rhododendron plantings

The rather slow-growing rhododendrons and their relatives develop a dense system of fine roots in the acid, humus-rich soil beneath the shelter of established trees. Here they may be combined with many of the woodland perennials, and with bulbs such as snowdrops, *Scilla bifolia* and the Turk's cap lily (*Lilium martagon*).

Rhododendrons grow best in the tree-sheltered environment of a mature garden. In moist and humid conditions, protected from the wind, they will also thrive in a new garden, but here the soil must be well enriched with peat.

Many of the perennials from lists 1.2.4 and 1.3.1 can be successfully combined with rhododendrons in the shade. In a sunny position it may be better to use the species from lists 1.1.1, 1.1.3 and 1.1.4.

No planting of perennials should be allowed to detract from the effect of the flowering shrubs, and in each case the final selection will depend on the particular rhododendrons that are present.

The following species can be recommended for general use.

Robust, evergreen species suitable for large plantings and public places

Ferns (especially *Dryopteris affinis* and *D. filix-mas*), goatsbeard (*Aruncus*) and hostas may all be combined with these to create thematic highlights.

Evergreen spindle	*Euonymus* spp.
Arrow-leaved ivy	*Hedera helix* 'Sagittaefolia'
Pachysandra	*Pachysandra terminalis*
Periwinkle	*Vinca* spp.

Evergreen and deciduous species, principally suitable for gardens

These may be combined with many of the perennials from the aforementioned lists and with the evergreens that are listed above.

Evergreen and semi-evergreen species

Japanese sedge	*Carex morrowii*
Copper fern	*Dryopteris erythrosora*
Bunchberry	*Cornus canadensis*
Barrenwort	*Epimedium* spp.
Partridge berry	*Gaultheria* spp.
Greater woodrush	*Luzula sylvatica*
Shield-fern	*Polystichum* spp.
Whortleberry, Huckleberry	*Vaccinium* and relatives

Deciduous species

Japanese anemone	*Anemone* Japonica hybrids and *A. hupehensis*
Goatsbeard	*Aruncus* spp.
Astilbe	*Astilbe* spp. and hybrids
	Astilboides tabularis
Bugbane, Cohosh	*Cimicifuga* spp.
Hosta	*Hosta* spp.
Candelabra primulas	*Primula japonica* and relatives
Rodgersia	*Rodgersia* spp.
Foam flower	*Tiarella* spp.

Species for special conditions and maintenance:

For sunny positions, in association with low, deciduous rhododendron species

Ling	*Calluna vulgaris*
Heather	*Erica carnea* and relatives
Autumn gentians	*Gentiana farreri* and *G. sino-ornata*

For the enthusiast

The perennials from list 1.3.2, many ferns (list 1.2.4) and some lilies, including *Lilium speciosum* (list 5.2.2) and the oriental hybrids (list 5.2.2) are all suitable for planting with rhododendrons.

1.3. Special sites in shade and semi-shade

The following perennials do particularly well under mature conditions. With a little extra maintenance, many will also flourish in a newly landscaped garden, where they need the shade of a wall or building. Some are better cared for in the shady parts of a rock garden.

1.3.1. Cool, partly shaded, mostly damp and humid sites

Plants with a preference for areas dominated by trees

Rodgersias, and astilbes such as *A. simplicifolia*, are the typical mountain woodland species for these conditions. Several of the lower-growing astilbe cultivars will do well in an open border, but the tall wild species, and the rodgersias with their exceptionally large and beautifully formed leaves and decorative inflorescences, all prefer a planting position beneath the trees of a mature garden. To be really effective they need a lot of space. Rodgersias in particular quickly attain large proportions. All species prefer a rich, damp soil in a cool and humid spot, though not a frost hollow. The majority of ferns make good neighbours; suitable grasses are given in lists 1.1.4 and 1.2.3. The more demanding, enthusiasts' perennials appear in list 1.3.2.

Goatsbeard	up to 2.00	VI–VII, large, pinnate leaves and sturdy flowering
Aruncus dioicus	white	stems; male (pure white) and female (yellowish white)
(*A. sylvester*)		inflorescences on separate plants; self-seeding where
Eur., Cauc., E Sib.,		both occur together but seldom troublesome; tolerates
N Am.		a fairly bright position; grows immense with good
		cultivation; not for raw soils.
		'Zweiweltenkind', (2.00), VI, late flowering; massive
		habit; compact inflorescence.
		'Kneiffii', (1.30), laciniate leaves; weak stemmed and
		falls over easily.
		A. d. var. *sinensis*, elegant variety of the species.
		A. d. americanus, (1.30), VI, brownish new foliage;
		early flowering.
		A. aethusifolius, (0.20), white; like a tiny astilbe; see
		list 4.5.3.
		A. astilboides, (0.50).
		A. parvulus 'Dagalet', (0.25).
Astilbe spp.		Lists 1.1.2, 2.1.4 & 5.1.

Astilbe davidii (*A. chinensis* var. *davidii*) Jap., N China	0.40/2.00 purplish-red	VIII, slim, decorative panicles on tall, erect stems. 'King Albert', white. 'Salland', carmine; both rare in the trade.
Astilbe grandis China	0.50/0.70 creamy white	V, broad, loose panicles of flowers up to 1 m long; large, 3-pinnate leaves.
Astilbe japonica Jap.	0.30/0.40 white	VI, squat, pyramidal inflorescences; glossy, dark green, divided foliage; good groundcover; old and crowded plants flower poorly; rare in the trade. Hybrids, see list 5.1.
Astilbe koreana Korea, N China	0.30/0.40 creamy white	VII–VIII, large, arching panicles of flowers; dark foliage; undemanding, but rare in the trade.
Astilbe simplicifolia Jap.	0.30 white	VII, graceful, arching panicles; shiny, dark green, lobed but undivided leaves; rare in the trade. 'Alba' (0.40), VIII, white to pale pink; commoner and less demanding than the type.

Astilbe Simplicifolia hybrids

'Aphrodite'	0.40 pale red	VIII, dark-leaved mutant of *A. s.* 'Atrorosea', (0.40), dark pink; fine arching panicles; very vigorous.
'Bronze Elegance'	0.40 dark pink	VIII, upright, slightly arched panicles.
'Dunkellachs'	0.40 salmon-pink	VIII, narrow heads of flowers on stiff, wiry, dark brown stems; dark green foliage. 'Rosea', dainty, pale pink, loose and arching panicles; bushy and vigorous.
'Elegans'	0.40 glowing pink	VIII, open, arching inflorescences; rare in the trade.
'Praecox-Alba'	0.45 white	VII, stiff, upright stems; very vigorous. 'Praecox', salmon-pink.
'Sprite'	0.40 white to pink	VIII, large, open panicles; dark green, bronze-tinted foliage.
Astilbe thunbergii		List 5.1.
Astilboides tabularis (*Rodgersia tabularis*) Manch., Korea	0.60/1.20 white	VI–VII, very large, round leaves; more demanding than the related rodgersias; needs damp soil.
Boykinia aconitifolia USA	up to 0.70 white	VI–VII, small flowers; lobed, maple-like leaves; spreads by means of rhizomes.
Cardamine trifolia		List 1.2.2.
Carex muskingumensis		List 2.3.1.
Hakonechloa macra		List 1.1.4.
Kirengeshoma palmata		List 1.3.2.
Liriope spp.		List 1.3.3.

Blue nettle *Meehania urticifolia* Jap.	up to 0.30 purplish-blue	IV–V, flowers in one-sided spikes on few-leaved stems; vegetative shoots with nettle-like leaves up to 10 cm long; not yet widely available.
Mondo grass *Ophiopogon japonicus* Jap.	0.15 whitish	VII, insignificant flowers followed by violet berries; narrow, arching, grassy leaves; evergreen ground-cover for small areas; light, acid soils away from the sun; somewhat tender. 'Minor', hardier; see list 4.5.2. *Ophiopogon planiscapus* 'Nigrescens' (0.25), lilac; arching, strap-shaped, purplish-black leaves. *O. p.* 'Arabicus', American cultivar, similar or identical to the above; needs long, warm summers. Other *Ophiopogon* spp. are widely grown in the southern half of the USA.
Patrinia triloba Jap.	0.30 golden yellow	V–VII, fragrant flowers in corymbose cymes on stiff, reddish stems; deeply lobed leaves; vigorous and un-demanding. *P. gibbosa* (0.20) (Jap.), rounded basal leaves.
Umbrella plant *Peltiphyllum peltatum* NW USA	1.00/0.40 reddish	IV–V, small flowers on tall stems before the leaves; large, round, very decorative, dark green leaves; moist or damp soils; grows wild in mountain streams.
Peltoboykinia *tellimoides* (*Boykinia tellimoides*) Jap.	0.20/0.70 greenish	VII–VIII, unspectacular flowers; fresh green, lobed, orbicular leaves; creeping rhizome; good groundcover for all but dry soils; rare in the trade.
May apple *Podophyllum* *hexandrum* 'Majus' Him.	0.40 white	V, upward-facing flowers; reddish-bronze patterned leaves which unfurl like an umbrella; large red fruits in summer; a prey to slugs and snails. *P. peltatum*, N Am. (0.30), V, white; deeply lobed, green leaves; yellowish fruits in August; vigorous, spreading rhizomes; undemanding plant for shade.
Polygonatum *commutatum*		List 1.2.2
Polygonum filiforme Jap.	up to 0.80 red	VII–VIII, loose, spreading habit when planted singly; pointed leaves with two maroon blotches; axillary spikes of flowers on long, thin, light brown pedicels; seeds itself in shade and semi-shade. 'Variegatum' (*Tovara virginiana* 'Painter's Palette'), broad, light green leaves, which are splashed with colour in summer like a painter's palette; spreads vegetatively.
Primula cortusoides W Sib.	0.30 pink	IV–V, crowded, many-flowered umbels; softly hairy leaves and stem. *P. saxatilis* (0.25), IV–V, violet-pink; similar to above; for light shade on humus-rich soils; see list 4.5.1.
Primula polyneura (*P. veitchii*) W China	0.30 deep pink, yellow eye	V–VI, variable species; whorled inflorescences; leaves round to broad-triangular, softly hairy, lobed.

Ranzania japonica (*Podophyllum japonicum*) Jap.	0.50/0.20 lilac-pink	IV, large, nodding flowers on forked stems; round, white berries; maple-like leaves; for light shade on humus-rich soils.
Reineckia carnea (*Sansevieria sessiliflora*) Jap., China	0.30/0.15 pink	VIII–X, well-hidden racemes; smooth, broadly linear leaves; creeping habit; not reliably hardy.
Rodgersia aesculifolia C China	up to 1.00 white	VII–VIII, horsechestnut-like leaves with leaflets over-lapped at the base.
Rodgersia pinnata Yunn.	up to 1.20 creamy white	VI–VII, dark green, pinnate leaves with 6–9 leaflets; broad panicles. 'Blickfang', similar. 'Superba', pale pink. 'Rubra', deep red.
Rodgersia podophylla Jap., Korea	1.00/1.60 creamy white	VI–VII, large, shining, coarsely serrate leaves; bronze-tinted new growth; very free-flowering. 'Pagode', pagoda-like inflorescences. 'Rotlaub', coppery-red leaves. 'Smaragd', emerald green leaves.
Rodgersia purdomii China	up to 1.00 pure white	VI–VII, long, pinnate leaves with 6–7 narrow leaflets; red-brown on emergence. 'Irish Bronze', 'Kupferschein', coppery leaves.
Rodgersia sambucifolia Yunn.	1.20 white.	VI–VII, very long, pinnate leaves with 3–5 pairs of matt, lanceolate leaflets. 'Rothaut', red stems and leaf veins; white flowers.
Alaska fringecup *Tellima grandiflora* W N Am.	0.20/0.40 greenish	V–VI, rounded, crenate, heart-shaped leaves; unde-manding; tolerates competition from tree roots in moist soil. 'Purpurea', compact habit; colours up in autumn and has wine-red leaves through the winter.
Thalictrum delavayi (*Thalictrum dipterocarpum* Hort.) W China	1.80 pink-violet	VII–IX, exceedingly graceful and decorative plant; delicate, light green columbine-leaves; large, open panicles of small flowers on strong stems; often needs support at flowering time; prefers a slightly acidic soil; rather short-lived. 'Album', beautiful, white-flowered cultivar. 'Hewitt's Double' (1.20), double flowers.
Toadlily *Tricyrtis macropoda* Jap.	0.50 creamy white and purple	VIII–X, small, spotted, lily-shaped flowers; glossy, oval leaves; vigorous and hardy. *T. hirta* (0.50), pale lilac; grey-hairy leaves; not as hardy as the above. *T. h.* 'Alba', white; rare in the trade.
Tricyrtis pilosa Hort. Him.	0.60/1.00 white blotched red	X–XI, flowers in corymbs on stiffly upright stems; elongated, heart-shaped leaves with clasping bases; undemanding clump-former.

Tricyrtis latifolia Jap.	0.50–0.80 white spotted red	VI–VII, upright habit; fresh green, glabrous leaves and stems. All *Tricyrtis* species thrive in acid soil.

Bugbane (Cohosh), *Cimicifuga*

Like all long-lived perennials, these decorative plants with their long-stemmed, narrow heads of small white flowers and large, attractive leaves develop slowly, requiring several years to reach their full potential. They prefer moist to damp conditions and are thankful for a site free from competition.

Low and middle-sized plants

Cimicifuga racemosa var. *cordifolia* (*C. cordifolia*) E USA	0.40/1.50 yellowish white	VIII–X, wand-like racemes on wiry, dark brown stems above low mounds of, overlapping foliage; tolerates a certain amount of sun.
Cimicifuga japonica Jap.	0.30/1.50 white	IX–X, glossy, finely divided leaves; leafless flower-stems; not for exposed positions.
Cimicifuga acerina 'Compacta' Jap.	0.20/0.80 white	VII–IX, stiff but very dainty inflorescences over low foliage; often sold as *C. acerina* (1.20).
Cimicifuga simplex (*C. racemosa* var. *simplex*) 'White Pearl' Jap.	0.40/1.30 white	IX–X, much-branched, slightly drooping panicles; sensitive to early frosts. 'Armleuchter' ('Candelabrum'), old cultivar. 'Frau H. Herms' (1.50), IX–X, white. 'Braunlaub', brown-tinted foliage.

Tall species

Cimicifuga racemosa N Am.	2.00 white	VII, large, elegantly divided leaves; slightly arching panicles with few or no branches.
Cimicifuga dahurica Jap., Sib.	2.00 white	VIII, flower heads like branching candelabras over large, clean-cut leaves with serrated leaflets; dioecious; female plants inferior.
Cimicifuga ramosa Kamtsch.	2.00 cream-white	IX, perhaps the most beautiful *Cimicifuga*; long, fragrant panicles wirth very little branching. 'Atropurpurea', (2.00), white flowers; red-brown leaves. 'Brunette', (1.50), pale, red-brown foliage.

1.3.2. Perennials for enthusiasts

Anemonopsis macro-phylla Jap.	up to 1.00 pale lilac	VII–VIII, loose racemes of waxy, nodding flowers on long stems; leaves similar to *Actaea*; fully hardy but rare in the trade.
Arisaema ringens Jap., China	0.30/0.50 grey-brown, white stripes	III–IV, inflorescence appears before the large, tri-foliate leaves; brownish spathe bent like a helmet over the flower spike; very hardy.

A. amurensis, light green, 5-foliate, pedate leaves.
A. consanguineum (up to 1.50), large flowers; glowing red, cone-like fruits in autumn.
A. triphyllum, E. N Am., red, club-shaped fruit clusters; for shady woodland humus; tubers 15 cm deep; may need protecting with dry leaves in winter.

Begonia grandis var. *evansiana* (*B. evansiana*) China	up to 0.50 pink	VII–X, large, pointed, asymmetrical leaves with reddish undersides; axillary bulbils; not completely hardy. 'Alba', white; hardy.
Giant lily *Cardiocrinum giganteum* (*Lilium giganteum*) Him.	up to 3.00 white	VII–VIII, up to 20, downward-facing, funnel-shaped flowers on a powerful stem with broad, cordate, dark green leaves; bulbs die after flowering but offsets flower again after 4–5 years; for moist or damp, humus-rich soils in a cool, lightly shaded position; bulbs should be set very shallow; may need winter protection; rare in the trade.
Cortusa matthioli		List 4.5.1
Cyrtomium fortunei		List 1.2.4
Deinanthe caerulea China	0.30 lilac-blue	VII–VIII, broad, bushy habit; large, nodding flowers; large, shiny, hydrangea-like leaves; brownish new growth sensitive to late frosts; creeping rhizomes; for loose, damp, humus-rich soils; rare in the trade.
Umbrella leaf *Diphyleia cymosa* E USA	0.70 white	V, white corymbs; large, prettily lobed leaves; blue berries in September; for light shade on moist, humus-rich, woodland soil; prone to slug damage; sensitive to extreme cold.
Snow poppy *Eomecon chionantha* China	0.30 white (flushed pink)	IV, open panicles of poppy-like flowers with yellow stamens; large, kidney-shaped leaves; forms long rhizomes in moist, well drained soil; for cool, shady postitions in mild regions; winter protection.
Wand flower *Galax urceolata* (*G. aphylla*) E USA	0.20/0.30 white	VI–VII, dense-flowered spikes on leafless stems over glossy, evergreen foliage; round, leathery leaves turn reddish bronze over winter; for moist, acid, humus-rich soils; good with rhododendrons.
Gentiana asclepiadea		List 4.6.1
Hepatica nobilis 'Plena' Eur.	0.07/0.10 blue	III–IV, loamy soil in a spot that is free from competition and handy for maintenance; red and white forms also (rarely) available.
Jeffersonia dubia (*Plagiorhegma dubium*) E. N Am.	0.15 lavender blue	IV–V, thin, rounded, shell-shaped leaves with a metallic sheen; turns bronze-brown in autumn. *J. diphylla* (Twinleaf) (0.40/0.20), V, white; two-lobed leaves; for moist, humus-rich soils.
Kirengeshoma palmata Jap.	0.80 yellow	IX–X, thick, waxy, nodding, bell-shaped flowers in loose clusters borne on elegant, arching stems; rounded, heart-shaped leaves with pointed lobes;

		damp but well drained, lime-free, humus-rich soils in semi-shade.
Bloodroot *Sanguinaria canadensis* E N Am.	0.20 white	IV–V, anemone-like flowers appear before the blue-green, kidney-shaped leaves; dies down in late summer; rhizomes have copious, orange-red sap. 'Major', large flowers. 'Multiplex', double.
Saxifraga cortusifolia var. *fortunei* Jap., China	0.10/0.25 white	IX–X, rounded, lobed leaves; flowers may need protection against early frosts; long-lived in a shady spot; thrives in moist, acid, humus-rich soil. 'Rubrifolia', IX, reddish-brown leaves and red stems; flowers earlier.
Shortia galacifolia		List 4.6.2
White mandarin *Streptopus amplexifolius* Eur., As., N Am	0.70 greenish-white	V–VII, unspectacular flowers; red berries on branched stems with heart-shaped, clasping leaves; eaten by slugs. *S. roseus* (Rose mandarin), (0.40), pale pink flowers; broad lanceolate leaves.
Symphytum rubrum	0.10/0.25 red	III–V, similar to *S. grandiflorum* (list 1.1.1) but somewhat tender.
Pick-a-back plant *Tolmiea menziesii* W N Am.	up to 0.30 greenish	V–VI, insignificant flowers in long racemes; similar to *Heuchera*; lobed basal leaves often carry bulbils and young plants; needs a little protection in winter.
Celandine poppy *Stylophorum diphyllum* E USA	up to 0.50 golden yellow	VI–VII, stems have a single pair of leaves at the tip; poppy-like flowers; light green, pinnate, roughly hairy leaves; for moist soils in semi-shade.
Synthyris stellata (*S. reniformis* hort.) W USA	up to 0.20 lilac-blue	III–IV, racemes of bell-shaped flowers as the foliage unfurls; glossy, serrate, kidney-shaped leaves; best left undisturbed; for humus-rich soils.

1.3.3. Special conditions for more difficult perennials

These appealing but somewhat capricious woodland perennials are often better accommodated in the shady parts of a rock garden rather than among trees and shrubs, where their special requirements are not easily met. Individual maintenance is required for many of the species.

Lady's slipper orchid, *Cypripedium*

The severely endangered, native yellow lady's slipper orchid (*Cypripedium calceolus*) is among the prettiest and most admired of all our wild flowers. Pot-grown specimens of this large-flowered terrestrial orchid with its yellow, slipper-shaped lower lip are sometimes available in nurseries. The removal of specimens from the wild is not only illegal but also senseless, for the plants are very sensitive and damaged root-tips do not regenerate.

In contrast to many other orchids, the native lady's slipper prefers an alkaline, loamy soil, well-drained but not too dry, and rich in woodland humus. All the following species require a sheltered spot in semi-shade. *C. calceolus* also flourishes in somewhat brighter conditions, in association with plants such as *Carex montana*.

Cypripedium calceolus var. *calceolus* Eur., Cauc., Sib.	0.30 reddish-brown and yellow	V, 3–5-leaved shoots with 1–3 flowers; prone to slugs; calcicole. *C. macranthon*, Jap., N China, (0.40), light rosy purple with a darker lip; larger in all its parts.
Cypripedium acaule E N Am	0.15 greenish pink with darker lip	V–VI, large flowers; stems with two basal leaves; for damp, lime-free, peaty or acid–sandy soils.
Cypripedium calceolus var. *parviflorum* E N Am.	0.30 dark brown and yellow	V–VI, smaller American variety of *C. calceolus* with strongly twisted sepals; easily cultivated on lime-free soils; forms good clumps.
Cypripedium reginae (*C. spectabile*) NE Am.	0.50 white with pink lip	V–VI, large flowers with inflated, almost spherical lips; for damp, lime-free, peaty soils; very imposing and easily cultivated.

Numerous other *Cypripedium* species grow in the north temperate zone, but only rarely are any of them cultivated for the trade.

Shooting star, *Dodecatheon*

The attractive and dainty shooting stars with their nodding, cyclamen-like flowers succumb only too readily to competition from neighbouring plants, especially since their leaves die down immediately after flowering. Their proper planting position is in a cool woodland glade under the eye of a gardener, or on a shady rock terrace with primulas, *Liriope* and low-growing *Epimediums*. They need a lot of moisture in spring but should be kept dry for the rest of the year.
    Only a few of the many species and varieties are available from nurseries.

Dodecatheon jeffreyi W N Am.	0.15/0.60 purplish-red, white base	VII, statelier and longer-lived than the others; smooth, ovate-lanceolate leaves; rare in the trade.
Dodecatheon meadia E N Am.	0.15/0.50 pink, white base	V–VI, very variable; 10–20-flowered umbels on slender stems; longish, oval leaves; widespread in nurseries. f. *alba*, white-flowered form. Wild plants divide into two distinct ecological forms, confined either to open prairie or to forest habitats; neither will survive in the other's habitat.
Dodecatheon pulchellum (*D. pauciflorum*) W N Am.	0.08/0.20 pink	VI, very dainty; smooth or downy, ovate-lanceolate leaves; 3–7-flowered umbels. 'Red Wings', bright-red flowers.

Liriope

These Asiatic woodland perennials love a warm but at least partially shaded site on moist, rich, well-drained, acid soils with plenty of humus. Their narrow, evergreen leaves can be damaged by the sun in winter and it is therefore a good idea to place them under the shelter of evergreen shrubs such as rhododendrons, where they combine well with species such as *Ophiopogon* and *Saxifraga cortusifolia* var. *fortunei*.

Liriope graminifolia Jap., China	0.30 pale violet	VII, tough, grassy, evergreen leaves; spreads to form a good groundcover under shrubs. Plants sold in

America as *L. graminifolia* are probably *L. spicata* var. *densifolia*.

Liriope graminifolia var. *minor* Jap., China	0.20 greenish white	VII, narrow, dark green leaves; good groundcover.
Liriope muscari (*L. platyphylla*) Jap., China	0.20/0.40 lavender-blue	VIII–IX, clump-forming; attractive, dense-flowered racemes in autumn; for a warm, shady spot. 'Curly Twist' broad leaved. 'Ingwersen', free-flowering; strong grower. 'Majestic', very vigorous. 'Monroe White', snow-white flowers; green leaves. 'Golden Banded', leaves with yellow margins. 'Lilac Beauty', particularly large and attractive inflorescences. 'Silver Dragon', pale lavender and white flowers; green and white striped leaves; some leaves all white. One American nursery lists more than eighty cultivars of this species.
Liriope spicata Jap., China	0.40/0.45 violet	VII–IX, hardiest species; narrow, dark green leaves; loose flowered inflorescences; foliage deteriorates in winter; spreads and quickly forms a dense carpet.

Blue poppy, *Meconopsis*

The proper planting site for these wonderfully beautiful poppies from Tibet and Nepal is a clearing under trees, 'where dew and raindrops drench the air' (Wocke), or a similarly bright but cool situation with a northerly or northeasterly aspect.

Well-drained, lime-free soil can be improved for meconopsis by the addition of needle litter and sandy loam. During the growing season the plants need a lot of moisture and should be sprayed over in dry weather. In winter, on the other hand, they should be kept as dry as possible. The beauty of these rare plants is best appreciated in a spacious setting. They are not well suited to regions with a warm, dry climate. In America they grow best on the Olympic Peninsula.

Meconopsis *betonicifolia* (*M. baileyi*) Tibet, Yunn.	0.30/1.20 sky-blue	VI–VII, leaves with brownish hairs; large, slightly nodding flowers with golden yellow anthers on sparse-leaved stems; long-lived on well-drained, loose, loamy soils.
M. grandis Tibet, Nepal	0.30/0.90 sky-blue	V–VI, rigid, upright, almost leafless stems; large basal leaves with red-brown hairs; not as hardy as *M. betonicifolia*; acid soil. *M. × sheldonii* (*M. grandis × M. betonicifolia*) (1.00), VI, intense blue flowers; elegant habit, resembling *M. betonicifolia* but with larger flowers; very long-lived.
Meconopsis cambrica		List 1.2.2

Biennial species, such as *M. napaulensis* (VI, wine-red flowers) and *M. regia* (VII–VIII, pure yellow flowers) are much admired in botanic gardens but not generally available from nurseries.

Primula capitata, P. sikkimensis and their relatives

These mostly short-lived but incomparably beautiful primulas thrive in a cool, humid spot with moist or damp, neutral to slightly acid soil. They associate well with ferns in the bright semi-shade of a woodland clearing but must be well protected from the midday sun. Their roots do not go deep and they tend to dry out quickly when planted too far apart or in unfavourable conditions. In spring the plants need plenty of moisture but prefer slightly drier conditions for the rest of the year. In winter they can be protected with conifer branches.

The following species grow best in dense stands, as they do in the wild, so any seedlings should be carefully nurtured. They are especially effective combined with dwarf shrubs and the perennials from list 1.3.3. The more robust, candelabra primulas have been assigned to the woodland edge (list 2.3.1).

Primula alpicola Tibet	0.50 yellow	VI–VII, funnel-shaped flowers; long, elliptic, somewhat leathery leaves; vigorous and comparatively long-lived. 'Alba', milk-white flowers. 'Luna', lemon-yellow. 'Violacea', violet.
Primula capitata E Him	0.20 blue-violet	VII–IX, capitate inflorescence on a slender, silvery-white, mealy stem; long, wrinkled, serrate leaves; short-lived. *P.c.* ssp. *mooreana*, leaf upper surfaces not mealy.
Primula chionantha Yunn.	0.40 white	V–VI, a very beautiful plant; fragrant whorls of flowers on tall stems; sensitive to damp in winter.
Primula secundiflora (*P. vittata*) Yunn., Tibet	up to 0.70 purple	V–VI, flattened rosettes; white, mealy stems with nodding, funnel-shaped flowers; short-lived.
Primula sikkimensis Tibet, Sikkim	up to 0.50 yellow	VI–VII, daintier version of *P. florindae*; sturdy, often mealy stems with nodding flowers. 'Crimson and Gold', colourful selection.
Primula vialii (*P. littoniana*) NW Yunn.	up to 0.60 pale lilac (red buds)	VI–VII, broad, lanceolate leaves; sturdy, mealy stems with dense, conical spikes of flowers; does not appear until May; perennates well on moist, loamy, humus-rich soil.

Roscoea

These plants resemble orchids but belong to the ginger family. Their home is the mountain woodlands of sub-tropical China, but given a protective blanket of peat or leaves they are reasonably hardy and develop into many-flowered clumps, which may even seed themselves. Roscoeas flourish in a sheltered, semi-shady position in well-drained soil that is rich in humus. Their shoots develop slowly, first appearing at the end of May but then speeding up to flower soon afterwards. When required, the plants can be forced. Roscoeas should be planted about 10 cm deep in spring.

Roscoea cautleoides NW Yunn.	up to 0.40 bright yellow	VI, large (4 cm), two-lobed flowers in spikes of 7–8; rigid stems; blue-green, lanceolate leaves up to 60 cm long.

Roscoea humeana W Yunn.	up to 0.30 purple to wine-red with yellow	VII, the most ornamental species; very large (7 cm) flowers in spikes of 4–8; stems up to 25 cm; broad, dark green leaves.
Roscoea purpurea Him.	up to 0.40 purple	VIII–IX, less spectacular than the other species; the flowers appear one at a time when the leaves are fully developed; robust and hardy. *R. p.* var. *procera* (up to 0.30), VII–VIII, lilac flowers striped with white.

Cautleya

A small genus of tender plants from the Himalayas that resemble both *Roscoea* and *Canna*. The hardiest species needs a sheltered, semi-shady spot with moist, humus-rich soil and a thick blanket of leaves in winter. Planting depth at least 10 cm.

Cautleya lutea (*C. gracilis*) Him.	0.25–0.40 golden yellow	VIII–IX, spikes of small flowers with red bracts; long, broad, pointed, fresh freen leaves.

1.3.4. Perennials for summer drought under deciduous trees (park-type maintenance)

These important perennials belong mostly to the woodland edge but are able to withstand much drier and shadier conditions. They thrive in full shade directly under trees, especially where the soil is rich and loamy. Of course, the majority of them prefer a more favourable position, but a few, such as *Cyclamen hederifolium*, actually grow better where the ground is permeated with tree roots. Others, such as *Euphorbia amygdaloides* var. *robbiae* and *Waldsteinia geoides*, grow almost as well in drought as in moisture. The same applies for most of the early-flowering bulbs, corms and tubers. Many of these, like *Chionodoxa luciliae* and *Crocus tommasinianus*, prefer a site which is dry in summer. *Eranthis* too grows well under these conditions, seeding itself prolifically. Among the woody plants the common ivy, *Hedera helix*, is suitable, particulary its cultivars 'Sagittaefolia' and 'Crispa'.

   The elegant but robust species from lists 1.3.5 and 1.3.6 are for the special soil conditions under mature trees.

Bergenia spp.	List 2.3.3	Light shade on loamy or sandy soils; the drought resistance of the different species and hybrids is variable, and none thrive in combined heat and drought.
Buglossoides purpurocaerulea	List 2.1.2	Prefers a loamy soil.
Cyclamen hederifolium	List 2.3.3	Not for sandy soils.
Cyclamen coum	List 2.3.3	Not for sandy soils.
Dryopteris filix-mas	List 1.2.4	Loamy and sandy soils.
Duchesnea indica	List 2.1.2	Not for sandy soils.
Epimedium alpinum & *E. pinnatum*	List 1.1.1	Rich, loamy, but also sandy soils.
Euphorbia amygdaloides var. *robbiae*	List 4.5.4	Nutrient-rich soils in mild regions.

Galium odoratum	List 1.2.1	Only on loamy, nutrient-rich soils; can become invasive.
Helleborus spp.	List 2.3.3	Only on loamy soils; the various species and hybrids have different requirements.
Hypericum calycinum	List 2.1.2	Sandy and loamy soils.
Galeobdolon luteum 'Florentinum'	List 1.1.1	Sandy and loamy soils.
Luzula pilosa & *L. sylvatica*	List 1.2.3 List 1.1.4	Humus-rich, sandy and loamy soils.
Poa chaixii	List 1.1.1	Loamy, intermittently moist soils.
Symphytum grandiflorum	List 1.1.1	Nutrient-rich, loamy soil.
Vinca minor	List 1.1.1	Sandy and loamy soils.
Waldsteinia geoides & *W. ternata*	List 1.1.1	Sandy and loamy soils.

1.3.5. Needle litter under mature conifers

The sparsely moss-covered needle litter under groups of tall conifers is generally inimical to the growth of perennials. However, the following species have proved effective on moist and dry soils.

Montia sibirica (*Claytonia sibirica*) NW USA	0.05/0.10 pink	VI–VIII, dainty, unassuming perennial with rhombic, semi-evergreen leaves; seeds itself prolifically.
Veronica 'Allgrün' (*V. allionii* × *V. officinalis*)		See list 4.5.3; can be smothered by fallen leaves under broadleaved trees. *V. allionii* (0.05), VII–VIII, evergreen carpeter; for rich, lime-free humus.
White butterbur *Petasites albus* Eur.	0.30 white	IV, branched, dome-shaped inflorescences; decorative, rounded, broad-triangular leaves with woolly grey hairs underneath; spreads even in deepest shade; rare in the trade.

1.3.6. Mor soils under mature broadleaves and conifers

These dainty, European species can be effectively established in the shade on moist, poorish, moderately acidic soils that are rich in mor humus. Given the right conditions they require only a park-type maintenance but cannot stand competition from strong-growing neighbours.

Avenella flexuosa		List 2.1.8; as groundcover.
Luzula pilosa		List 1.2.3; small groups.
May-lily *Maianthemum bifolium* Eur., Sib., E Asia	0.10 white	V–VI, like a dwarf lily-of-the-valley; spreads freely on acid, humus-rich soils; tolerates periodic drought. *M. canadense*, (0.20), more imposing; covers the ground well; rare in the trade.
Wood sorrel *Oxalis acetosella* Eur., Asia	0.05 white	IV–V, delicate, fresh green, clover-like leaves; for moist mor humus without competition; shade only.

Cowberry	0.20	V–VI, bell-shaped flowers; shiny, dark green, ever-
Vaccinium vitis-idaea	whitish pink	green leaves; edible red fruits.
Eur., N As., N N Am.		'Koralle', vigorous selection.
		'Minus', (0.07), dwarf, mat-forming cultivar.

For garden-type maintenance

Hard fern, Deer fern		List 1.2.4
Blechnum spicant		Singly or in small groups on peaty soils.
Eur., Cauc., China,		
Jap., N Am.		
Bunchberry	0.10	V–VI, very dainty flowers over whorled leaves; round,
Cornus canadensis	white	red fruits in autumn (X); calcifuge.
N Am.		
Twinflower	0.20	VI–VIII, delicate, bell-shaped flowers over creeping,
Linnaea borealis	white and	round-leaved stems; roots in cool, damp, acid, nutri-
Circumpolar	pink	ent-poor humus.
Chickweed wintergreen	0.15	VI–VII, very attractive and delicate; spreads by
Trientalis europaea	white	seeding on moist or damp, acid, peaty soils.
Eur., N Asia		
Soldanella montana		List 4.5.3
Eur.		
Saxifraga cuneifolia		List 4.1.3
S Eur.		

1.4.   Bulbs, corms and tubers for woodland areas

The following woodland edge species (list 2.4.2) will thrive and seed themselves in deciduous woodland too, wherever the soil is rich and moist enough in spring.

For dense summer shade

Winter aconite (*Eranthis hyemalis*)
Snowdrop (*Galanthus nivalis*)
Snowflake (*Leucojum vernum*), especially on damp or wet soils.

For light summer shade

Daffodil (*Narcissus pseudonarcissus*)
Scilla (*Scilla bifolia, Scilla siberica*)
English bluebell (*Hyacinthoides non-scripta*)

2 Woodland edge

The woodland edges of our parks and gardens are very variable in their structure and it is helpful to make a distinction between 'open' and 'closed' formations. The former have much in common with a thinly planted grove, offering niches for both woodland and meadow plants along with the perennials that are more specifically associated with the woodland edge. By contrast, a closed woodland edge is made up of densely growing twigs and branches and thus bears some resemblance to an annually cut hedge. In the absence of trimming, however, the trees and shrubs continue to grow and spread outwards until space runs out or the branches must be cut back.

There are many perennials that grow well on the woodland edge, each finding its own narrow niche among the varied ecological conditions to be found. Many of them are creeping, spreading or climbing species, well adapted to cope with the annual growth of the woody plants above them. Tall, sturdy, clump-forming perennials are typical for more open and brightly lit spaces, while all sorts of woodland plants fill the shady spots under trees and shrubs. In the lists that follow, these species have been ordered according to their growing requirements and the degree to which they are bound to the woodland edge proper.

In a small garden the areas of woodland edge are often intricately meshed with other garden habitats. The stone edging of a path might provide an opportunity to plant rock garden perennials, or there may be an area in front of a densely planted shrubbery or formal hedge where border perennials can be found a home. In the same way, the sloping ground between an area of woodland and a path might be suitable for growing meadow plants, and a ditch or stream would create additional planting positions for wetland perennials and tall herbs.

For the most part, woodland edge perennials must be able to cope with an annual covering of fallen leaves. Plants such as evergreen, sedums, saxifrages and *Cotula* spp., which are easily smothered, should rather be grown in the rock garden, though their use in intensively maintained gardens and on graves, in combination with evergreen trees and shrubs, may also be possible.

Competition between woody species and herbaceous perennials plays an important role on the woodland edge. Of course, in the first few years it is possible to grow almost anything beneath newly planted trees and shrubs. However, if tree roots later form a dense mat directly under the soil surface, then every sort of underplanting is at risk, even where the shade is not too intense. For this reason, perennial plantings develop poorly under false acacias, birches, poplars and willows. Similarly, on nutrient-rich and loamy soils, the roots of wild cherry (*Prunus avium*) and the related sweet cherries prevent any of the more demanding perennials from developing properly. Sea buckthorn (*Hippophaë* spp.), grey alder (*Alnus incana*), aspen (*Populus tremula*), lilac (*Syringa vulgaris*) and stag's horn sumach (*Rhus typhina*) are all unsuitable for underplanting because, like the false acacia, they tend to send up suckers, especially where their roots are injured by digging.

In the deep shade cast by trees such as horse-chestnuts, the only plants that will grow are spring flowering bulbs, such as winter aconites (*Eranthis*) and snowdrops (*Galanthus*). A planting under limes may be affected by sooty mildew, for these trees often play host to aphids, whose sticky secretions drop down onto the leaves below. Water droplets may also be a hazard for some plants. Heather (*Erica herbacea*) and ling (*Calluna*) are particularly sensitive in this respect and should therefore be planted in the open. Ling cannot tolerate the fallen leaves of deciduous trees but will put up with pine and larch needles, associating well with these conifers on an open woodland edge.

Professional and amateur gardeners alike often find themselves regretting the choice of lawn

Woodland edge: an open, sunny woodland edge.

Woodland edge: a shady woodland edge.

shrubs that allow a weedy undergrowth. If only the chosen species had a fuller skirt of low, dense branches then all the work of weeding would be saved. However, it is precisely these leggy, high-branching shrubs that are most suited to an underplanting of woodland edge perennials. The more ornamental among them are better combined with border perennials or else wild perennials with border character. For example, delphiniums may be planted to flower together with the upright growing *Philadelphus lemoinei* 'Erectus'. Nevertheless, there remains a place for true wild perennials in the area directly under ornamental shrubs, When flowering times coincide then even the most unassuming of plants may achieve an effect. A flowering currant (*Ribes sanguineum*), for instance, might be underplanted with blue-flowered *Brunnera macrophylla*, thus forming a harmonious colour combination with the yellow of a neighbouring *Forsythia*.

Convincingly combined with trees and shrubs, perennials attain an importance in the garden that is independent of any strong colours or mass effect. A scattering of snowdrops under limes or hazels, fragrant blue violets along a hawthorn hedge or the splendour of a delphinium among roses all bear witness to this.

The recreational value of a woodland edge is high, and ecologists emphasise the importance of this habitat as a home for many different species of plant and animal. Nevertheless, in public parks the woodland edges are often spoiled by the introduction of all kinds of exotic plants and even ornamental flowering shrubs. Within a few years, such intruders tend to form an unsightly collar around the woodland areas, disrupting the harmonious appearance of the park and preventing the development of a more natural flora. On top of this, the grass is often mown regularly right up to the trees and shrubs, leaving no room for a proper woodland fringe to develop. It is high time that woodland edge perennials achieved more recognition from landscape architects and planners. Many of them are not available as plants from the nursery trade but their seed may be sown out in places where patches of woodland adjoin a path or meadow, or in bright and airy groves of high-crowned trees. The prevailing ecological conditions and type of maintenance are both factors to be taken into account when choosing species. In some parks the twice-yearly hay-cut allows a very attractive woodland edge flora to develop. The same effect can be achieved in private gardens, wherever there is room to allow meadow flowers and grasses to grow up in front of trees and shrubs.

The great value of woodland edge perennials is seldom fully appreciated. In a newly landscaped garden they will tolerate both sun and shade, and a suitable combination with groundcover plants will prevent the emergence of troublesome weeds. They also include an unusually high proportion of species that are undemanding and hardly require any maintenance once established.

Left largely to itself, a woodland edge planting can develop into a valuable garden biotope, offering delightful surprises at almost every time of year. Bulbs flower in early spring beneath the bare twigs and branches, and are followed by a summer bounty of form and colour that reaches its climax with the warm tones of autumn.

The different species have been ordered as follows.

2.1 Perennials confined to the woodland edge.
2.2 Perennials more loosely bound to the woodland edge.
2.3 Perennials for special conditions, on or near the woodland edge.
2.4 Flowering bulbs, corms and tubers.

2.1.   Perennials confined to the woodland edge

These lists contain many important groundcover species for use in association with trees and shrubs, including some, such as *Anemone canadensis*, which only thrive under special growing conditions. The species in lists 2.1.7 and 2.1.8 form a transition to the perennials that are more loosely bound to the woodland edge. A few are also related to the perennials for open ground.

2.1.1. Groundcover perennials for shady woodland edge conditions

The following species are suitable for moist, loamy soils but will also tolerate periodic drought. Depending on the planting position, they may be combined with the undemanding woodland perennials from list 1.1.1, or with woody species such as ivy and *Symphoricarpus* 'Hancock'.

Yellow archangel	*Galeobdolon luteum* 'Florentinum'
Spotted dead-nettle	*Lamium maculatum*
Pachysandra	*Pachysandra terminalis*
Caucasian comfrey	*Symphytum grandiflorum*
Foam flower	*Tiarella cordifolia*
Periwinkle	*Vinca minor*

2.1.2. Widely spreading (and creeping) groundcover plants for sun and semi-shade on the woodland edge

These are typical woodland edge plants, able to adapt to the constantly changing conditions under advancing trees and shrubs. They thrive on nutrient-rich, predominantly moist but also intermittently dry soils, increasing by means of rhizomes, runners and stolons. Their lax stems sprawl out across the ground and may even scramble into overhanging shrubs. In the garden, they are simple to use. A few plants of a single species are often enough to create a weed-proof groundcover that also brings an annual harvest of flowers.

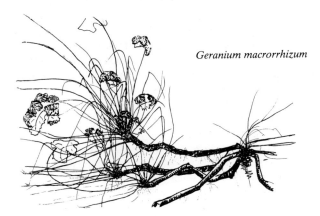

Geranium macrorrhizum

A capacity for vigorous spread is characteristic of many woodland edge species.

Newly planted trees and shrubs should be given time to get established before the soil beneath them is planted up. Woodland edge perennials should first be introduced after two or three years, when they serve to keep down aggressive weeds such as ground-elder (*Aegopodium podagraria*).

Species marked with an asterisk are especially suitable for use in public parks.

Blue gromwell *Buglossoides purpuro-* *caerulea* (*Lithospermum pur-* *purocaeruleum*) Eur., Asia Minor	0.20 gentian blue	V, grey-green leaves on long, rooting stems; prefers a warm, dry sunny position on limy soil; must be kept moist directly after planting.
Herbaceous *Clematis* spp.		List 2.1.5. Especially *C. × jouiniana*

Duchesnea indica Jap., China	0.10 yellow	V, strawberry-like leaves and (tasteless) fruits; thrives in a warm spot; spreads rapidly on light soils.
Wild strawberry Fragaria vesca Circumpolar	up to 0.20 white	IV–VI, the well known, small-fruited, wild strawberry; unfortunately, only the runnerless Alpine strawberry (*F. v.* var. *semperflorens*, list 5.7.1) is available in the trade. *F. viridis*, good groundcover plant.
Geranium endressii W Pyren.	0.35/0.55 pale pink	VI–VIII, fresh green foliage; very vigorous. 'A. T. Johnson', (0.30), silvery pink flowers. 'Claridge Druce', (*G. endressii* × *G. versicolor*), pink; evergreen; exceptionally vigorous and free-flowering; climbs up to 1.50 m into shrubs. 'Crimson Beauty', crimson. 'Rose Clair', similar to the next. 'Wargrave Pink', dark pink.
Geranium macrorrhi- zum SE Eur., S Alp.	0.25/0.30 magenta	VI, semi-evergreen, aromatic foliage; vigorous spreader. Selections: 'Biokovo', list 4.3.1. 'Ingwersen's Variety', delicate pink; semi-evergreen foliage; not so vigorous. 'Variegata', green and white leaves; not for extensive planting.
Geranium macrorrhi- zum 'Spessart'	0.25/0.30 whitish pink	VI, rounded, aromatic, semi-evergreen leaves; very vigorous but always presentable; seeds itself freely and comes true. Selection: 'Velebit', red flowers; semi-evergreen.

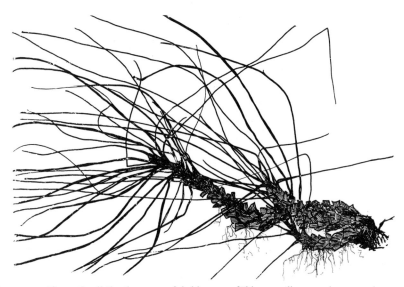

Geranium × magnificum: the distinctive, powerful rhizomes of this sprawling, weed-suppressing cranesbill.

Geranium × magni-ficum (*G. platypetalum* hort.)	0.35/0.70 violet-blue	VI–VII, leaves have fiery autumn colours; tolerates drought. *G. platypetalum* is similar but weaker, with smaller, purple flowers and no autumn colour.
Spotted cranesbill *Geranium maculatum* N Am.)	0.30 lilac	V–VI, free-flowering; hairy, palmately-lobed leaves with reddish autumn colour; thick rhizomes; still fairly uncommon.
Geranium renardii Cauc.	025/0.30 lilac-pink	V–VI, attractively corrugated, grey-green leaves; sensitive to extreme cold. Good selection: 'Walter Ingwersen'.
*Bloody cranesbill *Geranium sanguineum* Eur., Cauc.	0.15/0.25 magenta	VI–VII, open habit with large flowers and neat, dainty foliage; attractive, red autumn colour, seeds itself. 'Album', white. 'Lancastriense', list 4.3.1. 'Nanum', low; long-flowering. 'Elspeth', red; larger flowers than the type.
Geranium wallichianum 'Buxton's Variety' Him.	0.20/0.30 opal blue	VII, low-growing plant with brightly coloured flowers; thrives in warmth; not for covering large areas.
Siberian cranesbill *Geranium wlassovianum* C Asia	0.40 dark violet	VII, hairy, rounded leaves on long petioles; thrives in warmth; sprawling habit; prolific self-seeder.

Buglossoides purpurocaerulea

The arching shoots of this species need a lot of space in order to be properly effective.

Species that are also suitable for open ground

*Rose of Sharon *Hypericum calycinum* SE Eur., Turk.	0.30 yellow	VII–IX, semi-shrubby groundcover plant with rooting branches and spreading roots; evergreen in a sheltered location; large, yellow flowers; blue-green foliage often clashes with the dark green of neigh-

bouring plants; undemanding in shade or sun; suitable for covering steep slopes; usually needs cutting back in early spring.

Polygonum com- pactum 'Roseum' (*Reynoutria japonica* 'Compacta' Jap., China	0.50 white, then pink	VIII, flowers in dainty panicles over coarse, green foliage; emerges late and is unsightly in winter; moist or damp soils; dangerously invasive.

2.1.3.   Groundcover plants that tolerate mowing

These low-growing perennials thrive on the woodland edge and spread out into lawns or areas of long grass. They tolerate occasional, but not constant, mowing. (See also p. 245.)

Purple bugle *Ajuga reptans* 'Purpurea' Eur.	0.30/0.10 blue	IV–V, purplish-leaved cultivar of the native bugle; shallow rooted; requires a moist to damp, loamy, nutrient-rich soil in order to succeed as groundcover; susceptible to crown rot fungus where summers are warm. 'Palisander', similar to above. 'Alba', white; green leaves. 'Burgundy Glow', blue; purple, pink and white leaves. 'Multicolor', yellowish mottled leaves. 'Teppichrosa', pink; reddish-green leaves. 'Variegata', blue; white-variegated leaves.
Ground ivy *Glechoma hederacea* Eur., As., Jap.	0.15 violet	IV, low, undemanding meadow perennial for damp, fertile, humus-rich soils; spreads strongly and should be used with care. 'Variegata', green and white leaves; sometimes useful for troughs and containers.
Creeping Jenny *Lysimachia nummularia* Eur., Cauc.	0.05 yellow	VI, large flowers on prostrate, creeping stems; for damp, shady places; very vigorous and invasive in a warm climate. 'Aurea', rounded, golden-yellow leaves; somewhat tender; less vigorous. *L. nemorum*, (0.08), yellow; forms dense carpets, but short-lived and does not tolerate mowing.

2.1.4.   Low, undemanding groundcover plants for garden-type maintenance in shade and bright shade on the woodland edge

On moist, rich soils, the following perennials form plantings that hardly require any maintenance once established. They may also be combined with the species from lists 2.2.1 and 2.2.2.

Astilbe chinensis 'Pumila' Tibet	0.10/0.25 lilac-pink	VIII–IX, delicate, leafy plant with flowers in slender panicles; vigorous, spreading habit, covers the ground well, prefers cool and moist conditions. For similar but more demanding species, see list 5.1. *A. chinensis*, list 1.1.2.

Convallaria majalis 'Grandiflora' Eur., Cauc., E Asia	0.20/0.30 white	V, old, thick-stemmed, garden cultivar, with more abundant flowers than the species (list 1.1.2); red berries; for sun or shade under trees. 'Fortin's Giant', abundant large flowers. 'Plena', double white flowers; rare in the trade. 'Rosea', light pink flowers.
Blue-eyed Mary, Navalseed *Omphalodes verna* SE Alp. to N Apenn., C Rum.	0.15 bright blue	IV–V, forget-me-not flowers and ovate leaves; short rhizomes; covers the ground well on moist to dryish soils in semi-shade; may be smothered out under fallen leaves. 'Alba', white; not very vigorous. 'Grandiflora', blue; somewhat larger flowers than the type.
Saxifraga × urbium		List 4.1.3
Vinca minor		List 1.1.1
Woolly blue violet *Viola sororia* (*V. papilionacea*) N Am.	0.15 blue-violet	IV–V, large-flowered, scentless violet; vigorous, healthy foliage; groundcover plant; bare in winter; prolific self-seeder. 'Immaculata' ('Albiflora') (0.20), white; very vigorous on loam. 'Priceana' (0.15), white with porcelain-blue markings.

2.1.5. Climbing and sprawling perennials (without spreading rhizomes)

On the whole, these species are best planted singly, in sun or bright shade, directly on the woodland edge. (Figures in brackets refer to climbing height.)

Aconitum volubile 'Tenuisectum' Jap., E Sib.	1.50 violet	VII–IX, weakly twining stems with dangling racemes of flowers; leaves deeply lobed and divided; enthusiasts' plant for shade and semi-shade. Other *Aconitum* spp., see list 1.1.2.
Asparagus pseudo-scaber 'Spitzenschleier' (*A. officinalis* var. *pseudoscaber*) Rum.	up to 2.00	VI, insignificant flowers; deep green, feathery foliage; best planted with conifers. *A. verticillatus* (2.00), climber with branching stems; red berries; rare in the trade.
Clematis × bonstedtii		List 2.2.2
Clematis × bondstedtii 'Mrs. Robert Brydon'	0.50 (up to 2.00) pale lilac	VIII–IX, exceptionally vigorous cultivar; lax stems, making plants of up to 3 m diameter; attractive as a trained specimen.
Clematis heracleifolia N China	0.50 (to 0.70) blue	VIII–IX, clusters of dainty, nodding flowers over broad leaves. *C. h.* var. *davidiana*, *C. h.* 'Gentianoides', intensely blue flowers; more attractive than the type.
Clematis integrifolia SE Eur., Asia Minor, Altai	0.50 (to 1.00) blue	VII–VIII; more important is the hybrid with *C. × jackmanii*: *C. × durandii* (1.80), semi-woody perennial with bright blue flowers; can be rather short-lived; cut back hard in autumn or spring.

Clematis × jouiniana (*C. heracleifolia × C. vitalba*) 'Praecox'	0.30 (to 4.00) blue-white	VIII–IX, stems up to 2 m long, sometimes becoming woody; reliable groundcover for the woodland edge; cut back hard in autumn or spring.
Codonopsis clematidea C Asia	0.50 milky blue	VII–VIII, robust, leafy perennial, best appreciated from close range; flowers have a musky, animal odour; also suitable for training into rock garden shrubs. *C. ovata, C. convolulacea, C. mollis, C. vinciflora*, unspectacular, bell-shaped flowers; enthusiasts' plants. All species rare in the trade.
Perennial pea *Lathyrus latifolius* Eur.	up to 2.00 (3.00) magenta	VI–VIII, robust and hardy perennial that resembles a sweet-pea; climbs well and will cover an ugly wire fence; seeds freely and becomes rampant in regions with a warm summer. 'Rose Queen', mallow pink. 'Splendens', red. 'White Pearl', white.
Everlasting pea *L. grandiflorus* S Eur.	up to 2.00 pink-purple	VI–VIII, very large flowers in clusters of 1–3; less robust and shorter-lived than *L. latifolius*.
Hop *Humulus lupulus* Eur., As., N Am.	2.00–6.00	VII–VIII, dioecious; male flowers insignificant; female flowers in a cone-like inflorescence; winding stems with rough, yellowish green, entire or 3–5 lobed leaves; invasive and difficult to eradicate; rarely available in the trade. *H. scandens* 'Aureus', annual species.

2.1.6.   Perennials for shade and bright shade on moist, nutrient-rich soils

These woodland edge perennials are ecologically related to the woodland species from list 1.2.2 and may often be combined with them, particularly in a garden setting. Though all will grow in light woodland, they do better in the somewhat brighter conditions of the woodland edge.

Plants marked with an asterisk are more loosely bound to the woodland edge, and will tolerate fairly open, sunny conditions.

Allium paradoxum Cauc.	0.25 white	IV–V, umbels of drooping, long-stemmed flowers and ovoid bulbils; 3-angled stalks; rapid coloniser; rare in the trade. Similar: *A. triquetrum* (0.30), IV–V, white. *A. zebdanense* (to 0.50), IV–V, white; erect habit; abundant flowers. All die down after flowering.
Anemone canadensis N Am.	0.40 white	VI–VII, palmately divided leaves on upright petioles; creeping rootstock rapidly covers large areas in shade and semi-shade; intolerably invasive in warm regions. *A. cylindrica* (Thimbleweed) (0.80), VI–VII, white; also for bright shade.
Anemone trifolia Mts. of C & S Eur.	0.25 white	V, dark green, serrate, trifoliate leaves; shallow, spreading rhizomes similar to *A. nemorosa*; for woodland soils, also under pines; rare in the trade.

Aquilegia vulgaris		List 2.2.1 Not for massed planting; may be seeded out (800 seed/g), especially on sparse grass-covered slopes.
Astrantia maxima Cauc.	0.40 whitish	VII–VIII, similar to *A, major* (list 1.2.1) but with tripartite basal leaves; strongly spreading rhizomes; rare in the trade.
Cicerbita bourgaei Asia Minor	0.30/2.00 lilac	VII–VIII, racemes of abundant small flowers; basal leaves with heart-shaped terminal section; for moist, loamy soils in parks and large gardens. *C. macrophylla* (2.00), VIII, vigorous vegetative spread but flowers reluctantly. Both species are rare in the trade. See also list 4.6.1.
Corydalis nobilis Sib., Altai	0.30/0.50 yellow, with dark spots	V, abundant, large flowers in squat racemes; blue-green, deeply lobed or pinnate leaves; dies down soon after flowering; rare in the trade. *C. ophiocarpa* (0.50), V–VII, yellowish-green; short-lived; seeds itself abundantly.
Cyclamen purpurascens		List 2.3.3
Wood spurge *Euphorbia amygda-loides* Eur., Cauc.	up to 0.50 greenish yellow	IV–V, unspectacular flowers in terminal cymes on reddish, sparsely leafy stems; eye-catching, purplish leaves in winter; seeds itself; also colonises sunny areas. 'Purpurea', purplish leaves throughout the year.
Gentiana asclepiadea		List 4.6.1
Geranium nodosum Eur.	0.30 lilac-pink	VI–VII, upright habit; glossy, lobed leaves; spreads in deepest shade; prolific self-seeder
Mourning widow Geranium phaeum Eur.	up to 0.50 brown-violet	VI–VII, fairly upright habit; grows well in large groups on moist, nutrient-rich soils in bright shade. 'Album', white. 'Lividum', lilac.
Geranium himalayense (*G. meeboldii*) (*G. grandiflorum*) 'Johnson's Blue' Sikk.	0.30/0.40 lilac blue	V–VI, bowl-shaped flowers on branching stems; deeply cut leaves are cast off early; not for planting in large groups. *G.m.* 'Alpinum' (0.30), large flowers. *G. m.* 'Gravetye' (0.30), very large, blue-purple flowers. *G. rectum* 'Album', white; otherwise similar to the above.
Geranium sylvaticum Eur., W Sib.	0.60 red-violet	VI–VII, open, upright habit; many-flowered cymes over large, incised and lobed leaves; less invasive than many other *Geranium* species; for cool, bright shade and northern slopes. 'Compactum' (0.30), lower. 'Mayflower', light blue. 'Meran', dark blue. 'Roseum', pink. *G. versicolor*, (0.25), pink; flowers early.

Helleborus spp.   List 2.3.3

Lamium garganicum S Eur.	0.25 pink	V–VI, large flowers over hairy, green, nettle-like leaves; spreads and covers the ground well.
Lamium maculatum		List 1.1.1
Lamium orvala N Ital. to S Hung.	0.60 brownish red	V–VI, sturdy inflorescences over dark, nettle-like foliage; seeds itself in bright shade.
Lamium pyrenaicum Pyren.	0.30 light pink	VI–VII, leafy, upright plant with light green, nettle-like foliage; similar to *L. maculatum* (list 1.1.1).
Lathyrus gmelinii (*Orobus luteus*) Urals, C Asia	0.50 orange- yellow	V–VIII, open, spreading habit; leaves pinnate with 3–6 pairs of lanceolate leaflets; free-flowering, robust and reliable; prolific self-seeder in light shade. 'Aureus', orange or brownish.
*Lathyrus trans- *sylvanicus* (*Orobus trans-* *sylvanicus*) Rum.	up to 0.60 yellow and orange	V–VI, bushy habit; smooth, pinnate leaves. *L. laevigatus*, similar but with smaller, hairy leaves. Both for sunny positions.
Bastard balm *Melittis melissophyllum* Eur.	0.30 reddish and white	VI, large-flowered, nettle-like perennial; remains attractive till autumn; prefers a warm position.
*Oxlip *Primula elatior* Eur.	0.20 pale yellow	III–IV, scentless flowers in umbels; for moist or damp, loamy soils in sun or shade; seeds itself. Cultivars, see list 2.2.1.
*Primula veris		List 2.1.7
*Primrose *Primula vulgaris* (*P. acaulis*) Eur.	0.10 sulphur yellow	II–IV, whorls of scentless flowers in the centre of a leafy rosette; for predominantly lime-free, moist or damp, loamy, humus-rich soils; prefers semi-shade. Cultivars, see list 2.2.1.
Primula vulgaris ssp. *sibthorpii* (*P. acaulis* var. *rubra*) (*P. abchasica*) E Balk., Asia Minor, Cauc.	0.10 red, pink, purple	II–IV, early-flowering; tolerates limited summer drought; prolific self-seeder; naturalised plants hybridise with *P. vulgaris*, and the two will spread together into a lawn; unfortunately rather uncommon.
Narrow-leaved lung- wort *Pulmonaria angustifolia* 'Azurea' (*P. visanii*) Eur., Cauc.	0.10/0.30 gentian blue	IV–V, reliable and rewarding plant; long, green leaves spread to cover the ground after flowering; very long lived in a warm, bright or shady position on loamy soil. 'Alba', attractive white flowers. 'Blaues Meer', large flowers. Hybrid: 'Munstead Blue' (0.20), blue.
*Sweet violet *Viola odorata* W Eur., Med., Cauc.	0.10 blue-violet	III, popular old garden plant; fragrant flowers over broad, evergreen, heart-shaped leaves; spreads by means of runners. 'Königin Charlotte' ('Queen Charlotte'), large flowers.

White and reddish cultivars are also available.
All seed themselves prolifically on the woodland edge
or in grass.

Lesser celandine	0.05–0.15	III–V, dies down very early.
Ficaria verna	yellow	

Low-growing wild phloxes

The following plants cannot withstand much competition and tend to look rather exotic in
combination with other species from this list. It is often better to grow them with the rock garden
perennials from list 4.5.4, especially as they all thrive in (or at least tolerate) summer drought.

Phlox divaricata	up to 0.30	V–VI, flowers in cymes; open habit; creeping shoots
(*P. canadensis*)	pale purple	with upright flowering stems; rounded, ovate leaves;
N Am.	to pale violet	white-flowered forms also available.
		P. d. ssp. *lamphamii*, lavender blue, ovate leaves.
		Hybrids between *P. divaricata* and *P. paniculata*: see
		Phlox × arendsii, list 3.4.6.
Phlox ovata	up to 0.40	VI–VII, flowers in cymes on erect or decumbent stems
E USA	(0.90)	with oval leaves; basal leaves round or heart-shaped.
	purplish-pink	*P. o.* var. *pulchra*, pink.
Phlox stolonifera	up to 0.30	IV-VI, flowers in cymes; spathulate leaves; spreading
(*P. reptans*)	purplish-pink	roots; for well-drained, slightly acid soils; brightens
E USA	to violet	up a shady spot; intolerant of dry soil.
		'Ariane', white.
		'Blue Ridge', lavender blue.

2.1.7.   Perennials for sun or bright shade on an open woodland edge (moderately dry, loamy, alkaline soils)

The place for these attractive, mostly calcicole, European native species is on a sunny woodland
edge, particularly on a warm slope, often in combination with the dry grassland species from list
3.2.2. Once they are established they hardly require any maintenance apart from mowing in
autumn or the removal of old, brown stems in spring.
    The plants mentioned in the right-hand column are better combined with the perennials from
list 3.4.5.

Anemone sylvestris	0.15/0.40	VI, single flowers on erect stems over dark green
Eur., Cauc., Sib.	white	leaves; very robust; spreads strongly in mild areas.
		A. × lesseri (0.50), V–VI, red; requires more main-
		tenance; short-lived; rare in the trade.
St. Bernard's lily	0.50	VII, flowers in racemes over grass-like leaves; also for
Anthericum liliago	white	sandy soils.
Eur., Asia Minor		'Major', sturdier than the type.
		A. ramosum (0.60), white; branching, small-flowered
		inflorescences; open, graceful habit.
Aquilegia atrata		List 2.2.1
Aquilegia vulgaris		Lists 2.1.6 and 2.2.1

Asperula tinctoria Eur.	0.30 (to 0.50) white	VI–VII, loosely branched cymes over whorls of very narrow leaves; densely bushy and free-flowering in a sunny spot on well-drained soil.
Yellow ox-eye *Buphthalmum salici-* *folia,* Eur.	0.40 yellow	IX, chrysanthemum-like; undemanding; rare in the trade.
Peach-leaved bellflower *Campanula persicifolia* Eur., Asia	0.80 blue	VII–VIII, large bells on tall stems; vigorous and long-lived on porous, sandy soils; also thrives in shade. 'Grandiflora Alba', white. 'Grandiflora Coerulea', large flowered. 'Telham Beauty', short-lived and sensitive to damp. Cultivars are better combined with the perennials from list 3.4.5.
Carex montana		List 3.2.2
Centaurea ruthenica Rum., Cauc., Sib.	1.20/1.50 sulphur yellow	VI–VII, spherical flower heads on branched stems; dark green, serrate, pinnately cut leaves; forms large clumps. *C. nervosa*, list 3.3.4.
Chrysanthemum *corymbosum* Eur., Cauc., Med.	1.20 white	VII, corymbs of daisy-like flowers on rigid stems; may be cut down after flowering; for planting in small groups.
Clematis recta Eur., Asia	0.80–1.50 white	VI–VII, flowers in loose, terminal sprays; unassuming; often rather sparse. 'Grandiflora', large flowers. 'Purpurea', red-brown shoots.
Coronilla montana		List 4.4.1
Dittany *Dictamnus albus* (*D. fraxinella*) Eur., E As., Him.	0.70 pink	VI, flowers in terminal racemes on powerful stems; strongly aromatic in all its parts. 'Purpureus', red. 'Albus', white. *D. caucasicus*, (0.80), similar but with larger and more intensely coloured blooms.
Large yellow foxglove *Digitalis grandiflora* (*D. ambigua*) Eur., Cauc., Sib.	0.60 yellow	VI–VIII, long-lived (in contrast to the common foxglove); downy leaves. *D. lutea*, see list 1.1.2.
Erica herbacea		List 3.2.3
Cypress spurge *Euphorbia cyparissias* Eur.	up to 0.30 yellow	IV–VI, yellow bracts turn reddish as the season advances; yellowish-green, narrow, lanceolate leaves; invasive roots; rare in the trade. 'Waldsteinii' (0.50–0.60).
Lady's bedstraw *Galium verum* Eur., Nr East, N Afr.	up to 0.60 yellow	VI–IX, flowers in loose panicles; narrow, needle-like leaves; invasive roots; still rare in the trade.

Geranium psilostemon		List 3.5.1
Geranium sanguineum		List 2.1.2
Orange lily *Lilium bulbiferum* Eur.	0.80 orange-red	VI, large, erect, goblet-shaped flowers on stiff, upright stems; bulbils in the leaf axils; autumn planting. *L.b.* ssp. *croceum*, see list 3.4.1. Both of these can sometimes disappear without warning.
Buglossoides purpuro-caerulea		List 2.1.2
Molinia arundinacea		List 3.5.3 (Periodically dry or damp conditions)
Wild majoram, Oregano *Origanum vulgare* 'Compactum' Eur., Sib., Him., Asia Minor	0.20 lilac-pink	IX–X, forms dense, compact bushes with small, aromatic leaves; many-flowered, cymose inflorescences. 'Albiroseum', pink-white. 'Aureum', (0.15), golden-yellow foliage; dense bushes. 'Erntedank', (0.25), bright violet-purple.
Peucedanum cervaria C & S Eur., Cauc.	0.30/1.00 white	VI–VIII, attractive, stiffly branched umbellifer with grooved and nearly leafless stems; flowers reddish in bud; coarse, almost leathery, pinnate leaves.
Angular Solomon's seal *Polygonatum odoratum* (*P. officinale*) Eur., Sib., W Him.	0.15–0.30 white	V–VI, not so tall as *P. multiflorum*; nodding flowers, singly or in pairs, in the leaf axils; rhizomatous; best in large groups.
Cowslip *Primula veris* (*P. officinalis*) Eur., Sib., C Asia	0.20 yellow	V–VI, sweetly scented species with smaller flowers than *P. elatior*.
Tulipa sylvestris		List 2.4.1

Pioneer species for disturbed soil

These plants are particularly useful for clothing bare embankments. Here they may be associated with the powerful open ground perennials of list 3.4.3, and with annuals such as melilot (*Melilotus officinalis*, 0.90, yellow; *M. alba*, 1.20. white) and *Phacelia tanacetifolia* (0.70, blue-violet). Beekeepers grow these species as nectar plants and seed is available in the trade.

Crown vetch *Coronilla varia* S & C Eur., Cauc.	0.30 pink	VI–VII, flowers in spherical umbels; narrow leaflets; spreads strongly and smothers neighbours; available as plants or seed (300 grains/g).
Black medick *Medicago lupulina* Eur., Asia	up to 0.30 yellow	V–IX, heads of 10–50 flowers on angled stems; short-lived; kidney-shaped seed (560 grains/g).
Onobrychis viciifolia		List 3.2.1

2.1.8.   Perennials for an open woodland edge on dry to moist, sandy, silica-rich soils in sun and bright shade

The following, mostly calcifuge, perennials tolerate poor, acid soils and will seed themselves in an open grove under pines and birches. Ling (*Calluna*) and the various fine-leaved grasses (particularly *Festuca*) are key species that should always be included in a planting of this type. A well-conceived planting is attractive and requires very little maintenance.

Many gardens only allow space for a small planting of woodland edge perennials. Where this is so the shorter growing species will need a certain amount of attention to prevent them getting squeezed out. The same applies to the perennials listed separately for garden-type maintenance.

Dwarf shrubs

Ling, Heather *Calluna vulgaris* Eur., W Sib.	0.30 lilac	IX, densely branched evergreen; often brown in winter; cut back to a hand's breadth every two or three years in spring; will not grow in the drip zone under trees. Cultivars, see list 3.2.3.
Hairy greenweed *Genista pilosa* Eur.	0.25 yellow	V–VI, slender, green, slightly prostrate branches; forms extensive carpets. 'Procumbens', flat, spreading habit.
Winged greenweed *Genista sagittalis* Eur.	0.02/0.10 yellow	VI, prostrate, creeping, winged and partly woody stems; flowers in short, terminal racemes; rare in the trade.
Dyer's greenweed *Genista tinctoria* Eur., Cauc.	0.80 yellow	V–VI, upright habit; flowers in terminal racemes. 'Plena', common, double-flowered form. *G. germanica* (0.40), V–VI, yellow; thorny shoots with grass-green leaves; hardly available in the trade.

Herbaceous perennials

Ajuga pyramidalis Eur., Cauc.	0.05/0.20 pale blue	VI–VII, leaves in rosettes with dense spikes of flowers; does not spread; moist or damp soils near to trees. *A. reptans* × *A. pyramidalis* 'Rosa Kerze', pink.
Antennaria dioica		List 3.2.4
Briza media		List 3.2.4
Campanula rotundifolia		List 3.2.4
Festuca ovina		List 3.2.4; especially *F. tenuifolia*
Orange hawkweed *Hieracium aurantiacum* Eur., W Asia	0.40 orange- yellow	VI–VIII, 2–6 composite flowers on long, leafless, glandular-hairy stems; spreads rapidly at the roots and will colonise areas of grass; to be used with caution.
Hieracium pilosella		List 3.2.4
Creeping soft-grass *Holcus mollis* 'Variegata' Eur.	0.20/0.40	Dainty, light green leaves with white stripes; spreading roots; for poor, sandy soils in sun or shade; evergreen, very attractive in winter.
Luzula pilosa		List 1.2.3

Spignel *Meum athamanticum* Eur.	0.40 white	VI–VII, pretty umbels over finely divided, hairlike, grass-green leaves; for lime-free soils in sun and semi-shade.
Nardus stricta		List 3.2.4
Sedum acre		List 3.2.4
Sedum sexangulare		List 3.2.4
Sedum maximum (*Sedum telephium* ssp. *maximum*) Eur., Cauc.	0.30/0.50 yellowish- green	VII–IX, flowers occasionally pale red; sessile, ovate leaves in opposite pairs on upper part of stem. 'Atropurpureum', dark, red-brown foliage.
Golden rod *Solidago virgaurea* 'Nana' Eur., Asia	0.40 yellow	VII–IX, not to be compared with *S. canadensis* (list 5.3.4); clump-forming, does not spread; flowers in racemes on stiffly upright stems with elongate–elliptic leaves; plants cut down after flowering bloom again in autumn.
Betony *Stachys officinalis* (*Betonica officinalis*) Eur., Cauc.	up to 0.40 pink	VI–VIII, spike-like inflorescences on stiff, sparse-leaved stems; longish, ovate, round-toothed leaves; rare in the trade. 'Alba', (0.30), white; flowers abundantly; widely available in the trade.
Wood sage *Teucrium scorodonia* Eur.	0.50 Greenish yellow	VI–VIII, slender, open spikes of flowers; wrinkled, crenate, heart-shaped leaves; creeping rhizomes. 'Crispum' (0.20), VII–IX, leaves with ruffled edges; for the rock garden.
Thymus serpyllum and relatives		List 3.2.4
Verbascum nigrum		List 3.3.2

Plants requiring a little garden-type maintenance

Long-leaved thrift *Armeria elongata* (*A. maritima* var. *elongata*) Eur.	0.10/0.30 pale red	V–VIII, undemanding but seldom available. Cultivars, see list 4.1.1.
Armeria alliacea (*A. plantaginea*) W Eur., N It.	0.30 pink	VI–VII, broad leaves. 'Grandiflora', large flowers. 'Leucantha', white flowers.
Thrift *Armeria maritima* N Eur.	0.06/0.20 pale pink	V–VIII, shorter, more succulent leaves than other *Armeria* spp.; forms a rounded cushion. Cultivars, see list 4.1.1.
Dianthus seguieri ssp. *glaber* (*D. sylvaticus*) Eur.	0.05/0.30 pale red	VI–IX, forms an open turf; narrow, green, linear–lanceolate leaves; variable species.

Dianthus superbus ssp. *autumnalis* Eur.	0.50/0.80 lilac/pink	VIII–X, stiffly branching stems; narrow, linear, pale blue-green leaves; forms an open turf; rare in the trade. *D. superbus*, list 6.4.2.
Red hawkweed *Hieracium × rubrum* (*H. aurantiacum ×* *H. flagellare*)	0.50/0.20 orange-red	VI—VIII, small flower heads over hairy, green foliage; short rhizomes.
Birdsfoot trefoil *Lotus corniculatus* 'Plenus' Eur.	0.20 yellow	V–VIII, small umbels with 3–7 double flowers; green, clover-like leaves; full sun on moderately rich soils.
Potentilla recta Eur., C Asia	0.50 pale yellow	VI–VII, flowers in dense corymbs on upright stems; small leaves, shaped like those of a horsechestnut. 'Warrensi', canary-yellow flowers; undemanding; gravelly or sandy, lime-free soils. *P, arenaria*, for alkaline soils; list 3.2.2.
Spring cinquefoil *Potentilla taber-* *naemontani* (*P. verna*) (*P. neumanniana*) Eur.	0.15 golden yellow	III–IV, dense, spreading habit; grass-green, palmate leaves with 5–7 leaflets; undemanding groundcover plant for sandy or stony soils. 'Nana', 'Compacta', dwarf forms. Related species, see list 4.4.3.
Small pasque flower *Pulsatilla pratensis* Eur.	0.05–0.25 violet	IV–V, small flowers on tall stems; rare in the trade; does not tolerate mowing.
Spring pasque flower *Pulsatilla vernalis* Eur., Sib.	0.05/0.10 white and lilac	IV–V, very dainty, hairy pasque flower; rare in the trade; does not tolerate mowing.
Teesdale violet *Viola rupestris* 'Rosea' Eur.	up to 0.10 pink	IV–V, pale green, rounded, ovate leaves; for sun or bright shade; good on warm, dry, sandy or loamy soils on the edge of pines.

The following species form a disruptive element in most plant communities. They may occasionally find a use in large parks for covering extensive areas

Wavy hair-grass *Avenella flexuosa* (*Deschampsia flexuosa*) Eur., Cauc., Jap., N Am.	0.20/0.50	VI–VII, forms turf-like mounds of lax, bristly, ever-green leaves; massed stems have a graceful effect; for acid, peaty soils in the neighbourhood of birches and pines; dangerously prolific self-seeder. Selection: 'Mückenschwarm'.
Digitalis purpurea		List 1.1.2
Rose-bay willow-herb *Epilobium* *angustifolium* (*Chamaenerion angusti-* *folium*) Eur., As., N Am.	0.60–1.50 pink	VI–VII, flowers in terminal racemes on stiff, brittle, narrow-leaved stems; spreading roots; for disturbed ground with fertile, lime-free soil.

Lupin	1.00	VI–VII, tall spires of flowers; rounded, many-lobed
Lupinus polyphyllus	blue	leaves; for moist, lime-free, loamy soils.
Pacific N Am.		Hybrids with *L. perennis* and *L. arboreus*: see list 5.3.4.

2.2. Perennials more loosely bound to the woodland edge

These plants are among the oldest inhabitants of our gardens. Many of them (especially those with pronounced border character) will thrive on an open site away from trees, but most of the original species grow wild in woods and on the woodland edge. They are particularly effective in the neighbourhood of trees and shrubs, associated with the perennials from list 2.1.4, in areas where the soil is not too infested with tree roots.

2.2.1. Perennials with border character, for garden-type maintenance

The following, mostly clump-forming species and cultivars can be used to establish a link between a border planting and the adjacent woodland edge.

Together with the perennials from list 2.2.2 they have a marked preference for rich, moist soils and bright shade. Hostas (list 1.1.3) are suitable companions where the shade is particularly intense. Alternatively, they may be combined with crown imperials (list 5.2.3), tulips (list 5.4) and daffodils (list 2.4.3) in a sunny position, or with the bulbs from list 2.4 in areas of summer shade.

Columbine, *Aquilegia*

The old-fashioned and popular garden columbine (*Aquilegia vulgaris*) has been grown for hundreds of years in a variety of different forms and colours. The predominantly long-spurred hybrids of American species such as *A. caerulea, A. chrysantha* and *A. canadensis* are of more recent origin and have contributed greatly to the current assortment.

Columbines should be placed singly or in small groups so that their blooms can hover like butterflies above a mass of other perennials. In this way the plants remain hidden when they die down and become unsightly after flowering. *Aquilegia vulgaris* has a relatively short lifespan of about five years. The plants seed themselves abundantly but their colours do not always fall true.

Species

Aquilegia chrysantha	0.80	VI, elegant habit; flowers with exceptionally long
USA	pale yellow	spurs; seldom true in the trade.
		'Silver Queen', silvery-white flowers.

Aquilegia longissima	up to 1.00	VI–VII, scented, upward-facing flowers; very long,
Texas to Mex.	yellow	slender spurs; rare in the trade, often hybridised with
		A. chrysantha.

| *Aquilegia skinneri* | | List 3.3.5 |

Common columbine	0.60	V–VI, old garden plant with short, bent spurs; avail-
Aquilegia vulgaris	red, white	able in many different colours, including double-
Eur.	blue, violet	flowered selections.
		A. atrata (0.50), VI–VII, brown-violet; European species; rare in the trade.

Hybrids

Long-spurred hybrids	0.70–0.80	V–VI, elegantly shaped blooms with long, slightly
Aquilegia caerulea	red, white,	bent spurs on branching stems.
hybrids	yellow,	
	blue, violet	

Mixtures

'Benarys Spezialrasse' ('Benary's Special Strain') (0.75), very large, long-spurred blooms.
'Mc.Kana Hybrids' (0.80–1.00), many colours, including pastel tones.
'Dragon Fly', (0.40), short plants; rich spectrum of colours.

Single colours

'Blue Star' (0.60), light blue.
'Edelweiss' (0.60), white.
'Helenae' ('Haylodgensis') (0.50), blue and white; early flowering.
'Maxi-Star' (0.75), yellow.
'Olympic-Blue-White' (0.70).
'Olympic-Red-Yellow' (0.75).
'Olympic-Violet-Yellow' (0.75).
'Red Star' (0.40), blood red.
'Crimson Star' (0.60), crimson and white.

Aquilegia vulgaris hybrids

Aquilegia alpina hort.	0.40	V–VI, belongs to the *A. alpina* × *A. vulgaris* group of
'Superba'	pure blue	hybrids.
'Biedermeier'	0.30	V–VI, dwarf form with double, short-spurred flowers
	various	in many different colours.

Bleeding heart, *Dicentra*

Whether planted in small groups or used as an extensive groundcover, the low-growing dicentras create a pleasing effect throughout the growing season. Their ample, daintily cut foliage does not turn yellow after flowering but remains attractive until late in the autumn, unlike that of *D. spectabilis*. Their flowering season, especially that of *D. formosa*, is also exceptionally long.

    The following species come from mountain woods in N America and thrive in bright, cool shade on moist, humus-rich soils. A shady part of the rock garden may also provide a suitable home, particularly for the more demanding cultivars. (*D. spectabilis*: see list 5.2.1.)

Dicentra eximia	0.20/0.30	V–VIII, long flowering season; delicate, grey-green
E USA	pink	leaves; creeping habit; very robust on moist, humus-rich soils in bright semi-shade.
		'Alba', white.
Dicentra formosa	0.20/0.30	VII–VIII, ferny, blue-green foliage; moist, humus-rich
W N Am.	pale red	soils in bright semi-shade.
		'Bountiful' (0.25), V–IX, dark pink.
		'Luxuriant' (0.30), V–IX, dark pink.
		'Adrian Bloom' (0.35), cherry red.
		'Spring Morning' (0.40), pink.
		D. oregana, see list 4.5.2.

Leopardsbane, *Doronicum*

These early-flowering, yellow daisies are often grown in beds for cutting. However, the original species grow wild in mountain woods and are well suited to a woodland edge planting, where their unsightly summer foliage can be hidden away behind other perennials.

   The most suitable species for herbaceous borders is the late flowering *Doronicum plantagineum* 'Excelsum', whose wild ancestors grow among the tall herbs of open, scrubby areas in the Spanish mountains.

Doronicum orientale (*D. caucasicum*) 'Magnificum' SE Eur., Asia Minor, Cauc.	0.15/0.50 yellow	IV–V, heart-shaped leaves with toothed and scalloped edges; single daisies on stout stems; sometimes unsightly in summer. 'Finesse' (0.50), long, narrow, pointed ray-florets. 'Frühlingspracht' ('Spring Beauty') (0.40), double flower heads; for cutting. 'Gerhardt' (0.50), lemon yellow; double flowerheads. 'Goldzwerg' (0.30), vigorous. 'Riedels Goldkranz' (0.35), double row of ray-florets. 'Riedels Lichtspiegel' (0.50), flowers somewhat later.
Doronicum plantagineum 'Excelsum' W Eur.	0.10/0.70 yellow	V, large yellow daisy flowers on long stems, valuable for cutting; dies down after flowering. Selection 'Strahlengold' (0.80). *D. columnae (D. cordatum)* (0.20/0.50), V–VI, yellow; serrate, heart-shaped leaves with long petioles; rare in the trade.

Avens, *Geum*

The cultivated geums include the very ornamental but unfortunately rather short-lived *Geum* Chiloense hybrids (the parents come from Chile), together with a number of robust and long-lived perennials whose ancestors mostly grow wild in the damp mountain woods of SE Europe. The latter have evergreen rosettes and strawberry-like flowers on sturdy stems. Set together in small or large groups in areas of light shade (not in full sun), their dense, dark green foliage remains neat and attractive even after the flowers have faded.

Geum coccineum 'Borisii' Balk., Asia Minor	0.15/0.30 orange-red	V–VII, evergreen foliage; brilliantly coloured flowers.
Geum coccineum 'Feuermeer' ('Sea of Fire')	0.15/0.25 orange-red	V–VII, abundant, semi-double blooms; repeat flowering. 'Werner Arends', (0.25), orange-red; similar to above; good second crop of flowers.
Geum × heldreichii 'Georgenberg'	0.10/0.25 yellowish-orange	V–VII, similar but more graceful than the previous plants.
Geum montanum		List 4.4.3
Geum Chiloense hybrids Chile	0.20/0.60 yellow, brown, red	V–VII, taller and with larger flowers; rather short-lived. Numerous cultivars, including: 'Bernstein', golden yellow. 'Dolly North', dark orange; long-lived.

'Feuerball' ('Mrs. Bradshaw'), fiery red; double.
'Fire Opal', coppery red.
'Goldball' ('Lady Stratheden'), golden yellow; double.
'Princess Juliana', old gold; semi-double; long-lived.
'Red Wings', fiery red.
'Rubin', crimson; semi-double.

Garden primulas

Intensive hybridisation and selection among the familiar yellow primulas of meadow and wood-land (*P, vulgaris, P. veris, P. elatior* and their relatives) has produced a number of richly colourful but often short-lived strains of large-flowered plants that have largely replaced the older and more persistent cultivars. These so-called 'Polyanthus' primulas (*Primula* Elatior hybrids, *Primula × polyantha* hort.) gradually superseded the once popular auriculas (*P. × pubescens*), with their leathery leaves and muted colours, at the end of the eighteenth century. The current assortment of spring flowering garden primulas includes not only the stout stemmed *P.* Elatior hybrids but also the almost stemless *P. vulgaris* 'Grandiflora' cultivars, the short stemmed *P.* Juliae hybrids (*P. × margotae*, originating from a cross with the carpet-forming *P. juliae*), *P. × pruhoniciana* hort. and the various cultivars of *P. denticulata*. All these colourful, long-flowering perennials will thrive in a well-maintained flower bed, especially if they are given cool and lightly shaded woodland edge conditions. The older *P.* Elatior hybrids and *P. vulgaris* cultivars will seed themselves, but their colours do not always come true.
The wild species have been assigned to the following lists.

Primula elatior and *P. vulgaris*	List 2.1.6
Primula veris (P. officinalis)	List 2.1.7
Primula juliae	List 4.1.3
Primula auricula	List 4.3.1

Polyanthus *Primula* Elatior hybrids (*P. × polyantha*) 'Grandiflora'	0.08/0.25 yellow, white, blue, red	IV–VI, lush foliage; flowering often begins in autumn; many different strains available.
Primula vulgaris (*P. acaulis*) 'Grandiflora'	0.80/0.10 yellow, white, blue, red	IV–VI, flowers in almost stalkless umbels; popular pot plant in winter; few named cultivars but many different colours.
Primula Juliae hybrids (*Primula × margotae* hort.)	0.05/0.15 mostly reddish or lilac	IV–VI, distinguished from *P. × pruhoniciana* hort. by their shorter stems.
Primula Juliae hybrids (*P. × pruhoniciana* hort.) (*P. × helenae* hort.)	0.05/0.15 mostly reddish, white or lilac	IV–VI, stalkless umbels; long-lived in areas with an oceanic climate; clumps divide well; many named cultivars.
Drumstick primrose *Primula denticulata* 'Grandiflora' Him., W China	0.10/0.30 lilac-pink	III–IV, spherical inflorescences on stout stems; substantial leaf rosettes first develop after flowering.

Cultivars

Lilac/blue/violet:	Reddish violet:	White:
'Juno', pale lilac.	'Cachemiriana-Rubin'	'Alba'
'Amethystkugel', blue.	'Feuerkugel', red.	'Schneekugel' ('Snowball')
'Opalkugel', dark blue.		
'Atroviolacea', dark violet.		

Auricula	0.08/0.20	IV–V, old, formerly very popular, garden plant; smooth, leathery leaves; numerous cultivars in yellow, red and blue tones.
Primula × pubescens	various	

Primula sieboldii

The ornamental cultivars now available in the trade have little in common with this large, pink, phlox-flowered species from marshy meadows in Japan. Rosettes of crenate, heart-shaped leaves produce many-flowered umbels on 20 cm stems in May and June. The plants die down again in July, so it is advisable to set them in small groups interspersed with other perennials. The soil for these primulas should be damp in spring and rich in humus, with a porous structure and low lime content. The plants set little seed and propagation is by division.

Selections

Lilac:	Red:	White:
'Coshibori', lilac-pink.	'Hinomaru', crimson.	'Haruno Yuki', fringed petals.
'Kihino Yume', white centres.	'Itozakura', wine red, white	
'Kumoi', pale lilac-pink.	centres.	
'Sumizone Gawa', lilac-pink,	'Sangokuko', red-violet.	
pale centres.		
	Blue-violet:	
Pink:	'Shinkiro'.	
'Miyono Homare', pale pink.	'Yubi Sugata', pale blue.	
'Okinawa tomo', white veins.		
'Shishi-Funjin', dark pink.		

2.2.2. Further perennials loosely bound to the woodland edge

The following species are undemanding and will thrive in areas of light shade under trees. They are particularly effective associated with the perennials from list 2.2.1. Plants for moist to damp soils are marked with an asterisk.

Lady's mantle	0.30/0.40	VI, beautifully shaped, softly hairy leaves; small flowers in airy inflorescences; remove stems after flowering (troublesome self-seeder). Selection: 'Robustica', (0.50), valuable for cutting. *A. acutiloba*, slightly hairy leaves; no particular garden value.
Alchemilla mollis	pale yellow	
(*A. acutiloba* hort.)		
E Carp., W Asia		

*Elk clover	2.00	VII–VIII, loose, decorative panicles on stout stems; very large, mostly 4-pinnate leaves; shade tolerant specimen perennial for moist to damp, nutrient-rich soils; fully hardy. Similar but rarely available: *A. racemosa*, strongly invasive. *A. cachemirica*, large, 3-pinnate leaves. *A. cordata*, cordate leaves with veins hairy beneath.
Aralia californica	milk-white	
SW Oregon to Calif.		

White wood aster *Aster divaricatus* E N Am.	0.60 white	IX–X, very attractive, open inflorescences; leaves heart-shaped to lanceolate; particularly beautiful in semi-shade; also for dry, sandy soils. *A. ageratoides* var. *vesoensis* (0.60), X–XI, pale lilac; large flowers, broad, nettle-like leaves.
Big-leaf aster *Aster macrophyllus* W N Am.	up to 1.00 lavender blue	VIII, flowers in umbels; very large, glandular-hairy, heart-shaped leaves; spreads to form dense thickets; robust. *A. schreberi*, similar to above; whitish flowers; very large, heart-shaped leaves.
Siberian bugloss *Brunnera macrophylla* Cauc., W Sib.	0.25/0.40 blue	IV–V, clump-forming; branching sprays of flowers over heart-shaped leaves that stay green long into winter; seeds itself on soils that are not too dry. 'Blaukuppel', dense, upright domes of flowers. 'Variegata' ('Dawson's White'), leaves variegated white.
Campanula grandis (*C. latiloba*) (*C. persifolia* ssp. *sessiliflora*) Balk.	0.80 pale blue	VI, large, open, bowl-shaped flowers crowded on stiffly upright stems; flat rosettes of narrow, shining, wavy leaves; does not tolerate too much shade. 'Alba', white; also suitable for border plantings and for cutting; good between ornamental roses.
Campanula latifolia 'Macrantha'	List 1.1.2	
Mountain knapweed *Centaurea montana* 'Grandiflora' Eur.	0.50 blue	V–VI, large, solitary flower heads which should be removed after flowering to promote a second crop in autumn; bright shade. 'Alba', white. 'Rosea', pink. 'Parham', (0.60), purple-lavender; vigorous, with very large flowers; strong border character.
Clematis × *bonstedtii* 'Crepuscule'	0.80 pale blue	VIII–IX, upright habit; abundant flowers; very hardy in sun or bright shade; tolerates drip from trees.
Goat's-rue *Galega bicolor* Asia Minor, W Asia	0.70 whitish lilac	VI–VIII, open racemes on powerful, upright stems; pinnate leaves; a one-time fodder plant; for a warm position, also in sun; rare in the trade.
Sweet rocket *Hesperis matronalis* C & S Eur	0.70 lilac	V–VII, crowded, terminal inflorescences on rigid stems with elongated heart-shaped leaves; sweetly scented after dusk; short-lived but seeds itself well on moist, nutrient-rich soils. The following, double-flowered varieties are good for cutting but need more maintenance: 'Purpurea Plena', violet. 'Alba Plena', white.
Meconopsis cambrica	List 1.2.2 short-lived, seeds itself.	
Kalimeris incisa (*Aster incisa*) Sib., Jap., N China	0.70 white to pale lilac	VIII–IX, corymbose panicles with daisy-like flower heads; hairy, lanceolate, incised and remotely serrate leaves.

		K. *integrifolia*, similar to above, with softly hairy, remotely lobed leaves; very robust; also for shady sites; rare in the trade.
Polemonium reptans		List 5.3.5.
Jupiter's distaff *Salvia glutinosa* Eur., SW Asia	1.00 yellow	VII–IX, coarsely serrate leaves; ample, spreading habit; fragrant flowers; very long-lived; not invasive; rare in the trade.
Stachys grandiflora 'Superba' (*Betonica macrantha*) Cauc.	0.50 purple-pink	VII–VIII, forms dense clumps; large, bright flowers on rigid stems; wrinkled, crenate, heart-shaped leaves; strong border character.
Symphytum peregrinum E Cauc.	1.00 brilliant blue	VI–VII, vigorous plant with rough leaves; sprawling stems; for bright shade.
Telekia speciosa SE Alps, SE Eur., Cauc.	1.50 yellow	VII–VIII, big composite flowers with thread-like ray-florets; relatively short flowering season; large and beautiful leaves; undemanding and shade-tolerant in damp soil; prolific self-seeder.
Thalictrum aquilegi- folium Eur., Jap., Sib.	1.00 purple-lilac	V–VII, feathery flowers on stiff stems; columbine-like leaves; seeds itself; dies down soon after flowering. 'Album', white. 'Atropurpureum', violet. 'Thundercloud', soft mauve.
Thalictrum rochebruni- anum Jap.	1.00 purple-lilac	VII–VIII, daintier and later-flowering than the above.
Corn lily *Veratrum californicum* W USA	up to 2.50 white	VII–VIII, large inflorescences on stout stems with broad, glossy, spirally arranged leaves; very orna-mental but difficult to grow; a plant for the enthusiast; rare in the trade.
Vinca minor		List 1.1.1
Waldsteinia geoides		List 1.1.1

2.2.3. Invasive perennials loosely bound to the woodland edge

These vigorously colonising perennials are likely to be disruptive in a planting of species from lists 2.2.1 and 2.2.2. However, they can be invaluable for planting between the trees and shrubs of a bright, open woodland edge, even in a small garden.

Strongly invasive perennials for large parks and gardens are treated in list 2.3.5.

Leopardsbane *Doronicum pardalianches* W & S Eur.	0.10/0.60 yellow	VI, pale green leaves on stiff stems; very invasive; can be naturalised in grass under thinly planted trees; dies down soon after flowering.
Hemerocallis fulva Jap., China	1.20 tawny orange	VII–VIII, corymbs of unscented flowers on tall, sturdy stems; coarse foliage; very vigorous spreader; for a

		sunny (not too cool) position; appreciates a long, warm autumn. 'Kwanso', double flowers; slightly less vigorous.
Lysimachia punctata SE Eur., Asia Minor	0.60/0.80 yellow	VII–VIII, flowers and leaves in whorls on stiffly upright stems; spreads strongly on (damp) loamy soils, also under trees; very attractive, even after flowering.
Nepeta sibirica (*Dracocephalum sibiricum*) (*Nepeta macrantha*) S Sib., W China	0.80 lilac-blue	VII, broad, round-toothed, lanceolate leaves; spreads strongly. *N*. 'Blue Beauty' ('Andre Chaudron'), hybrid (?) with elongated heart-shaped leaves.
Chinese lantern *Physalis alkekengi* S Eur., W Asia	up to 0.60 yellow	V, similar to the next, but with spherical 'lanterns'; old medicinal plant; rare in the trade.
Physalis alkekengi var. *franchetii* (*P. bunyardii*) Jap., N China	1.00 whitish	Flowers insignificant; persistent sepals form large, bright, red, pointed, ovoid 'lanterns' in autumn; good for cutting.

2.2.4.   Tall perennials with border character for moist to damp soils

These stately perennials may be grown as specimen plants, especially near to water. Given sufficient moisture they will thrive in sun or bright shade, but do not tolerate planting directly under trees. In times of drought their leaves droop and they may need watering.

The plants have much in common with the moisture-loving perennials for open ground and associate particularly well with species from lists 3.5.4 and 3.6, or with some of the related border perennials from list 5.3.5.

Aconitum septentrionale 'Ivorine' N Eur., Asia	0.80 white	VI–VII, flowers in dense panicles on strong, branching stems; large, palmate leaves with 3–5 segments; for rich, moist soils. Other *Aconitum* spp., see lists 1.1.2 and 5.2.1.
Artemisia lactiflora W China	up to 1.60 white	VIII–X, fragrant, airy inflorescences covered for many weeks with small, spherical flowers; rather stiff stems; very leafy, deep-cut, pinnate foliage; long-lived on loamy soils.
Campanula lactiflora Cauc., W Asia	1.50 lilac-blue	VI–VII, wide, bell-shaped flowers in branching panicles; a vigorous and substantial plant. 'Alba' (0.90), white. 'Loddon Anna' (0.90), pink. 'Prichard's Variety' (0.50), violet.
Wild senna *Cassia marylandica* (*C. hebecarpa*) USA	2.00 yellow	VIII–IX, flowers with black anthers in short, erect, axillary racemes; spreading habit; dense, pinnate foliage; undemanding, but young plants need protection in winter; damp soils.
Deschampsia cespitosa		List 1.1.4

Ligularia dentata (*L. clivorum*) Jap., China	0.60/1.00 golden yellow	VIII–IX, large, round, entire leaves. 'Desdemona', 'Moorblut', 'Othello' (VII–VIII), leaves red-brown beneath. Green foliage: 'Orange Queen', pale orange. 'Sommergold', yellow.
Ligularia × *hessei*	0.60/1.60 golden-yellow	VIII–IX, tall, massive spikes of daisy flowers. 'Gregynog Gold', similar but with longer, more slender spikes. *L.* × *veitchiana* (0.40/1.60), leaves with solid petioles; uncommon.
Ligularia × *palmatiloba* (*L. dentata* × *L. japonica*)	0.60/1.60 golden yellow	VI, deeply divided leaves; flowers early. *L. japonica* (1.70), leaves deeply and narrowly lobed; a worthwhile but uncommon plant. *L. sachalinense*, (to 2.00), VII, tall, yellow flower spikes; undivided leaves; rare in the trade.
Ligularia przewalskii N China	0.40/1.60 yellow	VII, not so massive as the previous plants; tall, graceful spikes of flowers; incised and palmately divided foliage; immune to slugs! Recent selections: 'Gigant'. 'The Rocket' (1.80).
Ligularia stenocephala N China	0.50/1.80 yellow	VII–VIII, coarsely toothed, kidney- to heart-shaped leaves with red-brown petioles; fairly open spikes. 'Globosa' (to 1.00), fewer flowers and not so decorative.
Ligularia wilsoniana C China	0.60/1.60 golden yellow	VIII–IX, rounded leaves and tall strong stems; strikingly beautiful seed heads in late autumn. 'Zepter' (2.00), vigorous and early-flowering hybrid (*L. wilsoniana* × *L. przewalskii*).
Senecio doria C Russ., E Fr., Bulg., S Spain	up to 1.80 yellow	VII–IX, vigorous and long-lived, with smooth, serrate leaves and abundant flowers; reminiscent of *S. fuchsii*; attractive as a specimen plant.
Telekia speciosa		*List 2.2.2*

2.3. Perennials for special conditions on or near the woodland edge

The following lists contain plants which grow wild in conditions that are variously related to those of the woodland edge. The species from list 2.3.1 might also find a place in a large rock garden or at the edge of a pond or stream. In the same way, many of the shade and drought tolerant plants of list 2.3.3 also thrive in rock garden conditions. The sun-loving woodland-edge perennials from lists 2.3.4 and 2.3.5 form a transition to plants belonging to an open ground habitat.

2.3.1. Perennials for cool, damp, sunny or lightly shaded sites

Tall-growing primulas are particularly important perennials for these conditions. The wild plants come from wet meadows, streamsides and wooded valleys in East Asia. In a garden, they grow particularly well close to water. If the soil is damp enough they will even tolerate full sun. However, they are intolerant of hot summers, and fail in dry soil or on a windy site.

Primulas

Primula florindae SE Tibet	0.80 pale yellow	VI–VIII, long-lived species; sturdy stems with heads of fragrant, pendent flowers. *P. f.* × *P. waltonii* (0.60), VI–VIII, red, orange and pink hybrids; less robust.
Primula luteola E Cauc.	0.20 pale yellow	IV–V, many-flowered umbels; elliptic leaves; for very damp soils that are drier in winter.
Primula sieboldii	List 2.2.1	
Primula sikkimensis	List 1.3.3	

Candelabra primulas

Primula aurantiaca Yunn.	0.30 reddish orange	VII, thin, lanceolate leaves and red-brown stems; pink and orange coloured hybrids.
Primula beesiana Yunn.	0.60 pink	VI–VII, crimson-flowered forms predominate in the trade; broad, lanceolate leaves with red mid-ribs; small flowers on mealy stems. Hybrids, see *P.* × *bullesiana*. *P. burmanica* (0.70), VI, pale red.
Primula bulleyana NW Yunn.	0.60 orangey-reds and yellows	VI–VIII, ovate–lanceolate leaves with reddish veins and winged petioles; fragrant blooms.
Primula × *bullesiana* (*P. beesiana* × *P. bulleyana*)	0.50 various	VI–VIII, flowers in pastel tones; very vigorous; available in mixtures (e.g. Asthore Hybrids, Moerheimii Hybrids).
Primula × *chunglenta* (*P. chungensis* × *P. pulverulenta*) 'Red Hugh'	0.70 orange-red	V–VI, very vigorous; comes true from seed. Sterile hybrids: 'Ravenglass Vermilion', warm, red-brown flowers. 'Rowallane Rose', 'Wilbrook Seedling', similar to above, with orange-scarlet flowers; propagation by division in IX or III.
Primula helodoxa W Yunn.	0.70 golden yellow	VI–VII, finely toothed, ovate to ovate-lanceolate leaves with rolled margins; for very damp soils. *P. prolifera*, V–VI, similar but more demanding; large, yellow flowers.
Primula japonica Jap., Taiw.	0.60 purple-crimson, with brown or yellow eyes	V–VII, vigorous, rewarding species with glabrous stems; seeds itself. Many colour forms, including: 'Alba', white with red eyes. 'Rosea', pink. 'Fiery Red', red. 'Miller's Crimson', crimson. 'Postford White, white. 'Valley Red', red. 'Sanguinea', red.

Primula pulverulenta W Szechwan	0.70 dark red, with brown eyes	V–VII, very vigorous; toothed and wrinkled leaves; mealy stems and calyces.

Perennial herbs and grasses

Depending on the situation, the following species may be combined with the woodland plants from lists 1.1.4 and 1.3.1, or with the marsh and streamside perennials from list 6.3.

Anemone rivularis Him., Ind.	0.50 white	V–VI, small flowers in open inflorescences; long-stemmed leaves; rare in the trade.
Astilbe rivularis Him.	up to 1.80 yellowish-white	VIII, a well-proportioned plant with large, attractive leaves; flowers reluctantly. Selection: 'Grandiflora'.
Carex grayi		List 3.5.2
Carex muskingumensis N Am.	0.40–0.60	VII, compact inflorescences on graceful, leafy stems; long, narrow leaves; good in small groups.
Filipendula digitata 'Nana' (*F. palmata* 'Nana') Kamch.	0.30 deep pink	VII–VIII, low-growing; flowers in corymbose panicles over dainty, pinnate foliage.
Water avens *Geum rivale* 'Leonard's Variety'	0.10/0.30 coppery red	V–VI, few-flowered corymbs of small, nodding, bell-shaped flowers on russet stems. 'Lionel Cox', V, hybrid with large, pale yellow flowers. *G. coccineum*, list 2.2.1.
Pennisetum japonicum		List 3.5.3
Aconite-leaved buttercup *Ranunculus aconitifolius* 'Pleniflorus' C Eur.	0.70 white	V–VI, spherical, very double flowers over ample, spreading foliage. *R. platanifolius*, similar, with long flower stems.
Trollius × cultorum		List 5.3.5

Wild daylilies

These undemanding species thrive on moist to somewhat damp soils. Hybrids and cultivars are treated in list 5.2.1.

Hemerocallis citrina C China	1.00 lemon yellow	VI–VIII, vigorous clumps of dark green leaves; slender, elegant, lily-like flowers that open in the evening; fragrant after dark.
Hemerocallis lilio-asphodelus (*H. flava*) Sib., E Asia	0.70 pale yellow	V, old garden plant with lily-shaped, orange-scented flowers and lush green foliage. *H. aurantiaca*, VI–VII, orange-yellow flowers; rare in the trade.
Hemerocallis middendorffii Jap., W China	up to 0.50 deep yellow	VI–VII, scented, funnel-shaped flowers in clusters over slender, elegantly arching leaves; a valuable plant, which often flowers again in autumn.

		H. dumortieri, similar, with dark orange-yellow flowers. Both species rare in the trade.
Hemerocallis minor (*H. graminifolia*) E Asia	0.25/0.40 lemon yellow	V–VI, dainty, narrow, foliage; well-formed, funnel-shaped flowers.

2.3.2. Perennials for warm, sunny (or bright shady) corners, particularly on the woodland edge

Most of the following plants grow wild on fallow ground, field margins and sunny woodland borders. In the garden, they thrive in warm, sunny positions on rich, moderately dry to moist soils. Many of them are prolific self-seeders. They will also flourish on an open site, perhaps associated with the perennials from lists 3.4.4 and 3.4.8. The taller species can be particularly effective planted singly in front of trees and shrubs.

Campanula alliariifolia Cauc.	0.40 white	VII, robust, spreading plant with grey-haired, heart-shaped leaves; bell-flowers with pointed petals.
Creeping bellflower *Campanula rapuncu-* *loides* Eur., Asia Minor	up to 1.00 blue-violet	VI–VIII, abundant funnel-shaped flowers in one-sided racemes on stiff, slender stems; lanceolate leaves; very attractive in full sun but dangerously invasive; periodically dry, loamy soils; rare in the trade. *C. bononiensis*, similar but not invasive.
Perennial cornflower *Centaurea dealbata* 'Steenbergii' Cauc.	0.50/0.80 rosy purple	VI–VII, large cornflower-like flower heads; leafy, spreading habit; unsightly after flowering; best planted singly. 'Joan Coutts', (up to 0.80), bright pink; good for cutting.
Chrysanthemum *macro-* *phyllum* Carp. Cauc., Asia Minor	1.30 white	VI–VII, small, yarrow-like flowers in corymbose panicles on leafy stems; particularly good in mild areas.
Feverfew *Chrysanthemum par-* *thenium* Balk., Cauc., Asia Minor	up to 0.70 yellow with white ray florets	VII–IX, delicate, pale green, aromatic foliage; composite flowers; old ornamental and medicinal plant; short-lived but seeds itself freely; double forms available from seed merchants. 'Aureum', shoots emerge golden yellow.
Tansy *Chrysanthemum* *vulgare* (*Tanacetum vulgare*) Eur., Cauc., Sib.	up to 1.30 yellow	VII–IX, composite flowers, lacking ray florets; luxuriant, aromatic foliage with dark green, bipinnate leaves. 'Crispum', much dissected, ruffled, strongly aromatic leaves; old cottage garden plant; rare in the trade.
Galega bicolor		List 2.2.2
Lavatera thuringiaca C & SE Eur., W Asia	1.50 pale pink	VII–IX, branching growth and open, spreading habit; leaves 5-lobed below and 3-lobed above; short-lived (3–4 years) but valuable. *L. cachemiriana*, exceptionally large flowers.

Motherwort *Leonurus cardiaca* Eur., W Asia to Him., E Sib.	1.00 flesh-pink	VI–IX, small flowers in dense whorls in a spike-like inflorescence; branching, upright stems; softly hairy, coarsely toothed leaves with 3–5 lobes; decorative habit. *L. marrubiastrum*, (1.20), more vigorous, with smaller flowers.
Malva alcea Eur.	0.80 pink	VII–IX, branching stems with deeply lobed and serrate leaves; for a sunny spot on nutrient-rich soil; see also list 3.4.4. Selection: *M. a.* var. fastigiata.
Musk mallow *Malva moschata* Eur.	up to 0.70 pale pink	VI–IX, lush, green, finely divided leaves; branching stems; undemanding, tolerates bright shade; good for cutting. 'Alba', white flowers.
Melica altissima C & E Eur, As.	1.30	V–VI, white spikelets in long, slender panicles on tall and somewhtat fragile stems; green tuft of leaves; seeds itself freely. 'Atropurpurea', brownish-purple panicles.
Sweet cicely *Myrrhis odorata* W Balk. to Alb., Pyren., Alps, Apenn.	0.80 white	VI–VII, flowers in flat umbels; 2–4, large, soft, pinnately cut leaves; whole plant smells of aniseed; for rich, moist, loamy soils.
Catmint *Nepeta cataria* S, E & C Eur., W & C As. to Him.	0.50–1.00 yellowish or reddish	VII–IX, insignificant flowers in dense whorls on a spike-like inflorescence; hairy, pointed, serrate, triangular heart-shaped leaves; old ornamental and medicinal plant; rare in the trade.
Nepeta grandiflora 'Blue Beauty' Cauc.	0.60–1.00 violet-blue	VII–X, large flowers in whorls on a spike-like inflorescence; branching, upright stems; sparsely hairy, round-toothed, elongated heart-shaped leaves.
Nepeta nuda (*N. pannonica*) Eur., Cauc., Asia Minor, Altai, C & S Russ.	0.50–1.00 violet-blue or white	VII–VIII, flowers in whorl-like inflorescences on branching, upright stems; serrate or crenate, elongate-elliptic leaves with short petioles; rare in the trade.
Peucedanum alsaticum C & SE Eur., Cauc., Altai, C & S Russ.	up to 1.80 pale yellow	VII–IX, sturdy umbellifer with branching, angled stems and pinnate leaves; for sun and semi-shade on warm woodland fringes; dry, limy soils; long-lived pioneer species.
Pokeweed *Phytolacca acinosa* Jap., China	up to 1.50 white	VI–X, old garden plant; stately habit; large, erect spikes of white flowers; red berries that turn black upon ripening; huge, ovate leaves on red-flushed stems; seeds itself freely, especially in semi-shade. *P. americana*, N Am., nodding inflorescences.
Soapwort *Saponaria officinalis* 'Plena' Eur., Nr East, W Sib.	0.60/0.80 pale pink	VII–IX, flowers in terminal and axillary clusters on leafy, upright stems; invasive rhizomes; for a sunny woodland edge. 'Rubra Plena', dark pink.

Stachys germanica Eur., Med., SW Asia	0.60/1.20 red-violet	VI–VIII, whorled inflorescences on stout stems; hairy, round-toothed, blunted, oval leaves; for a warm, sunny woodland edge; rarely available in the trade.
Prickly comfrey *Symphytum asperum* Cauc.	up to 1.50 reddish to light blue	VI–VIII, nodding, tubular flowers with little ornamental value; leafy, spreading habit (fodder plant); stiffly hairy leaves and stems; not available from nurseries. *S.* × *uplandicum (S. asperum* × *S. officinale)* (1.00), blue.
Thalictrum flavum ssp. glaucum (*T. glaucum*) Spain, Port.	up to 2.00 sulphur yellow	VII–VIII, flowers in large, terminal panicles; blue-green bipinnate leaves; undemanding. 'Illumination', (1.20).
Peucedanum verticillare (*Tomassinia altissima*) SE Eur., C It.	up to 2.50 yellowish green	VI–VII, very ornamental umbellifer; finely grooved stems, up to 5 cm thick at the base; whorled branches; large, smooth, 2- or 3-pinnate leaves; often dies after flowering; for a sunny position on cool soil.

2.3.3. Perennials for moderate summer drought in bright to shady conditions, also under trees and shrubs

Plants that grow in these conditions are characterised by leathery leaves and thick rhizomes or tubers. *Lithospermum purpurocaeruleum* and some of the *Geranium* species (e.g. *G. sanguineum* and *G. renardii*) from list 2.1.2 also have sturdy rhizomes but tend to overwhelm their neighbours and are unsatisfactory in full shade.

Elephant's ears (Pigsqueak), *Bergenia*

Bergenias are extremely obliging perennials that will put up with almost any soil and situation. This makes them indispensable for planting under trees in places where the ground dries out in summer, though they actually prefer moister conditions and will thrive in sun or semi-shade among rocks. For this reason the hybrids and cultivars have been assigned to the rock garden (list 4.1.3).

  Plants offered for sale in European nurseries are mostly hybrids; in America the species are commoner. Among the species, *B. crassifolia* and *B. cordifolia* come from Siberia and Altai, where they grow especially luxuriantly on the sites of former fires or in clearings and on mountain pastures. Other species, such as *B. purpurascens* and *B. stracheyi*, grow wild in the Himalayas and are somewhat more demanding in their requirements. They flourish in moderate woodland edge conditions or among rocks and close to water, though not in wet soils.

  It may occasionally be necessary to cover the exposed rhizomes of bergenias with soil to prevent them growing out of the ground.

Robust species

Bergenia cordifolia Altai, Mongol.	0.30/0.35 violet and pink	IV–V, small, nodding flowers; coarse, thick, leathery, evergreen leaves; indestructible on moist soils, but does not tolerate wet conditions; a valuable plant for light shade under trees or on the rock garden. 'Alba', white flowers.

Bergenia crassifolia Sib., Mongol.	0.25/0.50 pink	IV, evergreen with coarse, elongate–oval leaves; old garden plant. *B. c.* var. *orbicularis*, pink; rounded leaves; low-growing. *B.* × *schmidtii*, IV, pink; exceptionally beautiful and abundant flowers; robust evergreen; thrives in sun.

Less robust but still reliable species

Bergenia ciliata Nepal, Kash., W Pak.	0.30/0.40 pink	III–IV, large, round, densely hairy leaves; frost-sensitive flowers and foliage. *B. c.* f. *ligulata*, one-sided inflorescences; leaves with hairy margins, easily damaged by frost.
Bergenia stracheyi Afgh., W Him.	0.20/0.30 whitish pink	III, a variable species; flowers appear very early and are often damaged by frost; otherwise hardy; very bold, glossy, semi-evergreen foliage; effective in a shady spot. *B. s.* var. *afganica*, (0.20), white. 'Alba', (0.20), white. 'Belvedere', (0.25), white. *B. acanthifolia* hort., pink; probably belongs here.

Wild cyclamen

With the exception of *C. purpurascens*, all of these dainty wild cyclamen come from areas with mild winters and hot summers, where they grow in moist to dry conditions, mostly under the protection of trees and shrubs. In the garden, their tubers will thrive and flower on heavy soils within a dense mat of tree roots on the woodland edge. Alternatively, they may be grown closer to eye-level, beneath the dwarf woody species of a rock garden.

The tubers of most species are best planted 3–5 cm deep in a limy, humus-rich loam. The shoot bases should on no account be exposed. A light covering of conifer branches may be beneficial in winter. All the species seed themselves freely and can be very effective in large drifts.

Cyclamen coum (*C. orbiculatum*) SE Eur.	0.05 red	II–III, thrives in the shade and protection of deciduous trees; flattened spherical tubers with tufts of roots beneath; roundish, dark green leaves; white- and pink-flowering forms are available in the trade. Subspecies: *C. c.* ssp. *alpinum (C. vernum)*. *C. c.* ssp. *caucasicum (C. ibericum, C. abchasicum)*. *C. c.* ssp. *hiemale (C. atkinsii)*. All are fairly similar.
Cyclamen purpurascens (*C. europaeum*) SE Fr., Alps, W Carp., C Yug.	0.08 pink	VII–IX, roots emerge from the top and sides of the tubers; evergreen leaves with scalloped edges and silvery-grey patterning; needs a moist (but not wet) soil that does not dry out in summer; associates well with the perennials from list 2.1.6.
Cyclamen hederifolium (*C. neapolitanum*) S Eur.	0.10 pink	IX–X, roots emerge from the top of the tubers; flowers appear before the attractively marked, ivy-like, overwintering leaves; the tubers become very large in old age. 'Album', white; comes true from seed.
Cyclamen repandum		List 4.5.5

Hellebores, *Helleborus*

All of the following species and hybrids flourish in the neighbourhood of trees and shrubs. In winter and spring they need plenty of moisture but do not tolerate wet conditions. They prefer a well-drained, loamy, alkaline soil and thrive in summer drought. Hellebores grow slowly. They are extremely sensitive to root damage and should not be disturbed by digging and cultivation. Given the right conditions they will attain a great age, developing and becoming ever more beautiful for decades without replanting.

Helleborus abchasicus hort. Cauc.	0.30 dark purplish-red	III–IV, dark, semi-evergreen leaves. Selection: 'Atropurpureus', rare in the trade.
Helleborus dumetorum ssp. *atrorubens* (*H. atrorubens* hort.) Yug.	0.50 purple-red	II–IV, glossy, fresh green leaves with long petioles. *H. purpurascens* (0.30), III–IV, misty purple flowers in threes; deciduous leaves.
Stinking hellebore *Helleborus foetidus* SW & W Eur.	0.30/0.50 pale green	II–IV, small, nodding, bell-shaped flowers with red-fringed petals on branching stems; attractive, fingery foliage; undemanding; short-lived, but seeds itself freely.
Helleborus × hybridus (*H. orientalis*)	0.20/0.30 greenish white and red	III–V, robust and long-flowering evergreen; seeds itself freely. Named colour forms are available but rare in the trade.
Christmas rose *Helleborus niger* Alps, Carp., Apenn., Yug.	0.20/0.25 white (flushing red)	III–IV, large, impressive blooms, beloved of flower arrangers; the evergreen foliage is less spectacular than that of other species.
Helleborus niger ssp. *macranthus* N Yug., It.	0.20/0.30 white (tinged green)	IV, vigorous subspecies with particularly large flowers and large, narrowly divided leaves. 'Altifolius', XI–XII, similar to above, with luxuriant foliage; flowers at Christmas.
Helleborus niger 'Praecox'	0.20/0.25 white	X–XII, valuable for its late autumn flowers; smaller flowers than the type; suitable for forcing; various selections available in the trade.
Helleborus odorus N It. to S Rum.	0.40	II–IV, fragrant, nodding, cup-shaped flowers; also thrives on dry soils in full sun. *H. cyclophyllus*, (0.40), Balk., large, upward-facing, green flowers; deciduous leaves.
Helleborus olympicus W Asia Minor	0.30 whitish	III–IV, large, cup-shaped flowers; decorative foliage.
Helleborus viridis W & C Eur., It.	0.30 green	III–IV, old garden plant, often naturalised; scentless, nodding flowers over deciduous, deeply divided leaves.

More or less tender species for moderate summer drought and bright shade on the woodland edge

Sometimes effective combined with the perennials from lists 4.5.4 and 4.5.5.

Euphorbia amyg- *daloides* var. *robbiae*		List 4.5.4
Helleborus lividus ssp. *corsicus* (*H. corsicus*) Cors., Sard.	up to 0.50 yellowish green	III–IV, semi-shrub with leathery, matt green, sharply serrate, tripartite leaves; branching inflorescences with nodding, bell-shaped flowers; prolific self-seeder; needs protection from winter sun.
Butcher's broom *Ruscus hypoglossum* N It to Crim. SW Turk.	up to 0.70 yellowish	III–IV, semi-shrub with unbranched, angled stems and evergreen, spineless cladodes; dioecious; flowers insignificant; spherical, red fruits on female plants. *R. aculeatus* (to 0.80), round, branching stems and spine-tipped cladodes; dioecious; hardly available from nurseries.

Sometimes useful

Erica arborea 'Alpina' W Sp.	0.70 white	III–IV, beautiful, delicate, needle-shaped foliage on upright, branching stems; somewhat tender but much hardier than *E. arborea*.
Erica erigena		List 3.2.3
Iris foetidissima		List 4.6.4 moist to damp soils
Paxistima canbyi		List 4.5.4

2.3.4.   Perennials for summer drought on a sunny woodland edge

Autumn crocus, *Colchicum*

In spring, colchicums develop large, broad leaves and seed capsules, which combine well with flowering tulips. These die back in June or July to be followed by crocus-like blooms in late summer and autumn. The flowers appear without leaves and often in great numbers over the bare soil.

These undemanding, though unfortunately poisonous plants thrive in cultivated, loamy soils, which may dry out completely in summer. For this reason, they grow well in the root-infested soil of a sunny woodland edge, though *C. autumnale* and its derivatives require somewhat moister conditions. The smaller species can be used in sunny parts of the rock garden. Wild forms seed themselves freely in open soil.

The corms are best planted during their summer dormant season. They should be set 5–20 cm beneath the surface, according to size.

Colchicum autumnale Eur.	0.20/0.10 lilac	IX, for soils that stay moist in summer (see list 6.4.2); more difficult than other *Colchicum* spp., the wild form is rarely available in the trade. 'Plenum', lilac-pink; double. 'Album', white. 'Album Plenum', white; double. *C. pannonicum* (0.15), IX, reddish-lilac; somewhat larger than the above species; rare in the trade.

Colchicum byzantinum Asia Minor, Gr.	0.20/0.10 lilac-pink	IX, abundant, smallish flowers; undemanding. *C. agrippinum*, VIII, lilac; chequered flowers; narrow, wavy leaves; rare in the trade.
Colchicum speciosum var. *bornmuelleri* (*C. bornmuelleri*) Asia Minor, Iran	0.30/0.20 pink-lilac with white centres	VIII, very large, early flowers; to be recommended. 'Magnificum', somewhat darker.
Colchicum *neapolitanum* W Med.	0.30/0.20 pink-lilac	IX, longer and more slender flowers than the previous species; not so robust.
Colchicum speciosum Cauc., Asia Minor	0.30/0.25 lilac with a white base	IX, large, open, goblet-shaped flowers. 'Album', rare white form.

Colchicum Hybrids

'Lilac Wonder', IX, lilac.
'Princess Astrid', IX–X, chequered ruby and cream.
'The Giant', IX–X, pink-lilac; very large flowers.
'Violet Queen', IX, dark violet; large flowers.
'Waterlily', IX, lilac; very double.

None of these seeds itself and all are relatively short-lived.

Further species for moderate summer drought

Autumn-flowering crocuses *Crocus speciosus* etc.		List 4.4.2
Euphorbia griffithii 'Fireglow' S Tibet	0.50 orange-red	V–VI, terminal umbels on rigid, upright stems set with lanceolate leaves; spreading rhizomes; red autumn colour; also for bright shade; sensitive to extreme cold.

Wild peonies, *Paeonia*

The following peony species can be used to good effect on a herbaceous border. However, their most natural planting position is an open woodland edge in sun or bright shade. By drawing on the nutrients and moisture stored in their thick, tuberous roots they are well able to withstand periods of drought. A few rarer and more difficult species have been appended to the end of the list. The ornamental cultivars are treated in list 5.2.3.

Paeonia anomala E Russ. to C Asia	1.00 pink	V, large, flat, open, nodding flowers; finely divided leaves with sunken, white-hairy veins. *P. a.* var. *intermedia*, VI–VII, light crimson; similar. *P. tenuifolia*, see list 3.4.4.
Paeonia mascula (*P. corallina*) S Eur. to C Fr., Cauc.	0.80 purplish-red	IV–V, flowers mostly solitary on hard stems with small, glossy, dark green, ternate leaves above; red fruits; old monastery garden plant.
Paeonia mascula ssp. *arietina* 'Northern Glory' E Eur., Asia Minor	1.20 crimson	V, magnificent silky flowers; leaves more strongly divided and with more pointed lobes than those of *P. mascula*. 'Mother of Pearl', pink.

Paeonia officinalis Fr., S Alps to Hung. & Alb.	0.60 purplish-red	IV–V, flowers solitary; 2- or 3-ternate leaves on upper part of stem; old garden plant; undemanding; descendants include the double flowered cottage peonies (see list 5.2.3). *P. mollis*, (0.50), pink; grey-green foliage; undemanding.
Paeonia peregrina (*P. lobata*) It., Balk.	0.90 deep crimson	V–VI, blooms somewhat later than the above species; glossy, dark green leaves with incised tips; brilliantly coloured flowers. Cultivars, see list 5.2.3.
Paeonia wittmanniana NW Cauc.	1.00 creamy-white	V, yellow buds expanding to large, whitish globes, opening into single flowers; needs a dryish, well-drained, loamy soil.

More difficult species

Paeonia delavayi Yunn.	to 1.50 (2.00) dark red	VI, shrubby species; small, bowl-shaped flowers; dark green, biternate leaves with blue-green undersides; bizarre habit.
Paeonia mlokose- *witschii* Cauc.	0.70 yellow	V–VI, blue-green leaves with reddish veins; not for heavy soils; does poorly in a wet summer and must be kept dry in winter.
Paeonia potaninii var. *trollioides* (*P. trollioides*) Tibet	0.80 yellow	V, shrubby species; flowers, like *Trollius*, never open properly; leaves incised, pinnately divided or lobed; spreading roots.
Paeonia veitchii W China	0.70 magenta	V–VI, large, nodding flowers; finely divided, light green foliage; red roots; robust in bright shade on soils that are not too dry. *P. emodi* and *P. japonica*, V, are rarely available in the trade.

2.3.5. Tall, highly invasive perennials for large parks and gardens

These exceptionally vigorous and highly invasive perennials are particularly luxuriant on rich, moist to damp soils. They may occasionally be useful for planting on embankments.

Polygonum poly- *stachyum* Him. to Sib.	2.00 white	IX, beautiful, fragrant flowers in autumn; long, pointed leaves; invasive but very ornamental.
Reynoutria sach- *alinensis* (*Polygonum sach-* *alinense*) Jap., Sachalin	up to 3.00 white	IX, small racemes of flowers hidden among the bold foliage; very invasive. *R. japonica* (*Polygonum cuspidatum*) (2.00), smaller leaves; to be used with great caution.
Polygonum weyrichii Sachalin	up to 2.00 white	VIII–IX, short-stemmed, oval leaves; not so invasive but still needs a lot of space; very ornamental.

Senecio tanguticus (*Ligularia tangutica*) N China	up to 1.50 yellow	VII, large, pinnate leaves; small flowers in broad, pyramidal inflorescences which open first at the top; grey-white seed heads, which remain until winter; prefers sun and a well-drained soil.

Bamboos

Bamboos are woody relatives of the grasses though some of the lower-growing species, with their fine stems and creeping habit, bear more resemblance to herbaceous perennials. Their luxuriant, evergreen and semi-evergreen foliage can be effectively combined with oriental trees and shrubs, particularly the more ornamental species such as Japanese cherries and some of the conifers. The clump-forming bamboos are easier to use in gardens than the more tender, creeping species, which need a protected position in a shady courtyard or beneath trees. All bamboos are more or less shade-tolerant and can therefore be assigned to woodland or woodland edge habitats. The clump-forming species may also be used to liven up an open, sunny site near to buildings or at the side of a pond.

Bamboos are foliage plants. Flowers seldom appear until plants are 10–20 years old or even 100–120 years, depending on the species. At Weihenstephan, plants of *Arundinaria variegata* flowered in 1979 and subsequently died. This behaviour is typical for bamboos in the wild, where large stands suddenly flower and die in spectacular fashion. The internal timing that controls this process is not yet fully understood.

The plants appreciate well-drained and nutrient-rich, moist to damp soils. They thrive in mild areas. Only a few species grow satisfactorily in a harsh climate, and these should always be given a sheltered site. Propagation is by division in spring. The stems of newly divided plants should on no account be cut away.

Hardy, clump-forming species

Sinarundinaria murielae (*Thamnocalamus spathaceus*) C China	3.00–4.00 (up to 4.50)	Arching stems with gently drooping, yellow-green branches; narrow, pointed leaves that roll up in frosty weather; sheaths not persistent; whitish bloom on stem internodes; tolerates sun.
Sinarundinaria nitida (*Arundinaria nitida*) C & W China	4.00 (to 6.00)	Upright habit; dark, reddish side branches; narrow, abruptly pointed leaves; sheaths persist over winter; best in semi-shade. Selections: 'Eisenach', (4.50), loosely arching habit. 'Nymphenburg', (to 4.50), very narrow leaves; forms loose clumps; tolerates shade.
Shibataea kumasasa Jap.	0.60	Compact habit; stems densely set with broad, ovate, glossy, dark green leaves whose pointed tips start to bleach in autumn; not invasive; prefers a damp soil.

Hardy, spreading species

Phyllostachys aureosulcata (*P. nevinii*) China	4.00 (to 7.00)	Zig-zag stems, with one side flattened and coloured golden yellow; narrow leaves, 3–12 cm long; still rare in the trade.

Phyllostachys boryana (*P. nigra boryana*) China	up to 5.00	Dainty, fresh green, evergreen foliage; open, branching habit; slightly arched, yellowish stems with one flattened side; produces occasional, far-reaching suckers, which are marbled brownish at the base.
Species for mild areas		
Arundinaria japonica (*Pseudosasa japonica*) Jap.	4–5 m	Leaves glossy, 20 cm long, 2–4 cm wide, narrowed at the base; broad, bushy habit; creeping roots.
Arundinaria pumila (*Sasa pumila*) Jap.	0.50–0.70	Slender, dainty-leaved stems; spreads strongly to form lawn-like colonies under trees or in the sun; dies back to the ground annually at Weihenstephan.
Arundinaria auricoma (*A. viridistriata*) Jap. (?)	1.20–1.50	Leaves green with golden yellow stripes, 10–20 cm long, 3 cm wide; slender, reddish-green stems; produces particularly colourful regrowth after cutting back.
Arundinaria fastuosa (*Semiarundinaria fastuosa*) Jap.	3.00–4.00	Narrow, upright habit; pointed leaves, 15 cm long, 2 cm wide; tender.
Arundinaria graminea Jap.	up to 3.00	Yellowish stems; very narrow (1 cm) leaves up to 20 cm long.
Arundinaria pygmaea (*Sasa pygmaea*) Jap.	0.20–0.50 (to 1.00)	Invasive groundcover plant for a sunny position; leaves 5–12 cm long; tolerates cutting or high mowing; dies back to the ground each winter at Weihenstephan.
Phyllostachys henonis (*P. nigra henonis*) China	up to 4.00	Gracefully arched and branching stems; leaves 10 cm long.
Phyllostachys viridi-glaucescens SC China	up to 5.00	Loose habit; robust and strongly invasive, but plants at Weihenstephan suffer on an open site in winter.
Sasa palmata 'Nebulosa' Jap.	up to 2.00	Very bold foliage; leaves up to 30 cm long, 7–8 cm wide, palmately arranged on unbranched stems.
Sasa tesselata Jap.	up to 1.20	Arching habit; leaves up to 60 cm long, 10 cm wide, on slender, unbranched stems.

2.4. Spring-flowering bulbs and their allies

These dainty spring flowers come from woodland, meadow and alpine plant communities, and can be broadly divided into warm- and cool-loving species. In gardens they thrive on the woodland edge where they can spread out under trees or into an adjacent lawn. Most will also do well on a rock garden, and those that set little or no seed have been assigned to lists 4.4.2 and 4.5.5.

Flowering bulbs get planted in all sorts of places, especially in a new garden. However, their true value first becomes apparent in a mature setting, where a modest number of initial plants can spread to form impressive carpets whose annual variations at flowering time are a constant source of delight. This sort of floral display can only develop in association with trees and shrubs. The intense summer shade under deciduous species prevents establishment of all but a sparse covering of vegetation, allowing seed of spring bulbs to germinate and grow on free of competition in the spring sunshine. As tree leaves unfurl and shade increases, the bulbs are already dying down and going into their summer dormancy.

Lawns tend to grow thin and full of moss wherever they are shaded by trees and shrubs. In such places spring bulbs can survive the competition of the weakened grasses and will spread freely, provided only that they are not disturbed by mowing. The same applies to sunny areas where tree roots grow in dense mats close to the surface. By avoiding early mowing and making careful use of fertilisers, species such as scillas, crocus and snowdrops can be encouraged to spread far out into the lawn, turning it into a sea of flowers in early spring.

Bulbs are often mistakenly planted in the middle of a lawn where the grass is dense and vigorous. It is much better to set them out under trees and shrubs or on the woodland edge, and to let them spread into the lawn from there. On the whole, they do not seed themselves well in perennial plantings, except among low-growing rock garden species.

Of course, bulbs, corms and tubers intended for naturalising must be capable of producing fertile seed. Most species germinate in winter and then require three years to reach mature size, flowering in their fourth year if left undisturbed. Sometimes, even sterile forms such as the double snowdrop (*Galanthus nivalis* 'Plenus') will multiply as if by seeding. As the vegetative clumps grow larger there is eventually no more room for the annually produced bulbets and these are then forced up to the surface. Here they may be collected and sown about, or the process may be left to birds and ants, which scatter seed and bulbets in their search for food.

Spring bulbs need abundant light and moisture during their short growing season. They thrive in rich, moist to damp soils, avoiding dry conditions in spring and responding well to an application of fertiliser in early or late winter.

2.4.1.   Spring-flowering bulbs, corms and tubers for warm, sunny positions

The following species thrive in woodland edge areas that are moist, warm and sunny in spring. In summer they will tolerate both shade and drought. A rock garden or steppe-type planting may also provide suitable growing conditions. The plants seed themselves freely in open soil or among sparse vegetation.

Chionodoxa gigantea Asia Minor	0.15 blue	III–IV, larger flowers than *C. luciliae*; very variable. 'Alba', white; rare. 'Blaustern', short and sturdy.
Chionodoxa luciliae Asia Minor	0.15 blue, with white centres	III–IV, narrow, grooved leaves; usually 4 flowers per stem; somewhat similar to *Scilla siberica*; vigorous spreader, thrives at the foot of a warm, sunny wall. 'Alba', white. 'Pink Giant,' pink. 'Rosea', pale pink-violet.
Chionodoxa sardensis Asia Minor	0.10/0.15 gentian blue, white stamens	III–IV, loose racemes of 6–7 flowers; does not always flourish and spread as well as *C. luciliae*; will often seed itself in thin grass.
Galanthus elwesii Asia Minor	0.15 white	II–III, large, broad-leaved snowdrop; seeds itself in a warm, sunny position, but increases less vigorously than *G. nivalis*. Many named forms, including:

'Whittallii', very large flowers; early.
'Maximus', large flowers; twisted leaves.
'Merlin', long, narrow flowers with green inner petals; starts to emerge in XII.

Muscari azureum (*Hyacinthella azurea*) (*Hyacinthus azureus*) Asia Minor	0.10 azure blue	II–III, blooms very early; hardy; multiplies rapidly; flowers not constricted at the mouth. 'Album', white.
Armenian grape hyacinth *Muscari armeniacum* Balk., Asia Minor, Cauc.	0.15 azure blue	IV–V, flowers constricted at the mouth, with a narrow white rim; narrow, arching leaves, which appear in autumn and are often damaged through the winter. 'Cantab', V, sky blue; somewhat tender and often unsightly foliage. 'Blue Spike', double flowers that last well. 'Early Giant', large, deep blue flowers. 'Heavenly Blue', very similar to the species.
Muscari botryoides C & S Eur., Asia Min.	0.15 azure blue	IV–V, flowers almost spherical; similar to the above, but leaves appear in spring; a rewarding plant and prolific self-seeder. 'Album', white; not so robust.
European grape hyacinth *Muscari neglectum* (*M. racemosum*) Sw & C Eur. to Nr East	0.10 dull blue	IV, plum scented; rare in the trade. 'Carneum', white, flushed red.
Muscari tubergenianum		List 4.4.2
Nodding star-of- Bethlehem *Ornithogalum nutans* SE Eur., Nr. East	0.30 white	V, large, nodding flowers on stiff stems; naturalises well on grassy slopes or in the shade of trees. *O. boucheanum*, similar to the above but leaves die back before flowering; not available in the trade.
Star-of-Bethlehem *Ornithogalum umbel-* *latum* Med., Cauc., Nr East	0.20 white	IV–V, stiff, umbellate inflorescences; long, very narrow leaves that wilt after flowering; the 'stars' open only in sunshine and in the morning; invasive and prolific self-seeder; to be used with caution; plants often do not flower.
Puschkinia libanotica Asia Minor	0.10 pale blue	III–IV, very dainty; petals have a white central stripe; seeds itself and spreads rapidly. 'Alba', white; not so vigorous.
Tulipa sylvestris Eur., Med., NW Iran	0.25 yellow	V, elegant habit with nodding buds; only flowers freely in sun; spreads widely underground; for a warm, sunny woodland edge or open soil on the rock garden; naturalised in E USA. 'Tabriz', (0.30), similar, but more abundant flowers; does not spread; flowers first appear in the second year after planting.

Crocus

Among the many different sorts of crocus, only the ornamental *C. vernus* cultivars and a few of the wild species are really suitable for naturalising on the woodland edge. Crocuses need sunshine and abundant moisture in spring but will tolerate dry and shady conditions in summer, making them ideal for planting in places where the lawn grows thin under established trees and shrubs. Their leaves only start to die back at the beginning of June, so planting should be confined to areas where the grass can be left to grow long without detracting from the overall garden picture. Alternatively, the corms may be found a suitable home on the edge of a sunny flower bed or around the base of an ornamental shrub.

In common with the majority of spring-flowering bulbs, corms and tubers, crocus corms can be planted out from the beginning of October onwards. They should be set at least three times their own depth in the soil, preferably scattered at random and then planted where they fall. It is worth bearing in mind that the corms are readily eaten by mice, in contrast to the bulbs of daffodils.

Garden crocus (Crocus vernus *cultivars*)

The original, white-flowered meadow plant, *C. vernus* ssp. *albiflorus*, is not available in the trade. (See list 4.4.4.)

Fifteen years of careful investigation by Hermann Müssel at Weihenstephan have established that most of the available cultivars, including those sold for forcing, will seed themselves in suitable areas of sparse, mossy grass. In the majority of cases the seedling colours come true.

The following cultivars are among those commonly offered in bulb catalogues. Sterile cultivars are listed separately.

white:	'Joan of Arc', 'Schneesturm'
lilac-blue:	'Excelsior', 'Queen of the Blues'
violet-striped:	'King of the Stripes', 'Pickwick'
dark plum-purple:	'Purpureus Grandiflorus', 'Remembrance'
dark violet:	'Nigger Boy', 'Paulus Potter'

The following, older cultivars also seed themselves well: 'King of the Blues' (dark violet), 'Pallas' (white, striped lilac) and 'The Sultan' (violet).

Sterile cultivars for selected spots on the woodland edge

(Propagation by division of the corm clusters just before the leaves die back; planting in October.)

golden yellow:	'Dutch Yellow' ('Large Yellow', 'Yellow Giant')
pale lilac:	'Haarlem Gem', very early.
lilac:	'Vanguard', very early.

Wild species for the woodland edge and thin grass

The following plants have large flowers and seed themselves freely. They can also be recommended for use in parks. Their corms are seldom eaten by mice.

Crocus tommasinianus	0.08	II–III, large, delicate flowers; fine, grassy leaves; unde-
Hung., Dalm.	pale lilac	manding; prolific self-seeder. The following selections
		flower rather later but also seed themselves:
		'Barr's Purple', reddish-purple.
		'Taplow Ruby', ruby red.
		'Whitewell Purple', reddish-purple.

| *Crocus vernus* ssp. *vernus* (*C. neapolitanus*) (*C. napolitanus*) It., Austria, Yug. | 0.10 lilac | III–IV, large flowered sub-species; seeds itself freely, especially in areas of high humidity (Black Forest) or in moist meadows; unfortunately still rare in the trade. |

Species that are commonly naturalised in parks in SE Europe

| *Crocus byzantinus* | List 4.4.2 autumn flowering |
| *Crocus heuffelianus* Herbert | List 4.4.2 |

Further wild species and their cultivars are treated among the rock garden perennials (lists 4.1.4, 4.4.2, and 4.4.4).

2.4.2. Spring bulbs, corms and tubers for bright but cool positions

The following species thrive in the cool shade of deciduous trees, which allow abundant light to fall at flowering time. They love rich, moist to damp, loamy soils that do not dry out in summer. They will seed themselves to form large populations on open soil or among thin vegetation under trees.

Care should be taken when buying the bulbs, corms and tubers, since not all will tolerate storage. *Eranthis, Erythronium, Fritillaria* and *Galanthus* are often delivered dry and incapable of further growth.

× *Chionoscilla allenii* (*Chionodoxa luciliae* × *Scilla bifolia*)	up to 0.20 violet-blue	III, dark blue or violet-blue flowers without a white centre; rare bigeneric hybrid for bright but not too dry conditions.
Eranthis cilicica Asia Minor	0.05 yellow	III, flowers over a collar of narrow, almost feathery leaflets; reddish stems; does not spread so rapidly as the following species. Hybrids, see list 4.5.5.
Winter aconite *Eranthis hyemalis* S Eur.	0.05 yellow	II–III, flowers earlier than the above species; collar of broad leaflets; green stems; seeds itself prolifically and quickly forms large populations under trees.
Dog's tooth violet *Erythronium dens-canis* Eur., Jap.	0.10 white and lilac	III–IV, nodding flowers with pointed petals; two, large, oval to oblong, basal leaves, with green and brown marbling; for humus-rich soils, out of the sun; tolerates lime. 'Little Wonder', light purple. 'Pink Perfection', delicate pink; early. 'Rose Beauty', dark pink. 'White Splendour', white. All seed themselves reluctantly. Further species, see list 4.5.5.
Corydalis cava	List 1.2.1
Snakeshead fritillary *Fritillaria meleagris* Eur., Cauc.	up to 0.30 wine-red, chequered white	IV–V, nodding, bell-shaped flowers on straight stems; a plant of damp meadows; may be naturalised in the garden on moist to damp soils in semi-shade on the woodland edge; tends to get squeezed out of sunny, waterside plantings.

'Alba', white.
'Charon', dark purple.
'Poseidon', very large, pink-chequered flowers.
'Saturn', reddish violet.

Snowdrop *Galanthus nivalis* W, C & S Eur.	0.10 white	II–III, popular garden plant with narrow, ovoid buds; some cultivars are sterile but nevertheless spread themselves vegetatively. 'Plenus', double flowers; sterile. 'Scharlockii', flower bracts erect like donkeys' ears. Other species, see list 4.5.5.
Spring snowflake *Leucojum vernum* C Eur.	0.20 white	II–III, resembles a large snowdrop with broad, bell-shaped flowers like tiny parachutes; seeds itself only on rich and continually damp soils.
Hyacinthoides hispanica (*Scilla hispanica*) (*S. campanulata*) W Med., Port	0.25 blue	V, nodding, bell-shaped flowers in pyramidal racemes; strong stems; broad, rich green leaves, which die down after flowering; thrives in sun or shade; only seeds itself freely in warmer regions; some robust and long-lived cultivars hardly set seed at all. 'La Grandesse', white. 'White Triumphator', white. 'Excelsior', light blue. 'Myosotis', early flowering. 'Blue Giant', blue; very early. 'Dainty Maid', pink. 'Rosabella', pink. 'Queen of the Pinks', dark pink.
Bluebell *Scilla non-scripta* (*S. nutans*) (*Endymion non-scripta*) W Eur.	0.25 blue	V, narrow, elongated bells in loose, almost one-sided racemes; similar to the above but with narrower leaves; seeds itself freely on damp, loamy soils; grows in large drifts in W European (especially British) woods and meadows.
Scilla bifolia C Eur., Asia Minor, Cauc.	up to 0.10 soft blue	III–IV, small, dainty flowers in loose racemes; seeds itself freely in bright, damp areas of woodland.
Scilla siberica Cauc., Nr East, C Russ.	up to 0.15 bright blue	IV, 1–3 broad, bell-shaped, nodding flowers on each stem; seeds itself prolifically, especially in open woodland or on lawns. 'Alba', white; rare in the trade. 'Spring Beauty', deep blue; larger than the type but does not seed itself. 'Taurica', brilliant light blue; flowers early.
Scilla tubergeniana		List 4.4.2

Species that require garden-type maintenance have been assigned to the rock garden (list 4.4.2). For the most part, these are plants which hardly seed themselves and must therefore be given a convenient site where their clumps can occasionally be lifted for division. Where no rock garden is available they may also be grown in selected positions on the woodland edge.

2.4.3.   Daffodils and other narcissi

Narcissi can often be found growing wild on meadows or in damp woods under oaks and alders. In the garden, however, it is advisable to plant them in groups on the woodland edge and in adjoining areas of lawn, where the grass must be left long and undisturbed until the leaves have died down some time in June or July. Alternatively, the bulbs may be set in a border planting, though here their bluish, wilting foliage is a disturbing factor, to be hidden away behind other perennials from the end of April until it dries and may be removed.

Narcissi thrive in any garden soil but do especially well in a damp, sandy loam. They must be planted as early as possible from the beginning of September to the end of October. Their bulbs should be set at 2–3 times their own depth in the soil, and at least 30 cm apart. When flowering diminishes, the clumps can be lifted and divided just before they die down.

The best sorts for naturalising on the woodland edge or at the edge of a lawn are the early-flowering daffodils or yellow trumpet narcissi, and in brighter places the white, late-flowering *N. poeticus*. The more brightly coloured cultivars, particularly those belonging to the Large-cupped, Small-cupped, and Tazetta groups, are better given planting positions where they have less competition, such as on a perennial border. Apart from a few dainty wild species (see lists 4.2.4, 4.4.4 and 4.6.6), the bulbs that are offered in the trade are all cultivars. The following review of some common and reliable selections hardly conveys the variety of the complete assortment.

Tall cultivars (0.30–0.40 m) with single-flowered stems

Trumpet narcissi (Daffodils) (Narcissus pseudonarcissus), S Eur.

(III–) IV, very robust; the trumpet (corona) is as long as, or longer than, the perianth segments (petals).
'Dutch Master', 'Golden Harvest', (early), 'King Alfred', Rembrandt, 'Unsurpassable', all yellow.
'Magnet', yellow trumpet, white petals.
'Mount Hood', white.
'Texas', yellow with orange streaks; double.

Large-cupped narcissi (N. × incomparabilis) (N. poeticus × N. pseudonarcissus)

IV, large, cup-shaped coronas.
'Carlton', golden yellow; early and robust.
'Helios', yellow cup, pale yellow petals.
'Flower Record', orange-yellow cup, white petals.
'Scarlet Elegance', orange cup, dark yellow petals.

Short-cupped narcissi (N. × barrii)

IV, somewhat delicate; corona approximately one third as long as the perianth segments.
'Barret Browning', orange cup, white petals; early.
'La Riante', dark orange cup, white petals.
'Birma', red cup, pale yellow petals.

Poet narcissi (Narcissus poeticus), S Eur.

IV–V, very robust; corona is a very small, red-rimmed cup.
'Actaea', (to 0.40), white petals; particularly for moist or damp soils.

Cultivars with many-flowered stems

The following narcissi are mostly shorter-lived than the single-flowered varieties. They are best planted in open soil.

Tazetta narcissi	0.30–0.45	IV–V, robust; normally 4–8 flowers per stem.
Narcissus × medio-luteus		'Laurens Koster', yellow corona, white petals.
		'Geranium', orange corona, white petals.
(*N. × poetaz*)		'Scarlet Gem', orange corona, yellow petals.
(*N. poeticus ×*		'Cheerfulness', creamy white; double.
N. tazetta)		'Yellow Cheerfulness', yellow; double.
Triandrus narcissi		V, normally 3–6, large, nodding flowers per stem; a
Narcissus Triandrus hybrids		few hardy cultivars.
		'Thalia', (to 0.60), white; flowers late; very long-lived.
		'Silver Chimes', (up to 0.40), yellow corona, white petals; somewhat tender.
		N. × johnstonii 'Queen of Spain' (0.25), lemon yellow.
Jonquils		V, tender; normally 2–4, intensely fragrant flowers per
Narcissus jonquilla		stem; cylindrical leaves.
W Med., Nr East		'Suzy', (0.40), orange corona, light yellow petals.
		'Trevithian', (0.50), delicate yellow; reliable cultivar.

Low-growing cultivars

Low-growing (0.20–0.30) *Narcissus* cultivars have been assigned to the ornamental rock garden (list 4.1.4), but they may also be suitable for planting in woodland edge conditions together with plants such as *Muscari*.

3 Open ground

Open ground comprises all those parts of a garden that are free from trees and shrubs. Normally speaking, these areas are largely taken up by lawn, and it is debatable to what extent this important utility and structural element may be sacrificed to make way for perennials and groundcover plants. The edges of a lawn are often dominated by trees and shrubs, creating conditions that are only suitable for woodland edge species. Perennials for open ground are more useful in association with architectural features such as buildings and areas of paving, where it is comparatively easy to create the right conditions for attractive communities of steppe (prairie) or other sun-loving plants. Used in this way, wild perennials can form an effective alternative to the more labour intensive border perennials that are often grown in similar situations.

It should always be borne in mind that a mistaken or poorly conceived planting can destroy the effect of even the most beautiful design. In view of this, open ground perennials should only be considered for areas that have no conflicting structural function, and where a planting of trees and shrubs would be inappropriate.

Some of the species or groups of species contained in this section may also find a use in other garden habitats. Various possibilities are mentioned in the text.

3.1. Perennials as a lawn substitute

An extensive, monotypic planting of low, densely growing perennials or dwarf shrubs can sometimes fulfil the visual and structural functions of a mown lawn, at least during the summer months. Generally speaking, these plantings should not be trodden and are less robust than other lawn substitutes such as wildflower meadows or mixed plantings of dry grassland species. Their use is thus more or less restricted to special situations in well-tended parts of a park or garden.

Since they do not require mowing, such plantings constitute a practical alternative to small patches of lawn in a front garden or among the graves of a cemetery. Here they may contribute substantially to the structure of the design, particularly if they are combined with appropriate groups of woody species.

The following lists contain many examples of perennials from rock garden and woodland habitats, which have nevertheless proved successful as extensive groundcover in open situations.

Groundcover plantings using a single species

3.1.1. Perennials and dwarf shrubs for extensive lawn-like areas

There are few plants that will reliably cover large tracts of ground to make a durable and weed-proof lawn substitute. Pure stands of a single species are rare in the wild, occurring most often where pioneer plants quickly colonise an area of disturbed soil before a more varied vegetation becomes established. Nevertheless, there are many perennials that grow wild in more or less extensive groups and colonies, and these have been adopted for use as groundcover plants by gardeners and landscape architects.

The behaviour of these species in gardens is varied. Some of them grow much more strongly at the edge than in the middle of a planting, some go bare in the centre (*Achillea tomentosa*), and others get too crowded and mound up, growing out of the ground (*Festuca scoparia, Saxifraga × arendsii* and its relatives). A good lawn substitute must grow evenly and vigorously over a long period with just an occasional application of fertiliser, only requiring thorough maintenance at intervals of 8–10 years.

The species listed here have proved reliable and long-lived on rich, moist, predominantly loamy soils. It is important to begin with soil that is free of perennial weeds. Sterilisation of the soil by steaming can be recommended before planting in public areas, and a mulch of coarse peat is beneficial until the plants are well established. In a large planting it may be worth laying narrow paths so that the initial maintenance can be carried out without too much treading. A good groundcover plant will have hidden the paving by the time no more maintenance is required.

Planting distances are important when using perennials as groundcover. Widely spaced individuals need more maintenance at first, but create a more durable groundcover than densely set plants that cover the ground quickly. A rough figure for planting density is given in the following lists but much depends on the size and quality of the available nursery stock.

Evergreen species for shade (e.g. the north side of a building.)

Plants that are more suitable for use in woodland areas, such as *Euonymus fortunei* and its cultivars, are not listed here.

Ivy *Hedera helix*		Also for use under trees; rooted cuttings can be planted at 15–20 plants/m².
Pachysandra terminalis	List 1.1.1	Sensitive to treading; prefers slightly acid soils; 8–12 plants/m².
Lesser periwinkle *Vinca minor*	List 1.1.1	Very robust; also grows on sandy soils; 7–16 plants/m².

Evergreen and semi-evergreen species for sun and semi-shade (e.g. the east or west side of a building)

Cotoneaster dammeri W China	0.20	Dwarf shrub, suitable for rock gardens; 8 plants/m², or 3–4 plants/m² with intensive maintenance. 'Eichholz' (0.30), very vigorous. 'Major' (0.20), larger leaves than the type. The following make a less lawn-like groundcover: *C. dammeri* 'Coral Beauty'. *C. salicifolius* 'Parkteppich', 'Gnom', 'Saldam'.
Geranium macrorrhizum 'Spessart'	List 2.1.2	Semi-evergreen, unlike *G. endressii* and *G. × magnificum*, which can also be used in this way; best planted in association with trees and shrubs; 4–12 plants/m².
Hypericum calycinum	List 2.1.2	Very robust; stays green in winter wherever the climate is not too harsh; 5–9 plants/m².

Deciduous perennials

The following species favour a sunny site with rich, moist, preferably loamy soil. Widely spaced *Sedum* spp. (8–10/m²) require intensive maintenance until they have grown together, but are much longer-lived than crowded plants (16/m²), which cover the ground more quickly. The soil must be free from weeds before planting.

Polygonum affine & *P. a.* 'Superbum'	List 4.1.3	Flowers long and abundantly; 6–12 plants/m².
Reynoutria japonica var. *compacta* 'Roseum'	List 2.1.2	Emerges late; very invasive; 4–9 plants/m².
Sedum kamtschaticum var. *ellacombianum* (*S. ellacombianum*) Jap	0.20/0.25 yellow	VI–VII, unbranched stems; broad, light green, some-what crenate leaves; sometimes turns red in autumn.
Sedum floriferum 'Weihenstephaner Gold' NE China	0.10/0.20 golden yellow	VI–VII, dark green, lanceolate–spathulate leaves on prostrate stems; very tidy, even after flowering; attractive, purple autumn colour; see list 4.1.1.
Sedum hybridum C & S Urals, Sib., Manch.	0.10/0.20 yellow	VII–VIII, elongated, wedge-shaped leaves with crenate tips; also for semi-shade. 'Immergrünchen', evergreen.
Sedum kamtschaticum E Asia	0.10/0.15 orange yellow	VI, open heads of flowers on branching stems; dark green, denticulate, spoon-shaped leaves; see list 4.1.1. 'Variegatum', colourful leaves; striking cultivar.
Sedum midden- *dorfianum* 'Diffusum' E Sib., Manch.	0.10/0.20 pale yellow	VII, more vigorous than the type (list 4.2.1); narrow, dark green leaves on sturdy, prostrate stems; spent inflorescences are attractive throughout the winter; see list 4.1.1.
Sedum spurium 'Album Superbum' Cauc., Arm., Kurd.	0.10/0.15 whitish	VII, very few flowers; oval to rhombic, slightly glossy leaves; forms dense green carpets; for warm, moist soils.

3.1.2. Species for small lawn-like areas

Depending on the situation, plants from the previous list may sometimes also be used for covering smaller areas. Alternatively, the following species will all form dense carpets on a small scale and are therefore popular for terraces, grave plantings and the like. The plants mentioned here for semi-shade differ from woodland edge species in that they do not tolerate a covering of fallen leaves, and must therefore be kept free in autumn.

Many woodland and woodland edge species may also be used in small, lawn-like patches under trees (*Asarum, Waldsteinia, Tiarella, Duchesnea, Ajuga*). However, only those species that are suitable for growing on open ground have been listed here.

Low, turf-forming perennials with shallow roots have been given a list on their own. They are mostly rather sensitive and best suited to planting in special situations such as on a rock garden.

Semi-shady areas with moist to damp soils

Arabis procurrens Carp., Balk.	0.03/0.15 white	IV–V, evergreen; also grows in full sun; see list 4.1.1. *A.* × *suendermannii*, (list 4.3.1), reliable groundcover for the rock garden (8–20 plants/m²); flowers a second time in October.
Azorella trifurcata S Chile	0.08 yellowish	V, hard, glossy, fresh green rosettes; also for full sun; 8–20 plants/m². *A. umbellata,* similar; rather tender.

× *Heucherella tiar-elloides*	0.10/0.25 pink	V–VII, forms dainty-leaved carpets; abundant flowers; 10–12 plants/m²; see list 4.1.3.
Awl-leaved pearlwort *Sagina subulata* Eur.	0.02/0.02 white	VI–VIII, forms dark green, mossy carpets; tiny white flowers; for stony, but not too dry soils in bright shade; almost maintenance-free between paving stones or on gravel; occasional treading or rolling helps flatten the carpets; sieved compost can be scattered lightly over the plants in spring as a top-dressing; clumps should be divided before planting; 10–15 plants/m². 'Aurea', very prone to sun damage.
Saxifraga × *geum*		List 4.1.3
Saxifraga × *urbium* 'Elliott'		List 4.1.3

Low-growing species with shallow roots, for moist to damp soils

The following species may also be used on a rock garden (lists 4.1.3 and 4.5.1). Planting density 8–10/m² in a well-tended garden, and 15–20/m² elsewhere.

Golden saxifrage *Chrysosplenium oppositifolium* var. *rosulare* Eur.	0.03 greenish yellow	IV, dense green mats of rounded leaves; for damp, lightly shaded sites.
Cotula dioica N.Z.	0.02	Forms small carpets of dark green, bluntly toothed leaves; insignificant flowers; shallow roots; long-lived in bright shade among rocks.
Cotula potentillina N.Z.	0.05	Finely divided, olive green to brownish-violet leaves; forms a dense turf on sunny sites; robust; tolerates periodic drought but no extremes of heat.
Cotula squalida N.Z.	0.05	Brownish-green, pinnate leaves; forms an attractive turf in sun or shade on damp soils.
Rupture-wort *Herniaria glabra* Eur. to W Sib., Nr. East	0.02–0.07 greenish	VII–IX, very small flower clusters; ovate-lanceolate leaves up to 1 cm long; forms dense, springy, fresh green carpets; for sandy, nutrient-rich, lime-free soils in full sun; thrives in rock crevices; short-lived but seeds itself. *H. pyrenaica* (*H. latifolia*), similar but lower-growing and longer-lived. *H. serpyllifolia caucasica*, very prostrate; small leaves.
Creeping Jenny *Lysimachia nummularia* Eur., Cauc.	0.03 yellow	V, only reliable on constantly moist soils in shade; see list 2.1.3.

Tender, low-growing species

Not to be recommended for outdoors in regions where frost enters the soil.

Frogfruit *Phyla nodiflora* (*Lippia repens*) N Am.	0.05 pink–white	VII, forms a dense turf of long leaves.
Mentha requienii Cors., Sard.	up to 0.02 pale violet	VI, minute, round leaves which are scented when brushed.
Pratia angulata NZ	up to 0.05 white	V–IX, rounded leaves; red berries; vigorous.
Helxine, baby's tears *Soleirolia soleirolii* Cors., Sard., Elba	up to 0.05	Minute, rounded, deciduous leaves.

Species for moist or moderately dry soils in full sun

Woody species

Dwarf bamboo *Arundinaria pumila* (*Sasa pumila*) Jap.	0.30–0.50	For warm sites in mild areas, on damp but porous soil; some sort of protection is advisable in winter; see list 2.3.6. *A. pygmaea* (to 1.00), also grows in shade. Both species are very vigorous and to be used with caution; 3 plants/m².
Cotoneaster dammeri 'Streibs Findling'	up to 0.10	V–VI, very prostrate, small-leaved, semi-evergreen groundcover plant; grows more slowly than either the wild species or the cultivars in list 3.1.1; also for bright shade; 12–15 plants/m².
Cytisus decumbens C Fr. to S It., Alb.	0.20 golden yellow	V–VI, prostrate habit; slowly covers a large area; also for alkaline soils; 1–2 plants/m²; see list 3.3.1.
Genista pilosa 'Procumbens' Eur.	0.20 golden yellow	V–VII, densely branched semi-evergreen for sandy loam; 3 plants/m².
Muehlenbeckia axillaris	List 4.3.2	Slow-growing species for enthusiasts; 12–15 plants/m².

Herbaceous perennials

Acaena buchananii	List 3.3.3	Grey-green leaflets remain through the winter; 7–12 plants/m².
Acaena microphylla	List 3.3.3	Brownish leaflets remain through the winter; 7–12 plants/m².
Ceratostigma plum-baginoides	List 4.1.1	For dry positions on porous, alkaline soils in fairly mild areas; invasive in regions with warm summers; 8–10 plants/m².
Cerastium tomentosum var. *columnae*		Suitable as a lawn substitute; 7–12 plants/m². Species for walls: see list 4.1.1.

Stachys byzantina 'Silver Carpet'	List 4.1.1	Can be used extensively; reliable, does not flower; 7–12 plants/m².
Teucrium chamaedrys 'Nana'	List 4.2.1	Forms a dense, moderately flowering turf; 8–16 plants/m².
Thymus × *citriodorus* 'Golden Dwarf'	List 4.1.1	Forms dense carpets that must be cut back from time to time; 8–10 plants/m².

3.1.3.   Species for full sun on specially prepared soil

The following open ground and rock garden perennials may be used as a lawn substitute for small areas of specially prepared soil.

Moist, loamy soils, improved with crushed rock and gravel

Aster andersonii	List 4.3.1	Forms low green carpets on somewhat poor, gravelly soils; rare in the trade; 8–10 plants/m².
Aubrieta hybrids	List 4.1.1	*A.* 'Tauricola' forms an especially dense and robust carpet; 5 plants/m².
Campanula poschar-skyana	List 4.1.1	Very vigorous with long, leafy shoots; 3–5 plants/m².
Dianthus gratiano-politanus 'Nordstjernen'	List 4.4.1	Pink flowers; forms dense, turf-like carpets, unlike the many cushion-forming varieties; 7–12 plants/m².
Dianthus plumarius	List 4.1.1	The cultivars 'Altrosa' and 'Diamant' form attractive, loose carpets; 5–8 plants/m².
Dryas octopetala	List 4.1.1	Evergreen carpets; 9–12 plants/m²; more reliable than the very vigorous *D.* × *suendermanii*; 8–10 plants/m².
Phlox subulata	List 4.1.1	Most cultivars form a dense carpet; 7 plants/m².

Moderately dry soils, improved with sand and gravel

These low-growing, carpet-forming perennials can be combined with drought resistant species such as *Sedum acre, S. gracile, S. bithynicum, S. sexangulare, Jovibarba sobolifera* and robust *Sempervivum* spp. They will thrive almost without soil on a flat rooftop.

Antennaria tomentosa	List 4.4.1	Forms dense, silvery-grey carpets; reliable; 10–20 plants/m².
Anthemis nobilis 'Treneague'	List 3.3.3	Rather tender, non-flowering cultivar, which forms dense, green mats; 12 plants/m².
Sedum album	List 4.2.1	Extremely undemanding on gravelly soil; 15–18 plants/m².
Sedum album 'Coral Carpet'	List 4.2.1	Forms dense, purple carpets; 15–18 plants/m².
Sedum album 'Murale'	List 4.2.1	Quickly forms a dark red carpet on gravelly soil; 15–18 plants/m².

Sedum sexangulare	List 4.2.1	Also thrives on loamy soils, in contrast to *S. acre*; good groundcover; 15–18 plants/m^2.
Thymus balcanus		Similar to *T. serpyllum*; particularly vigorous; 8–10 plants/m^2.
Thymus doerfleri 'Bressingham Seedling'	List 4.4.1	Forms robust, stable carpets; 8–10 plants/m^2.
Thymus pseudo-lanuginosus	List 4.4.1	Grey-leaved carpets; particularly vigorous in mild areas; 8–10 plants/m^2.

3.2.   Flowering meadows and other types of grassland

In places where a lawn need not be trodden or where slopes make mowing difficult, it is possible to create flowering grassland areas that need little maintenance and bring a new and exciting dimension into a park or garden. A large lawn may contain small areas where the grass can be left to grow long without disrupting the overall design. Wild flowers start to appear spontaneously wherever mowing is reduced, particularly if a potassium- and phosphate-rich fertiliser is applied. The effect may then be improved by the addition of further species (spring-flowering bulbs; see list 2.4).

It is comparatively easy to convert an old, established lawn into a wildflower meadow by restricting mowing and avoiding all herbicides and nitrate fertilisers. Before proceeding, however, it is worth considering the extra work involved in hay-making and the possible need for protection against trampling.

The creation of a new wildflower meadow by seeding onto bare ground poses more problems. Seed mixtures for flowering meadows are available in the trade but the results are often disappointing. Grasses tend to suppress other plants wherever they are sown too densely, while sparse sowings give weeds the chance to dominate. The species contained in a wildflower mixture are often ecologically unrelated to one another and to the conditions where they have to grow. Soils in a new garden are often so badly disturbed that it is difficult to choose the right plants anyway.

The most appropriate species for moderately dry to moist conditions have been assigned to list 3.2.1. Plants for dry, calcareous grassland can be found in list 3.2.2, and those for sandy soils in list 3.2.4. All of these can be used to create attractive meadows and grasslands. Experience shows that planting is mostly more effective than sowing. A sown meadow often takes years to settle down properly in combination with the spontaneously occurring vegetation. Purely planted meadows have yet to be attempted on the large scale required for parks.

Sowing

Many meadow wild flowers germinate and develop more slowly than grasses and are therefore set at a considerable disadvantage by mixed sowing. A wildflower meadow should on no account be sown too densely. The seed mixture may consist of about two thirds grasses, but the sowing rate should not exceed 10 000 grains/m^2. Seed should be stored in a cool, dry, airy place until it is needed. Germination is never 100%, especially when the storage time is long. Some wild flowers germinate more quickly and reliably if they are given a cold treatment first: the seed is mixed with about an equal volume of slightly moistened sand in a tight container, and kept in a refrigerator at 1–4 °C for about four weeks before sowing. Preparation of the ground and distribution of the grass seed is the same as for a normal lawn. It is a good idea to sow the grasses first and rake them over, before turning to the wildflower seed, which can be mixed with a little sand for ease of handling. Plants with coarse seed such as red clover (3–5 grains/m^2), sainfoin and other legumes are best dealt with separately. After sowing, the ground should be firmed with a roller.

It may be possible to sow some seeds in selected areas where they can be given a little attention as they develop. Many species will spread themselves gradually over the whole meadow from a limited sowing of this kind. During its first year, the meadow can be cautiously mown to about 5 cm, whenever weeds and grasses threaten to overwhelm more valuable species.

Wildflower seed is obtainable from specialist suppliers, or it may also be collected from suitable habitats in the wild. Rare species should be left undisturbed to help conserve their stands. On the whole they do not thrive in newly created grassland anyway.

Planting

The costs and labour involved in planting a large wildflower meadow far exceed those of direct seeding. For this reason, it may sometimes be advisable to grow the necessary plants oneself, preferably using peat pots, which provide the best chances of establishment on planting out. Seed may be either purchased or collected. It is usually sown in early spring in a mixture of equal parts weed-free, humus-rich soil and sand. The resulting seedlings should be kept in cool, bright conditions, protected at first with a glass sheet, and carefully sprayed over to prevent drying out. Soon after germination they should be thinned out, leaving 2–3 plants in each pot. These can then be grown on until the autumn or following spring for planting out into their final positions in weed-free turf or open soil.

Plants for dry calcareous grassland or other extreme conditions should be set out very densely in open soil, rather than into existing turf. Ordinary turf grasses are unsuitable for plantings of this type; the following lists include several weak-growing grasses that can be used instead. In less extreme conditions, it is best to start by sowing a grass mixture in spring or early autumn, mowing regularly to keep down weeds and waiting to introduce flowering perennials at a later date. Subsequent planting is best carried out in dry weather: sites are marked out across the whole area to be planted and turves of about 20 cm diameter removed from each site. The exposed soil is then loosened and improved where necessary before planting. Several plants may be set at each site; young plants may be set more closely than mature specimens. The new plants should be kept well watered and free from competition until they are established. Cared for in this way, they develop well and soon fill the gaps in the turf, requiring little or no maintenance after the first season. Mown at the proper time of year, they will set seed and spread, gradually turning the whole area into a flowery meadow.

It is difficult to alter the basic growing conditions for a large-scale planting, but in a small garden it may be possible to make some improvements to the soil. If the subsoil is stony and alkaline then it is possible to work crushed rock and gravel into the topsoil to provide suitable conditions for dry grassland or sunny woodland edge species (lists 3.2.2 and 2.1.7). A poor, sandy soil can also be improved to support a wider range of plants, though the rather limited natural vegetation is well worth encouraging in a park setting and may even be effective in a garden, given the right surroundings.

Encouraging wild flowers in an existing lawn

Even without special sowings and plantings it is possible to maintain an existing lawn in such a manner that it becomes populated with a variety of attractive wild flowers, which are resistant to treading and being cut. By mowing every 2–6 weeks, any area of grass can be converted into a flowering lawn that is especially colourful in spring and summer. The work involved is significantly less than would be required to keep the lawn permanently short or to turn it into a wildflower meadow. This sort of species-rich lawn develops particularly well on poor, well-drained, alkaline soils. Nutrient levels are critical, and it is therefore advisable to have the soil analysed before applying any fertiliser. It should contain the equivalent of approximately 10 mg P_2O_3 and 10 mg K_2O per 100 g, together with the usual trace elements and sufficient calcium. If excess phosphate and potassium are present then white clover tends to dominate. Similarly, if too much nitrate is present then the grasses grow too strong. If there is insufficient nitrate in the soil then a maximum of $10 \, mg/m^2$ should be given in two applications between July and September.

A powerful mower is required to cut the grass. The height of cut should be about 4 cm. All mowings must be removed, but it is as well to let them dry off first for ease of composting. All manner of resistant and beautiful wild flowers will find their own way into this sort of lawn. Examples are (in Europe): yarrow (*Achillea millefolium*), bugle (*Ajuga reptans*), daisy (*Bellis perennis*), mouse-ear chickweed (*Cerastium holosteoides*), ground ivy (*Glechoma hederacea*), selfheal (*Prunella vulgaris*), clover (*Trifolium dubium* and *T. repens*) and speedwell (*Veronica filiformis*). Of course, unwanted species may also start to appear. Dandelions, for instance, can be kept in check by dusting their rosettes with a calcium nitrate preparation, or spot-treating with a systemic herbicide.

3.2.1. Species for a wildflower meadow on moist to moderately dry soil

The following perennials are suitable for wildflower meadows on loamy, slightly sandy or gravelly soils that occasionally dry out in summer. Plant material is rarely available in the trade, but seed may be purchased, or collected from nearby sunny slopes and meadows, along with that of other species such as lady's smock (*Cardamine pratensis*) and cowslip (*Primula veris*). Heavy soils must be improved with sand and gravel before sowing.

Yarrow *Achillea millefolium*	0.40 white	VI–IX, composite flower heads with white ray-florets in flattened umbels; finely divided, pinnate leaves; spreading rhizomes; seed available in the trade (6700 grains/g). Pink and red cultivars, see list 3.4.5.
Kidney vetch *Anthyllis vulneraria*	0.60 yellow	V–VI, flowers in large clusters; pinnate leaves with large terminal leaflets; undemanding; seed available in the trade (400 grains/g). *A. montana*, reddish flowers; mat-forming semi-shrub.
Clustered bellflower *Campanula glomerata*	0.50 violet	VII, large terminal bells; rough, broad-lanceolate leaves; *C. g.* 'Superba' (0.60) may be planted if seed of the type is unavailable (8000 grains/g). Further cultivars, see list 3.4.5.
Greater knapweed *Centaurea scabiosa*	0.70 reddish purple	VI–IX, large composite flower heads on stout, branching stems; pinnate foliage; seed available in the trade (600 grains/g).
Brown-rayed knap- weed *Centaurea jacea*	0.70 purple	VI–X, stiff habit; composite flowers; basal leaves often scalloped or pinnately divided, stem leaves entire; 500 grains/g.
Ox-eye daisy *Chrysanthemum leucan- themum*	0.40 white	VI, white ray-florets around a golden yellow disc; most commonly available as a cultivar for cutting (see list 5.5); seed also available in the trade (1500 grains/g).
Orange hawkweed *Hieracium aurantiacum*	0.05/0.35 orange-red	VII–VIII, composite flower heads on rigid stems with blackish hairs; green basal rosettes; invasive; see list 2.1.8.
Bird's-foot trefoil *Lotus corniculatus*	0.10 golden yellow	V–VIII, flowers in loose umbels on round stems; leaves pinnate, composed of 5 short-stemmed, obovate leaflets; seed available in the trade (970 grains/g).

Medicago lupulina	List 2.1.7	Short-lived but seeds itself freely; seed available in the trade (500 grains/g).
Sainfoin *Onobrychis viciifolia*	up to 0.50 red	V–VII, broad, ovoid flower clusters; pinnate foliage; for a sunny spot on dry (or moist), alkaline, loamy soil; 50 grains/g.
Burnet saxifrage *Pimpinella saxifrage*	0.50 white	VI–IX, dainty umbellifer with pinnate leaves; old medicinal plant; seed available in the trade (2200 grains/g).
Hoary plantain *Plantago media*	0.03/0.30 lilac anthers	V–VII, fragrant, decorative inflorescences on long stems; basal rosettes of ovate–elliptic leaves; seed available in the trade (2500 grains/g).
Meadow clary *Salvia pratensis*	0.50 blue-violet	VI–VII, flowers in branched, spike-like inflorescences over rosettes of wrinkled, ovate–lanceolate leaves; seed available in the trade (550 grains/g). 'Rosea', pink. 'Alba', white.
Salad burnet *Sanguisorba minor*	0.40 greenish, with. red anthers	V–VIII, dainty, spherical heads of flowers; pinnate foliage with rounded, serrate leaflets; old medicinal plant; for dry (or moist) loamy soils; seed available in the trade (250 grains/g).
Red clover *Trifolium pratense* var. *serotinum*	up to 0.30 purple-red	VI–X, late-flowering variety of the well-known fodder plant; for moist soils; seed available in the trade (500 grains/g).
Alsike clover *Trifolium hybridum*	0.40 whitish pink	V–VIII, flowers on ascending stems; for moist to damp soils; seed available in the trade (1400 grains/g).

Grasses

Widely available, vigorous lawn grasses, suitable for a wildflower meadow

Common bent *Agrostis tenuis*	up to 0.40	Airy panicles; short rhizomes; 16 000 grains/g.
Sheep's fescue *Festuca ovina*	up to 0.30	Grey-green, bristle-leaved, clump-forming grass; 2000 grains/g.
Red fescue *Festuca rubra* ssp. *commutata* (*F. r. fallax*)	up to 0.60	Dense, dark green clumps of fine leaves; 1300 grains/g.
Smooth-stalked meadow grass, Blue-grass *Poa pratensis*	up to 0.50	Dark green, rhizomatous species; 3300 grains/g.
Yellow oat-grass *Trisetum flavescens*	up to 0.60	Loose panicles of yellow-green spikelets; not invasive; 2000 grains/g.

Non-invasive meadow grasses, rarely available in the trade

Sweet vernal grass *Anthoxanthum odo-* *ratum*	0.10–0.40	Dainty, clump-forming grass for bright semi-shade; hay-scented; indicator plant for poor soils; 1700 grains/g, but not available in the trade.
Quaking grass *Briza media*	0.20–0.40	Attractive species with rounded heart-shaped spike-lets on thin pedicels; forms loose tufts; needs plenty of light; indicator plant for poor soils; 1400 grains/g; very rarely available in the trade.
Crested dog's tail *Cynosurus cristatus*	0.20–0.40	Narrow, comb-like inflorescences; prefers nutrient-rich, alkaline soils; may be pastured; 1700 grains/g.
Fine-leaved fescue *Festuca tenuifolia*	0.15–0.25	Dense clumps of hairlike leaves, which bleach in winter; for sandy soils; 2500 grains/g.
Timothy *Phleum bertolonii*	up to 0.50	Stems with swollen bases; flowers in dense, cylindrical, spike-like panicles over broad, pale blue-green leaves; 2000 grains/g.

3.2.2. Species for dry calcareous grassland and meadow steppe (prairie)

The following grassland perennials thrive on sunny terraces and stony, south-facing slopes with loamy, alkaline soils that dry out in summer. In the neighbourhood of trees and shrubs they may also be combined with the plants from list 2.1.7. Such plantings are by no means always green, and do not associate well with patches of maintained lawn. If they are not mown down in autumn then various dwarf shrubs can be most effective, sparsely distributed amongst the herbaceous plants.

Once established, the plantings only require occasional attention, although intensive maintenance and protection from competition encourages the individual plants to develop more luxuriantly than if they are left to fend for themselves. An extensive approach is better on slopes, where a dense plant cover helps to prevent soil washing away in persistent rain. All plantings need a clean-up in spring, and may also be mown or burned off in autumn if desired.

Grasses are an important constituent. The characteristic feather grasses (*Stipa*), with their long, silvery awns, are only satisfactory in the long term when they are protected from competition. In many cases they need proper garden-type maintenance in order to hold out against their neighbours. Clump-forming grasses (see the lists) are to be preferred to rhizomatous species, which often prove too invasive in the course of time.

Plants such as *Anthericum liliago, Anemone sylvestris* and *Campanula persicifolia*, which have been assigned to the woodland edge (list 2.1.7) but whose natural distribution includes open, sunny slopes, may also be considered for this type of planting. The same goes for some rock garden species such as *Gentiana verna, Helianthemum* spp. and *Iris pumila*.

Adonis vernalis Eur., Altai, Sib.	0.10 (0.30)/0.25 golden yellow	IV–V, very large flowers; feathery foliage; slow-growing and sensitive to disturbance.
Italian aster *Aster amellus* Eur., Cauc., Sib.	up to 0.40 blue	VIII–X, flowers in corymbose panicles; roughly hairy, broad-lanceolate leaves; many garden forms (see list 5.3.2).
Goldilocks aster *Aster linosyris* Eur.	0.30 golden yellow	IX, flowers in umbels on stiffly upright stems; fine, linear leaves. 'Golden Dust', compact habit.

Campanula sarmatica Cauc.	0.05/0.30 blue	VII, large, nodding bells; grey-green leaves; undemanding and very attractive.
Carlina acaulis Eur.	0.08/0.15 silvery	VIII–X, large, silvery grey flower heads; short-lived. 'Bronze', coppery flowers; seeds itself. *C. a.* var. *caulescens,* somewhat taller than the type.
Carthusian pink *Dianthus carthusian-* *orum* Eur.	0.40 red	VI–IX, terminal clusters of 3–8 flowers; grass-like leaves; rare in the trade.
Dropwort *Filipendula vulgaris* (*F. hexapetala*) Eur., Cauc., Asia Minor, W Sib.	0.05/0.30 white	V–VII, dainty rosettes of pinnately divided leaves with toothed and incised leaflets. 'Plena', double-flowered form; more widely available than the type.
Cross gentian *Gentiana cruciata* Eur., Cauc., Asia Minor	0.30 blue	VII–VIII, ascending stems, densely set with opposite pairs of leaves; undemanding and free-flowering, but short-lived.
Globularia punctata (*G. willkommii*) (*G. elongata*) Eur.	0.20 blue-violet	IV–VI, small flower heads on leafy stems; modest, undemanding perennial; rare in the trade; see also list 4.3.1.
Horseshoe vetch *Hippocrepis comosa* Eur.	0.10 yellow	V–VII, dainty flower clusters; horseshoe-shaped pods; delicate, pinnate foliage; forms small carpets; rare in the trade.
Inula ensifolia Eur., Cauc.	0.20/0.40 golden yellow	VII–VIII, dense, bushy plant; deep green, lanceolate leaves.
Inula hirta Eur., Cauc.	0.30 golden yellow	VI–VIII, large single flower heads with yellow ray-florets; bushy habit; roughly hairy, broad-lanceolate leaves.
Inula salicina Eur., Cauc.	0.40 yellow	VI–VIII, flowers in clusters of 1–5 on rigid stems with almost hairless, clasping leaves.
Perennial flax *Linum perenne* Eur., W Asia	0.50 blue	VI–VII, stiff, open habit; needle-like leaves; best planted in loose clusters. 'Album', white. *L. austriacum* (0.60). *L. narbonense* 'Six Hills', (0.40); large violet flowers; for light soils.
Lychnis viscaria		Lists 3.2.1 and 3.4.2
Round-headed rampion *Phyteuma orbiculare* Eur.	0.25 blue-violet	VI–VII, spherical flower heads; toothed, heart-shaped basal leaves; rare in the trade.

White cinquefoil *Potentilla alba* Eur.	0.50/0.10 white	IV–VI, silvery green foliage; open habit; old, isolated plants can form dense groundcover.
Grey cinquefoil *Potentilla cinerea* (*Potentilla arenaria*) Eur.	0.03/0.06 yellow	IV–V, attractive, grey-green leaves; can be used as groundcover for small areas.
Prunella grandiflora		list 4.4.3
Pasque flower *Pulsatilla vulgaris* Eur.	0.05/0.20 violet	IV, leaves appear after the flowers; beautiful, feathery seed heads; white, pink and red forms available in the trade (see list 4.4.1). *P. grandis,* large flowers; erect, bushy foliage. *P. halleri* ssp. *slavica,* very early-flowering.
Bulbous buttercup *Ranunculus bulbosus* 'Pleniflorus' Eur., W Asia	0.30 golden yellow	IV–VII, dainty rosettes of tripartite leaves; undemanding but not invasive; rare in the trade.
Stachys nivea (*Betonica nivea*) Cauc.	0.20/0.30 white	VI–VII, flowers in loose whorls; wrinkled, crenate, ovate–lanceolate leaves. *S. recta* (0.30), VI–X, narrow leaves; rare in the trade.
Spiked speedwell *Veronica spicata* Eur., Cauc.	0.05/0.30 lilac	VII, stiffly upright, mostly unbranched stems; flowers in slender, terminal, spike-like racemes; coarsely toothed, blunt, lanceolate leaves. Cultivars, see list 4.1.1.
Large speedwell *Veronica teucrium* (*V. austriaca* ssp. *teucrium*) Eur.	0.15/0.20 blue	VI, flowers in long-stalked racemes; strongly toothed, ovate–lanceolate leaves; insignificant and weedy after flowering; best planted in loose clusters. Cultivars, see list 4.1.1.

Grasses

Many of the most characteristic dry grassland species, such as upright brome (*Bromus erectus*), hair grasses (*Koeleria gracilis* and *K. pyramidata*) and the highly invasive tor grass (*Brachypodium pinnatum*), are not available from nurseries. *Festuca ovina* (list 3.2.4), *Sesleria varia* and *Melica* spp. (list 3.3.4) may all be suitable in addition to the species listed below.

Briza media		List 3.2.4
Carnation sedge *Carex flacca* Eur., Asia Minor	0.05/0.20	V–VI, elegant stems with drooping inflorescences; broad, grey-green leaves; spreading roots; also for periodically damp or wet soils.
Humble sedge *Carex humilis* Eur., Cauc.	0.15	III–IV, dainty, dark green tufts of narrow, rolled, bristle-like leaves. *C. umbrosa* (0.20), IV–V, small, flattened, semi-evergreen clumps.
Mountain sedge *Carex montana* Eur., Cauc., Sib.	0.20	III–IV, neat-looking tufts of arching leaves; colours light brown in autumn.

Festuca amethystina	List 3.3.4	
Phleum phleoides (*P. boehmeri*) Eur., Sib., Turk.	0.40	VI, flowers in long, dense, cylindrical, spike-like racemes on rigid stems; dainty tufts of foliage; seeds itself freely; rare in the trade.
Stipa spp.	List 3.3.4	Sensitive to competition; best in open soil or among rocks (stony steppe).

Dwarf shrubs

Cytisus austriacus Eur., Cauc.	0.80 yellow	VI, flowers in terminal panicles on upright stems; stays green long into winter; reasonably hardy and tolerates lime.
Cytisus supinus Eur., W Ukr.	0.50 yellow-brown	VI, similar to the previous species; fully hardy and tolerates lime.
Cytisus ratisbonensis Eur., Cauc., Altai, Urals	0.30 pale yellow	VI, spreading, almost prostrate habit; rare in the trade.
Garland flower *Daphne cneorum* Eur. to C. Ukr.	0.25 pink	V, very abundant, scented flowers. *D. blagayana,* white flowers; prostrate habit; rare in the trade.
Spring heath *Erica herbacea* (*E. carnea*) Eur.	0.30 pink	XII–IV, green, needle-like foliage; often turns brownish in autumn; see list 3.2.3.
Burnet rose *Rosa spinosissima* (*R. pimpinellifolia*) Eur., W Asia	0.80 (1.20) cream white	V, hardy, invasive shrub with dainty foliage; resistant to the diseases of ornamental roses.

3.2.3.   Heaths and heathers, *Erica* and *Calluna*

The most important heather species for garden use are the early-flowering spring heath, *Erica herbacea* (*E. carnea*), and the autumn-flowering ling or heather, *Calluna vulgaris.* There are several other *Erica* species that flower in spring and summer but these are only suitable for growing in mild areas.

Wild heather species may be planted in sunny woodland edge conditions, but the cultivars are best confined to open ground, where they are already used extensively in well-tended parks and gardens, mostly combined with an unconvincing mixture of other woody species and herbaceous plants.

Enthusiasts often set different forms and species together in soil enriched with coarse peat. Although such plantings thrive, it is more effective to take account of the character and origins of the different species and to use them accordingly. Spring heath is best combined with plants from dry, basic, grassland communities, while ling and the other *Erica* species associate better with plants for acid, sandy soils (lists 2.1.8 and 3.2.4).

Planting should be carried out in spring or early autumn. A suitable density is 8–10 plants to the square metre. Vigorous, spreading varieties of *Calluna* can be set at 6–8/m², dwarf forms at up to 16/m². A dense planting covers the ground quickly and needs little maintenance. However, it may be necessary to thin out the plants after a few years to an average spacing of 50–60 cm to ensure longevity.

Spring heath, *Erica herbacea* (*E. carnea*), and its relatives

Spring heath is a dwarf shrub that grows wild in the European Alps and surrounding regions. The flowers of all but the earliest varieties are extremely frost-resistant, with buds that are already starting to colour and swell in late autumn among the brownish-green, needle-like foliage.

The plants thrive on soils enriched with coarse peat, but are not fussy about lime content. On the whole, they do better associated with pines and dwarf conifers than with broadleaved trees, whose drips they cannot tolerate. They also flourish among rocks, where the extra warmth can encourage them to flower before Christmas. Seslerias (*Sesleria* spp.), alpine sedges (particularly *Carex montana*) and the dry grassland species from lists 2.1.7 and 3.2.2 are all suitable companions.

It is seldom necessary to cut back plants. Vigorous hybrids may be lightly trimmed immediately after flowering.

Flowers in winter and spring (*Erica herbacea*)

White:

'Springwood White', I–III, flowers scattered amongst the light green foliage; more vigorous than *E.h.* 'Alba'.
'Snow Queen', I–III, flowers stand free of the foliage.
'Cecilia M. Beale', II–IV, abundant, large flowers.

Pale pink:

'December Red', I–III, robust habit; early flowering.
'C. J. Backhouse', III–IV, paler than the previous selection (white with a pink flush).

Deep pink:

'Winter Beauty', abundant flowers start appearing in XI.
'King George', fresh pink flowers start appearing in II.

Magenta:

'Atrorubra', reliable; starts flowering in III.
'Rubinteppich' (0.20), vigorous new selection; starts flowering in II.

Dark red:

'Vivellii' (0.20), I–III, popular, late-flowering selection; leaves dark green or brown in summer, red-brown in winter.
'Ruby Glow', III-IV, similar to the previous plant, but with flowers of a paler red; dark green leaves, bronze in autumn.

Wine red:

'Myreton Ruby', III–V, dark green foliage; valuable cultivar.

Orange-yellow leaves:
'Anne Sparkes', magenta flowers; reddish-yellow leaves.
'Foxhollow', delicate pink flowers; intense yellow leaves.

Flowers in spring

(*Erica erigena* and hybrids)		
Erica erigena (*E. mediterranea* hort.) (*E. purpurascens*) SW Eur.	0.60 (to 2.00) dark pink	III–V, similar to *E. herbacea* but stronger and taller; often damaged by frost.
Erica × *darleyensis* (*E. erigena* × *E. her-* *bacea*)	0.40 pink	III–V, more vigorous than *E. herbacea* but sensitive to frost. 'Erecta' (0.50), dark pink; open, upright habit; frost sensitive. 'Ghost Hills', pink. 'Darley Dale' (0.50), pink; bushy, spreading habit. 'Silberschmelze' (0.35), white with dark brown anthers; spreading habit; hardy.
Erica arborea 'Alpina'		List 2.3.3

Flowers in summer and autumn

The following *Erica* species grow wild in the milder parts of Western Europe. The cultivars that are listed here are among the hardiest, but they cannot be relied upon in harsh climates. Vigorous plants may be cut back like *Calluna* (see p. 207) in spring.

Bell heather *Erica cinerea* W Eur.	0.30 pink	VI–VIII, clusters of needle-like leaves; extremely lime-sensitive; for sandy, peaty soils. 'Coccinea' (0.30), dark red. 'Splendens' (0.50), magenta.
Dorset heath *Erica ciliaris* W Eur.	0.30 pink	VI–VIII, appealing, large-flowered, almost prostrate species; extremely frost-sensitive.
Cornish heath *Erica vagans* W Eur.	0.30 pink	VIII–IX, flowers in cylindrical racemes; hardier than the above. 'Mrs D. F. Maxwell' (0.50), pink. 'Lyonesse' (0.40), white. 'St Keverne' (0.30), salmon pink.
Erica × *williamsii* (*E. vagans* × *E. tetralix*) 'P. D. Williams'	0.25 pink	VII–IX, yellowish new foliage, which colours green in summer; flowers in terminal inflorescences.
Erica × *watsonii* (*E. ciliaris* × *E. tetralix*) 'H. Maxwell' *E. tetralix:* see list 4.6.2.	0.25 pale pink	VII–X, hardy.

Ling (Heather), *Calluna vulgaris*

A planting of ling (*Calluna*) on sandy soil, with its associated junipers, brooms, Scots pine and birches, has an entirely different but equally attractive character to that of the heath gardens dealt with above, with their larches and mountain pines (*Pinus nigra* and *P. mugo*) set amongst rocks and scree. *Calluna vulgaris* thrives in a sunny spot on sandy, peaty, lime-free soil, flowering in August and September. The wild species can also be grown in dry woodland edge conditions (see list 2.1.8), beyond the drip of trees, but its cultivars need open ground and full sun. Tall-growing varieties should be cut back 5–10 cm annually in early spring.

Tall cultivars (0.50/0.80):

'Alba Erecta' (0.50), white.
'Alba Plena' ('White bouquet') (0.50), white; double flowers.
'Alportii' ('Atrorubens') (0.70), red.
'C. W. Nix' (0.80), red.
'Elegantissima' (0.50), white.
'Elsie Purnell' (0.60), pale pink; double flowers.
'Finale', X–XI, purple violet.
'Frejus', X–XI, lilac.
'Hammondii' (0.50), white.
'H. E. Beale' (0.60), pink; double flowers; branching habit.
'Long White' (0.60), white.
'Peter Sparkes' (0.60), dark pink; double flowers.
'Plena' (0.60), lilac-pink; double flowers.
'Schurig's Sensation', pink; double flowers; tender.

Middle-sized cultivars (0.20/0.40):

'Alportii Praecox', red.
'Aurea', pale violet; bronzey foliage, golden yellow in summer.
'Darkness', red; dense, upright habit.
'Dark Star', dark red; double flowers; low-growing.
'Darleyensis', pinkish red; brownish foliage.
'Davis Eason', pink; late flowering; always in bud.
'Golden Feather', pale red; feathery, golden yellow shoots.
'Loch Turrett', VI, white.
'Lyall's Late White', white; very late.
'Robert Chapman', red; foliage yellow in summer, bronzey orange in winter.
'Silver Knight', pink; grey leaves.
'Silver Queen', violet; grey leaves.
'Underwoodii', silvery pink; always in bud.

Low-growing cultivars with prostrate shoots (0.10/0.15):

(*Calluna vulgaris* var. *ericae*)
'Decumbens Alba', white.
'Golden Carpet', pink; yellow foliage.
'Heidberg', reddish-violet.
'Kuphaldtii', pale violet.
'Multicolor', bronze-yellow foliage.
'Sandwood Bay', white.

Dwarf cultivars (0.10/0.25):

'County Wicklow', pink.
'Cuprea', (0.35), violet; foliage yellowish-green in summer, red-brown in winter.
'Foxii Nana', pale violet; forms turf-like cushions.
'J. H. Hamilton', salmon pink; double flowers.
'Mullion', violet; forms turf-like cushions.

3.2.4.   Heathland perennials for sandy soils

Ling (*Calluna vulgaris*) is an indispensable structural element in any large-scale planting on dry to moist, slightly acid, sandy soil. A heathland planting requires an open, sunny site, whose surface can be carefully modelled to enhance the effect of spaciousness. Peat must be added to the soil wherever *Calluna* is planted.

Smaller plantings may be enriched with woodland edge perennials (list 2.1.8) or the various cultivars from list 3.2.3.

The following species are all tolerant of acid conditions.

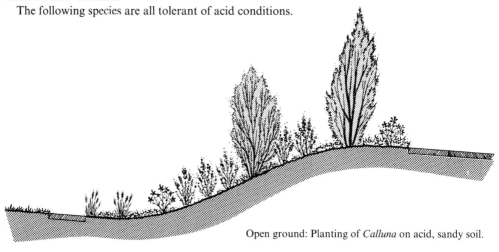

Open ground: Planting of *Calluna* on acid, sandy soil.

Cat's foot, Pussy-toes *Antennaria dioica* Eur., Cauc.	0.03/0.10 pink	V–VI, spoon-shaped leaves with white-hairy undersides forming dainty, silver carpets; male plants have pink flowers. 'Rubra', red. Further species, see list 4.4.1.
Arnica *Arnica montana* Eur.	0.03/0.50 orange- yellow	VI, daisy-like flowers; flattened rosettes of opposite, pointed, ovate leaves; for poor, lime-free, periodically moist soils; intolerant of fertilisers; short-lived. *A. longifolia,* long-lived and vigorous. Both rare in the trade.
Harebell *Campanula rotundifolia* Eur., Sib., N Am.	0.03/0.20 blue	VI–VIII, dainty, bell-shaped flowers on delicate, wiry stems; round basal leaves and narrow, linear stem leaves; spreads loosely at the roots; thrives in combination with grasses; rare in the trade.
Dianthus arenarius C Eur., Russ.	0.15 white	VI–VII, fragrant flowers with deeply cut petals; long, narrow, pointed, green leaves; forms a loose turf. 'Weibull' (0.20), white.

Maiden pink *Dianthus deltoides* Eur., Asia	0.03/0.15 pink	VI–IX, forms green, turf-like carpets in the absence of competition; small, linear-lanceolate leaves. Red cultivars: 'Brilliancy', 'Splendens', 'Vampir', 'Leuchtfunk', 'Wisley'. All spread and seed themselves quickly.
Genista pilosa		List 2.1.8
Sand strawflower *Helichrysum arenarium* Eur., Asia, Sib.	0.30 golden yellow	VIII, open habit; white-hairy, linear-lanceolate leaves; spherical flower heads; tolerates lime; rare in the trade. *H.* × 'Schwefellicht', VIII, sulphur yellow.
Mouse-ear hawkweed *Hieracium pilosella* Eur., Asia Min., Sib.	0.03/0.08 yellow	V–VII, green, entire leaves with matted grey hairs beneath; forms small carpets; rare in the trade. 'Niveum', silvery leaves; spreads strongly; more widely available than the type.
Sheep's bit *Jasione perennis* (*J. laevis*) Eur.	0.30 blue	VII–IX, creeping rosettes. Selection: 'Blaulicht'. *J. montana* (0.20), VI–VIII, branched habit; does not spread; rare in the trade.
Biting stonecrop *Sedum acre* Eur., Asia	0.05/0.05 yellow	VI–VII, small, fleshy, sessile, ovoid leaves; forms loose cushions; can be invasive.
Sedum sexangulare (*S. boloniense*) (*S. mite*) Eur.	0.05/0.05 yellow	VII–VIII, small, linear-cylindric leaves with blunt spurs at the base; forms large, dense, unbroken cushions. *S. telephium,* see list 3.4.4.
Wild thyme *Thymus serpyllum* Eur., Sib.	0.03/0.05 lilac	V–VIII, long, creeping stems with small, linear-elliptic leaves; forms attractive carpets on soils leavened with sand and gravel. Selections (partly *T. pulegioides*): 'Coccineus', magenta. 'Carneus', pink. 'Coccineus-Major', deep red. 'Albus', white. Further creeping *Thymus* spp., see lists 3.1.3 and 4.4.1.

For damp, to wet, acid, sandy soils:

Cranberry *Vaccinium macrocarpon* N Am.	0.05 pale purple-red	VI–VIII, evergreen, mat-forming shrub; much cultivated in the USA for its thick, red fruits; peaty soils on level ground or in shallow depressions.

Grasses

Wavy hair grass *Avenella flexuosa* (*Deschampsia flexuosa*) Eur., Cauc., Jap., N Am.	0.20/0.50	VI–VIII, long, lax, wiry, semi-evergreen leaves; open panicles with sinuous branches; seeds itself prolifically (list 2.1.8); thrives on peat.
Quaking grass *Briza media* Eur., Asia Minor, Cauc.	0.10/0.30	V–VII, rounded, heart-shaped spikelets on slender pedicels; not for planting in large groups.

Sheep's fescue *Festuca ovina* Eur., Sib.	0.20/0.30	VI–VII, grey-green clumps of mostly bristle-like leaves; very variable species. Selections, see list 3.2.1.
Fine-leaved fescue *Festuca tenuifolia* (*F. ovina capillata*) Eur.	0.15/0.25	VI–VII, stiff, upright stems; fine green leaves, which bleach in autumn, providing contrast in the brown, heathland landscape (see list 3.2.1).
Festuca trachyphylla		List 3.3.4
Koeleria glauca		List 3.3.4
Mat-grass *Nardus stricta* Eur., Asia, N Am.	0.10/0.20	V–VI, forms dense, turf-like clumps of bristle-like leaves; unassuming, one-sided spikes of flowers; rare in the trade.

Corynephorus canescens (Silver grass) (0.25), has silvery-grey, fine, bristle-like leaves and daintily branched panicles. it is very short-lived and only suitable as a pioneer plant on bare sand and wind-blown dunes. *Molinia caerulea* (list 6.4.2) can be recommended for moist to damp soils enriched with peat.

3.3   Plants from hot, dry, stony steppes (prairie)

The often exotic-looking plants that are dealt with in this section grow wild in dry, rocky areas of steppe vegetation. Although they respond well to the less stringent growing conditions in a garden, their true character and beauty first become apparent in plantings designed to resemble their natural habitat. Rocks are not essential for their growth, so they are best regarded as plants for open ground, though many species will grow just as well on a rock garden.

The planting medium should consist of a fertile soil mixed with crushed rock, sand and gravel. The surface should be at least partly covered with the same materials, and a few larger pieces of rock may be strategically sited among the plants. Much depends on the skill of the designer. It is important to bear in mind that steppe plants do not like to be shaded at the base, and must therefore be sparsely distributed to ensure their optimal development.

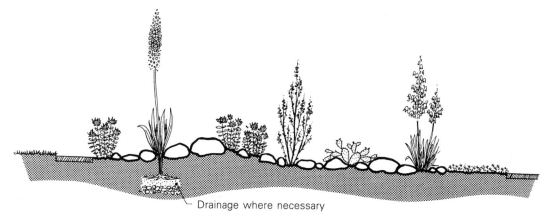

Drainage where necessary

Open ground: stony steppe planting.

It is an exciting challenge to find the right position and neighbours for exotic and contrasting species such as foxtail lilies, yuccas, hardy cacti, mulleins and ornamental alliums. Steppe shrubs such as *Halimodendron halodendron*, *Caragana jubata* and *Lonicera spinosa* 'Alberti' can also be useful, particularly on a gently undulating, south-facing slope, or in a terrace planting. Elsewhere, the dwarf and semi-shrubs listed below might have a role to play. Annuals such as *Verbena peruviana*, *Portulaca grandiflora* and *Gazania* spp. may occasionally be set between the loosely scattered perennials.

Many of the following species associate well with the less drought-resistant plants from list 3.4.1 or with dry grassland species (list 3.2.2). Though they may also be grown on a rock garden, many of them become quite large and are thus unsuitable for small designs.

3.3.1.   Drought-resistant dwarf and sub-shrubs

The following woody and semi-woody species may sometimes be included in a steppe planting. Many of them also associate well with the species from list 3.4.1.

Wormwood *Artemisia absinthium* Eur., Asia, W Med.	0.80	Silvery grey sub-shrub with strongly aromatic leaves and insignificant flowers; old medicinal plant; thrives on dry, basic, nitrate-rich soils; lifespan of about 10 years; best planted in groups.
Southernwood *Artemisia abrotanum* SE Eur., W Asia	0.60	Dainty, dark green foliage; strongly aromatic; yellowish, insignificant flowers.
Berberis thunbergii 'Atropurpurea Nana'	0.40 yellow	Very attractive red foliage; grows slowly.
Cytisus decumbens C Fr. to S It., Alb.	up to 0.20 yellow	V–VI, abundant large flowers; spreads horizontally over the ground to form plants up to 1 m across; fairly hardy.
Daphne cneorum		List 3.2.2
Daphne blagayana		List 3.2.2
Ephedra distachya S Eur., NE Asia, Manch.	0.90	Bizarre-looking shrub with stiff, matt bluish-green, *Equisetum*-like branches; sensitive to damp. *E. gerardiana* (0.05), Him., China; slender, dark green, finely striped branches with scale-like leaves. *E. major* var. *procera* (0.40), Med.; smooth, dark green branches; dense habit. *E. minuta* (0.20), W China; slender, dull green branches; spreading rhizomes. All species rare in the trade.
Genista lydia E Balk., Syr.	0.40 (to 0.80) golden yellow	V–VI, dainty, wide-spreading, spiny branches; not very hardy; for mild areas; also for rock gardens.
Hebe armstrongii NZ	0.40 white	V–VI, unusual shrub with an open habit; small white flowers on leafless, coppery-yellow branches; fairly hardy.
Hebe pinguifolia NZ	0.40 white	V–VI, small, stiff shrub with overlapping, blue-green leaves; hardier than other similar *Hebe* spp.
Hyssop *Hyssopus officinalis* S Eur., W & C Asia	0.60 violet	VIII, flowers in leafy, whorled spikes; aromatic, narrow-lanceolate leaves; often sprawls across rocks. 'Roseus', pink.

Lavender *Lavandula angustifolia* (*L. vera*) Med.	0.30/0.60 lavender	VII, strongly aromatic, grey-leaved dwarf shrub; it is advisable to trim plants immediately after flowering or in early spring. 'Grappenhall' (0.70), broad leaves; very vigorous but tender. 'Hidcote Blue' (0.40), dark violet; flowers early. 'Hidcote Giant' (0.60), very vigorous. 'Munstead' (0.40), very reliable. 'Nana Alba' (0.20), white. 'Rosea' (0.40), pale rose; flowers early.
Perovskia abrotanoides Transc. to W Him.	1.00 bluish	VIII–IX, silvery, finely divided foliage on erect, grey stems; roots sucker freely; invasive on sandy soils. *P. atriplicifolia*, falls apart easily and needs a lot of space.
Dwarf almond *Prunus tenella* (*Amygdalus nana*) E. C Eur. to E Sib.	1.00 (to 1.50) pink	IV, upright shrub with slender branches; suckering roots; flowers very early; white and red flowered varieties are available in the trade.
Sage *Salvia officinalis* Med.	0.50 lilac	VI–VIII, strongly aromatic, evergreen sub-shrub; old medicinal and kitchen-garden plant; vigorous in mild areas. 'Aurea', golden yellow leaves. 'Berggarten', broad leaves; bushy. 'Purpurascens', dull red leaves. 'Sturmiana', green and white leaves. 'Tricolor', grey-green, yellowish white and flesh coloured variegation. 'Variegata', leaves variegated yellow and green.
Small-leaved sage *Salvia officinalis* ssp. *lavandulifolia* Spain	0.40 lilac	VII–VIII, similar to the above but with narrower leaves; not quite as hardy; good groundcover for warm, sunny sites; plants benefit from cutting back lightly in spring.
Cotton lavender *Santolina chamae-* *cyparissus* W Med.	0.40/0.50 yellow	VII–VIII, bushy, silvery grey sub-shrub with green, leafy flower stems; tolerates cutting but is sensitive to frost and damp. 'Dwarf Form' (0.20). *S. × lindavica*, grey-green foliage; particularly abundant flowers.
Santolina pinnata (*S. chamaecyparissus* ssp. *tomentosa*) Pyren. to C It.	0.40/0.50 whitish	VII–VIII, sub-shrub with fine, green leaves. *S. rosmarinifolia* (*S. viridis, S. virens*), similar but with mostly prostrate stems; strongly aromatic foliage. Both species are fairly tender.
Wall germander *Teucrium massiliense* (*T. chamaedrys* hort.) (*T. lucidrys*) W Med.	up to 0.30 pinkish- purple	VII–VIII, stiff, upright habit; evergreen foliage; does not spread at the roots; occasionally damaged by frost. *T. chamaedrys* L., deciduous, serrate or crenate leaves; spreading rhizomes; rarely available from nurseries.

Thymus × *citriodorus*   Lists 3.1.2 and 4.1.1
'Golden Dwarf'

3.3.2. Dominant, eyecatching perennials for stony steppe plantings

Yucca

The hardy yuccas, with their tufted, leathery leaves and massive inflorescences, are among the most showy of all steppe perennials. The following commonly available species grow wild in dry, rocky areas of SE North America, often associated with tall prairie grasses and other flowering perennials. All are herbaceous except for *Y. glauca*, which forms a short, woody stem like the more tender yuccas in list 3.3.5. Given a well-drained, alkaline soil in full sun, and protected from persistent damp in winter, the plants can attain a great age. Appropriate neighbours include *Acaena* spp., silver-leaved *Stachys*, low-growing euphorbias and (a little further removed) hardy *Opuntias*.

Spent inflorescences should be cut off low down to encourage the formation of new leaf rosettes. In a harsh climate it may be advisable to cover the plants with conifer branches in winter.

Yucca filamentosa SE USA	0.50/1.50 white	VII–VIII, decorative, imposing heads of large, bell-shaped flowers; large clumps of tough, dark green, glaucous leaves. Selections: 'Eisbär' (1.50), graceful, slender inflorescences; abundant flowers. 'Elegantissima' (1.30), exceptionally attractive clumps of leaves. 'Fontäne' (1.20), creamy yellow flowers; low-growing. 'Herkuleskeule', inflorescences almost columnar. 'Rosenglocke', flowers flushed pink; large, attractive clumps of leaves. 'Schellenbaum' (1.80), broad, open inflorescences; large, bell-shaped flowers. 'Schneefichte' (1.50), narrow inflorescences. 'Schneetanne' (1.50), very symmetrical in habit. 'Variegata' leaves striped with creamy yellow.
Yucca flaccida SE USA	0.40/1.20 yellowish white	VII–IX, flowers longer and broader than those of the otherwise similar *Y. filamentosa,* with which it is often hybridised; thin, lax leaves which droop at the ends or bend in the middle; relatively tender. 'Glaucescens', broad, glaucous leaves. 'Grandiflora', larger, statelier inflorescences.
Yucca glauca C USA	0.40/1.00 greenish- white	V, bizarre clumps of rigid, narrow, blue-green leaves with sharply pointed tips; old plants form short, almost prostrate, woody stems; for very dry sites; some wild forms have dark rose sepals. *Y.* × *karlsruhensis* (*Y. filamentosa* × *Y. glauca*), broader leaves; flowers white, flushed pink; rare in the trade; see also list 3.3.6.

Hardy cacti, *Opuntia* (Prickly pear)

Several of the many different *Opuntia* species from the prairies, plains and mountains of North and Central America have proved to be very tough and hardy, requiring no protection against extremes of cold. The plants form dense, prickly colonies, which are rather unsightly in winter, when their otherwise swollen segments contract and shrivel. Nevertheless, small groups of plants can be very effective scattered amongst rocks and scree (limestone, basalt, tuff or pumice).

Opuntias have shallow roots but will thrive in dry, sunny, sheltered conditions on any sort of soil that is not too rich. Good drainage and ample moisture in spring are important requirements. The former can be provided by a layer of rubble or stone chips buried beneath the surface. It is better to start with a weed-free soil than be compelled to weed between the spines.

Planting is best carried out in spring. It is advisable to cover the ground around new plants with a layer of dark gravel or expanded clay pellets to trap and conserve heat. Occasional watering does no harm during a summer drought, but the plants must be kept as dry as possible in winter.

The following species have rounded to oval segments, more or less densely set with spines. The flowers are 6–10 cm in diameter and rather short-lived, but appear in succession from the end of June to the end of July.

Opuntia humifusa (*O. compressa*)	Pale yellow flowers, often with reddish centres; segments round to ovate.
Opuntia engelmannii var. *discata*	Yellow flowers; large, circular segments with black spines.
Cholla *Opuntia fragilis*	Very dainty, but seldom produces its yellow to pale red flowers; very spiny, cylindrical segments.
Opuntia phaeacantha	Yellow flowers with orange centres; oval segments (up to 15 cm) with long spines. Recommended cultivars: 'Albispina', pale yellow with brownish centres. 'Pallida', creamy white with greenish centres. 'Longispina', pale yellow. *O. p. camanchica* 'Rubra', dark vermilion.
Opuntia polyacantha var. *erythrostemma*	Deep yellow flowers, reddish on the outside; prostrate, almost circular segments.
Opuntia rafinesquei	Abundant sulphur yellow flowers; segments up to 10 cm long and 6 cm wide; now considered to be a form of *O. humifusa*.
Opuntia rhodantha	Reddish-brown flowers; needs good drainage. 'Köhlein', dark red; extremely resistant to damp.
Opuntia utahensis	Dainty species with crimson flowers; sensitive to damp; obovate to elliptic segments.

Species of several other cactus genera are also quite tolerant of extreme cold.

Mulleins, *Verbascum*

The mulleins are an ornamental genus with large, basal leaf rosettes and tall spikes of flowers. Although the plants are comparatively short-lived, they seed themselves abundantly and are always popping up unexpectedly to enrich a planting (see also list 3.4.3).

The tall, yellow-flowered, European species, *Verbascum thapsus* (up to 2.00) and *V. thapsiforme* (up to 1.80), are rarely available from nurseries but will thrive in stony, disturbed soils and are well worth growing in gardens. They both make such large plants that it can sometimes be difficult to find suitable neighbours for them. In view of this, they are best sown or planted out in a warm, sunny spot of their own.

Tall species, over 1.50 m

Verbascum longifolium var. *pannosum* (*V. pannosum*) Balk., It.	0.25/1.60 yellow	VI–VIII, immense, unbranched inflorescence and long leaves with matted grey hairs.
Verbascum olympicum (*V. speciosum*)	0.30/2.00 yellow	VI–VIII, powerful, candelabra-like inflorescence, branched almost to the tip. 'Silberkandelaber', leaves with silvery-white hairs; broad, pyramidal inflorescence; comes true from seed.
Verbascum hybrid 'Densiflorum' (*V. vernale* hort.)	0.25/1.70 yellow	V–VI, dense, green foliage; sometimes long-lived.

Species up to 1.50 m

Verbascum bombyciferum (*V. lagurus*) Asia Min.	1.40 golden yellow	VI–VIII, matted, silvery-white hairs on leaves and stems. 'Polarsommer', very attractive, furry white cultivar.
Verbascum Cotswold hybrids 'Cotswold Queen'	0.70/1.30 yellow– bronze	VI–IX, one of a number of widely available hybrids, including: 'Blushing Bride' (0.70), white. 'Gainsborough', pale yellow; pubescent. 'Golden Bush' (0.50), bright yellow; low-growing. 'Harkness', yellow. 'Pink Domino', pink.
Dark mullein *Verbascum nigrum* Eur., Sib., Altai	0.80 yellow	VI–VIII, leaves green with grey undersides; for a sunny position on moist soil. *V. chaixii* (to 1.00), pale yellow; much-branched panicles.
Purple mullein *Verbascum phoeniceum* E & SE Eur., Iran, Altai	0.60 violet	V–VI, green leaves; dainty habit; long-lived on sandy soils. *V. wiedemannianum* (to 1.00), VI–VIII, similar but with grey-white foliage.

Foxtail lilies, *Eremurus*

These strongly architectural plants belong to the lily family. Their thick, horizontally spreading, starfish-shaped rootstocks are best planted in deep, rich, porous soil that dries out completely in summer. After flowering, they remain dormant until the following spring. Although the plants are hardy, their emerging shoots can be severely damaged by late frosts in spring, and it is therefore advisable to protect them on cold nights with a cardboard box or upturned flowerpot.

It is important that the plants are given good drainage, particularly on a heavy soil. The roots should be set 10–15 cm deep on a 5 cm layer of coarse sand, with at least 10 cm of stones or rubble underneath. Planting may be carried out in summer or autumn.

It is helpful to distinguish between massive, tall-growing species, which are best used in isolated groups among the rocks of a steppe planting, and daintier, middle-sized species, which can be combined with the perennials from lists 3.4.1, 3.4.4 and 5.3.1. These latter are mostly quite robust and not so dependent on open soil above their roots.

Massive, tall-growing species

Eremurus × elwesii (*E. himalaicus ×* *E. robustus*)	up to 2,00 light pink	V, flowers very early; tall inflorescences; light green leaves up to 1 m long. 'Alba', white.
Eremurus himalaicus Him.	1.20–2.00 white	V–VI, lush green leaves up to 50 cm long.
Eremurus robustus Turkest.	2.50/3.00 light pink	IV–VII, broad, blue-green leaves with rough edges; racemes more than 1 m long; foliage dies down during flowering.

Dainty, middle-sized species

Eremurus stenophyllus (*E. bungei*) SW Asia	0.70/1.00 lemon yellow	VI–VII, narrow leaves; multiple flowering stems; more robust than the foregoing species; very long-lived; valuable for cutting. *E. × tubergenii* (*E. s. × E. himalaicus*), VI, light yellow.
Shelford hybrids (*Eremurus ×* *isabellinus*) (*E. stenophyllus* *× E. olgae*)	1.00/1.50 warm, pastel shades	VI–VII, stiffly upright stems; attractive inflorescences in many different colours; valuable and long-lasting as a cut flower. Ruiter hybrids: early-flowering; colours even more varied.
Eremurus olgae SW Asia	1.00 pink	VII–VIII, very variable in height and colour; narrow, blue-green leaves; rare in the trade. *E. altaicus* (0.80), VI, pale yellow flowers. *E. tauricus* (0.80), white flowers with a green central vein.

Ornamental alliums, *Allium* (see also list 4.2)

The following species flourish in full sun on warm, porous, well-drained, mineral-rich soils that tend to dry out in summer. They may also be combined with the border perennials from list 5.3.1. In contrast to the dainty rock garden alliums of list 4.4.2, these plants die down immediately after flowering. Early autumn is the best planting time but potted specimens may also be put out in spring. Small bulbs should be set at 3–5 cm below the soil surface, larger ones at 8–10 cm.

Low-growing species

Allium karataviense Turk.	0.20 pale purplish- pink	IV–V, large, spherical heads of flowers on very short stems; broad leaves; seeds itself freely; also suitable for rock gardens.
Allium oreophilum (*A. ostrowskianum*) Cauc., E Turk.	0.10 magenta	VI–VII, spherical umbels of large flowers; also suitable for rock gardens. Selection: 'Zwanenburg'.

Stately, middle-sized and tall species

Allium christophii (*A. albopilosum*) Asia Minor, N Iran	0.40 lilac	VI–VII, flower heads up to 15 cm across; blue-green, strap-like leaves; attractive seed heads persist until winter; sometimes seeds itself; also reliable on loamy soils.
Allium giganteum Him., C Asia	1.20–1.50 purplish-pink	IV, large, spherical inflorescences (up to 10 cm across) on tall, smooth stems; glabrous leaves; protection with conifer branches is advisable in winter. *A rosenbachianum* (*A. jesdianum*) (up to 1.00), similar, but shorter and leaves are hairy beneath.
Allium stipitatum Turk.	0.80–1.50 purple-lilac	VI–VII, very large, spherical inflorescences; narrow-lanceolate leaves with rough hairs beneath; plants turn pink as they die down; pleasantly scented; fairly hardy.
Round-headed leek *Allium sphaerocephalon* Eur., Med., Cauc.	0.70 dark purple	VII–VIII, dense, ovoid to spherical flower heads, up to 3 cm across; stiff, wiry stems; fully hardy.

3.3.3. Further perennials for stony steppe plantings (and rock gardens)

Species for moderately dry, loamy soils

The following plants grow well among rocks and scree, and are thus also suitable for rock gardens. They have much in common with the species in list 3.4.1, and are best planted in similarly loose formations. The bulbs from list 4.2.4 often make good companions.

Achillea tomentosa S Eur., Cauc.	0.05/0.15 golden yellow	VI–VII, grey foliage; clumps commonly deteriorate after two or three years in cool, damp climates; not to be used in extensive patches, except in warm regions. *A. aurea,* V–VII, mossy green foliage; also goes bare in the middle.
Sheepburr *Acaena buchananii* NZ	0.05	V, grey-green, feathery foliage; spherical flower heads on short stems; greenish calyx spines; long-lived; covers the ground well; more reliable than *A. microphylla* in a continental climate.
Sheepburr *Acaena microphylla* NZ	0.05	VI, brownish, feathery foliage; spherical flower heads with bright red calyx spines; more reliable than the previous species in an oceanic climate. 'Kupferteppich', daintier and less vigorous; red-brown flower heads. *A. pulchella,* brighter red-brown than the former; attractive fruits.
Sheepburr *Acaena caesiiglauca* (*A. glauca* hort.) NZ	0.05	V, silky, matt blue-grey leaves on short, prostrate, woody stems; less invasive than the previous two species. *A. magellanica* (*A. glaucophylla*), steel blue foliage; less vigorous and not so hardy.

Spiny bear's-breeches *Acanthus spinosus* S Eur.	0.50 pale purple	VIII, makes a very decorative plant; deeply incised and spiny leaves. *A. caroli-alexandri* (0.40), large, green leaves; whitish-brown flowers; tender. Further species, see list 3.4.8.
Alyssum murale (*A. argenteum* hort.) SE Eur.	0.15–0.04 yellow	VI–VII, flowers in umbels on upright, partly woody stems with rough, grey-green leaves; forms silver-grey cushions that mostly disappear after 3–4 years; seeds itself freely; also for sandy soils.
Cinnamon everlasting *Anaphalis cinnamomea* Him.	0.40 white	VIII, stiff habit; similar to *A. margaritacea*; leaves cinnamon-brown beneath; very vigorous.
Pearl everlasting *Anaphalis triplinervis* Him.	0.30 white	VIII–IX, silvery, white-hairy leaves that are greenish above; vigorous and leafy but not invasive. 'Silberregen' (0.40), IX–X, valuable, late flowering cultivar. 'Sommerschnee' (0.40), VII–IX, flowers early.
Pearl everlasting *Anaphalis yedoensis* (*A. margaritacea* var. *yedoensis*) Him., Jap.	0.15 white	VIII–IX, cymose inflorescences; narrow-lanceolate leaves with matted white hairs; spreading rhizomes; for sites that are not too dry.
Dusty miller *Artemisia stelleriana* NE Asia, E N Am.	0.30 yellowish	V, insignificant flowers; deeply divided, almost palmate leaves with matted white hairs; stems mostly decumbent; for very well-drained soils; likes to sprawl over rocks.
Asparagus tenuifolius S Eur.	0.30 (0.50) greenish- white	VII, insignificant flowers; fine foliage on upright shoots; golden yellow in autumn, with large red berries.
Asphodel *Asphodeline lutea* Med.	0.20/0.70 golden yellow	VI, neat, grass-like clumps of blue-green foliage in winter; attractive seed heads. *A. l. subalpina*, shorter than the type. *A. liburnica* (1.00), yellow; graceful habit; flowers open at night. *A. taurica* (0.30), white, V–VI.
Astragalus centralpinus (*A. alopecuroides*) SW Alps, S Blg.	0.80 yellow	VII–VIII, decorative, upright, woolly perennial; long, pinnate leaves with spine-tipped leaflets; flowers freely; thrives on limestone soils.
Winecup *Callirhoe involucrata* USA, Mex.	0.15 magenta pink	VII–IX, large mallow flowers on lax green stems; palmate leaves with 5–7 segments; for a sunny position on dry soil.
Campanula ochroleuca Cauc.	0.10/0.70 yellowish- white	VII, large, toothed bells on lax, leafy stems; light green, heart-shaped leaves; good in the neighbourhood of trees and shrubs.
Campanula grosseckii Hung.	1.20 whitish-blue	VII, rough, nettle-like leaves; abundant flowers on sturdy stems; seeds itself freely; good in the neighbourhood of trees and shrubs.

Red valerian *Centranthus ruber* Med.	0.60 pink	V–VII(–X), blue-green foliage; very long flowering season; seeds itself abundantly, even into rock crevices. 'Coccineus', red. 'Albiflorus', white.
Ceratostigma plum- baginoides		List 4.1.1
Hairy golden-aster *Chrysopsis villosa* var. *ruteri* N Am.	0.20 yellow	VIII, daisy-like flowers; slightly serrate, grey-hairy, lanceolate leaves; stout tap root.
Colewort *Crambe cordifolia* Cauc.	0.60/1.60 white	VI, very large, rounded green leaves; thick rhizomes; immense, spherical inflorescences up to 1 m across; very long-lived; needs a lot of space.
Hound's tongue *Cynoglossum nervosum* Him.	0.50 gentian blue	VI–VII, forms broad clumps of pointed, lanceolate leaves with short, bristle–like hairs.
Eriogonum spp.		List 4.2.3
Eriophyllum lanatum		List 4.1.1
Euphorbia capitulata Balk.	0.05 yellowish	VII, dense, low mats of grey-green foliage; small heads of flowers.
Euphorbia myrsinites S Eur., Asia Minor, Crim.	0.15/0.20 yellow	V, large inflorescences; cylindrical, prostrate shoots, densely set with blue-green leaves; also suitable for rock gardens. *E. polychroma*, see list 4.1.1.
Gypsophila paniculata		List 4.1.1
Helichrysum thian- shanicum (*H. lanatum*) Turkest.	0.05/0.25 yellow	VI–VII. forms woolly, turf-like cushions; aromatic foliage. Selection: 'Goldkind'. *H. plicatum*, VII–VIII, golden yellow; shorter.
Helichrysum hybrid 'Schwefellicht' ('Sulphur Light')	0.05/0.25 sulphur yellow	VII, woolly, grey-green leaves; flowers in dense corymbs; tender.
Iris crocea (*I. aurea*) Kashm.	1.20 golden yellow	VII–VIII, stiff, sword-shaped leaves, which die down in autumn; steppe species. *I. halophila*, VI–VII, pale yellow flowers; sometimes blooms again in autumn. *I. h. sogdiana*, VI–VII, pale blue; thrives in dry soil.
Iris germanica Barbata–Elatior group	List 5.3.1	Robust (diploid) varieties are suitable for extreme steppe-like conditions.
Iris pumila S C Eur., SE Eur., Asia Minor, Cauc., Sib.	0.10/0.15 blue and yellow	IV, delicate species; a single flower on each stem; rare in the trade. Hybrids, see list 4.1.1.
Iris ruthenica (*I. caespitosa*) SE Eur., NW Afr.	0.20–0.30 violet and white	V–VI, flowers nestle among the leaves; dense, over-arching, grass-like clumps.

Marrubium supinum Spain, NW Afr.	0.20 lilac	VI–VII, forms compact cushions; soft, woolly, ovate leaves; insignificant flowers in whorls. *M. vulgare,* see list 5.7.1
Morina longifolia Nepal	0.10/0.70 white then pink	VII–VIII, ornamental habit; flowers in whorls on stout stems; needs a deep soil for its powerful tap-root. *M. persica,* dark pink. *M. kokanica,* violet Both less hardy than the above.
Catmint *Nepeta × faassenii* (*N. mussinii* hort.) (*N. mussinii × N. nepe-tella*)	0.20/0.30 light blue	V–VII, (IX), small, bushy, silver-grey perennial; blooms again in autumn if cut back after flowering; particularly long-lived on sandy soils in mild areas; also suitable for rock gardens. 'Blauknirps' (0.20), spherical dwarf form.
Nepeta × faassenii 'Six Hills Giant' (*N. gigantea*)	0.50 lilac blue	VI, vigorous, grey-leaved plant; also thrives in less extreme conditions. 'Superba', V, early flowering; shorter, but with larger blooms; rounded, grey-green leaves.
Missouri evening prim-rose *Oenothera missouriensis* E USA	0.10/0.20 yellow	VI–IX, very large flowers; shiny green leaves; sprawls horizontally over rocks or soil.
Penstemon pinifolius and similar species		List 4.2.1
Phlomis samia Gr., Asia Minor	0.15/1.00 yellow	VI–VII, attractive, whorled seed heads decorate the plants far into winter; not for areas with an oceanic climate. *P. tuberosa* (up to 1.50), pink; does not spread so rapidly. *P. herbaventi* (0.60), VI, lilac; flowers in whorls on slender stems; rare in the trade.
Rhodiola kirilowii (*Sedum kirilowii*) NW China, Him.	0.30 greenish-yellow	IV–V, hemispherical flower heads on erect, leafy stems; irregularly sharp-toothed, linear-lanceolate leaves; dies down after flowering. 'Rubrum', red-brown flowers. *R. rosea,* see list 4.3.2.
Rhodiola semenowii (*Sedum semenowii*) C Asia	0.40 greenish-white	VI–VII, flowers in long, upright racemes on erect, unbranched, leafy stems; green, entire, linear leaves, up to 5 cm long.
Sedum aizoon (*S. maximowiczii*) Jap., Sib.	0.30–0.45 yellow	VII, very leafy, upright stems; deciduous; propagation from seed. 'Aurantiacum' (0.20), orange-yellow.
Sedum anacampseros		List 4.2.1
Sedum ewersii		List 4.2.1
Sedum midden-dorffianum		List 4.2.1

Sedum populifolium Sib.	0.30 pale pink	VIII, open, upright habit; broad, irregularly toothed leaves; deciduous.
Sedum spectabile		List 5.3.1
Sedum telephium		List 3.4.4
Stachys byzantina		List 4.1.1
Thermopsis fabacea Sib., W N Am.	0.50 yellow	V–VI, lupin-like species; drought resistant by virtue of its deep roots. *T. lanceolata* (*T. lupinoides*) (to 0.30), VI–VIII, yellow.
Tulipa sylvestris	List 2.4.1	See list 4.2.4 for other suitable tulip species.

Species for sandy soils

The following perennials all thrive in warm, sunny, open situations with fertile, well-aerated, moist to moderately dry, sandy soils. All have spreading roots, and some are highly invasive. Species such as *Gypsophila paniculata*, *Oenothera missouriensis* and *Thermopsis* spp. from the previous list may sometimes be combined with them.

Pearl everlasting *Anaphalis margaritacea* N Am., NE Asia	0.50 white	VII–VIII, narrow, silvery leaves; spreading roots; flowers good for drying. Selection: 'Neuschnee' (0.50).
Common chamomile *Chamaemelum nobile* (*Anthemis nobilis*) SW Eur.	0.05/0.15 white	VII–X, small daisy-like flowers; dainty, pinnate leaves covered in downy hair; forms evergreen mats; old medicinal plant; rare in the trade. 'Plena', double flower heads; spreads well. 'Treneague', see list 3.1.3.
White sage *Artemisia ludoviciana* var. *albula* 'Silver Queen' N Am., Mex.	0.70	VIII–IX, matted white hairs on leaves and shoots; open, many-stemmed habit; rhizomatous, sometimes invasive roots; a better plant than the narrow-leaved *A. purshiana*. 'Silver King', common cultivar in the USA.
Roman wormwood *Artemisia pontica* C & E Eur. to W Sib.	0.50	VIII, a dainty plant with dense, grey-green, feathery foliage; very invasive; good groundcover for warm, sandy, nutrient-rich soils. *A. austriaca* (0.25), similar but shorter.
Lyme-grass *Elymus arenarius* (*E. glaucus* hort.) C & N Eur., Sib., N Am.	0.50/1.50	VI–VII, steel blue, slightly glaucous leaves; strongly spreading rhizomes; to be used with caution. *E. giganteus* (1.50), broad, green leaves. *E. glaucus* (to 1.00), glaucous blue leaves; hardly spreads. *E. racemosus* (1.50), green leaves.
Elymus canadensis (*E. robustus*) N Am.	0.40/1.10	VII–VIII, rough, green (sometimes bluish) leaves; broad and often drooping inflorescences; rare in the trade.

3.3.4.   Grasses for stony steppe plantings and similar sites

Steppe grasses are just as varied and exotic as other steppe perennials. Further appropriate species may be found in list 3.4.1.

Achnatherum pekinense (*Stipa extremiori-entalis*) Sib., China, Jap., Korea, Manch.	0.50/1.70	VIII, rigid stems with loose, narrow panicles; decorative in winter; sparse tufts of foliage; rare in the trade. *A. calamagrostis,* see list 3.4.1.
Mosquito grass *Bouteloua oligostachya* (*B. gracilis*) N Am., Mex.	0.10/0.30	VII–IX, flower spikes extend laterally from the graceful stems. *B. curtipendula,* (0.80), dropping, racemose inflorescences; rare in the trade.
Carex buchananii NZ	0.40	VII, rusty-red foliage all year round; very beautiful in frost; for not too dry soils. 'Viridis', greenish yellow foliage. *C. comans,* shorter.
Chrysopogon gryllus Med., Asia Minor	1.00–1.20	VII–VIII, very attractive, particularly as a specimen plant; well-formed clumps of rough, elegantly overarching leaves; stiff stems; panicles of almost horizontal spikelets on long pedicels, each with a basal crown of golden yellow hairs.
Elymus sibiricus Sib., China, Kamch.	0.80	VII–IX, clump-forming species; drooping, long-awned inflorescences on powerful stems; seeds itself freely; still rare in the trade.
Eragrostis curvula Afr., Argent.	up to 1.00	VII–IX, decorative clumps of hard, narrow, grey-green leaves; narrow panicles on lightly arching stems; seeds itself freely; still rare in the trade. *Sporobolus heterolepis,* similar.
Festuca punctoria Asia Minor	0.10/0.15	VI–VII, hard, piercing, grey-green leaves; loose tufted habit.
Helictotrichon sempervirens		List 3.4.1
Koeleria glauca Eur., Asia	0.20/0.30	VI–VII, broad, blue-green leaves; plants can be unsightly after flowering; does not flower every year; for porous, alkaline soils in dry areas.
Melica ciliata Eur., SW Asia	0.70	VI, spikelets in loose, one-sided panicles over grey-green clumps of foliage; the straw-yellow fruiting stems fall apart easily in damp conditions; for dry, chalky, gravelly soils.
Melica transsylvanica W Fr. to SE Eur, Cauc.	0.80	VI, graceful habit; attractive, cylindrical, silky inflorescences; green leaves.
Poa glauca (*P. caesia*) N Eur., Pyren., S Alps, Gr.	0.20	VI–VII, short, dense panicles; firm cushions of blue-green foliage; see also list 4.4.1.

Sesleria autumnalis N Yug.	0.30/0.80	IX–X, powerful clumps of fine, light green leaves with rough edges; also decorative in winter. *S. argentea,* very similar.
Sesleria heufleriana (*S. heuffeliana*) SE Eur.	0.30/0.50	IV, rigid stems over clumps of glaucous, dark green leaves.
Sesleria nitida Balk., It.	0.50/0.80	V, smooth, broad, rigid, grey-blue leaves; numerous tall, stiff stems.
Sesleria rigida Balk.	0.15	III–IV, green, lance-like leaves; dark purple inflorescences; also suitable for rock gardens.
Sesleria caerulea (*S. uliginosa*) Eur.	0.50	III, long, narrow, grooved, slightly glaucous leaves; dark, almost spherical inflorescences.
Sesleria albicans (*S. varia*) Eur., N Med.	0.25	III, coarse, broad, linear leaves; blades glaucous above and green below; short, oval, whitish inflorescences. Selections: 'Blaureif'. 'Blauzwerg' (0.15), dwarf form.
Needle-and-thread *Stipa capillata* C & S Eur., S Russ., Sib., Turk., Cauc., Iran	0.80	VII–VIII, consistently attractive clumps of narrow, stiffly upright leaves; panicles of spikelets with long, straight (but not feathery) awns, which curl later. Related species: *S. grandis* (0.60). *S. tenacissima* (1.00), imposing clumps.
Golden oats, Giant feathered grass *Stipa gigantea* (*Macrochloa arenaria*) Pyren., Port., It.	1.80	VI–IX, tall, graceful habit; old plants form large clumps, which bear numerous, rigid stems and remain decorative until autumn; divides well.
Green needle-grass *Stipa viridula* USA	0.60/1.30	VII–VIII, clumps of overhanging leaves; long, slender, dense-flowered panicles with bristle-like awns; diagonally held stems.

Long-awned feather grasses, *Stipa*

These spectacular grasses do not live long if they are subject to competition. They are best planted in an isolated position where their long awns can play freely in the wind.

Stipa barbata W Med.	0.80	VI–VII, sparse, open tufts of leaves; very long, drooping, silvery, feather-like awns; unsightly stems should be removed after the seed is shed. *S. joannis* (0.50), similar.
Stipa pennata (*S. eviocaulis*) C & SE Eur., W Asia	0.80	V–VI, similar to the previous species; sets fruit very early; beautiful, long, feathery awns. *S. ucrainica,* flowers and fruits even earlier. *S. tirsa* (*S. stenophylla*), seeds itself prolifically. Somewhat rarer are: *S. nudicostata, S. pulcherrima* and *S. papposa* (0.30).

It is advisable to combine early- and late-flowering species in plantings.

Blue fescues and their relatives

The blue-leaved fescues are longer-lived in steppe and dry grassland (prairie) conditions than in rich, peaty garden soils, where their clumps grow up out of the ground and need regular division. It is best not to use them in extensive patches. The beauty of their foliage and wind-blown stems is most apparent when just a few tufts are grouped among other plants such as iris and lavender. The stems remain bluish-green until the end of June, when they slowly turn yellow or brown before bleaching entirely in autumn. This may detract from a formal, intensively maintained planting, in which case the stems should be removed. Breeders are trying to produce forms with intensively coloured foliage and as few flowers as possible.

Cultivars of *Festuca glauca* are listed here, together with a few other *Festuca* species that are particularly suitable for steppe, dry grassland and rock garden plantings.

Festuca amethystina Alps, SE Eur., Asia Minor	0.30/0.40	VI, spine-tipped, awnless lemmas; clumps of long, fine, hair-like, blue-green leaves; overarching leaves and stems; planting distance not less than 50 cm. 'Herms', green leaves; good with *Erica herbacea* in a dry, sunny spot under pines.
Festuca rupicola (*F. sulcata*) Eur., Asia	0.15–0.30	V–VI, hairy lemmas with awns 1–3 mm long; compact, upright panicles at flowering time; clumps of somewhat erect, slightly bristly, dark green leaves; long-lived in dry grassland on stony, loamy soils.
Festuca trachyphylla (*F. longifolia*) C Eur.	0.35/0.50	V–VII, smooth, glaucous, blue-green leaves; few flowers; stems arch far out over the clumps; awns 1–2.5 mm long; long-lived in dry grassland on lime-free, sandy soils.
Festuca valesiaca S, C & E Eur.	0.15–0.30	VI–VII, dainty clumps of rough, flexible, hair-fine, slightly glaucous, blue-green leaves; long-lived on alkaline, rocky soils.
Festuca valesiaca 'Glaucantha'	0.10/0.25	Very showy steel-blue foliage; low, brush-like clumps; quite variable.
Blue fescue *Festuca glauca* (*F. cinerea*) S, C & E. Eur.	0.20/0.40	Many different microspecies with sturdy clumps of variable, glaucous blue leaves; awns more than 1 mm long.

Blue fescue cultivars (Festuca glauca *and relatives*)

Silvery blue, glaucous leaves:
'Blausilber' (0.20/0.50).
'Blaufink' (0.25/0.60).
'Blauglut' (0.30/0.80).
'Krähenwinkel' (0.30/0.60).

Low clumps (under 20 cm):
'Eisvogel'.
'Silbersee'.

Dark blue-green leaves:
'Harz' (0.25/0.40).

Blue leaves
'Frühlingsblau' (0.20/0.50).
'Meerblau' (0.25/0.60).

Blue-green leaves:
'Aprilgrün' (0.25/0.60).

Flowerless; Blue-green leaves:
'Silberreiher' (0.25)
'Solling' (0.25).

Flowerless; dark green leaves:
'Grünling' (0.25).

3.3.5. Slightly tender perennials and dwarf shrubs for rocky, steppe-like plantings

The following species are suitable for warm, sunny positions on a rock garden or at the foot of a sheltering wall, particularly in mild areas. They all thrive in summer drought, and many can be long-lived if they are given a little protection in winter.

Italian alkanet *Anchusa azurea* (*A. italica*) S Eur., Iran	1.20 blue	VI–VII, short-lived species; very large heads of abundant bright blue flowers; rough, dark green leaves; fully hardy; seeds itself prolifically. 'Morning Glory', lobelia blue. 'Pride of Dover', azure blue. 'Dropmore', gentian blue. 'Little John', (0.50), deep blue. 'Lodden Royalist', (0.70), deep blue. 'Royal Blue', (0.50), gentian blue. The plants perennate better if they are cut back into the crown, below the root junction, immediately after flowering.
Milkweed, Butterfly weed *Asclepias tuberosa* USA, N Mex.	0.60 light orange	VIII, numerous umbellate cymes at the top of each stem; valuable for cutting; elongate–lanceolate leaves; tuberous rootstock; needs protection against damp in winter.
Aquilegia skinneri Calif., C Mex.	up to 0.60 red	VII–IX, abundant, slender, brightly coloured flowers; only for warm, sunny sites; short-lived and needs protection in winter; rare in the trade.
Asphodel *Asphodelus albus* S Eur.	up to 1.00 white, with brown central vein	V–VI, flowers in panicles or unbranched racemes on stiff, leafless stems; narrow, grey-green leaves, triangular in cross-section; for mild areas. *A. aestivus* (*A. microcarpus*), daintier; branching, pyramidal inflorescences; rare in the trade.
Ballota pseudo-dictamnus (*Marrubium pseudo-dictamnus*) S Eur.	0.50 white, with mauve blotches	VI, a bushy plant with small flowers in whorls; stems densely set with rounded, white-hairy leaves up to 2 cm long; ornamental, rosette-like tips to the shoots; for dry, south-facing walls in mild areas; needs protection in winter.
Rock rose *Cistus laurifolius* SW Eur., It.	up to 1.00 white, with yellow blotches	VI–VIII, evergreen shrub with green, ovate leaves that are grey-hairy underneath; hardly needs protection in winter. Other *Cistus* spp. are more tender.
Crassula milfordiae		List 4.2.3
Cardoon *Cynara cardunculus* S & W Med.	up to 1.50 blue	VIII–X, huge flower heads with immense, star-shaped buds; decorative habit; very large, pinnately incised and spiny, silvery-green leaves; for rich, loamy soils; needs a little protection in winter. 'Altilis' (to 2.50). *C. humilis* (0.50), small flowers; rare in the trade.

Artichoke *Cynara scolymus*	to 1.50 blue-violet	VIII–X, similar to the previous species but with even larger flower heads; smaller, less incised and almost spineless leaves with fleshy ribs and petioles; grown as a vegetable; needs protection in winter.
Delosperma cooperi S Afr.	0.10 red	VI–IX, large, bright flowers with many thread-like petals; thick, cylindrical leaves; prostrate, branching stems; sensitive to damp in winter. *D. aberdeenense,* forms green mats; red flowers. *D. sutherlandii,* pink flowers with a yellow centre. All species require dry conditions in winter; the flowers only open in sunshine.
Delphinium nudicaule Calif.	0.30 orange-red	VI–VII, racemes of flowers with straight spurs; branching stems with swollen bases; for dry, porous soils in full sun; the fleshy rootstock must be lifted in autumn or given protection through the winter, particularly against damp.
Diascia cordata 'Ruby Field'	0.10 salmon pink	VII–IX, very free-flowering over a long period; flowers in terminal racemes on long, decumbent stems; needs protection in an exposed position; also suitable for rock gardens.
Grassy bells *Dierama pendulum* S Afr.	0.60 pink	VI–IX, flowers in pendulous, one-sided racemes; stiff, narrow leaves; needs protection in winter.
Wand flower *Dierama pulcherrimum* (*Sparaxis pulcherrima*) S Afr.	0.30 pink	IX–X, stiff, grassy, evergreen leaves and arching, pendulous inflorescences; for warm, sunny sites and not too dry soils; cormaceous plant for mild areas; needs protection in winter.
Dorycnium hirsutum S Eur.	0.70 white and pink	VI-IX, semi-shrub with large flowers and white-hairy foliage; red-brown clusters of seed pods.
Gaura lindheimeri S USA	0.80 white	VII–IX, long flowering season; flowers in long racemes on stiffly branched stems with few, narrow, grey-green leaves; for dry soils; sometimes short-lived, but seeds itself prolifically; needs protection in winter.
Delosperma nubigenum (*Mesembryanthemum othonna*) S Afr.	up to 0.10 yellow	VI–IX, forms shiny green carpets, which turn reddish in winter; covered with glossy, yellow, daisy-like flowers in summer.
Penstemon campanulatus Mex.	0.30–0.50 pink to violet	VII–IX, loose racemes of flowers; sharply serrate, linear leaves; semi-evergreen. 'Evelyn', pink. 'Richardsonii', flowers prolifically.
Penstemon erianthus (*P. cristatus*) USA	0.30 violet	VII–VIII, forms small, stemmy, evergreen bushes; basal leaves spathulate; needs protection in winter.
Phygelius capensis		List 5.6.1

Californian poppy *Romneya coulteri* Calif., Mex.	up to 1.50 (2.50) silvery white	VII–IX, smooth, branching, grey-green stems with papery, blue-green leaves; large, terminal flowers; for a warm, sunny position in front of a south-facing wall, with deep, porous soil; not to be watered, even in drought; needs winter protection, particularly against damp.
Rosemary *Rosmarinus officinalis* Med.	0.50–1.00 pale blue	V, evergreen shrub with long, linear, often shiny leaves, grey-hairy beneath; flowers in short, axillary racemes on the previous year's wood; kitchen herb. *R. lavandulaceus* (*R. prostratus*), prostrate, mat-forming shrub; more tender than the above; needs protection in winter.
Senecio bicolor 'White Diamond' Med.	0.50 yellow	VII–IX, flowers in dense, corymbose racemes; pinnately divided, white-hairy leaves; semi-shrubby species for mild areas; needs a little protection in winter.
Themeda triandra Jap., China	0.50	IX–X, clump-forming grass; broad, arching, red-flushed leaves; coppery in winter; rarely flowers; for mild areas; needs protection against cold and damp in winter.
Thyme *Thymus vulgaris* W Med.	up to 0.25 rosy red	VII–IX, small, aromatic shrub with ovate leaves; flowers in whorled clusters; kitchen herb; needs protection in winter. 'Compactus', see list 4.2.3.
Yucca recurvifolia S USA	up to 1.50 creamy white	VII–IX, massive, grey-green clumps of leaves on short woody stems; open, branching inflorescences; hardy in a sheltered spot. *Y. gloriosa* (1.50), more tender than the previous species; compact inflorescences; nodding, bell-shaped flowers, striped purple on the outside. Hardy *Yucca* spp., see list 3.3.2.
Epilobium canum spp. *latifolium* (*Zauschneria cali-* *fornica* spp. *latifolia*) W USA	up to 0.30 bright red	VII–X, fuchsia-like flowers on lax stems with sparsely grey-hairy, ovate–lanceolate leaves; for a sunny position on well-drained sandy loam; mild areas; needs protection in winter.

3.3.6. Somewhat tender bulbs, corms and tubers

Hardy bulbs for steppe plantings can be found in lists 4.2.4 and 4.4.2. The following species may also be used, in regions where frost does not penetrate the soil, or where the planting can be protected in winter.

Anemone coronaria Med., W Asia	0.25–0.40 various	IV-VI, large, single flowers on hairy, unbranched stems; fresh green, tripartite leaves; widely grown in many different colours as a cut flower; for a warm, sunny position on dry to moist soil; where summers are rainy, tubers must be lifted after flowering and stored in a dry place until autumn; tender and short-lived. *A. × fulgens*, scarlet flowers with pointed, narrow-lanceolate petals; hardier than the above.

Bletilla striata China, Jap.	0.30–0.50 magenta pink	V, 3–7 small, *Cymbidium*-like flowers on slender, wand-like stems; arching, reed-like leaves; tuberous rhizomes; for well-drained, loamy, mineral soils in full sun; also on limestone soils; plants should be set 7–10 cm deep in spring; spreads slowly; water during dry weather; needs a generous covering of leaves in winter. 'Alba', white.
Gladiolus italicus (*G. segetum*) S Eur., Med.	0.30–0.60 red-violet	IV–V, loose spikes of flowers. *G. byzantinus* (0.60), VI–VII, purplish-red; one-sided flower-spikes; flattened or spherical corms. 'Albus', white. Both species need a covering of leaves in winter.
Ixiolirion tataricum Asia Minor	up to 0.40 violet-blue	V–VI, large, trumpet-shaped flowers loosely arranged on tall, thin stems with narrow, linear leaves; for porous soils in full sun; hardy; bulbs should be planted 10 cm deep; may be used for cutting.
Muscari moschatum (*M. muscarini*) Asia Minor	0.20 olive red or yellow	IV–V, murky flowers on stout stems; very strongly scented; only perennates in warm areas.
Ornithogalum balansae Asia Minor	0.15 white	III–IV, large flowers; for mild areas.
Ornithogalum arabicum Med.	up to 0.45 white	V–VI, stout stems with up to 12 white flowers and blackish pistils; reliable only in mild areas. *O. thyrsoides* (Chincherinchee), S Afr., tender species for cutting; plant in spring to flower in VII–VIII.
Ornithogalum pyren-aicum (*O. latifolium*) S. C & S Eur., Cauc., Nr East	up to 0.60 white	VI, racemes of starry, white flowers on long stems; hardy. Other hardy species, see list 2.4.1.
Ornithogalum nar-bonense Fr. to SE Eur., Cauc.	up to 0.45 white	IV–V, many small, green-striped flowers in terminal, corymbose panicles. *O. pyramidale* (0.80), V–VI, taller and more robust. Both species hardy.
Oxalis adenophylla Chile, Arg.	0.08–0.10 lilac-pink	VI–VII, large flowers over dense, grey-green foliage; for sandy, lime-free, humus-rich soils in full sun; dies down after flowering; will perennate if kept dry in summer and given a good covering in winter; also suitable for rock gardens.

3.4.   Perennials for warm, sunny sites with moderately dry to moist soils

The perennials contained in the following lists (3.4.1–3.4.5) have many characteristics in common, and associate well with one another. The species from lists 3.4.1 and 3.4.2 may also be used in steppe plantings or on a rock garden. They thrive in any dryish or moist soil that is well drained and not too poor in nutrients. These plants do not form a dense turf (in contrast to the dry grassland perennials from lists 3.2.2 and 2.1.7) but cover the ground loosely and need not be kept apart like the stony steppe plants from list 3.3.

   Wild perennials with border character (list 3.4.5) may be planted more densely but still appreciate an open soil around their clumps.

3.4.1. Wild perennials for well-spaced planting

These drought- and heat-tolerant species have requirements similar to but not so extreme as those of steppe plants. Like them, they are best planted rather sparsely. Bulbs such as wild tulips or the alliums from list 4.2.4 may be planted in the gaps between them.

Adenophora liliifolia	List 4.5.4	
Allium sphaeroce-phalum	List 4.4.2	
Anthemis marshalliana (*A. biebersteiniana*) Cauc., Asia Minor	0.10/0.20 yellow	VI, silvery grey, silky-haired leaves; unfortunately, the attractive cushions decline in vigour after a few years. 'Tetra', robuster and with larger flowers than the type.
Aster linosyris	List 3.2.2	
Asphodeline lutea	List 3.3.3	
Carlina acanthifolia S Eur., Balk.	0.15/0.10 bronze-yellow	VII–VIII, immense, golden yellow, thistle-like flowers appearing directly at ground level; already attractive in bud. *C. acaulis*, see list 3.2.2.
Cupid's dart, Blue Cupidone *Catananche coerulea* W Med.	0.60 lilac-blue	VI–VIII, cornflower-like blooms on long, usually leafless stems; narrow-lanceolate basal leaves; for warm, porous soils; not very long-lived; good for cutting.
Centaurea bella Cauc.	0.15/0.25 pink	VI–VII, forms dainty cushions of silvery foliage. *C. axillaris* (0.15). blue; silvery grey leaves. *C. simplicicaulis* (0.20), pale pink flowers on long stems; feathery leaves; forms dainty, silver-grey carpets.
Centaurea pulcherrima (*Aethiopappus pul-cherrimus*) Cauc., Asia Minor	0.40 pink	VI–VII, delicate cornflower-like species; fine, grey leaves with matted grey hairs underneath; rare in the trade. *C. hypoleuca* (0.50), VII–X, pink; pinnately cut leaves with matted white hairs underneath; rare in the trade.
Chrysanthemum mille-foliatum (*Tanacetum millefolium*) SE Eur., Cauc., Asia Minor	0.10/0.50 yellow	VII–IX, stiff, upright habit with attractive, silvery foliage; rare in the trade. *C. cinerariifolium* (Pyrethrum) (0.30), VII–VIII, white flowers; pinnately lobed leaves; best-known source of natural pyrethrum; rare in the trade.
Dianthus cruentus Balk.	0.05/0.50 blood-red	VI–VII, narrow green leaves; small, bright flowers in clusters on tall, rigid stems.
Large purple storksbill *Erodium manescavii* Pyren.	0.30–0.50 magenta	VII–IX, Strongly fragrant; fresh green, pinnate leaves; rare in the trade *E. chamaedryoides* 'Roseum', very low-growing; tender.

Eryngium alpinum Alps to Balk.	0.60 violet	VII–VIII, exceptionally beautiful thistle-like plant with colourful bipinnate sepals and bluish, filigree foliage; not very long-lived in gardens; needs a damp soil in spring. 'Amethyst' (0.80), VII–VIII, silvery blue. 'Blue Star' (0.80), steel blue. 'Opal' (0.70), VI–VII, silvery lilac. 'Superbum', large flowers.
Eryngium amethys- *tinum* SE Eur.	0.80 blue	VII–VIII, leathery, pinnately incised leaves; whorled branches; ovoid to spherical heads of flowers; rare in the trade.
Eryngium bourgatii SW Eur.	0.30 blue	VII–VIII, blue flower heads; much-divided, leathery leaves with white markings; long-lived.
Eryngium giganteum		List 3.4.2
Eryngium hybrids (*E. × zabelii*)	0.50–0.80 steel blue	Decorative, large-flowered but mostly short-lived plants. 'Juwel' (0.70), dark blue. 'Robustum' (0.50), steel blue. 'Violetta' (0.80), violet.
Eryngium planum C & SE Eur., C As, Nr East	0.90 pale blue	VII–VIII, abundant small, steel-blue flower heads on tall, rigid, almost leafless stems; sometimes needs staking. 'Blauer Zwerg' ('Nanum') (0.50). *E. palmatum* (1.00), steel-blue flower heads on branching stems; good for cutting; still rare in the trade.
Eryngium tricuspidatum Med	0.30 silvery blue	VIII–IX, striking, white-veined rosettes; lasts long when cut (like all *Eryngium* spp.). *E. variifolium*, similar but tender. Species for damp soil: see list 3.5.2.
Euphorbia griffithii		List 2.3.4
Euphorbia polychroma		List 4.1.1
Ornamental fennel *Foeniculum vulgare* 'Atropurpureum' (*F. v.* var. *consan-* *guineum*) Med., N Asia	1.50 yellow	VIII, relatively short-lived umbellifer; very fine, graceful, feathery, reddish-brown flushed foliage; seeds itself freely in warm climates.
Gladiolus communis Med., Cauc., Iran	0.70–1.00 purple-red	V–VI, sturdy stems with up to 10 flowers; long leaves; overwintering corms; hardy.
Iris aphylla C & SE Eur., Cauc., Asia Minor	0.30 deep violet	V, very abundant flowers; sword-shaped leaves, which die down after flowering. 'Autumn King', V (IX), flowers a second time in autumn.
Iris cengialti S Alps, Dalmat.	0.30 pale lavender blue	V–VI, bluish grey-green, sword-shaped leaves; brown, papery sepals. *I. pallida,* similar, but taller.

		I. p. var. *dalmatica* (0.80), reliable cottage garden plant.
Iris germanica	Lists 5.3.1. & 4.1.1	Less demanding Barbata–Elatior and Barbata–Nana cultivars.
Plum-scented iris *Iris graminea* N Spain to S Russ., Cauc.	0.40/0.30 purple-blue	VI, attractive tufts of slender, grass-like leaves; plum-scented flowers nestling amongst the foliage; medicinal and cottage garden plant. *I. humilis,* E C Eur., Cauc.; similar but shorter and with larger flowers.
Iris kochii Dalmat.	0.40–0.60 purple-violet	IV, large flowers; sword-shaped leaves; robust and long-lived.
Iris sintenisii SE Eur., Asia Minor	0.20 violet and white	V–VI, flowers in pairs; violet standards, falls white with lilac veins; evergreen, linear leaves; also suitable for rock gardens.
Iris variegata C Eur., N Balk., S Russ.	0.15–0.40 yellow	V–VI, purple-veined flowers, with yellow standards and creamy-yellow falls; sword-shaped leaves; undemanding species; parent of many hybrids.
Orange lily *Lilium croceum* (*L. bulbiferum* ssp. *croceum*) S Alps	0.40–1.00 reddish-orange	VI–VII, very similar to *L. bulbiferum* (list 2.1.7) but with statelier, heavily spotted flowers and no bulbils; longer-lived than *L. bulbiferum.*
Sea lavender *Limonium latifolium* (*Statice latifolia*) 'Violetta' Bulg., Rum., SE Russ.	0.20/0.50 violet	VII–VIII, much branched, almost spherical, veil-like inflorescences. Good selections: 'Blauschleier', 'Blauwolke'.. *L. vulgare* (0.40), VII–VIII, not so showy; rare in the trade.
Goniolinum tataricum (*Limonium tataricum*) SE Eur., C Russ., Cauc.	0.20/0.30 white	VII–IX, attractive domes of flowers; widely grown for dried flower arrangements. *L. gmelinii,* bluish flowers; larger in all its parts; very broad inflorescences.
Yellow flax *Linum flavum* C & SE Eur., C Russ.	up to 0.30 clear yellow	V–VII, flowers in cymes on stiff stems; long, spathulate leaves. 'Compactum' (0.20). 'Goldzwerg' (0.10), blue-green leaves.
Paeonia tenuifolia		List 3.4.4
St Bruno's lily *Paradisea liliastrum* Switz., N It., Pyren.	0.70 white	V–VI, grassy leaves; flowers like a miniature Madonna lily; dies down after flowering; for rich, loamy soils. 'Major', more vigorous than the type.
Rhazya orientalis Gr., Turk.	0.50 violet-blue	VI–VIII, open corymbs with abundant starry flowers; dark green, oval to lanceolate leaves; spreading roots; thrives in heat.
Rue *Ruta graveolens* Balk., It.	0.30–0.60 murky yellow	VI–VIII, densely bushy plant with aromatic, blue-green, pinnately divided foliage; small flowers; old medicinal and kitchen herb; thrives in heat. Selection: 'Jackman's Blue', blue leaves.

Serbian sage *Salvia jurisicii* Maced	0.30 pale violet	VII–VIII, silver-grey, hairy, pinnately incised leaves; very attractive; best grown as an isolated specimen.
Scabiosa graminifolia		List 4.3.1
Veronica spicata ssp. *incana* (*Veronica incana*) E & C Eur.	0.50 dark blue	VI–VII, dense, spike-like racemes; silvery-white to grey foliage; basal rosettes of broad-lanceolate leaves; only vigorous in loose, sandy soils. Selections: 'Silberteppich'. 'Rosea' (0.30), pink.

Grasses

These ornamental, clump-forming grasses have much in common with the perennials listed above,
but may also find a use in steppe plantings, on rock gardens or in a formal border.

Achnatherum calama- *grostis* (*Stipa calamagrostis*) (*Lasiagrostis calama-* *grostis*) C, S & SE Eur.	1.00	VI–IX, well-proportioned clumps of arching leaves; panicles turn brownish after flowering. 'Lemperg' (0.60), similar but more compact.
Helictotrichon semper- *virens* (*Avena sempervirens*) (*A. candida* hort.) W med.	0.60/1.20	VI–VII, decorative, blue-green clumps; dry stems should be removed in summer. 'Pendula', longer, drooping stems; planting distance 1 m. 'Saphirsprudel', apparently resistant to rusts. *H. parlatorei* (0.40/0.80), grey-green foliage.
Atlas mountain fescue *Festuca mairei* Morocco	0.40/1.20	VI–VII, imposing clumps of stiff, narrow, green leaves; for use wherever blue grasses are inap- propriate; the slender flower heads dry up in summer and should be removed.
Panicum bulbosum		List 3.4.7
Pennisetum com- *pressum* E Asia	0.50/0.70	VIII–X, sturdy clumps of stiff leaves; flowers in autumn. 'Weserbergland' (0.25/0.40), very short.
Pennisetum com- *pressum* 'Hameln'	0.25/0.60	VII–IX, sturdy, low clumps of foliage; abundant, early flowers; leaves turn rusty brown in autumn. Selection: 'Herbstzauber'.
Pennisetum japonicum		List 3.5.3
Pennisetum orientale N Afr., SW Asia	0.60	VI–VII, graceful, light green species; leaves turn pale greenish-brown in drought; loose, violet-flushed heads of flowers.
Stipa spp.		List 3.3.4

3.4.2. Short-lived species for warm, sunny positions

The following, mostly biennial, species fit well into a well-spaced planting of perennials from lists 3.4.4, 3.4.5 or 3.3. Some of them seed themselves regularly without becoming a nuisance. Not all are available from perennial nurseries.

Woolly thistle *Cirsium eriophorum* W & C Eur., N It., Balk.	1.00 purple-violet	VII–VIII, large flower heads, which remain beautiful as they go to seed; calyces spun-over with white, woolly hairs; ornamental rosettes of spiny, deeply incised or pinnately divided leaves.
Cirsium diacanthum S Eur., Asia Minor	0.05/0.20 reddish	VIII, decorative, flattened rosettes of spiny leaves with silvery-white veins; unfortunately, the plants lose their charm at flowering time.
Delphinium grandi- *florum* E Sib., W China	0.30–0.50 gentian blue	VI–VII, erect, loosely branching stems; much divided leaves; seeds itself occasionally. 'Blauer Spiegel' ('Blue Mirror'), large flowers without spurs. 'Album', white.
Delphinium tatsienense China	0.40–0.60 cornflower blue	VI, similar to the previous species; very finely divided leaves; loose panicles of somewhat slenderer, long-spurred flowers.
Delphinium semi- *barbatum* (*D. zalil*) (*D. sulphureum*) Iran, Afgh.	1.00 light yellow	VI–VII, open, thin-stemmed inflorescences; finely divided foliage; dies down after flowering; sensitive to damp. All of these short-lived *Delphinium* spp. thrive on well-drained, humus-rich soils.
Eryngium giganteum Cauc., Iran	0.70 bluish white	VI–VIII, very decorative thistle-like plant with stiff, strong, branching stems; cylindrical flower heads; seeds itself prolifically; attractive flowers for drying.
Caper spurge *Euphorbia lathyris* E & C Med.	up to 1.00 pale yellow	VII–VIII, flowers in false umbels; leaves in opposite pairs arranged at right angles up the rigid stems; explosive seed capsules; old medicinal plant, thought to provide protection against moles; also for bright shade.
Horned poppy *Glaucium flavum* S & W Eur., Med.	0.15/0.50 yellow	VI–VIII, greenish grey foliage; unusual, long, horn-like fruit capsules; flowers sometimes ochre coloured. *G. squamigerum* (0.30), VII–VIII, orange; seeds itself prolifically.
Linaria genistifolia Balk., Med.	up to 1.00 yellow	VII–VIII, short-spurred flowers in slender racemes on widely branching, grey-green, leafy stems; rare in the trade.
Dusty miller, Rose campion *Lychnis coronaria* SE Eur., Asia Minor, Him.	0.60 bright red	VI–VIII, silvery foliage; mostly biennial but seeds itself freely. *L.* × *walkeri* (*L. coronaria* × *L. flos-jovis*) 'Abbotswood Rose', more compact and longer-lived.
Flower of Jove *Lychnis flos-jovis* W Alps	0.50 pale red	V–VII, flowers in dense, cymose inflorescences; matted, silky, white hairs on the leaves; usually long-lived; seeds itself freely; white- and purplish-flowered forms also occur.

Lychnis × haageana (*L. fulgens × L. coron-* *ata* var. *sieboldii*)	0.40 fiery red	VI–VIII, large-flowered hybrid; short-lived; dies down after flowering; good for cutting. *L. × arkwrightii* (*L. chalcedonica × L. × haageana*), orange-red; longer lived than *L. × haageana*; also good for cutting.
German catchfly *Lychnis viscaria* (*Viscaria vulgaris*) 'Atropurpurea' Balk., Rum.	0.40 dark red	V–VI, basal tufts of lanceolate leaves; sticky stems; rare in the trade. *L. viscaria,* pink; rarely available from nurseries; see list 3.2.2. *L. v.* 'Plena', pale magenta; double flowers. Selection: 'Fontaine', vigorous; good for cutting.
Salvia argentea S Eur.	0.70 white	VI–VII, large rosettes of silvery-white, hairy leaves; widely branched inflorescences; plants perennate if the stems are removed immediately after flowering.
Salvia haematodes (*S. pratensis* var. *haematodes*) Eur.	0.80 lavender blue	VI–VII, attractive, branching habit; ovate to heart-shaped leaves. Selection: 'Mittsommer'.
Clary *Salvia sclarea* Med., Nr East	1.00 pink and pale lilac	VI–VIII, green, wrinkled leaves; flowers with pink bracts in sturdy, branching panicles on stout, upright stems; aromatic; old medicinal plant and kitchen herb; seeds itself in mild areas.
Garden catchfly *Silene armeria* C S & E Eur.	0.30 pale red	VI–IX, abundant flowers in almost umbelliferous cymes on stiffly upright stems; seeds itself prolifically.

3.4.3.   Short-lived species for special uses

These powerful, eye-catching plants cannot easily be fitted into a perennial planting. However, if they are sown out onto bare, stony embankments and waste areas, they will seed themselves abundantly and quickly form impressive stands. After a few years they are usually crowded out by other species, but will often hold on in one or two places.

Sometimes it helps to scatter a little humus-rich soil over the area where seed is to be sown.

Musk thistle *Carduus nutans* Eur., Sib., Asia Minor, Cauc.	0.80 purple-red	VII–VIII, large, nodding flower heads; coarsely spined leaves; unsightly after flowering; biennial; rare in the trade. In the USA, this species has naturalised in dense colonies, making previously valuable pasture land unusable. To enforce eradication, several states now impose severe fines on landowners who allow these plants to grow.
Teasel *Dipsacus sylvestris* (*D. fullonum* ssp. *sylvestris*) Eur., Asia Minor, Cauc.	1.50 lilac	VII–VIII, decorative, imposing habit; stem-leaves fused into cups at their bases; cone-shaped inflorescences; popular for dried flower arrangements. *D. sativus* (*D. fullonum* ssp. *fullonum*) (1.80); long, cylindrical seed heads used for carding wool. *D. pilosus* (1.20), spherical, white-flowered inflorescences.

D. strigosus (2.00), similar.
All *Dipsacus* spp. thrive on rich and not too dry soils.

Viper's bugloss *Echium vulgare* Eur., W Asia	1.00 blue	VI–VIII, green leaves with bristle-like hairs; attractive habit; brightly coloured flowers; rarely available from nurseries; pink-, purple- and white-flowered forms available as seed.
Scotch thistle *Onopordum acanthium* Eur., Nr East	2.00 rosy red	VII–VIII, large, grey-green rosettes; attractive flower heads on powerful, branching stems; needs a lot of space. *O. tauricum* (0.50), deeply incised leaves with silvery white undersides.
Holy thistle *Silybum marianum* Med., Asia Minor, Cauc.	up to 1.50 purple-pink	VII–VIII, broad, scalloped, white-variegated leaves with yellow spines; inflorescences less ornamental; stems may be cut to prevent flowering; biennial; often naturalised; once a valued medicinal plant.
Verbascum spp.		List 3.3.2

3.4.4. Plants for well-spaced or dense planting

The following warmth- and sun-loving perennials grow best on moist or intermittently dry, nutrient-rich soil. Their appearance and requirements match those of the wild perennials with border character, and they associate well with these. In spring they are well complemented by vigorous varieties of tulip (list 4.1.4).

Achillea clypeolata Balk.	0.20/0.60 golden yellow	VII–VIII, silvery-grey foliage; long flowering season; blooms again in IX if cut back after flowering. Hybrid: 'Schwellenburg' (0.30), lemon yellow.
Achillea × taygetea	0.10/0.40 yellowish	VI–VII, silvery-white leaves; not very long-lived; needs frequent division; may be a pure species. 'Moonshine', pale lemon yellow.
Aster mongolicus N Asia, Jap.	0.70 lavender- blue, yellow disc	VII–IX, flowers in loosely branched, corymbose panicles; coarsely serrate, sessile, broad-lanceolate leaves. *A. sibiricus*, similar species with shorter stems and creeping rhizomes.
Centaurea uniflora ssp. *nervosa* (*C. nervosa*) Alps, N Appen., Balk.	0.40 pink	VI–VII, large composite flowers; hairy, coarsely serrate, broad-lanceolate leaves; rare in the trade.
Costmary, Bible-leaf *Chrysanthemum bal- samita* (*C. b.* var. *majus*) Asia Minor, Iran	0.80 yellow	VIII–IX, small, insignificant flowers; long, entire, balsam-scented leaves; spreading roots; sometimes needs staking; old medicinal and culinary herb.
Inula hybrida 'Garden Beauty'	0.30–0.40 golden yellow	VII–VIII, densely leafy, almost spherical habit; similar to *Buphthalmum salicifolium* but with larger flowers.

Malva alcea		List 2.3.2
Nepeta grandiflora 'Blue Beauty'		List 2.3.2
Nepeta nervosa Kashm.	0.40 pale blue	VII–VIII, dense spikes of flowers on stiffly upright stems; blue-green, crenate leaves; forms an open, bushy plant. Further *Nepeta* spp.: see list 3.3.3.
Origanum laevigatum Asia Minor	0.40 purple-red	VIII–X, narrow, glaucous leaves; dainty, erect panicles. 'Nymphenburg' (*O. vulgare* × *O. laevigatum*) (0.50), dark pink. 'Erntedank', 'Herrenhausen', similar; valuable for cutting.
Paeonia tenuifolia SE Eur., Asia Minor, Cauc.	0.60 fiery red	V–VI, finely dissected leaves; very ornamental in bud. 'Plena', red; double flowers. 'Rosea', pink. *P.* × *smouthii* (0.80), red; very long flowering season. Further *Paeonia* spp.: see list 2.3.4.
Phlomis samia		List 3.3.3
Balloon flower *Platycodon grandiflorus* China, Jap.	0.50 deep blue	VII–VIII, balloon-like buds; large, open bell-shaped flowers; stems branched near the top; emerges late; carrot-like roots; for moist, well-drained soils. 'Album' (0.50), white with blue veins. 'Apoyama' (0.20), blue (list 4.5.4). 'Mariesii' (0.40), blue. 'Perlmutterschale' (0.50), pink.
Potentilla argyrophylla W Him.	0.30 yellow	VI–VII, stiff, upright habit; basal leaves with matted white hairs. *P. megalantha* (*P. fragiformis*) (0.20), VI, golden yellow; coarser; attractive habit. Both species are rather short-lived. Also for bright semi-shade.
Potentilla atro- *sanguinea* Nepal	0.40 red	VI–VII, silvery leaves. 'Gibson's Scarlet', bright red flowers; green leaves. 'Scharlachkönigin', deep red; green leaves. 'Splendens', V–VI, blood-red; green leaves.
Potentilla nepalensis W Him.	0.30/0.50 pink to crimson	VI–VIII, green, strawberry-like leaves; red stems. 'Miss Willmott', pink. 'Roxana', coppery pink with a red eye. 'Flammenspiel', VII–IX, red with a yellow eye.
Potentilla hybrids	0.40/0.50	VI–VIII, similar to the above; green foliage; more upright habit; not very long-lived. Widely available cultivars: 'Flamenco', bright red. 'Yellow Queen', pure yellow; double. 'William Rollison', orange and yellow; semi-double. 'Emilie', blood-red; semi-double.
Potentilla recta		List 2.1.8

Orpine *Sedum telephium* (*S. purpurascens*) Eur., Cauc., Sib.	0.40 purple-red	VII–IX, flowers in terminal and axillary cymes; sessile, green, obovate, weakly serrate leaves. 'Atropurpureum' (0.50), purple-red; red leaves and stem. 'Munstead Red' (0.40), reddish brown; red-brown leaves.
Sedum cauticolum	List 4.3.1	
Sedum fabaria	List 4.3.1	
Sedum maximum	List 2.1.8	
Sedum spectabile	List 5.3.1	
Verbascum nigrum	List 3.3.2	
Veronica gentianoides	List 4.1.1.	

3.4.5.   Wild perennials with border character for sunny sites

These robust and sun-loving perennials for rich, well-drained, moist or intermittently dry soils have requirements that lie midway between those of wild and border perennials. Consequently, they may be combined with either the wild perennials from list 3.4.4 or the border perennials from list 5.3.2 (together with the tulips from list 5.4).

The species and cultivars that come from North America (list 3.4.6) are best used in plantings on their own.

Achillea millefolium 'Sammetriese' Eur., W Asia, Cauc.	0.80 deep red	VI–VIII, large, flat umbels on stout stems; fine, pinnately divided, grey-green leaves. Good selections: 'Kelwayi', 'Red Beauty' (0.40), red. 'Cerise Queen' (0.40), pink. 'Apfelblute' ('Appleblossom') (0.60), pale rose. 'Hoffnung' ('Great Expectations') (0.60), pale yellow. 'Lachsschönheit' ('Salmon Beauty') (0.60), salmon pink. 'Schwefelblute' ('Flowers of Sulphur') (0.60), pale lemon yellow. 'Wesersandstein' (0.80), coppery red.
Achillea filipendulina 'Parker' Cauc., Asia Minor	up to 1.20 golden yellow	VI–VIII, flat, sturdy umbels on powerful stems set with grey-green, pinnate leaves; removal of the first, exceptionally large inflorescences promotes a long flowering season; good for dried flower arrangements. 'Gold Plate', similar to the above. 'Altgold' (0.60), open habit; good for cutting.
Achillea 'Coronation Gold'	0.70 golden yellow	VI–VIII, somewhat greyer foliage than the previous varieties; reliable and indispensable plant. 'Neugold' (0.50), shorter.
Achillea sibirica N Asia, Jap., N Am.	up to 1.00 white	VII–IX, straight stems; flowers and leaves larger and coarser than those of *A. millefolium*.
Aster sedifolius (*A. acris*) 'Nanus' E C & E Eur., N Asia	0.20/0.30 lavender-blue	IX–X, erect stems with dense, narrow, linear leaves; does not flop over like the species (*A. sedifolius*, 0.80). 'Nanus Roseus', pink; still rare in the trade.

Aster tongolensis (*A. subcoeruleus*) W China	0.10/0.50 violet orange disc	VI, large blooms on long stems over flat carpets of long, sturdy, oval, entire leaves; not very long-lived, must be transplanted every 3–4 years; good for cutting. Large-flowered selections: 'Leuchtenburg' (0.50). 'Berggarten' (0.50). 'Wartburgstern' (0.40). 'Sternschnuppe' (0.40). 'Elfriede' (0.40). 'Napsbury' (0.50), probably *A. yunnanensis*.
Aster amellus cultivars		List 5.3.2
Clustered bellflower *Campanula glomerata* 'Superba' Eur., Cauc., Iran	0.50 violet	VII, terminal clusters of large, stalkless bells; rough, broad-lanceolate leaves; unsightly after flowering; see also list 3.2.1. 'Acaulis' (0.10), violet. 'Dahurica' (0.60), dark violet. 'Joan Elliott' (0.40), violet; early. 'Schneehäschen' (0.15), white. 'Schneekrone' (0.50), white.
Campanula persicifolia cultivars		List 2.1.7
Great golden knapweed *Centaurea macrocephala* Arm., Cauc.	1.00 yellow	VI–VII, exceptionally large flower heads on strong, leafy, unbranched stems; not very attractive after flowering; best as an isolated specimen.
Centaurea glastifolia Asia Minor	1.00 yellow	VI–IX, branching stems; long, lanceolate leaves; valuable, long-lasting cut flower.
Coreopsis verticillata		List 3.4.6
Globe thistle *Echinops banaticus* 'Taplow Blue' SE Eur.	1.10 blue	VII–IX, spiny, spherical inflorescences; forms a massive, densely leafy plant; does not flop. 'Blue Globe' (1.50), deep violet. *E. ritro* 'Veitch's Blue' (0.80), intense blue inflorescences. Further species, see list 3.4.8.
Elecampane *Inula helenium* W Asia	up to 1.50 yellow	VII–VIII, large flowers on thick, branching stems; large, serrate, elliptic leaves with matted hairs beneath.
Inula hookeri Sikkim	0.60–1.00 yellow	VIII–IX, abundant large flowers in loose corymbs; bushy habit; hairy, broad-lanceolate leaves; very robust and long-lived. *I. royleana* (0.50), orange-yellow; very large flowers; hairy, ovate leaves; sensitive to damp; seldom true in the trade.
Inula orientalis (*I. glandulosa*) Cauc., Asia Minor	0.50 (to 1.00) orange-yellow	VII–VIII, large flowers on strong, leafy, unbranched stems; hairy, lanceolate leaves; flowers quickly fade.
Knautia macedonica C Balk.	1.80 blood-red	VI–VIII, small flowerheads on stiff, loosely branching stems; very long flowering season.

Leuzea rhapontica (*Centaurea rhapontica*) S Alps	0.40/1.50 lilac-pink	VII–VIII, large, silvery grey, onion-shaped buds on tall, sturdy, little-branched stems; large, matt green leaves, grey-green beneath; good for cutting; needs a rich, open soil.
Maltese cross *Lychnis chalcedonica* C, SW & SE Russ.	0.70/0.80 brick-red	VI–VIII, flowers in umbels on rigid, densely leafy stems; blooms again in autumn if cut back to about 30 cm after flowering.
Salvia nemorosa 'Ostfriesland' SE Eur., SW Asia	0.50 dark violet	VI–VII, reliable, bushy plant. 'Superba' (*S. n.* × *S. amplexicaulis*) (0.70), pale violet; taller than the previous variety; reddish-violet bracts remain attractive when the flowers have faded; blooms again in autumn if cut back after flowering. 'Blauhügel' (0.60), lavender-blue; blooms again in autumn if cut back after flowering. 'Blaukönigin' (0.50), dark violet. 'Wesuwe', taller than 'Ostfriesland'. 'Primavera' (0.60), dark violet; very vigorous.
Salvia 'Mainacht' (*S. pratensis* × *S. nemorosa*)	0.50 deep blue	VI–VII, intense blue-black flowers appearing very early in the season; stiff, upright habit. 'Viola Klose' (0.40), V–VI, deep blue; very early. 'Laurin' (0.30), VI–IX, violet-blue. All bloom again in autumn if cut back after flowering.
Scabiosa caucasica		List 5.3.2
Yellow scabious *Scabiosa ochroleuca* Eur., W Asia, Sib.	0.60 pale yellow	VI–X, flowers on long, much-branched stems; grey-green, pinnate or bipinnate leaves; up to 80 cm tall on moist soils; not very long-lived.
Skullcap *Scutellaria incana* (*S. canescens*) C & SE USA	0.80 light blue	VIII–IX, upright plant with grey-green foliage; valuable on loamy soils; uncommon.
Sedum telephium 'Herbstfreude'		List 5.3.1
Verbena hastata N Am.	0.80 violet	VII, attractive, slender habit; seeds itself well; rare in the trade. 'Alba', white flowers.
Veronica subsessilis (*V. longifolia* 'Subsessilis') (*V. hendersonii* hort.) Eur., Asia	up to 0.50 dark blue	VII–IX, luxuriant spires of flowers on stiff stems; short-lived.

Grasses

Achnatherum cala-magrostis	List 3.4.1
Achnatherum pekinense	List 3.3.4
Molinia arundinacea	List 3.5.3

Sesleria autumnalis		List 3.3.4
Stipa viridula		List 3.3.4

3.4.6.   North American wild perennials with border character

The following species thrive on sunny sites with nutrient-rich, moist or intermittently dry soil. The list also includes several border perennials that associate particularly well with the wild species.

Aster laevis N Am.	1.50 lavender-blue	IX, healthy, vigorous, reliable and incomparably beautiful species with elegant, slightly overhanging shoots; abundant flowers; often grows wild in woodland edge habitats, especially on steep banks; rare in the trade.
Wild indigo *Baptisia australis* E USA	1.00 violet-blue	VI–VII, bushy habit; dense, glaucous green foliage; very reliable and healthy; rare in the trade.
Boltonia asteroides		List 3.4.8
Green-and-Gold *Chrysogonum virginianum* E USA	0.25 yellow	VII, zinnia-like flowers; compact, leafy habit; undemanding and easy to propagate; forms lush plants in mild areas.
Coreopsis grandiflora		List 5.5
Coreopsis lanceolata 'Goldfink' N Am.	0.25 golden yellow	VII–IX, compact habit; abundant flowers. 'Lichtstadt' (0.25), golden yellow with a brown eye. 'Rotkehlchen' (0.30). 'Sterntaler' (0.30). All rather short-lived. Varieties for cutting: see list 5.5.
Coreopsis tripteris		List 3.5.4
Coreopsis verticillata 'Grandiflora' ('Golden shower') SE USA	0.70 yellow	VIII, dark green, needle-like foliage; very long-lived; remains neat and attractive after flowering. 'Zagreb' (0.25), golden yellow; vigorous dwarf form. 'Moonbeam' (0.40), pale yellow.
Fleabane *Erigeron speciosus* 'Mrs E. H. Beale' N Am.	0.40 pale lilac	VI, fine-rayed, daisy-like flowers; stiff, low habit; flowers early and long. Border varieties: see list 5.3.4.
Erigeron pulchellus N AM.	0.30 violet	V–VI, leaves with long, soft hairs; spreading roots.
Helenium hoopesii W USA	0.60 golden orange	VI, large flowers on strong, branching stems; long, glossy leaves in whorl-like clusters.
Liatris pycnostachya USA	0.81–1.20 rose-purple	VII–IX, tiny composite flowers in spikes up to 40 cm long; dense, linear leaves. *L. elegans* (0.70), red flowers; heavily spotted leaves. *L. cylindrica* (0.30), purple-violet; large individual flowers.

Gay feathers *Liatris spicata* C & E USA	0.80 rose-purple	VII–X, important plant for cutting; unusual, club-like spikes of flowers, opening downwards from the top. 'Kobold' (0.40). 'Alba' (0.60), white. 'Floristan Violett' (0.90), violet. 'Floristan Weiß' (0.90), pure white. 'September Glory' (0.90), light purple. 'Picador' (0.90), deep purple; intense autumn colour. *L. scariosa* (0.70), broad, open, almost racemose inflorescences. 'Magnifica' (0.70), white; large individual flowers. 'Snow White' (0.70), white; large inflorescences. All *Liatris* spp. are sensitive to damp in winter, but tolerate extreme drought and thrive in sandy soil.
Lobelia siphilitica		List 3.5.4
Evening primrose *Oenothera tetragona* (*O. glauca*) (*O. glabra*) 'Fyrverkeri' S Appal.	0.40 golden yellow	VI–VIII, bronze-coloured leaf rosettes; red flower-buds. 'Hohes Licht' (0.60), yellow; especially free-flowering. 'Sonnenwende' (0.50), golden yellow; dark foliage.
Oenothera fruticosa 'Yellow River' C & E USA	0.40 golden yellow	VII, large blooms on reddish stems which are branched above. Particularly large-flowered selections: 'Moonlight' (0.70), bright yellow. 'Silvery Moon' (0.70), pale yellow.
Oenothera speciosa USA, Mex.	0.10/0.40 white or pink	VII–IX, invasive but does not thrive everywhere; flowers until autumn; rare in the trade. *O.* × *arendsii* 'Bowles', pink.
Penstemon barbatus (*Chelone barbatus*) Utah to Mex.	0.80–1.00 vermilion	VII–IX, narrow, bell-shaped flowers in loose inflorescences on stems that are prone to flop; lanceolate leaves; popular for cutting; short-lived; larger-flowering, violet, white and pink cultivars also available.
Penstemon barbatus 'Praecox Nanus'	0.40–0.50	VII–IX, similar to the type but shorter in growth; slender racemes in red, pink, violet, etc.; short-lived.
Penstemon confertus W USA	0.40 yellowish white	VII, dense, whorled inflorescences; smooth, broad-lanceolate leaves; forms turf-like mats; native to dry, sandy pinewoods.
Penstemon hirsutus (*P. pubescens*) 'Pygmaeus' N AM.	0.20/0.30 whitish	VI–VII, abundant, bearded flowers in open inflorescences; long flowering season; grey foliage; reliable and fully hardy.
Penstemon digitalis (*P. laevigatus digitalis*) E USA	0.20/0.60 white	VII–VIII, stiff, upright inflorescences; healthy and long-lived. 'Nanus' (0.30), V–VI; semi-evergreen.
Penstemon ovatus N–AM.	1.00 blue-purple	V–VI, flowers in dense whorls; oval basal leaves; short-lived.

Phlox Arendsii hybrids (*P. divaricata* × *P. paniculata*) (*P. arendsii* hort.)	0.40–0.60 various	VI–VII, early-flowering phlox hybrids with generous, broad umbels on hard, wiry stems; formerly more popular than today; fit well into plantings of wild perennials with border character; not for dry, sunny sites; prefer dry shade. Available selections: 'Anja', purple-red. 'Hilda', pale lavender with a pink eye. 'Susanne', white with a red centre.
Phlox Maculata hybrids (*P. carolina* × *P. maculata*)	0.70–1.50 white, pink, lilac-pink	VI–VIII, border perennials with growth requirements similar to *P. paniculata*; somewhat smaller flowers in narrower panicles on stiff, purple-spotted stems; smooth, long pointed, broad-lanceolate leaves. Early cultivars (VI–VII) with narrow panicles: 'Magnificence' (0.70), pink. 'Miss Lingard' (0.80), white. Late cultivars (VII–VIII) with long, cylindrical panicles: 'Alpha' (to 1.00), lilac-pink. 'Rosalinde' (1.00), pink. 'Schneelawne' (1.00), white.
Rudbeckia laciniata		List 3.5.4
Rudbeckia fulgida var. *speciosa* (*R. newmannii*) USA	0.50 golden yellow rays, black disc	VIII–X, prolifically flowering, robust and beautiful wild species; hairy, ovate–lanceolate leaves in dense clusters; somewhat overshadowed by the vigorous and large-flowered *R. fulgida sullivantii* 'Goldsturm' in the trade.
Salvia azurea 'Grandiflora' C & E USA	1.00 deep blue	X–XI, stiff, upright stems; grey-green foliage; valuable flower for late autumn; well-drained, loamy soils; sensitive to frost on sand.
Sidalcea × *cultorum*		List 5.5
Solidago cutleri (*S. brachystachys* hort.) 'Robusta'		List 5.3.4
Wreath goldenrod *Solidago caesia* N Am.	0.90 yellow	VIII–IX, dainty, arching, wiry stems; flowers in the leaf axils. *S. graminifolia* (up to 1.00), IX, linear-lanceolate leaves; yellow terminal inflorescences on stiff, branching stems; not available in the trade.
Solidago rigida N Am.	up to 1.50 white, with yellow centres	VIII–X, comparatively large, white ray-florets; decorative, domed inflorescences on sturdy, brown stems; oval, hairy leaves; rhizomatous and often invasive; still rare in the trade.
Solidago virgaurea (*S.* × *hybrida*) 'Praecox'	0.40 yellow	VII and IX, early flowering selection with slender, rigid stems and narrow panicles; blooms again if cut back after flowering. Further *Solidago* spp: see list 5.3.4.

Culver's root, Bowman's root *Veronica virginica* (*Veronicastrum virginicum*) N Am.	1.50 white to pale blue	VII–VIII, stiff, attractive habit; whorled leaves; flowers in terminal and axillary racemes. 'Alba', white. 'Rosea', pink.
× *Solidaster luteus* (*Aster ptarmicoides* × *Solidago* sp.)	0.60 pale yellow	VII–IX, flowers in much-branched inflorescences; narrow, linear leaves; valuable for cutting; long flowering season; stems tend to sprawl; invasive, to be used with caution.

3.4.7. Grasses

The following species are suitable for planting with either wild perennials (especially those with border character) or border perennials. Several more compact, clump-forming species appear in list 3.4.1.

Achnatherum calamagrostis		List 3.4.1
Calamagrostis × *acutiflora* 'Karl Foerster'	1.70	VI–VIII, similar to *C. epigeios,* but clump-forming and not invasive; dark brown, stiffly upright stems; slender inflorescences, which turn yellow on ripening; remains attractive into winter; very undemanding.
Bottlebrush grass *Hystrix patula* E USA	0.80	VII–IX, stiff, clump-forming habit with stiff-looking flower heads; seeds itself prolifically.
Panicum bulbosum SW USA to Mex.	0.50/1.20	VII–VIII, many straight stems with swollen bases; panicles of reddish-brown spikelets; powerful, leafy, *Molinia*-like clumps of narrow, blue-green leaves; seeds itself prolifically; rare in the trade.
Switch grass *Panicum virgatum* 'Strictum' N Am., Mex.	1.70	VIII–IX, vigorous, upright clumps with many stems; graceful, open panicles; stiffer and more rain-proof than the type. *P. maximum,* seldom produces flowers; tender.
Panicum virgatum 'Rehbraun'	1.20	VIII–IX, reddish-brown leaves; shorter-growing than the previous cultivar. 'Hänse Herms' and 'Rotstrahlbusch' are very similar.
Pennisetum spp.		List 3.4.1
Indian grass *Sorghastrum nutans* (*Chrysopogon nutans*) N AM., Mex.	1.20	IX–X, clumps begin growth late and do not flower until September; stiff, slender habit; brownish stems and amber-gold flower heads; beautiful in winter.

Tall, attractive, but strongly invasive grasses

The following are best used in special situations where their invasive character is of no consequence. They need a sunny site with moist or intermittently dry soil.

Elymus arenarius	List 3.3.3

Amur silver grass *Miscanthus sacchari-* *florus* 'Robustus' Jap., N China, Korea		IX–XII, reed-like leaves, which turn brown in autumn; large, silky, silvery-white inflorescences; very vigorous in damp or wet soils; sensitive to drought. Further *Miscanthus* spp.: see list 3.6.1.
Pennisetum incomptum (*P. flaccidum*) Him., Manch.	1.00	VII–X, dense grass with invasive rhizomes; flowers from July onwards; needs a lot of space.

3.4.8.   Tall, specimen perennials

These powerful, mostly rather invasive species, for rich, moist soils in full sun, can seldom be combined with plants from the previous lists. They function well as specimen plants grown against walls or on a sunny woodland edge.

Bear's breeches *Acanthus longifolius* (*A. balcanicus*) (*A. hungaricus*) Balk.	0.80–1.20 pink and white	VII, stately spikes of flowers; ornamental, pinnately lobed and divided leaves; spreads strongly in the course of time; for nutrient-rich soils; sensitive to extreme cold. 'Stele' (0.80), attractive selection. *A. mollis,* hairy leaves up to 60 cm long; less hardy. *A. spinosus:* see list 3.3.3.
Common milkweed *Asclepias syriaca* (*A. cornuti*) N Am.	up to 2.00 pale pink or, greenish white	VII–IX, honey-scented flowers in large umbellate cymes on very sturdy stems; hard, broad, oval leaves with white, woolly hairs beneath; cucumber-shaped fruit capsules with seeds bearing long, silky hairs; rhizomatous; very invasive on sandy soils; fully hardy.
Boltonia asteroides var *latisquama* C USA	2.00 bluish white	IX–X, fine-rayed composite flowers in large, loosely branching panicles; normally needs staking in a cool, damp climate; rare in the trade. *B. asteroides* 'Nana' (0.90), VIII–IX, rewarding plant; good for cutting.
Cephalaria gigantea (*C. tatarica*) Cauc.	2.50 pale yellow	VII, very imposing plant, with bold foliage; sometimes needs staking. *C. alpina* (1.60), VI–IX, pale yellow. *C. ruthenica* (1.50–2.00), VII–VIII, sulphur yellow; see list 2.1.7.
Globe thistle *Echinops exaltatus* E C Eur., N It., N Balk.	1.70 blue	VIII–IX, more widely available than *E. ritro*; tall, stately plant; very long-lived and undemanding.
Echinops sphaer- *ocephalus* Eur., Sib., Cauc.	1.80 whitish	VIII–IX, similar to the previous species. Selection: 'Niveus'. All *Echinops* spp. are good bee plants.
Echinops ritro S, SE & C Eur.	1.10 steel-blue	VII–VIII, very hardy and robust; spreads strongly on porous, nutrient-rich soils. Shorter forms: see list 3.4.5.
Inula magnifica Cauc.	2.00 whitish	VIII, bold leaves with matted hairs beneath; large flowers; spreading habit but stems do not flop; see also list 3.4.5.

Plume poppy *Macleaya cordata* (*M. yedoensis*) Jap., China	2.50 whitish	VII–VIII, formerly *Bocconia*; feathery panicles; very decorative and sturdy; blue-green foliage; extremely invasive, especially on sandy soil.
Macleaya microcarpa China	2.50 ochre	VII, similar to the previous species and just as invasive; flowers somewhat earlier; leaves hairy beneath; bronze coloured inflorescences. 'Coral Plume' ('Korallenfeder'), very decorative selection.

3.5.   Perennials for sun or bright shade on moist to damp soils

Perennials that grow wild in wet meadows and other waterside habitats are usually dependent on damp soils in the garden. Some grow particularly well close to water, but many others thrive in damp woodland edge conditions (see lists 2.2.4 and 2.3.1) or in a cultivated bed with border perennials (see list 5.3.5).

In the following lists, the different species have been classified according to their flowering season. This reflects the most appropriate grouping for parks and large gardens, where the plantings should be designed to flower at just one time of year. Though this entails long periods without flowers, it should be remembered that a planting is always neat and attractive before it starts to flower. In a small garden, the spring-, summer- and autumn-flowering species might well be set together to create a longer season. Nevertheless, it is worth arranging the plants in groups that bloom simultaneously, thus creating the right effect at flowering time and making it easier to cut down the stems afterwards with a sickle or scythe.

3.5.1.   Species that flower in spring and early summer (meadow perennials)

The following are primarily plants for damp soils, though many will also thrive in moist loam. Most of them are unsightly once flowering is over, and the plantings must then be cut down like a meadow. Often they will flower again in autumn.

Low, creeping, meadow plants can be found in list 2.1.3. Combined with the species that are listed here, they require considerable maintenance. If the planting is extensively maintained (e.g. by mowing twice a year), then such low-growing plants are swallowed up in the dense cover, and are hardly noticeable after a couple of years.

The selected forms of perennials such as *Trollius* and *Polemonium* have been assigned to list 5.3.5. If the early summer cut is postponed, then undemanding *Narcissus* spp. (list 2.4.3) may also be grown.

Lady's smock *Cardamine pratensis* 'Plena' Eur., C Asia, N AM.	0.30 lilac	IV–VI, erect stems and pinnate foliage; flowers reminiscent of stocks; rare in the trade. *C. pratensis,* single flowers; seeds itself prolifically.
Brook thistle *Cirsium rivulare* C, E & SE Eur.	1.40 purple-red	VI–VII, 1–5 composite flowers on stems that are leafy below; decorative species.
Meadowsweet *Filipendula ulmaria* 'Plena' Eur., W Asia, N Sib.	1.00 white	VI–VII, very robust; green, irregularly pinnate leaves; double flowers. *F. u.* 'Aurea', pale yellowish foliage.

Meadow cranesbill *Geranium pratense* Eur., N Asia, Cauc., Him.	0.70 blue-violet	VI–VII, flowers in branched inflorescences; best propagated from seed; mostly double-flowered forms in the trade. 'Album', white. 'Birch Lilac' (0.70), VII; blue-flowered hybrid. 'Kashmir Purple', purple.
Geranium psilostemon Arm.	0.90 cherry red	VI–VII, forms broad clumps of upright stems; unimposing once the flowers have faded. 'Bressingham Flair' (0.60), cherry red.
Geum rivale 'Leonard's Variety'		List 2.3.1
Jacob's ladder *Polemonium caeruleum* N & C Eur., Yug., S Russ., C Asia, Sib.	0.20/0.70 blue	V–VI, bell-shaped flowers; elegantly pinnate leaves; blooms again in VI–VIII if cut back after flowering; short-lived but seeds itself prolifically. Cultivars: see list 5.3.5.
Bistort *Polygonum bistorta* 'Superbum' Eur., Asia	1.00 reddish white	V–VII, dense, cylindrical inflorescences on straight stems; elongate–ovate leaves, blue-green below; robust and very invasive.
Polygonum sericeum Sib.	0.60 (1.50) white	V–VI, bushy; not invasive; flowers long and prolifically.
Double buttercup *Ranunculus acris* 'Multiplex' Eur., Asia, N AM.	0.60 yellow	VI, very long flowering season; stiff, open habit.
Great burnet *Sanguisorba officinalis* 'Rubra' Eur., Asia	up to 1.00 dark red	VII–VIII, short, cylindrical inflorescences on long stems; very attractive in a meadow; rarely available in the trade; to be sown *in situ* or raised from seed.
Sanguisorba obtusa (*Poterium obtusum*) Jap.	1.00 pink	VII, rather floppy stems but stays upright in a meadow; distinctive spikes of flowers; robust.
Thalictrum aqui-legifolium		List 2.2.2
Globe flower *Trollius europaeus* Eur., Cauc., Arct. N Am.	0.50 light yellow	V–VI, globe-shaped flowers; lush green, palmately divided leaves. 'Superbus' (0.60), VI–VII, pale lemon yellow; late flowering. Hybrids: see list 5.3.5.
Chinese globe flower *Trollius chinensis* NE China	0.25/0.70 orange	VII, bowl-shaped flowers. 'Golden Queen', common in the trade; see list 5.3.5.

Direct sowings in moist to damp, grassy areas (in W Europe)

There have been few systematic attempts to sow meadow perennials into damp, sparse areas of lawn. Nevertheless, the results are encouraging. Suitable species include *Cardamine pratensis, Cirsium rivulare, Geranium pratense, Polemonium caeruleum, Sanguisorba officinalis* and *Thalictrum aquilegifolium,* though it is sometimes difficult to obtain seed of these. If the grass is subsequently mown twice a year (VI–VII and X) then the area may be turned into a flowering meadow.

3.5.2. Species that flower in late spring and summer

The distinctive and often somewhat bizarre-looking perennials in the following list tolerate longer periods of drought than meadow plants. In contrast to the species from list 3.5.1, they need not be cut down during the growing season.

Marsh mallow *Althaea officinalis* Eur., Sib., Nr East	1.40 (2.00) pale lilac	VII–IX, axillary clusters of rather insignificant flowers; grey-hairy leaves; bushy habit; medicinal plant.
Amsonia tabernae- montana E USA	0.80 pale blue	VI–VII, abundant, small, starry flowers, borne terminally on leafy stems; smooth, oval–lanceolate leaves; rare in the trade. *A. illustris,* slightly taller, with larger, brighter flowers.
Swamp milkweed *Asclepias incarnata* N Am.	1.10 red or pink	VII, vanilla-scented flowers in umbellate cymes on sturdy stems with smooth, elongate-lanceolate leaves; short rhizomes. 'Alba', white.
Boltonia asteroides USA	0.80 (2.00) white, pink or lavender	VIII–IX, daisy-like flowers in large, open inflorescences on rigid, upright stems; narrow, glabrous, blue-green leaves; undemanding.
Camassia cusickii Oregon	1.00 pale blue	V–VI, bulbous species with long, linear leaves and imposing spikes of flowers; dies down in August; uncommon; fully hardy. *C. leichtlinii* (0.80), Br. Col. to Calif.; large, creamy-white flowers. *C. l.* ssp. *suksdorfii,* bright blue. 'Atrocaerulea', deep blue-violet. 'Alba', white.
Camassia quamash (*C. esculenta*) 'Orion' W N Am.	0.30–0.60 deep blue	IV–V, flowers in racemes on slender stems; leaves up to 30 cm long; edible bulbs. 'Purpureocaerulea', violet-blue; needs a winter covering of leaves in cold areas.
Carex grayi E N Am.	0.60	VI, clumps of decorative, bright green leaves; large, star-shaped seed heads; undemanding and long-lived.
Eryngium yuccifolium USA	0.70 whitish	VII–IX, lush, green basal leaves with bristly-spiny edges; for moist to damp, loamy soils. *E. aquaticum* (0.90), VII–VIII; similar to the above; long, entire leaves, toothed at the tips; somewhat tender; must be kept dry in winter.

Yellow gentian *Gentiana lutea* Alps, Pyren., Carp., Balk.	up to 1.00 yellow	VI–VIII, starry flowers; whorled bracts on sturdy, upright stems; opposite, glabrous, blue-green, broad-elliptic leaves; decorative as an isolated specimen; for periodically moist, loamy soils.
Gladiolus imbricatus E & SE Eur., Sib., Cauc.	0.30–0.80 purple-red	VII, fairly crowded, one-sided inflorescences; large flowers; corms 2 cm across. *G. illyricus* (up to 0.50), V, smaller flowers in loose inflorescences; very hardy; rare in the trade. See also list 6.4.2 (*G. palustris*).
Hemerocallis spp.		List 2.3.1
Iris chrysographes Yunn.	0.30/0.50 deep purple-violet	VI, very dainty, finely marked flowers with golden yellow streaks; reed-like leaves. Selection: 'Stjerneskud', dark violet and golden yellow. *I. × chrysophor* (0.50), unusual, spotted and marked flowers.
Iris ensata (*I. lactea*) China, Jap.	0.80/0.40 light blue	VI–VII, variable species; narrow, bluish, grass-like leaves up to 80 cm long; unbranched stems.
Iris brevicaulis (*I. foliosa*) USA	0.40/0.15 bright blue and white	VI, leafy, zig-zag stems; enthusiasts' plant for dryish soils.
Iris fulva × I. brevicaulis 'Dorothea K. Wil- liamson'	0.70 reddish purple, yellow centre	VII, spreading habit; broad leaves; refined flowers; spreads strongly.
Iris forrestii Yunn.	0.30/0.50 yellow	V–VI, very dainty and beautiful foliage; upright standards, brown-veined falls.
Iris koreana Korea, Manch.	0.50/0.40 mid-blue	VI, narrow leaves; abundant large flowers; vigorous.
Iris pseudacorus	List 6.2.2	Attractive, vigorous, shallow-water species; also for moist to damp soils.
Iris sanguinea		List 5.3.5
Iris sibirica C & E Eur., Cauc., Sib.	0.80 blue	VI, clumps of narrow, dark green leaves, which turn russet brown in autumn. Selections: see list 5.3.5.
Iris versicolor N Am.	0.60 reddish-purple	VI, broader leaves than the previous species; robust, with spreading rhizomes; terminal inflorescences of 2–3 flowers; grows less tall in dry conditions. 'Kermesina', intense red flowers; vigorous. *I. delavayi* (1.00), Yunn., violet; rarely available in the trade.
Iris wilsonii W China	0.30/0.50 yellowish-white	V–VI, leaves up to 1 cm wide; flowers with a dark blotch and red-brown veins; somewhat tender.
Leucojum aestivum		List 6.3

Lythrum virgatum 'Rose Queen' SE & E Eur., W Asia	0.70 pink	VIII, attractive, dainty habit; lanceolate to linear leaves, narrowed at the base; similar to *L. salicaria* (list 3.5.4) but more freely branched and with somewhat smaller flowers.
Orange mint *Mentha × citrata* (*M. × piperita citrata*) (*M. odorata*)	0.30 rosy-purple	VII–VIII, flowers in short, rounded spikes on branching stems; rounded, broad-oval, lemon-scented leaves; for a sunny position on damp soil; invasive,
Penny-royal *Mentha pulegium* S, W & C Eur., Nr East	0.30 blue	VII–IX, flowers in axillary whorls; strongly aromatic; decumbent stems; ovate leaves with short petioles; spreads mostly by means of stolons; old medicinal plant.
Apple mint *Mentha × rotundifolia* W Eur., W Med.	0.60 pale blue	VII–IX, dense, spike-like inflorescences; grey-hairy, ovate, round-toothed leaves; invasive.
Mentha × rotundifolia 'Variegata'	0.50 pale blue	VII, very vigorous and invasive; spreads by means of stolons; flowers in dense, spike-like inflorescences on erect stems; softly hairy, wrinkled, white-variegated, broad-ovate leaves. 'Bowles' Variety' (to 0.30), green and white leaves.
Spearmint *Mentha spicata* SW Fr. to Dalm.	0.30–0.80 lilac	VII–IX, terminal, spike-like inflorescences; strongly aromatic; fresh green, glabrous, elongate-ovate leaves; stems often flushed red; invasive; old culture plant; thrives in warmth. *M. longifolia* and *M. crispa*: see list 7.2
Polygonum carneum Iran, Turk.	0.60 Pink	V–VI, masses of cylindrical inflorescences over compact clumps of foliage; not invasive.
Polygonum milletii W China, Him.	0.40 dark red	VI–VII, similar to the previous species but with narrower leaves; still rare in the trade.
Rudbeckia maxima S USA	2.00 yellow	VIII–IX, striking, tall black cones in the centre of each large composite flower; sturdy, almost leafless stems over large, smooth, bluish, entire basal leaves; for periodically damp soils; thrives as an isolated specimen.
White false helleborine *Veratrum album* Eur., Sib., E Asia, Alaska	up to 1.50 whitish	VI–VIII, abundant, starry flowers in upright panicles on powerful stems; green, glaucous, alternate, broad-oval leaves, hairy beneath; decorative as an isolated specimen in a sunny position; for moist to wet, nutrient-rich soils; rarely available in the trade.
Zigadenus elegans N Am.	0.80 greenish-white	VI–VIII, star-shaped flowers in loose racemes on stiff, leafless stems; long, grooved, linear, grey-green leaves; bulbous species; very poisonous.

3.5.3. Tall grasses for more or less damp, sunny places

Miscanthus sinensis 'Purpurascens' Him.	1.00	Clumps of reed-like foliage which turn reddish brown in summer; rarely produces flowers. Further *Miscanthus* spp.: see list 3.6.1.

Molinia arundinacea 'Karl Foerster' Eur.	0.50/1.80	VI–VIII, makes large clumps; smooth, leafless stems; golden autumn colour in October. Further selections: 'Bergfreund'; 'Fontäne'; 'Transparent', fine panicles; 'Windspiel' (2.00); 'Moorfeuer' (0.40/0.80). For periodically damp to dry soils.
Panic grass *Panicum clandestinum* N Am.	up to 1.20	VII–VIII, broad, oval leaves; slightly reminiscent of bamboo; brownish inflorescences hidden among the foliage.
Fountain grass *Pennisetum alope- curoides* (*P. japonicum*) Jap.	1.00/1.50	VIII–IX, imposing clumps of long, elegantly arching leaves; cylindrical, white-tipped inflorescences; for a warm position. Further *Pennisetum* spp.: see list 3.4.1.
Spartina michauxiana		List 3.5.4
Spodiopogon sibiricus Sib., Jap., China	up to 1.50	VII–IX, rigid-leaved stems arising from dense clumps; stiff panicles; good for cutting.
Uniola latifolia (*Chasmanthium lati- folium*)	1.00	IX–X, dark green, leafy clumps; large, flattened spike- lets in loose panicles; useful for dried flower arrange- ments; thrives in a warm summer.

3.5.4.   Species that flower in high summer and autumn (tall herbs and grasses with border character)

The following mostly robust and vigorous perennials grow wild in waterside and meadow-like habitats. In gardens they grow best in a sunny position on moist to damp, nutrient-rich soil, but will also tolerate bright semi-shade and short periods of drought. With a certain amount of maintenance they will thrive in damp woodland edge conditions, together with the perennials from list 2.2.4. Alternatively, they might be used in a border planting (list 5.3.5) or in the vicinity of water (list 6.3). In a large-scale planting, it is best not to mix them with earlier-flowering species, which tend to be unsightly if they are not cut down after flowering. Nevertheless, it is possible to liven up a small planting with spring-flowering narcissi, which are quickly hidden by emerging foliage once they start to fade.

Turtle head *Chelone obliqua* E USA	0.80–1.00 pink	VIII–IX, dense, terminal spikes of flowers; ample, dark green foliage; pointed, broad-lanceolate leaves. 'Alba', white; not so vigorous.
Autumn marguerite *Chrysanthemum ser- otinum* (*C. uliginosum*) SE Eur.	1.50 white	X, very erect habit; beautiful, large daisy-like flowers on tall stems. 'Herbststern', yellow, as opposed to green, discs.
Tall tickseed *Coreopsis tripteris* E USA	up to 2.00 light yellow	VIII–IX, upright stems with well-spaced foliage; bran- ched above; ornamental, slender habit; impressive as an isolated specimen; grows naturally in woodland edge conditions in the southern part of its range.
Hemp agrimony *Eupatorium can- nabinum* 'Plenum' Eur., Asia Minor, Cauc., W Sib.	1.20 reddish	VII–IX, imposing, leafy clumps; dense-flowered, corymbose panicles; undemanding. 'Album', white.

White snakeroot *Eupatorium rugosum* (*E. ageratoides*) N Am.	1.00 white	VIII–IX, green, sharply dentate, ovate leaves; double white flowers; long-lived; seeds itself freely. *E. coelestinum* (0.90), VIII–IX, blue.
Filipendula palmata 'Elegans' E Asia	1.00 white, with red stamens	VII–VIII, rigid, dark green, leafy stems.
Queen-of-the-Prairie *Filipendula rubra* 'Venusta' E USA	up to 1.50 pink	VII, tall, leafy stems; very long-lived; remains attractive after flowering. *F. r.* 'Venusta Magnifica', magenta. *F. ulmaria*: see list 3.5.1.
Veronica virginica		List 3.4.6
Ligularia spp.		List 2.2.4
Great blue lobelia *Lobelia siphilitica* N Am	0.80 blue	VIII–X, ridged stems with somewhat hairy, oval to lanceolate leaves; indispensable prolifically flowering, autumn perennial; good for cutting. 'Alba', white.
Lobelia × *vedrariensis* (*L. fulgens* × *L. siphilitica*) 'Blauzauber'	0.50 purple-violet	VIII–IX, narrow spikes of flowers on stiff stems; broad-lanceolate leaves; somewhat tender and not very long-lived. *L.* × *gerardii* (0.70), violet. 'Rosenkavalier' (0.50), magenta.
Lysimachia clethroides Jap., China	up to 1.00 white	VII–IX, slightly arching, white-flowered inflorescences over healthy-looking, broad-ovate foliage; long flowering season; stems lose their leaves early and are best hidden behind other plants; long-lived; thrives in semi-shade. *L. brachystachys* (0.50), VII–VIII, white; similar to the above; small flowers in nodding racemes; elongate–lanceolate leaves, bluish beneath.
Purple loosestrife *Lythrum salicaria* Eur., Asia	0.80 purple-red	VII–IX, also suitable for reedswamp conditions (list 6.2.2); sturdy, branching stems with inflorescences up to 30 cm long. 'Feuerkerze' (1.20), bright pink. 'Morden's Pink' (0.70), deep pink. 'Rakete' (1.50), pink. 'Robert' (0.80), crimson. 'Stichflamme' (1.00), bright wine-red. 'Zigeunerblut' (1.20), deep red.
Mountain fleece *Polygonum amplex- icaule* 'Atropurpureum' Him.	0.90 ruby red	VIII–IX, full, bushy habit; clasping, deep green, ovate-lanceolate leaves; flowers in long spikes; indispensible. 'Speciosum' ('Firetail'), salmon red.
Polygonum campanu- latum W Him.	0.80 pink	VIII–X, broad, bushy habit; flowers in erect or nodding racemes; abundant and long flowering; sometimes frost-sensitive in a damp, mild climate. 'Rosenrot', red flowers.

Polygonum campanu- *latum* var. *lichiangense* (*P. lichiangense*) W Him.	0.80 white	VII–IX, long-pointed leaves with wavy edges; very abundant flowers; panicles appearing from almost every node; rare in the trade.
Rudbeckia laciniata E USA	1.80 yellow	VIII–X, stiff, upright habit; dainty leaves; composite flowers with yellowish green discs; does not flop like the double flowered 'Goldball' ('Goldenglow') (list 5.3.4).
Oriental burnet *Sanguisorba tenuifolia* 'Alba' Jap., E Sib.	up to 1.80 white	VIII, slender, drooping, cylindrical inflorescences on upright stems; pinnate leaves with narrow-lanceolate, serrate leaflets; warmth-loving species. *S. sitchensis* (1.50), deep red; still very uncommon.
Valeriana alliariifolia E Gr., Asia Minor, Cauc.	up to 1.50 pink	VII–VIII, large, pointed, heart-shaped leaves; widely branching inflorescences; very imposing in autumn, with graceful, downy seed heads.
Ironweed *Vernonia crinita* (*V. arkansana*) USA	1.50 red-violet	IX–X, stiff, upright, aster-like species. *V. noveboracensis* (1.90), IX–X, dark purple-red flowers; rarely available in the trade. Vernonias hybridise freely. Their flower heads are unsightly when faded.
Veronica longifolia 'Blauriesin' Eur., Sib., E Asia	0.80 blue	VII–VIII, upright, little-branched stems; vigorous; the original species (1.00) is rarely available in the trade. Free-flowering cultivars: 'Blauer Sommer', deep blue. 'Schneeriesin', white. 'Romiley Purple' (0.60), purple.
Veronica virginica		List 3.4.6

Variegated grasses

Unvariegated forms of the following species may also be recommended. However, their strongly invasive character makes them poor neighbours and they are not normally available in the trade.

Glyceria maxima 'Variegata' Eur., Sib., Asia Minor	0.40/1.50	VII–VIII, erect, reed-like stems; crowded panicles; leaves striped yellow and white; spreads strongly. 'Pallida', pale yellow autumn colour; very vigorous.
Gardener's garters, Ribbon grass *Phalaris arundinacea* 'Picta' Eur., Asia, N Am.	1.00	VI–VII, white-striped, reed-like leaves; robust and very invasive; formerly popular in flower arrangements. 'Tricolor', leaves striped reddish violet and white. 'Superba' and 'Elegans' are similar but rare in the trade.
Variegated cord grass *Spartina pectinata* (*S. michauxiana*) 'Aureomarginata' N Am.	1.50	VIII–IX, picturesque habit; long, green, drooping leaves with wide, yellow borders; invasive; resistant to drought.

3.6. Large ornamental herbs and grasses for sunny sites on damp soils

The following species cannot be assigned to any particular community of perennials. Their most appropriate companions are determined by the character and growing requirements of the individual species, and depend largely on aesthetic considerations. (Further large perennials: see list 3.4.8.)

3.6.1. Hardy species

Boltonia asteroides var *latisquama*		List 3.4.8
Joe Pye weed *Eupatorium purpureum* E USA	2.00 wine-red	VIII–X, immense, decorative plant; red-brown stems with leaves in whorls; does not flop. 'Atropurpureum': see list 5.3.5. *E. maculatum* (to 1.50), similar but shorter.
Filipendula kamts-chatica (*Spiraea gigantea* hort.) Jap., Kamch.	2.00–2.50 white and pink	VIII–IX, broad leaves; very decorative; remains tidy until autumn; does not flop.
Willow-leaved sun-flower *Helianthus salicifolius* C USA	2.50 yellow	X; the rather small flowers are unimportant; tall, sinuous stems set with long, willow-like leaves.
Giant hogweed *Heracleum mante-gazzianum* SW Asia	3.00 white	VII–VIII, gigantic, coarsely serrate leaves; umbels up to 1 m across on powerful, pole-like stems; 2–3 year lifespan; plants die after flowering but seed themselves prolifically on sandy or loamy soils; skin contact during humid, sunny weather can produce a nasty rash. *Peucedanum verticillare,* similar but not phototoxic; see list 2.3.2.
Heracleum lanatum N Am., Sib.	1.80 white	VI–VII, longer-lived but not so immense as the previous species. *H. villosum* (*H. laciniatum*) (2.50); very beautiful but rare in the trade; densely hairy.
Petasites japonicus 'Giganteus' Jap., China	1.00/0.15 whitish	III, immense leaves, more than 1 m across; sweetly scented flower heads like Victorian posies appear at ground level before the leaves; also for semi-shade; very invasive; to be used with caution. *P. hybridus* (*P. officinalis*), reddish flowers; not available from nurseries.
Ornamental rhubarb *Rheum palmatum* W China, E Tibet	2.50 creamy white	V–VI, powerful leaves with pointed lobes; stout stems; flowers in slender panicles.
Rheum palmatum 'Tanguticum' NW China, NE Tibet	2.00 red	V–VI, beautiful emerging foliage; very large, dark green leaves with pointed lobes; stout stems; red fruits; dies down after flowering.

Giant grasses, *Miscanthus*

The following species and cultivars quickly form huge, impressive plants with lush green, arching, reed-like leaves. They are particularly beautiful on nutrient-rich, moist to damp soils. The plants turn yellow in winter and may shed some of their leaves. The stems should be cut down in autumn or early spring.

Miscanthus floridulus (*M. sinensis* 'Giganteus') (*M. japonicus*) Jap.

Hardy, reed-like grass, over 2 m tall; seldom flowers in temperate regions; loses its leaves in winter, and should therefore be cut down in December; may need winter protection.

Maiden grass *Miscanthus sinensis* 'Gracillimus' Jap., China

Hardy, graceful, upright-growing grass, up to 1.70 m tall; flowers only in warm summer regions; best as an isolated specimen; dried stems are more ornamental than those of other *Miscanthus* spp. New selections: 'Sirene' (3.00), feathery, red-brown inflorescences. 'Rotfeder' (1.80). 'Roland' (3.50). 'Graziella' (1.50), flowers early; open habit.

Miscanthus sinensis 'Silberfeder' ('Silver Feather') Jap., China

Hardier than the type; flowers regularly in September, even in exposed positions; large, feathery inflorescences on 2.00 m stems. *M. s.* 'Condensatus' (1.80), compact habit; dense foliage; feathery, wavy inflorescences.

Tiger grass, Zebra grass *Miscanthus sinensis* 'Zebrinus'

Yellow-banded foliage; arched, drooping leaves on tall stems (1.50); attractive inflorescences in a good year. 'Zebrinus-Strictus', similar but with stiffer, more upright leaves.

Striped eulalia *Miscanthus sinensis* 'Variegatus'

Leaves striped silvery white along their length; taller (1.60) but less vigorous than the previous variety; does not flower. *M. s.* 'Purpurascens': see list 3.5.3. 'Silberpfeil' (1.30).

3.6.2.   More or less tender species

Gunnera

Gunnera manicata (Brazil) and *G. tinctoria* (Chile) are both immense, rhubarb-like foliage plants, with huge, rounded leaf blades, up to 2 m across, on powerful, thorny petioles. Their unspectacular flowers are crowded in brownish, club-shaped inflorescences, which appear in May (*G. manicata*) or July (*G. tinctoria*).

   Gunneras need a lot of space and careful attention. A damp, nutrient-rich soil is needed to support the massive leaves in summer. The planting site should be well manured and the soil loosened to a depth of a metre. Further manure may be applied around the roots each year in spring. The plants must be watered copiously in dry weather. As winter approaches, they should be cut down and their roots covered with a thick layer of peat or dry leaves. It is best to invert a wooden box over the crown to keep it as dry as possible until spring. New shoots must be protected against late frosts once the coverings have been removed.

Giant reed, *Arundo donax*

The giant reed is a Mediterranean species with tall (3–4 m), powerful stems and elegantly drooping, grey-green leaves. Flowers are only produced in a hot summer. The plants favour moist to damp soils and will grow to majestic proportions in mild areas. Their stems should be cut down in autumn and the roots covered over with leaves. In America, these plants have become naturalised along the Mississippi river as far north as St Louis.

A. donax 'Versicolor' has white-striped leaves. It is shorter (2 m) and slightly less hardy than the type; except in mild climates, it is best grown in a tub that can be moved indoors in winter.

Pampas grass, *Cortaderia selloana*

The showy, silvery-white inflorescences of these popular, clump-forming grasses from South America often develop as late as September or October. The foliage is a dense clump of long, narrow, elegantly arching leaves.

Pampas grasses need a lot of moisture in summer but must be kept as dry as possible in winter. Their evergreen leaves should be bound together at the end of autumn and mounded up with peat or dry leaves to protect them against the cold. A wooden box can then be inverted over the whole plant to keep it dry. The clumps are uncovered at the end of April or in May, and any dead leaves removed, taking care not to damage the remaining foliage. Spring is also the time to plant new specimens, or divide those which have gone bare in the middle.

The plants are dioecious. Females are commoner in the trade; their panicles are more luxuriant than those of the male plants. The following are among the more readily available cultivars:

'Aurea', brownish panicles.

'Pumila' (1.00), white dwarf form.

'Rendatleri', very vigorous; delicate pink panicles.

'Rosea', murky pink panicles; rather tender.

'Sunningdale Silver', abundant, large, open, silvery-white panicles on strong stems.

4 Rock gardens

The rock garden habitat can be taken to include all those places where rocks and stones are built into the garden, providing favourable conditions for a range of alpine and other rock-loving plants. The construction of such features has been dealt with in a previous chapter (p. 58). Careful consideration at the planning stage makes it possible to provide planting sites for a great variety of rock garden species, especially where walls and terraces are included in the garden design. The addition of a substantial rock garden to an existing design can easily spoil the overall effect. Nevertheless, it is usually possible to find room for an unassuming mound or wall in a secluded corner of the garden, or for a formal rock garden bed somewhere near the house.

Rock garden perennials have very varied requirements, though most of them are in some way dependent on rocks, scree or gravel for their well-being. The roots of many plants thrive only in the cool, damp conditions to be found under stones during the hottest part of the day. Other, warmth-loving, species appreciate the heat stored in rocks that are exposed to the sun. Cushion- and mat-forming plants thrive on a stone or scree surface, where they do not have to contend with damp. More delicate, weak-growing species find refuge in tiny cracks and crevices, and are thus protected from the competition of their neighbours. Many alpine plants and mountain woodland species need the cool, bright shade cast by rocks and dwarf shrubs. The same conditions are favoured by a variety of delicate perennials from woodland and wetland habitats that are not strictly dependent on rocks but require a special site where they can be kept under the eye of a gardener.

Some sort of classification is necessary to clarify the proper use of these diverse perennials. A large assortment of vigorous, striking, predominantly Mediterranean species and their often very numerous cultivars have been listed as 'species for the decorative, formal rock garden' (lists 4.1.1—4.1.4). These are undemanding plants, tolerant of a wide range of growing conditions, making them particularly suitable for use in a formal, architectural style of garden. Of course, the classification is not a rigid one, and the same plants may sometimes also be used in a natural setting. Conversely, many of the more specialised species from other lists can often be found an appropriate niche amongst the rocks of a formal design.

Rock garden perennials for special conditions have been ordered into numerous lists according to various factors, including their degree of dependence upon rock, soil requirements, demands on light (and warmth) and moisture preferences. It is worth mentioning that drought-tolerant species may also be planted in moist soils but that species for moist and damp soils will not survive in dry conditions.

In order to avoid disappointments with rare and difficult perennials, the more demanding species have been listed separately under the heading of 'enthusiasts' plants'. In a sense, every rock garden demands the dedication of an enthusiast. Rock gardens need constant, knowledgeable attention, and wherever appropriately skilled maintenance is not available (e.g. in most parks), it is probably better to plant dwarf rock garden shrubs rather than perennials. The true enthusiasts' plants need particular care and understanding in addition to this specialised maintenance.

The cultivation of plants in a rock garden implies a readiness to devote detailed attention to their observation and upkeep. This need for attention characterises the many species listed here that are not dependent upon the rock itself. For such plants, the special world of the rock garden is the place where individual requirements can most readily be accommodated (see lists 4.6.1–4.6.6).

4.1. The decorative, formal rock garden

The following lists contain a selection of widely available species and cultivars that are suitable for the creation of showy, formal rock gardens. These are vigorous, undemanding, free-flowering plants, which thrive in any moist and mineral-rich soil. All will tolerate a wide range of conditions, though some have individual preferences. Plants such as *Aubrieta, Cerastium* and *Phlox subulata* grow especially well if they are planted to grow out over a stone or hang down the face of a wall. Planted in this way, they will grow very old and attain impressive proportions. In open soil, they are short-lived and prone to rotting, while the weeds that grow up inside their cushions entail a great deal of extra maintenance.

It is impossible to make a sharp distinction between these species and the more specialised perennials in the subsequent lists. Of course, there are occasions where both types of plant can be used together. However, the lush growth and striking flowers of the decorative species are often difficult to combine with the more subdued charms of other rock garden perennials, and their vigorous spread is often a danger to weaker-growing neighbours.

The terraces of a formal rock garden may also provide appropriate planting positions for steppe plants (lists 3.3 and 3.4), dry grassland species (list 3.2.2) or even low-growing border perennials (list 5.3).

4.1.1. Vigorous, colourful cushion- and carpet-forming perennials for sun or bright shade among rocks

Carpeting and cushion plants for sunny positions: planting behind the stone.

Carpeting and cushion plants for sunny positions: planting in cracks between the stones.

Achillea serbica	List 4.3.1	
Gold dust, Basket-of-gold *Alyssum saxatile* (*Aurinia saxatilis*) C & SE Eur., Asia Minor	0.25 golden yellow	IV–V, grey-leaved semi-shrub; flowers in paniculate racemes; plants will hang down for more than a metre if planted on top of a wall. Proven cultivars: 'Citrinum', sulphur yellow. 'Compactum', (0.20), low-growing. 'Dudley Neville', ochre. 'Plenum', golden yellow; double flowers.
Arabis caucasica (*A. albida*) Med. to Cauc. & C Asia	0.05/0.15 white	IV–V, flowers in racemes; grey-green, hairy, broadly toothed leaves; turf-like habit; pink-flowered cultivars are mostly short-lived. 'Variegata', white-variegated foliage.

White flowers:
'Bakkely'
'Grandiflora Superba'
'Plena', double flowers
'Schneehaube' ('Snowcap')
'Schneewolke'

Pink flowers:
'Compinkie', (0.10)
'Hedi'
'Monte Rosa'
'Rosea la Fraicheur'
A. × *arendsii* 'Rosabella'

Arabis procurrens Balk.	0.03/0.15 white	IV, vigorous, free-flowering species; stoloniferous; smooth, shiny, broad-lanceolate leaves; evergreen groundcover; also thrives in bright shade. 'Neuschnee', IV–V, particularly long flowering season.
Armeria latifolia 'Bee's Ruby' Port.	0.10/0.20 ruby red	VI–VIII, luxuriant cushions of grey-green, fleshy, grass-like leaves. 'Ornament' (*A. maritima* 'Laucheana' × *A. latifolia*) (0.30), white and dark pink; particularly valuable cultivar.
Thrift *Armeria maritima* 'Splendens' N Eur.	0.10/0.20 pink	V–VII, dense, rounded cushions of fresh green foliage. Selections: 'Alba', white. 'Düsseldorfer Stolz' ('Dusseldorf Pride'), bright red. 'Rosea Compacta', magenta. 'Vindictive', rose-pink.
Aster × *alpellus* (*A. alpinus* × *A. amellus*) 'Triumph'	0.15 violet-blue	VI–VII, large daisy-like flowers over dense foliage; more persistent than *A. alpinus* (list 4.1.2).
Aubrieta Hybrids (*A.* × *cultorum*)	0.05–0.10 blue-violet or pink	IV–V, popular cushion plant with grey-green foliage; pink- and red-flowered cultivars are mostly weak-growing and short-lived; the following do not include strains that are propagated by seed.

Blue-violet:
'Blaumeise', violet; very compact.
'Blue Emperor', dark blue.
'Bob Sanders', violet; large flowers.
'Carnival', violet purple; large flowers.
'Dr Mules', dark violet.
'Greencourt Purple', purple; semi-double flowers.
'Gurgedyke', deep purple.
'Lodge Grave', violet; semi-double flowers.
'Neuling', lavender blue; very vigorous.
'Schloß Eckberg', almost pure blue.
'Tauricola', lilac; low-growing; forms good cushions.

Pink or red:
'Barker's Double', red; double flowers.
'Bordeaux', wine-red.
'Bressingham Pink', pink; late.
'Crimson Bedder', red.
'Daybreak', pink.
'Red Carpet', deep red.
'Rosengarten', pink.
'Rotkäppchen', crimson.
'Vesuv', ruby red.
Variegated foliage:
'Argenteo-variegata', creamy-white variegation; lavender-pink flowers.
'Aureo-variegata', yellow variegation, purple flowers.
'Variegata', yellow variegation; blue flowers.

Campalula carpatica Low-growing cultivars (*C. c. turbinata* × *C. carpatica*)	0.15 (to 0.25) pale blue, violet or white	VI–VIII, cushion-forming plants with upturned flowers on rigid stems; for sun or bright shade on moist, humus-rich soils among rocks; prone to slugs. The wild species has long-stemmed flowers and grows best in rock crevices (see list 4.1.3).

Blue:
'Blue Clips'
'Blue Moonlight'
'Karl Foerster'
'Karpatenkrone'

Violet:
'Blaumeise'
'Jewel'
'Wheatley Violet'
C. c. var. *turbinata*

White:
'White Clips'
'Bressingham White'
'Zwergmöve'
C. c. var. *turbinata* 'Alba'

Campanula porten-schlagiana Dalm.	0.15 violet	VI–VII, vigorous and exceptionally long-flowering species; indispensable for dry-stone walls; funnel-shaped flowers; fresh green, sharply toothed, rounded heart-shaped leaves in dense clusters on prostrate stems; for sun or bright shade on well-drained, loamy soils. 'Birch Hybrid', (0.20), purple-blue; very vigorous; large flowers. 'Major', (0.15), purple-blue; forms dense cushions.
Campanula poscha-rskyana S Dalm.	0.10/0.15 pale lilac	VI–IX, very vigorous species; densely leafy shoots with coarsely toothed basal leaves; covers the ground well; spreads very strongly in cracks and crevices; also thrives in bright shade. The following cultivars are mostly hybrids with *C. garganica*: 'Blauranke', long shoots; very vigorous. 'Blue Gown' (0.10), blue; dainty, less vigorous selection. 'E. H. Frost' (0.25), white with a blue eye; very vigorous. 'Werner Arends' (0.15), dark lilac. 'Glandore' (0.20), lilac. 'Lisduggan' (0.15), lavender pink. 'Stella' (0.15), blue; large, starry flowers; not invasive.
Centranthus ruber	List 3.3.3	
Taurus chickweed *Cerastium biebersteinii* Crim.	0.15/0.20 white	V, silvery grey foliage; very invasive; best grown over a wall, with plenty of space to spread.
Snow-in-summer *Cerastium tomentosum* S It.	0.10/0.15 white	V, silvery white foliage; lower-growing than the previous species; vigorous but not invasive. *C. t.* var. *columnae*, small leaves with silvery hairs; very popular and widely available.
Leadwort *Ceratostigma plumba-ginoides* W China	0.15/0.25 blue	VIII–IX, flowers in terminal inflorescences; smooth, green, obovate leaves; far spreading roots; red autumn colour; thrives in a sunny position but will tolerate semi-shade; good groundcover in mild areas.
Arctic daisy *Chrysanthemum arcticum*	0.25 white	IX–X, large daisy-like flowers which fade pink as they age; smooth, light green, coarsely toothed leaves; reliable perennial.

N. Arctic Zone		'Roseum' (0.40), delicate pink; very vigorous and free-flowering. 'Schwefelglanz' (0.40), yellow. *C. zawadskii* (0.30), IX, whitish pink; rare. *C. z.* var. *latilobum*: see list 5.2.3.
Cheddar pink *Dianthus gratiano-* *politanus* (*D. caesius*) W & C Eur. to Ukr.	0.08/0.15 pink	V–VII, dainty, glaucous, grey-green cushions; very abundant flowers; for walls and rock crevices in full sun. Many different cultivars with single, semi-double or double flowers in shades of red, pink, white, purple or crimson.
Common pink, Clove pink *Dianthus plumarius* (*D. P.* Hybrids) E C Eur.	0.10/0.30 various	V–VI; the showy, scented garden cultivars bloom earlier than the wild species (list 4.2.1). Many different cultivars with mostly double flowers in shades of red, pink and white.
Mountain avens *Dryas octopetala* Eur., Asia, N Am.	0.05/0.10 white	V–VI, very free-flowering; feathery seed heads; blunt, oval, coarsely crenate leaves; forms dense mats over rocks and scree. *D.* × *suendermannii* (to 0.15), more vigorous than the above; larger leaves and flowers. *D. o. lanata* (0.10), grey-green, hairy leaves.
Eriophyllum lanatum (*E. caespitosum*) N Am.	0.30 yellow	VI–VII, daisy-like flowers on loosely branching, leafy stems; grey-green, pinnately-cut leaves, silvery when young; for dry, sunny positions among rocks; undemanding.
Euphorbia myrsinites		List 3.3.3
Euphorbia polychroma (*E. epithymoides*) C & SE Eur.	0.40 greenish yellow	IV–V, forms decorative, bushy, almost spherical clumps; bright yellow bracts; robust. Selections: 'Sonnengold', 'Major'. *E. niciciana* (0.40), VII–IX, similar to the above; fine, evergreen foliage.
Gentiana lagodechiana (*G. septemfida* var. *lagodechiana*) E Cauc.	0.15 blue	VII–IX, upward-facing, mostly solitary flowers at the ends of prostrate, leafy shoots; undemanding. 'Doeringiana', abundant large flowers. *G. septemfida* (0.20–0.30), VII–VIII, flowers in dense, terminal clusters on more or less erect, leafy shoots; seldom true in the trade.
Geranium dalmaticum SW Yug.	0.08/0.10 pale pink	VI–VII, dense cushions of dainty foliage; spreads like turf, especially among rocks; red autumn colour; indispensable. 'Bressingham Pink', pink. 'Album', white.
Geranium meeboldii		List 2.1.6.
Gypsophila pacifica Sib., C Asia	1.00 white	VII–VIII, robust, expansive plants; larger flowers and less branched panicles than *G. paniculata*; long-lived in cold, heavy soils.

Baby's breath *Gypsophila paniculata* SE Eur., Cauc., W-Sib.	1.00 white	VII–VIII, billowing inflorescences in summer; similar to the previous species but with smaller flowers and daintier, more branching panicles; linear-lanceolate leaves; undemanding; valuable for cutting; propagation from seed.
Gypsophila paniculata 'Bristol Fairy'	1.00 white	VII–VIII, double flowers in open, veil-like panicles; for a warm, sunny position with well-drained soil. 'Bristol Fairy Perfect', large, double flowers. 'Flore Pleno', smaller, double flowers; comes true from seed. 'Compacta Plena' (0.50), whitish pink; double flowers. 'Flamingo' (1.20), pink; double flowers. 'Schneeflocke' (0.80), white; single and double flowers; comes true from seed.
Gypsophila hybrid 'Rosenschleier' ('Rosy Veil')	0.30 delicate pink	VI–VIII, forms domed bushes up to 1 m across; very free-flowering over a long period; for a sunny position on well-drained soil; more reliably perennial then the other tall cultivars. 'Pink Star' (0.30), dark pink; double flowers.
Creeping baby's breath *Gypsophila repens* C & S Eur.	0.05/0.10 white	V–VI; forms a dense, low turf; grey-green, linear leaves; decumbent stems. The following selections have a less turf-like habit: 'Dorothy Teacher', clear pink. 'Letchworth Rose', pink; vigorous growth. 'Rosea', pink. 'Rosa Schönheit' ('Rose Beauty') (0.15), pink. *G.* × *monstrosa* (0.25), white.
Rockrose *Helianthemum* hybrids (*H. nummularium* × *H. apenninum*)	0.20/0.25 various	V–VII, dwarf shrubs with green (g) or silvery grey (sg) leaves; cultivars exhibit various degrees of hardiness, and it is advisable to protect grey-leaved plants with conifer branches in winter; individual flowers close or break up at midday during sunny weather but the plants are covered in bloom again the following morning; repeat flowering often occurs in summer; see also lists 4.3.2 and 4.4.1. Proven selections:

Red:
'Fire Dragon' (sg).
'Mrs C. W. Earle' double.
'Cerise Queen' (g), double.
'Ben Hope' (g).
'Supreme' (g-sp).

Magenta pink:
'Lawrenson's Pink' (g).
'Pink Double' (g), semi-double.
'Rose of Leeswood' (g), double.
'Wisley Pink' (sg).

Yellow:
'Praecox' (sg).
'Golden Queen' (g).
'Sterntaler' (g), very hardy.
'Jubilee' (g), double.
'Wisley Primrose' (sg).

Orange-red:
'Henfield Brilliant' (sg).

White:
'The Bride' (g-sg).
'Snowball' (sg), double.

Evergreen candytuft *Iberis sempervirens* It.	0.25–0.30 white	V, broad, densely bushy, evergreen semi-shrub with leathery, lanceolate leaves. Tall cultivars (up to 0.30):

'Elfenreigen', large flowers; very vigorous.
'Findel', vigorous and healthy.
'Gracilis', small flowers; luxuriant growth.
'Nana', sturdy, rounded habit.
'Snowflake' ('Schneeflocke'), popular selection.
'Winterzauber', occasional flowers in winter.
Low-growing cultivars (0.10–0.20):
'Little Queen' (0.15), rounded habit.
'Weißer Zwerg' ('Little Gem') (0.10).
'Zwergschneeflocke' (0.15).
I. saxatilis, see list 4.2.1.
I. candolleana (*I. pruithii*), (0.30–0.15), white flushed with lilac; fleshy, spathulate leaves; very variable; rare.

Nepeta × *faassenii*   List 3.3.3

Phlox douglasii   List 4.3.1

Phlox subulata   0.10/0.15   V–VI, abundant flowers; needle-like leaves; carpets
USA   various   the ground on warm, well-drained, nutrient-rich soils. Proven selections:

'White Delight', white.   'Beauty of Ronsdorf', red.
'Nivalis', white; small flowers.   'Chuckles', red.
'Schnee' ('Snow'), pure white.   'Marjory', rose-pink.
'G. F. Wilson', slate-blue.   'Atropurpurea', purple-red.
'Lilakönigin', lilac-blue.   'Temiscaming', dark red.
'Daisy Hill', pink.   'Scarlet Flame', brilliant red.

Phuopsis stylosa   0.20   VI–VII, small, strongly scented flowers in terminal
(*Crucianella stylosa*)   pink   inflorescences; whorled, lanceolate leaves on prostrate
Cauc., Iran   stems; for moist, loamy soils; needs sun; also thrives in woodland edge conditions; do not plant too densely. 'Rubra', purple-pink.

Potentilla 'Goldrausch'   List 4.4.3

Rock soapwort   0.20/0.20   VII, flowers in densely compressed cymes; dainty,
Saponaria ocymoides   pink   ovate to spathulate leaves; undemanding.
SW Eur., S Alps, It.   'Rosa Königin' and 'Splendens', flowers in foaming masses. 'Rubra Compacta', dark red.

Saponaria × *lempergii*   0.30   VIII–IX, dense, dark green foliage; vigorous, strongly
(*S. cypria* ×   magenta–   branching, prostrate shoots; irreplaceable for its
S. hausknechtii)   pink   abundant flowers in autumn.
    'Max Frei', VI–IX, pink; similar but flowers earlier and longer.

Sedum species

The following *Sedum* species are often used for extensive groundcover plantings (see list 3.1.1) but are not invasive and can also be planted singly or in small groups among rocks or in crevices. Along with cultivars of *S. spectabile* and *S. telephium* (list 5.3.1) they may be used to create colourful plantings on sunny rock garden terraces.

Sedum ellacombianum		List 3.1.1
Sedum floriferum 'Weihenstephaner Gold'		List 3.1.1
Sedum kamtschaticum		List 3.1.1
Sedum midden-dorffianum 'Diffusum'		List 3.1.1
Sedum spurium Cauc., Iran, Arm.	0.05–0.20 pale purple	VII–VIII, funnel-shaped (as opposed to open, star-shaped) flowers; prostrate, rooting stems; obovate leaves with wedge-shaped bases and crenate, ciliate tips; forms a turf-like groundcover; grows up vertical walls; sometimes naturalised in warm sites on dry, alkaline soils; rare in the trade. 'Album Superbum', important, widely available cultivar; forms a dense turf even in semi-shade; few flowers; see list 3.1.1.
Sedum spurium 'Schorbuser Blut' ('Dragon's Blood')	0.03/0.10 red	VII–VIII, flowers in cymes on decumbent stems with dark, brownish leaves; best planted in groups, but not in extensive patches; thrives in bright shade. 'Splendens' ('Coccineum'), red flowers and foliage. 'Fuldaglut', red; dark, red-brown leaves. 'Purpurteppich' ('Purple Carpet'), magenta; dark purple leaves. 'Tricolor', green and red leaves with yellow borders.
Sedum stoloniferum Cauc., Iran, Asia Minor	0.10 red-pink	VII–VIII, similar to *S. spurium* but with open, star-shaped flowers and glabrous, light green, entire leaves; slightly pink-coloured, creeping stems; forms a loose turf; also for bright shade; seeds itself freely; currently rare in the trade.
Sea campion *Silene maritima* 'Weißkehlchen' W Eur., N Afr.	up to 0.20 white	VII–VIII, flowers with inflated calyces; forms an open, grey-green turf; broad-lanceolate leaves; very long flowering season. 'Plena', white; double flowers. 'Rosea', pink.
Silene schafta 'Splendens' Cauc.	0.10 deep red	VIII–IX, large, stemless flowers; pointed, lanceolate leaves; forms a loose turf.
Lambs' ears *Stachys byzantina* (*S. lanata*) 'Silver Carpet' Cauc., N Iran	0.10	Thick leaves with matted white hairs; turf-like habit; seldom produces flowers. *S. byzantina* (0.25), VI–VII, pink; spent flowerheads are unsightly and must be removed; still commonly used but 'Silver Carpet' is mostly better. 'Byzantinus', large leaves.
Thymus × citriodorus 'Golden Dwarf'	0.10/0.15 lilac-pink	VI–VII, seldom produces flowers; forms gold-variegated carpets that are very persistent; occasional trimming encourages a dense, low growth.

Thymus rotundifolius 'Purpurteppich'	0.08 purple-red	VII–VIII, similar to *T. serpyllum* (list 3.2.4) but with larger, rounded leaves; forms a green turf. *T. balcanus,* very vigorous; forms dark green carpets. Further *Thymus* spp.: see list 4.4.1.
Trifolium repens 'Purpureum'		List 4.4.3
Veronica gentianoides Cauc., SW Asia	0.30 light blue	V–VI, crowded, upright stems; green foliage; reliably perennial but sensitive to competition; cut back after flowering. 'Variegata', white-variegated leaves.
Veronica prostrata		List 4.4.1
Spiked speedwell *Veronica spicata*	0.05/0.30 lilac	VII, see list 3.2.2. Selections:

Pale blue:
'Spitzentraum' (0.50).

Wine-red:
'Heidekind' (0.20).

Dark blue:
'Blaufuchs' (0.40).
'Nana' (0.15).

Pink:
'Baccarole' (0.25).
'Erica' (0.30).
'Minuett' (0.30).

Red:
'Rotfuchs' ('Red Fox') (0.40).

White:
'Alba' (0.30).

Veronica teucrium (*V. austriaca* var. *teucrium*)	0.15/0.20 blue	VI, see list 3.2.2. Selections: 'Knallblau', 'Royal Blue', 'Shirley Blue', 'True Blue', 'Kapitän'.

Dwarf and intermediate bearded iris, *Iris germanica*

Just like the tall bearded iris, whose wild ancestors come from dry grassland, stony slopes, vineyard walls and rocky outcrops, these low-growing cultivars prefer a warm position on gravelly loam among rocks or on open ground.

The assortment is in a constant state of flux. The following lists contain some of the commoner and more recent selections, arranged according to height. Dwarf varieties flower as early as March or April and are important plants for the spring garden. Intermediate iris flower in May, before the majority of tall cultivars. They have the character of border perennials and may be used accordingly.

Miniature iris (5–10 cm)

Blue:
'Blue Beret', mid-blue standards; violet falls with white beards.

Yellow:
'Little Sunbeam', lemon yellow standards; paler falls.
'Christine', mid-yellow standards; golden yellow falls.
'April Accent', golden yellow with white beards.

Red:
'Three Cherries', wine-red with yellow beards.
'French wine', dark wine-red with blue beards.

Dwarf iris (0.15–0.20 cm)

Blue:
'Coerulea', sky blue.
'Cyanea', violet-blue.
'Mitternacht', violet.

Yellow:
'Lemon Puff', pale lemon yellow; white falls.
'Sulphurea', sulphur yellow.
'Path of Gold', golden yellow.
'Excelsa', ochre.

Red:
'Little Rosy Wings', ruby red.

White:
'Die Braut', white.
'Crispy', white.
'Knick-Knack', white with blue margins.

Short intermediate iris (0.20–0.40 m)

Blue:
'Blue Denim' (0.30), pale blue; white beards.
'Tinker Bell' (0.30), intense light blue; exceptionally vigorous.
'Silkie' (0.20), violet.

Yellow:
'Baria' (0.30), pale sulphur yellow.
'Stockholm' (0.35), clear pale yellow; blue beards.
'Laced Lemonade' (0.30); pale, two-tone yellow; petals with wavy margins.
'Golden Fair' (0.25), golden yellow.
'Orange Caper' (0.30), orange-yellow.

Red:
'Cherry Garden' (0.30), wine-red.
'Jerry Rubin' (0.30), ruby red.

White:
'Schneekuppe' (0.30), snow white.
'Green Spot' (0.30), white with green veins.
'Cotton Blossom' (0.30), ivory white.
'Cherry Spot' (0.25), creamy white with brown-violet margins.
'Dale Dennis' (0.35), white with pink margins.

4.1.2. Short-lived species

These undemanding and free-flowering perennials quickly bring life into a new rock garden but do not live for very long. Some of them seed themselves freely, especially in cracks and crevices, and thus make a more permanent contribution to the planting. Unwanted seedlings are easily removed.

Alpine aster	0.05/0.20	V–VI, large daisy-like flowers; rosettes of grey-hairy
Aster alpinus	violet-blue	leaves; cultivars do not seed themselves.
Eur. to C Asia, Sib.,		'Abendschein', pink.
W N Am.		'Albus Giganteus', white.
		'Dunkle Schöne' ('Dark Beauty'), violet.

'Frühlicht', pink.
'Goliath', delicate blue.
'Happy End', pink.
'Susanne', white; double flowers.

Erigeron aurantiacus Turkest.	0.25 orange	VII–VIII, large single, daisy-like flowers; oval-spathulate leaves.
Dwarf fleabane *Erigeron karvinskianus* var. *mucronatus* Mex. to Venez.	0.05/0.15 pink	VI–X, large, graceful, daisy-like flowers; flattened, ground-hugging habit; seeds itself freely in mild areas; needs protection in winter.
Fairy foxglove *Erinus alpinus* Mts. of Spain to Austria	0.05/0.08 purple-pink	V–X, forms dainty cushions; flowers freely from May to October; seeds itself; undemanding. 'Albus' white. 'Dr Hähnle', red. 'Mrs Charles Boyle', clear pink.
Erysimum arkansanum 'Golden Gem' N Am.	up to 0.25 yellow	IV–V, vigorous cultivar; stiff, erect habit; abundant and long-flowering; seeds itself prolifically; taller seedlings should be removed.
Purple toadflax *Linaria purpurea* It.	0.80 purple	VII–XI, tall, slender, crowded racemes; seeds itself freely. 'Canon Went', pink.
Papaver monanthum Cauc.	0.05/0.40 orange	VI–VII, short-lived poppy flowers on tall stems; reliably perennial. *P. pseudocanescens,* bright lemon yellow; seeds itself prolifically.
Iceland poppy *Papaver nudicaule* Arct. & Subarct. Asia & N Am.	0.15/0.30 white, red and yellow	IV–IX, flowers long and abundantly; biennial; seeds itself freely; prone to slugs; mostly available in mixed strains such as Goldzwerg (0.20). Good named cultivars: 'Golden Monarch' (0.40); large yellow flowers. 'Giganteum Matador' (0.40), scarlet. 'Kardinal' (0.40) red.
Horned pansy *Viola cornuta* hort. Pyren.	up to 0.25 blue-violet	V–X, leafy plant with large flowers on long stems; blooms until autumn; persists for several years in cool, mild regions; adaptable in use. Many different cultivars in yellow blue, violet, red and white.
Viola × floraiensis	0.15 pale blue	V–X, similar to *V. cornuta:* flowers from March to November; short-lived, but seeds itself without becoming a nuisance; not invasive; indispensable rock garden plant.

4.1.3. Vigorous cushion- and carpet-forming perennials for bright shade and semi-shade

The following, vigorous and widely available species and cultivars have been divided into plants which grow best in cracks and crevices, and those which thrive in less confined situations among rocks and on terraces. These latter may often be combined with perennials from woodland

and woodland edge habitats, such as *Astilbe chinensis,* low-growing *Dicentra* spp., *Omphalodes, Polemonium reptans, Tiarella* and *Primula* spp.

Less common perennials for shade and bright shade have been ordered according to their special requirements in lists 4.5.1–4.5.4. Low-growing groundcover and turf-forming plants are treated in list 3.1.2.

Plants for bright shady cracks and crevices

Campanula carpatica Carp.	up to 0.30 blue-violet	VI–IX, large, open flowers over bushy foliage; loose clumps which fall apart after a few years, unlike those of more short-stemmed, cushion-like cultivars (list 4.1.1); pretty amongst stonework; very undemanding and easy to grow; prone to slug damage. 'Isabel' (0.40), dark blue. 'Kobaltglocke' (0.30), dark violet. 'Violetta' (0.40), dark violet. 'White Star' (0.30), white.
Chiastophyllum oppo- sitifolium Cauc.	0.10/0.20 yellow	VI–VII, abundant flowers in drooping panicles; fleshy, rounded, blunt-toothed leaves; thrives on walls.
Yellow fumitory *Corydalis lutea* S Alps	0.20/0.30 yellow	V–IX, flowers throughout the growing season; dainty and undemanding; sometimes seeds itself excessively on shady or partly sunny walls. *C. ochroleuca* (0.40), creamy-white; similar to the above but seeds itself sparingly.
Ivy-leaved toadflax *Cymbalaria muralis* (*Linaria cymbalaria*) S Alps, It., Yug., W Asia	0.05 lilac-blue, yellow lip	VI–IX, small axillary flowers; lobed, rounded heart-shaped leaves; loosely covers semi-shady rocks and walls; rare in the trade.

Plants for shady rock garden terraces

Bergenia **hybrids**

The exceptionally undemanding and sun-tolerant *Bergenia* species from list 2.3.3, with their coarse, leathery foliage, are best suited to planting in dry woodland edge conditions or in the shade of a building. The following hybrids are more effective for rock garden use. All flower freely in a sunny position but will also tolerate shade. The predominantly pink- and red-flowered cultivars have been ordered according to the colour of their leaves in winter. The following six cultivars can be especially recommended.

'Abendglocken'	0.40 magenta	III–IV, flowers abundantly; foliage turns deep brownish red in winter; sometimes flowers again in summer.
'Admiral'	0.40 red	IV–V, flowers on tall, sturdy stems; exceptionally bold foliage; deep brown-red in winter.
'Morgenröte' ('Morning Red')	0.30 pink	IV–V, the only cultivar that regularly flowers again in summer; comparatively small, rounded, semi-ever-green leaves.
'Oeschberg'	0.30 fresh pink	IV–V, much-branched inflorescences up to 60 cm tall; erect, long-stemmed leaves, which turn red in autumn.

'Schneekönigin' ('Snow Queen')	0.35 pale pink	III–IV, very free-flowering; leaves mostly green in winter; often flowers a second time.
'Silberlicht' ('Silverlight')	0.40 white	III–IV, flowers often flushed pink; vigorous and free-flowering; prostrate leaves.

Further cultivars (according to their foliage in winter):

Deep red-brown:
'Ballawley', pink; large flowers.
'Bressingham Beauty', pink.
'Margery Fish', purple-red.
'Pugsley's Pink', pink.
'Abendglut' ('Evening Glow'), purple; double flowers.

Brownish:
'Glockenturm', pink; free-flowering.
'Purpurglocke', magenta; sometimes flowers again in IX; leaves with long petioles.
'Sunningdale', reddish-pink; good groundcover plant.
'Walter Kienli', lilac-red; attractive foliage; vigorous.

Mostly green:
'Baby Doll', pink; dainty selection.
'Schneekissen', pale pink; slightly wavy leaves.

Bergenia pacifica (*B. crassifolia* var. *pacifica*) E Sib.	0.10/0.20 magenta	IV, flowers sparingly; comparatively small, rounded leaves, very beautifully coloured in autumn and winter; turf-like habit.
Bergenia purpurascens 'Wintermärchen' Sikkim to W Tibet	0.40 red	IV–V, narrow, oval, leathery leaves that turn a striking red-brown in winter.
Dicentra eximia (i.a.)		List 2.2.1
Epimedium grandi- *florum* (i.a.)		List 1.1.1

Coral flower, *Heuchera*

Heucheras are adaptable plants. The hybrids grow well and thrive for many years on bright, shady rock garden terraces with moist soil. The plants have a tendency to grow up out of the ground and therefore need occasional replanting or a top-dressing of humus-rich soil.

Heuchera × *brizoides* 'Gracillima'	0.10/0.50 white to pale pink	VI–VII, graceful, finely branched panicles; rounded heart-shaped leaves; cushion-like habit.
Heuchera hybrids	0.50–0.70	VI–VII, flowers in panicles on wiry, often rigid stems. Proven selections: 'Schneewittchen' (0.50), white. 'Silberregen' (0.60), white. 'Jubilee' (0.50), pale pink. 'Scintillation' (0.50), bright pink. 'Pruhoniciana' (0.70), pink; powerful growth. 'Weserlachs' (0.60), salmon pink. 'Rakete' (0.60), bright red.

		'Red Spangles' (0.50), scarlet. 'Widar' (0.50), bright red. 'Ricard' (0.50), bright red.
Heuchera sanguinea 'Splendens' USA	0.10/0.50 pink	V–VII, rounded, kidney-shaped leaves; may be propagated from seed. Improved new selection: 'Leuchtkäfer'.
Heuchera sanguinea 'Bressingham Hybrids'	0.10/0.60 salmon pink	VI–VII, similar to the above; may also be propagated from seed.
× *Heucherella tiarel-* *loides* (*Heuchera* × *Tiarella*)	0.10/0.25 whitish pink	VI, abundant flowers in dainty racemes; dense carpets of coarsely lobed, rounded heart-shaped leaves. 'Bridget Bloom', bright pink.

Hosta (Low-growing species and cultivars)		List 1.1.3
Polygonum affine Nepal	0.05/0.25 deep pink	VI–X, dense spikes of piebald flowers; broad-lanceolate leaves which turn bronze in winter; turf-like habit; for moist to damp soils; less common in the trade than its cultivars.
Polygonum affine 'Darjeeling Red'	0.05/0.15 deep pink	VII–IX, narrow, erect flower spikes over deep green, lanceolate leaves; compact habit; old plants are reluctant to flower.
Polygonum affine 'Donald Lowndes'	0.05/0.20 bright pink	VII–IX, thick, sturdy spikes of flowers over broad-lanceolate leaves; cushion-like habit; short-lived.
Polygonum affine 'Superbum'	0.05/0.25 pink	VI–X, similar to the wild species but statelier and more luxuriant in growth; much used as groundcover; for sun or bright shade on moist to damp soils.
Clover knotweed *Polygonum capitatum* N India	0.03/0.15 pink	VIII–X, short-lived, prostrate, mat-forming species; round, clover-like heads of flowers; dark green, brown-banded, oval-elliptic leaves; tender in the open but seeds itself freely; perennates in a cool glasshouse. Selection: 'Afghan'.
Primula juliae Transcauc.	0.06 violet-red	IV, flowers very prolifically; dense, turf-like habit; rounded, kidney-shaped leaves; spreads in lawn-like patches on moist to damp soils in bright shade; old plants should be lightly top-dressed with weed-free compost in winter. Hybrids: see list 2.2.1.
Prunella grandiflora		List 4.4.3
Tiarella cordifolia		List 1.1.1

Drought-sensitive, evergreen mossy saxifrages

Saxifraga Arendsii hybrids (*S.* × *arendsii*)

The fresh to dark green cushions of these hybrids are made up of impressively uniform, star-shaped rosettes of pinnately cut leaves. In May and June these disappear under a multitude of flowers borne on wiry stems.

On the whole, the plants prefer a cool spot in bright shade with continually damp, humus-rich but well-drained soil. They are longer-lived among rocks or on a semi-shady wall than in an ordinary bed.

The following cultivars are available from European nurseries:

White:
'Schneeteppich', robust and very persistent.
'Frühlingsschnee', forms a very persistent turf.

Pink:
'Blütenteppich'
'Feuerwerk'
'Purpurteppich'
'Rosenkönigin'

Pale red:
'Dornröschen'
'Spätlese'

Dwarf selections:
'Peter Pan' (0.10), dark red.
'Rosenzwerg' (0.03), dark pink.

Magenta:
'Farbenkissen'
'Purpurmantel'

Red:
'Ingeborg'
'Triumph'
'Leuchtkäfer'
'Luschtinez'

Yellow:
'Schwefelblüte'

Saxifraga hypnoides var. *egemmulosa* (*S. klingii* hort.) 'Gemmifera'	0.08–0.15 white	V–VI, forms dense, fresh green mats, which turn bronze-red in autumn. 'Purpurea', pink.
Saxifraga muscoides hort. (*S. cespitosa*) 'Findling'	0.10 white	V, forms dense, dark green cushions. 'Purpurea', red.

Evergreen saxifrages for shade

The following species and hybrids are rewarding plants, spreading by means of stolons to make a robust and very attractive groundcover for small, bright-sunless to shady areas on moist, mineral-rich soils. They will thrive in a variety of sites in shady, well-tended gardens, and are particularly effective for covering graves.

Less common species are included in lists 4.5.1 and 4.5.3.

Saxifraga cuneifolia Pyren., Alps, Carp.	0.05/0.15 whitish	VI–VII, porcelain-like inflorescences; small, glabrous, leathery, wedge-shaped leaves with horny edges; dense, evergreen rosettes; for shady rock slopes and places under trees. Selections: 'Multicaulis' (0.10), white. 'Capillipes' (0.10), white flowers with red spots.
London pride *Saxifraga × urbium* (*S. umbrosa* hort,) (*S. spathularis* × *S. umbrosa*)	0.05/0.30 white, with red spots	V–VI, popular old garden plant; flowers in loose panicles over dark green rosettes; elongate to obovate, blunt-toothed leaves that taper into broad, flat petioles, hardly longer than the blades. 'Aureopunctata', similar to the above but with yellow-spotted leaves.

Saxifraga × *urbium* 'Serratifolia'	0.05/0.30 white, with red spots	V–VI, similar to the above but with evenly toothed leaves. 'Serratifolia Morrisonii' (0.30), larger, oval, serrate leaves; vigorous.
Saxifraga × *urbium* 'Elliott'	0.05/0.15 pink	V–VI, evergreen rosettes of small, rounded, daintily crenate leaves; very persistent. 'White Elliot', white.
Saxifraga × *geum* (*S. hirsuta* × *S.* × *urbium*)	0.08/0.35 cream, with red spots	VI–VII, loose, evergreen rosettes; similar to *S.* × *urbium* but somewhat hairy leaves with cordate bases and long, slightly rounded petioles; spreads strongly over the years and forms a dense ground-cover.
Saxifraga trifurcata		List 4.2.1

Sedum species for bright shade

All *Sedum* species thrive in full sun. The following also tolerate bright shade.

Sedum ellacombianum		List 3.1.1
Sedum hybridum 'Immergrünchen'		List 3.1.1
Stringy stonecrop *Sedum sarmentosum* Jap., N China	0.02/0.08 yellow	VII, flowers in flattened cymes; long, creeping stems with yellowish green, lanceolate leaves; forms a sparse groundcover; not always reliable.
Sedum spurium 'Album Superbum'		List 3.1.1
Sedum stoloniferum		List 4.1.1

4.1.4. Bulbs and corms

The terraces of a formal rock garden provide good planting positions for a variety of spring-flowering bulbs, corms, and tubers particularly the cultivated forms of plants such as *Chionodoxa, Muscari* and *Scilla*. The following, colourful species and cultivars also have an important role to play. All need an open soil in order to thrive. The plants should be lifted and divided when their flowering diminishes.

Crocus Chrysanthus hybrids

Crocus chrysanthus is a variable species from SE Europe, producing rounded, pale orange-yellow flowers in February and March. It is the parent of many cultivars and hybrids, some of which are listed here. The cultivars seed themselves freely in open soil but the colours do not come true.

White:
'Ladykiller', purple exterior.
'Snow Bunting', dark-veined exterior.
'Warley White', dark purple exterior.

Yellow:
'Advance', violet exterior.
'Cream Beauty', delicate matt yellow.

'Gipsy Girl', purple-striped exterior.
'Nanette', violet exterior.
'Saturnus', brown exterior; early flowering.
'Zwanenburg Bronze', dark bronze exterior.

Lilac-blue:
'Blue Bonnet', dark exterior.
'Blue Bird', white edges.
'Blue Giant', pearl blue.
'Blue Peter', purple and white exterior.

The large garden crocuses (*C. vernus* and its cultivars) have been assigned to the woodland edge along with *C. tommasinianus* and *C. neapolitanus* (list 2.4.1). Wild species for summer drought are dealt with in list 4.4.2.

Miniature narcissi, *Narcissus*

The following cultivars are reliable garden plants, unlike the more demanding wild species (list 4.2.4).

Narcissus pseudo-narcissus 'W. P. Milner'	0.20 pale yellow	IV, very long-lived dwarf daffodil.
Narcissus triandrus 'April Tears'	0.20 pale yellow	IV, several dainty, nodding flowers on each stem. 'Thalia' (0.30), IV, white flowers; very persistent cultivar; suitable for rock gardens (list 2.4.3).
Narcissus cyclamineus hybrids	(up to 0.30) yellow	'February Gold' (to 0.30), II–III, golden yellow. 'Garden Princess' (to 0.30), IV, larger than the above. 'Little Witch' (0.20), IV, golden yellow. 'March Sunshine' (0.30), II–III, clear yellow. 'Peeping Tom' (0.30), III–IV, deep yellow; very slender flowers. 'Tête-à-Tête' (to 0.30), III–IV, lemon yellow; two flowers on each stem.

Vigorous wild tulips, *Tulipa*

Selected cultivars of the following species can be found among the garden tulips in list 5.4. The lower-growing wild tulips have been assigned to list 4.2.4.

Tulipa acuminata (0.30–0.40), IV.
Remarkable, almost grotesque flowers, with long, narrow, reddish or yellow petals; origin unknown.

Tulipa eichleri (*T. persica*) (0.30), IV–V; Turkest., N Iran, Buchara.
Large, well proportioned, scarlet-coloured flowers; slightly wavy leaves.

Tulipa fosteriana (0.45), IV; C Asia.
Very large red flowers; only available as one of its many cultivars (list 5.4), of which 'Mme Lefeber' ('Red Emperor') is closest to the wild species.

Tulipa greigii (0.25/0.60), IV–V; Turkest.
Large, globular, orange-scarlet flowers; blue-green leaves, striped and spotted with red; numerous cultivars (list 5.4).

Tulipa kaufmanniana (0.25), III–IV; Turkest.
One of the earliest and most beautiful of tulips; creamy yellow flowers, sometimes flushed red; the wild species is finer than many of its cultivars (list 5.4).

Tulipa lanata (0.50), IV; C Asia.
Very large, bright scarlet, goblet-shaped flowers; rare in the trade; spreads by means of rhizomes; only for warm, sheltered sites.

Tulipa marjolettii (0.40), IV–V.
Colourful, middle-sized, yellow and red flowers on tall stems; very persistent; origin unknown.

Tulipa praecox (0.40), IV–V; Iraq, S Eur.
Middle-sized, vermilion flowers; triangular buds; large, blue-green leaves; spreads by means of rhizomes.

Tulipa praestans (−0.40), IV; C Asia.
Several scarlet-vermilion flowers on each stem. Widely available selections: 'Fuselier', 'Van Tubergen's Variety', 'Zwanenburg'.

Tulipa sprengeri (0.40), V–VI; Arm.
Mahogany-coloured flowers with dark brown bases and golden anthers; long, narrow green leaves; often flowers as late as June; rare in the trade.

Rock garden perennials with special requirements: Species that are more or less dependent on rock

4.2.   Plants for gritty soil in dry, sunny positions among rocks

Unlike the majority of enthusiast's plants in list 4.2.3, the more widely available of the following drought-tolerant species will also grow under moist conditions. This is borne out by experience in Weihenstephan and the Munich Botanic Garden, where some of the plants have developed into imposing and worthy specimens in spite of an annual rainfall that often exceeds 800 mm. Whether this applies to regions with a more oceanic climate is a question that can only be answered by international trials.

The grey-hairy, sometimes bluish or red-brown coloured plants, with their often fleshy or finely divided foliage, are particularly effective in combination with stone. Like all drought-tolerant species, they appreciate the wide spacing that comes about naturally when planting among rocks. On the other hand, they do not require a full-blown rock garden in order to flourish. They are just as happy in a dry-stone wall, on scree- and gravel-beds, or on a normal sunny slope with stony, mineral-rich soil. Enthusiasts might even try growing them (and especially the plants from list 4.2.3) on a warm, sunny, covered site next to the house. Where space is available, drought-tolerant rock garden species may be effectively incorporated into a planting of steppe (prairie) perennials (list 3.3), though not where the growing conditions are too extreme.

Individual preferences, such as for limestone or igneous rock, crevice-planting or stony soil, are all mentioned in the text. With few exceptions, the plants will tolerate damp in winter and spring, thriving wherever they are given a warm sunny, relatively dry and well-drained position among rocks. Planted in the right place, they require hardly any maintenance or special attention.

4.2.1.   Commonly available, mostly vigorous species

Prickly thrift	0.10	VII–VIII, dense, dark green cushions of piercing,
Acantholimon glu-	pink	needle-like leaves; old plants are broad and imposing;
maceum		calyx tubes with white margins and dark violet veins.
Cauc., Arm.		*A. androsaceum* (0.15), white; gradually forms large, spiny, grey-green cushions.

A. olivieri (*A. venustum*) (0.15), abundant pink flowers; rigid, blue-green cushions.
For dry soil and full sun in cracks or between stones, preferably hanging down the face of a rock.

Achillea ageratifolia C Balk.	0.15 white	VII–VIII, ascending stems with solitary flower heads; greyish white, deeply scalloped leaves; on rocks and scree; for the enthusiast.
Achillea ageratifolia var. *aizoon*	0.15 white	IV–VII, similar to the above but with flower heads in clusters; linear to tongue-shaped, finely crenate leaves; available in various forms, including: *A. conjuncta* (0.10/0.15), vigorous; doubtful species.
Achillea umbellata Greece	0.05/0.15 white	VI–VIII, attractive cushion-forming species; narrow, pinnately divided leaves with matted white hairs; not very hardy. 'Argentea' (0.20), widespread cultivar. *A. serbica*: see list 4.3.1.
Aethionema grandi- *florum* Cauc., Iran, Asia Minor	up to 0.25 purple-pink	V, flowers in racemes on erect stems with almost needle-like foliage; often disappears after 3–4 years. Hybrids: 'Warley Ruber', red. 'Warley Rose', pink. *A. oppositifolia* (0.03), IV, lilac-pink; forms blue-green cushions; for the enthusiast.
Alyssum arduinii SE Eur.	0.20 lemon yellow	IV–V, flowers in panicles; grey-green, spathulate leaves; more compact than *A. saxatile* (list 4.1.1).
Alyssum serpyllifolium SW Eur.	up to 0.05 golden yellow	V, abundant flowers on prostrate stems; leaves elliptic above, round below; forms dainty, grey-green mats. *A. repens* (up to 0.15), orange-yellow; forms a dense turf among rocks.
Arenaria grandiflora S Eur.	0.10–0.12 white	VI–VIII, large flowers over green, needle-like foliage; forms extensive carpets; variable species.
Arenaria montana SW Eur.	0.02/0.08 white	V–VI, abundant, exceptionally large flowers over a flat, green turf; for limy soils. *A. purpurascens* (to 0.10), VII–VIII, pink; also for bright shade.
Arenaria rigida S Russ., Balk.	0.10 white	VII–IX, many-flowered inflorescences; slender shoots with needle-like leaves; grows quickly and forms extensive, turf-like patches; for sun or bright shade on sandy, humus-rich soil.
Athamanta haynaldii (*A. matthioli*) W Yugo., Alban.	0.30 white	VII–VIII, numerous umbels over graceful mounds of dark green, hair-like foliage; long-lived in dry-stone walls. *A. cretensis* (0.30), V–VI, white; finely divided, grey-green foliage; often short-lived; seeds itself freely.

Wild pinks, *Dianthus*

Wild *Dianthus* species are at their most attractive planted in crevices or on dry-stone walls and rocky mounds in full sun. Further species have been assigned to lists 4.1.1 and 4.2.3.

Dianthus banaticus (*D. giganteus* ssp. *banaticus*) Rum.	0.30 dark red	VI, clusters of mostly 6 flowers; leaves broadening at the base, not grass-like.
Meadow pink *Dianthus campestris* Rum., E & S Russ.	0.30 red	VII, small flowers on much branched stems; lax, narrow leaves; bushy habit; undemanding.
Dianthus cruentus		List 3.4.1
Dianthus knappii W Yugo.	0.30 yellow	VI–VII, short-lived; flowers on long, rigid stems; green, grass-like leaves. *D. atrorubens,* red; similar to the above.
Fringed pink *Dianthus monspessulanus* var. *sternbergii* E Alps	0.06/0.20 pink	VI–VII, scented flowers with feathery, laciniate petals on tall, arching stems. *D. monspessulanus* (0.40), white (to pink) flowers with fringed petals.
Dianthus petraeus ssp. *noeanus* Bulg.	0.05/0.20 white	VII–VIII, small, scented flowers with finely laciniate petals; domed, blue-green cushions; stiff, piercing leaves; also for roof plantings.
Dianthus petraeus ssp. *petraeus* (*D. spiculifolius*) Balk.	0.05/0.20 white	VII–VIII, finely fringed petals; forms large, flat, grey-green mats.
Common pink *Dianthus plumarius* E C Eur.	0.05/0.30 pink and white	VI–VII, very fragrant flowers with feathery, laciniate petals on stiff, branching stems; forms a dense, blue-green turf; to be recommended, but rare in the trade. (Garden cultivars: see list 4.1.1.)
Wood pink *Dianthus sylvestris* Alps, Jura, Fr., It., Balk.	0.05/0.20 pink	VI–VIII, stems with 1–4 large flowers; dense, sea-green, grassy cushions; seeds itself freely; very amenable to cultivation.

Further commonly available and vigorous species

Euphorbia capitulata		List 3.3.3
Euphorbia myrsinites		List 3.3.3
Festuca pallens (*F. glauca* ssp. *glauca*) C, S & E Eur.	0.20–0.30	VI, arching, glaucous, blue-green leaves; for sunny crevices and in groups between rocks.
Festuca rupicaprina 'Laggin' Alps	0.10–0.20	VI–VII, small cushions of very fine, bristle-like leaves; deciduous; turns foxy red in autumn; thrives in rock crevices and among dry rubble.

Geranium cinereum 'Ballerina' Pyren., It., Balk., Cauc.	up to 0.15 pale lavender, with dark veins	VI–IX, very long flowering season; rounded, lobed, hairy leaves with long petioles.
Geranium farreri China	up to 0.15 clear pink	VI, large, dark-veined flowers; prostrate, daintily lobed leaves.
Geranium subcaulescens 'Splendens' S & W Balk., It.	up to 0.15 magenta, black centre	VI–VII, flowers long and abundantly; rounded, deeply lobed, grey-green, hairy leaves.
Hieracium villosum Mts of Eur.	up to 0.25 golden yellow	VI–VII, large flowers on sturdy stems; elongate–lanceolate leaves; plant covered with silvery, woolly hairs; for dry or moist soil in sun.
Hypericum olympicum Asia Minor, Balk.	0.20 yellow	VI–VII, large flowers in cymes on upright stems; glossy, grass-green, opposite leaves; undemanding. 'Citrinum', lemon yellow.
Hypericum polyphyllum Nr East, Asia Minor	up to 0.15 yellow	VI–VII, abundant large flowers in cymes; dainty, blue-green, cushion-like clumps; undemanding. 'Schwefelperle' (0.10), pale yellow. 'Zitronenfalter' (0.15), pale yellow.
Hypericum cerastoides (*H. rhodoppeum*) Balk.	0.10 brilliant yellow	VI–VII, large flowers in small cymes; low, bushy habit; grey, hairy leaves; undemanding; for stony places among rocks.
Rock candytuft *Iberis saxatilis* S Eur.	0.05/0.10 white	IV–V, reliable species; forms firm, dainty cushions; thrives in rock crevices. 'Pygmaea' (0.03), dwarf selection for trough gardens. Further *Iberis* spp.: see list 4.1.1.
Micromeria croatica (*Satureja croatica*) Yugo.	0.10 pink	VI–VII, thin, ascending stems, woody at the base; small, ovate leaves; for holes in the rock; seeds itself well on tufa; undemanding. *M. pygmaea*: see *Satureja* (list 4.3.1).
Minuartia graminifolia (*Alsine rosanii*) Balk., Yugo.	0.02/0.08 white	VI–VII, grassy leaves; forms large patches of dense, flat, green turf; old plants rarely flower. *M. stellata*, similar. *M. juniperina*, *M. imbricata* and *M. rupestris* all form large, flat, green carpets.
Minuartia laricifolia S Alps, Spain	0.15 white	VII–VIII, flowers abundantly; dull green, needle-like leaves; undemanding; forms large patches of turf on rocks and boulders. *M. l. kitaibelii* (0.10), flowers very abundantly; turf-like habit.

Beard-tongue, *Penstemon*

These striking and free-flowering North American perennials thrive in warm, dry, sunny, lime-free conditions. They need some protection against damp, but are hardier and more persistent than the species from lists 3.3.5 and 4.2.3. The mountain species fail in hot, humid summers.

Penstemon linarioides ssp. *coloradoensis* SW USA	0.08/0.15 blue-lilac	VI–VII, spreading cushions of pointed, lanceolate leaves.
Penstemon humilis Mts of W USA	0.05/0.30 dark blue	VI–VII, luxuriant in bloom; erect racemes of narrow, funnel-shaped flowers; elongate–lanceolate leaves; forms an extensive green turf.
Penstemon menziesii (*P. davidsonii* ssp. *menziesii*) NW N Am.	0.15 pale violet	V–VIII, abundant flowers; creeping stems with small, semi-evergreen, entire or serrate, ovate–lanceolate leaves.
Penstemon pinifolius SW USA, N Mex.	up to 0.20 glowing red	VII–VIII, erect racemes of brilliantly coloured, tube-shaped flowers; needle-like leaves; best planted next to rock; fully hardy.

Further common, mostly vigorous species

Pink cinquefoil *Potentilla nitida* S Alps, N Apenn.	0.05 delicate pink	VI–VIII, solitary flowers on very short stems over dense, shiny carpets of silvery foliage; ternate leaves; for a sunny position on poor soil among rocks. 'Rubra', rosy red. 'Alba', white. Flowers reluctantly in lowland gardens but may be grown for its attractive foliage alone.
Pterocephalus perennis (*P. parnassii*) Greece	0.15 pink	VII–VIII, forms spreading, grey-green cushions; thrives on dry, stony, well-drained, limy soils.
Ptilotrichum spinosum (*Alyssum spinosum*) S Spain, S Fr., N Alps	0.20 white	V–VI, very dense, intricately branched, spiny dwarf shrub, with silvery, ovate–lanceolate leaves; old plants have a broad, spreading habit. 'Coccineum', red.
Saponaria × *olivana* (*S. pumila* × *S. caespitosa*)	0.05 pink	VI–VII, large, firm cushions with large flowers; small, lanceolate leaves; undemanding and free-flowering. *S.* × *olivana* × *S. ocymoides* 'Bressingham' (0.03), large, mallow-coloured flowers; softly hairy. *S. pulvinaris* (0.03), Turkest.; red flowers on dense, flat cushions; hardy.
Stachys lavandulifolia Cauc., Asia Minor, Iran	up to 0.15 lavender-pink	VI–VII, cylindrical heads of flowers; lanceolate leaves with shaggy, silk-like hairs; forms carpets on dry, stony soil. *S. citrina* (0.20), VII–VIII, lemon yellow; silver-grey leaves. *S. spicata* (0.20), pink; dark green leaves.
Teucrium chamaedrys hort. 'Nana'	up to 0.10	VII, low, spreading, turf-like form of *T. chamaedrys* hort.; pink flowers.
Tunic flower *Petrorhagia saxifraga* (*Tunica saxifraga*) S & C Eur., Cauc., Iran	0.05/0.15 pink	VI–IX, graceful veils of flowers; needle-like leaves. 'Alba Plena', white; double flowers. 'Rosette', pink; double flowers; blooms until October.

Veronica cinerea Asia Minor	0.08 blue	VI–VII, forms a loose turf of grey, velvety, linear leaves; small racemes of flowers; for dry rocks.
Veronica surculosa Asia Minor	0.08 pink	VI–VII, flowers sometimes blue; thick, prostrate mats of rounded, coarsely crenate leaves with matted grey hairs.

Drought-tolerant mossy saxifrages (Section Dactyloides)

These are undemanding, drought-tolerant species, which grow wild in the Spanish mountains. In the absence of competition they form large, dark green cushions among rocks or on bright, stony slopes, protected from the midday sun.

Saxifraga camposii ssp. *leptophylla* SE Spain	0.20 white	V–VI, forms loose, domed, turf-like cushions; somewhat sticky, much-divided, semicircular leaf-blades with lanceolate tips; slender petioles; difficult in cultivation; rare in the trade.
Saxifraga canaliculata N Spain., GB	0.15 white	VII, broad, green, domed cushions; very sticky, flat, pointed, deeply incised, lanceolate leaves; calcicole.
Saxifraga cuneata N Spain	0.15 white	VI, forms glaucous, turf-like cushions; rosettes of shiny, leathery, wedge-shaped leaves, divided up to one third of their length into 3–5 broad, triangular lobes; also for sunny positions; undemanding.
Saxifraga trifurcata N Spain	0.15 white	VI, loosely domed cushions, which turn dark green in autumn; long-stemmed, three-lobed leaves, with lobes further divided into pointed, lanceolate segments; undemanding; also for sunny sites; can be used for edging. *S.* 'Berner Moosteppich', related to the above; finer foliage.

Encrusted saxifrages (Section Euaizoonia)

The following species have silvery-grey rosettes of tongue-shaped, lime-encrusted leaves that often appear fused with the rock. They are undemanding plants, thriving on moist to dry soils in sun or bright shade. For the most part, their flowers are borne in long, white panicles. Like the century plant (*Agave*), the individual rosettes die away after flowering, but the plants are continually forming new rosettes and any gaps are quickly filled.

Further species can be found in lists 4.3.1 and 4.3.2. Tender species have been assigned to list 4.2.3.

Saxifraga paniculata ssp. *paniculata* (*S. aizoon*) Cauc., Asia Minor	up to 0.20 white	V–VI, variable but undemanding species; dense, grey-blue rosettes of erect, tongue-shaped leaves; flowering stems branch above into slender panicles; forms dense turf-like cushions; also for bright shade. Selections (some of which may be attributable to another subspecies): 'Balcana', white with red spots. 'Baldensis', white; very small rosettes; reddish stems. 'Esther', yellowish white. 'Lutea' ('Lutescens'), sulphur yellow. 'Rosea', delicate pink. 'Splendens', magenta.

Saxifraga paniculata ssp. *cartilaginea* (*S. cartilaginea*) Cauc.	0.25 white	V–VI, flowers prolifically; finely pointed leaves. 'Minor' (0.10), dainty plant for trough gardens. 'Portae' (0.20), VI, yellowish; dense, firm, stone-like cushions.
Saxifraga paniculata ssp. *kolenatiana* (*S. kolenatiana*) Cauc.	0.25 pink	V–VI, growth similar to the previous species. 'Atropurpurea', dark red flowers.
Saxifraga paniculata var. *carinthiaca* Austria	0.15 creamy-white	V–VI, sparse, open rosettes of stiff, heavily encrusted leaves. *S. p. brevifolia* (0.15), white; very small rosettes.
Saxifraga × *burnatii* (*S. paniculata* × *S. cochlearis*)	0.05/0.35 white	VI, small, neat, silvery rosettes; forms gently domed cushions; for rock crevices.
Saxifraga callosa ssp. *callosa* (*S. lingulata*) Pyren., SW Alps	0.05/0.35 white with red blotches	VI, drooping inflorescences; blue-grey rosettes of linear leaves with lime-encrusted margins and (often) dark red bases; for dry positions on rocks and walls. 'Albert' (0.60), inflorescences like ostrich plumes. 'Superba' (0.60), large rosettes. *S. c. lantoscana* (*S. c. australis*) (0.20), white leaf-tips bent strongly back. *S. c. latonica* (0.25), compact, stocky habit.
Saxifraga callosa ssp. *catalaunica* (*S. catalaunica*) NE Spain, SW Fr.	0.20 yellowish-white	VI–VII, rigid, grey-white rosettes of short, tongue-shaped leaves.
Saxifraga cochlearis SW Alps	0.05/0.20 white	V–VI, dainty panicles of large flowers with pearl-like buds; domed rosettes; spathulate leaves with club-like thickening at the tips; for cracks in the rock. 'Farreri' (0.20), very narrow leaves. 'Minor' (0.10), white flowers; red stems; dwarf habit. 'Pseudovaldensis', even more compact than 'Minor'. *S. valdensis,* see list 4.2.3.
Saxifraga cotyledon		List 4.3.1
Saxifraga hostii (*S. altissima*) S Alps	up to 0.40 milky white and reddish	V–VI, flowers in tall, stately panicles; very large, star-shaped rosettes up to 15 cm across; ash-grey, tongue-shaped leaves that colour reddish in autumn; forms large, flattened mats. *S. h. altissima* (0.60), white with red spots; erect, grey, tongue-shaped leaves. *S. h. rhaetica* (0.20), cream-white flowers. *S. crustata* (0.20), cream white flowers; densely crowded, very narrow, white-encrusted leaves. 'Rosea', pale pink flowers.
Saxifraga longifolia		List 4.2.3

Sedums

The popular, sun-loving, fleshy-leaved sedums feel at home in any soil that is not too damp. Plants listed below are particularly tolerant of dry conditions. Miniature, turf-forming species have been listed separately.
See also steppe (list 3.3.3), open ground (list 3.1.1), border (list 5.3.1), rock garden (lists 4.1.1 and 4.2.3) and water's edge (list 4.6.5).

Sedum anacampseros Pyren. to SW Alps	up to 0.5 purple	VII–VIII, crowded heads of flowers; prostrate shoots with dense, rounded, grey-green leaves; stems sometimes root to form a small semi-evergreen turf; for rocks and scree; undemanding.
Sedum ewersii W Him.	up to 0.10 purple-pink	VIII–IX, crowded heads of flowers on decumbent stems; dense, opposite, blue-green, rounded-oval leaves; turf-forming; deciduous. 'Nanum', low, compact selection. 'Homophyllum', smaller in all its parts. 'Turkestanicum', dark pink flowers.
Sedum forsterianum ssp. *elegans* (*S. rupestre*) Morocco	0.15 yellow	VI–VIII, cylindrical leafy shoots forming a loose turf; similar to *S. reflexum,* but with thin, crowded leaves on the tips of sterile shoots.
Sedum midden-dorfianum E Sib.	0.15 yellow	VII–VIII, flowers in umbels; upright habit; narrow-lanceolate leaves, which turn brownish in summer; hardly spreads but will live for decades if kept free from shade and competition; thrives on dry to moist, loamy soils. 'Diffusum', coarser, broader leaves; much more vigorous; see list 3.1.1.
Sedum ochroleucum (*S. anopetalum*) 'Centaurus' S Eur. to C Fr.	0.10 pale yellow	VII, flowers on slender, upright stems; dark (grey-) green, narrow, linear, spine-tipped leaves; creeping stems form loose cushions.
Sedum reflexum (*S. rupestre* ssp. *reflexum*) C & S Eur., Norw., Ukr.	0.20 yellow	VII–VIII, flowers in loose, nodding cymes on leafy stems; thick, spindle-shaped leaves. 'Cristatum', monstrous form. 'Elegant' (0.25), yellow flowers; fine, bluish leaves. 'Viridis', grass-green foliage; old kitchen herb.
Sedum sediforme (*S. nicaeense*) Med., Asia Minor	up to 0.40 whitish	VII–VIII, decumbent shoots with erect, rounded inflorescences; coarse, grey-blue, lanceolate leaves (similar to *S. reflexum*).
Sedum stribrnyi (*S. sartorium* ssp. *stribrnyi*) Bulg., Greece	0.05–0.12 bright yellow	VII, ascending, branched flowering stems; neat, leafy, blue-green shoots similar to *S. reflexum*; turns bleached pink when starved.
Sedum tatarinowii N China	up to 0.15 reddish white	VII–VIII, flowers on erect stems; coarsely and irregularly toothed (or almost entire), linear–lanceolate leaves; swollen rootstock like *S. telephium*; undemanding.

Dainty, cushion- and turf-forming Sedum *species*

The following, low-growing sedums will colonise rocks, walls and flat, gravel rooftops, almost without soil. In a rock garden they will complement the plantings without requiring extra maintenance, though it may sometimes be necessary to remove sections of cushion to protect other plants from competition.

Biting stonecrop *Sedum acre* Eur., Asia, N Afr.	0.05/0.05 yellow	See list 3.2.4; thrives on dry walls, rocks and rooftops as well as on sand.
Sedum acre var. *majus* (*S. maveanum* hort.)	0.10 yellow	VI, taller and statelier than *S. acre*; larger, pallid green, elongate–ovate leaves; more densely leafy, particularly the flowering stems. *S. a.* 'Aureum', similar but not so tall; yellow shoot tips in spring. *S. a. krajinae:* see *S. krajinae.*
White stonecrop *Sedum album* Eur., Asia, N Afr.	0.03/0.10 white	VI–VIII, very variable species; forms an open turf of thick, sometimes almost spherical, sometimes club-shaped or elongate leaves with flattened upper surfaces. 'Murale', 'Rubrifolium', red-brown leaves. 'Coral Carpet', pink. 'Micranthum', very small brownish leaves; for the enthusiast. 'Micranthum Chloroticum', pale green leaves. 'Laconicum', sturdy, thick, blunt, brownish leaves; rarely true.
Sedum dasyphyllum C & S Eur.	0.02/0.05 whitish	VI–VII, starry flowers from pink buds; small cushions of grey-green, almost spherical leaves which turn pink in drought; shoots and leaves break away easily and root themselves in moist soil; thrives in sun and moderate summer drought. 'Suendermannii', VIII, coarser, hairy leaves.
Sedum gracile Cauc., N Iran	0.05/0.07 white-pink	VI, small green (or brownish) plants which do not form a closed cushion; cymes with 2 or 3 branches; succulent, narrow-linear leaves; not invasive; rarely grown.
Sedum hispanicum Alps, S & SE Eur., Asia Minor	0.10 pink	VI, small, bushy, fast-growing, grey-green cushions, which die completely after flowering; little importance in gardens.
Sedum hispanicum var. *minus*	0.05 whitish pink	VI, small, dense, blue-green cushions which turn reddish in drought; often used for bedding; widely available as *S. lydium glaucum.*
Sedum bithynicum Asia Minor, Balk.	0.05	VI, very similar to the previous species; individual shoots die after flowering but the plants perennate by means of small, densely leafy, self-rooting, sterile shoots; forms dense carpets on soils that are not too poor and dry.

Sedum krajinae S Czech.	up to 0.10 yellow	VI–VII, similar to *S. acre* and often hybridised with it; characterised by its dense foliage; almost club-like shoots; seldom true in the trade.
Sedum lydium Asia Minor	0.03/0.10 white	VI, tiny, dense, dark green or bronzy cushions; linear, often reddish-tipped leaves; for the enthusiast.
Sedum sexangulare C Eur., Greece, C Fr.	0.05/0.05 yellow	See list 3.2.4; more attractive than *S. acre* in winter; thrives on dry walls, rocks and rooftops as well as on sand; seeds itself freely. 'Weiße Tatra', yellow; finer leaves; forms dense mats. 'Montenegrinum', shorter than the above; very dense; rarely available in the trade.

4.2.2.   Houseleeks, *Sempervivum* and *Jovibarba*

A comprehensive treatment of these popular, rosette-forming succulents is hardly possible within the scope of this book. Along with an abundance of false names and synonyms, a multitude of natural and artificial hybrids makes it difficult to classify all of the plants available from nurseries. In many catalogues *Jovibarba* species are still listed under the old name *Sempervivum*, thus contributing to the general confusion. In the lists that follow, the most widespread species, forms and hybrids have been arranged according to the size and colour of their rosettes and the possibilities for their use. It is worth noting that the rosettes of established plants may be much smaller than those of specimens grown in nursery beds.

Houseleeks are very undemanding and tolerate extremes of drought, except in very hot regions. They are best planted in a gravelly, mineral-rich soil in cracks and crevices. Species with large rosettes, such as *S. tectorum,* are particularly suitable for decorating the crown of a wall. Formerly they were planted on thatch and wooden rooftops as a protection against fire. Today they are increasingly important for colonising flat roofs that will only support a thin layer of substrate.

Sempervivum

Small, silvery-white rosettes for narrow cracks and joints in stonework

Cobweb houseleek *Sempervivum arachnoideum* Pyren. to Carp.	VI, ovoid to spherical rosettes up to 1.5 cm across; starry pink flowers. *S. a.* var. *bryoides* and *S. a.* var. *doellianum* have very tiny rosettes.
Sempervivum arachnoideum ssp. *tomentosum*	Slightly flattened, densely silver-hairy rosettes 1.5–2 cm across. Old cultivars: 'Hookeri', 'Laggeri' (reddish), 'Webbianum' (silvery white rosettes up to 3 cm across). More recent cultivars: 'Silberkarneol', 'Jubilee', 'Rheinkiesel', 'Zinal Rothorn'.

Small and medium-sized (1–3 cm), brownish to purple rosettes

Sempervivum arachnoideum
hybrids
(Leaf tips with cottony hairs.)

Natural hybrids:
S. × fauconnetti, purple-brown.
S. × schnittspahnii, green, flushed shiny red.
S. × thomayeri, grey with velvety hairs.
Cultivars:
'Alpha', bluish green; red-brown hairs.
'Beta', dark purple-brown.
'Gamma', brown to olive green.
'Rauhreif', reddish.
'Zirkon', dark purple-brown.

Large and medium rosettes, suitable for crowning walls and rocks:

Sempervivum tectorum N & C Alps	VII–VIII, open green rosettes 3–12 cm across; glabrous leaves with ciliate margins; red flowers; old rooftop and cottage garden plant.
Sempervivum marmoreum (*S. schlehanii*) Balk., E Eur.	VII, similar to *S. tectorum* and just as variable, but generally smaller; open, greenish rosettes 3–10 cm across; green leaves with red-flushed bases; young leaves are hairy but become glabrous; pinkish-purple flowers with white edges.

A selection of cultivars and hybrids:

Large rosettes (3–15 (20) cm):
Dark purple to reddish-brown:
'Donarrose'
'Othello'
'Rotkopf'
'Lady Kelly'

Glaucous blue- to violet-purple:
'Atropurpureum'
'Atroviolaceum'
'Athen'
'Metallicum Giganteum'

Reddish-brown with green tips:
'Commander Hay'
'Zackenkrone'

Green with brown tips:
S. tectorum 'Monstrosum'
'Berggeist'
'Rotspitz'
'Wunderhold'

Olive green (flushed purple):
S. tectorum
'Bicolor'
'Glaucum'

Medium rosettes (2–7 cm):

'Granat'
'Rubin'
'Shotrold's Triumph'
'Spinell'

'Nocturno'
'Noir'
'Triste'
'Violascens'

'Grünschnabel'
S. marmoreum 'Rubicundum'

S. t. calcareum and cvs.
'Adlerhorst'
'Norne'
'Smaragd'
'Zwielicht'

'Mondstein'
'Mahogany'
'Topaz'
'Turmalin'

Further species with small to medium rosettes

Sempervivum ciliosum Bulg., Yugo.	VI, spherical, finely hairy, grey-green rosettes 3–5 cm across; cord-like, spreading stolons; yellow flowers. 'Ali Botusch', reddish tint; short hairs. 'Borisii', long hairs, giving the rosettes a whitish centre.
Sempervivum montanum Alps, Carp.	VII–IX, tight, spherical, glandular hairy, olive green rosettes 1–3 (–4) cm across; light purple flowers. *S. stiriacum* (*S. m.* ssp. *stiriacum*), VII–VIII, similar to the above but with flat, open rosettes; brown leaf tips; red-violet flowers. *S. m.* ssp. *minimum,* dwarf subspecies.
Sempervivum kosaninii Yugo.	VII, flat, open, dark green rosettes with dense downy pubescence; brown leaf tips; daughter rosettes on long stolons; forms an extensive, closed turf; red flowers. *S. ossetiense* 'Excaliber', open rosettes of very fleshy, green, densely hairy leaves with brown tips; stolons up to 15 cm long; mottled, white and red flowers.

Jovibarba

Jovibarbas closely resemble *Sempervivums* in their succulent, rosette-forming habit and preference for dry, sunny conditions among rocks. They are distinguished by their yellow, bell- or tube-shaped flowers with 6 or 7 fringed or ciliate petals appearing in July and August. In addition, some species are capable of forming daughter rosettes among the leaves of their existing rosettes. Hybrids with *Sempervivum* species and within the genus *Jovibarba* have recently been reported. All species prefer a limy soil.

Jovibarba allionii (*J. hirta* ssp. *allionii*) SW Alps	VII–VIII, form, spherical, hairy, pale green rosettes about 2 cm across; daughter rosettes on short, fragile stems; greenish-white flowers.
Jovibarba arenaria (*J. hirta* ssp. *arenaria*) E Alps	VIII, small (0.5–2 cm), spherical, light green rosettes, which turn reddish in autumn; sharply pointed leaf tips; daughter rosettes break off and roll to the ground, eventually forming an attractive turf.
Jovibarba heuffelii SE Eur.	VII, flat, open, brownish rosettes 5–7 cm across; creamy-white flowers; the rosettes divide but do not form stolons.
Jovibarba hirta SE Eur., E Alps	VII–VIII, open, star-shaped, green rosettes 2–5 cm across; reddish leaf tips; yellowish greenish-white flowers; forms small, spherical daughter rosettes which break off and root easily.
Jovibarba sobolifera (*J. hirta* ssp. *sobolifera*) E & C Eur.	VII–VIII, spherical, green rosettes up to 2 cm across, turning reddish in winter; small, spherical daughter rosettes that break off and root quickly; yellow flowers; particularly suitable for colonising extreme sites with very little substrate (e.g. rooftops).

4.2.3.   Plants recommended for enthusiasts

Achillea × kellereri	0.15/0.25 white	V–VII, open, umbel-like inflorescences; ferny, silver-grey foliage; needs to be dry in winter.
Actinella scaposa N Am.	0.12 yellow	V–VI, small daisy flowers over felted grey rosettes; for narrow holes in the rock; needs protection in winter.
Alyssoides utriculata SW Alps, It., Balk.	up to 0.40 yellow	V–VI, flowers on stiff, grey-hairy stems set with lanceolate leaves; large, spherical or ellipsoidal seed capsules; thrives in scree.
Amaracus		See *Oreganum*
Atlas mountains daisy *Anacyclus depressus* Morocco	0.01/0.05 white	IV–V, daisy-like flowers; rays red beneath; finely divided, silvery-grey foliage; turf-like habit; needs protection against damp in winter and in wet summers.
Andryala agardhi S Spain	0.10 yellow	VI–VIII, small, hawkweed-like flowers over silvery-grey rosettes; for rocks in full sun; needs protection against damp.
Arenaria tetraquetra Pyren., SE Spain	0.03 white	VI–VII, flowers scattered singly on firm, rigid, scaly-leaved, grey-green cushions; for a warm, dry spot. *A. t. granatensis* (0.02), for deep rock-crevices.
Artemisia laxa (*A. mutellina*) (*A. umbelliformis*) Alps, N Apenn.	0.10–0.20 yellow	V–VI, insignificant flowers; finely divided, aromatic, silky-haired foliage; very sensitive to damp.
Asarina procumbens (*Antirrhinum asarina*) Pyren., Switz., Hung.	0.05 pale yellow, dark lip	IV–IX, shoots up to 1 m long with strongly crenate leaves; flowers in the leaf axils; best in sun or bright shade in dry-stone walling; for mild areas; seeds itself freely; rare in the trade. *A. glutinosa* (to 0.20), V–VIII, creamy-white; for sunny positions.
Asperula arcadiensis Greece	0.05 pink	V, small, elongated, tube-shaped flowers on fine, grey-green cushions; for sunny holes and cracks in the rock. *A. suberosa* (0.05), pink; similar to the above; tender.
Asperula nitida Greece	0.03 whitish pink	VII, cushions of fine, green, lanceolate leaves with white, aristate tips; needs protection against damp in winter. *A. lilaciflora* var. *caespitosa* (0.05), pink; dense green cushions of needle-like leaves.
Astragalus angustifolius Balk., Asia Minor	0.10 creamy-white	V–VI, gradually forms large, dense, firm, grey-green carpets; evergreen, pinnate leaves with very fine leaflets; long-lived in dry-stone walling and on rocks in full sun. *A. exscapus* (0.05), yellow; grey, silky hairs.
Calandrinia umbellata Chile, Peru	0.10–0.15 red-violet	VII–IX, *Portulaca*-like flowers over roughly hairy, succulent, narrow-linear leaves; forms a dense turf; seeds itself freely; needs protection against damp in winter. 'Amaranth', magenta red.

Campanula × *warleyensis* 'Flore Plena' (*C. cochleariifolia* × *C. carpatica*)	0.05/0.10 light blue	VI–VIII, dainty, double, bell-shaped flowers; for limestone scree in full sun; needs to be dry in winter.
Carduncellus mitissimus Spain, Fr.	0.10 lilac	VI, thistle-like flower heads over rosettes of deeply pinnately lobed, mostly prostrate leaves; fully hardy. *C. rhaponticoides*, large, coarse, dark green leaves in flattened rosettes; more tender than the above; for warm, dry positions on well-drained soil.
Campanula versicolor		List 4.3.2
Rusty-back fern *Ceterach officinarum* Med., W Eur., Cauc., Nr East to Him.	up to 0.20	Warmth-loving, drought-tolerant fern; longish, grey-green fronds with rounded pinnae; for dry rock crevices with humus-rich soil, especially in mild areas.
Chaenorrhinum crassifolium (*C. origanifolium* ssp. *crassifolium*) S & E Spain	0.05 lilac and yellow	VI–VIII, like a dwarf snapdragon; small cushion plant with rounded, grey-green leaves; for sunny rocks; seeds itself prolifically on tufa; needs protection in winter. *C. glareosum*, lilac. *C. villosum*, violet; densely hairy leaves.
Chrysanthemum haradjanii (*Tanacetum haradjanii*) Syria	0.20 yellow	VII–VIII, cymes of composite flowers, lacking ray-florets; white-felted shoots; silvery white, filigree leaves; semi-shrubby; hardy but very sensitive to damp.
Convolvulus cantabrica S & SE Eur.	0.30 pink	V–VII, clusters of large bindweed flowers on erect (not winding) stems; hairy, lanceolate leaves; for stony, loamy soils; quite tender.
Convolvulus lineatus Med., Nr East, S Russ.	0.05 pink	V–VI, bowl-shaped flowers 2–3 cm across; vigorous, silvery mats of foliage; for dry, stony sites; not hardy where the soil freezes. *C. nitidus*, V–VI, pale pink; silvery mats. *C. suendermannii*, VII–VIII, similar to the above, but less hardy; for cracks in the rock.
Crassula milfordiae S Afr.	0.05 white	VI–VII, starry flowers over small, brownish-green, sempervivum-like rosettes; forms dense, low mats; particularly suitable for troughs and urns; must be kept dry in winter.

Rock pinks, *Dianthus* (see also lists 4.2.1 and 4.3.2)

Dianthus anatolicus Turk.	0.20 white and pink	VI–VII, good, vigorous cushion plant.
Dianthus × *avernensis* Fr.	0.10 pink	V–VI, like a dwarf *D. gratianopolitanus*; forms dense blue-green cushions; flowers on thin pedicels; for dry-stone walls. Selection: 'Graukissen'.

Dianthus erinaceus Asia Minor	up to 0.15 pink	VIII, clusters of 2–3 flowers on short stems; stiff, spiny cushions; for dry, sunny joints in stonework.
Dianthus suendermannii Bosnia	up to 0.20 white	VI–VII, closed, spherical, scented flowers; very loose, green cushions; for dry-stone walling.

Edraianthus

Dwarf cushion plants with campanula-like flowers and narrow-linear leaves. For sunny rock crevices and scree slopes. Sensitive to damp. All species require a poor, stony, well-drained but humus-rich soil.

Edraianthus pumilio W Yugo.	0.03 violet	VI–VII, large, sessile flowers over a flat turf; common. *E. dinaricus* (0.05), VII–VIII, forms a silvery green turf.
Edraianthus tenuifolius W Balk.	0.10 blue	VI–VII, small clusters of flowers on short stems; clump-forming habit. *E. graminifolius* (0.12), VI–VII, rosy-violet. *E. dalmaticus* (0.10), VI–VIII, violet.

Sulphur flower *Eriogonum umbellatum* E USA	0.20/0.30 light yellow	VI–IX, semi-shrubby relative of the knotweeds; flowers in umbels; grey-green cushions of ovate-spathulate leaves; sensitive to damp. *E. allenii* (Umbrella plant) (0.30), VII–VIII, yellow; leathery, green, ovate-lanceolate leaves; for gritty soil, dry in winter; full sun. *E. racemosum,* reddish-white flowers in racemes.
Erodium macradenum Pyren.	0.15 pale pink, with violet veins	VI–VII, large storksbill flowers; green, finely pinnate leaves. *E. cheilanthifolium* (0.15), very dainty species; pale pink flowers with red veins; pinnate leaves with dense, white-woolly hairs; for dry places, also in walls.
Geranium argenteum S Alps	0.10–0.15 pink	VII–VIII, large, dark-veined flowers; whitish, silky, rounded, deeply lobed to divided leaves with long petioles; for sites on gritty soil.
Geranium sessiliflorum 'Nigricans' S Am. to Austral.	0.01/0.02 white	VII, dainty, flattened habit; blackish-green, rounded, lobed or crenate leaves; seeds itself prolifically in carpets of low-growing sedums; for dry to moist sites.
Geranium stapfianum 'Roseum' China	0.15 pink	V–VI, long-stemmed flowers in pairs on decumbent stems; light green, incised, three-lobed leaves; for dry sites.
Globularia nana (*G. repens*) SW Eur.	0.03/0.04 dark blue	V, creeping shoots with ovate leaves. *G. pygmaea* (0.02), forms dense carpets; for dry sites, especially in trough gardens.
Gypsophila aretioides N Iran	0.03–0.05 white	VI–VIII, tiny white flowers on firm, dense, grey-green cushions; for holes in the rock. *G. cerastioides,* white flowers with pink veins; forms hairy cushions.

Gypsophila petraea Carp.	0.03 whitish pink	VII–VIII, flowers in dense clusters over grey-green cushions; short, thick leaves; for sunny holes and crevices; undemanding.
Gypsophila tenuifolia Cauc., Asia Minor	up to 0.15 pink	VII–VIII, flowers in loose cymes; light green, narrow-linear leaves; turf-like habit; similar to *Minuartia*; for dry-stone walls in sun and bright shade. *G. × suendermannii* (*G. repens × G. petraea*), VII–VIII, white; creeping stems form a dense turf; flowers in loose cymes; undemanding.
Helianthemum mace-donicum Greece	0.05 golden yellow	VI–VII, silvery-grey rockrose with prostrate shoots; thrives on limy soils; needs to be dry in winter; not very hardy. Further species, see lists 4.3.2 and 4.1.1.
Helichrysum milfordiae S Afr.	0.03–0.05 white	VI–VII, large everlasting flowers from magenta-pink buds; small, dense cushions covered in grey, wavy hairs; for east-facing crevices; sensitive to damp. Further species: see list 3.3.3.
Hypericum coris S Alps, It.	0.20 pale golden yellow	VII–VIII, dwarf shrubby species; flowers in terminal panicles; heather-like foliage; for warm, sunny positions.

Iris (Juno section)

Iris bucharica Buchara	0.40 white and yellow	III–IV, elegant axillary flowers on leafy stems; bold, shiny foliage; for open sites in sun or bright shade; hardy and persistent.
Iris graeberiana Turkest.	0.30 pale violet	IV, similar to the above; narrow, sickle-shaped leaves; hardy.

Iris (Onocyclus and Regelia sections)

These choice, but difficult and somewhat tender bearded iris (see also list 5.3.1) are mostly rare in the trade, but plants of *I. hoogiana, I. korolkowii, I. stolonifera* and some of the less demanding Regeliocyclus hybrids are occasionally available. They must be kept completely dry in summer and need protection against cold in winter. Plants such as the well known, blue-grey mourning iris, *I. susiana,* only develop properly in an alpine house in the temperate zone. All these irises grow well (replacing the tall and intermediate bearded irises) in the hot climate of Arizona and S. California.

Lithodora diffusa (*Lithospermum diffus-um*) SW Eur.	up to 0.15 bright gentian blue	V–VI, prostrate dwarf shrub with rough, lanceolate leaves; for sunny rock crevices; calcifuge; not reliably hardy. Large-flowered selections: 'Heavenly Blue', 'Grace Ward'.
Moltkia petraea Yugo. to Greece	0.40 violet-blue	V–VII, semi-shrub with dark green, linear, silky-haired leaves; flowers in branched racemes. *M. × intermedia* (0.20), VI, bluish-green, linear leaves; abundant, dark blue flowers; for very sunny, dry sites; thrives in walls and crevices; needs to be dry in winter.

Onosma taurica SE Eur.	up to 0.20 pale yellow	VI–VII, club-shaped flowers in drooping inflorescences; narrow, very hairy, green leaves; for sunny crevices in well-drained, gritty, alkaline soil. *O. alborosea*, V–VI, white and pink. *O. sieheana*, VI–VII, salmon pink; tender.
Origanum amanum Turk.	0.05–0.10 pink	VII–VIII, tube-like flowers up to 4 cm long; densely bushy, domed habit; ovate leaves; long flowering season; for dry, sheltered positions among rocks on well-drained soil.
Dittany of Crete *Origanum pseudo-* *dictamnus* (*Amaracus dictamnus*) Crete	0.15 violet-pink	VII, erect spikes of flowers on stems that are leafy below; small, broad-oval leaves with matted white hairs; not very hardy.
Origanum scabrum (*Amaracus scaber*) Greece	up to 0.40 pale violet	VII–VIII, nodding spikes of flowers arranged in loose panicles; smooth, aromatic, oval to rounded, sessile leaves.
Orostachys spinosus (*Umbilicus spinosus*) Sib., W Tibet	0.03/0.30 yellow	VII–VIII, sempervivum-like rosette plant; grey-green, linear to spathulate leaves with long, white spines at the tips; for bright shade; thrives on tuff.
Pelargonium endlich- *erianum* Asia Minor	0.30 lilac-pink, with red veins	VI–VII, two-petalled flowers in umbels; rounded, finely hairy, crenately lobed leaves; for warm stonework, sheltered from the rain; needs protection against damp in winter.

Penstemon

These striking and prolifically flowering North American perennials and dwarf shrubs are suitable for warm, sunny, dry positions on lime-free soil. Protection is needed against cold and damp in winter.

Penstemon cardwellii	up to 0.25 lilac-pink	V, very large flowers; thick, blunt, elongate leaves.
Penstemon caespitosus	up to 0.10 turquoise	VI–VII, striking flowers; narrow-lanceolate leaves.
Penstemon davidsonii	up to 0.15 lilac-pink	VI–VIII, large flowers on upright stems; spreading rhizomes; evergreen, entire, ovate leaves.
Penstemon hallii	up to 0.20 blue-violet	VI, short, spike-like racemes; thick, bluish green, linear leaves.
Penstemon linarioides	0.15–0.40 lilac	VII–IX, leafy, thread-like stems; flowers in racemes; very narrow, linear-lanceolate leaves.
Penstemon scouleri (*P. fruticosus*)	0.15 purple-violet	V–VI, dense, turf-like cushions of matt green, ovate leaves.
Petrocallis pyrenaica Pyren., Alps, Carp.	0.01/0.02 pale lilac	IV–V, small cushions of tiny, grey-green rosettes; similar to *Draba*; for limestone rocks and scree. 'Alba', white; more amenable to cultivation than the type.

Plantago nivalis Spain	0.01/0.10 dark brown	V–VI, ovoid inflorescences over flattened, snow-white rosettes; for sunny rock crevices and scree; undemanding.
Rosularia pallida (*R. chrysantha*) Turk.	0.02/0.15 creamy white	VI–VII, similar to *Sempervivum*; flowers in cymes; grey-hairy, spathulate leaves; daughter rosettes spread to form turf-like cushions; for a sunny site that is dry in winter.
Saponaria caespitosa Pyren.	0.02/0.08 pink	V–VI, flowers in compact cymes; linear-lanceolate leaves; gradually forms large, flat cushions on limestone rocks.

Encrusted saxifrages (Section Euaizoonia)

(Robust species: see list 4.2.1.)

Saxifraga × *calabrica* (*S. callosa latoscana* × *S. longifolia*) 'Tumbling Waters'		VII, for steeply sloping and vertical rock faces; immense, overhanging inflorescences up to 60 cm; very large, regular, silvery rosettes of narrow leaves; forms lateral rosettes (unlike *S. longifolia*) by means of which it can perennate after flowering.
Saxifraga longifolia Pyren.	white	VII, for east-facing limestone rocks and stonework; regular, silvery grey-green, narrow-leaved rosettes up to 15 cm across; slightly arching, conical to cylindrical inflorescences up to 70 cm long; dies after flowering.
Saxifraga valdensis SW Alps	0.02/0.10 white	VI, tiny, stone-hard, hemispherical rosettes, heavily encrusted with lime; for narrow joints in stone walling and miniature trough gardens.

Alpine skullcap *Scutellaria alpina* Spain, Greece, Rum.	0.20 blue-violet and white	VI–VIII, large skullcap flowers arranged cross-wise in terminal spike-like inflorescences; bushy habit; green, crenate, ovate leaves; thrives on limy soils in sun. 'Alba', white. 'Rosea', pink.
Sedum bellum (*S. farinosum*) Mex.	0.03 white	IV–V, similar to *S. acre*; glaucous purple leaves; frost-sensitive.
Sedum nevii E USA	0.03/0.05 white	VI–VII, forms a loose turf of small rosettes; pale green, spathulate leaves; for moist (not too dry) soils in bright shade; calcifuge; needs to be dry in winter.
Sedum oreganum Alaska to N Calif.	0.05/0.07 yellow	VII–VIII, cushion-forming species; prostrate shoots with rosettes of erect, glossy, dark or brownish-green, broad-spathulate leaves; calcifuge; needs to be dry in winter; protection against cold in harsh climates. 'Metallicum', coppery-bronzy leaves.
Sedum pachyclados Him.	0.10	VI, insignificant flowers; light blue-green, evergreen rosettes.
Sedum pilosum Asia Minor, Cauc.	0.03/0.10 pink	V–VII, biennial species; forms a dense, hemispherical rosette of narrow, hairy, grey-green leaves in the first

year; flowers on densely leafy stems; seeds itself freely; for dry planting niches and troughs.

Sedum sempervivoides Asia Minor, Cauc.	0.10 whitish pink	VII–VIII, attractive biennial species; reddish, sempervivum-like rosettes; for mild areas; seeds itself occasionally.
Sedum spatulifolium W Can. to Calif.	0.05/0.07 yellow	V–VI, evergreen rosettes with lateral offsets; fleshy, spathulate, whitish grey-green leaves, which turn reddish in drought; turf-like habit on well-drained, stony, lime-free soils that are dry in winter; may be grown in bright shade in a harsh climate; needs protection in winter; top-dress with light soil after rain-showers. 'Cape Blanco', yellow; miniature white rosettes. 'Purpureum', yellow; whitish rosettes turning wine-red with age. 'William Pascade', yellow; silvery-grey leaves, tinged with red.
Sideritis glacialis S Spain	0.25 pale yellow	VI, small flowers in dense, spike-like inflorescences; resembles a slender *Stachys*; small, green, hairy leaves; densely bushy habit; undemanding in a dry spot.
Teucrium marum W Med. (islands)	0.20 purple	VII. grey-white, aromatic sub-shrub; tender.
Thymus × *citriodorus* 'Aureus'	up to 0.20 lilac	VII–VIII, upright-growing thyme with yellow-margined leaves; lemon-scented. 'Argenteus', leaves with silver margins; needs protection in winter. 'Silver King', similar to the previous selection; very leafy; only for mild areas.
Thymus villosus SW Spain	up to 0.08 pink	VII–IX, ascending, branched stems; leaves with matted silvery hairs; sensitive to cold and damp. *T. villosus* hort. (0.03), V–VI, pink; forms dense, silvery grey carpets; sensitive to damp.
Thymus vulgaris 'Compactus' W Med., It.	0.15 pale lilac	VII–IX, insignificant flowers; small, strongly aromatic, grey-green leaves on upright stems; needs protection in winter. *T. vulgaris*: see list 3.3.5.
Townsendia exscapa (*T. wilcoxiana*) N Am., Mex.	up to 0.05 blue-violet, yellow disc	V–IX, large, daisy-like flowers on short stems; narrow, hairy basal leaves; for deep, dry, stony soil and rock crevices in sun or bright shade; short-lived.
Verbascum dumulosum Asia Minor	0.20–0.30 lemon yellow, reddish anthers	VI–VII, bushy semi-shrub, covered with large flowers; felted, round–elliptic leaves; for a dry spot in full sun; sensitive to damp; attractive plant for the alpine house. 'Letitia' (*V. dumulosum* × *V. spinosum*) (0.30), pale lemon yellow; similar but with very large flowers.

Veronica poliifolia Syria, Iran	up to 0.15 blue	VI–VIII, small speedwell flowers in terminal racemes; lance-like leaves with matted, silvery-grey hairs; long-lived on soils that are not too rich.
Veronica saturejoides Balk.	0.02/0.05 cobalt blue	V, flowers in racemes; evergreen, glabrous, ovate leaves; spreads loosely over the soil. 'Kellereri', more vigorous; turf-like habit.
Veronica turilliana E Balk.	up to 0.10 light blue	V–VI, flowers in slender racemes; leathery, crenate, elliptic leaves; for well-drained, stony soils.

4.2.4. Bulbous species

The following species from stony steppes and dry mountain swards need a warm, sunny site on well-drained, mineral-rich soil in order to remain truly perennial. On soils that stay moist or damp in summer the bulbs may sometimes flower a second time but do not survive for very long.

The plants may sometimes be combined with species from list 4.4.2.

Iris (Section Reticulata)

These are very early-flowering, hardy, dwarf species with netted tunics and rush-like leaves. The bulbs should be planted 6–10 cm deep (according to size) in early autumn.

Iris bakeriana Asia Minor	0.10–0.15 purple-violet	II, horizontal falls with a white central stripe; variable in colour; slender habit; angled leaves; tender, short-lived plant for the enthusiast.
Iris danfordiae Asia Minor	0.10 lemon-yellow	II–III, leaves appear with the flowers; fully hardy; bulbs often break up after flowering and need 2–3 years before they can flower again.
Iris histrio Asia Minor	0.10–0.15 bluish to reddish purple	II–III, variable species; not as hardy or vigorous as *I. histrioides*. *I. h. aintabensis* (0.10), commoner and hardier than the above; matt blue petals with an orange mid-rib; protection advisable in winter; propagation by means of offsets.
Iris histrioides N Asia Minor	0.10 brilliant blue	II–III, falls with a white central stripe and golden mid-rib; more adaptable than the previous species and quite resistant to bad weather; needs a little protection in winter. 'Major' (0.10), blue; very early. 'Katherine Hodgkin', creamy yellow.
Iris reticulata Cauc.	0.20 blue-violet	III, narrow leaves grow to 30 cm when the flowers have faded; very persistent and particularly garden-worthy; increases to form large, free-flowering clumps on well-drained soils; many cultivars available in the trade, including:

Sky-blue:
'Blue Veil'
'Cantab'
'Clairette'
'Harmony'
'Joyce'

Blue-violet:
'Jeannine'
'Royal Blue'
'Springtime'
'Violet Beauty'
'Wentworth'

Reddish purple:
'Herkules'
'J. S. Dijt'
'Krelagei'
'Pauline'

Ipheion uniflorum (*Triteleia uniflora*) (*Brodiaea uniflora*) Brazil, Uruguay, Arg.	up to 0.15 blue-lilac	IV–V, erect, starry flowers; narrow, flat, linear leaves, which appear in autumn; seeds itself prolifically in mild areas; needs winter protection in a harsh climate. Selections: 'Wisley Blue', blue. 'Froyle Mill', deep violet.
Leucojum autumnale Port., N Afr.	up to 0.20 white	IX, petals often flushed pink; narrow, thread-like leaves, which appear after the flowers; quite tender, especially when damp; for warm, sandy soil and full sun in mild areas.

Dwarf narcissi (and *Sternbergia*) for summer drought

The following wild species need a slightly raised position, free from competition, in order to look their best. Species for soils that are moist to damp in summer are dealt with in list 4.4.4. The more robust hybrid dwarf narcissi can be found in list 4.1.4.

Narcissus asturiensis (*N. minimus*) Pyren., Port.	0.08	II–III, yellow flowers; dwarf version of the larger trumpet narcissi; very robust.
Narcissus canaliculatus Spain	0.15	III–IV, yellow petals with a white corona; several flowers on each stem.
Narcissus juncifolius Pyren.	0.12	III–IV, up to 4 golden-yellow flowers on each stem.
Narcissus minor Spain, Port.	0.15	III, golden-yellow petals and pale yellow trumpets; blue-green leaves.
Narcissus minor var. *conspicuus* Spain, Port.	0.20	III–IV, sulphur-yellow petals and yellow trumpets. *N. nanus*, similar but smaller in all its parts.
Narcissus rupicola Spain, Port.	up to 0.15	V, yellow flowers; similar to *N. juncifolius* but with solitary flowers.
Sternbergia lutea Med.	0.05–0.10	IX–X, golden yellow, crocus-like flowers; dark green, strap-shaped leaves, which grow to 15 cm after flowering; hardy on well-drained soil in a sunny position with summer drought, especially in mild areas; best planted in July or August; seeds itself in regions with hot, dry summers.

Low-growing wild tulips, *Tulipa*

Dwarf tulips are typical rock garden plants. They are particularly effective combined with low-growing alpine perennials but must always be given an open soil above their roots. Like the taller wild tulips from list 4.1.4, they are most persistent in a warm spot that dries out in summer. They may also be cautiously combined with the species from list 4.1.1.

Tulipa batalinii Buchara	0.10	III–IV, pale yellow-ochre flowers; salmon and apricot colour forms are also available.
Tulipa biflora Cauc.	up to 0.15	III–IV, small, white flower with a reddish exterior; several flowers on each stem; similar to *T. turkestanica* but smaller and with glabrous stems.
Tulipa chrysantha (*T. clusiana* var. *chrysantha*) Mts of India	0.15	IV, orange-yellow flowers with reddish exteriors; narrow petals; a relative of *T. stellata*.
Tulipa clusiana Iran	0.15–0.30	IV, white and red striped flowers with pointed petals; naturalised in Northern Mediterranean countries; rhizomatous.
Tulipa orphanidea (*T. hageri*) 'Splendens' Greece, Asia Minor	0.20	III–IV, red-brown flowers with greenish exteriors.
Tulipa kaufmanniana		List 4.1.4
Tulipa kolpakowskiana C Asia	0.20	IV, yellow flowers with darker exteriors, solitary or in pairs; wavy leaves.
Tulipa linifolia Buchara	0.20	V, dainty, bright scarlet flowers; narrow, wavy leaves.
Tulipa pulchella Asia Minor	0.10	III, violet-pink, funnel-shaped flowers; related to the purple-flowered *T. violacea*.
Tulipa sylvestris		List 2.4.1
Tulipa tarda (*T. dasystemon* hort.) Turkest.	0.15	IV, yellow flowers with whitened tips, several on each stem; brownish-green leaves; undemanding.
Tulipa turkestanica Turkest.	0.15	III–IV, white flowers with greenish-yellow exteriors, several on each stem; many grey lanceolate leaves; see also *T. biflora*.
Tulipa urumiensis Iran	0.15	IV, bright yellow flowers with reddish exteriors; green, strap-shaped leaves.
Tulipa wilsoniana (*T. montana*) Elbrus Mts., Caspian	0.15	V, ovoid, scarlet flower with black basal blotch, appearing very late in the season.
Tulipa whittalli (*T. orphanidea* var. *whittalli*) Izmir	0.25	IV, ovoid, bronzy orange-red flowers with yellowish exteriors.

4.3. Species for moist, gritty soils in sun or bright shade among rocks

Although most of the drought-tolerant species from the previous lists (4.2.1–4.2.4) also thrive on moist soils, the following moisture-loving perennials are better adapted to a rainy, temperate climate.

It is important to distinguish between species that grow naturally on rocks and in crevices, and those that come from stony slopes and scree, particularly when dealing with the more difficult enthusiasts' plants. Preferences for limestone or silicaceous rock must also be taken into account.

Many of the free-flowering species from list 4.1.1 may also be combined with these plants.

4.3.1. Common, vigorous species

Achillea rupestris S It.	0.10–0.20 white	VII–VIII, simple umbels of 4–8 composite flowers; green, entire, spathulate leaves; spreads at the roots; rare in the trade.
Achillea serbica Alps, C Apenn.	0.15 white	VI–VII, up to 3 composite flowers per stem; forms silvery-grey cushions of finely cut leaves; variable species. The drought tolerant *Achillea* spp. from list 4.2.1 also thrive in a moist, sunny position; see also list 4.3.2.
Alpine calamint *Acinos alpinus* (*Calamintha alpina*) (*Satureja alpina*) C & S Eur., Asia Minor	0.10–0.30 red-violet	VI–VIII, flowers in dense whorls on decumbent stems; small, ovate to elliptic leaves; for poor, stony soils.
Alchemilla hoppeana N Alps, Jura	0.10 yellowish	VI–VIII, forms dense cushions with insignificant flowers; palmately lobed leaves (7–9 segments) with silvery hairs beneath. *A. alpina erythropoda* (to 0.10), yellowish; similar to the above; very vigorous; forms small patches of turf; undemanding plant for gritty soils.
Mountain alyssum *Alyssum montanum* Eur., Asia Minor	0.10–0.20 golden yellow	III–V, flowers in umbels, elongating into racemes; grey, narrow-lanceolate leaves on decumbent stems. Selection: 'Berggold', V. *A. moellendorfianum* (0.15), V, light yellow; similar to the above with silvery, elongate-spathulate leaves; undemanding; for warm, stony (also dry) soils.
Androsace primuloides W Him.	up to 0.12 light pink	V–VI, umbels of small, primrose-like flowers on stiff stems above neat rosettes of narrow-lanceolate, silver-hairy leaves; spreads to form small mats, as do the following species.
Androsace sarmentosa W China	up to 0.12 pink	VI, often confused with *A. primuloides,* to which it is very similar; more intensely coloured flowers; broader, mostly elliptic, silky haired leaves. 'Watkinsii', (0.10), cherry-red; flowers profusely.
Androsace sempervi- *voides* Tibet	up to 0.03 pink	V–VII, small umbels on stems that occasionally grow to 7 cm; the overwintering rosettes resemble those of a tiny *Sempervivum tectorum*; more demanding than the previous two species; see also list 4.3.2.

Arabis ferdinandico-burgi Maced.	0.03/0.10 white	V, dainty species; hairy, obovate leaves; good groundcover for small areas in sun or bright shade. 'Variegata', white-variegated leaves. *A.* × *suendermannii* (*A. f.-c.* × *A. procurrens*) (0.15), IV–V, firm green cushions of hairy leaves; abundant and repeat flowering (see list 3.1.2).
Arabis vochinensis SE Alps	0.02–0.05 white	V, abundant flowers in crowded racemes; creeping habit; forms small, evergreen patches; glabrous, elongate-spathulate leaves. *A. scopoliana,* similar but with dark green, ciliate leaves; for a lightly shaded spot.
Armeria juniperifolia (*A. cespitosa*) Spain	0.05/0.10 pink	V, spherical flower heads over domed cushions of needle-like foliage. 'Alba', white. 'Rubra', red. *A.* × *suendermannii,* pink; not so tender as the above; needs protection against damp in winter; also for bright shade.
Silvermound wormwood *Artemisia schmidtiana* 'Nana' Jap.	0.25	VII, insignificant flowers; silvery-white cushions of fine, deeply cut leaves; for sunny, not too dry positions among rocks and on scree. *A. nitida* (−0.20), VII–VIII, S Alps; grey-white, coarsely pinnate, aromatic foliage; more tender than the above.
Aster andersonii W N Am.	0.03/0.05 blue	V–VI, creeping habit; spathulate leaves; gradually forms dense carpets.
Calamintha nepeta (*C. nepetoides*) C Eur., Asia Minor	up to 0.50 light blue	VIII–X, small, thyme-like flowers; free-flowering over a long period; incised and dentate, broad-oval leaves; compact, upright habit; nectar plant.
Fairy's thimble *Campanula cochleariifolia* (*C. pusilla*) Mts of Eur.	0.05/0.15 light blue	VI–VIII, delicate, free-flowering plant that spreads vigorously across scree and stonework; very amenable to cultivation. 'Alba', white. 'Seibertii', deep blue.
Mouse-ear chickweed *Cerastium arvense* 'Compactum' Eur., Asia, N & S Am.	0.10 white	IV–VII, forms dense green cushions of linear-lanceolate leaves; not invasive; dry to moist soils.
Dianthus spp.		List 4.2.1
Yellow whitlow-grass *Draba aizoides* Cauc.	0.02/0.10 golden yellow	III, flowers in small umbels over domed cushions of stiff, ciliate leaves; full sun between rocks; also for sandy soils.
Draba bruniifolia (*D. olympica* hort.) Cauc.	0.01/0.03 golden yellow	IV, tiny flowers on moss-like cushions; grows best on rocks; rewarding and free-flowering species.

Draba sibirica (*D. repens*) Cauc., Sib.	0.02/0.10 yellow	IV–VI, long, green, leafy, procumbent stems forming a loose turf; for small niches between rocks; becomes weedy and invasive on nutrient-rich soils. Further *Draba* spp.: see list 4.3.2.
Dragon's head *Dracocephalum ruys-chiana* Eur. to E Asia	0.40 steel blue	VII–VIII, dense, bushy habit; dark green, linear leaves; steel-blue flowers in false whorls; for planting between rocks. 'Nanum' (0.20).
Erysimum pumilum (*E. helveticum*) Alps, Pyren., Balk.	0.10 yellow	V–VI, small, bushy plant; very free-flowering; green, linear leaves; reliably perennial; for planting among rocks. *E. kotschyanum* (0.06), VI, forms a dense, miniature turf; uncommon.
Alpine fescue *Festuca alpina* Alps, Croat.	0.07/0.15	Rounded green cushions of hair-fine leaves, which turn brown in winter; for rock crevices; robust; not always true in the trade.
Festuca scoparia Pyren.	0.10/0.25	VI, dense, turfy cushions of very fine, deep green leaves; long-lived only among rocks and on coarse scree; each plant can cover a square metre; also for bright shade. 'Pic Carlit', low-growing form.
Geranium dalmaticum		List 4.1.1
Geranium 'Biokovo' (*G. macrorrhizum* × *G. dalmaticum*)	0.20 pink and white	VI–VII, striking, large flowers; deep green, rounded, lobed leaves; semi-evergreen; short rhizomes; not at all invasive; also for bright shade and woodland edge conditions.
Geranium sanguineum 'Lancastriense'	0.10 pale pink	V–IX, very free-flowering; green carpets of small, deeply lobed and divided, matt green leaves. 'Drake's Strain', pink. 'Prostratum', VI–VII, deep purple-pink.
Globularia cordifolia Alps., Pyren., It., Balk.	0.03/0.05 blue	V–VI, globular heads of flowers over dense, dark green mats of woody, rooting stems.
Globularia trichosantha 'Suendermannii' Balk., Asia Minor, Cauc.	0.20 blue	V–VI, free-flowering cultivar; dark bluish green rosettes of long, blunt-tipped leaves; stoloniferous; spreads vigorously to form evergreen carpets. *G. nudicaulis* (0.12), V–VI, pale blue; does not spread; also for bright shade. *G. punctata*: see list 3.2.2.
Helianthemum spp.		Lists 4.1.1 and 4.3.2
Silene alpestris (*Heliosperma alpestre*) Pyren, to Carp., Balk.	0.03/0.15 white	VI–VIII, delicate, starry flowers over a loose turf; undemanding. 'Pleniflorum' ('Flore Pleno'), double flowers. 'Heidi', white to delicate pink. For moist, rich, well-drained soils.

Hieracium bombycinum Spain	0.10/0.25 yellow	VI–VII, branched inflorescences; thick cushions of elliptic, felted, grey-green leaves; for rocky scree slopes in full sun; undemanding. *H. villosum*: see list 4.2.1.
Hutchinsia auerswaldii N Spain	0.05/0.10 white	V–VI, dainty dark green cushions; for moist crevices in scree and rubble. *H. alpina* (Chamois cress), V–VI, similar but not so luxuriant; enthusiasts' plant.
Linum dolomiticum S Alps	0.40 yellow	VI–IX, large flowers in umbel-like inflorescences; elongate-spathulate leaves; undemanding; for warm, sunny positions, also on dry soil.
Papaver nudicaule		List 4.1.2
Paronychia kapela Med.	0.01	V–VI, silvery inflorescences; covers rocks and soil with a dense, bluish-green turf. *P. k.* var. *serpyllifolia* (0.01), tiny, green, rounded leaves; also forms a dense turf.
Phlox douglasii 'Georg Arends' USA	0.08/0.10 pink-lilac	V–VI, forms dainty, evergreen cushions of needle-like foliage; for gravelly soils. 'Apollo', intense violet-pink. 'Boothman's Variety', violet-pink, dark centre. 'Crackerjack', crimson. 'Eva', pink, crimson centre. 'Iceberg', bluish white. 'Lilac Queen', lilac. 'Maysnow', white. 'Red Admiral', red. 'Waterloo', red.
Phlox subulata cultivars		List 4.1.1
Auricula *Primula auricula* Alps, Carp.	0.05/0.20 bright yellow	IV–VI, umbels of scented flowers over smooth, fleshy, white-mealy leaves; for limestone rocks in sun; prefers mild winters and cool, damp summers. *P. a.* ssp. *bauhinii*, S Alps, particularly large inflorescences; very mealy.
Primula marginata W Alps	up to 0.20 lilac	III–IV, umbels of flowers with white throats; strongly denticulate, elongate-ovate leaves; for rocky outcrops, particularly with an easterly or westerly aspect; plants need an occasional dressing of earth. Many free-flowering cultivars, such as 'Beatrice Lascaris', 'Clear's Variety', 'Drake's Form', 'Pritchard's Variety' and 'Linda Pope'. *P.* × *wockei* (*P.* × *arctotis* × *P. marginata*), dark lilac; luxuriant green leaves.
Winter savory *Satureja montana* Spain to S Alban.	up to 0.40 white	VIII, flowers may also be pale pink or lilac; semi-shrubby species with dark green, slightly hairy, linear-lanceolate leaves; similar to the annual kitchen herb *S. hortensis* (Summer savory).
Satureja montana ssp. *illyrica*	0.10/0.15 blue-lilac	IX, indispensable autumn-flowering perennial; forms attractive cushions on stonework and scree; green,

(*S. subspicata*) Balk.		lanceolate leaves; aromatic fragrance. *S. repandens* (0.15), VIII–IX, dark green, lanceolate leaves on prostrate shoots; for gritty soils. Both species will also grow in dry conditions.
Pyramidal saxifrage *Saxifraga cotyledon* Eur.	0.10/up to 0.50 white	VI, for moist to damp conditions in bright shade on igneous rock; many-flowered panicles, branching from the base; flat, shiny, grey-green rosettes up to 10 cm across; coarse, elongate-spathulate leaves. 'Pyramidalis', probably a hybrid with *S. hostii*; good for cutting; up to 60 cm tall on cultivated, nutrient-rich soil.
Scabiosa graminifolia S Eur.	0.40 lilac	VI–VIII, attractive, vigorous, semi-shrubby species; narrow leaves with silvery, silky hairs; flowers on slender, wiry stems; for dry-stone walls.
Scabiosa lucida Pyren., Alps, Carp.	0.40 red–lilac	VII–VIII, solitary involucrate flower heads; smooth, shiny leaves; for stony soils.
Scabiosa japonica var. *alpina* Jap.	0.20 pale lilac	VII–IX, very free-flowering; decorative, finely pinnate leaves; also for bright shade.
Scutellaria amana Turk.	0.15 lilac–blue	VIII, small flowers; grey-green leaves widening at the base; bushy habit; rhizomatous; for moderately dry (also sandy) soils among rocks; rare in the trade.
Yellow skullcap *Scutellaria orientalis* var. *pinnatifida* SE Spain, Asia Minor, Iran	0.10 pale yellow	VII–IX, large flowers over deeply incised, silvery grey leaves; forms loose carpets of decumbent stems.
Scutellaria scordifolia Sib.	0.20 violet-blue	VI–VIII, short spikes of large flowers; dark green, elongate-cordate leaves; spreads at the roots; undemanding; for stonework and among rocks.
Sedum cauticolum Jap.	0.10 deep magenta	VIII–IX, many-flowered cymes; blue-green leaves with reddish-purple edges on prostrate stems up to 30 cm long; for well-drained soil among rocks. 'Lidakense' (0.15), VII–IX, red; similar to the type but with slate-grey leaves. Hybrids (*S. c.* × *S. telephium*): 'Robustum' (0.20), IX–X, magenta; larger in all its parts. 'Ruby Glow' (0.25), VII–IX, ruby red; reddish blue-green leaves. 'Vera Jameson' (0.20), VII–IX, deep pink; silvery grey-blue leaves.
Sedum telephium ssp. *fabaria* (*S. fabaria*) W & C Eur.	0.15–0.40 pink	VI–VII, similar to *S. telephium* ssp. *telephium* (list 3.4.4) but with pointed, blue-green, elongate leaves with wedge-shaped bases and short petioles; for moist (to damp) stony soils and rock crevices.
Sedum spectabile		List 5.3.1

Sedum cyaneum (*S. pluricaule*) Jap.	0.10 deep pink	VIII–IX, flowers in corymbose racemes; prostrate shoots with fleshy, grey-green, round to oval leaves; thrives on well-drained soil. 'Rosenteppich', bright magenta-pink.
Senecio abrotanifolius C & E Alps, NW Yugo.	0.25 golden-yellow	VI–VII, flowers in clusters over dark green, finely pinnate foliage; for stony, humus-rich soils. *S. a. tirolensis* (0.20), orange-red flowers.
Senecio adonidifolius S Fr.	0.20–0.30 pale yellow	VI, similar to the previous species but with smaller flowers; paniculate inflorescences over dark green, finely pinnate foliage; old plants develop a turf-like habit; undemanding species for humus-rich soil.
Teucrium pyrenaicum N Spain, SW Fr.	0.05 pale yellow	VII–IX, abundant flowers in loose terminal clusters; attractive, compact habit; prostrate stems densely set with rounded, irregularly crenate leaves; reliable and fully hardy.
Veronica armena Asia Minor	0.05 light blue	V, green, needle-like foliage; dainty but often short-lived perennial; for sunny, stony places among rock. 'Rosea', pink.
Veronica cuneifolia Nr East	0.10 white and blue	VI–VII, prostrate shoots with dense grey foliage; for poor, dry slopes and cracks in stonework.
Veronica prostrata		List 4.4.1

Edelweiss, *Leontopodium*

These popular, silvery-white, starry-flowered alpines grow wild in intense sun on poor, stony, mountain grasslands. In a lowland garden they grow best among rocks in full sun. If the location is too exposed, they may fall victim to periodic drought. If the soil is too rich or even lightly shaded, the plants become grey and unsightly.

Leontopodium alpinum Cass. Alps, Pyren., Carp., N Balk.	up to 0.15 yellowish-white	VI–VII, white-felted, starry bracts around insignificant composite flower heads; for a sunny position on poor, moist, well-drained, alkaline, loamy soil; not very suitable for lowland gardens; very variable. *L. a. nivale* DC (0.05), Yugo.; early-flowering; densely hairy; for planting on rocks.
Leontopodium palibianum Beauv. (*L. sibiricum* DC.) Sib.	0.25 (yellowish) white	VI–VII, abundant, large, rounded starry heads; green young shoots; long, grey-felted leaves; clump-forming habit; also for dry, stony sites.
Leontopodium souliei Beauv. Yunn.	0.15 silvery-grey	VI (–VII), reliable and very free-flowering; abundant small flower heads; greyish white-felted leaves; forms a dense turf; grows wild in bogs. *L. calocephalum* Diels (*L. himalayanum* DC) (0.30), silvery-woolly flower heads on stiffly erect stems; leaves with grey-silver hairs above; very free-flowering. *L. japonicum* Miq., VII–VIII, small flower heads; leaves glossy green above; turf-like habit.

| Leontopodium stracheyi Hook SW China | 0.30 yellowish-white | VI (–VII), very large, fingery flower heads; thin, crowded, silvery-grey leaves. |
| Leontopodium × lindavicum (L. calocephalum × L. japonicum) | 0.15 white | VI–VII, dainty flower heads on stiff stems; long flowering season, extending sometimes into autumn. 'Bergsilver' (0.20), forms dense cushions. 'Mignon' (0.10), silvery-white; vigorous and free-flowering. 'Sterntaler' (0.25), large white stars; particularly good for cutting. |

4.3.2. More demanding species, for enthusiasts

| Achillea clavenae E & C Alps, W Balk. | 0.20 white | VI–VIII, composite flowers in simple or compound umbels; narrow, pinnately incised leaves with matted, silky hairs; several less demanding cultivars are also available; for low, turf-like plantings among rocks on loamy soil. Free-flowering hybrids: A. × kolbiana (A. clavenae × A. umbellata), white. A. × jaborneggii (A. clavenae × A. moschata), white. A. × wilczeckii (A. lingulata × A. ageratifolia) (0.30), creamy yellow. Widely cultivated Achillea spp.: see lists 4.2.1 and 4.3.1. |

Rock-jasmine, Androsace

In addition to the robust, stoloniferous rock-jasmines from list 4.3.1, a number of mostly rather difficult, cushion-forming species are available from specialised nurseries. Only a few of these plants are mentioned here.

Androsace carnea var. laggeri C Pyren.	up to 0.10 pink	IV–V, rosettes of needle-like foliage; for scree and rubble.
Androsace carnea var. brigantiaca W Alps	up to 0.15 white	IV–V, dense cushions of open rosettes; for turf-like plantings among rocks. A. c. var. rosea, pink flowers.
Androsace lactea N Balk.	up to 0.10 white	VI–VII, delicate green rosettes; for humus-rich soil in the shade of rocks.
Androsace lanuginosa Him.	up to 0.10 pale red	V–VII, branching, prostrate stems with grey-green leaves; for semi-shade.
Androsace strigillosa Sikkim	up to 0.30 magenta	V–VII, flowers in large umbels on tall stems; broad, hairy leaves; for bright shade among rocks.
Androsace villosa var. arachnoidea It., SE Eur.	0.05 pale pink	VI–VII, dense, turf-like cushions of blunt, lanceolate leaves with grey hairs; for open turf-like plantings among rocks.
Arabis androsacea Asia Minor	0.05 white	VII, dwarf species of rock-cress; forms dense, grey-green cushions of silver-hairy leaves; for small niches in bright shade on limestone rock.

Arabis blepharophylla 'Frühlingszauber' Calif.	0.02/0.10 dark crimson	IV, flowers in crowded racemes; sharply dentate leaves; for porous, moist soils; tender; calcifuge. *A. billardierii* (0.15), silvery-pink.
Prophet flower *Arnebia echioides* (*Echioides longiflorum*) (*Arnebia pulchra*) Asia Minor, Cauc., N Iran	0.10/0.25 yellow	VI, leafy plant with rough foliage; yellow flowers marked with five black spots; for warm, well-drained soils in sun or bright shade; short-lived and not very hardy.
Callianthemum anemonoides NE Alps	up to 0.20 white	IV–V, large, anemone-like flowers; pinnate basal leaves, which are not fully developed at flowering time; for well-drained, humus-rich soils with plenty of moisture in spring; also for bright shade; fails in regions with hot summers.
Campanula barbata Alps, Norw., Czech.	up to 0.30 pale blue	VI, hairy, bell-shaped flowers in one-sided racemes; rough-hairy leaves; short-lived; for lime-free soils.
Campanula fenestrellata W Yugo., E Alban.	up to 0.10 blue	V–VI, similar to *C. garganica* but daintier and more compact; star-shaped flowers; rhombic leaves with pointed lobes; for rock crevices and stonework in sun and bright shade.
Campanula garganica SE It., W Greece	up to 0.10 lilac with white centre	VI–VII, open, starry flowers; shoots grow flat against the rock; evergreen, crenate, kidney-shaped basal leaves; heart-shaped stem leaves; forms a clump and does not spread; for rocks and walls in sun and semi-shade. 'Blue Diamond', violet; vigorous and undemanding. 'Hirsuta', domed cushions of grey-hairy foliage.
Campanula pulla NE Alps	0.02/0.10 dark violet	V–VI, drooping, broadly funnel-shaped bells; bluntly serrate, spoon-shaped basal leaves; for moist, cool positions in bright shade on stony, alkaline soil; often difficult to grow; sometimes forms turf-like patches; thin rhizomes terminating in rosettes.
Campanula × pulloides 'G. F. Wilson' (*C. pulla × C. turbinata*)	0.05/0.15 violet	V, large bells over grey-hairy clumps of foliage; spreading rhizomes; vigorous and more amenable to cultivation than the previous species.
Campanula raddeana Cauc.	0.10/0.20 violet-blue	V–VI, dark green cushions of dentate, heart-shaped leaves with long petioles; branching, red-brown stems.
Campanula raineri S Alps	0.03/0.05 lilac	VII–VIII, large, inflated bells; crenate, elliptic leaves; for rock crevices in bright shade with well-drained soil.
Campanula tomasiniana NW Yugo.	0.20 lilac-blue	VII, nodding, tubular bells; pointed, lanceolate leaves; slender, more or less drooping stems; for rocks and stonework in bright shade.
Campanula versicolor Balk., SE It.	up to 0.50 violet-blue and white	VII–VIII, related and similar to *C. pyramidalis*; bowl-shaped flowers with whitish tips; stiff, unbranched stems; sun- and warmth-loving rock plant; not very hardy.

Campanula wald-steiniana Croat.	up to 0.10 blue-violet	VI–VII, bushy, free-flowering dwarf species; small, erect, bell- to funnel-shaped flowers; lanceolate leaves; hardly spreads; for sunny rock crevices; thrives in limestone soils.
Carex baldensis E Alps	0.10–0.25	VII, white flower heads; clumps of long, narrow, grey-green leaves; for sunny but not too dry, turf-like plantings among limestone rocks.
Carex firma Alps	0.03/0.10	VI, turf-like carpets of rigid, shiny rosettes; for moderately dry, limy soils; also for shady sites among rocks. 'Variegata', yellow-striped leaves.
Cerastium alpinum Arctic zone	0.05 (–0.15) white	V, dainty, prostrate-growing species with hairy, ovate to elongate leaves; fails in hot summers. *C. villosum* (0.15), V, upright flowering stems; silvery-woolly foliage and stems; for gritty soil among rocks.

Rock garden pinks, *Dianthus*

The following are highly treasured but sometimes rather difficult dwarf species for cool positions in bright shade among rocks. Further rock garden pinks may be found in list 4.2.3. The less difficult species are covered in list 4.2.1.

Dianthus pavonius (*D. neglectus*) SW & E Alps	up to 0.10 red, yellowish beneath	VI, large, solitary flowers; forms flat, grey-green cushions; for moist, stony to loamy soils. 'Inshriach Dazzler', red; even more robust than the type.
Dianthus subacaulis SW Alps, Spain, Port.	0.05/0.10 pale pink	VI, small flowers over dense, flat, grey-green cushions. *D. freynii* (0.02), V–VI, pink; forms small, dense, turf-like cushions; for moist, gritty, alkaline soils in sun.
Dianthus alpinus E Alps	0.05–0.10 magenta-pink	VI–VIII, flowers on short stems; green, turf-like cushions of broad leaves; for a cool position on limestone rubble in bright shade; difficult in cultivation. *D. callizonus* (to 0.15), VII–VIII, pink flowers with dark and light spots; similar to the above; only for rock crevices. *D. glacialis* (0.05), V–VI, pink; forms a dense turf of fine leaves; for gravelly, lime-free soils in bright shade.
Dianthus grisebachii Maced.	up to 0.10 magenta	VI, dainty species; small flowers; forms dense, greenish cushions.
Draba bryoides var. *imbricata* Cauc.	0.01 yellow	IV, forms flat, green cushions; sensitive to drought in spring; for rocks in full sun.
Draba dedeana Spain	0.01/0.03 white	IV, finely hairy, domed cushions. *D. × suendermannii,* more abundant, larger flowers than the above.
Draba haynaldii Rum.	0.01/0.10 golden yellow	IV, flowers in tiny racemes; dark green, turf-like cushions; bristle-tipped leaves; for planting on rocks.

Eritrichium rupestre (*E. strictum*) Kashmir	0.10–0.20 sky blue	VI–VIII, upright stems, branched above; loose rosettes of grey-green, linear-lanceolate leaves; for stony soils. *E. nanum* (King of the Alps) (0.02–0.05), much more sensitive than the above; impossible to grow in lowland gardens.
Festuca glacialis Pyren.	0.05/0.15	VI, flattened cushions of fine, bluish leaves; needs frequent division on all but the poorest soils.
Helianthemum oelan- *dicum* ssp. *alpestre* (*H. alpestre*) 'Serpyllifolium' C & S Eur.	0.05 yellow	VI–VII, green, ovate–lanceolate leaves in false whorls; forms dense carpets on limy, stone- and rubble-filled soils; fully hardy.
Hoary rock-rose *Helianthemum canum* C, W & S Eur., Asia Minor	up to 0.15 yellow	V–VI, dwarf shrubby species with ascending stems; green (to grey), linear leaves, grey beneath; gradually forms large, flat, dense cushions on limestone rubble and scree. *H. lunulatum,* VI–VII, W Alps, golden yellow; rounded, grey-green leaves; forms small, dense cushions; difficult. Further *Helianthemum* spp.: see list 4.1.1.
Alpine toadflax *Linaria alpina* Mts of Eur.	up to 0.10 blue-violet, orange lip	VI–IX, dwarf species with loose terminal racemes on decumbent, blue-green, leafy stems; short-lived but seeds itself freely among rocks in sun.
Lychnis alpina (*Viscaria alpina*) N Eur., Alps, Pyren.	0.10 deep pink	V–VI, flowers in dense clusters over bushy rosettes of lanceolate leaves; for a sunny position on moist to dry, lime-free soil; seeds itself freely.
Mertensia echioides W Him., Tibet	0.20–0.30 dark blue	V–VI, dense cymes of nodding flowers; elongate-spathulate leaves; turf-like habit; calcifuge; for moist, humus-rich soils in bright shade; short-lived. *M. primuloides* (0.15), V–VII, short, crowded racemes of gentian-blue flowers; small, hairy, elliptic leaves; difficult and often short-lived.
Muehlenbeckia axillaris NZ	0.03–0.05 greenish	VII, insignificant flowers; slow-growing, mat-forming dwarf shrub with thin, wiry stems; brownish, rounded leaves; for planting in groups; good groundcover for a sunny site on not too dry soil.
Myosotis decora NZ	0.05 white	V, dwarf forget-me-not with small, silver-hairy rosettes; for gritty soils.
Papaver burseri (*P. alpinum*) Alps, Carp.	up to 0.15 white, yellow or orange	VI–VIII, delicate alpine poppy; mostly available as a hybrid or as one of the following closely related microspecies: *P. kerneri*, golden yellow; fine foliage. *P. rhaeticum*, orange-yellow; fine foliage. *P. sendtneri*, white; broad, blue-green, pinnate leaves; thrives in limestone rubble and scree.

P. nudicaule, see list 4.1.2; larger and more robust in all its parts.

Petrocoptis lagascae (*P. glaucifolia*) N Spain	up to 0.15 pale pink and white	VI–VIII, similar to *Lychnis*; glabrous, blue-green leaves. *P. pyrenaica* (0.10), blue-green, spathulate leaves; calcicole; for sun and bright shade among rocks and on stony soil.
Phyteuma comosum (*Physoplexis comosa*) S Alps	up to 0.15 bluish white and violet	VI–VII, flowers in clusters on short stems; forms dark green cushions; for narrow rock crevices or holes in tufa; bright shade; difficult in cultivation.
Horned rampion *Phyteuma scheuchzeri* S Alps	up to 0.25 deep blue	VI–VII, spherical heads of flowers; pointed, ovate–lanceolate leaves; for rock crevices.
Potentilla ambigua Him.	0.10 bright yellow	VI–VIII, large flowers over dark green, ternate foliage; forms spreading, rhizomatous carpets; for rocky or stony sites on poor, moist soils in sun.
Potentilla nevadensis S Spain	0.05 pale yellow	V–VI, leaves with 5 segments covered in silky, silvery-grey hairs; for a sunny position among rocks.
Raoulia hookeri (*R. australis*) NZ	0.01 whitish	V–VI, tiny sessile flower heads among miniature, silky-haired, ovate–spathulate leaves; forms dense, flat, silvery mats; for a sunny position on well-drained, sandy to loamy soil among rocks. *R. glabra* (0.01), VII, NZ; white flower heads; forms extensive green mats. *R. lutescens* (*R. subsericea*), NZ; flat, shiny, yellowish grey-green mats. None of these plants grows in regions where winters are very cold or summers very hot.
Roseroot *Rhodiola rosea* (*Sedum roseum*) Circumpol., Pyren. to Carp.	0.10–0.35 yellowish	VI–VII, flowers in dense, hemispherical cymes; elongate–oval leaves somewhat toothed at the tips; roots have a pleasant rose scent; for moist soils in bright shade among rocks.
Schivereckia podolica Rum., W Ukr.	0.20/0.15 white	III–IV, flowers in squat racemes; basal rosettes of grey-green., ovate leaves; forms a dense turf; undemanding. *S. bornmuelleri* (0.02/0.10), Asia Minor; grey-green cushions. *S. doerfleri* (0.07), Asia Minor; particularly free-flowering; rare in the trade.
Scutellaria alpina Spain, Greece, Rum.	0.20 blue-violet, white lip	VI–IX, variable flower colour; erect spikes on prostrate stems; for limestone soils. *S. a.* var. *lupulina*, Russ., Altai; yellowish flowers.
Sedum sieboldii Jap.	0.15–0.20 pink	X, flowers in spherical cymes; very decorative, blue-green, rounded, spathulate leaves on arching stems; widely used for hanging baskets; needs protection in cold, wet winters.

'Mediovariegatum', leaves with a yellowish-white central blotch.

Sempervivella alba Him.	0.03 white	VII–VIII, large (1.5 cm) flowers on short stems emerging from the sides of fleshy, light green rosettes; finely hairy, remotely dentate, elongate–ovate leaves; needs protection against damp in winter; for mild areas. *S. sedoides,* larger and more abundant flowers.
Moss campion *Silene acaulis* Alps	0.02 pink	V–VI, solitary flowers on dense, flat, green cushions; sometimes reluctant to flower; needs frequent division and replanting.
Tufted catchfly *Silene saxifraga* S Eur., Switz.	0.20 white	VI–VII, small flowers on slender stems; *Minuartia*-like habit; graceful tufts of linear–lanceolate leaves; for rocks and stonework in semi-shade; seeds itself.
Pyrenean snowbell *Soldanella villosa* Pyren.	0.05 violet-blue	IV, 3–4 flowers on each stem; rounded, hairy leaves; robust and undemanding, rhizomatous species; for bright shade behind rocks; see also lists 4.5.3 and 4.6.4.
Stachys densiflora (*S. monnieri*) Alps, Pyren.	0.25 deep pink	VI–VII, flowers in short spikes; glossy, dark green, somewhat wrinkled, crenate leaves. *S. nivea*: see list 3.2.2.
Stokesia laevis USA	0.25 lilac-blue	VIII–IX, large, bright, cornflower-like blooms on branching stems over smooth, broad-lanceolate leaves; sensitive to damp and extremes of cold; for a sunny position on mineral-rich, well-drained but not too dry soil. 'Blue Moon', light blue. Purple-, pink- and white-flowered forms are also available.
Ring bellflower *Symphyandra hof-mannii* Yugo.	0.40 whitish	VI–VIII, large, fat, nodding bells in regular, candelabra-like inflorescences; green rosettes of elongate leaves; for rock crevices; seeds itself freely.
Thalictrum alpinum Arctic, Alps, E Carp.	0.15 yellowish-green	VII–VIII, elegant species; small, bipinnate leaves with rounded leaflets; for lime-free, even moory soils. *T. klusianum* (0.10), lilac; dainty, fern-like foliage; for moist, humus-rich soils in bright shade.
Thymus pseudo-lanuginosus 'Pygmaeus' W Eur.	up to 0.05 violet	VII–IX, small, firm, deep green cushions; flowers reluctantly; does not tolerate extremes of cold.
Trachelium jacquinii ssp. *rumelianum* (*T. rumelianum*) Bulg., Maced.	up to 0.25 violet-blue	VII–VIII, dense heads of small flowers with long corolla tubes; elongate–ovate leaves; for narrow rock crevices in sun or bright shade; calcicole; sensitive to damp.
Rock speedwell *Veronica fruticans* (*V. saxatilis*) Eur.	up to 0.10 azure blue, with a red blotch	V–VI, flowers in short racemes on long stems; glabrous, glossy, dark green, ovate leaves; for stony, humus-rich soils in sun or bright shade.

Veronica repens Spain	up to 0.05 white to light blue	V–VI, flowers in short axillary racemes; glabrous, glossy, round to ovate leaves; turf-like habit; for moist (not too dry) soils in sun; needs protection in winter.
Viola bertolini W Alps, It.	0.15 violet	V–VI, large pansy-like flowers; forms a loose cushion. 'Lutea', smaller, yellow flowers.
Viola jooi Rum.	0.05–0.10 peach-red	IV, bluish-green, heart-shaped leaves, often somewhat leathery after flowering; forms a clump and does not spread; for rocks in bright shade.
Vitaliana primuliflora (*Douglasia vitaliana*) Alps	0.03/0.05 golden yellow	V, forms flattened, fresh green mats on gritty soil. *D. v.* ssp. *cinerea,* cushions of grey-green rosettes. *D. praetetiana* (0.05), golden yellow; cushions of grey-green rosettes.

Lewisia

These lime-hating rock plants from western North America belong to the purslane family. Under normal soil conditions they must be kept dry throughout their dormant period, from August until early spring, and for this reason they are most often cultivated in an alpine house. Abundant moisture and nutrients must be available in spring to encourage flowering. The plants need strong light or even direct sun but cannot tolerate heat. They must be well protected from the sun in winter (possibly by using mats). The following species thrive in warm, well-drained, gravelly, mineral-rich soil (equal parts loam, sand and peat) in well lit, north-facing rock crevices, or on free-draining rocky terraces strewn with sand and grit. It is worth putting a collar of quartz sand around the root crowns to guard against rotting. *Lewisia cotyledon* and its close relatives and hybrids can be particularly recommended for garden use.

Lewisia cotyledon	0.20 white, with red stripes	V–VI, branching inflorescences; large, evergreen, blue-tinted rosettes of broad, spathulate leaves; robust, particularly the white-flowered 'Alba'. *L.* Cotyledon hybrids (up to 0.30), various shades of pink to purple. Sunset Strain, orange, pink and yellow hybrids.
Lewisia heckneri (*L. cotyledon* var. *heckneri*)	0.25 pink, unstriped	VI, abundant large flowers; evergreen rosettes of pointed, serrate leaves. Large Flowered Strain, particularly large flowers.
Lewisia cotyledon var. *howellii* (*L. howellii*)	0.15 pink, with pale stripes	VI–VII, many-flowered stems; evergreen rosettes of narrow, spathulate leaves with ruffled edges; rarely true in the trade.
Lewisia nevadensis	0.05 white	V–VI, rosettes with almost sessile flowers; for gritty, loamy soils on igneous rock; deciduous; dies down after flowering.

Early-flowering saxifrages (sections Porphyrion and Porophyllum)

The range of different cushion- and carpet-forming saxifrages belonging to the sections Porophyllum (including the Kabschia and Engleria saxifrages) and Porphyrion (including the very difficult *S. oppositifolia*) is very much greater than conveyed by the following list, which contains only proven species and hybrids obtainable from specialist nurseries.

With few exceptions, these are lime-loving, or at least lime-tolerant, rock dwellers for bright, shady conditions, out of direct sun. The carpet-forming species and cultivars are best planted on steep slopes, while cushion-forming plants belong in holes and crevices within the rock itself. The planting medium should be a free-draining compost of rubble or gravel mixed with garden soil and a little peat. All species benefit from high humidity during the growing season and sometimes appreciate a light spraying-over in the early morning or evening. In winter they should be protected with conifer branches against the sun.

The special characteristics of the different species correlate well with their flower colour, thus making the following classification possible.

Small, cushion- and carpet-forming species with red or pink flowers (section Porphyrion)

Purple saxifrage	magenta	III–IV, sessile, cup-shaped flowers on dense mats of
Saxifraga oppositifolia		foliage; particularly sensitive to drought; for moist,
N Eur., N Sib., N		somewhat loamy soils in semi-shade among rocks.
N Am.,		'Splendens', deep purple.
Mts of C Eur.		'Latina', large flowers; more amenable to cultivation than the foregoing.

Section Porophyllum, subsection Kabschia

Saxifraga lilacina	pale lilac,	III–IV, solitary flowers on 2 cm stems over grey-green,
W Him.	with	turf-like cushions; calcifuge and difficult to please; for
	purple veins	moist, lightly shaded sites. The following hybrids are not so demanding:

S. × *gloriana* 'Amitie', pale pink.
S. × *arco-valleyi* 'Arco' (*S. l.* × *S. marginata*), pale lilac to pink; vigorous miniature cushions.
S. × *anglica* 'Cranebourne' (*S. l.* × *S. luteo-purpurea*), pink-lilac.
S. × *angelica* 'Myra', pink flowers; grey-green cushions.
S. × *irvingii* (*S. l.* × *S. burseriana*), pink with red centres.
S. × *irvingii* 'Jenkinsae', pale pink.
S. × *irvingii* 'Mother of Pearl, delicate pink; large, solitary flowers.

Red- and pink-flowered species with flat cushions of rosettes (section Porophyllum, subsection Engleria)

The following plants have reddish-leaved, mostly nodding inflorescences, and require little space for their growth.

Saxifraga grisebachii	magenta	IV, stems up to 15 cm with nodding, red-coloured
Balk.		racemes over flat, grey rosettes of spathulate leaves; for rocky slopes in bright shade; easily grown. 'Wisley', particularly vigorous selection.

Saxifraga stribrnyi	magenta-pink	IV, similar to the previous species but with squat,
N Greece		branching inflorescences (0.08) and broader leaves. Selections:

'Tristan', pink; lime-encrusted.
'Isolde', whitish flowers.
S. × *kellereri* (*S. burseriana* × *S. stribrnyi*), III, pink;

early-flowering; long, branching stems; silvery rosettes.

Saxifraga sempervivum f. *stenophylla* (*S. thessalica*) Balk.	blood red	IV, nodding inflorescences (0.10); pointed, lanceolate leaves. 'Waterperry' and 'Minor' are two elegant selections.

Hybrids

Saxifraga × biasolettii (*S. grisebachii* × *S. sempervivum*)	magenta	IV, free-flowering; attractive in bud; long rosette leaves. 'Phoenix' (to 0.15), pretty rosettes; slightly nodding inflorescences.
Saxifraga × hoer-hammeri (*S. grisebachii* × *S. marginata*)	pale pink	IV, flowers in nodding racemes (0.10); tough, firm rosettes.
Saxifraga × kellereri 'Suendermannii' (*S. suendermannii* 'Purpurea')	pink	IV, firm, grey-green cushions; flowers sessile at first, then on stems up to 10 cm. 'Major', pale pink; forms larger cushions than the above.

Small, dainty, cushion-forming species with white or pale yellow flowers (*section Porophyllum, subsection Kabschia*)

Saxifraga burseriana E Alps	white	III, open flowers with red stems; blue-green cushions of fine, needle-like foliage; for rocks in bright shade; somewhat difficult; needs high humidity. The following selections are less demanding: 'Crenata', white; particularly compact cushions. 'Gloria', large white flowers; dark brown stems. 'Magna' (*S. b.* var. *tridentata*), white flowers on salmon-pink stems. *S. × paulinae* 'Franzil' (*S. b.* × *S. ferdinandi-coburgii*), pale yellow. *S. × elizabethae* 'Carmen' (*S. b.* × *S. sancta*).
Saxifraga marginata var. *coriophylla* Balk.	white	IV–V, large flowers in corymbose racemes (up to 0.05); dense, grey-green, lime-encrusted cushions. *S. × borisii* 'Margaretta' (*S. m. c. lutea*), pale yellow; vigorous.
Saxifraga marginata var. *rocheliana* It.	white	IV–V, flowers in corymbose racemes (to 0.10); more robust and vigorous than the above; rosettes of lime-encrusted, spathulate leaves; for sunny sites. *S. × salmonica* 'Marie Louisa', white. *S. × boydii* 'Aretiastrum' (*S.* 'Valerie Finnis'), pale yellow. *S. × boydii* 'Faldonside', pale yellow. *S. × pseudokotschyi*, pale yellow.

Undemanding species with extensive, turf-like cushions and yellow flowers (section Porophyllum, subsection Kabschia)

Saxifraga × apiculata (*S. marginata × S. sancta*)	pale yellow	IV, free-flowering hybrid; inflorescences up to 8 cm; forms dense, green, turf-like cushions; vigorous and undemanding. Selections: 'Gregor Mendel'. 'Alba', white.
Saxifraga ferdinandi-coburgii Maced.	yellow	IV, flowers in finely branched racemes (0.08); firm, blue-green cushions. *S. f.-c.* var. *pravislavii* (var. *radoslavovii*), red-brown flower stems; more robust and vigorous than the above.
Saxifraga × eudoxiana 'Haagii' (*S. ferdinandi-coburgii × S. sancta*)	dark yellow	IV, very vigorous and undemanding hybrid; forms dark green mats; inflorescences up to 8 cm.
Saxifraga juniperifolia Cauc.	yellow	IV, forms a vigorous, dark green, mossy turf; flowers reluctantly (0.08).
Saxifraga sancta Greece	yellow	III–IV, small flowers (0.08); not always free-flowering; forms stiff, green, mossy cushions.

4.4.   Plants that are not closely dependent on rock

The following perennials combine well with species from lists 4.2 and 4.3, but may also be planted in positions away from the rock. They are best set in groups on open rock garden terraces, where they develop into spreading mats of varied vegetation.

4.4.1.   Species for sunny positions on moderately moist soils that dry out in summer

These undemanding, warmth- and sun-loving perennials mostly grow wild in dry grassland. In the garden they will thrive on hot slopes or on patches of open ground between the stones of a rock garden. Depending on the particular species, the soil may be improved by the addition of gravel, sand, grit or loam. The majority also tolerate moister conditions and may thus be combined with species from list 4.4.3. The dry grassland perennials from list 3.2.2 often thrive in similar situations.

Alyssum montanum		List 4.3.1
Cat's foot, Pussy-toes *Antennaria dioica* var. *dioica* Eur., Asia	0.02/0.10 white and pink	See list 3.2.4. 'Minima', V–VI, dwarf cultivar, particularly suitable for troughs. 'Baltrum', very similar. 'Nyewood' (to 0.08), V–VI, pink; silvery-grey leaves; vigorous.
Antennaria parviflora (*A. aprica*) W N Am., Mex.	0.02/0.10 white	VI, silvery-grey, spathulate leaves; very vigorous.

Antennaria dioica var. *borealis* (*A. tomentosa* hort.) N Subarctic Zone	0.02/0.10	VI, silvery foliage; forms low, firm, reliably dense carpets.
Antennaria plantagini-folia N Am.	0.05/0.20	VI, leafy species; green leaves, silvery beneath; forms small turf-like patches.
Squinancywort *Asperula cynanchica* Eur., Med., Cauc.	0.20 white to pink	VI–VII, small flowers in branching inflorescences; prostrate habit; green, narrow-linear leaves.
Coronilla montana (*C. coronata*) Eur., Asia Minor, Cauc.	0.30–0.40 golden yellow	V–VI, umbels of 12–20 nodding flowers on upright stems; pinnate leaves; also for dry, sunny, woodland edge conditions and under pines (list 2.1.7).

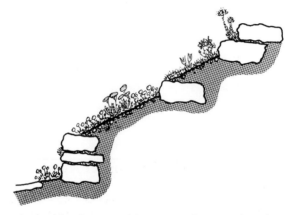

Rock garden: turf-forming perennials among rocks on a rather gritty soil.

Small scorpion vetch *Coronilla vaginalis* C Eur., Alps, Apenn., Balk.	0.15 yellow, marked with brown	V–VI, prostrate stems with umbels of 4–10 flowers; thickish, blue-green, pinnate leaves. *C. cappadocica* (0.20), VI–VII, yellow. *C. minima* (0.10), VIII–IX, yellow. Both more tender than the above. Must be kept dry in winter.
Dianthus gratiano-politanus		List 4.1.1
Dianthus gratiano-politanus 'Nordstjernen'	0.05/0.15 pink	VI, steel-blue foliage; for warm soils in full sun; dense, spreading, turf-like habit, in contrast to the cushion-forming cultivars of list 4.1.1.
Geum triflorum N N Am.	0.05/0.30 reddish white	V–VI, nodding, bell-shaped flowers on upright stems; silky-haired, pinnate basal leaves; undemanding species for dry, sunny positions.
White rockrose *Helianthemum apen-ninum* S & W Eur., Med., Asia Minor	0.20 white	V–VIII, dwarf shrub with low-spreading branches; silvery-green foliage; moderately hardy; seeds itself freely. 'Roseum', pink flowers.

Common rockrose *Helianthemum num- mularium* (*H. chamaecistus*) Eur., Asia Minor, Cauc.	0.05/0.10 yellow	V–VI, prostrate habit; hairy, green leaves; robust and fully hardy. *H. n. grandiflorum,* exceptionally large flowers. (Used for breeding.) Further *Helianthemum* species and hybrids: see lists 4.1.1 and 4.3.2.
Iris pumila and hybrids		Lists 3.3.3 and 4.1.1
Linum altaicum	0.15 light blue	VI, large flowers; light green, lanceolate leaves; rare in the trade.
Linum campanulatum W Med.	up to 0.30 yellow	VI–VII, large flowers; domed habit; grey-green, spathulate leaves; thrives on limy soils; rare in the trade.
Linum capitatum It., Balk, Asia Minor	up to 0.30 yellow	VI–VII, semi-shrubby species; tongue-shaped rosette leaves; linear–lanceolate stem leaves; spreading roots; rare in the trade.
Poa caesia		List 3.3.4
Potentilla arenaria		List 3.2.2
Pasque flower *Pulsatilla vulgaris* (*Anemone pulsatilla*) Eur.	0.05–0.20 violet	See list 3.2.2. The following cultivars have large flowers covered with fine hairs: 'Alba', white. 'Rödde Klokke', glowing red. 'Rubra', red.
Sweet scabious *Scabiosa canescens* (*S. suaveolens*) C & W Eur.	0.30 (0.50) light blue	VII–X, scented flowers on pinnately leaved stems; undivided, grey-hairy, lanceolate basal leaves; for dry, sandy loam in sun.
Low-growing *Sedum* spp.		List 4.2.1
Mountain germander *Teucrium montanum* C & S Eur., Med., Asia Minor	0.05–0.15 pale yellow	VII–VIII, flowers in terminal clusters; forms cushions of narrow-linear leaves with matted grey hairs beneath; for dry limestone grassland and rocky slopes.
Thymus doerfleri Alban.	up to 0.05 pink	V–VI, small, grey-hairy leaves; forms dense cushions. 'Bressingham Seedling' (0.08), V–VI, pure pink; vigorous selection; forms luxuriant grey carpets. *T. balcanus,* very vigorous. *T. ciliatus* var. *pubescens* (0.05), grey foliage; dainty.
Thymus pannonicus (*T. marschallianus*) Cauc., Balk.	0.20 lilac-pink	V–VIII, upright, bushy species without long creeping shoots; linear–lanceolate leaves with ciliate margins.
Thymus praecox var. *pseudolanuginosus* (*T. lanuginosus* hort.)	up to 0.05 pink	VI–VII, few flowers; small, hairy, grey-green leaves; forms a dense, grey turf; very vigorous. *T. procumbens* (0.05), similar but with a more compact habit.
Thymus serpyllum		Lists 3.2.4 and 4.3.2

Veronica prostrata	0.05/0.10	V, flowers in erect racemes on decumbent stems; crenate, bluntly lanceolate leaves; unsightly after flowering; not for planting in large patches. Many garden cultivars, including:
'Coerulea'	deep blue	
C Eur., Sib., Asia		
Minor		

'Alba', white.
'Coelestina', bright blue.
'Flexuosa', more prostrate.
'Heavenly Blue', light to mid-blue.
'Mrs Holt', bright pink.
'Pallida', pale blue.
'Rosea', pink.
'Spode Blue', light blue.
V. rupestris hort. (0.10), blue; similar to the foregoing cultivar.
V. r. 'Rosea', bright pink.

Veronica spicata Lists 3.2.2 and 4.1.1

4.4.2. Bulbs, corms and tubers

These are mostly rather dainty species which thrive in sunny positions on mineral-rich, sandy to loamy soils. They need plenty of moisture in spring but should be kept dry (to moist) in summer.

Spring-flowering species

Glory of the snow, *Chionodoxa*

Chionodoxas flourish in warm, open soils between rocks, but have nevertheless been assigned to the woodland edge (list 2.4.1) on account of their considerable invasive tendencies.

Spring crocus, *Crocus*

The following wild crocuses come from the mountains of southern Europe, flourishing in full sun on soils that dry out in summer. Species that require a moist soil in summer are dealt with in lists 2.4.1 and 4.1.1.

White
Crocus biflorus var. *weldenii* 'Albus', II–III, S Eur., Asia Minor, Cauc.
Crocus versicolor 'Picturatus', IV, SE Fr., It.; flowers feathered with violet.

Pale violet
Crocus etruscus 'Zwanenburg', III, It.; lavender-blue flowers with grey-blue exteriors.
Crocus heuffelianus, III, red-violet, E C & S Eur.; seeds itself prolifically; spreads also by means of stolons.
Crocus imperati, II–III, S It.; reddish-lilac flowers; buff exteriors with purple stripes and feathering.
Crocus sieberi, II–III, Greece, Crete; white to purple; very early-flowering.
'Firefly', pinkish-lilac.
'Violet Queen', violet.

Yellow

Crocus ancyrensis, II, Turk; orange-yellow; early flowering.
Crocus flavus (C. aureus), III, SE Eur., Asia Minor; golden yellow; seeds itself freely in open soil.
'Golden Yellow', large-flowered sterile hybrid, commoner in the trade.
Crocus balansae, II, Asia Minor; yellow flowers with brown-striped exteriors.
Crocus chrysanthus, Bulg., Greece, Asia Minor, Nr E.; see list 4.1.4.
Crocus angustifolius (C. susianus), II–III, Cauc.; golden yellow flowers with brown exteriors.

Grape hyacinth, *Muscari*

The following species hardly seed themselves and are thus particularly suitable for rock gardens, where they thrive in a sunny position on nutrient-rich soil. The undemanding woodland edge species from list 2.4.1 also flourish in these conditions.

Muscari comosum 'Monstrosum' S Eur., Asia Minor	0.40	V–VI, sterile flowers with bushy, violet-blue stigmas; the wild species has reddish-blue, sterile flowers above and greenish, fertile ones below; for the enthusiast.
Muscari latifolium Asia Minor	up to 0.40	V, racemes of gloomy, violet-blue flowers; bulbs usually produce a single, broad, green leaf; rare in the trade.
Muscari paradoxum N Iran, Cauc.	up to 0.30	V–VI, blue-black flowers with greenish interiors; strap-shaped leaves up to 45 cm long; rare in the trade.
Muscari tubergenianum hort.	0.20	IV, sky-blue flowers with white margins; crowded inflorescences, darker at the base; clumps divide well after flowering. *M. aucheri,* Turk., probably the original wild species; rarely available in the trade.
Scilla tubergeniana (*S. mischtschenkoana*) NW Iran	0.10	II–III, large, light blue flowers with darker stripes; bulbs often produce several stems; broad, pale green leaves; persistent but does not seed itself freely. Further *Scilla* spp.: see list 2.4.2.

Summer- and autumn-flowering species

Ornamental leeks, *Allium*

Strong, tall-growing alliums have been assigned to the steppe perennials in list 3.3.2. The following undemanding species also require a spacious setting to be properly effective. They are best planted in autumn.

Allium caeruleum SE Eur., Asia	0.30–0.50 sky blue	VII, dense, globular heads of flowers; narrow, grey, three-angled leaves persist through the winter.
Allium cernuum N Am.	0.30 pink to purple	VI–VII, loose umbels of nodding flowers; strap-like, semi-evergreen leaves; seeds itself without becoming a nuisance.
Allium cirrhosum (*A. pulchellum*) (*A. carinatum* ssp. *pulchellum*) S Eur., W Asia	0.30 pink-violet	VII–VIII; inflorescence resembles an exploding firework; glaucous blue stems. 'Album', white. 'Superbum' (0.40), very vigorous.

Allium cyaneum W China	0.20 steel-blue	VI–VII, spherical heads of flowers; thread-like leaves; often forms turf-like clumps.
Small yellow onion *Allium flavum* C & S Eur., Med., Cauc.	0.30 yellow	VII–VIII, sulphur-yellow flowers in firework-like inflorescences; stiff, glaucous blue stems; semi-ever-green; seeds itself freely. 'Minus' (0.05), yellow; dwarf cultivar.
Yellow onion, Lily leek *Allium moly* Med.	0.25 yellow	VI, flowers in broadly domed umbels; exceptionally broad, blue-green leaves; seeds itself prolifically and often becomes a nuisance. 'Luteum', clear yellow. *A. narcissiflorum:* see list 4.5.4.
Rose garlic *Allium roseum* S Eur.	0.50 pink	VI–VII, flowers in spherical umbels; broad-linear leaves up to 3 cm across; seeds itself prolifically in some areas.
Round-headed leek *Allium sphaerocephalon* C & S Eur, Asia Minor, Cauc.	up to 0.80 purple-red	VII–VIII, spherical heads of flowers, 3 cm across; stiff stems; good for cutting.
Chinese chives *Allium tuberosum* 'Glaucum' Jap., China, Nepal	0.50 white	VIII–IX, free-flowering umbels; semi-evergreen.

Autumn crocus, *Colchicum*

The various *Colchicum* species with a southerly distribution all flourish in summer drought on a rock garden or in a stony steppe (prairie) planting. In a small garden, they may also be used successfully in sunny woodland edge conditions (list 2.3.4).

True autumn crocus, *Crocus*

These fragile-looking but vigorous perennials are seldom encountered in our gardens, not least because they require competition-free planting positions on a rock garden or on a warm, bright, dry woodland edge (see list 2.3.4) for their long-term success. Most of the species that are currently available in the trade flower before their leaves are developed.

Species that flower before their leaves emerge

Iris-flowered crocus *Crocus banaticus* (*C. byzantinus*) (*C. iridiflorus*) E Carp.	X–XII, large, sky-blue, cup- or bowl-shaped flowers with long corolla tubes; also for lightly shaded sites under trees; seeds itself prolifically; without a doubt the finest autumn-flowering crocus.
Crocus kotschyanus (*C. zonatus*) Asia Minor	VIII–X, finely veined, rose-lilac flowers with a yellow ring at the base of the cup; seeds itself prolifically. *C. k.* var. *leucopharynx* (*C. karduchorum* hort.), blue-lilac with a creamy-white throat.
Crocus speciosus Asia Minor, Iran, S Russ.	IX–X, large, light blue flowers with darker veins. 'Albus', pure white. 'Artabir', blue-violet.

'Cassiope', blue with a yellow throat.
'Conqueror', deep sky blue.
'Globosus', blue; very late.
'Oxonian', deep violet-blue.
'Pollux', delicate violet with a silver-grey exterior.

Species that flower after the leaves emerge (uncommon, sometimes tender)

Crocus asturicus 'Atropurpureus' N Spain	IX–X, dark mauve.
Crocus medius W Alps	X–XI, lilac to purple with a white throat and purple veins; leaves barely emerge in autumn.
Crocus pulchellus Greece, Asia Minor	X, lilac-blue with darker veins; yellow throat. 'Zephyr', white with a yellow throat.
Saffron *Crocus sativus* Med.	IX–X, blue-violet flowers with darker veins; long, orange stigmas (kitchen herb and dye). *C. cartwrightianus* 'Albus', pure white with orange-red stigmas.

4.4.3.   Species for sun (or bright shade) on moist soils

Although the following species normally grow together to form dense mats in the wild, not all of them will tolerate close planting and strong competition in a garden. Some thrive only in open soil, and are therefore best planted among stones and rubble. Many are very adaptable, including Edelweiß, which prefers a warm site next to a large stone in lowland gardens and has therefore been assigned to list 4.3.1. By contrast, the trumpet gentians (*Gentiana acaulis* hort.) thrive on moist, loamy soil in bright shade.

Trumpet gentians, *Gentiana acaulis* hort.

The trumpet gentians have deep green rosettes of elliptic to lanceolate leaves, producing large, deep blue, funnel-shaped flowers on short stems in May and June. Plants sold as *Gentiana acaulis* in the trade are mostly vigorous, robust, lime-tolerant hybrids and selections from the following, often wrongly named species.

Gentiana angustifolia Vill. SW Alps, Jura, Pyren.	V–VI, flowers on long stems; linear–lanceolate leaves.
Gentiana clusii Perr. et Song. C & S Eur.	V–VI, flowers without green blotches on the inside; calyx teeth appressed; glossy, somewhat leathery leaves.
Gentiana dinarica G. Beck SW Yugo., Alban., It.	Flowers without blotches on the inside; glossy, broad-elliptic leaves. 'Fronleiten', V–VI, very vigorous.
Gentiana kochiana Perr. et Song. (*G. acaulis*) Alps, Carp., NE Spain, It., Yugo.	V–VI, flowers with green blotches on the inside; calyx teeth not appressed; ovate–elliptic leaves; calcifuge.
Gentiana acaulis hort.	V–VIII, commonly available in the trade; deep blue, funnel-shaped flowers; forms flat cushions; for damp, loamy soils; needs occasional division after flowering.

Cinquefoil, *Potentilla*

The remaining plants from this list all make good partners for trumpet gentians. The following *Potentilla* species are low-growing perennials with strawberry-like flowers and palmate or pinnate foliage.

Golden cinquefoil *Potentilla aurea* N Spain to Sudet., Balk., Asia Minor	0.10/0.15 golden yellow	V–VI, forms loose cushions of dark green, five-finge-red leaves with silver-hairy margins. 'Goldklumpen', particularly free-flowering. 'Rathboneana', VI–VII, golden yellow; semi-double flowers.
Potentilla aurea ssp. *chrysocraspeda* (*P. chrysocraspeda*) (*P. ternata*) Carp., Balk.	0.10–0.15 yellow, with orange spot	VI–VII, several large flowers on each stem; very hairy, tripartite basal leaves. 'Aurantiaca' (0.10), orange-flowered dwarf form.
Potentilla crantzii W Eur., N Asia, N N Am.	0.05–0.15 golden yellow	VI–VIII, variable species; five-fingered leaves with erect hairs; forms large, dark green carpets. 'Goldrausch', natural hybrid (?); very vigorous; very long and free-flowering, often starting in autumn and early spring.
Potentilla taber- *naemontani* (*P. verna*) 'Nana'	0.03–0.05 golden yellow	III–VII and IX–XI, very long flowering season; dark green, five- to seven-fingered leaves; forms small, turf-like patches. Further low-growing *Potentilla* spp.: see lists 4.3.2 and 2.1.8. *P. arenaria:* see list 3.2.2.
Potentilla × tonguei (*P. anglica ×* *P. nepalensis*)	0.10 apricot- yellow, with red eye	VII–VIII, shiny, dark green, five-fingered leaves; groundcover plant for small areas on moist soil.

Further species for sun or bright shade on moist soil

Anemone narcissiflora Eur., Asia	up to 0.30 white	V–VI, loose umbels of 3–8 flowers; palmate basal leaves; rare in the trade.
Anthyllis montana 'Rubra' S Eur., Alps	0.10 wine-red	V–VI, clover-like heads of flowers; grey-green, pinnate leaves; weak-growing at first but robust later; not very long-lived; thrives in gritty soil; rare in the trade. Other selections: 'Carminea', 'Rosea'.
Campanula collina Cauc.	up to 0.20 violet	IV, large, drooping, solitary flowers on upright stems; petiolate, oval to lanceolate leaves; rhizomes spread to form dense mats; for moist soils in bright shade. *C. rotundifolia:* see list 3.2.4.
Golden hawksbeard *Crepis aurea* Alps, It., Balk.	0.05/0.20 orange-red	VI–VII, flowers solitary; dentate leaves; for loamy soils, also in shade.

Spring gentian *Gentiana verna* Eur., Cauc., Iran, Sib.	0.10 azure blue	III–V, flat, open flowers with long corolla tubes; rosettes of elliptic leaves; often grows in small colonies. *G. angulosa,* similar but more amenable to cultivation; lanceolate leaves; enthusiast's plant for not too dry soil.
Alpine avens *Geum montanum* C & S Eur.	0.10/0.20 yellow	V–VI, large, solitary flowers; irregularly pinnate leaves; clump-forming species. *G. bulgaricum* hort. (*G. coccineum × G. montanum?*) (up to 0.25), V, large, orange-yellow flowers.
Hieracium villosum		List 4.2.1
Dragonmouth *Horminum pyrenaicum* Pyren., Alps	up to 0.25 blue-violet	V–VII, flowers in one-sided whorls; short-stemmed, wrinkled, crenate, obovate basal leaves, undemanding species for sun and semi-shade; white, pink and red forms are available but all are rare in the trade.
Lotus corniculatus 'Plenus'		List 2.1.8
Lychnis viscaria (*Viscaria vulgaris*) 'Kugelblitz'	0.10 pink	VI, very short-stemmed cultivar; for moist, alkaline but not too limy soils.
Matricaria caucasica (*Tripleurospermum caucasicum*) Cauc., Bulg., Asia Minor	0.03/0.15 white	VI–VII, daisy-like flowers; finely divided, dark green foliage; covers the ground densely on poor, stony soils; for a sunny position. *M. tschihatschewii* and *M. oreades* are very similar.
Phyteuma betonici- folium (*P. michelii*) Alps	0.20 blue-lilac	VI–IX, dense, cylindrical spikes on stiff stems; weakly crenate, broad-lanceolate leaves; rare in the trade.
Phyteuma charmelii SW Eur., Alps, Apenn.	0.20 blue	VI–VII, spherical heads of flowers; crenate, heart-shaped leaves; rare in the trade.
Phyteuma orbiculare		List 3.2.2
Large self-heal *Prunella grandiflora* Eur.	0.05/0.20 violet	VI–VIII, terminal spikes of large flowers; lush green, elongate-ovate, sometimes pinnately lobed leaves. The following selections grow more luxuriantly than the wild species: 'Alba', creamy-white. 'Rosea', pink. 'Loveliness', pale lilac. 'Pink Loveliness', pink. 'White Loveliness', white. 'Rotkäppchen' ('Little Red Riding Hood'), red. *P. × webbiana,* deep violet. For planting in groups but not in extensive patches.
Ranunculus gramineus SW Eur., Switz.	up to 0.30 yellow	V–VI, brilliant flowers on stiff, upright stems; linear–lanceolate leaves; dies down after flowering but usually forms new shoots again; undemanding.

Mountain buttercup *Ranunculus montanus* N & C Alps, Jura	0.10–0.20 yellow	V, variable species; large flowers; dark green, deeply three-lobed basal leaves; not invasive.
Trifolium repens 'Purpureum' Eur., Asia	up to 0.10 white	V–VI, red-brown clover leaves; forms small carpets and is invasive but not quite so vigorous as the type; undemanding.
Trollius europaeus		List 3.5.1
Wulfenia carinthiaca SE Alps	0.15–0.30 blue-violet	V–VI, dense, one-sided racemes on leafy stems; glossy green, crenate, obovate leaves; for moist to damp, humus-rich soils in bright shade. 'Alba', white.

Grasses and sedges

Quaking grass *Briza media* Eur., Asia Minor, Cauc.	0.30	V–VII, forms sparse clumps; elegant, open inflorescences with flattened, heart-shaped spikelets; see list 3.2.4.
Evergreen sedge *Carex sempervirens* Alps	up to 0.40	VI–VII, clump-forming habit; occasional rhizomatous spread; shiny leaves and upright stems; rarely available in the trade. *C. baldensis* and *C. firma*: see list 4.3.2.
Festuca scoparia		List 4.3.1
Poa alpina Mts of Eur., Asia and N Am.	0.10–0.30	VI–VIII, stems with swollen bases; dark green leaves; spikelets mostly viviparous; rare in the trade.
Sesleria varia		List 3.3.4

4.4.4. Bulbs, corms and tubers for sun and bright shade on soil that stays moist in summer

Bulbocodium vernum Pyren., Alps, Balk., Cauc.
III–IV, crocus-like species with overwintering corms; reflexed, lilac-pink perianth segments; strap-shaped leaves appear after the flowers; for moist (not too dry and not too damp), sandy to loamy soils; needs frequent replanting; quite hardy.

Spring crocus, *Crocus vernus* ssp. *albiflorus* (*C. albiflorus*)
Pyren., Alps, It., Yugo.
IV–V, covers moist, nutrient-rich mountain meadows and pastures with its white or occasionally violet flowers; the wild species is rarely available from nurseries. The closely related, lilac-flowered *C. v.* ssp, *vernus* (including *C. neapolitanus* and *C. heuffelianus*) is dealt with in list 2.4.2. Both deserve to be more widely planted, especially since they seed themselves freely in the right conditions. *Crocus* spp. for soils that are dry in summer: see list 4.4.2.

Fritillary, *Fritillaria*
Fritillaria meleagris: see list 2.4.2. Also to be recommended:
F. pyrenaica (0.20), IV–V, Pyren., C Fr.; purplish-brown flowers with yellow interiors; hardy and adaptable species for not too dry soil; thrives on the woodland edge.
Species that tolerate summer drought: see list 4.5.5.

Brimeura amethystina (*Hyacinthus amethystinus*)
Pyren.
V–VI, loose racemes of pale blue flowers (0.20); blooms unusually late in the season; easy to grow but rare in the trade.

Hoop petticoat, *Narcissus bulbocodium* (*Corbularia bulbocodium*)
SW Eur.
IV–V, broad, funnel-shaped, yellow flowers (up to 0.15); very narrow, almost cylindrical leaves; thrives where the soil does not dry out in summer.
'Citrinus', (0.15), IV–V, pale lemon-yellow flowers; very easy to grow.

Narcissus cyclamineus	List 4.6.6
Narcissus Cyclamineus hybrids	List 4.1.1

Angel's tears, *Narcissus triandrus* var. *albus*
III–IV, 1–3 creamy white, nodding flowers on each stem (0.10–0.20/0.30); very variable; tall and short, yellow- and white-flowered forms available; the hybrids (list 4.1.1) are more robust.

4.5.   Shade, semi-shade and bright shade on the rock garden

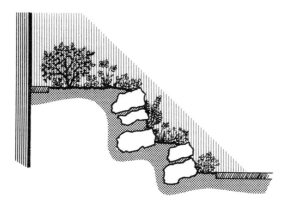

Rock garden: semi-shade and shade among rocks.

Shade-loving rock garden perennials may be divided into plants for moist to damp soil among rocks (lists 4.5.1 and 4.5.2), plants for woodland conditions (list 4.5.3) and plants for woodland edge conditions with summer drought (lists 4.5.4 and 4.5.5). The robust and widely available, shade tolerant species for decorative formal rock gardens appear in list 4.1.3. Dainty, carpet-forming species are dealt with in list 3.1.2. Some of the more demanding woodland perennials from list 1.3.3 may also find suitable planting positions on a shady rock garden.

4.5.1.   Perennials for bright to full shade on moist to damp soil among rocks

Most of the following species do not tolerate full sun and require damp, humid conditions with fertile, humus-rich soil for their optimal development. The more difficult and tender among them have been put into a separate list.

Dwarf columbines, *Aquilegia*

These very dainty plants require a cool site, sheltered from the midday sun. They thrive in rocky niches or under the protection of dwarf trees and shrubs.

Aquilegia discolor N Spain	0.12–0.15 light blue and white	V, flowers on short, branching stems; bifid leaves; loose, bushy habit. *A. bertolonii* (0.15), large, nodding, blue-violet flowers.
Aquilegia einseleana Alps	0.20 blue-violet	V, small, short-spurred flowers on branching stems; dense tufts of foliage; thrives in limestone rubble; also tolerates full sun. *A. thalictrifolia,* similar but with sticky leaves; very persistent; grows wild on limestone Alps.
Aquilegia flabellata Jap.	0.15–0.20 lilac-blue and white	V, flowers with short spurs; coarse-textured, blue-green leaves. 'Nana Alba' (0.20), V–VI, white.
Aquilegia flabellata var. *pumila* (*A. akitensis*) Jap.	0.15 blue and white	V–VI, large, rounded flowers with short spurs; grey-green leaves. Selection: 'Ministar'. 'Alba', large white flowers. 'Kurilensis' (0.07–0.10), dwarf form.
Aquilegia pyrenaica N Spain	up to 0.20 violet-blue	V–VI, large flowers over basal rosettes of delicate green foliage.

Further plants for bright to full shade

Aster bellidiastrum (*Bellidiastrum michelii*) Jura, Alps to Carp., Apenn.	0.05/0.15 white	IV–V, like a large daisy; leaves in rosettes; easy to propagate from seed; rarely available in the trade.
Alpine bells *Cortusa matthioli* C & E Russ., Carp. SW Alps	0.10/0.40 magenta	V–VI, primula-like species; umbels of small, nodding bells on tall stems; hairy, lobed and serrate leaves with long petioles. *C. m.* var. *pekinensis,* larger flowers and densely hairy, lobed leaves; valuable plant for shady niches on humus-rich soil.
Corydalis cheilanthifolia W China	up to 0.30 yellow	V–VI, flowers in ascending racemes; brownish-green, pinnately incised, fern-like leaves; thrives on damp, shady walls; hardy.
Dicentra eximia		List 2.2.1
Dicentra formosa		List 2.2.1
Hosta (dwarf species)		List 1.1.3
Mossy sandwort *Moehringia muscosa* Mts of S & C Eur.	0.15 white	V–IX, flowers like tiny, four-pointed stars scattered over a loose cushion of narrow, linear leaves; undemanding species for cool, damp conditions in shade or bright shade on humus-rich soil; sometimes offered as *Alsinopsis, Arenaria* or *Minuartia* in the trade.

Primula frondosa C Bulg.	0.10 pink	V, small umbels over dainty rosettes of leaves with mealy undersides; more luxuriant than *P. farinosa* (list 6.4.2); for damp, lightly shaded soils or shady rock crevices; undemanding.
Primula saxatilis Manch.	0.15–0.25 pink-violet	IV–V, umbels of flowers with pedicels up to 5 cm long; leaves incised or lobed, often with ruffled margins. *P. cortusoides* (0.30), IV–V, pink; similar to the above; many-flowered umbels on tall stems; pedicels up to 1 cm long; downy leaves. Both species thrive in shady, humus-filled rock crevices.
Saxifraga × andrewsii (*S. paniculata × S. hirsuta*) Ireland	0.20 white	VI, flattened rosettes of fleshy, green, remotely dentate leaves, broadening towards the tip; for bright shade; forms small, turf-like patches; hardy.
Saxifraga cortusifolia		List 1.3.2
Saxifraga cuneifolia		List 4.1.3
Saxifraga cymbalaria ssp. *huetiana* E Med., Cauc.	0.03–0.10 yellow	V–IX, attractive, fresh green, three-lobed leaves; short-lived but seeds itself freely in damp soil and on walls in bright shade; enthusiast's plant.
Saxifraga rotundifolia Alps, Cauc., Arm., Mts of S Eur.	0.10/0.50 white, with red and yellow spots	VI–IX, abundant flowers in open panicles; variable species; bluntly toothed or crenate, rounded to orbicular leaves; seeds itself freely on tufa in the shade. *S. r.* var. *heucherifolia,* similar to the above; large flowers; almost lobed leaves.
Strawberry-geranium *Saxifraga stolonifera* 'Cuscutiformis' China	0.10–0.20 white, with red spots	VII–VIII, loose rosettes of brownish green, pale veined, rounded to kidney-shaped leaves, reddish beneath, with long petioles; red, thread-like stolons; also for planting on shady walls; hardier than the houseplant *S. stolonifera* (*S. sarmentosa*).
Saxifraga veitchiana China	0.20 white	VI–VII, flowers reluctantly; pink blotches on the petals; rounded, lightly crenate, long-stemmed, dark green, hairy leaves, reddish-brown beneath; forms dense mats over and among rocks; seeds itself freely on tufa in the shade.
Wulfenia baldaccii Alban.	0.10/0.15 violet-blue	V–VI, sparse, open inflorescences; elongate, deeply crenate, dentate or almost lobed leaves. *W. × suendermannii* (*W. carinthiaca × W. baldaccii*) (0.25), V–VI, violet-blue. *W. amherstiana* (0.15/0.20), VI–VII, lilac-blue; small flowers; wrinkled, coarsely dentate leaves; for moist to damp rock crevices in bright shade.

4.5.2.   Plants for the enthusiast (mostly tender species)

The following perennials are all sensitive or difficult in one way or another. Most are only available from specialised alpine nurseries.

Astrantia minor SW Alps, Pyren., Apenn.	0.20 white	VI–VII, 3–4 flower heads on each stem; basal leaves divided into 7–9 coarsely serrate, narrow-lanceolate segments; calcifuge; for moist soil in bright shade or semi-shade; difficult.
Calceolaria biflora Chile, Arg.	0.10 yellow, with red spots	VI–VII, flowers in pairs on upright stems; small, flattened rosettes of glossy, spathulate leaves; for a cool position with continually damp, humus-rich soil among rocks in bright shade; needs protection in winter (needle litter). *C. polyrrhiza* (0.15), yellow; turf-like habit; elongate–ovate leaves; somewhat hardy but intolerant of summer heat. 'John Innes', large-flowered cultivar; less hardy than the above; needs protection in winter.
Cymbalaria aequi- triloba (*Linaria aequitriloba*) W Med.	0.05 pink	VI–IX, similar to *C. muralis* (list 4.1.3); fleshy, hairy leaves; for damp rocks or joints in stonework; needs protection in winter.
Cymbalaria pallida (*Linaria pallida*) It.	0.03 blue-violet	VI–IX, glossy dark green, rounded leaves; forms dense cushions; somewhat invasive.
Dicentra formosa ssp. *oregana* USA	0.25 whitish	V–VII, variable in colour; similar to D. f. ssp. *formosa* but more tender; bluish leaves. Further *Dicentra* spp.: see list 2.2.1.
Haberlea rhodopensis Balk.	0.02/0.15 lilac-blue	V–VI, small, *Gloxinia*-like flowers in loose panicles over rosettes of rough, fleshy, coarsely serrate, broad-lanceolate leaves; for damp, shady rocks and joints in stonework; humus-rich, limy soil; needs a little protection in winter. 'Virginalis', white.
Mimulus cupreus Chile	0.10 coppery-red	VI–IX, prostrate, rooting stems; small, dentate leaves; turf-like habit; for moist to damp soils in semi-shade; needs protection in winter. 'Roter Kaiser', scarlet; tender.
Mondo grass *Ophiopogon japonicus* 'Minor' Jap., China	0.05 purple to white	VI–VII, very small, nodding, bell-shaped flowers; deep blue fruits; narrow, arching, dark green, grassy leaves; rhizomatous spread; forms small, dense, turf-like patches; for shady niches; somewhat tender.
Polygonum vaccinii- folium Him.	0.05/0.15 pink	IX–X, spreading, creeping habit; small, glossy green leaves.
Ramonda myconi C & E Pyren.	0.05/0.10 pale violet, with yellow anthers	VI, flowers like African violets on weakly branched stems; flattened rosettes of matt green, ovate leaves; for damp, shady rocks and stonework, north-facing stony slopes and rock-faces. *R. nathaliae,* V, Yugo., N Greece; early flowering; glossy green, crenate, broadly ovate leaves.

> *R.* × *regis-ferdinandii* (*R. myconi* × *R. nathaliae*), V–VI, vigorous but rare garden hybrid.

Roscoea alpina Nepal	0.10–0.20 pink–white	VII–VIII, small flowers opening in succession; variable species; for moist soils among rocks in bright shade; see list 1.3.3.
Semiaquilegia ecalcarata (*Aquilegia ecalcarata*) W China	up to 0.20 violet-purple	V, small flowers without spurs; delicate, finely divided, grey-green foliage; for cool, damp soils in semi-shade.
Tanakaea radicans Jap.	up to 0.20 white	VI–VII, like a miniature *Astilbe*; spreads by means of stolons to form small, evergreen carpets; small flowers in pyramidal panicles; for humus-rich, slightly acid soils; needs protection in winter.
Pleione limprichtii (*P. bulbocodionides*) E Tibet	0.15 lilac-pink	IV–V, large, solitary flowers (6–7 cm across) appearing in spring from bottle-shaped pseudo-bulbs; grows wild in areas of winter drought.

Pleiones need a very humus-rich soil (peat, sand, a little loam and bone meal) in a semi-shady position among rocks. They are sensitive to extremes of frost. The plants should be kept moist in spring and summer but do not tolerate being sprayed from above. In autumn and winter they must remain completely dry, hidden under a layer of dry peat and covered with a sheet of glass or an upturned flower-pot. Occasional application of an easily soluble fertiliser in summer encourages growth and flower production.

Pleione limprichtii is hardier than its relatives, such as *P. formosana* (pale pink), *P. hookeriana* (delicate lilac) and *P. humilis* (white with a dark-spotted lip), which are better suited to cultivation in an alpine house.

Rock-dwelling *Primulas*

The following are sensitive European alpine species for small pockets of soil and damp rock crevices. On a rock garden they will flourish in well-drained, evenly moist, stony, humus-rich soil. The correct pH is important for their well-being.

Lime-loving species

Primula carniolica	up to 0.25 rose to lilac	IV–V, bell-shaped flowers with a white throat; glabrous leaves.
Primula clusiana	up to 0.10 pink	III–IV, flowers fade to lilac; shiny, pale green, pointed, oval leaves with narrow, horny, white margins.
Primula glaucescens ssp. *calycina*	0.05–0.15 purple–lilac	IV–V, narrow, glossy, pointed, broad-lanceolate leaves with horny, white, serrulate margins.
Primula marginata		List 4.3.1
Primula spectabilis	0.15 deep magenta-pink	IV–V, spreading, funnel-shaped, rosettes; slightly sticky, glossy green leaves; only flowers well on poor, damp, limestone rubble. *P. wulfenia* (0.15), dark pink; similar to the above but with non-sticky, blue-green leaves. Both species form turf-like patches.

Primula tirolensis	0.03 pink and violet	IV, small rosettes of dark green, remotely denticulate, rounded leaves; forms turf-like patches in semi-shade.

Lime-hating species

Primula glutinosa E Alps	0.07 blue-violet	V, turf-like habit; dull-glossy, remotely denticulate, lanceolate to ovate leaves.
Primula hirsuta C Alps	0.08 lilac-pink white throat	IV–V, very free-flowering, variable species; fleshy, dentate, rounded oval leaves with sticky glandular hairs; for rock crevices. Hybrids with the lime tolerant *P. auricula* (list 4.3.1): *P. × pubescens* (Auricula), list 2.2.1. *P. × arctotis* (0.15), III–IV, reddish; tends more to the low-growing *P. hirsuta*.
Primula integrifolia C Alps, Pyren.	0.05 red-violet	IV–V, turf-like habit; soft, grass-green, elliptic leaves with slightly inrolled margins (1–2 cm long and 1 cm across); for a damp spot.
Primula minima E Alps, Carp.	0.03 pink	V–VI, large flowers; often blooms again in autumn; turf-like habit; small rosettes of glossy, wedge-shaped leaves, toothed at the tips; thrives in rock rubble.
Primula oenensis SE Tyrol	0.08 pink and rose-lilac	III–IV and VIII, umbels of 1–7 flowers; elongate, wedge-shaped leaves.
Primula pedemontana SW Alps	up to 0.20 pink, white throat	IV–V, glossy leaves with densely ciliate margins; for north-facing rock crevices; grows easily, also in deep, humus-rich soil. *P. apennina* (0.03–0.05), III–IV, large flowers; needs little moisture after flowering.
Primula villosa Noric Alps	0.15 pink	III–IV, rounded–ovate to elongate–oval leaves covered in dense, fine hairs.
Primula viscosa W Alps, Pyren.	0.18 dark violet, purple	IV–V, one-sided umbels of nodding, funnel-shaped flowers; sticky, sinuate, elongate–ovate leaves; difficult in cultivation.

Small ferns for shady walls and rock crevices

These dainty species can be of great importance for the rock garden enthusiast, especially since they will spread unaided in the right conditions, without becoming troublesome. It is good to see that plants are now being offered by specialist nurseries, along with rare and unassuming species such as *Asplenium ruta-muraria* and *Ceterach officinarum* for warm, bright positions among rocks. Ferns for damp, shady areas and rock garden terraces can be found in list 4.5.3.

Black spleenwort *Asplenium adiantum- nigrum* Eur., Transcauc., S China	up to 0.30	Elegant, shiny, semi-evergreen, leathery fronds; calcifuge; somewhat warmth-loving species for sun to semi-shade; protection in winter is advisable.

Asplenium septen-trionale Eur., Asia Minor, Cauc. Him., USA	up to 0.15	Narrow, grassy fronds with toothed, wedge-shaped tips, for bright positions on lime-free walls and rocks.
Maidenhair spleenwort *Asplenium trichomanes* Cosmopol.	up to 0.20	Almost linear, pinnate fronds; sessile, rounded pinnae on blackish, shining stalks; for shady rocks and walls.
Green spleenwort *Asplenium viride* Eur., Cauc., Him., Sib., N Am.	up to 0.20	Similar to the previous species but with green stalks; for shady, moist to damp, limestone rocks.
Parsley fern *Cryptogramma crispa* Asia Minor, Cauc.	up to 0.20	Tufts of pinnate fronds, reminiscent of parsley; for cool positions in bright shade on igneous rock.
Brittle bladder-fern, Fragile fern *Cystopteris fragilis* Cosmopol.	0.25	Thin, finely pinnate, lanceolate fronds on short stems; for cool, damp, mostly shady rocks and walls; also on the ground.
Woodsia obtusa N Am.	0.30	Light green, finely pinnate, broad-lanceolate fronds; for rock crevices in bright shade. Smaller species: *W. alpina* (up to 0.15), *W. ilvensis* (to 0.20) and *W. polystichoides* (to 0.20).

4.5.3. Perennials for shady and semi-shady woodland conditions on the rock garden

The following list contains a small number of dainty herbs and ferns for moist to moderately damp soils. Many woodland species, especially those from list 1.2.2, may also find a use under rock garden trees and shrubs. Examples are the blue-flowered anemones (*A. blanda* and *A. apennina*), dwarf astilbes and low-growing epimediums. Exotic perennials such as *Cautleya*, *Liriope* and *Roscoea* (list 1.3.3) are also easily catered for in these conditions.

Aruncus aethusifolius		List 1.3.1.
Astilbe × crispa 'Perkeo'	0.10/0.15 dark pink	VII, glossy, dark green leaves; dwarf habit. 'Liliput' (0.20/0.25), white and pink; dense, beautiful, glossy, dark green foliage.
Astilbe glaberrima 'Sprite' Jap.	0.30/0.40 pale pink	VIII, very graceful, glossy green leaves; compact, low habit. 'Inrish Pink' (0.20), pink. 'Saxatilis' (0.10/0.25), VIII, very pale pink; lower-growing than the above; very decorative.
Enchanter's nightshade *Circaea × intermedia* (*C. alpina ×* *C. lutetiana*) Eur.	up to 0.30 white	VII–VIII, rhizomatous; similar to *C. lutetiana* (list 1.2.1) but shorter and not quite so invasive; shiny, glabrous leaves; for moist to damp soils in shade; to be used with great caution; only for large rock gardens; rare in the trade.
Epimedium grandi-florum		List 1.1.1

Epimedium × *youngianum*		List 1.1.1
Hosta (Dwarf species)		List 1.1.3
Polygonum tenuicaule Jap.	0.10 white	IV, dainty species; erect spikes of flowers reminiscent of May-lily (*Maianthemum*); dull green, broad, ovate–lanceolate leaves, purple beneath; thrives on moist, humus-rich soils in shade.
Saxifraga cortusifolia		List 1.3.2
Saxifraga cuneifolia		List 4.1.3
Saxifraga × *geum*		List 4.1.3
Saxifraga × *urbium*		List 4.1.3
Saxifraga × *polita* (*S. hirsuta* × *S. spathularis*)	0.20 white	VI, rounded, long-stemmed, regularly deeply toothed leaves; for shade or bright shade; enthusiast's plant, rarely available from nurseries.
Saxifraga spathularis Spain, Port., Ireland	up to 0.20 white, with red spots	VI–VII, similar to *S. umbrosa* (list 4.1.3); erect, long-stemmed, dentate leaves with translucent margins; also for rock crevices; enthusiast's plant, rarely available from nurseries.
Soldanella carpatica W Carp.	0.01–0.15 violet-blue	IV, free-flowering; 1–5 flowers on each stem; dark green, entire, almost orbicular leaves; all *Soldanella* spp. thrive in cool, damp, humus-rich soils in shade, and appreciate applications of needle-litter compost.
Soldanella montana E Alps, Carp., Balk.	0.02/0.10 (0.20) violet-blue	V, 3–6 flowers on each stem; rounded, kidney-shaped leaves; easily grown but lime-sensitive. *S. villosa*: see list 4.3.2.
Veronica 'Allgrün' (*V. allionii* × *V. officinalis*)	0.02/0.07 pale blue	VI, prostrate, leavy stems with semi-evergreen, elongate-oval leaves; colours reddish in winter; does not tolerate fallen leaves.
Viola labradorica N Am.	0.15 blue	IV–V, almost orbicular, purple-violet-flushed leaves; seeds itself freely. 'Viridis', light green leaves.

Plants for the enthusiast

(Continually damp but not stagnant conditions in shade and semi-shade.)

Golden saxifrage *Chrysosplenium alternifolium* Eur., Asia, N Am.	0.15 yellowish	IV–V, insignificant flowers, but an attractive, open habit; deeply crenate, alternate leaves; for humus-rich, loamy or clayey soils; thrives, as does the following, on the banks of woodland streams; rare in the trade.
Chrysosplenium oppositifolium W & C Eur.	0.10 yellowish	IV–V, similar to the previous species but more delicate; opposite, rounded, scalloped or crenate leaves; forms a dense, turf-like groundcover. *C. o.* var. *rosulare,* common in the trade; see list 3.1.1.

Small ferns for shade and semi-shade

In addition to woodland ferns (list 1.2.4) and rock crevice ferns (list 4.5.2), there are a number of small fern species for damp, shady, sheltered areas, especially in the neighbourhood of trees and shrubs, which thrive particularly well on a rock garden. Woodland ferns such as *Phyllitis, Gymnocarpium* and *Adiantum* spp. may also be grown in the same conditions but are less dependent on the extra shelter and detailed maintenance that a rock garden provides.

Adiantum pedatum var. *aleuticum* N Am.	0.15–0.20	Very dainty, but stiffer than *A. pedatum* (list 1.2.4); also available as *A. p.* 'Imbricatum', *A. p.* 'Aleuticum', *A. p.* 'Nanum' and *A. p.* 'Minor' in the trade.
Adiantum venustum Him.	0.15	Graceful, delicate, deciduous fronds with a triangular outline; turf-like habit; young plants need a covering of leaves in winter until they are established; for soils rich in raw humus.
Blechnum penna-marina S S Am., S Austral., NZ	0.20	Similar to *B. spicant* but much smaller and daintier; turf-like habit; slightly tender. 'Dura' (0.25), particularly hardy form. *Asplenium platyneuron* (0.15–0.30), S N Am., similar species.
Cystopteris montana Mts of Eur., N Asia, & N Am.	0.35	Finely divided fronds on long stalks; creeping rootstock; thrives on damp, limestone rubble.
Dryopteris abbreviata		List 1.2.4
Dryopteris villarii (*D. rigida*) W, C & S Eur.	0.25–0.45	Small, light green mountain fern with dense, bipinnate, elongate–lanceolate fronds; lower pinnae are spine-tipped; for limestone scree and rock crevices in bright shade; for the enthusiast.
Gymnocarpium robert-ianum		List 1.2.4
Phyllitis scolopendrium		List 1.2.4
Polypodium vulgare		List 1.2.4
Polystichum lonchitis Eur., Asia, N Am.	0.30–0.40	Narrow, pinnate, evergreen fronds with slightly sickle-shaped pinnae.
Thelypteris decursive-pinnata		List 1.2.4

4.5.4. Species for moist soils that are moderately dry in summer, particularly in woodland edge conditions on the rock garden

These are robust and predominantly hardy perennials from mountain woodland areas. They do not spread vigorously like other woodland edge species but thrive in bright shade and semi-shade, and most will also tolerate sun. They are particularly suited to soils that are somewhat dry in summer. Although they are by no means dependent upon rocks for their well being, they are best planted on a rock garden where they can readily be given the special attention they require. The woodland edge species from list 2.1.6 may also be effective under similar conditions.

Lily-leaf ladybells *Adenophora liliifolia* C Eur. to Sib.	0.80 blue	VII, tall, *Campanula*-like racemes densely set with bell-shaped flowers; mostly serrate, elliptic–lanceolate leaves.

Taller species: *A. bulleyana* (up to 1.20), *A. potaninii* (1.00).
A. tashiroi (0.70), light blue.

Whorled ladybells *Adenophora triphylla* (*A. verticillata*) E Asia	1.20–1.50 blue	VII–VIII, flowers in terminal racemes on upright, branching stems; leaves in whorls. *A. confusa* (*A. farreri* hort.) (0.60), VII, bell-shaped flowers on upright stems.
Adonis amurensis Amur., Jap., Sachal.	0.20 golden yellow	III, finely cut foliage; dies down in June and is easily displaced by other plants; thrives on moist soils in areas of summer shade. 'Pleniflora', greenish-yellow, double flowers.
Allium narcissiflorum SW Alps to Balk.	0.25 pale pink	VI–VII, large, funnel-shaped flowers in drooping umbels; grassy leaves; thrives on moist soil in semi-shade; undemanding.
Aquilegia glandulosa Altai	0.30 deep blue, paler centre	V–VI, 1–3 large, pendant flowers on each stem; very short spurs; seldom true in the trade. 'Jucunda' (0.25), white.
Bearberry *Arctostaphylos uva-ursi* Arctic & N Temp. zone	0.05–0.20 white	IV–V, creeping shrubby species; forms evergreen mats across rocks and soil; glossy dark green leaves; small flowers in terminal racemes; for light, humus-rich, dry to moist, stony and lime-rich soils in semi-shade; an easily propagated, narrow-leaved form is available as *A. nevadensis* in the trade.
Bergenia spp. and hybrids		Lists 2.3.3 and 4.1.3
Campanula poschar- skyana		List 4.1.1
Codonopsis spp.		List 2.1.5
Delphinium cashmer- ianum Him., Afgh.	up to 0.40 dark violet	VI–VII, loose, branching, few-flowered inflorescences; funnel-shaped flowers with blunt spurs; rounded, 3–5-lobed leaves; easily grown; thrives in bright shade. *D. brunonianum* (to 0.30), VII, pale violet; hairy, bell-shaped flowers; more demanding and sensitive than the previous species; rare in the trade. Both species are high mountain plants.
Dodecatheon spp.		List 1.3.3
Dragon's head *Dracocephalum rupe- stre* Sib.	up to 0.30 brilliant blue	VII–VIII, large flowers in whorls on false spikes; ascending stems; fresh green, crenate, elongate–ovate basal leaves; for a stony spot on moist, humus-rich, loamy soil in sun or bright shade; mostly offered in the trade as *D. grandiflorum,* but this species is not in cultivation.
Euphorbia amygda- loides var. *robbiae*	0.60 green	IV, flat, umbel-like cymes of large flowers over dark green rosettes; evergreen in mild areas; spreading rhizomes; for sun or shade; thrives on limy soils that dry out frequently.

Gentiana cruciata var. *phlogifolia* Asia Minor to NW China	0.25 blue	VII–VIII, small, four-lobed flowers in axillary and terminal clusters on ascending stems; narrow-lanceolate leaves; upper leaves sessile and clasping; for a sunny position; short-lived.
Geranium nodosum		List 2.1.6
Geranium renardii		List 2.1.2. The more sprawling *Geranium* spp. from list 2.1.2 may also find good use in similar situations.
Helleborus spp.		List 2.3.3. *H. niger* thrives in sunnier and drier positions on limy soil, also between rocks.
Incarvillea delavayi Yunn.	up to 0.60 pink	VI–VII, trumpet-like flowers with yellow throats on strong stems; dark green, composite leaves with lanceolate leaflets; carrot-like rootstock; very robust and hardy.
Incarvillea mairei 'Grandiflora' (*I. grandiflora* var. *brevipes*) Tibet, Nepal, W China	0.15–0.30 magenta	V–VI, large flowers; wrinkled, pinnate leaves with few leaflets. *I. compacta* 'Bee's Pink' (0.15), VI–VII, delicate pink; for moist, nutrient-rich, limy soils in warm, bright shade under trees; needs a little protection in winter.
Lagotis stolonifera Cauc.	0.10 lilac-blue	VI–VII, small flowers in erect spikes; loose rosettes of glossy, dark green, lanceolate leaves; spreading stolons; forms a loose groundcover; undemanding, particularly in bright shade.
Lilium pumilum & *L. pyrenaicum*		List 5.3.3
Mandrake *Mandragora officin- arum* N It., W Yugo.	up to 0.30/0.50 whitish-green	III–IV, large, dark green, elongate–ovate leaves; carrot-like rootstock; enthusiast's plant for shade and semi-shade.
Omphalodes cappa- docica Asia Minor, Cauc.	0.15 clear blue	IV–VI, flowers in loose racemes over long-stemmed, dark green, pointed, oval–lanceolate leaves; for sun or bright shade; frost-sensitive in a harsh climate; thrives on humus-rich soils; seeds itself prolifically in mild areas.
Omphalodes verna		List 2.1.4
Cliff green *Paxistima canbyi* (*Pachistima canbyi*) USA	up to 0.25 reddish- brown	IV–V, evergreen dwarf shrub with insignificant flowers and whitish fruits; small, crowded, elongate leaves; for bright shady positions on dryish, well-drained soil in mild areas; spreads vegetatively on loamy, nutrient-rich soils.
Fragrant butterbur *Petasites fragrans* C Med.	0.20/0.06 whitish pink	I–III, small, vanilla-scented, posy-like inflorescences appear before the rounded, finely toothed leaves; to be used with caution; spreads strongly underground; for moist, nutrient-rich soils in semi-shade; may need some protection in winter.

Dwarf balloon flower *Platycodon grandiflorus* 'Apoyama'	0.20 blue	VII–VIII, dwarf habit but large flowers; carrot-like rootstock; for sun and bright shade on not too dry soils; see also list 3.4.4.
Phlox divaricata, *P. ovata & P. stolonifera*		List 2.1.6
Polygonatum falcatum Jap., Korea	0.15 greenish- white	V, dwarf Solomon's seal with oval leaves; for the enthusiast.
Rubus calycinoides Taiw.	0.05 white	V–VI, creeping dwarf shrub with insignificant flowers and scattered red fruits; wrinkled, evergreen, three-lobed leaves with matted grey hairs beneath; prostrate, rooting stems; groundcover plant for shade; needs some protection in winter in harsh areas.
Calamintha grandiflora (*Satureja grandiflora*) S C Eur., Med., Asia Minor, Cauc.	0.50 pink	VI–VIII, large, axillary flowers on upright, mostly unbranched, sparsely leafy stems; coarsely serrate, ovate leaves with long petioles; for humus-rich, not too dry soils; also on rocks in light shade.
Scutellaria baicalensis (*S. macrantha*) E Sib.	up to 0.40 dark blue	VII–IX, flowers with pale centres in dense, terminal racemes; lanceolate leaves; undemanding; also for sunny positions. 'Coelestina', bright blue.
Thalictrum coreanum N Asia	0.20 pale pink	V, wiry stems; attractive, finely divided foliage; spreads strongly to form dense colonies; for humus-rich soils in bright shade, especially on the woodland edge.
Vaccinium vitis-idaea		List 1.3.6

4.5.5. Bulbs, corms and tubers for woodland edge conditions with intermittently dry to moist soils in summer

The bulbs and corms from lists 2.4.1 and 4.4.2 will also thrive in bright shady areas of the rock garden and in the neighbourhood of trees and shrubs, provided they receive the right amount of light.

Bulbocodium vernum	List 4.4.4
Colchicum spp.	List 2.3.4

Wild cyclamen, *Cyclamen*

Hardy, self-seeding wild cyclamen species have been assigned to the woodland edge (list 2.3.3). With the exception of *C, purpurascens* (list 2.1.6), they will also flourish in shade or bright shade on the rock garden, in places where the soil dries out in summer. These are suitable conditions for the somewhat tender, pink-flowered *C. repandum* (*C. vernale*) (III–IV), with pointed, triangular leaves, which can be particularly recommended for mild areas. Its tubers should be planted at least 10 cm deep.

Winter aconite, *Eranthis*

The large, golden-yellow-flowered hybrid *E.* × *tubergenii* is more vigorous than either of its parents (*E. hyemalis* and *E. cilicica*). It flowers a little later and longer (III–IV), as do its cultivars 'Glory' and 'Guinea Gold' (with slightly bronze-coloured leaves). Sadly, these hybrids can only be propagated vegetatively. They are better planted on a rock garden where they can be protected from competition, than in woodland or on the woodland edge, where the prolifically self-seeding parent species (list 2.4.2) can develop and spread to better advantage.

Dog's-tooth violet, Trout-lily, *Erythronium*

Erythronium dens-canis and its cultivars have been assigned to the woodland edge (list 2.4.2) though they can also be recommended, along with the following species, for planting on a rock garden. These lively perennials flourish in semi-shade on humus-rich, lime-free soils with plenty of cool moisture at flowering time. Once the plants have died down in summer, the soil should remain rather dry and on no account damp or wet.

Trout-lily *Erythronium revolutum* W USA	up to 0.25	IV–V, large, nodding flowers; very variable flower colour from white to pink. 'Johnsonii' and 'Pink Beauty' (0.35), pink; particularly strongly marbled leaves. 'White Beauty' (to 0.25), white with a yellow throat; large flowers.
Erythronium tuolum-nense Calif.	0.30	IV–V, up to three golden yellow flowers on each stem. 'Pagoda' (0.40), golden yellow; 4–5 flowers per stem; easily cultivated; also for shade. *E. americanum* (yellow), *E. albidum* (greyish-white) and *E. mesochoreum*, from the eastern USA, all thrive in American gardens but do less well in cool, wet, European summers.

Fritillary, *Fritillaria*

Fritillaries are graceful but rarely grown members of the lily family, with curiously marked, nodding, bell-shaped flowers. Apart from *F. meleagris* and *F. pyrenaica*, they are most effective planted singly rather than in masses, reflecting their natural occurrence in the wild. In areas of high rainfall the bulbs require a well-drained soil in order to ripen properly. A variety of other, daintier species are sometimes offered for sale, but these are mostly too tender for cultivation outdoors and are better grown in pots in an alpine house.

Fritillaria acmopetala Asia Minor, Syr.	0.40 green-brown	IV, 1–3 nodding, urceolate bells on long, arching stems; increases and forms colonies; hardy.
Fritillaria persica Nr East	0.60–0.90 glaucous violet	IV, many-flowered terminal racemes on stiff, leafy stems; spirally arranged, dark grey-green foliage. 'Adiyaman', taller, with larger flowers.
Fritillaria pallidiflora C Sib.	0.40 whitish yellow	IV, abundant bell-shaped flowers, mostly arranged in two whorls up the sturdy stem; hardy; seeds itself freely.
Fritillaria pontica Balk., E Turk.	up to 0.40 yellowish green to brownish red	IV, up to 3 bell-shaped flowers on each stem; easily cultivated.

Fritillaria verticillata	up to 0.60	IV–V, up to 6 broad, nodding bells on each strong
C Asia, China	pale green	stem; leaves curled at the tip; hardy; also for semi-
	to cream	shade.

Snowdrop, *Galanthus*

The less prolific and less common snowdrop species are safer planted on a rock garden than in a more competitive woodland or woodland edge environment. The commoner species treated in list 2.4.2 also thrive under the same conditions. All of the following are hardy but uncommon species for summer shade in the neighbourhood of trees and shrubs.

Galanthus byzantinus Turk.	II, white flowers with a dark green blotch at the base of each inner petal; broad leaves.
Galanthus plicatus Crim.	III, large white flowers with a small, dark green blotch on each inner petal, not extending to its base; broad leaves with rolled-back margins.
Galanthus caucasicus Cauc., Russ.	II, green, horseshoe-shaped blotches on the inner petals; broad green leaves.
Galanthus elwesii & cvs.	List 2.4.1

English iris, *Iris xiphioides* (*Xiphium latifolium, Iris anglica* hort.)

Iris xiphioides is an elegant, hardy species from the Pyrenees. Its violet-blue flowers with yellow blotches are carried on stems up to 60 cm tall in June. The narrow, grooved, blue-green leaves appear in early spring, unlike those of the related Spanish iris (*I. xiphium*), which emerge in autumn. Both species are available in many forms. They are particularly important as cut flowers but are also popularly grown as garden plants. The bulbs of *I. xiphioides* (though not of *I. xiphium*) may be left in the ground over winter. It is as well to give them a light covering of peat in a harsh climate. The plants are best grown in a sunny or bright shady position on soil that dries out in summer. Lists of cultivars can be found in catalogues.

4.6. Special planting positions for species that are not dependent on rock

The following perennials have special growing requirements which are most readily satisfied on a rock garden. The species from list 4.6.1 form an exception, needing no particular soil preparation for their cultivation.

4.6.1. Sub-alpine tall herbs for large rock gardens

These middle-sized and tall-growing perennials from sub-alpine herb communities can be used to form a link between a rock garden and its surroundings. They require moist to damp, nutrient-rich soil, and may be grown on the approaches to a rock garden or on a woodland edge, in sun or bright shade.

Apart from a few, rarely available but very characteristic species most of these plants have been assigned primarily to other garden habitats. Perennials from lists 2.2.4 and 2.2.1 may also be found good planting positions in the same conditions.

Aconitum spp.		Lists 1.1.2 & 5.2.1
Adenostyles alliariae Pyren., Alps, Carp.	up to 1.00 lilac-pink	VII, small composite flower heads in compound umbels; long stems; coarsely serrate leaves up to 50 cm across with web-like hairs beneath.
Adenostyles glabra (*A. alpina*) Alps, Apenn., Jura	up to 0.70 lilac-pink	VII, regularly serrate leaves with hairy veins beneath; more amenable to cultivation than the previous species.
Astrantia carniolica SE Alps	up to 0.70 pale green	VI–VII, flowers in cymes on slender stems; leaves with 5 broadly ovate lobes. 'Rubra' (0.30), daintier selection.
Athyrium distentifolium		List 1.2.4
Alpine sow-thistle *Cicerbita alpina* (*Mulgedium alpinum*) (*Lactuca alpina*) Eur.	0.40/1.40 blue-violet	VII–IX, racemose to paniculate inflorescences; large, pinnate leaves; does not spread vegetatively; some-what difficult to grow; rare in the trade.
Cicerbita plumieri Pyren., W Alps, Bulg.	0.30/1.30 light blue	VII, composite flowers in a loose corymb; coarsely pinnate leaves; not invasive; rarely available in the trade; see list 2.1.6.
Doronicum austriacum C & S Eur., Asia Minor	1.00 orange- yellow	VI, corymbs of large, daisy-like flowers on sturdy stems; clasping, elongate–spathulate stem leaves.
Eupatorium canna- binum		List 3.5.4
Willow gentian *Gentiana asclepiadea* S & C Eur., Cauc.	0.40 dark blue	VII–IX, regularly leafy, erect or arching stems; large, bell-shaped flowers with pointed petals in the upper leaf axils; for damp, moory, lime-free soils. 'Alba', white. 'Knightshayes', deep blue with a whitish throat.
Gentiana lutea		List 3.5.2
Geranium sylvaticum		List 2.1.6
Lilium martagon & relatives		List 5.2.2
Ranunculus aconiti- folius		List 2.3.1
Thalictrum aquilegi- folium		List 2.2.2
Thelypteris limbo- sperma		List 1.2.4
Trollius spp.		Lists 3.5.1 and 5.3.5
Veratrum album		List 3.5.2

4.6.2. Enthusiasts' plants for sites enriched with peat and moory soil

The following attractive but demanding perennials and dwarf shrubs are more easily grown on specially prepared rock garden beds than anywhere else in the garden. They need a moist, lime-free and very humus-rich soil (see p. 132), combining well with dwarf rhododendrons. Like the gentians from list 4.6.3, they are frequently offered for sale but are rarely given the chance to develop properly in a garden.

Lime-tolerant species from marshland plant communities have been assigned to the water's edge (list 6.4.2).

Cassiope tetragona N Eur., Sib., N Am.	0.20 white	IV–V, attractive, dense-growing dwarf shrub with dark green scale-like leaves and nodding, bell-shaped flowers on long pedicels; for peaty, gritty soils.
St Dabeoc's heath *Daboecia cantabrica* N Port., Ireland	0.25 purple	VII–IX, prostrate dwarf shrub; loose racemes of nodding, urceolate flowers; small, dark green, elongate-ovate leaves with matted white hairs beneath. 'Alba', large white flowers; particularly vigorous selection. 'Cinderella', delicate pink. 'Wijnje' pink. *D. × scotica,* rose-violet; somewhat hardier than the above. All need moist, lime-free soil and a little protection in winter.
Crowberry *Empetrum nigrum* N Eur., N Asia., N Am., Pyren., C It., Bulg.	0.30 purplish-pink	V, dwarf shrubby species; insignificant flowers and black, pea-sized fruits; small, needle-like leaves. *E. hermaphroditum,* similar but coarser species; erect habit; enthusiast's plant for a sunny position; rare in the trade.
Cross-leaved heath *Erica tetralix* N & W Eur.	0.30 pink	VI–VII, urceolate flowers; for moist to damp, peaty, lime-free soils, particularly in an oceanic climate. 'Alba', white; very robust. 'Con Underwood' (0.30), red. 'Silver Bells' (0.20), white; see list 6.4.3.
Checkerberry *Gaultheria procumbens* N Am.	up to 0.15 white	VI–VIII, dwarf shrubby species; nodding, solitary flowers sometimes grouped in racemes; glossy, dark green, elliptic leaves up to 5 cm long; spherical red fruits; spreads underground and makes a good groundcover; also for sandy soils in an oceanic climate.
Shallon *Gaultheria shallon* N Am.	up to 1.00 white and pink	V–VI, flowers in one-sided racemes; rounded, ovate leaves up to 10 cm long; thick, spherical, red-black fruits; suckering shrubby species; good groundcover plant for damp, shady sites in an oceanic climate.
Partridge berry *Mitchella repens* N Am., Mex.	0.05 white	IV–VII, small, funnel-shaped flowers; prostrate, rooting stems with opposite pairs of oval, dark green leaves; red berries; forms low mats in cool, semi-shady or shady positions with pure humus soil; rare in the trade.

Mountain heath *Phyllodoce caerulea* Arctic & alpine regions of Eur., N Asia & N Am.	up to 0.20 purple-red	VI–VII, bushy dwarf shrub with small, dark green, linear leaves; large, nodding, urceolate flowers in terminal clusters; for rich, peaty, lime-free soils in bright shade; needs a little protection in winter.
Ranunculus amplexi-caulis N Spain	up to 0.20 white	V–VI, large flowers on branched stems; clasping, grey-green, glabrous, entire, ovate–lanceolate leaves; enthusiast's plant for moist to damp, loamy, moor-like soils.
Arctic bramble, Crimson bramble *Rubus arcticus* N Eur., N Am., N Asia	0.15 pink	VII, solitary flowers followed by edible red fruits in autumn; tripartite leaves; spreads by stolons to form a dense groundcover; lime-free, sandy moor-like soils.
Cloudberry, Salmon-berry *Rubus chamaemorus* Circumpol.	up to 0.20 white	V, unbranched stems with solitary, terminal flowers; large, edible, orange fruits; kidney-shaped leaves with 5–7 lobes; spreading rhizomes; rarely available in the trade.
Oconee bells *Shortia galacifolia* USA	0.15 white, pink or blue	IV–V, large, funnel-shaped flowers, held horizontally on slender stems; glossy green, leathery, rounded leaves; thrives only in continually damp soil; tender, enthusiasts' plant for semi-shady sites under rhododendrons; rare in the trade. *S. uniflora* 'Grandiflora', large white flowers; pink in bud.

4.6.3.   Autumn gentians, *Gentiana*

The autumn gentians, with their indescribably lovely flowers and fine, fresh green, almost grass-like foliage, belong in the neighbourhood of the foregoing species for peaty, moor-like soils.

These long-flowering perennials, together with their countless cultivars and hybrids of often complex ancestry (only the commonest and most proven of these are listed here) need a cool, and humid planting position in sun or bright shade with moist (to damp), slightly acid, sandy loam, to which a generous measure of coarse peat has been added. Fine peat would destroy the necessary open pore structure of the soil.

Gentiana farreri Tibet, China	0.10 sky blue	VIII–IX, flowers striped white and green on the outside; prostrate, rooting stems with light green, almost needle-like leaves; lime-tolerant; for continually damp soils; thrives in bright shade; numerous calcifuge hybrids.
Gentiana veit-chiorum × G. farreri 'Coronation'	0.10 deep blue	VII–X, free-flowering; large flowers with dark spots; regular, compact growth.
'Inverleith'	0.10 dark blue	VIII–XI, creeping, prostrate stems with very large trumpet-shaped flowers; vigorous and long-flowering; needs a lot of space; parent of many cultivars.
Gentiana farreri × G. lawrencei 'Caroli'	0.10 brilliant sky blue	VII–IX, dainty; needs little space; abundant flowers, but smaller than those of 'Inverleith'.

Gentiana farreri × G. sinoornata 'Macaulayi'	brilliant blue	IX–X, wide open trumpet-shaped flowers with white throats; somewhat difficult.
'Admiral'	intense azure blue	VII–IX, early, middle-sized flowers; reliable and hardy.
'Kingfisher'	dark blue	VIII–IX, abundant flowers at the tips of short, upturned stems; dark green leaves; very vigorous.
Gentiana sinoornata × G. veitchiorum 'Midnight'	pure indigo	VIII–IX, very vigorous.
Gentiana sinoornata NW Yunn.	0.10–0.15 azure blue	IX–XI, flowers with light and dark striped exteriors; grassy leaves; for moist to damp, acid, peaty soils. 'Alba', middle-sized, white flowers, often flushed blue. 'Azurhimmel', densely striped, brilliant blue flowers; vigorous and larger than the type. 'Brin Form', clear dark blue; vigorous, popular garden cultivar. 'Praecox', VIII–XI, radiant blue; somewhat paler than the type; flowers freely; important for cutting. Numerous hybrids available from specialist nurseries (see also *G. farreri*).

4.6.4. Plants for damp (to wet) sites on the rock garden

The first plants to be listed here are dainty perennials for small, damp, frequently flooded or even boggy areas on the banks of streams and ponds. These conditions often produce an abundance of weeds; on the whole, such plantings can be maintained most effectively on a rock garden. Plants that are unavailable from perennial nurseries have not been listed here. Plants for damp, gravelly sites and wet scree are listed subsequently.

Perennials for a rock garden pond should be chosen from list 6.3. If sufficient space is available then other plants, such as candelabra primulas and similar species from list 2.3.1, or water-meadow perennials such as *Trollius* (list 3.5.1) and low-growing plants like *Lysimachia nummularia* and *Ajuga reptans* (list 2.1.3), or even the species from list 3.1.2, may all find a suitable planting position.

Small, dainty species for slightly boggy sites (or wet spring soils)

Caltha palustris 'Alba'		List 6.3
Bluets, Quaker ladies *Houstonia caerulea* (*Hedyotis caerulea*) E N Am.	up to 0.20 light blue, white centre	VI, free-flowering; forms small tufts of thyme-like foliage; also for damp, lime-free soils in bright shade. *H. serpyllifolia* (0.05), E USA, sky blue; creeping, turf-like habit; solitary flowers on slender stems; calcifuge.
Chrysosplenium oppositifolium var. *rosulare*		List 3.1.2
Mazus stolonifera (*M. miquelii*) Jap.	0.02/0.03 lilac-purple	IV–V, short-stemmed flowers with a large lip; pale green, spathulate leaves; slender, hairy stolons. *M. pumilio* (0.05), NZ, V–VI, pale blue, bell-shaped

flowers; rhizomatous cushion plant; needs protection in winter.

M. radicans (0.01) NZ, large white flowers with a yellow centre; brown, oval leaves; creeping habit; moist to damp soils in semi-shade.

M. japonicus and *M. reptans* are both available in the USA (often confused). *M. reptans* is smaller and more colourful. Both are naturalised in favourable locations.

Whitecup *Nierenbergia repens* Arg., Chile	0.03/0.05 white	VI–IX, bowl-shaped flowers on short stems; creeping, turf-like habit; spathulate leaves with long petioles; for damp soils; needs protection in winter.
Parnassia palustris		List 6.4.2
Primula farinosa		List 6.4.2
Primula frondosa		List 4.5.1
Primula rosea Him.	0.15 pink	III–IV, flowers appear before the elongate–ovate leaves. Various selections, including: 'Grandiflora', large flowers. 'Gigas' (0.20), tall stems.
Primula warshenew- *skiana* Afgh.	up to 0.10 pink	III–IV, similar to *P. rosea* but with spreading rhizomes; flowers with white and yellow bands in the throat; branching inflorescences; fleshy, tongue-shaped, irregularly dentate leaves; still rare in the trade.
Selaginella helvetica Eur., Sib., N China, Jap.	0.03	Moss-like lower plant; forked shoots, which turn reddish-brown in autumn; thrives in continually damp conditions, especially on moor-like soils. *S. douglasii* (0.10), dark green, scale-like leaves.
Blue-eyed grass *Sisyrinchium angusti-* *folium* N Am.	0.20 blue	V–VI, small tufts of grassy leaves; small, upward-facing, crocus-like flowers; hardy; seeds itself freely; for moist to damp soils. *S. graminifolium* (0.20), V–VI, Chile, yellow; sword-like leaves; needs protection in winter. *S. bermudiana* (0.20), violet-blue; fairly hardy.
Soldanella alpina Alps, Pyren.	0.08 lilac	III–IV, from snowy alpine valleys; dainty, nodding flowers with fringed petals; rounded leaves; enthusiasts' plant; see also lists 4.3.2 and 4.5.3.
Trollius acaulis Him.	0.03/0.15 lemon-yellow	V, solitary flowers on leafy stems; leaves with five segments. *T. laxus,* American globeflower (0.15), IV–V, yellowish; N American species; rarely available in the trade.
Trollius pumilus Him.	0.20 golden yellow	VI–VII, shallow, bowl-shaped flowers; small, distinctively ruffled leaves; plant for the enthusiast.

Crowsfoot globeflower *Trollius ranunculinus* (*T. patulus*) Asia Minor, Cauc.	0.40 golden yellow	V–VI, bowl-shaped flowers; palmately incised leaves; rare in the trade.
Trollius yunnanensis W China	0.40 light orange	VI–VII, open flowers with sometimes green-tipped petals; denticulate, spine-tipped stem leaves. *T. stenopetalus* (0.50), China, VII, pale yellow; closely related to the previous species; flowers later; rare in the trade.

Iris species for moist to damp soils, also in bright shade

Iris cristata SE USA	0.20/0.15 pale lilac	IV–V, usually two flowers per stem; crested falls; long, broad leaves; for humus-rich, lime-free, damp but not too wet soils in bright shade among rocks; also for full sun on loamy soils. 'Alba', white.
Gladdon, Gladwin *Iris foetidissima* S & W Eur.	0.70 lilac	VI, unspectacular flowers followed by brilliant orange-red seeds when the fruit capsules open; dark green, linear, evergreen leaves; for damp soils in semi-shade, not just on the rock garden; mild regions.
Iris gracilipes Jap.	0.20/0.25 pink-lilac	V–VI, several graceful blooms on each stem; clump-forming habit; short, branching rhizomes; pale green, grassy, overhanging leaves; from mountain woods in Japan. 'Alba', white; very dainty flowers.
Iris lacustris C N Am.	0.15/0.10 light blue	V, similar to *I. cristata* but smaller and more robust; falls with a yellow blotch; mat-like spread on moist soils and damp, rocky streamsides.
Roof iris *Iris tectorum* China	0.20/0.25 lilac	V–VI, broad, somewhat papery flowers on branching stems; pale green, sword-like leaves; for moist soils in sun or bright shade among rocks or on a streamside; tolerates long periods of drought.
Iris verna E C USA	0.10/0.15 pale violet	IV–V, erect standards; ovate falls with a central orange stripe; sword-shaped leaves; similar to *I. pumila* but somewhat difficult; for moist to damp, lime-free soils in semi-shade; from damp pinewoods in the Appalachians, westward to central Arkansas.

4.6.5. Plants for damp, gravelly places and wet scree, particularly at the edge of a pond or stream

Armeria alpina Mts of N Spain to Balk.	0.05/0.25 magenta	V–X, similar to *A. maritima*; flat green leaves; for a sunny waterside position on calcareous, gravelly or silty soil; rare in the trade.
Epilobium fleischeri Alps	up to 0.40 pink	VII–IX, flowers in loose racemes on upright stems with narrow, grey-green leaves; not invasive. *E. dodonaei* (to 0.50), VI–IX, large, pale pink flowers; for a sunny position; strongly invasive rhizomes.

Myosotis rehsteineri Alps	up to 0.10 blue	IV–V, large flowers; dwarf, turf-like habit; for sandy or gravelly, calcareous soils, particularly where the ground is wet in summer.
Primula rosea		List 4.6.4
Yellow mountain saxifrage *Saxifraga aizoides* Mts of Eur., N Asia & N Am.	up to 0.15 orange-yellow	VI–VII, loose, free-flowering cushions of fleshy, horny-tipped leaves; for wet rocks and stony soils; enthusiasts' plant; rare in the trade.
Sedum pulchellum E USA	0.10–0.15 pink	VII–VIII, flowers on upright stems with 3–5 horizontally spreading branches; linear leaves with a small, forked spur at the base; thrives in damp soil by water; enthusiasts' plant.

4.6.6.   Bulbs for periodically damp sites on the rock garden

Chionodoxa tmolusii S Turk.	0.10 brilliant blue, white centre	IV; unlike the commoner *Chionodoxa* species (list 2.4.1), this plant thrives on soils that are moist to damp in summer; rare in the trade.
Fritillaria meleagris		List 2.4.2
Leucojum aestivum		List 6.3
Leucojum vernum		List 2.4.2
Narcissus cyclamineus Spain, Port.	up to 0.15 bright yellow	III, flowers with a long, narrow trumpet and reflexed petals; thrives in semi-shade on soils that are damp or even wet and boggy in summer; easily displaced by competition.
Scilla litardieri (*S. pratensis*) W Balk.	0.20 amethyst blue	V–VI, flowers in pyramidal racemes; for a sunny position with moist to damp soil in summer; rare in the trade. *S. amethystina* hort. (0.20), V–VI, Dalm., a vigorous variety of the above with sky-blue flowers; not a valid species.

5 Border perennials

Border perennials are colourful, free-flowering plants that have been bred and selected for culture in an intensively maintained bed. Even well-established specimens will only flourish in cultivated soil and thus require the same sort of continuous and detailed attention as vegetables or hybrid roses (see p. 72 for soil preparation before planting). This being so, they are best grown in easily accessible borders where they can be conveniently weeded, fed and watered. Occasionally some plants may also need staking or cutting down. The old cottage gardens with their maze of tiny pathways provided an ideal environment for these maintenance-demanding perennials. Given a choice site they may still form the decorative highlights of a modern garden.

Although border perennials can be grown in fertile soil almost anywhere in the garden, subject only to their special requirements for light or shade, individual plants are most effective grown in an environment that corresponds to their original wild character. For the purpose of this book, it might have been possible to assign each of the border perennials to the garden habitat appropriate to its wild ancestors, and there to group them with the wild perennials with border character. However, the latter, though they respond well to cultivated soil and look good in combination with true border plants, have requirements and characteristics that relate them more closely to wild perennials than to the highly selected and more demanding border perennials. In view of this, border perennials have been treated separately, classified primarily according to their warmth and moisture requirements into groups closely related to the garden habitats of wild perennials. The intention thereby is to provide an aid to creating good plant associations. It would be wrong to consider these beautiful plants only in terms of their height, colour and season of flower, ignoring their intrinsic nature and relationship to the environment.

Some sort of perennial border is an essential component of every small garden. Plants should be set singly or in small groups and given plenty of room for their growth. In a densely planted, 'perpetually flowering' border the perennials are faced with intense mutual competition after only a few years. Repeated division and replanting is needed to preserve the rhythm and colour composition of the design, thus preventing the plants from ever attaining their mature beauty. Broadly spaced, the individual specimens and small groups can develop into imposing features, which combine to make a colourful and luxuriant display. The open soil around the clumps of perennials can be filled with tulips or other ornamental bulbs, and then planted over with annuals when these die down in May. In a public park this sort of planting is more economical to maintain than pure summer bedding. At the end of the season, the annuals are removed and the perennials cut down to the ground. Surrounded by blooming annuals, few of the perennials need to be cut down earlier in the year. The only other job is to gently loosen the soil in winter, taking care not to damage any dormant bulbs. Experience in the perennial trials garden at Weihenstephan has shown that certain annual grasses and herbs with perennial-like character (listed as 'ornamental elements' in the text) are particularly suitable for combining with various of the border perennials, forming a decorative feature with a long season of flower. Used in this way, border perennials can achieve an effect in even the most confined of spaces.

The design of herbaceous borders has already been described on pp. 53 ff. Much depends on the particular situation. Flowering shrubs can bring colour to the planting in spring, perhaps associated with the early-flowering woodland edge perennials from lists 2.2.1 and 2.2.2. On the whole it is better to use bulbs rather than a great number of early-flowering border perennials, thus leaving more room for a sumptuous display in summer.

Along with a high level of regular maintenance, most border plantings will need periodic readjustment, particularly when plants cease to flower properly or go bare in the middle, or when the rhythm and composition of the design is spoiled by plants that have died or spread too vigorously. The combination of widely spaced perennials and annual plants described above allows all the necessary operations to be carried out with ease.

Border perennials do not thrive when wild perennials are planted to fill up the spaces between them. Moreover, the association of wild and border perennials is mostly dissatisfactory from an aesthetic point of view, seldom producing a harmonious combination or evocative contrast.

Ornamental elements

Short lists of 'ornamental elements' have been appended to the descriptions of some of the main groups of border perennials. A carefully thought out combination of long- and free-flowering annual plants with certain border perennials can be most effective, particularly in a small garden.

5.1.   Border perennials derived from woodland species

The following garden cultivars thrive in a well-maintained border on moist to damp, nutrient-rich soil in light shade. Their ancestors come from woodland fringes and clearings in cool regions of forest vegetation. The cultivars themselves have requirements very similar to those of woodland and woodland edge (list 2.2.1) perennials and may be combined with some of them in a border-type planting, examples being *Cimicifuga, Aruncus, Hosta, Carex morrowii* and the species from lists 1.1.2–1.1.4, 1.2.4 and especially 1.3.1.

Japanese anemones, *Anemone* Japonica hybrids and their relatives (*A. hupehensis* and *A. tomentosa*)

These graceful, tall anemones, with ternate leaves and large, saucer-shaped blooms on elegant stems, are in flower from the beginning to the end of autumn. With the exception of *A. tomentosa* they are somewhat sensitive to frost and it is therefore advisable to cover young plants with a layer of peat or loose, dry leaves in winter, especially in regions without snow cover. Once the plants are established they can live to a great age. Even small sections of root will produce new shoots, so that when the plants are dug up they will nearly always reappear in their old position. Named cultivars are propagated by means of root cuttings.

Proven selections

White:
'Honorine Jobert' (1.20), IX–X, single flowers.
'Frau Marie Maushard', similar to the foregoing but with a stiffer habit; rare in the trade.
'Whirlwind' ('Wirbelwind') (1.00), IX–X, semi-double flowers.

Silvery-pink:
'Königin Charlotte' ('Queen Charlotte') (1.20), IX–X, semi-double flowers.
'Lady Gilmour' (0.60), VIII–X, nearly double flowers.
'September Charm' (0.70), VIII–IX, large flowers.

Rosy-pink:
A. hupehensis 'Splendens' (1.00), VIII–IX.
A. hupehensis 'Praecox' (0.80), VIII–IX, very early.
'Bressingham Glow' (0.50), VIII–IX, low-growing.

Carmine pink:
'Rosenschale' (0.70), IX–X.

Red:
'Prinz Heinrich' ('Prince Henry') (0.80), IX–X, semi-double flowers.

Anemone tomentosa (*A. vitifolia*) 'Robustissima'	0.40/1.00 pink	VIII, expansive habit; early flowering and absolutely hardy.

Astilbe Arendsii hybrids (*A.* × *arendsii*), A. Japonica hybrids (*A. japonica*) and their relatives

Georg Arends used a combination of the dainty *Astilbe japonica*, *A. astilboides*, and *A. simplicifolia* with the tall-growing *A. davidii* and *A. thunbergii* to produce this range of ornamental hybrids. The plants thrive in cool, moist to damp soil in semi-shade or shade, though in cool climates, if conditions are damp and humid enough, they will also grow in sun. Well-rotted horse manure will do wonders but cow manure should rather be avoided as a fertiliser. The wild species have been assigned to woodland (list 1.3.1), and woodland edge (list 2.1.4) conditions.

Astilbes are an attractive sight even when they are not flowering, thanks to their beautifully divided foliage, which may be tinted reddish or bronze when young. The feathery, erect or (depending on the parentage) gently drooping panicles only develop to their full beauty when conditions are exactly right. Even the most intensive maintenance cannot compensate for the hot, dry microclimate of an urban garden in regions with warm summers and a low rainfall.

The clumplike rootstocks are easily divided with a knife in either spring or autumn, though in the latter case it is better to heel-in the divisions for planting out in spring.

In the following lists the low-growing and early flowering Japonica hybrids (Jap.) have not been treated separately from *A.* × *arendsii*. Where the flowering season has not been characterised as either early or late, the cultivars can be assumed to flower from mid-July to mid-August. Early varieties are in flower from the end of June to the end of July and late ones from the end of July to the middle of September (at Weihenstephan).

Arendsii and Japonica hybrids

White:
'Brautschleier' ('Bridal Veil') (0.70), early; loose, drooping inflorescences.
'Deutschland' (Jap.) (0.50), early.
'Irrlicht' (0.50), early, dark foliage.
'Weisse Gloria' ('White Gloria') (0.70).
'Bergkristall (1.00), erect, open inflorescences.

Pale pink:
'Bressingham Beauty' (1.20), bright pink; early; expansive habit.
'Cattleya' (1.10), late; vigorous and leafy.
'Grete Püngel' (0.80).
'Straussenfeder ('Ostrich Plume') (*A. thunbergii*) (1.00), particularly showy cultivar.

Dark pink:
'Anita Pfeifer' (0.70).
'Bonanza' (0.70), dark foliage.

Brilliant red:
'Feuer' (0.80).
'Fanal' (0.65), early.
'Else Schluck' (0.75).

'Glut' ('Glow') (0.80), late.
'Montgomery' (Jap.) (0.60–0.70), dark red.
'Spinell' (0.80), 'Rotlicht' (1.00), dark foliage.

Carmine pink:
'Koblenz' (Jap.) (0.60).
'Federsee' (0.70).

Crimson:
'Obergärtner Jürgens' (0.70).
'Red Sentinel' (Jap.) (0.50).

Violet:
'Mainz' (Jap.) (0.60), early.
'Amethyst' (1.10), early to middle.

Tall-growing species

Astilbe thunbergii 'Moerheimii'	0.30/1.20 white	VII–VIII, stiff, upright habit; elegant, drooping panicles on reddish stems. 'Elegans', similar. 'Elegans Rosea', pink. *A. t.* var. *hachiioensis* (0.80), VI–VII, white; loosely branched panicles.
Astilbe Thunbergii hybrids 'Prof. van der Wielen'	0.30/1.20 white	VII–VIII, broad, powerful, loosely branched inflorescences.

Species suitable as groundcover

Astilbe chinensis	0.30/0.50 red-violet	VIII–IX, vigorous; spreading roots; still rare in the trade; see list 1.1.2.
Astilbe chinensis 'Pumila'	0.10/0.025 lilac	List 2.1.4; undemanding; also for warm and dry sites.
Astilbe taquetii 'Superba'	0.40/1.00 purple-pink	List 1.1.2; very undemanding; also for difficult sites. 'Purpurlanze' ('Purple Lance') (0.90–1.20), bright rose-purple.

Astilbe Chinensis hybrids

'Finale'	0.30/0.40 fresh pink	VIII–IX, vigorous groundcover plant with spreading roots.
'Veronica Klose'	0.30/0.40 dark pink	VIII–IX, similar to the foregoing; feathery panicles.

Further astilbes: see lists 1.1.2, 1.3.1, 2.1.4 and 2.3.1.

Ornamental elements

The following annual and biennial plants associate well with astilbes in bright shade: *Digitalis purpurea*, *D.* Excelsior hybrids and 'Dropmore Yellow'. *Impatiens balfourii*, *Nicotiana × sanderae*, *N. sylvestris*.

5.2. Border perennials derived from woodland edge species

The majority of these very decorative border perennials are in no way dependent on the woodland edge conditions required by their wild ancestors. Nevertheless, they are particularly effective in association with ornamental trees and shrubs, and it is worth bearing this in mind when considering their use. The woodland edge perennials from lists 2.2.1, 2.2.2 and 2.2.4 may all be combined with them.

We can make a broad distinction between species for:

Cool, sunny or bright shady places with moist to damp soil in summer (lists 5.2.1 and 5.2.2)
Aconitum, Delphinium, Dicentra, Hemerocallis and various lilies.

Warm, sunny places with moist to dry soil in summer (lists 5.2.3 and 5.2.4)
Fritillaria imperialis, Paeonia, Chrysanthemum × hortorum and various lilies.

5.2.1. Cool, sunny or bright shady places with moist to damp soil in summer

Depending on the situation, many of the species from lists 2.2.1–2.2.4 can be used in combination with these plants.

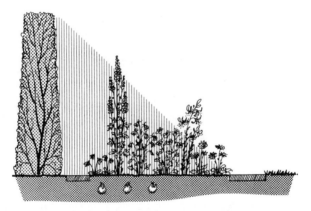

Herbaceous border: cool, sunny or bright shady positions.

Monkshood, *Aconitum*

The parents of these greedy, poisonous, strong-stemmed perennials, with palmately incised leaves and very distinctive, hood-like flowers, come from open alpine pastures and sparse mountain woodland, particularly in the neighbourhood of springs and streams. All species, including those from lists 1.1.2 and 2.2.4, grow best in very rich, loamy, moist to damp soil. Their tuberous rootstocks commonly fall apart when lifted, making the plants easy to divide.

Common monkshood	0.60–1.50	VI–VII, helmet-like flowers in occasionally branched
Aconitum napellus	violet	racemes; leaves incised almost to the base.
Eur.		

A. n. ssp. *neomontanum* (*A. n.* ssp. *pyramidalis*) is the most important subspecies, generally available in the form of the following selections.

Aconitum napellus	1.50	VI–VII, early-flowering; stiffly upright racemes, some-
'Newry Blue'	dark blue	what branched at the base.
		Even earlier:
		'Bergfürst, brilliant blue.
		'Gletschereis', 'Album', somewhat dirty white.

Aconitum napellus ssp. *tauricum* 'Bressingham Spire'	0.90 violet	VII–VIII, very slender, condensed, upright habit. 'Blue Sceptre', similar, but with blue and white flowers.
Aconitum × *cammarum* 'Bicolor'	1.30 blue and white	VIII, popular old cultivar; one of a number of sterile hybrids.
A. × *cammarum* 'Franz Marc'	1.30 blue-violet	VIII, branching inflorescences. 'Coeruleum', similar, but daintier and with smaller flowers. 'Doppelgänger' (1.60), large, glossy dark blue flowers; similar to *A. variegatum* with very tall 'helmets'.
Aconitum henryi 'Spark's Variety' W China	1.50 dark violet	VII–VIII, loose, widely branched inflorescences.

Autumn-flowering species

Aconitum × *arendsii* (*A. carmichaelii* × *A. wilsonii*)	1.10 dark violet-blue	IX–X, powerful habit; unusually large flowers; glossy green leaves; good for cutting. sometimes injured by frost.
Aconitum carmichaelii (*A. fischeri*) Manch. to Kamch.	0.80–1.00 blue-violet	IX–X, sturdy, upright habit; densely crowded inflorescences; exceptionally late-flowering.
Aconitum wilsonii (*A. carmichaelii* var. *wilsonii*) C China	1.60 amethyst-blue	VIII–X, well-proportioned inflorescences on sturdy stems; leathery, glossy green leaves. Selections: 'Barker's Variety', comes true from seed. 'Kelmscott' (to 1.80), blue-violet; massive habit.

Delphinium hybrids (*Delphinium* × *cultorum*)

Tall-growing delphiniums are among the most beautiful of all garden perennials. Foremost among them are the robust, healthy hybrids produced by the great German perennial breeder Karl Foerster. These plants do not need staking (unlike British and American cultivars), only falling over when they are given too much fertiliser. Moreover, they seldom fall prey to mildew. Signs of attack may appear during bad weather around the time of their second flowering but these confine themselves to the leaves and hardly ever affect the flowers. Foerster's cultivars are derived in large part from *Delphinium elatum*, which grows wild in mountain woods and meadows in eastern Europe. They have retained much more of their wild character than the showy and often double-flowered British and American selections. Of these, the Pacific hybrids make healthy plants but are raised from seed of varying quality and do not stay entirely true to type. Unfortunately, the Foerster delphiniums are not well known outside Germany, and are rarely available in Britain and North America.

Delphiniums need a lot of space. The plants will flower twice a year (June/July and again in September/October) but only if they are cut back to about 10 cm immediately after the first flowering. In autumn the soil around them should be gently loosened, taking care not to disturb the roots. The clumps respond badly to covering with peat.

Old plants are best divided with a spade in spring. There is little point in replanting large divisions; small sections of rootstock with two or three shoots quickly develop into strong, healthy specimens.

Delphinium Elatum hybrids, (VI–VII; IX–X)

Reliable, vegetatively propagated German selections, arranged into five colour groups.

Dark violet-blue:
'Finsteraarhorn' (1.70), VII, dark eye; sometimes needs staking; good for cutting; middle.
'Sommernachtstraum' (1.50), VI, dark eye; low-growing; early.
'Waldenburg' (1.50), eye almost black; middle to late.

Pure, brilliant blue:
'Abgesang' (1.80), white eye; latest-flowering cultivar; sometimes needs staking.
'Adria' (1.40), gentian blue with a white eye; graceful habit; middle.
'Azurriese' (1.80), white eye; sturdy, upright habit; middle to late.
'Berghimmel' (1.80), white eye; leafy; early.
'Blauwal' (2.00), brown eye; early to middle.
'Fernzünder' (1.50), white eye; stiff habit; middle to late.
'Jubelruf' (1.70), radiant blue with a white eye; slender panicles.
'Lanzenträger' (2.00), gentian blue with a white eye; robust selection; middle to late.
'Polarnacht' (1.50), deep gentian blue with a white eye.
'Zauberflöte' (1.80), mid-blue with a pink gloss; white eye; long panicles; middle.

Light blue:
'Frühschein' (1.70), somewhat pinkish with a dark eye; very early.
'Gletscherwasser' (1.80), white eye; early to middle.
'Junior' (1.50), dark eye; middle.
'Merlin' (1.80), white eye; middle to late.

Pink tones:
'Ouverture' (1.60), somewhat pinkish; black eye; early.
'Perlmutterbaum' (1.80), somewhat pinkish; brown eye; middle to late.
'Werratal' (1.50), pale bluish pink; middle.

White:
'Schneespeer' (1.30), white with green tips; white eye; middle.
'Ulrike zur Linden' (1.60), white; semi-double.

The tall (up to 2.40), spectacular, British large-flowered hybrids also belong here, but most of them need staking and are prone to disease. They are generally unavailable outside Britain.

Delphinium Pacific hybrids (VI–VIII; IX–X)

These opulent, large-flowered hybrids are raised from seed and are therefore somewhat variable. Care should be taken when placing them since their 1.60–1.80 m stems sometimes need staking and the colours often do not come true. The flowers last longer than those of other hybrid delphiniums and are very suitable for cutting, particularly if they are sprayed to keep them fresh. New plants flower in the autumn of the year they are sown. The usual flowering times are VI–VII and IX–X. All are relatively short-lived.

Widely available colour strains:

White: 'Galahad', 'Parzival', 'Weisser Herkules'
Pink: 'Astolat', 'Guinevera'
Dark violet: 'Black Knight', 'King Arthur'
Mid-blue: 'Blue Bird'
Light Blue: 'Summer Skies'
Various: 'Blue Springs' (0.80), dwarf form.

Delphinium Belladonna hybrids

These are low-growing hybrids (under 1.20 m) with loosely branching panicles of mostly long-spurred flowers. The plants are sterile and thus have a long flowering season, particularly if the spent stems are removed as they fade. They are shorter-lived than Elatum hybrids.

'Capri' (1.20), pale blue with a white eye; early to middle.
'Moerheimii' (1.00), white.
'Connecticut Yankee' (up to 1.00), VII-IX, shades of blue–violet; can be propagated from seed.
'Kleine Nachtmusik' (0.80), dark lilac; early to middle.
'Piccolo' (1.00), pure blue; dense habit; particularly sturdy; very long flowering season.
'Völkerfrieden' (1.00), VI–IX, gentian blue with a white eye.

Delphinium × *ruysii* 'Pink Sensation'

This is a hybrid between *D. nudicaule* and *D.* × *cultorum*, produced by B. Ruys in 1935. As the first delphinium to exhibit pink flowers (with lilac centres) it aroused a lot of interest in the horicultural world. It has a similar habit (up to 0.80) and flowering season (VI, VII and X) to some of the Belladonna hybrids, with short, open panicles. The plants grow well in mild, wet conditions but are insufficiently sturdy and long-lived to be of any importance for planting, requiring more frequent lifting and division than most other delphiniums. More recently, pink-flowed Pacific hybrids have been developed that come reliably from seed. A further group of pink- and red-flowered hybrids is currently being developed by the Royal Horticultural Society in Britain.

Ornamental elements

Perennials: *Calamagrostis* × *acutiflora* 'K. Foerster';
Chrysanthemum serotinum
Annuals: *Cosmos sulphureus* 'Sunset' (1.00), coppery orange; *Salvia patens* (up to 0.60), blue.

Bleeding Heart, *Dicentra spectabilis*

This lovely woodland plant was first introduced into Europe from East Asia at the beginning of the nineteenth century but quickly became one of the best loved of garden perennials. Graceful, sinuous stems with long rows of rosy, heart-shaped flowers adorn the plants in May. The blue-green foliage turns yellow and dies back soon after flowering, so it is best to set the plants singly or in small groups that do not leave a large gap in summer. A sheltered, semi-shady position is ideal, especially since the new shoots can be damaged by late frosts in spring.

Dicentras can attain a great age without requiring replanting. The roots are easy to divide but should not be set too deep in the ground. It is interesting to note that plants raised from cuttings flower freely but never produce seed.

Dicentra spectabilis	0.70	V–VI, rare and sought-after white-flowered cultivar;
'Alba'	white	invaluable for cutting.
		Low-growing *Dicentra* species are treated in lists 2.2.1 and 4.5.2

Daylily, *Hemerocallis* hybrids

Hybrid daylilies are characterised by powerful clumps of lush green leaves, which often remain attractive until late in the autumn, and trumpet-like flowers of various shapes and sizes in many tones of yellow, amber, apricot, orange, brown and dark red. In mild regions, several cultivars retain their leaves throughout the winter. As the name implies, the individual flowers last for just a single day, but each stem has many buds opening successively to keep the plants in bloom for several weeks at a time. At Weihenstephan, the earliest sorts begin flowering in May and the late ones go on until the end of August or even into September. In parts of North America, the season can extend from April to November. The parent species grow wild in East Asia and have been assigned to the woodland edge (list 2.3.1). Some of them (e.g. *H. lilioasphodelus*) flower very early, while others, such as the trusty *H. citrina* and the old, invasive, red-brown *H. fulva* (list 2.2.3), flower at the same time as the main flush of hybrids. Late-flowering species such as *H. multiflora* and *H. thunbergii* are hardly grown nowadays but have played an important part in the creation of some modern hybrids.

All daylilies thrive on moist to damp, nutrient-rich soil in full sun. Some of them (e.g. *H. fulva*) will also tolerate warmth and drought in summer, while others flower just as well in semi-shade. The plants are easy to propagate by division.

The modern assortment of daylilies is in a constant state of flux. The trend is increasingly towards tetraploid cultivars, which have stout stems and flowers with a more substantial, leathery texture. The following lists contain a selection of relatively recent introductions along with some older, well-tried and widely available cultivars.

Daylilies may be classified into:

Wild species (lists 2.3.1 and 2.2.3)
Early-flowering hybrids
Large-flowered hybrids
Miniature hybrids

Early-flowering hybrids

The following beautiful and undemanding cultivars flower together with some of the more graceful wild species (see list 2.3.1) at the end of May and beginning of June, several weeks before the main flush of hybrids.

'Aureola' (0.80), coppery orange; flowers abundant and refined.
'Brunette' (0.50), small brown flowers; very early.
'Daily Bread' (0.60), small, golden-yellow flowers; very long season.
'Earliana' (0.90), large, yellow, well-poised blooms; invariably flowers a second time.
'Judge Orr' (1.00), orange-yellow; very early; flowers a second time.
'Queen of May' (0.60), orange-yellow; attractive green foliage until December.
'Sunny Face' (0.60), yellow with brown reverse; free-flowering.
'Sovereign' (0.60), golden yellow; wild in character; similar to *H. lilioasphodelus*.

Large-flowered hybrids

The following is a selection of particularly beautiful, reliable or widely available cultivars. Their flowering season lasts from July to September and all thrive in full sun. The yellow flowered daylilies retain their lush green foliage until late in the autumn but many of the more intensely coloured cultivars start to die down earlier, especially if the soil is cool and damp. Those plants that stay green until December are marked with an asterisk (*).

Iris sibirica, *Miscanthus* ssp., *Molinia* ssp., *Polemonium foliosissimum* and *Veronica longifolia* are among the wild perennials that may sometimes be combined with these hybrids.

*Pale yellow:
'Atlas' (1.10), large, lemon yellow flowers on stiff stems.
'Hyperion' (1.00), pale yellow; beautiful, old, free-flowering selection; one of the few strongly fragrant cultivars.
'Prairie Moonlight' (0.70), yellowish-green, squat habit.
'Shooting Star' (1.20), lemon yellow; late; refined in flower and habit.

'Vespers' (1.20), pale lemon yellow; elegant flowers.

Golden yellow to light orange:
'August Orange' (1.00), golden yellow; late.
'Burning Daylight' (0.60), deep orange-yellow; late; large flowers.
'Cartwheels' (0.80), large, flattened, golden (orange) yellow blooms; sturdy, compressed habit.
'Felice' (1.10), pale golden yellow; late; large, starry, narrow-petalled ('spider') flowers.
'Golden Sceptre' (1.20), golden yellow; stiff, leafy habit.
*'Jake Russell' (0.80), golden yellow; broad petals.
'President Rice' (0.80), deep golden yellow; sturdy habit.

Red-brown:
'Bess Ross' (0.70), very bright red.
'Bruno Müller' (0.80), brilliant orange-red.
'Buzz Bomb' (0.70), brilliant red-brown flowers with a yellow throat.
'Crimson Glory' (1.10), crimson, early; free-flowering.
'Crimson Pirate' (0.60), small, starry, red-brown flowers; leaves sometimes turn yellow immediately after flowering.
'Red Perfect' (0.70), red-brown flowers with an orange reverse; stiff, upright stems.
'Regal Air' (0.70), matt blood-red with a greenish-yellow throat; late.
'Resplendent' (1.00), red-brown with golden yellow mid-ribs; starry flowers.
'Sammy Russell' (0.80), brick-red; late.
'Summer Interlude' (0.70), broad, blood-red flowers; late.
*'Wideyed' (0.60), yellow with mahogany red stripes and eye; mid-late; flowers a second time.

Pink and pale maroon:
'Bed of Roses' (0.60), rose to salmon pink; late; middle-sized flowers.
*'Evelyn Claar' (0.50), maroon-pink; late.
'Luxury Lace' (0.90), pale bluish-pink; graceful flowers.
'Pink Damask' (0.80), pink; vigorous.

Salmon pink and melon:
'George Cunningham' (0.90), orange-pink; late; dark stems.

Bicoloured and multicoloured:
'Frances Fay' (0.50), pale yellow and pink; late.
'Frans Hals' (1.00), ochre and brown, mid-late; vigorous.

Miniature hybrids

These are dainty plants, but their flowers are by no means small when compared to their stature. The following cultivars have already proved reliable and free-flowering.

*Pale yellow:
'Bitsy' (0.50), early, but flowers long into summer.
'Lemon Bells' (0.70), dark stems and buds.
'Renée' (0.50), rounded flowers with wavy margins.

Golden yellow:
'Corky' (0.70), dark stems; elegant habit.
'Golden Chimes' (0.70), similar to the previous.
'Stella de Oro' (0.40), pale golden yellow; flowers from early summer to the end of autumn.
'Thumbelina' (0.40), orangey golden yellow; dainty.

Striped:
'Sweet Harmony' (0.50), brownish pink with mahogany stripes.

Red:
'Cherry Ripe' (0.80), starry flowers with a greenish yellow throat.
'Little Tramp' (0.50), brightly coloured; well branched.
'Little Tyke' (0.50), greenish-yellow throat.

Lavender:
'Little Wart' (0.50), fragrant.

Salmon and pink:
'Lady Inara' (0.80), sturdy, rounded flowers.
'Lula Mae Purnell' (0.60), yellowish salmon pink; long flowering.
'Toyland' (0.70), small, melon coloured bells.
'Vivacious' (0.60), silvery-pink with a greenish throat.

Pale tones:
'Border Queen' (0.50), apricot-yellow with pink mid-ribs.
'Little Rainbow' (0.50), creamy-yellow with a pinkish gleam.

5.2.2. Lilies for cool positions in sun and bright shade

(See pp. 78 ff. for the planting and care of lilies.)

European Turk's cap lilies, *Lilium martagon*

These beautiful and undemanding lilies have long been grown in gardens, where they thrive and seed themselves on moist, humus-rich, basic, loamy soils on the edge of woodland or under a light canopy of trees. The plants grow wild in Europe and Asia, both in woodland and on mountain pastures in full sun. Their powerful stems grow up to 1.20 m and bear characteristic whorls of leaves. Large, nodding, dull pink, turban-shaped flowers appear in June and July, and are followed by distinctive seed capsules in autumn.

Lilium martagon 'Album Superbum'	pure white	More vigorous and with larger flowers than the wild species; comes true from seed.
Lilium martagon var. *cattaniae*	dark wine-red	Very vigorous variety from Yugoslavia; tall, stiff flowering stems.

Both these forms are less commonly seen than their hybrids with *L. hansonii*.

Lilium hansonii

This strongly scented Turk's cap lily comes from Korea. Its shoots emerge very early in the year and often require protection against late frosts. Brown-speckled, orange-yellow flowers start appearing at the end of June. The almost umbel-like racemes are held on stems up to 1.50 m tall, with leaves arranged in whorls. In a lightly shaded spot on moist to damp, humus-rich soil, these lilies can attain a great age. The plants tolerate lime and are resistant to disease. The best time to plant them out is in autumn (as with *L. martagon*), from the middle of September to the end of October.

Lilium Hansonii hybrids

The following vigorous, free-flowering hybrids flourish reliably on even the most unpromising of soils. In time they form sturdy clumps which can persist for decades without replanting, though not in regions with hot, dry summers. Although they thrive in sun, the plants also do well in light shade in the neighbourhood of trees and shrubs. They are easily propagated by division in autumn.

Lilium × dalhensonii (*L. m.* var. *cattaniae* × *L. hansonii*)		VI–VII, dark, chestnut-brown flowers with orange centres in pyramidal inflorescences, on stems up to 1.50 m.
L. Marhan Hybrids (*L, m.* 'Album' × *L. hansonii*)	up to 1.30	VI–VII, paler, orange and yellow flowers, speckled with brown; very robust and reliable but may be injured by late frosts. Selections: 'Jacques S. Dijt', brown-speckled, creamy yellow flowers on stems up to 1.00 m. 'Mrs R. O. Backhouse' (1.20), brown-speckled, orange-yellow flowers.

Oriental lilies

Oriental lilies are among the most beautiful but also the most difficult of garden lilies. Their parents, including the incomparable golden-rayed lily (*Lilium auratum*) and the late-flowering *L. speciosum*, are particularly demanding species, growing wild in the Japanese mountains near the sea, on porous, lime-free, humus-rich, sandy or volcanic soils. The various selections and hybrids are somewhat more obliging than their parents, which usually disappear after one or two years wherever conditions are not exactly right for them. Nevertheless, they are sensitive to damp in winter, and easily fall prey to virus infections or the basal rot that affects many lilies. Both parents and hybrids combine well with rhododendrons, which share their preference for sandy soils, rich in peat and leaf compost. The plants grow best in a mild, humid, coastal climate. In Europe, their bulbs are best planted in spring (possibly from containers), as they are not normally ripe enough in autumn.

Species

These grow best in sunny woodland edge conditions on acid, sandy soil with plenty of peat and leaf compost. The plants should be shaded at the base.

Golden-rayed lily *Lilium auratum* Jap.	1.00–1.50	VIII–IX, beautiful but delicate lily with large, fragrant, bowl-shaped flowers, whose white petals are speckled red and have a golden yellow central stripe; only to be recommended for experienced gardeners.
Lilium speciosum Jap., Taiw.	0.80–1.00 (2.00)	VIII-IX, large, fragrant, nodding flowers in loose racemes on rigid stems; petals pink, speckled red, with ruffled white margins. Selections: 'Grand Commander', larger and more sturdy in all its parts. 'Uchida' (0.90–1.00), dark crimson; particularly robust. 'Album', white with a greenish base. 'Rubrum', white, flamed with crimson.

Hybrids (*L.* Auratum hybrids)

'Black Beauty' (1.50), VIII, crimson with a dark red centre; reflexed petals.
'Crimson Beauty' (1.80), VIII, white with crimson stripes.
'Jamboree' (strain) (1.00–1.80), VIII–IX, speckled, crimson flowers with white margins.
'Pink Glory' (strain) (1.30), VII–VIII, salmon pink; thin but sturdy stems.
'Sunday Best' (1.30), VIII, white flushed with crimson; purple-red central stripe.

5.2.3. Warm, sunny places with moist to dry soil in summer

Border perennials do not thrive under extreme conditions. This applies to the following plants, whose requirements are otherwise related to those of the wild perennials from lists 2.2.2, 2.2.3 and 2.3.4.

Outdoor florists' chrysanthemums, *Chrysanthemum* Indicum hybrids

Florists' chrysanthemums are the descendants of the old Far Eastern culture plant *Chrysanthemum indicum*. The majority are tender, indoor plants. The hardy, outdoor varieties probably have *C. indicum* var. *koreanum* or some of the *C.* Koreanum hybrids in their blood. These colourful hybrids are no longer dependent on the woodland edge conditions required by their wild ancestors. They grow best in full sun on porous, nutrient-rich soils, particularly where the climate is mild and humid. In harsher regions they are best planted against a house wall. When frost threatens it is even possible to dig up plants in full bloom for transferring into large pots, where they will carry on flowering for many weeks in bright, frost-free conditions. It is advisable to choose early- rather than late-flowering varieties for an exposed position, and to lightly cover the plants with conifer sprays in winter. The clumps are easily divided with a knife in spring. Lists of reliable, outdoor cultivars may be obtained from catalogues. Each country produces its own large assortment of hybrids.

Flowering times: Early, VIII–IX; Mid, IX–X; Late, X–XI. The early-flowering chrysanthemums known as *C. rubellum* in the trade (*C. zawadskii* var. *latilobum*) are hardier than the above. Proven selections:
Pink: 'Clara Curtis' (0.70), single; early.
Wine-red: 'Duchess of Edinburgh' (0.60), VII–VIII, semi-double; very early.

Ornamental elements

Ageratum houstonianum 'Schnittwunder' (up to 0.50), blue; together with *Tagetes* (0.30–0.80), particularly the lemon-yellow sorts.

Crown imperial, *Fritillaria imperialis*

Crown imperials grow in open mountain woodland from Iran to the Himalayas. Whorls of leaves extend half way up their strong, fleshy stems. At the top there is a further tuft of leaves from which several large, coppery-red, bell-shaped flowers hang down, creating one of the most impressive appearances among spring-flowering perennials.

The first bulbs were introduced into Europe in 1576 and the plants have long been cottage garden favourites. Their strong, musky odour is said to repel mice and voles. Crown imperials grow best in a rich, porous soil that does not get too dry in summer. Their shoots emerge very early in the year, flower in April and are already beginning to die back by Whitsun. Their yellowed foliage should be cut down rather than pulled out of the ground. From time to time, when flowering diminishes, it may be necessary to lift the clumps and separate the bulbs. This is best done as soon as the plants have died down, though new bulbs can also be set out in early autumn. The planting depth should be about 25 cm;

Vigorous selections (ca. *1.00*)

'Aurora', reddish orange.
'Orange Brilliant', very large, orange-brown flowers.
'Rubra Maxima', broad, orange-red flowers.
'Lutea Maxima', large yellow flowers.

'The Premier', large, deep orange flowers.
'Inodora', (0.80), similar to the species but odourless.

Peonies, *Paeonia lactiflora, P. officinalis* and *P. peregrina*

Various forms of the southern European *Paeonia officinalis* have been grown for many centuries in European gardens. *P. lactiflora* has an even longer history, with plants being selected in Chinese gardens more than 1000 years ago. The Japanese took up the breeding of *P. lactiflora* to produce lighter and more graceful, single and semi-double flowered varieties. European cultivars only started to appear in the latter part of the nineteenth century, to be followed by selections from America.

The popular garden cultivars of *Paeonia lactiflora* and *P. officinalis* all need a very rich and preferably loamy soil in full sun. They thus differ from wild peonies, which, with the exception of *P. tenuifolia* (list 3.4.4), all grow best on nutrient-rich but not too damp soils in warm, bright, woodland edge conditions (list 2.3.4), flowering there longer than they would in an open bed. Although the garden cultivars are no longer bound to the woodland edge in this way, they nevertheless remain particularly effective planted in association with trees and shrubs.

The peculiar tuberous roots of peonies contain reserves of nutrients and moisture that allow the plants to survive during the long dry season in their natural habitat. Planted in the right spot, these extraordinarily long-lived perennials can flourish for decades, flowering each year with undiminished vigour. Old plants must be kept well fed, requiring up to $100 \, g/m^2$ of artificial fertiliser each spring and then again immediately after flowering.

Peonies are propagated in September by division with a spade or knife. Tubers of *P. officinalis* will form new shoots like a sprouting potato but *P. lactiflora* only grows well from divisions that include ready-formed buds from the base of an old stem. Peonies are typical hemicryptophytes: species with overwintering buds only half covered with soil. The plants should therefore on no account be set too deep in the ground, particularly where the soil is heavy. Chinese peonies develop very slowly and their flowers only assume their characteristic form after several years, making it almost impossible to identify newly planted specimens.

Peonies are best planted singly and at rhythmic intervals along a border. Each plant should be allowed at least one square metre for its development. It is worth bearing in mind that the foliage turns an attractive reddish brown in autumn, associating well with warm colours among the late-flowering perennials.

Chinese peonies, *Paeonia* Lactiflora hybrids

These emerge as attractive red shoots in spring and develop into leafy clumps. Their powerful flowering stems can grow to more than 1 m, each bearing several buds that open successively in June. Several of the double-flowered cultivars, particularly those grown for cutting, have a tendency to fall over in rainy weather and must therefore be supported. The foliage of many cultivars turns an attractive red-brown in autumn. The following are proven selections.

Deep red, double:
Early: 'Adolph Rousseau'
Mid: 'Mons. Martin Cahuzac', 'Karl Rosenfeld'
Late: 'Inspecteur Lavergne'

Crimson, double:
Mid: 'Bunker Hill', 'Kansas'
Late: 'Félix Crousse'

Pink, double:
Early: 'Noémie Demay', 'Reine Hortense'
Mid: 'Triomphe de l'Exposition de Lille' (silvery pink), 'Walter Faxon'

Late: 'Sarah Bernhardt', 'Miss Eckardt'

Pale pink, double:
Early: 'Mons. Jules Elie', 'Wiesbaden'
Mid: 'Lady Alexandra Duff', 'Baroness Schroeder'
Late: 'Claire Dubois', 'Le Perle'

White, double:
Early: 'Fesival Maxima', 'Le Cygne', 'Mme. de Vernéville', 'Duchesse de Nemours', 'Primevère' (cream)
Mid: 'Avalanche', 'Solfatare' (cream), 'Laura Dessert'
Late: 'Marie Lemoine', 'Alma Hansen', 'Couronne d'Or'

Single:
Red: 'Bandmaster', 'Hogarth', 'King of England', 'Rembrandt'
Pink: 'Holbein', 'Murillo', 'Schwindt', 'Thoma', 'L'Etincelante'
White: 'Angelika Kauffmann', 'Clairette', 'Watteau' (cream)

Single and semi-double Japanese cultivars (see also catalogues)

Red: 'Surugu', 'Okinawa', 'Some Ganoko', 'Torpilleur'.
Pink: 'Petite Renée', 'Bowl of Beauty', 'Globe of Light', 'Tokio'.
White: 'Jean van Leuwen'.

Ornamental elements

The following annuals can sometimes be appropriate in large plantings: *Tithonia speciosa* (up to 2.00), red–orange; *Verbena bonariensis* (1.20), blue–violet.

European peonies, *Paeonia officinalis* and *P. peregrina*

Paeonia officinalis is an old medicinal plant, which produces its single red blooms in May, one to two weeks before the Chinese peonies. The plants bear only one flower on each stem. Apart from the dark red, double-flowered 'cottage peony', the species and its forms are seldom to be found in gardens.

Double-flowered cultivars:
Paeonia officinalis (SW Eur., Hung., Alban.)
'Rubra Plena' (0.60), dark red; the old cottage garden peony.
'Rosea Plena' (0.60), pink.
'Alba Plena' (0.60), white; delicate pink buds.
'Mutabilis Plena' (0.60), delicate pink, turning white.
'Starlight' (0.60), creamy white; semi-double.

Single-flowered cultivars:
(Also for partly shaded positions on the woodland edge)

Paeonia officinalis
'Anemonaeflora' (0.30), flattened, deep pink flowers; very early.
'Anemonaeflora Aurea-Ligulata (0.50), dark red; very early.
'China Rose' (0.60), brilliant salmon pink.
'Cyntherea' (0.60), cherry red.
'J. C. Weguelin' (0.60), large, crimson blooms.

Paeonia peregrina (*P. lobata*) (It. Balk.), upturned flowers; glossy green, biternate leaves.
'Crimson Globe' (0.70), brilliant salmon pink globes.

'Sunshine' (0.70), orangey salmon pink flowers (see list 2.3.4).
'Fire King' 'Otto Froebel', 'Sunbeam', similar; all salmon pink.
'Rubinschale' (0.30), ruby red; golden yellow anthers.

Wild species and hybrids: see lists 2.3.4. and 3.4.4.

Paeonia hybrids

The hybridisation of Asiatic and European wild peonies with *P. lactiflora* has produced a range of mostly early, single-flowered plants with large but sadly short-lived blooms. These hybrids have retained a measure of their wild character and are particularly effective planted in a slightly shady border on the woodland edge. The following selections are for the most part only available from specialist nurseries.

'Alexander Steffen' (1.00), V, vigorous; large, single, dark pink flowers.
'Burma Ruby' (0.80), IV, bright red; large, bowl-shaped flowers.
'Chalice' (1.00), V, very large, creamy flowers.
'Claire de Lune' (0.70), V, pallid yellow, semi-double flowers.
'Gertrud Allen' (0.70), V, ivory white, bowl-shaped flowers; fused, lemon-yellow stamens.
'Hoffnung' (0.70), IV–V, pink, semi-double flowers; very early; stiff habit.
'Mai Fleuri' (0.60), V, cream with pink; dark, almost bronzy foliage.
'Le Printemps' (0.80), V, pale creamy yellow.
'Ludovica' (0.80), IV, semi-double, salmon pink flowers; very early.

5.2.4.   Lilies for sunny positions

(Planting and maintenance, see pp. 78 ff.)

Trumpet-flowered lilies

The trumpet-flowered lilies include a number of exceptionally sturdy and free-flowering garden plants with large, showy, strongly scented blooms. The Aurelianense hybrids (*L.* × *aurelianense*) are derived from *L. sargentiae* and the orange-flowered Chinese Turk's cap lily, *L. henryi*, back-crossed with *L. regale* and other white and yellow, Chinese, trumpet-flowered species. They form a vigorous and healthy race, thriving on any well-drained fertile soil. Most of them flower just after the delphiniums, making a useful splash of colour, particularly in combination with grasses. Both species and hybrids are best planted in spring from March onwards.

Species

Lilium regale China	0.80–1.50	VII, one of the easiest sun-loving lilies; large, white, fragrant, funnel-shaped flowers with a maroon-pink interior; emerges early and should be protected against late frosts; forms a clump.
Lilium henryi China	1.20–2.00	VIII–IX, large, brown-speckled, orange, Turk's cap flowers on sturdy, slightly over-arching stems; reliable and long-lived in porous, basic, sandy soils; loathes peat. 'Citrinum', IX, lemon yellow.

Hybrids

The following lists contain several seed strains that vary somewhat in colour and habit, unlike vegetatively propagated cultivars.

Funnel-shaped flowers:
'African Queen' (strain) (1.50–1.80), VII, apricot.
'Black Magic' (strain) (1.50–2.00), VII–VIII, white with a bronze reverse.
'Black Dragon' (1.80), VII, white, with a white-marked, purple-brown reverse.
'Damson' (1.50), VII, dark fuchsia red.
'Dillenburg' (1.50), VII, lemon-yellow.
'Golden Clarion' (strain) (1.40), VII, golden lemon-yellow.
'Golden Splendour' (strain) (1.20–1.80), VII, dark golden flowers with a reddish reverse.
'Green Magic' (strain) (1.50), VII–VIII, white with a green reverse.
'Green Dragon' (1.50), VII–VIII, open, greenish-yellow funnels.
'Limelight' (1.60), VII, chartreuse yellow with a green reverse.
'Moonlight' (strain), VII, chartreuse yellow.
Olympic Hybrids (1.60), VII–VIII, large white trumpets.
'Pink Perfection' (strain) (1.80), VII, dark pink and white.
'Royal Gold' (1.00–1.50), VI–VII, golden yellow.
'Verona' (1.80), VII, fuchsia red.

Bowl-shaped flowers:
'Life' (1.50), VII, golden yellow with a bronze reverse.
'Sentinel' (1.50), VII, pure white with a pale yellow throat.

Flat, starry flowers:
'Copper King' (strain) (1.50), VI–VII, orange with a reddish brown reverse.
'Golden Showers' (strain) (1.60), VII–VIII, butter yellow to orange.
'Golden Sunburst' (strain) (1.50–1.80), VII–VIII, golden yellow with a yellow reverse.
'Pink Sunburst' (strain) (1.50–1.80), VII–VIII, fuchsia pink.
'Stardust' (1.50–1.80), VII–VIII, silvery white with an orange centre.
'Thunderbolt' (1.50), VII–VIII, melon yellow.
'White Henryi' (1.50), VII–VIII, white with a slightly yellowish throat.

Nodding flowers:
'Honeydew' (1.50), VII, long, greenish-yellow trumpets with a green reverse.

5.3.   Border perennials derived from open ground species

Like their wild ancestors, the following widely grown and free-flowering border perennials have little or no affinity with trees and shrubs. They are most effective grown in an open site, particularly in combination with summer annuals. In the confined space of a small garden it is important to give them as much room as possible for their development. Their suitability for use in intensively maintained public areas deserves wider recognition from planners and landscape architects.

The combination of these plants with wild perennials from open ground habitats, particularly those that display some border character, is also worthy of consideration. Various possibilities are mentioned within the following classification.

Warm, sunny sites with soil that is mostly dry in summer:
Iris, Lilium, Papaver, Sedum (list 5.3.1).
These may be combined with many of the steppe species from list 3.3.

Warm, sunny sites with moderately dry to moist soil:
Aster amellus, Lilium, Scabiosa caucasica (list 5.3.2).

These may be combined with many of the species from list 3.4.4 and particularly the wild perennials with border character from list 3.4.5.

Sunny sites with moderately moist to moderately damp soil:
Aster, Helenium, Helianthus, Heliopsis, Rudbeckia, Solidago, Erigeron, Lupinus, Phlox (list 5.4.4). These are closely related to the North American wild perennials with border character (list 3.4.6).

Sunny (or bright shady) sites with moist to moderately damp soil:
Achillea ptarmica, Iris sibirica, Lilium, Polemonium, Trollius, Eupatorium, Monarda, Physostegia, Tradescantia (list 5.4.5).
These can sometimes be combined with wild perennials for more or less damp conditions (list 3.5).

Wild species of lily have been listed together with their hybrids. Their particular requirements and proper garden habitat are mentioned in the text.

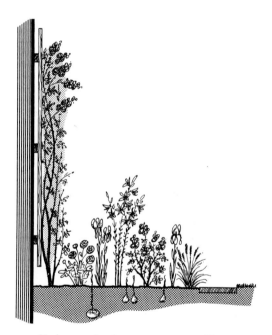

Herbaceous border: warm, sunny positions.

5.3.1.   Warm, sunny sites with soil that is mostly dry in summer

Rather few perennials are suitable for a border planting in these conditions. Among the steppe plants from list 3.3, it is particularly the less overpowering foxtail lilies, such as *Eremurus bungei* and the Shelford and Ruiter hybrids, together with some of the larger *Allium* species, that associate best with the border perennials listed below. Large gypsophilas (list 4.1.1) can also be appropriate, especially where they tumble down the front of a terrace. Further possibilities may be found among the species in lists 3.4.1 and 3.4.2.

Tall and intermediate bearded iris, *Iris* Barbata Elatior and Barbata Media hybrids

The assortment of these beautiful bearded irises is intractably large and in a constant state of flux. Modern cultivars are the product of a gradual development, starting with robust, undemanding selections from drought– and warmth-loving plants such as *Iris pallida* and *I. variegata*, and incorporating other southern European wild species together with the old garden hybrids *Iris florentina* and *I. germanica* to form an immensely varied range of more or less demanding border perennials whose large, uncommonly graceful flowers are reminiscent of orchids in the splendour and indescribable diversity of their colours. The early-flowering dwarf irises (list 4.4.1) have a different pedigree whose most important component is *Iris pumila* from the dry grasslands of central Eurasia.

In common with their wild ancestors the modern hybrids need a warm, well-drained, relatively dry and limy soil. A mineral-rich loam is particularly suitable and requires only moderate applications of a low-nitrate fertiliser. Too much nitrate is harmful, promoting soft, succulent tissues, which are prone to bacterial and fungal diseases. Older cultivars, with smaller flowers and a more modest range of colours, are mostly less demanding in their requirements and more resistant to disease. For this reason they have been listed separately. Given an open soil these long-lived and free-flowering plants will survive for decades on a sunny, stone-covered slope or along the crown of a wall, becoming ever more beautiful as the years go by.

Irises must not be planted too deeply. Their rhizomes should be pressed firmly into the ground upon planting but only lightly covered with soil. Should their flowering diminish over the years, they are best divided and replanted during the dormant season in late summer.

Intermediate bearded iris, *Iris* Barbata Media hybrids

These attractive, sturdy, undemanding, comparatively low-growing (0.40–0.50) hybrids between dwarf irises and tall bearded irises flower abundantly in May, before the main flush of tall irises gets under way.

Some representative cultivars

White:
'Cloud Fluff'
'Cutie'

Light blue:
'Andalusian blue'
'Blue Denim'

Dark blue:
'Maroon Caper'

Lilac-pink:
'Rose Harmony'

Yellow:
'Moonbeam'
'Findelkind'
'Alaskan Gold'
'Sunbeam'

Grey-lavender:
'Lichtelfe'

Wine-red:
'Cherry Garden'

Ornamental elements

Annuals: *Asperula orientalis* (0.20), blue; *Eschscholzia californica* (up to 0.30), yellow to orange-red.
Perennials: *Sedum* spp.; lavender.

Tall bearded iris, *Iris* Barbata Elatior hybrids

(Robust, undemanding selections that also tolerate extreme conditions.)

These are very beautiful and undemanding, mostly diploid irises with comparatively small but abundant flowers. In contrast to the more recent large-flowered hybrids (see following list) they will tolerate extreme conditions on warm, dry, stony soil. At Weihenstephan, their flowering season extends from May to June.

White:
'White Knight' (0.60)

Blue/white and violet/white:
'Rheinnixe' (1.00)
'Toelleturm' (0.60)

Blue and pale blue:
'Corrida' (0.80)
'Meissner Porzellan' (0.70)
'Bonnie Blue' (0.80)

Predominantly blue and pale blue:
'Rheintraube' (0.90)

Predominantly dark blue-violet:
'Parc de Neuilly' (0.70)
'Tom Tit' (0.50)

Pale yellow:
'Yellow Moon' (0.60)
'Ellen' (0.50)

Pale golden yellow:
'Phebus' (0.80)

Yellow and brown:
'Kupferhammer' (0.60)

Light red and pink:
'Rota' (0.70)
'Favori' (0.70)

Lilac-pink:
'Rheingauperle' (0.90)

Brown:
'Stardom' (0.70)
'Impromptu' (0.90)

Tall bearded iris, *Iris* Barbata Elatior hybrids
(Fairly recent, highly selected, large-flowered cultivars.)

These truly magnificent early summer perennials abhor damp conditions, needing plenty of sunshine and a dry soil in summer to achieve their full potential. In a cold climate they are best planted on rich, loamy soil in a warm, sunny, sheltered position next to the house. Even in the coldest areas, any sort of covering in winter is not only unnecessary but positively harmful. At Weihenstephan, the plants flower in May and June.

Some representative cultivars:

Pure white:
'New Snow' (1.20)
'Cliffs of Dover' (0.80)

White and blue:
'Bright Hour' (0.80)
'Miss Indiana' (0.80)

White with blue margins:
'Blue Petticoats' (0.70)
'Wiener Walzer' (0.90)
'Stepping Out' (0.80)

White with yellow margins:
'Radiant Apogee' (0.70)

Off-white:
'Wedding Bouquet' (0.80)

Yellowish:
'Lugano' (0.80)

White with yellow falls:
'Pinnacle' (0.80)

White with red margins:
'Crinoline' (0.70)

Yellow with brown markings:
'Cayenne Capers' (0.70)

Light blue:
'Jane Phillips' (0.80)
'Sparkling Waters' (0.75)

Mid-blue:
'Tyrolean Blue' (0.70)

Black-violet:
'Tuxedo' (0.80)
'Black Taffeta' (0.70)
'Licorice Stick' (1.00)

Red-brown:
'Vitafire' (0.70)
'Bang' (0.70)
'Captain Gallant' (0.65)

Coppery brown:
'Starburst' (0.80)
'Rusticana' (0.80)

Lemon yellow:
'Buttercup Bower' (0.80)
'Green Quest' (0.75)
'Soaring Kite' (0.95)

Dark yellow:
'Goldfackel' (0.90)
'West Coast' (0.60)
'Ola Kala' (0.90)
'Granada Gold' (0.80)

Two-tone, blue-violet:
'Helen Collingwood' (0.90)
'Lord Baltimore' (0.80)

Lilac-pink:
'Camelot Rose' (0.70)
'Amethyst Flame' (0.80)

Flamingo pink:
'One Desire' (0.70)

'Esther Fay' (0.80)
'Karin von Hugo' (0.70)

Yellow and brown:
'Lambent' (0.90)
'Accent' (0.80)
'Kingdom' (0.80)
'Mystic Melody' (0.90), two-tone.

Oriental poppies, *Papaver orientale* and *P. bracteatum*

Oriental poppies are characterised by their large, hairy, pinnately divided leaves and massive buds, which open into enormous flowers in brilliant tones of red. The modern assortment includes a number of more subdued, pink- and white-flowered forms, with petals that may be wavy or fringed. The plants die down completely after flowering, only resuming growth in late summer and autumn.

These poppies have much in common with some of the steppe perennials from list 3.3 and associate well with them on suitable, nutrient-rich soils. In common with their wild parents from the mountain steppes of Armenia and the southern Caucasus, they need a warm, loose, rubbly soil for their long tap roots to develop properly. On cold, heavy soils, they are somewhat unreliable and even the most robust cultivars may suddenly dwindle or disappear. The clumps can be divided either in early spring or when the leaves die down in summer. Nurseries propagate them by means of root cuttings.

Papaver bracteatum 'Beauty of Livermere'	0.30/1.00 deep red	VI–VII, dense, green, hairy foliage; stiff habit; effective flower colour; a healthy and sociable plant, more reliable on cold, clayey soils than other oriental poppies.
Papaver orientale 'Feuerriese'	0.30/0.90 fiery red	VI–VII, silver-hairy foliage; stiff habit. Low-growing cultivars: 'Sturmfackel' ('Stormtorch') (0.50), VII. 'Border Beauty' (0.50), double.
Papaver orientale 'Marcus Perry'	0.25/0.70 orange– scarlet	VI–VII, silver-hairy foliage; very large flowers. 'Aladin' (0.80), VI, wavy petals. 'Allegro' (0.70), VI–VII, bright scarlet. 'Arwide' ('Pinnacle') (0.80), very distinctive flowers patterned orange and white. 'Frührot' (0.80), V–VI, brilliant red; very early. 'Indian Chief' mahogany-red. 'Türkenlouis' (0.60), fringed petals.
Papaver orientale 'Catharina' ('Elizabeth')	0.25/0.90 salmon pink with a black blotch	VI–VII, hairy leaves. 'Corinna' (0.70), salmon pink with red blotches; late. 'Derwisch' (0.70), salmon pink; late. 'Kleine Tänzerin' (0.50), salmon pink. 'Mrs Perry' (0.90), salmon pink. 'Picotee' (0.70), V–VII, salmon pink and white; frilled petals. 'Salmon Glow' salmon pink; double flowers.
Papaver orientale 'Fatima'	0.25/0.80 whitish, pink margins	VI–VII, grey-green leaves; wavy petals. 'Springtime' (0.80), white, merging with salmon pink. 'Karine' (0.60), pale pink with red blotches.

Papaver orientale	0.25/0.80	VI–VII, dark purple blotches at the base of the petals.
'Perry's White'	white	'Baron von der Glotz' (0.75), similar to the above. 'Black and White' (0.70), large white flowers with a black centre.

Numerous local cultivars are available in each country.

Ornamental elements

Argemone mexicana (0.60), yellow.
Cladanthus arabicus (to 0.50), yellow.
Eschscholzia californica (to 0.30), yellow to orange-red.
Glaucium flavum (0.30), yellow.
Galtonia candicans (to 1.00), white; see list 5.8.

Tall *Sedum* species

The following tall, showy sedums may be regarded as border perennials, though they are just as effective in a wild planting on a sunny, open site. Old plants tend to lose stature and flower less freely. They may be taken up and divided with a knife in spring.

Sedum alboroseum	0.40–0.60	IX, unbranched stems with pale blue-green, slightly
(*S. japonicum* hort.)	greenish	toothed, ovate leaves; red carpels.
E As.	white	'Mediovariegatum', creamy-white leaves with broad green margins; also for bright shade.
Sedum telephium		List 3.4.4
Sedum spectabile	0.40	VIII–X, large, flat-domed inflorescences on rigid
Korea, Manch.	pale pink	stems with fleshy, pale grey-green, scalloped, broad-oval leaves; old garden plant in China. Intensely coloured selections: Magenta: 'Brilliant', 'Carmen', 'Meteor', 'Rosenteller' ('Pink Plate'). Dark purple: 'Septemberglut' ('September Glow').
Sedum × telephium	0.60	IX–X, attractive, bushy habit with stiffly erect,
'Herbstfreude'	rust red	unbranched stems; reliable and persistent autumn per-
(*S. spectabile ×*		ennial.
S. telephium)		

Lilies for warm, sunny conditions (including brief summer drought)

(Planting and maintenance, see pp. 78 ff.)

Lilium Maculatum hybrids (*L. × hollandicum, L. × umbellatum*)

These lilies are descended for the most part from *Lilium bulbiferum* (list 2.1.7), formerly a weed of Central European arable land, together with its close relative *L. bulbiferum* ssp. *croceum* from mountain pastures in Italy, France and Switzerland (list 5.3.3), and the rarely grown *L. dauricum* from NE Asia (list 5.3.3). The hybrids used to be known under the names of *L. × hollandicum* and *L. × umbellatum* but are now classified as *L.* Maculatum hybrids and are grouped together with the Asiatic hybrids (list 5.3.3).

The following, particularly undemanding and widely available garden lilies need little maintenance. They thrive in a warm, sunny position on porous, limy soil, producing up to 30 flowers per stem when the plants are well nourished.

The more difficult hybrids have been assigned to list 5.3.3.

'Erect' (0.70), VII, orange-red.
'Grandiflorum' (0.75), larger and darker flowers than the foregoing.
'Invincible' (up to 0.80), VI–VII, deep orange.

Madonna lily, *Lilium candidum*

The Madonna lily is an old garden cultivar from the eastern Mediterranean, with dense racemes of large, scented, pure white, funnel-shaped flowers on stems 0.80–1.20 m tall in late spring or early summer. It is unique among garden lilies in producing a vigorous, green basal rosette of overwintering leaves in September. The bulbs are best planted out during their dormant season in August. Unlike other lilies, they should not be set deeper than 3 cm in the soil.

Madonna lilies thrive best in a porous, alkaline loam that is warm and fairly dry in summer. Once planted, they should be left undisturbed and kept free from competition. In a well-tended cottage garden the plants will often persist for many years.

Among the hybrids it is worth mentioning *L.* × *testaceum*, whose nodding, yellow flowers (often flushed pink) appear in June and July on stems up to 1.20 m tall. The plant originated in 1836 as an accidental cross between *L. candidum* and the rarely grown *L. chalcedonica* from Greece. It requires a porous, limy, humus-rich soil that does not get too dry in summer. The stems are incapable of forming roots, and the bulbs should only be planted about 10 cm deep in the soil. Like *L. candidum*, *L.* × *testaceum* is very susceptible to lily disease (*Botrytis*). The bulbs are best planted in August.

5.3.2. Warm, sunny sites with moderately dry to moist soil

The following plants are here regarded as border perennials though their growing requirements are in many respects similar to those of the open ground perennials from lists 3.4.4 and 3.4.5. In plantings they associate well with these latter wild perennials, especially with selected forms of *Achillea filipendulina*, *Campanula glomerata*, low-growing *Echinops*, *Paeonia tenuifolia* and *Salvia nemorosa*, together with *Lychnis chalcedonica*, *Scutellaria incana* and *Lychnis viscaria* 'Plena' (list 3.4.2).

Italian aster, *Aster amellus*

These large-flowered, single asters begin flowering at the end of June and carry on until well into September. The original species grows wild in dry limestone grassland and sparse pine woods, thriving on warm, limy, moderately dry and loamy soil. The following selections share the same requirements and have all retained enough wild character to be incorporated into wild plantings in the appropriate conditions.

The plants are not so easily propagated as other asters. They are generally raised from cuttings taken as the new shoots appear in April and May. They respond poorly to planting in autumn and should therefore be set out in spring.

Pale violet to lavender:
Early: 'Praecox Junifreude' (0.50); 'Hermann Löns' (0.60).
Mid: 'Dr. Otto Petschek' (0.60); *A. pyrenaeus* 'Lutetia' (0.60); *A.* × *frikartii* 'Wunder von Stäfa' ('Stäfa Miracle') (0.70), open habit; *A.* × *frikartii* 'Mönch' (0.75).

Late: 'Sternkugel' (0.50).

Dark violet:
Early: 'Breslau' (0.50).
Mid: 'Kobold' (0.40); 'Sonora' (0.40).
Late: 'Veilchenkönigin' ('Violet Queen') (0.50); 'Blütendecke' (0.50).

Pink:
Mid: 'Heinrich Siebert' (0.40); 'Lady Lindlip' (0.60).
Late: 'Rosa Erfüllung' ('Pink Zenith') (0.50).

Scabiosa caucasica

These are somewhat unruly, clump-forming plants with leaves that are elongate and entire basally, but pinnately divided on the stem. Large, predominantly light blue flowers on long, rigid stalks decorate the plants throughout the summer (VI–X), especially if the old stems are regularly removed. The plants are sensitive to damp, especially in winter, and do not tolerate extremes of heat or cold. They transplant badly in autumn and are best divided in spring. Their flowers are invaluable for cutting.

Dark blue:	Pale blue:	White:
'Blauer Atlas' (0.70)	'Clive Greaves' (0.80)	'Ivory Queen' (0.80)
'Moerheim Blue'	'Perfecta' (0.70)	'Miss Willmott' (0.80)
'Nachtfalter' (0.80)		
'Stäfa' (0.70)		

Ornamental elements

Grasses: *Acnatherum calamagrostis, Hystrix patula.*
Annuals: *Dracocephalum moldavica* (to 0.50), violet-blue; together with *Hibiscus trionum* (0.60), pale yellow with a dark basal blotch.

5.3.3.   Lilies for sunny and bright shady sites with moderately dry to moist, well-drained soil

Species

The following lilies have all played a role in the development of the Asiatic hybrids. The different species have different growing requirements which cannot always be adequately dealt with in the text. The safest time to plant them is in early autumn.

Lilium amabile Korea	0.40–1.00	VII, glossy, orange-red Turk's cap flowers with black spots; leafy stems; short-lived but easily raised from seed; prefers a porous, loamy soil.
Lilium bulbiferum ssp. *croceum* (*L. croceum*) S Alps	0.40–1.00 orange	VI–VII, very similar to *L. bulbiferum* (list 2.1.7); upturned, cup-shaped flowers with numerous dark blotches; leaves velvety with a dull glossy upper surface; seldom produces axillary bulbils; undemanding on warm, dry to moist soils.
Lilium cernuum Korea, Manch.	0.30–0.80	VI–VII, drooping, scented, lilac coloured flowers; grassy leaves; short-lived but easily raised from seed; for sandy soils, particularly in sunny woodland edge conditions.

Candlestick lily *Lilium dauricum* (*L. pensylvanicum*) E As.	0.30–0.70	VI–VII, upright, goblet-shaped, orange to scarlet flowers on stiff stems; for moist to damp, loamy, lime-free soils; parent of the popular Maculatum hybrids (see list 5.3.1).
Lilium davidii N China	1.50	VI–VII, orange-red Turk's cap flowers speckled with brown, on long, horizontally held pedicels; leafy stems. *L. d.* var. *willmottiae*, more vigorous and free-flowering. 'Maxwill', striking, many-flowered, pyramidal inflorescences on very sturdy stems. All of the above are easily raised from seed; they thrive on well-drained, loamy soil in light shade, particularly in sunny woodland edge conditions; very persistent.
Caucasian lily *Lilium monadelphum* N Cauc.	0.60–1.20	VI; early; large, open funnel-shaped flowers, pale yellow with dark blotches and a reddish reverse; petals reflexed for half their length; often short-lived; for very well-drained, loamy soils, rich in leaf compost; bright shade; prone to *Botrytis*. *L. szovitsianum* (Cauc.), very similar, but somewhat paler and earlier; for heavy soils; needs a light covering of leaves in winter.
Coral lily *Lilium pumilum* (*L. tenuifolium*) E As.	0.40–0.50	VI–VII, sealing-wax red; small, Turk's cap flowers on delicate, wiry, grassy-leafed stems. 'Golden Gleam', yellow flowers. Both are short-lived but easily raised from seed; for well-drained soils in full sun; particularly suitable for associating with rock garden shrubs.
Tiger lily *Lilium tigrinum* (*L. lancifolium*) Jap., China	1.00–1.50	VIII–IX, nodding flowers with strongly reflexed, orange-red petals, speckled with black; strong stems; propagation from axillary bulbets which break off in autumn; short-lived in continental regions but otherwise very robust, and long-lived; healthy-looking plants may carry virus infections that are spread by insects and may damage more delicate lilies. Widespread, early flowering selections for slightly acid soils: 'Splendens' 'Fortunei', IX, orange-pink; vigorous.

Further species, not involved in the ancestry of the Asiatic hybrids

Lilium pyrenaicum Pyren., SW Fr.	0.30–1.20	V–VI, racemes of small, nodding, yellow, Turk's cap flowers; linear–lanceolate stem-leaves; for well-drained, loamy soils or limestone rubble in full sun; naturalised in many gardens.
Lilium tsingtauense China, Korea	0.40–0.90	VI, upright, sessile, starry, fiery orange-red flowers with reddish speckles; lightly marbled leaves in whorls; for damp sites in light shade.

Asiatic hybrids

Many excellent garden plants have been produced by hybridising the foregoing lilies with other species, including the N American *L. philadelphicum*. The hybrids are grouped according to the posture of their flowers:

(a) Plants with upward-facing flowers.
(b) Plants with outward-facing flowers.
(c) Plants with nodding flowers.

The position of the flowers determines the plants' appearance and thus their mode of use. Lilies with upright and outward-facing flowers are most effective in an open, sunny position, while those with nodding flowers also tolerate the association with woody plants in sun or bright shade.

Bulbs are best planted out in early autumn. The plants have a strong tendency to break dormancy too early in the year, and the success of any spring planting is therefore dependent on cool storage. The lily specialist C. Feldmaier recommends placing a trowel-full of sharp sand below and above the bulbs, which should be taken up and replanted every two or three years.

(a) Proven garden cultivars with upward-facing flowers

'Chinook' (1.20), VII, yellow ochre; flattened, bowl-shaped flowers; all borne at the same height.
'Connecticut King' (0.80), VI–VII, cadmium yellow; large, starry flowers.
'Connecticut Morn' (1.00), VII, orange-red.
'Croesus' (0.80), VI–VII, pale golden yellow.
'Destiny' (0.80), VI–VII, intense lemon yellow.
'Discus' (1.00), VII, orange-red; umbel-like inflorescences.
'Enchantment' (1.00), VI–VII, nasturtium orange; common.
'Firecracker' (0.80), VII, red.
'Harmony' (0.80), VI–VIII, orange-red.
'Joan Evans' (0.60), VI–VII, yellowish orange.
'Obrist' (1.40), VII, red-orange; large, flat, starry flowers.
'Pepper' (0.80), VII, blackish red.
'Pirate' (0.80), VI, glowing orange-red.
'Prince Charming' (0.50), VII, rosy-lilac with an ivory centre.
'Prosperity' (0.60), VI, lemon yellow.
'Ralph' (1.40), VII, currant red.
'Roter Prinz' (1.50), VII, fiery brick red; pyramidal inflorescences.
'Sonnentiger' (1.20), VII–VIII, intense lemon yellow with brown speckles; open flowers with broad, reflexed petals.
'Sunray' (1.00), VII, greenish lemon yellow.
'Treues Herz' (1.00), VII–VIII, reddish orange; flattened, bowl-shaped flowers.

(b) Proven garden cultivars with outward-facing, Turk's cap flowers

'Agnes Bernauer' (1.20), VII–VIII, blood-red with dark speckling; flowers in racemes.
'Brauner Bär' (1.60), VII–VIII, apricot with reddish veins; flowers in racemes.
'Crimsonia' (0.60), VII, antique red.
'Dunkirk' (0.80), VI, glossy mahogany red.
'Feuer und Rauch' (0.80), VII–VIII, dark red with orange-red shading.
'Fireking' (1.50), VI–VII, red.
'Lemon Glow' (1.20), VII, canary yellow.
'Ming Yellow' (0.90), VII, golden yellow.
'Schützenlisl' (1.20), orange.
'Sutter's Gold' (1.20), VII, golden yellow.

(c) Proven garden cultivars with nodding flowers

'Citronella' (strain) (1.00), VII, lemon yellow.
'Edith Cecilia' (0.80), VII, creamy orange and pink.
'Hesperus' (1.20), VII, chrome yellow.
'Nutmegger' (1.20), VII–VIII, canary yellow; starry flowers.
'Panamint' (1.20), VI–VII, lemon yellow.
'Schellenbaum' (2.00), VI, dark cayenne red with an orange centre.
'Troika' (1.00), VII, orangey red-brown.

5.3.4. North American border perennials for sunny sites with moderately moist to moderately damp soil

One might imagine that plants such as goldenrod, coneflowers, perennial sunflowers, Michaelmas daisies and lupins, all of which are so often to be seen naturalised along embankments and on wasteland, would also play a large part in determining the characteristic appearance of our gardens. Their innumerable cultivars dominate the catalogues of several perennial nurseries, but the majority of gardens do not contain enough space for these generously proportioned plants to achieve their full effect. All of them should be given plenty of room to spread. The bare soil around their clumps can be planted up with annual flowers, which turn even the smallest planting into a colourful ornament for many weeks at a time.

The various species have been intensively selected in several European countries, especially Britain, Holland and Germany. The cultivars mentioned here are sturdy, weather-proof and largely resistant to disease, though some of the *Aster novi-belgii* and *Phlox paniculata* selections leave something to be desired in this latter respect, being rather prone to a variety of pests and diseases under certain climatic conditions.

It is sometimes possible to combine cultivars from the lists below with the wild perennials from list 3.4.6.

Dwarf Michaelmas daises, *Aster* Dumosus Hybrids

These are low-growing, free-flowering hybrids between selected forms of *Aster novi-belgii* and *A. dumosus* from meadows and damp hollows (swales) in eastern North America. Their domed cushions normally remain attractive throughout the growing season but older plants are sometimes affected by mildew and other diseases, and should therefore be taken up and replanted before they start to deteriorate. This applies particularly to some of the dwarf selections (under 0.25), which tend to be rather short-lived. Extensive plantings occasionally need thinning out in places but will thrive for many years with an annual application of compost in spring, followed by an all-round fertiliser before the end of June. Such plantings are particularly effective punctuated by isolated specimens of *Panicum virgatum* 'Rehbraun'.

Dwarf asters are easily divided in autumn or spring.

'Audrey' (0.30), light blue.
'Herbstgruss von Bresserhof' (0.40), VIII–X, pink.
'Heinz-Richard' (0.30), VIII–IX, bright pink.
'Jenny' (0.40), VIII, reddish-purple; double.
'Kassel' (0.40), VIII–IX, bright crimson; semi-double.
'Kristina' (0.30), large, white, semi-double flowers.
'Lady in Blue' (0.25), VIII–IX, pure blue; semi-double.
'Little Pink Beauty' (0.40), pink; semi-double.
'Mittelmeer' (0.30), IX, pure blue; semi-double.
'Prof. Anton Kippenberg' (0.40), IX, pure blue.
'Pacific Amaranth' (0.50), VIII–IX, blue-violet; very vigorous.

'Rosemarie Sallmann' (0.30), X, lilac-pink; late flowering.
'Rosenwichtel' (0.15), VIII–IX, dark pink; very persistent.
'Silberblaukissen' (0.25), VIII–IX, pale blue.
'Silberteppich' (0.40), X, pale blue; very vigorous.
'Starlight' (0.40), IX, wine-red.

New England aster, *Aster novae-angliae*

These are tall (up to 1.80), sturdy, very healthy, autumn-flowering perennials, with masses of semi-clasping, softly hairy, lanceolate leaves. Their powerful clumps associate well with vigorous, moisture-loving grasses (especially *Panicum* spp.) and make robust theme perennials for border plantings. Modern selections are mostly shorter than the old cultivars and better suited to the scale of today's gardens. Their colours are strikingly brilliant against the mostly subdued wine-red and blue-violet tones of autumn. With the exception of 'Andenken an Paul Gerber' and 'Herbstschnee', they all close their flowers at night.

The wild species grows in damp hollows (swales) and at the edge of prairie wetlands in the eastern, central and southwestern USA. The garden cultivars need a well-drained but continually moist and fertile soil in full sun. They may prove unreliable in areas of summer drought with light, sandy soils.

Proven selections:
'Alma Pötschke' (0.80), IX–X, salmony red; low-growing.
'Andenken an Paul Gerber' (1.50), IX–X, wine-red; good for cutting.
'Barr's Blue (1.60), IX, deep blue; early.
'Harrington's Pink' (1.20), IX–X, pink.
'Herbstschnee' ('Autumn Snow') (1.40), IX–X, white; large flowers.
'Rubinschatz' ('September Ruby') (1.20), IX–X, ruby-red; early.
'Rosa Sieger' (1.30), IX–X, salmon-pink; Karl Foerster's selection from 'Harrington's Pink'.
'Rudelsburg' (1.20), IX–X, brilliant salmon-pink; early.

New York aster, *Aster novi-belgii*

The descendants of this smooth-leaved aster from damp meadows on the east coast of North America are generally not so robust and disease resistant as those of *Aster novæ-angliae* from the prairies. Even some of the more recent cultivars tend to suffer from mildew and other diseases in a bad year. In spite of this, their colourful flowers are an indispensable part of the autumn scene, decorating the garden from September till November. The plants thrive in a sunny position on moist to damp, limy, nutrient-rich soil. It is advisable to keep them well fed and watered, and to divide the clumps regularly. The less sturdy cultivars of both *A. novi-belgii* and *A. novæ-angliae* may be prevented from falling apart by cutting back the stems to half their length at the beginning of July. Alternatively, remove half the shoots in spring when they are 25 cm high and pinch out the tips of those remaining at about 40 cm.

Proven selections:
'Blaue Nachhut' (1.20), X–XI, light blue; healthy; very late.
'Bonningdale White' (1.00), IX–X, white.
'Brigitte' (1.00), IX–X, lavender-blue.
'Climax' (1.50), IX–X, light blue.
'Crimson Brocade' (1.00), IX–X, red; semi-double.
'Dauerblau' (1.50), IX–X, dark blue; healthy.
'Erica' (1.00), IX, red–violet; early.
'Fellowship' (1.00), IX–X, pale pink; double.
'Harrison's Blue' (1.00), IX–X, deep blue; double.

'Lady Frances' (0.90), IX, deep pink; good for cutting.
'Maria Ballard' (0.90), IX, light blue; double.
'Patricia Ballard' (1.20), IX–X, magenta; double.
'Royal Ruby' (0.50), IX–X, dark purple.
'Royal Blue' (1.00), IX–X, deep blue.
'Royal Velvet' (1.20), IX–X, deep violet.
'Sailor Boy' (0.90), VIII–IX, deep blue; semi-double.
'Schöne von Dietlikon' (0.80), IX–X, dark blue with a yellow centre.
'Weisses Wunder' ('White Miracle') (1.20), IX–X, white.
'Winston S. Churchill' (0.80), IX–X, ruby-red.

Ornamental elements

Rhynchelytrum repens (Natal grass); *Penstemon* hybrids (0.60–0.80).

Dainty, small-flowered asters

The following, elegant, fine-leaved asters have retained much of the wild character of their parent species from the prairies and woodlands of North America, but are nevertheless best grown on a perennial border in evenly moist and fertile soil. In the wild, *Aster ericoides* is an invasive weed, quickly colonising disturbed soil by windblown seed. *A. laevis* is a prairie and open woodland species, growing best on open woodland slopes. *A. lateriflorus* and *A. vimineus* both grow on wet ground, subject to seasonal inundation. Several of these asters are susceptible to various wilts and mildews in a bad season. They associate well with species from list 3.4.6.

White:
Aster ericoides 'Schneetanne' (1.00), IX–X.
A. e. 'Herbstmyrthe (0.90), IX.
A. e. 'Novembermyrthe' (1.10), X.
A. pringlei 'Monte Cassino' (1.20), X–XI.

Light blue:
Aster cordifolius 'Ideal' (1.00), VIII–IX.
Aster ericoides 'Erlkönig' (1.20), IX–X.
Aster laevis (1.50), IX; see list 3.4.6.

Pink:
Aster cordifolius 'Silver Spray' (1.20), VIII–IX.
Aster ericoides 'Ringdove' (0.90), IX–X.
Aster vimineus 'Lovely' (0.50), IX.
Aster lateriflorus 'Finale' (1.20), X–XI.

Fleabane, *Erigeron* hybrids

These low-growing (under 0.60), aster-like perennials will flower a second time in September if they are cut down to the ground immediately after their first flowering in June and July. Their wild parents (*E. speciosus* and *E. s.* var. *macranthus*) are wasteland plants from the mountains and prairies of western North America. Hybrids with *E. aurantiacus* from the mountains of Turkestan have proved too short-lived to be worthwhile in cultivation.

Erigerons thrive on an annual application of fertiliser; their clumps need rejuvenation by division every 5–7 years.

'Adria' (0.70), bright violet.
'Charity' (0.60), light pink.

'Dignity' (0.45), violet-blue.
'Dimity' (0.35), mauve-pink.
'Dunkelste Aller' ('Darkest of All') (0.60), dark violet.
'Foerster's Liebling' (0.60), carmine pink; semi-double.
'Lilofee' (0.60), dark violet; semi-double.
'Märchenland' (0.60), delicate pink; semi-double.
'Rosa Triumph' ('Pink Triumph') (0.60), bright pink; semi-double.
'Rotes Meer' (0.60), intense dark red; double.
'Schwarzes Meer' ('Black Sea') (0.60), intense dark violet.
'Strahlenmeer' (0.70), pale violet.
'Sommerneuschnee' (0.60), white.
'Violetta' (0.70), dark violet; double.
'Wuppertal' (0.60), dark lilac.

Ornamental elements

Pennisetum setaceum (0.70).
Penstemon spp. and hybrids (0.60–0.80), in various colours.

Sneezeweed, *Helenium* hybrids

These plants, with their immense domes of flowers in warm shades of red, brown, orange and yellow, are the supreme embodiment of summer opulence and colour in the herbaceous border. Modern cultivars are derived from a number of different wild species, particularly *Helenium autumnale* and *H. bigelovii* from damp meadows in North America. Karl Foerster was one of the foremost breeders, aiming to produce sturdy, large flowered, drought-resistant plants, blooming in succession from July until September.

Heleniums should not be planted in masses but given plenty of space for their development. Properly fed and looked after (and watered in dry weather) the plants can reach a great age. Should they start to deteriorate they must be taken up and divided before replanting.

Early (low-growing):
H. bigelovii 'Superbum' ('The Bishop') (0.70), VI–VII, large yellow flower heads with a black disc.
H. × hybridum:
'Goldene Jugend' ('Golden Youth') (0.80), VI, golden-yellow.
'Moerheim Beauty' (0.80), VI–VII, velvety copper-red.
'Waltraut' (0.90), VI–VII, golden-brown; particularly large flower heads.

Mid:
'Blütentisch' (0.90), VII–VIII, golden-yellow with a brown disc.
'Coppelia' (1.00), VII–VIII, coppery-orange.
'Flammendrad' (1.50), VII–VIII, brownish yellow.
'Kanaria' (1.10), VII–VIII, yellow.
'Kupfersprudel' ('Copper Spray') (1.10), VII–VIII, coppery-brown.
'Pumilum Magnificum' (0.70), VII–VIII, deep yellow.
'Wyndley' (0.60), VII–IX, orange-yellow.
'Zimbelstern' (1.30), VII–VIII, old gold flamed with brown.

Late:
'Baudirektor Linné' (1.00), VIII–IX, red-brown.
'Bruno' (1.20), VIII–X, crimson-mahogany.
'Butterpat' (1.00), VIII–X, deep yellow.
'Goldrausch' (1.50), VIII–IX, yellow flamed with red-brown.

'Margot' (1.20), VIII–IX, red-brown with yellow margins.
'Riverton Gem' (1.40), VIII–IX, crimson streaked with yellow.
'Septembergold' (1.10), VIII–IX, bright yellow.

Ornamental elements

A combination of:

Cosmos sulphureus 'Sunset' (to 1.00), coppery.
Lonas inodora (0.30), yellow.
Tagetes patula 'Rusty Red' (0.30), reddish-brown.
Tithonia rotundifolia (1.50), yellowish-orange.
Verbena bonariensis (up to 1.00), lilac-blue.
Verbena rigida (to 0.30), violet.

Perennial sunflowers, *Helianthus*

Among the various perennial sunflowers available in the trade, only *Helianthus decapetalus* from prairies and open woodlands in the USA, and its (probably hybrid) cultivars, are really suitable for growing on a herbaceous border. The natural varieties of *H. rigidus* (*H. × laetiflorus* var. *rigidus*), a rough-leaved prairie species, have invasive, creeping rhizomes that crowd out neighbouring plants, and are seldom of use in a border planting.

Perennial sunflowers need rich, well-fertilised soil. Their clumps are long-lived but grateful for occasional division and transplanting.

Non-invasive sunflowers (moisture-loving)
Helianthus decapetalus:

'Capenoch Star' (1.20), VII–IX, large, refined, lemon-yellow flowers; invaluable.
'Grandiplenus' (probably *H. decapetalus × H. annuus*) (1.50), VIII–IX, very double, golden-yellow flowers.
'Lodden Gold' (1.50), VII–IX, yellow; double.
'Meteor' (1.50), VIII–IX, golden-yellow; semi-double.
'Soleil d'Or' (1.50), VIII–IX, pure yellow; double.
'Triumph von Gent' (1.50), VIII–IX, golden-yellow; double.
'Multiflorus Maximum' (1.70), VIII–IX, large, single, golden-yellow flowers.

H. microcephalus (1.60), VII–IX, open habit and dainty flower heads; thin, green, ovate–lanceolate leaves; grows wild on woodland streambanks; not quite so hardy as *H. decapetalus*.

Invasive sunflowers (tolerate dry soil)

Helianthus rigidus:

'Miss Mellish' (1.40), VIII–IX, single, yellow flowers with a black disc.
'Oktoberstern' (1.50), IX–X, single, golden-yellow flowers with a black disc.
'Latest of All' (1.50), X–XI, similar to the foregoing.

Helianthus salicifolius: see list 3.6.1.
H. atrorubens: see list 5.5.

Ornamental elements

See under *Heliopsis*.

Oxeye, *Heliopsis helianthoides* ssp. *scabra*

This leafy, sturdy, clump-forming perennial comes from the central prairies of North America. Its cultivars are free-flowering and have a longer season (VI–IX) than any other tall, yellow herbaceous plant in summer. Heliopsis are long-lived, especially on adequately moist and fertile soil. Their spent flowerheads must regularly be removed and it is therefore advisable to set them in an accessible position towards the edge of the border. If blooms are required for cutting, the clumps must be taken up and divided every five years in spring or autumn.

Single-flowered cultivars:

'Jupiter' (1.70), orange-yellow; enormous flower heads.
'Karat' (1.30), golden-yellow; large flower heads.
'Mars' (1.50), yellow-orange.
'Orion' (1.30), golden-orange.
'Sonnenglut' (0.80), golden-orange.

Semi-double-flowered cultivars

'Hohlspiegel' (1.20), golden yellow.
'Lohfelden' (1.30), golden orange.
'Spitzentänzerin' (1.20), orange yellow.

Double-flowered cultivars:

'Goldgefieder' (1.20), deep golden-yellow.
'Goldgrünherz' ('Golden Greenheart') (0.90), yellow with a greenish centre.
'Sonnenschild' (1.40), golden-yellow; large flower heads.
'Summer Sun' (1.10), golden-yellow; double and semi-double flower heads.

Ornamental elements

Ageratum houstonianum 'Schnittwunder' (0.50), blue.
Verbena rigida (0.30), blue-violet.
Verbena 'Mammut Caerulea' ('Mammoth Blue') (1.20), blue.

Garden lupins, *Lupinus* Polyphyllus hybrids

The tall, stately, often bicoloured racemes of garden lupins are available in nearly every colour of the rainbow, making a gorgeous display when the plants start to flower at the end of May. Of the original species, the mostly blue-flowered *Lupinus polyphyllus* (with varieties in shades of blue, indigo, rose, pink and white) grows wild in western North America, on open mountain meadows from British Columbia to California. Another parent is the slightly tender, yellow- or occasionally white-flowered *L. arboreus* from California. George Russell produced the celebrated Russell hybrids by crossing both of these with *L. perennis*, a hardy blue-, or sometimes white- or pink-flowered species from the eastern USA.

It is a temptation to grow lupins in masses, in the same way that *L. polyphyllus* can sometimes be seen naturalised on embankments. However, the plants tend to be unsightly after flowering and they are therefore best planted in small groups behind other perennials that will grow up and hide them in summer and autumn.

Lupins thrive on well-drained, slightly acid soil with plenty of moisture in spring. Too much humus and fertiliser only shorten their already limited lifespan. Yellow-flowered cultivars are particularly short-lived.

Stems should be cut back after flowering to just above the young side-shoots, thus ensuring a good repeat flowering later in the year. Plants are propagated commercially from seed or cuttings. The sturdy, nitrogen-fixing rootstock can seldom be divided successfully.

Selected seed strains, whose colours fall true but not always uniform (0.80–1.00, VI–VII)

'Edelknabe', shades of crimson.
'Fräulein', white or creamy.
'Kastellan', shades of blue, with white standards.
'Kronleuchter', shades of yellow.
'Minarette' (0.60), various colours.
'Mein Schloss', red and brick-red.
'Roggli Rot', wine-red.
'Schlossfrau', pink with white standards.

Vegetatively propagated cultivars (0.80–1.00, VI–VII)

'Blue Crest', dark blue with white standards.
'Blushing Bride', white, flushed pink.
'Heather Glow', reddish purple.
'Lady Fayre', antique pink with paler standards.
'Lady Gay', pale yellow.
'President Landold', salmon.
'Rhapsody', deep pink.
'Rita', wine-red with matt red standards.
'Rosenquarz', pink.
'Thundercloud', violet with purple standards.

Ornamental elements

Polygonum orientale (1.50), magenta-pink.

Border phlox, *Phlox* Paniculata hybrids

Border phlox are characterised by the colourful opulence of their fragrant panicles, whose magic transforms the garden at flowering time. Their leafy green columns create an orderly effect even when the plants are not in bloom.

The wild species is a modest plant, growing in eastern, wooded regions of North America with an average yearly precipitation of 800–1500 mm. Although the summers are hot and dry, the plants are often found growing along rivers and small streams. It is therefore no surprise that garden cultivars tend to languish in dry conditions but will sometimes grow quite satisfactorily in a well-tended border in semi-shade. The plants grow best of all in areas that have an abundance of both sun and rain. In wet mountain regions they are so strong and healthy that they can often be seen growing semi-naturalised outside a garden fence. Poorly maintained and weak-growing specimens easily fall victim to eelworms, producing a stunted growth with narrow, twisted leaves and brittle stems. Adequate feeding and watering, together with the timely removal of any infected shoots as far down on the rootstock as possible and, where necessary, the use of pesticides such as Temik, can all help to alleviate the problem.

Small groups of phlox can grow very old if they are kept free of competition in a thoroughly moist and nutrient-rich soil. Old plants tend to grow up out of the ground and therefore need a regular mulch of compost. Alternatively, the crowns may be carefully pared away with a sharp knife in winter to encourage the production of healthy new shoots from the surrounding roots.

Phlox are easily propagated from root cuttings. If the clumps start to deteriorate they should be divided into pieces with 3–4 shoots for replanting.

   Todays cultivars are largely the work of breeders such as G. Arends, P. Pfitzer, B. Ruys, A. Schöllhammer and B. Symons-Jeune. Karl Foerster deserves special mention for the strong, healthy plants he raised on the sandy soil of his nursery in Bornim/Potsdam. The following selections are not all equally robust. Those that have proved particularly healthy and vigorous in the course of trials in Weihenstephan have been marked with an asterisk. Early varieties flower from the end of June; late ones from the middle of August to the end of September. The early-flowering Arendsii and Maculata hybrids have been assigned to list 3.4.6 on account of their strong wild character.

White, or red and white

'Fujiyama' (1.20), white; late.
'Kirmesländler (1.20), white with a red eye; late.
'Mia Ruys' (0.40), white; early.
*'Nymphenburg' (1.40), white; late.
*'Pax' (1.00), white; late.
*'Schneeferner' (1.00), white; mid.
'White Admiral' (0.80), white.

Pink to red

'Balmoral' (1.00), light, clear pink; mid.
'Bornimer Nachsommer' (1.00), salmon pink; late.
*'Dorffreude' (1.20), pink with a dark red eye; mid.
*'Frauenlob' (1.20), pale pink with a red eye; early.
*'Landhochzeit' (1.40), pale pink with a red eye; mid.
'Mother of Pearl' (0.80), very pale rose pink.
*'Sommerfreude' (0.90), pink with a red eye; mid.
*'Württembergia' (0.80), bright pink with a pale eye; early; for loamy soils.
'Pastorale' (1.00), salmon pink; mid; robust.
'Sandringham' (0.75), cyclamen-pink with a darker centre; mid.

Brilliant red to salmony orange

'Brigadier' (1.10), orange-red.
'Frau A. von Mauthner' ('Spitfire') (0.90), salmony orange-red with a crimson eye; mid.
*'Kirchenfürst' (1.00), dark crimson; mid.
'Prince of Orange' (0.90), orange-red.
'Starfire' (0.90), brilliant red; dark foliage; mid.
*'Spätrot' (1.00), orange-scarlet; late.

Bluish to violet

'Border Gem' (0.90), violet-blue.
'Norah Leigh' (0.80), pale purple; white-variegated leaves.
*'Violetta Gloriosa' (0.90), red-violet; mid.
'Sternhimmel' (0.90), pale violet with a white eye; mid.

Red-violet to lilac

'Aida' (0.90), red-violet; mid.
*'Düsterlöhe' (1.20), dark red-violet; early.
'Furioso' (1.00), dark lilac-red; mid.
'Prospero' (0.90), pale lilac and white.
*'Wilhelm Kesselring' (0.80), red-violet with a white eye; early.
'Windsor' (0.80), carmine-pink with a darker eye.

Ornamental elements

Grasses: *Panicum virgatum* 'Strictum', *Pennisetum compressum, P. japonicum.*
Annuals: *Penstemon hartwegii* and its hybrids, *Godetia grandiflora* (see also pp. 392 ff.)

Coneflower, *Rudbeckia*

Rudbeckias are well-proportioned, undemanding and generally healthy garden plants with showy, brilliant yellow daisy-like flowers. Selection has partly altered their original wild character: the double-flowered *R. laciniata* 'Golden Glow' is less sturdy than its parent species, which can sometimes be seen naturalised in masses along rivers. The lower-growing 'Goldquelle', on the other hand, has lost none of its sturdiness but is more demanding and somewhat shorter-lived.

The majority of cultivated species grow wild in wetland areas and along rivers in the USA. They all tolerate a wide range of conditions but prefer an adequately moist and nutrient-rich soil. Thus, although they associate well with the open ground perennials from list 3.4.6, they are better suited to cultivation in a herbaceous border, where they benefit from an occasional application of fertiliser, and irrigation during dry weather. Rudbeckias are easily propagated by division with a spade or knife. The purple-flowered *Echinacea purpurea* (*Rudbeckia purpurea*) and its cultivars are more difficult in this respect and may be short-lived. They have therefore been assigned to list 5.5.

Tall species and cultivars

Rudbeckia nitida 'Herbstsonne' ('Autumn Sun')	2.00 primrose-yellow, greenish cone	VIII–IX, sturdy, rigid stems with numerous large flowers; glossy, light green foliage; hardier than the wild species, but not for harsh climates; possibly a hybrid with *R. laciniata*.
Rudbeckia nitida 'Juligold'	1.80 golden-yellow	VII–VIII, earlier than the previous cultivar; important for areas with a cold autumn and early frosts.
Rudbeckia laciniata 'Golden Glow' ('Hortensis')	2.00 golden-yellow	VII–IX, widespread and popular cultivar; double flowers; deeply incised basal leaves; robust, but sadly prone to flop; spreads strongly. *R. laciniata*: see list 3.5.4.
Rudbeckia maxima		List 3.5.2

Middle-sized species and cultivars

Rudbeckia fulgida var. *deamii* (*R. deamii*)	0.80 golden-yellow, black disc	VIII–X, graceful habit; finely hairy, coarsely crenate, ovate leaves; roughly hairy stems; very free-flowering; valuable for cutting.
Rudbeckia laciniata 'Goldkugel'	1.30 golden yellow	VIII–IX, double flowers; similar to 'Golden Glow' but sturdier and not so tall; does not spread strongly.

Rudbeckia laciniata 'Goldquelle'	0.70 lemon yellow	VIII–IX, double flowers; shorter than the previous cultivar; sturdy and non-invasive; important as a cut flower.
Rudbeckia sub-tomentosa	1.50 pale yellow, dark disc	VII–IX, grey-hairy, deeply three-lobed or tripartite leaves; abundant flowers; very hardy prairie perennial.

Low-growing species and cultivars

Rudbeckia sullivantii (*R. fulgide* var. *sullivantii* 'Goldsturm'	0.70 golden-yellow, dark brown disc	VII–IX, very abundant large flowers; broadly spathulate to lanceolate basal leaves. *R. fulgida* var. *deamii*, similar but taller; see above. *R. fulgida* var. *speciosa*, shorter and with smaller flowers; see list 3.4.6.

Ornamental elements

Grasses: *Panicum virgatum* 'Strictum'
Annuals: *Ageratum houstonianum* 'Schnittwunder' (0.50), blue.
Verbena rigida (0.30), blue-violet.

Goldenrod, *Solidago* hybrids

North American species of goldenrod (particularly the descendants of *Solidago canadensis* with hairy stalks and *S. gigantea* with glabrous stalks), with their narrow, willow-like leaves and small yellow flowers on tall stems, are an all too familiar weed of riversides, wasteland and railway embankments in Europe. Perhaps for this reason, the many attractive, non-invasive cultivars that are now available from nurseries receive less attention than they really deserve. The wild parents of these garden hybrids mostly come from scrubby grassland areas on moist or dry soils in the USA. Older, taller-growing selections spread rapidly at the roots and seed themselves dangerously about. However, there are now a number of vigorous, sturdy and comparatively low-growing cultivars that only gradually develop into large clumps. All are easily propagated by division. Some may be slightly affected by mildew in a bad year.

Cultivars with a stiff, columnar habit

The following selections are given a columnar appearance by the mantle of leaves hanging down on their stiffly upright stems.

Solidago × *hybrida* 'Strahlenkrone' ('Crown of Rays')	0.70 golden-yellow	VIII–IX, healthy, dark green foliage; horizontally held inflorescences. 'Goldstrahl' ('Peter Pan') (0.80), flowers later, till the middle of September. 'Spätgold' (0.70), similar to the foregoing; stiff, columnar habit.

Cultivars with an open habit and loose inflorescences

Solidago × *hybrida* 'Goldwedel'	0.90 golden yellow	VI–VIII, bushy habit; free-flowering; blooms again in August if cut back at the end of July. 'Federbusch' (0.80), dense, feathery inflorescences.

'Ledsham' (0.80), VIII–IX, pale yellow flower heads in loose panicles.
'Lemore' (0.60), IX, large, intensely yellow flower heads.
'Cloth of Gold' (0.50), VII–IX, golden yellow flower heads in dense panicles.

Mimosa-like cultivars

These are characterised by their rounded, mimosa-like clusters of flower heads and very pale green foliage, which becomes almost yellow at the top of the stem. Exceptionally good for cutting.

Solidago × *hybridus* 'Golden Shower'	0.80 golden-yellow	VIII–IX, broad, branching, loosely overarching inflorescences. 'Goldenmosa' (0.80), pale yellow; small flower heads. 'Golden Gates' (0.90), lemon yellow. None of these is invasive.

Dwarf cultivars

Solidago cutleri 'Robusta' (*S. brachystachys* hort.)	0.30 pale yellow	IX, short, branching inflorescences; compact habit; undemanding.
Solidago canadensis 'Nana'	0.50 yellow	VIII, dense, low habit; rare in the trade.
Solidago hybrid 'Golden Thumb' ('Queenie')	0.30 golden yellow	VIII–IX, forms dense, rounded clumps.

Ornamental elements

Salvia farinacea (0.60), violet-blue.

5.3.5. Sunny (or bright shady) sites with moist to moderately damp, nutrient-rich soil

Most of the following perennials come from wetland areas and are therefore most effective planted near to water (though not in wet soil). Many of them have retained their wild character to a far greater extent than other border perennials, associating very well with *Filipendula* cultivars and the other wild perennials with border character from lists 3.5.1–3.5.4, and occasionally with those from list 2.2.4.

In view of their natural habitat, it is astonishing how well these plants will flourish in gardens on soil that is merely moist and somewhat loamy.

Double-flowered sneezewort, *Achillea ptarmica* 'The Pearl'

The double-flowered sneezewort forms characteristic mounds of narrow, deep green, serrate leaves, covered in masses of tiny, spherical, snow-white flower heads in July and August. It is a well loved garden plant, especially in areas of high humidity and rainfall, and its flowers are also widely grown for cutting. Although the wild species mostly occurs naturally on poor, damp, lime-free meadows, double-flowered forms will thrive on any ordinary, moist to damp garden soil. On dry soils plants are rather prone to mildew. In a herbaceous border, the plants must be taken up and divided every few years because their invasive rhizomes soon begin to threaten neighbouring plants. Specimens grown for cutting achieve about 1 m, but ordinary garden plants are a little shorter.

Double-flowered forms of *Achillea ptarmica* have been recorded since the sixteenth century. In catalogues they often appear simply as 'Plena' hort. 'The Pearl' is a sturdy, large-flowered cultivar raised by Lemoine in France and originally called 'Boule de Neige'. The English selection 'Perry's White' is similar but less sturdy and with a more open habit. A low-growing (0.30) form called 'Nana Compacta' is also sometimes available.

Eupatorium purpureum Atropurpureum

Few autumn perennials can compete with the colour and opulence of these reliable and sturdy plants, whose flowers are borne in enormous umbel-like inflorescences on stems set with bold, regular whorls of leaves. 'Atropurpureum' is a broad but compact (1.80) form of the tall, vigorous, rosy-purple flowered *Eupatorium purpureum* (list 3.6.1), characterised by its larger and more intensely coloured inflorescences and striking dark stems. Similar cultivars have appeared more recently under names such as 'Glutball'.

The plants are easily divided and very long-lived, thriving on moist to damp, loamy soils in full sun or bright shade, though not directly under trees. Other *Eupatorium* spp. can be found in list 3.5.4.

Iris sibirica and its relatives

These pretty, slender, mostly blue-flowered irises have long been cultivated in gardens. The original species, with dark-veined, blue or whitish petals, grows naturally in reedswamps and water meadows, but thrives just as well in garden on drier soil, making an ideal partner for *Hemerocallis flava*. In recent years, this undemanding wild plant has been crossed with other species, especially *I. sanguinea* (*I. sibirica* var. *orientalis*) from Siberia, to produce a race of large-flowered hybrids for the herbaceous border. The older, taller selections have retained much of their wild character and may be used in ecological plantings along with the species from lists 3.5.2. or 6.1.

Tall cultivars in particular are very long-lived, but their flowers soon start to diminish in size if they are not divided and transplanted. Older specimens of the low-growing, large-flowered hybrids tend to bloom reluctantly if they are not grown in damp soil.

The following cultivars associated very well with all forms of *Molinia caerulea* and *M. arundinacea*. Their flowering stems are generally taller than usual in the year following division.

Tall cultivars (I. sibirica)

'Caesar's Brother'	1.00 deep blue-violet	VI, beautiful, well proportioned plants; large, clear coloured flowers with rounded, drooping petals; vigorous and free-flowering.
'Elmeney' ('Uso') (*I. setosa × I. sibirica*)	1.20 blue-violet	VI, incomparable appearance; uniformly pale-veined flowers with horizontally held petals; attractive clumps of foliage; extremely drought-tolerant.
'Perry's Blue'	1.00 light blue	VI, well-proven, free-flowering selection; similar in habit to the older cultivars 'Strandperle' (pale blue), 'Phosphorflamme' (dark blue with light blue standards) and 'Superba' (dark blue).
'Blue Celeste'	1.00 light blue	VI, dark-veined flowers; very vigorous.

'Elfe'	1.00 violet-blue	VI, very vigorous.
'Dragonfly'	1.20 pale blue	VI, graceful habit; small flowers with elegantly droop-ing falls. 'Perry's Pygmy', shorter.
'Mrs Rowe'	0.90 silvery-pink	VI, old plants have exceptionally small, pale flowers.
'Schwan'	1.00 white	VI, powerful clumps; larger flowers than the otherwise similar 'Möwe'.

Middle-sized cultivars (hybrids)

Flowers in June with 'floating', horizontal falls; bluish leaves.

'Blue Brilliant' (0.60), mid-blue; abundant large flowers.
'Blue Mere' (0.60), light blue.
'Blue Moon' (0.80), dark blue with paler standards; green leaves.
'Cambridge' (0.70), turquoise with a green throat; exceptionally beautiful and free-flowering.
'Dreaming Spires' (0.80), violet-blue with a darker throat.
'Emperor' (0.90), dark blue.
'Helen Astor' (0.60), reddish lilac-pink.
'Mountain Lake' (0.50), mid-blue with paler standards.
'My Love' (0.70), light blue with fine markings; occasionally flowers a second time.
'Ottawa' (0.50), deep blue, flecked white; early.
'Sea Shadows' (0.70), light, luminous, inky blue; abundant large flowers.
'Snow Crest' (0.60), white.
'Tropic Night' (0.80), blue-violet.
'White Swirl' (0.80), white; leaves with ruffled margins.

Iris sanguinea (*I. sibirica* var. *orientalis, I. orientalis*)

Iris sanguinea grows wild on mountain meadows in Siberia, Manchuria, Korea and Japan. It has rather shorter flowering stems and narrower, more linear leaves than *I. sibirica*. Its large, noble, deep blue flowers with yellowish- or white-veined centres are enclosed by reddish spathes in bud. The species has been much used for hybridising with *I. sibirica* (see above). The following selections are sometimes available from nurseries:

'Snowqueen' (0.60), VI–VII, white; very persistent.
'Weißer Orient' (0.80), white; very abundant large flowers.

Iris spuria and its relatives

The following hardy irises flower a little later than *Iris sibirica* and most other ornamental irises, producing large, decorative blooms reminiscent of the florist's *I. × hollandica*. Their tall, stiff, grey-green clumps of foliage can dominate a planting until late in the autumn, though some forms of *I. spuria* die down somewhat earlier.

Iris spuria itself is a very variable species from periodically damp meadows in Europe and Western Asia. The plants thrive in full sun on loamy, well-drained soils that are thoroughly moist in spring but drier in summer. Their clumps are best divided in early autumn.

Iris spuria C Eurasia, Iran, Alger.	0.70 pale to mid-blue	VI–VII, rare in the trade, as are the following selec-tions: 'Archie Owen' (1.00), golden yellow. 'Cherokee Chief' (0.80), bronze and yellow.

'Dorothy Foster' (1.00), mid-blue.
'Dutch Defiance' (1.10), light blue and yellow.
'Premier' (1.00), violet and light blue.
'Shelford Giant' (1.50), white with golden yellow.
'Thrush Song' (1.00), dark violet-purple with yellow.

Iris crocea (*I. aurea*)		List 3.3.3
Iris monnieri Crete	1.00 yellow	VI–VII, robust and very persistent on loamy soils that dry out in summer; many flowers on each stem.
Iris × *monspur*	1.20 light blue with a yellow blotch	VI–VII, powerful, upright clumps of bluish foliage; vigorous and very persistent.
Iris orientalis 'Gigantea' (*I. ochroleuca,* *I. gigantea*) Asia Minor, Syria	1.20 ivory white, yellow blotch	VI–VII, strong, grey-green clumps of foliage; very robust and vigorous. *I. orientalis* (1.00), white and yellow.
Iris orientalis 'Gigantea Alba'	1.50 very pale yellow	VI–VII, reed-like leaves; very vigorous.

Bergamot, *Monarda* hybrids

These densely leafy, aromatic and very long-flowering (VI–IX) perennials are hybrids between the moisture-loving *Monarda didyma* from woodland and meadows in North America, and the more drought-loving *M. fistulosa*. Not all cultivars are equally vigorous. Some spread rapidly by means of powerful rhizomes to form impenetrable clumps, while others, such as 'Cambridge Scarlet', prefer a moist and humid climate, achieving only modest proportions in drier, continental regions.

The following hybrids all thrive on moist, nutrient-rich soils in full sun. Some of them will carry on flowering beautifully for many years without moving; others must be taken up and replanted every now and then. All are easily propagated by division.

'Adam' (1.00), VII–IX, crimson.
'Beauty of Cobham' (0.90), VII–IX, pale pink.
'Blaustrumpf' ('Blue Stocking') (1.40), VIII–IX, dark lilac; massy and vigorous.
'Cambridge Scarlet' (1.00), VI–VIII, brilliant red.
'Croftway Pink' (1.20), VII–IX, salmon-pink.
'Donnerwolke' (1.00), VII–IX, deep wine-red.
'Morgenröte' (1.00), VI–VIII, salmony-red.
'Präriebrand' (1.20), VII–IX, deep, salmony-red.
'Prärienacht' ('Prairie Night') (1.30), VIII–IX, dark lilac.
'Schneewittchen' ('Snow Maiden') (1.20), VII–IX, white; smaller flower heads.
'Sunset' (1.00), VI–IX, purple-red; reddish foliage.

Ornamental elements

Verbena bonariensis (up to 1.00), lilac-violet.
Verbena rigida (0.30), violet.

Obedient plant, *Physostegia virginiana*

This is an effective plant for late summer and autumn, with whorls of narrow leaves, and crowded flowers usually arranged in four rows. The individual flowers have hinged stalks and can be set in almost any position, so giving rise to the common name. The plants have long, vigorous rhizomes but cannot tolerate competition, making them rather difficult as garden subjects. They thrive in sun on nutrient-rich, moist to damp (not too cold or wet) soils, but need a lot of space, disappearing rapidly if they are not regularly divided.

The pink-flowered wild form comes from the USA and grows to 1 m, flowering in August and September. The following are well proven selections:

'Bouquet Rose'	0.70 lilac-pink	VIII–IX, strongly branching inflorescences; large, coarsely toothed leaves.
'Summer Snow'	0.90 white	VII–IX, big, long inflorescences; early; good for cutting. Recent selection: 'Schneekrone'.
'Summer Spire'	1.10 violet-rose	VII–IX, vigorous; well branched inflorescences; good for cutting.
'Variegata'	0.50 lilac-pink	VII–IX, leaves boldly edged with white.
'Vivid'	0.60 wine-red	IX–X, low, compact habit; more sociable than other cultivars. 'Frühe Vivid', VI–VIII, early form; rare in the trade.

A white-flowered cultivar with white-variegated foliage is marketed under various different names in America.

Several other *Physostegia* species are sometimes grown in the USA.

Jacob's ladder, *Polemonium caeruleum* **and its relatives**

The special attraction of these undemanding and orderly perennials is their exceptional compatibility with plants such as *Trollius*, early *Hemerocallis*, *Aquilegia*, *Geum* and other spring and early summer-flowering species. *Polemonium caeruleum* is a woodland edge and meadow plant from north and central Eurasia, while *P. reptans* and *P. foliosissimum* both come from the USA. All thrive best on a border with moist to damp soil in sun or semi-shade (see also lists 2.2.1 and 2.2.2).

The various species and hybrids are all relatively short-lived but seed themselves prolifically. Named cultivars are propagated by division. Plants that are cut back immediately after flowering often bloom again in July and August.

Polemonium caeruleum	1.00 blue	VI–VIII. see list 3.5.1
Polemonium × richard-sonii hort. (*P. × jacobaea*)	0.40 blue	V–VI and VIII, dainty, fresh green foliage; erect habit; sturdy inflorescences of nodding, bell-shaped flowers; more compact than *P. caeruleum*. 'Album' (0.40), white. 'Pallidum' (0.40), pale blue. 'Superbum' (0.50), dark blue. *P. carneum* (0.40), pale pink flowers; dense habit; tender.
Polemonium reptans USA	0.30 blue or white	V–VI and VIII, coarsely pinnate leaves; spreading habit; loose inflorescences on wiry stems; flowers early and blooms again if cut back.

'Album' (0.30), white.
'Blue Pearl' (0.30), blue.
'Firmament' (0.40), light blue.
'Pink Dawn' (0.30), pink.
'Sapphire' (0.35), light blue.

Polemonium folios-issimum USA	0.70 lavender blue or white	VI–VIII, upright stems; leaves with winged petioles; long-flowering; rare in the trade.

Spiderwort, *Tradescantia × andersoniana*

These stocky, lush green, 40–50 cm hybrids are robust and persistent perennials. They have an exceptionally long flowering season (VI–IX), but their modest, three-petalled flowers are partly hidden among grassy foliage and tend to close up at midday in sunny weather. The parent species come from water meadows and other wetland areas in the USA, and the hybrids rapidly turn yellow and die back when exposed to drought. Spent flowering stems should continually be removed to avoid the otherwise abundant, predominantly lilac-blue-flowered seedlings which grow up and frequently suppress the parent plant. The following is a selection from many available cultivars. All are easily propagated by division.

Violet: 'Purple Dome', 'Leonora', 'Marianne' (very intense colour).
Dark blue: 'Zwanenburg Blue', 'Blue Stone', 'Isis'.
Light Blue: 'I. C. Weguelin'.
White: 'Gisela', 'Eva', 'Osprey' (blue stamens), 'Innocence'.
Red: 'Karminglut', ('Carmine Glow'), 'Purewell Giant', 'Karin'.

Globe-flower, *Trollius* hybrids (*Trollius × cultorum*)

These vigorous, lush green hybrids with large, spherical, golden-yellow flowers make an important contribution to the spring border after the tulips have finished their display. Their most important parent is *Trollius europaeus* from poor, wet meadows in Europe and Arctic North America. This has been crossed with the more slender *T. asiaticus*, with orange, half-open flowers and deeply cut and divided leaves, and the tall, late flowering *T. chinensis*, to produce the modern garden hybrids.

Globe-flowers thrive in damp, loamy, humus-rich soil in sun or bright shade. Grown in a well-tended border and cut back hard after flowering, they will often bloom a second time in autumn. Plants are propagated by division in spring or autumn.

Pale yellow:
'Earliest of All' (0.50), V, free-flowering; by far the earliest.
'Maigold' (0.50), squat habit.

Yellow:
'Goldquelle' (0.80), V–VI, powerful, well proportioned plants; large flowers.
'Hohes Licht' (1.00), large flowers; incomparably strong and beautiful, but rare in the trade.
'Miss Mary Russell' (0.60).
'Yellow Beauty' (0.60).

Lemon-yellow:
'Lemon Queen' (0.60), VI, very vigorous.
'F. Smith' (0.70), vigorous and free-flowering.
'Byrne's Giant' (0.70), large flowers.
'Alabaster' (0.50), creamy white; not very vigorous.

Orange:
'Baudirektor Linne' (0.70), V–VI, sturdy habit; intense colouring.
'Fireglobe' (0.80), dark orange.
'Orange Globe' (0.80), orange-yellow.
'Orange Princess' (0.50), yellow-orange.
'Prichard's Giant' (0.80), deep golden orange.
'Meteor' (0.60), dark orange.

Trollius chinensis (*T. ledebourii* hort.) 'Golden Queen' NE China	0.90 orange	VI–VII, large, bowl-shaped flowers; commonly available in nurseries. *T. asiaticus* (NE Russ., Sib.) (to 0.60), V–VI, usually orange; rare in the trade.
Trollius europaeus		List 3.5.1

Further *Trollius* spp.; see list 4.6.4.

5.3.6.   American hybrid lilies for moist to damp soils in sun or bright shade

Lilium harrisianum (*L. pardalinum* var. *giganteum*) and the Bellingham hybrids (*L. humboldtii* × *L. pardalinum*) are invaluable plants for heavy, poorly drained soils, flourishing in conditions that no other lily would tolerate and eventually forming large, free-flowering clumps, which persist for many years.

The plants increase steadily by means of rhizomatous extensions of their bulbs. Sections of rhizome may be set out in the autumn and develop slowly into new plants. Once established, they are best left undisturbed.

Parent species

Meadow lily *Lilium canadense* E N Am.	0.60–1.50	VI–VII, moisture-loving species with orange-yellow, bell-shaped flowers in graceful, open umbels; large leaves in whorls up the stem; thrives in well-drained, acid, moory soil; may need irrigation; for the enthusiast.
Sunset lily *Lilium harrisianum* (*L. pardalinum* 'Giganteum') N Calif.	1.50–2.00	VI–VII, large, crimson. Turk's cap flowers with chrome yellow markings; develops into large, free-flowering clumps; undemanding on loamy, mineral- and humus-rich, moist to damp soils; grows best in full sun but shaded at the base; good in woodland edge conditions, as are the following hybrids.

Hybrids

Bellingham hybrids	1.20–2.00	VI–VIII, leaves in whorls up the stem; pyramidal racemes of up to 30 Turk's cap flowers in shades of red, orange and yellow; very robust and rewarding.
'Shuksan'	1.80	VI–VII, light orange with darker spots; Turk's cap flowers.
'Afterglow'	1.80	VI–VII, crimson with brown spots and a golden yellow throat.
'Buttercup'	1.50	VI–VII, golden yellow with brown spots.

5.4. Tulips and hyacinths

The right choice of these spring-flowering bulbs can bring seasonal flower and colour to almost any planting of border perennials. The only exceptions are plantings in semi-shade (list 5.1) or on moderately moist or damp soils (list 5.3.5), where various sorts of *Narcissus* (list 2.4.3) can perform a similar role.

Bulbs can be protected against fungal attack by watering with a solution of 1 g Ronilan (or other suitable fungicide) per litre of water. Mice are best kept at bay by thoroughly dusting the planting holes and surrounding earth with Toxaphene, where available. In the USA, County Extension Agents supply appropriate recommendations.

Garden tulips

These are typical border perennials, dependent on an open, nutrient-rich and adequately limy soil in order to grow properly. Many of them will flower freely in the same position for 5–10 years without replanting, provided their spent flowers are promptly removed and their leaves left to die down naturally. It is important that the surrounding soil should be kept cultivated in summer or else planted over with annual flowers. Tulip bulbs do not survive long in areas of lawn or in a dense planting of perennials.

The best time to plant bulbs is from September to the beginning of November. Large, mature specimens should be set 15–20 cm deep, bedded where necessary on 2–3 cm of coarse sand to protect them against damp in winter. Small clusters of 3–15 bulbs set 15–20 cm apart, scattered among the sparsely planted perennials of a herbaceous border, can create a most pleasing effect at flowering time. It is worth bearing in mind that a single group of colourful Breeder or Parrot tulips can contribute more to a small garden than a whole parade of varieties more suited to massed planting.

Established tulips are grateful for an annual application of an all-round fertiliser in autumn (e.g. Nitrophoska, 70 g/m²) or, better still, a liquid feed when shoots emerge in spring. Weak-growing specimens are mostly starved of nutrients. They should be taken up and sorted so that the largest bulbs can be replanted in rich soil elsewhere. Peat-based fertilisers should be avoided.

The following lists contain an assortment of reliable and widely avilable cultivars. In a mild, oceanic climate the differences in flowering time are much more pronounced than in continental regions where spring often appears very suddenly, causing early and late varieties to flower almost simultaneously.

Kaufmanniana tulips
(*T. kaufmanniana*) selections and hybrids

These colourful, low-growing (under 0.25) tulips have little more in common with the wild *T. kaufmanniana* (list 4.1.4). In terms of their requirements and possibilities of use, they are closely related to the more highly bred garden tulips. Nevertheless, they still associate well with plants from list 4.1.1 on a rock garden site. The earliest start flowering in March.

Red:
'Alfred Cortot' (0.25), bright red.
'Daylight' (0.20), orange-scarlet.
'Heart's Delight' (0.20), pale pink, flushed crimson outside.
'Scarlet Elegance' (0.15), scarlet.
'Shakespeare' (0.20), salmon-pink, flushed crimson outside.
'Showwinner' (0.20), red.

Yellow:
'Berlioz' (0.20), dark yellow.

'Primrose' (0.20), sulphur yellow.

Bicoloured:
'Cesar Frank' (0.20), yellow, magenta exterior.
'Goldstück' (0.25), yellow, scarlet exterior.
'Stresa' (0.20), yellow, red exterior.
'Gaiety' (0.10), white, pink exterior.
'Johann Strauss' (0.20), white, red and yellow exterior.
'The First' (0.20), creamy white, pink exterior.

Forsteriana tulips
(*T. forsteriana* hybrids)

The following medium-sized cultivars (0.25–0.45) are characterised by their large flowers in brilliant tones of red. Like the Kaufmanniana tulips they combine well with rock garden species from list 4.1.1. Their flowers are borne in April.

Red:
'Cantate' (0.20), scarlet.
'Madame Lefeber' ('Red Emperor') (0.40), vermilion.
'Princeps' (0.20), scarlet; late.
'Rockery Beauty' (0.20), vermilion.
'Pink Emperor' (0.35), cherry pink.

Golden yellow:
'Golden Emperor' (0.40).

Tulipa greigii selections and hybrids

Although the wild species (list 4.1.4) grows best on a warm, sheltered, rock garden site with porous, gravelly soil, the following selections and hybrids are less demanding and quite suitable for planting on a herbaceous border. All have beautifully marked leaves with reddish-brown stripes and blotches. They are mostly rather short-lived, flowering at the end of April and beginning of May.

Multicoloured:
'Cape Cod' (0.25), bronze-yellow with yellow margins, apricot exterior.
'Compostella' (0.25), golden yellow flamed with orange, magenta exterior.
'Donna Bella' (0.25), creamy yellow with cream margins, magenta exterior.
'Engadin' (0.35), golden yellow with red stripes and yellow margins, blood red exterior.
'Oriental Splendour' (0.30), lemon yellow, crimson exterior.

Red:
'Large Copper' (0.25), vermilion and violet.
'Margeret Herbst' (0.25), vermilion; large flowers; early.
'Oriental Beauty' (0.25), orange-red.
'Red Reflection' (0.25), scarlet.
'Rotkäppchen' (0.20), crimson.

Garden tulips

Single early tulips

These are erect, low-growing tulips (0.20–0.30), whose flowers are borne in early April. The various cultivars are much used for forcing and flowering indoors, but are also suitable for outdoor cultivation in areas with an early spring. The double-flowered forms tend to fall over in rainy weather and cannot be recommended for outside.

Particularly early:
'Bellona', pure yellow.
'Brilliant Star', scarlet.
'Christmas Marvel', dark pink.
'Diana', white.
'Ibis', magenta-pink and white.
'Joffre', yellow.

Early to mid:
'Charles', crimson.
'Dr Plesman', orangey red.
'General de Wet', golden orange.
'Kaiserkrone', red with yellow margins.
'Prinz Karneval', yellow, flamed red.
'Prinz von Österreich', scarlet orange.
'Weihnachtsgold', golden yellow.

Late (early May):
'Couleur Cardinal', crimson.
'Prinzess Irene', deep orange, flamed purple.
'Yokahama', dark yellow; pointed petals.

Mendel tulips

These elegant, large-flowered hybrids bloom at the end of April, along with the last of the early tulips. Their slender stems attain 40 cm. They may also be used for forcing.

'Athlete', pure white.
'Orange Wonder', orange-bronze flushed scarlet.
'Pink Trophy', pink; often with several flowers.
'Van der Eerden', bright red.

Triumph tulips

These are sturdy, thick-stemmed plants (up to 0.50), flowering shortly after the Mendel tulips at the end of April or beginning of May. They are much used in spring bedding schemes with forget-me-nots and pansies, where their early flowering season allows them to be cleared away in good time for the summer display.

White:
'Pax', pure white.
'Garden Party', white with broad pink margins.

Yellow:
'Levant', lemon yellow.
'Reforma', bright yellow.

Pink:
'Meissner Porzellan', pink and white.
'Peerless Pink', pure pink.
'Preludium', pink with a white base.

Red:
'Albury', cherry red.
'Bing Crosby', scarlet.
'Cassini', blood red.
'Fidelio', crimson with orange margins.
'Prominence', dark red.
'Robinea', scarlet.

Red with white margins:
'Edith Eddy', crimson.
'Elmus', pale red.
'Lucky Strike', dark red.
'Lustige Witwe' ('Merry Widow') dark red.
'Miriam', crimson.

Red with yellow margins:
'Golden Eddy', red.
'Kees Nelis', blood red.
'Madam Spoor', mahogany.
'Paris', scarlet.
'Rheinland', crimson.

Orange-red:
'Coriolan', yellow margins.
'High Society', orange margins.
'Orange Wonder', bronze-orange and scarlet.
'Prinzessin Beatrix', golden margins.

Violet and lilac:
'Attila', pale purple-violet.
'Don Quixote', bluish purple-violet.
'First Lady', reddish violet.

Darwin hybrid tulips

These are tall (0.70), vigorous hybrids, first raised by Lefeber from *T. fosteriana* and the Darwin tulips. Large and strikingly beautiful flowers appear at the end of April or in May. Their brightly coloured flowers have a velvety sheen, when the sun catches them.

Orange-red:
'Apeldoorn', orange-scarlet.
'Holland's Glory', orange-scarlet.
'Königin Wilhelmina', orange-scarlet.
'My Lady', orange-pink.
'Orange Sun', orange.
'Oxford', orange.
'Parade', scarlet.
'Red Matador', crimson with scarlet feathering.
'Spring Song', red.

Yellow:
'Golden Apeldoorn', golden-yellow.
'Golden Parade', yellow.

Pink:
'Big Chief', buff pink.
'Elisabeth Arden', rose-purple.

Multicoloured:
'Apeldoorn Elite', yellow with cherry red feathering.
'Beauty of Apeldoorn', crimson with golden yellow margins.
'Striped Apeldoorn', yellow with scarlet feathering.
'Tender Beauty', pure white with broad pink margins.
'Vivex', carmine-pink with orange-yellow margins.

Darwin tulips

These flower later than the Darwin hybrid tulips, beginning in May. They are tall plants (0.70), with angular buds opening into almost spherical flowers. Greatly valued for cutting.

Yellow:
'Mamasa', golden yellow.
'Yellow Giant', golden yellow.
'Sweet Harmony', lemon yellow, white margins.

Pink:
'Aristocrat', violet-pink.
'Clara Butt', salmon pink.
'Copland's Record', deep pink.
'Queen of Bartigons', salmon pink.

Red:
'Campfire', blood red.
'Cordell Hull', light red, striped with white.
'Lansealde's Supreme', cherry red to orange.
'Paul Richter', geranium red.

Black:
'Queen of Night'.

Lily-flowered tulips

Elegant and charming tulips with pointed, reflexed petals. Their flowers are produced on tallish stems (0.50–0.70) together with the Darwin hybrids in April and May.

White:
'White Triumphator', pure white.

Yellow:
'Westpoint', primrose yellow.
'Golden Duchess', golden yellow.

Pink:
'China Pink', pink.
'Jacqueline', deep pink with a yellow base.
'Marietta', satin pink.

Red:
'Aladdin', scarlet, yellow base.
'Captain Fryatt', ruby-purple.
'Dyanito', orange-red.
'Marjolein', orange-pink, red inside with a yellow base.
'Queen of Sheba', chestnut red.
'Red Shine', dark red.

Reddish violet:
'Maytime', narrow white margins.

Cottage tulips

The following, middle-sized and tall-growing cultivars (0.40–0.80) closely resemble Darwin tulips. Their elongate to ovoid flowers are mostly produced in May.

White:
'Sigrid Undset', creamy white; large flowers.

Yellow:
'Golden Harvest', lemon yellow.
'Mrs John T. Scheepers', pure yellow.
'Mother's Day', delicate yellow.

Pink:
'Rosy Wings', salmon pink; large flowers.
'Smiling Queen', purple pink.

Red:
'Balalaika', brilliant red, yellow base.
'Halcro', carmine red.
'Kingsblood', cherry red, scarlet margins.
'Lincolnshire', dark red; late.
'Marshal Haig', scarlet with a yellow centre.
'Renown', pale carmine.

Tulips for the enthusiast

The following tulips have no importance for the usual decorative plantings in public parks and other open spaces. They are oddities to be appreciated for themselves, reminders of the almost inconceivable wealth of genetic potential hidden within every living plant. The fascination that these tulips (especially Parrot tulips) exerted on seventeenth century Dutch artists has been immortalised in their glorious paintings. The immense diversity of bizarre and even monstrous modifications gives some indication of the possibilities that further breeding may still reveal.

Fringed tulips

These are tallish plants (0.60), bearing slightly fringed flowers at the end of April and beginning of May.

'Bellflower', salmon-pink.
'Burgundy Lace', wine-red.
'Maja', pale yellow.
'Swan Wings', white with a greenish tinge.

Parrot tulips

Parrot tulips have large, exotic flowers with fringed and incised (often flamed) petals borne at the end of April and in May. Unlike earlier cultivars, modern plants have sturdy, 40–60 cm stems that rarely break in heavy rain.

Yellow:
'Texas Gold', golden-yellow.
'Texas Flame', deep yellow, flamed with red.

Pink:
'Fantasy', salmon-pink.

Red:
'Karel Doorman', cherry-red, narrow yellow margins.
'Firebird', dark red.

Orange:
'Orange Favourite', orange with a yellow centre.

Blue:
'Blue Parrot', pale violet.

Multiflowered tulips

These produce clusters of 3–6 flowers on 50 cm stalks in May.

'Georgette', yellow, orange margins.
'Orange Bouquet', light orange, yellow base.

Breeder tulips

These tall (0.70) cultivars flower together with the Darwin tulips and are basically similar, differing in their more ovoid flowers and characteristic, hazy colour schemes. Their olive-brown, coppery-bronze and purple-blue tones are ineffective at long range. They are best enjoyed in more intimate areas of the garden and will tolerate a site in bright shade. Modern catalogues list them with the Late Single and Darwin tulips..

'Bacchus', dark purple with a violet shimmer.
'Dillenburg', orange and terracotta; late.
'Louis XIV', bluish violet with bronze-brown margins.
'President Hoover', orange-scarlet.

Rembrandt tulips

Originally, Rembrandt tulips were the highly prized 'broken' or 'flamed' forms of Darwin tulips, but the classification has now been extended to include similarly modified cultivars of Breeder and Cottage tulips. Colour breaking is induced by a virus transmitted by aphids, and can prove very troublesome if it spreads. Infected plants, however beautiful, are less vigorous and shorter-lived than healthy specimens. They are mostly sold in mixed assortments.

Well-known cultivars:
'American Flag', dark red with white.
'Clara', dark pink, striped with scarlet and white.

'Cordell Hall', white with blood red.
'Mme. de Pompadour', white with purple.
'Union Jack', white with red, blue base.

Double late tulips

These bear long, double, peony-like flowers at the end of May, but their stems break easily in rain and they cannot be recommended for general use.

Green tulips

The following green-flowered cottage tulips are treasured by flower arrangers. The plants grow 30–50 cm tall and flower at the end of May.

'Artist', salmon pink and green interior, purple and salmon exterior.
'Golden Artist', golden-yellow with green stripes.
'Greenland', green with pink margins.
'Hollywood', red with a green tinge.
'Hummingbird', primrose-yellow with green feathering.
'Spring Green', white with broad green markings.

Garden hyacinth, *Hyacinthus orientalis*

These fragrant, showy, spring-flowering plants are best grown in beds next to the house or at the foot of a warm wall, tucked in between widely spaced border perennials or on the sunny side of a slow-growing ornamental shrub. Their large bulbs should be planted in little clusters (of 5–7) in autumn, 10–15 cm deep in fertile, well-drained garden soil, preferably bedded on a thin layer of sand. Many different colours are available, but it is advisable to stick to a single colour within each cluster. Although the plants will survive for many years undisturbed in soil that is not too wet or hungry, it is nevertheless beneficial to lift the bulbs when their leaves have yellowed, clean them, rub away any offsets and store them in a dark, dry place for replanting in autumn. Double-flowered cultivars tend to fall over in rainy weather, and it is therefore better to plant well-tried garden cultivars that are not intended for forcing. Cheap bulbs tend to produce small, scanty inflorescences.

The following can be recommended for garden use:

Single-flowered hyacinths (IV–V)

White:
'Carnegie', late.
'L'Innocence', early.

Yellow:
'City of Haarlem', pale yellow; early.
'Yellow Hammer', garden yellow; late.

Pink:
'Anne Marie', pale pink; early.
'Lady Derby', pale pink; late.
'Pink Pearl', dark pink; early.
'Queen of the Pinks', pink; late.

Red:
'Amsterdam', glossy red; mid.
'Jan Bos', dark crimson; early.
'La Victoire', scarlet; early.

Blue:
'Bismarck', light blue; early.
'Blue Jacket', deep dark blue.
'Delft Blue', porcelain blue; early.
'Ostara', deep blue; early.

5.5.   Short-lived border perennials

The following are short-lived but showy perennials, whose flowers are often invaluable for cutting. They may be used to bring colour, warmth and plenty to a newly planted herbaceous border, while longer-lived plants are still developing to their full beauty. North American species are particularly effective in combination with their compatriots from list 5.3.4.

Hollyhocks and mallows, *Alcea, Lavatera, Malva* and *Sidalcea*

Hollyhocks (*Alcea rosea*) and mallows have long been popular as garden plants, grown in a variety of different forms and colours that are now almost symbolic of the cottage gardens of yesteryear. In contrast to the marsh mallow (*Althaea officinalis*, list 3.5.2), the species listed below are all short-lived, seldom persisting for longer than 2–3 years. Their value for cutting is very limited. Hollyhocks can be sown outdoors in March and are then planted into their final positions at the beginning of August, flowering in the following year. Some forms, such as *A. rosea* 'Indian Spring', will flower from seed in their first summer, but these seldom survive to flower again.

Mallows thrive in sunny positions on rich, moist, crumbly soils, preferably in the rainshadow of a house. Hollyhocks are particularly susceptible to rust, but this can be prevented by systematic treatment with a fungicide (Thiram). Individual plants will survive for several years if they are regularly dead-headed and cut down immediately after flowering.

Fig-leaf Hollyhock *Alcea ficifolia* Sib., Near East	2.00 yellow	VIII–X, erect, stately habit; green, fig-like leaves; longer-lived than hollyhocks; occasionally needs staking; forms hybrids with *A. rosea*.
Hollyhock *Alcea rosea* (*Althaea rosea*) 'Pleniflora'	2.00 pink	VII–IX, similar to the previous species but with matt green, wrinkled, 5–7-corned leaves; old garden plant, widespread in many different colours; single-flowered forms are especially recommended, and hardly ever need staking.
Lavatera olbia 'Rosea' Port.	up to 2.00 purple–pink	VII–IX, typical mallow flowers; freely branching stems, woody at the base; soft, lobate leaves; only reliably persistent in mild areas; sterile cultivar, but easily raised from cuttings. *L. thuringiaca*: see list 2.3.3.
High mallow, Cheeses *Malva sylvestris* var. *mauritiana* NW Afr., Asia, Eur.	up to 1.50 purple, violet veins	XII–X, dense clusters of large flowers on strong, leafy, branching stems; flowers until the first frosts if sown in April; mostly annual but seeds itself prolifically. *M. alcea* and *M. moschata*: see list 2.3.3.

Checkerbloom	0.70	VII–VIII, free-flowering cultivar with graceful, open,
Sidalcea × cultorum	pink	branching habit, should be cut back after flowering
'Brilliant'		or it may not perennate; for sandy, lime-free soils that
USA		are not too dry. Widely available selections:

'Elsie Heugh' (0.80), pink.
'Loveliness' (0.75), shell pink.
'Rose Queen' (1.20), rose.
'Rosy Gem' (0.60), lilac-pink.
Starks hybrids (0.80–1.00), pink to red.
'William Smith' (1.00), salmon-pink.

Yellow chamomile, *Anthemis tinctoria*

Anthemis tinctoria has large, solitary, fine-rayed, golden yellow, daisy-like flowers on tall stems (0.60), with grey-green, comb-like divided foliage. In common with several other of these short-lived garden perennials, it is a pioneer species of bare, gravelly soils on warm, dry slopes and embankments. In the trade it is only represented by its cultivars.

Anthemis tinctoria	up to 0.70	VII–IX, abundant large flowers over a long period;
'Grallagh Gold'	yellow	good for cutting; plants should be cut back in early
Eur., W Asia		autumn to encourage the formation of overwintering
		buds.
		'Kelwayi', similar but with finer-cut leaves.

Anthemis sancti-	0.40	VI–VIII, similar to the previous; not always true in
johannis	orange-	the trade; propagation by division, as for *A. tinctoria*.
SW Bulg.	yellow	

Ox-eye daisies and pyrethrum, *Chrysanthemum leucanthemum* and *C. coccineum*

Pyrethrums (painted daises) grow wild in regions of summer drought in the mountains of Asia Minor and the Caucasus. In a garden they require a moist (not too dry), slightly acid, loamy soil. The cultivars listed below are not too prone to fall apart upon flowering, and some of them make very robust and healthy perennials. Their clumps can be divided immediately after flowering in May.

Similar requirements are shared by cultivated varieties of the ox-eye daisy, a common European grassland species widely naturalised in North America, which is commonly associated with moist or moderately dry meadows and grassy slopes (see list 3.2.1). The plants differ from pyrethrum in forming a loose turf of creeping shoots. Both, however, should be taken up and divided every 2–3 years.

Chrysanthemum coccineum (*C. roseum*), V–VI

Red:
'Alfred' (0.60), dark red; double.
'Brenda' (0.80), cherry red; single.
'Dolly' (0.60), dark red; single.
'James Kelway' (0.80), scarlet, single.
'Regent' (0.80), brilliant red; single.
'Robinson's Red' (0.80), crimson; single; seed strain.

Pink:
'E. M. Robinson' (0.70), pink; single.
'Robinson's Pink' (0.80), pink; single; seed strain.
'Rosabella' (0.70), dark pink; double.

Chrysanthemum leucanthemum, V–VI (white)

'Maistern' (0.50), single.
'Maikönigin' (0.70), single.
'Rheinblick' (0.60), single.

Shasta daisy, *Chrysanthemum maximum*

Chrysanthemum maximum comes from sunny meadows and stony, grass-covered slopes in the Pyrenees. Its cultivars are popular border perennials whose large flowers are invaluble for cutting. Double-flowered forms are short-lived and must therefore be divided every 2–3 years. Single-flowered cultivars are best divided every 3–5 years, and unselected seedlings can sometimes be left even longer provided that growing conditions are suitable. None will thrive in wet soil.

Nurseries offer a combination of vegetatively propagated clones and more or less reliable seed strains such as 'Dieners Riesen', 'Marbecker Riesen', 'Polaris', 'Stern von Antwerpen' and 'Universal', which vary slightly from plant to plant.

Single-flowered

'Harry Pötschke' (1.00), VII-IX, huge flowers on rigid stems; also for cutting.
'Beethoven' (0.80), VI–VII, large flowers; ideal for both garden and cutting.
'Bishopstone' (0.90), VII–IX, large flowers with laciniate ray-florets.
'Silberprinzesschen' (0.30), VII–IX, medium-sized flowers; low-growing.
'Snowcap' (0.50), VI–VIII, intensely white flowers.

Double-flowered

'Christine Hagemann' (0.80), VI-VII, loosely double; suitable for cutting.
'Esther Read' (0.80), VI–VIII, fully double white.
'Heinrich Seibert' (0.80), VII–VIII, semi-double; ruffled flowers.
'Schwabengruss' (1.00), VII–IX, semi-double; elegant; invaluable for cutting.
'Wirral Supreme' (0.90), VII–VIII, densely double; short-lived; excellent for cutting.

Recent double-flowered cultivars

'Margrit' (0.80), 'Perlenkranz' (0.70); 'Grünberg' (0.60), white centre.

Recent single-flowered cultivars

'Eisrevue' (0.60); 'Polaris' (1.00), large flowers on sturdy stems.

Coreopsis

A number of short-lived species and cultivars of *Coreopsis* are available from the nursery trade, in addition to long-lived perennials such as *Coreopsis tripteris* (list 3.5.4) and *C. verticillata* (list 3.4.6). Of these, *C. lanceolata* is widely distributed in the USA in both dry and damp conditions, while *C. grandiflora* is found on damper soils in the southern states. Both are clump-forming species with fresh green leaves and flowers on long stems, popular for cutting. The plants thrive in gardens on rich, moist soils in full sun. Cultivars may be propagated from basal cuttings but most stocks are raised from seed. It is difficult to assign cultivars definitely to either *C. grandiflora* or *C. lanceolata*.

Coreopsis grandiflora 'Badengold'	0.70 golden yellow	VII–IX, lush green, pinnately lobed and divided leaves; large flower heads on long, smooth stems. 'Goldfink' (0.25), deep yellow; single. 'Sunray' (0.60), golden yellow; double. 'Tetragold' (0.60), yellow; single. Plants should be cut back hard in September to improve their chances of overwintering.
Coreopsis lanceolata 'Sonnenkind' ('Baby Sun')	0.40 golden yellow	VI–VIII, dainty habit; lanceolate leaves. 'Domino' (0.40), flowers with a dark disc. 'Golden Queen' (0.60). 'Schnittgold' ('Golden Gain') (0.60). 'Louis d'Or' (0.90). Plants exhaust themselves if they are allowed to bloom unchecked, so timely cutting back is necessary; annual lifting and division can be recommended. Other low-growing sorts: see list 3.4.4.

Purple coneflower, *Echinacea purpurea* (*Rudbeckia purpurea*)

These rather stiff, tall-stemmed, sun-loving perennials are popular garden plants, with flowers that are valuable for cutting. The genus *Echinacea* is native to North America *E. purpurea* is found on moist, mineral-rich soils in the eastern USA, while its rarely seen relatives *E. angustifolia*, *E. pallida* and *E. paradoxa* all grow wild in drier, prairie conditions. Named cultivars are propagated vegetatively from root cuttings. Plants that are raised from seed (and then frequently offered as hybrids on account of their variation) also make attractive and useful specimens.

Echinacea purpurea (*Rudbeckia purpurea*)	1.00 crimson to purple	VII–IX, coarse, ovate leaves; large composite flowers on stiff stems; ray-florets often droop and become umbrella-like with age; the following cultivars are particularly valuable: 'Abendsonne' (0.70), purple-crimson with an orange-brown centre. 'The King' (0.80), dark purple-crimson. 'Leuchtstern' (0.80), carmine-pink. 'White Swan' and 'White Lustre', white.

Blanket flower, *Gaillardia* hybrids

The following cultivars are chiefly descended from *Gaillardia aristata* (*G. grandiflora*) and *G. pulchella*, from the dry, sunny prairies of North America. Each bears a long succession of abundant, colourful, mostly red and gold, daisy-like flowers from July to September, and all are very suitable for cutting.

Gaillardias are mostly raised from seed, but propagation from root-cuttings is also possible and may sometimes be preferred. Individual plants can be long-lived in well-drained, sandy soils, but they must be cut back hard in September to promote the formation of new basal shoots.

The following named cultivars are available, along with a variety of seed strains.

Tall selections for cutting:
'Bremen' (0.50), red and yellow.
'Burgundy' (0.70), red-brown.
'Fackelschein' ('Torchlight') (0.70), dark red with yellow margins.
'Mandarin' (0.60), orange-red.

Dwarf selections:
'Büble' (0.15), red with yellow margins.
'Goldkobold' ('Golden Goblin') (0.25), golden yellow.
'Kobold' ('Goblin') (0.30), red and yellow.

Dark-eyed sunflower, *Helianthus atrorubens* (*H. sparsifolius*)

This is probably the most elegant and beautiful of all the sunflowers, growing wild in light, dry woodland in south eastern parts of the USA. Its sturdy stems (up to 2 m) with roughly hairy, ovate–lanceolate leaves are not entirely windproof, and may therefore need staking. The plants are somewhat tender but will perennate reliably in mild areas under a protective layer of leaves. Elsewhere the thick rhizomes should be taken up in autumn and kept in sand or potted up in a cool place until the spring. Selections: 'Gullick's Variety' (1.80), 'Monarch' (2.00).

Beard-tongue, *Penstemon*

These very decorative and long-flowering North American perennials are rather tender in cultivation and therefore mostly treated like annuals to be raised each year from seed or cuttings. Their long, raceme-like panicles of funnel-shaped or bell-shaped flowers are somewhat reminiscent of foxgloves.

Penstemon *heterophyllus* 'Züriblau' Calif.	0.50 gentian blue	V–VII, long- and free-flowering; inflorescences on upright or ascending stems; narrow, grey-blue, linear leaves; often confused with *P. azureus*. 'Blue Spring', pure blue. 'Enzianblau', gentian blue. All come true from seed. *P. barbatus*: see list 3.4.6.
Penstemon hartwegii Mex.	0.40–0.60 various	VII–X, several stems of large bell-shaped flowers; green, oval–lanceolate leaves; seed almost always in mixtures; sadly rare in the trade nowadays; sometimes sold as *P. gentianoides*.
Penstemon hybrids (*P. hartwegii* × *P. cobaea*)	up to 0.80 reddish	VI–X, very long- and free-flowering; large flowers on mostly upright stems with glossy green, lanceolate to oval–lanceolate leaves; cut flowers do not last well; only perennial on sheltered sites in mild areas; propagation from cuttings. 'Andenken an Hahn' (0.70), small, deep red flowers. 'Brilliant' (0.60), large, brilliant red, bell-shaped flowers. 'Paul Schoenholzer' (0.70), dark red. 'Scharlachkönigin ('Scarlet Queen') (0.80), red with a striped throat. 'Southgate Gem' (0.60), large red flowers.

Short-lived coneflowers, *Rudbeckia*

A few forms of these annual and biennial coneflowers from the USA can sometimes be encouraged to perennate by intensive cutting, particularly on damp soils.

Gloriosa daisy *Rudbeckia hirta* 'Gloriosa'	0.60–1.00 yellow with brown markings, black centre,	VII–IX, exceptionally large flowers, invaluable for cutting; entire, hairy, spathulate leaves; rough-hairy, unbranched stems. The following selections are usually annual: 'Irish Eyes', yellow with an olive-green cone. 'Marmalade', golden-yellow with a black cone. 'Rustic Dwarfs', shades of bronze, chestnut and yellow. 'Tetragold', golden-yellow.
Rudbeckia triloba	1.20 deep yellow, black centre	VIII–IX, three-lobed leaves; unusually abundant flowers; very good for cutting; annual to biennial; seeds itself freely in warm summer regions; annual propagation from late-ripening seed.

5.6.   Tender border perennials

The following, mostly South African or South American herbaceous perennials will survive any normal western European winter with just a little protection from the cold. They do not need to be taken up and stored in frost-free conditions like dahlias and gladioli. All thrive on warm, porous, loamy, moist soils in sun or (in most cases) semi-shade.

5.6.1.   Plants for the enthusiast

Agapanthus *campanulatus* S Afr.	0.30/0.80 (up to 1.00) blue	VII–X, many-flowered umbels on thick stems; short, upright, mostly grey-green, linear leaves; differs from *A. praecox* (*A. umbellatus* hort.) in being deciduous; hardy to zone (7B) 8. *A. c.* var. *patens* (to 1.20), spherical umbels.
Agapanthus Headbourne hybrids		Hardy descendants of *A. campanulatus* (Zone 7B). 'Blue Globe' (to 1.00), pale blue. 'Isis' (0.70), deep blue. 'Profusion' (0.80), dark blue. Further hybrids, of uncertain origin: 'Blue Giant' dark blue; broad leaves. 'Umbellatus Albus' (0.70), white.
Alstroemeria *aurantiaca* 'Orange King' Chile	0.80 orange with purple stripes	VI–VIII, umbels of irregular, mottled, funnel-shaped flowers; lanceolate leaves, often twisted to expose their grey-green undersides; very sensitive, fleshy roots; for warm, porous soils; needs protection with a covering of leaves in winter; hardy to zone 7. 'Aurea', yellow flowers.
Alstroemeria Ligtu hybrids	0.50 pink, salmon and yellow	VI–VIII, similar to the foregoing but less demanding and more persistent; should be planted from a pot in spring; need protection in winter; hardy to zone (7B) 8.
Belamcanda chinensis (*Pardanthus chinensis*) Jap., China, N India	0.40/0.60 orange-red	VII–VIII, large, bowl-shaped flowers on forked stems; sword-shaped leaves; large fruit capsules with black, pea-sized seeds; rootstock should be covered in winter or lifted and kept inside; easily raised from seed; tolerates winter temperatures to −25°C in regions wih long, hot summers.

Crinum × powellii (*C. bulbispermum ×* *C. moorei*) S Afr.	0.50/1.00 pink	VIII–IX, large, nodding, funnel-shaped flowers on tall stems; long, broad, strap-like, overhanging leaves; for rich soils that stay moist in summer; bulbs should be planted with their tips just showing; needs a covering of leaves in winter; hardy to zone 6B. 'Album', white. 'Harlemense', delicate pink. 'Krelagei', deep pink.
Montbretia *Crocosmia masoniorum* S Afr.	0.90 orange- yellow	VII–VIII, large, upward-facing flowers on a horizontally held rachis; strong, wiry stems, branched above; broad, stiff or drooping leaves; bright and long-flowering; needs a covering of leaves in winter in harsh districts; hardy to zone 6B.
Hybrid montbretia *Crocosmia ×* *crocosmiiflora*	0.40 orange- yellow	VII–X, flowers in short, crowded spikes; light green leaves; rhizomatous corms form dense colonies; fully hardy to zone 6B under a deep layer of leaves; it is safest to overwinter a few corms of any large-flowered cultivars in plastic bags or moist sand under frost-free conditions.
Pineapple flower *Eucomis punctata* S Afr.	0.60 yellowish- green	VII–VIII, spikes of large, fragrant flowers on stout, purple-spotted stems; tender; best grown in a plot, to be kept bright and cool in winter; should be planted out in spring.
Galtonia candicans S Afr.	0.60–1.40 white	VII–IX, large spikes of drooping, bell-shaped flowers on sturdy stems; long, fleshy, grey-green leaves; often hardy if planted deep enough (10 cm); bulbs may be lifted in autumn for frost-free storage; thrives in rich soil; hardy to zone (6B) 7.
Hibiscus moscheutos		List 6.2.3.
English iris *Iris* Anglica hybrids	0.60/0.60 shades of blue and white	VI–VII, ovoid bulbs; narrow, grooved, blue-green leaves; strikingly large flowers; hardy in many areas; shoots emerge in early spring. *I. xiphioides* (*I. anglica* hort.) (list 4.5.5), blue flowers with a yellow zone on each fall; hardy to zone 5B–6.
Spanish iris *Iris* Hispanica hybrids	up to 0.50 various	VI, shorter and daintier but also more tender than the previous hybrids; rounded falls with a long, nail-like haft; shoots emerge in autumn and are often damaged by frost. *I. xiphium* (*I. hispanica* hort.), violet flowers with an orange zone on each fall.
Dutch iris *Iris* Hollandica hybrids	0.60/0.60 various	VI–VII, large, elegant flowers on stiff stems; long, grooved, often bluish leaves; invaluable for cutting or forcing indoors; shoots emerge in autumn and need protection in winter; it is advisable to lift the bulbs (of these and the previous hybrids) when their leaves have died down, and store them in dry sand for replanting in October.

Lobelia fulgens 'Queen Victoria' Mex.	0.80 (1.20) scarlet	VIII–IX, brilliant flowers in large, branching racemes; red stems with dark red leaves; only perennates in very mild areas with protection against frost.
Cape figwort *Phygelius capensis* S Afr.	0.80–1.20 vermilion	VIII–X, nodding, tubular flowers in long panicles; powerful stems with opposite, crenately toothed leaves; old plants are particularly impressive; for rich, loamy soils in sun; needs protection in winter in cold districts; hardy to zone 7.
Sisyrinchium striatum Arg., Chile	0.50 pale yellow	VI–VII, decorative but short-lived species with relatively large flowers; evergreen, iris-like leaves, which turn black in winter after a frost; somewhat tender; seeds itself; hardy to zone (7) 7B.
Verbena bonariensis Arg.	up to 1.00 lavender blue	VII–X, small flowers in upright, terminal cymes; erect, stiffly branching, apparently almost leafless stems; rough, point, grey-green, elongate leaves; persistent in mild areas; spreads by seeding; mostly treated as an annual; hardy to zone (8) 9B.

5.6.2. Red hot poker, *Kniphofia* hybrids

These decorative South African perennials, with their showy, club-shaped inflorescences, lush green foliage and brilliant colours, have an exotic appearance that does not fit comfortably in the framework of a temperate garden. They are most effective combined with geographically related plants, such as *Agapanthus*, *Phygelius capensis* and *Galtonia candicans*, and set against a background of *Miscanthus sinensis*, perhaps with the scarlet *Lobelia fulgens* planted at a safe distance.

A great number of different cultivars are available but these have been difficult to assess in Weihenstephan, where they mostly prove rather tender and short-lived. The hardiest cultivars are several unspectacular descendants of *Kniphofia uvaria* and *K. tuckii*, such as 'Elegans Multicolor' and 'Earliest of All', which have now almost disappeared from the trade. The height of the plants varies considerably with age. Their exact flowering season depends on the weather and on the extent of any damage suffered in the preceding winter. Generally speaking, the assortment flowers from June to October.

Kniphofias need moist to moderately damp conditions in summer, particularly at flowering time. They cannot tolerate extremes of cold or a wet soil in winter. In a harsh climate it is necessary to protect them with a layer of peat or fallen leaves. It is advisable to bundle the plants' own leaves together in autumn and then cut them back by about one third of their length in spring. Kniphofias are easily propagated by division, but new plants should only be set out in spring.

Heights vary considerably from year to year. Those cultivars that are generally taller and more powerful have been listed separately below.

Species

Kniphofia galpinii	0.60–0.90 orange-yellow	VIII–X, dainty, free-flowering species; narrow, grassy leaves; widely available; easily raised from seed.
Kniphofia tuckii	0.80 pale yellow	VI–VII, sturdy leaves and inflorescences; pale red buds; relatively hardy; once very common but now rather rare in the trade.

| *Kniphofia uvaria* (*K. praecox*) | 1.00 yellow, red above | VII–X, thick, dense racemes on powerful stems; grey-green leaves; variable, hardy species; much used for hybridisation; normally available as *K. u.* 'Grandiflora'. |

Hybrids

Low and medium-sized cultivars

(Often taller than recorded here in the first year after planting)

'Canary' (0.80), VII–VIII, lemon-yellow.
'Gold Else' (0.70), VII–VIII, golden-yellow; good for cutting.
'Little Maid' (0.60), VI–X, ivory-white.
'Bronzeleuchter' (0.60), VII–X, light bronze.
'Alcazar' (0.90), VI–VIII, orange.
'Corallina' (0.70), VII–IX, yellow; orange and red buds.
'Express' (0.90), VI–VII, pale to dark orange; early.
'Comet' (0.50), VI–VIII, orange with red tips.
'Strawberries and Cream' (0.60), VIII–IX, creamy-white, flushed red at the tips.
'Safranvogel' (0.90), VI–IX, salmon-pink; light green leaves.

Cultivars over 1 m tall

'Golden Amber' (1.30), VII–VIII, golden-yellow.
'Lemon Ice' (1.30), VIII–IX, pale lemon-yellow.
'Luna' (1.50), bright yellow with an orange tip.
'Maid of Orleans' (1.00), delicate creamy-white with a hint of pink.
'Fiery Fred' (1.20), VI–VIII, fiery orange.
'Green Jade' (1.20), VIII–X, jade green.
'Ada' (1.10), VII–IX, deep orange-yellow.
'Saturn' (1.00), VI–IX, dark orange-red; early.
'Evered' (1.60), VIII–IX, brilliant red; late.
'John Benary' (1.50), VI–IX, coral-red.
'Red Brilliance' (1.00), VI–IX, brilliant red.
'Scarlet Cap' (1.00), VI–IX, scarlet.
'Atlanta' (1.00), VI–VII, yellow and red.
'Mars' (1.20), VI–VII, orange-yellow below, turning red.
'Royal Standard' (1.10), VII–VIII, sulphur-yellow and red; grown for cutting.

5.7.   The rural herb garden and its perennials

The small, neatly enclosed, rural herb garden with its geometrical beds of vegetables, herbs and medicinal plants has maintained an unbroken tradition over much of the European countryside since the middle ages. Herbaceous perennials played a small but increasingly important role in these gardens until the sixteenth century, when the rapid introduction of new species and double-flowered cultivars resulted in an almost baroque extravagance of planting that has been retained in some English cottage gardens to this day, though most rural gardens still reserved a place for herbs and medicinal plants alongside the more expressly ornamental species.

Geometrical layout with rondell. Box edgings accentuate the structural effect. Surrounding border with border perennials, small ornamental shrubs, roses, bulbs, dahlias, flowers for cutting and annuals.

Since the beginning of the twentieth century the picture has changed dramatically. Many rural gardens have been transformed into typical urban plots, full of ornamental trees and shrubs, while those that have retained their traditional lay-out are often very neglected or lacking in flowers. It is time that the old patterns and concepts were revived, providing as they do a simple but attractive way of growing a variety of both decorative and useful plants. There is no reason why roses and border perennials should not again be planted within the classical structure of crossed paths, emphasised where appropriate with a small round bed or 'rondell' in the centre. Such enclosed features are easily integrated into a larger open space, their box edgings providing interest even in the depths of winter. They attain a special beauty when annual and biennial flowers are set between the roses and perennials, in the time-honoured manner that has already been recommended for modern border plantings (see page. 57 ff.).

These small gardens can strongly influence the character of a village, particularly if traditional herbs and medicinal plants are included in their design. They could also provide a home for old-fashioned forms of our modern herbaceous cultivars, thus contributing to the conservation of some rare garden plants. Generally speaking, any border perennial can be used to good effect in geometrically laid out plots of this kind. However, the lists below exclude all those species and cultivars that have only become important within the last couple of centuries (e.g. delphiniums, phlox, Michaelmas daisies, rudbeckias and other easily divided species).

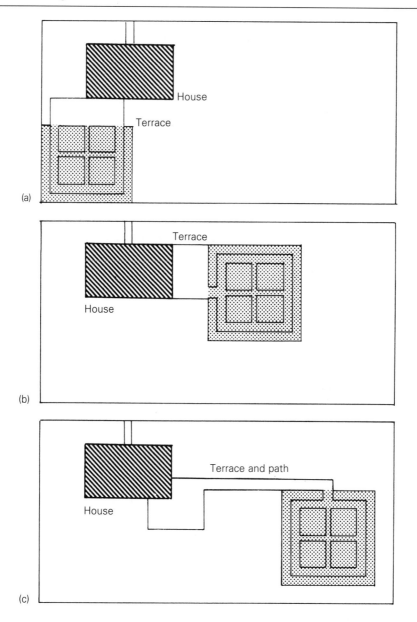

(a)

(b)

(c)

Sketches to illustrate the siting of a herb garden within a larger garden. In (a) and (b) the terrace forms a direct connection; in (c) a path is necessary.

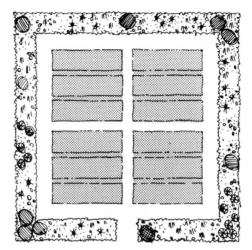

Plan of a small, simple garden for herbs and vegetables, surrounded by a border of perennials, roses, ornamental shrubs, annuals and flowers for cutting.

5.7.1. Herbaceous perennials and sub-shrubs

Plants for the outer beds

The narrow outer beds of a traditional herb garden were planted with vigorous perennials for display and cutting, together with scattered rose bushes, annual flowers and a selection of the following herbs and medicinal plants.

Horse radish	*Armoracia rusticana*
Costmary	*Chrysanthemum balsamita*
Licorice	*Glycyrrhiza glabra*
Lovage	*Levisticum officinale*
Gardener's garters	*Phalaris arundinacea* 'Picta'
Pokeweed	*Phytolacca acinosa*
Rhubarb	*Rheum rhabarbarum*
Spinach dock	*Rumex patientia*

Plants for full sun at the foot of a house wall

These warmth-loving herbs and medicinal plants will also thrive in a sunny position away from the house.

Sub-shrubs

Wormwood	*Artemisia absinthium*
Southernwood	*Artemisia abrotanum*
Hyssop	*Hyssopus officinalis*
Lavender	*Lavandula angustifolia*
Rue	*Ruta graveolens*
Sage	*Salvia officinalis*
Germander	*Teucrium chamaedrys*

Herbaceous perennials

Cottage pinks	*Dianthus plumarius*
Orris-root, iris	*Iris germanica, I. florentina*
White horehound	*Marrubium vulgare*
Grape-hyacinth	*Muscari botryoides*
Catmint	*Nepeta cataria*
Wild marjoram	*Origanum vulgare*
Stonecrop	*Sedum reflexum*
Wild tulip	*Tulipa sylvestris*

In mild areas and as a pot plant

Myrtle	*Myrtus communis*
Rosemary	*Rosmarinus officinalis*
Thyme	*Thymus vulgaris*
Lemon scented thyme	*Thymus × citriodorus*

On walls and rooftops

Sun plant, Rose moss	*Portulaca grandiflora*
Houseleek	*Sempervivum tectorum*

Perennials for a sunny position

With a bit of care and forethought, the following old garden plants may be effectively combined with modern border perennials. The spaces between them should be planted with annual herbs and bedding plants.

Herbaceous perennials

(*particularly in the neighbourhood of trees and shrubs)

Chives	*Allium schoenoprasum*
Marsh-mallow	*Althaea officinalis*
Birthwort	*Aristolochia clematitis*
Costmary	*Chrysanthemum balsamita*
Feverfew	*Chrysanthemum parthenium*
Cut-leaf tansy	*Chrysanthemum tanacetum* 'Crispum'
Dittany	*Dictamnus albus*
Crown imperial	*Fritillaria imperialis*
Daylily	*Hemerocallis fulva* and *H. lilioasphodelum*
Dame's violet, Sweet rocket	*Hesperis matronalis**
Elecampane	*Inula helenium*
Plum-scented iris	*Iris graminea*
Orange lily	*Lilium bulbiferum*
Madonna lily	*Lilium candidum*
Candlestick lily	*Lilium × hollandicum*
Tiger lily	*Lilium lancifolium*
Maltese cross	*Lychnis chalcedonica*
Hollyhock mallow	*Malva alcea**
Lemon balm	*Melissa officinalis*
Spignel	*Meum athamanticum**

Peony	*Paeonia officinalis* cvs.
Lantern plant	*Physalis alkekengii* and *P. franchetii**
Auricula	*Primula × pubescens*
Madder	*Rubia tinctorium*
Salad Burnet	*Sanguisorba minor*
Winter savory	*Satureja montana*

Tender, tuberous-rooted perennials

| Dahlia | *Dahlia variabilis* |
| Gladiolus | *Gladiolus* hybrids |

Perennials for sun or bright shade in the vicinity of trees and shrubs

The characteristic trees and shrubs of a traditional rural herb garden were elders (mostly self-sown), soft fruit bushes and small trees such as quince, plum and morello cherry, together with medlar, mock orange, shrub roses (e.g. *Rosa centifolia*), lilac and the poisonous *Juniperus sabina*. Typical climbing plants would be honeysuckle and grapevine. The following somewhat shade-tolerant perennials grow perfectly well in open positions but are particularly effective in association with trees and shrubs.

Columbine	*Aquilegia vulgaris*
Lily-of-the-valley	*Convallaria majalis* 'Grandiflora'
Bleeding heart	*Dicentra spectabilis*
Alpine strawberry	*Fragaria vesca* var. *semperflorens*
Snowdrop	*Galanthus nivalis*
Sweet woodruff	*Galium odoratum*
Christmas rose	*Helleborus niger* and *H. viridis*
Hepatica, Liverleaf	*Hepatica nobilis*
Spring snowflake	*Leucojum vernum*
Turk's cap lily	*Lilium martagon*
Dame's violet, Sweet rocket	*Hesperis matronalis*
Garden primulas	*Primula elatior* and *P. veris*
Lungwort	*Pulmonaria officinalis*
Valerian	*Valeriana officinalis*
Periwinkle	*Vinca minor* and *V. major*
Sweet violet	*Viola odorata*

Perennial kitchen herbs for damp soil

(Particularly between border perennials)

Tarragon	*Artemisia dracunculus*
Peppermint	*Mentha × piperita*
Penny royal	*Mentha pulegium*
Apple-mint	*Mentha × rotundifolia*
Spearmint	*Mentha spicata* 'Crispen'
Sorrel	*Rumex acetosa* var. *hortensis*

5.7.2.   Annuals and biennials

The following are distinctive and formerly very popular annual and biennial garden plants. Those that regularly seed themselves are marked with an asterisk.

Biennials

Hollyhock	*Alcea rosea*
*Fennel	*Foeniculum vulgare*
Angelica	*Angelica archangelica*
Yellow rocket	*Barbarea vulgaris*
*Canterbury bells	*Campanula medium* (seeds itself in mild areas)
Wallflower	*Cheiranthus cheiri*
*Treacle mustard	*Erysimum × allionii* (seeds itself in mild areas)
*Spurge	*Euphorbia lathyris* and *E. marginata*
Houndstongue	*Cynoglossum vulgare*
Sweet William	*Dianthus barbatus*
*Honesty	*Lunaria annua* (also in bright shade)
*Forget-me-not	*Myosotis sylvatica* cvs (also in bright shade)
*Clary	*Salvia sclarea* (seeds itself in mild areas)

Annual flowers

*Snapdragon	*Antirrhinum majus*
*Red-leafed orache	*Atriplex hortensis* 'Rubra'
*Candytuft	*Iberis umbellata* and *I. amara*
Garden balsam, Touch-me-not	*Impatiens balsamina*
*Marigold, Calendula	*Calendula officinalis*
China aster	*Callistephus sinensis*
*Red goosefoot	*Chenopodium purpurascens*
Sunflower	*Helianthus annuus*
Everlasting, Strawflower	*Helichrysum bracteatum*
Sweet pea	*Lathyrus odoratus*
*Love-in-a mist	*Nigella damascena*
*Mallow	*Malva verticillata* and *M. mauritiana*
Stock	*Matthiola incana* var. *annua*
*Opium poppy, Christmas poppy	*Papaver somniferum*
Mignonette	*Reseda lutea*
African marigold	*Tagetes*
*Nasturtium	*Tropaeolum majus*
Zinnia	*Zinnia*

Annual kitchen herbs

*Dill	*Anethum graveolens*
*Chervil	*Anthriscus cerefolium*
*Borage	*Borago officinalis*
Coriander	*Coriandrum sativum*
Roquette	*Eruca sativa*
Garden cress	*Lepidium sativum*
Basil	*Ocimum basilicum*
Parsley	*Petroselinum sativum*
Anise	*Pimpinella anisum*
*Winter savory	*Satureja hortensis*
Fenugreek	*Trigonella foenum-graecum*
Bread-clover	*Trigonella coerulea*

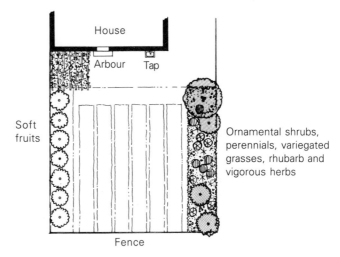

Simple division into beds for vegetables, flowers and herbs

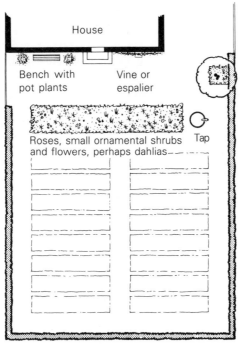

Beds for vegetables, flowers and herbs.

5.7.3. Variegated grasses

Invasive species

Glyceria maxima 'Variegata'	List 3.5.4
Phalaris arundinacea 'Picta'	List 3.5.4; formerly very popular for flower arrange-ments; typical for the outer beds of traditional herb gardens (see list 5.7.1). 'Tricolor', similar.

Clump-forming species

It is advisable to renew the following plants every few years by dividing them in spring. Cut off all seed heads before they are ripe!

Alopecurus pratensis 'Variegatus'	0.30/0.70	V–VI, vigorous; yellowish green striped leaves; for moist to damp soils; very short rhizomes.
Arrhenatherum elatius ssp. *bulbosum* 'Variegatum'	0.25/0.60	VI–VII, glassy root tubers; white-banded leaves; very persistent on moist (to dry) soils; cut back at flowering time or becomes unsightly in summer.
Dactylis glomerata 'Variegata'	0.25/0.60	V–VI, clump-forming; striking, white-banded leaves, not very persistent; rare in the trade.
Holcus lanatus 'Albo-Variegatus'	0.25/0.50	V–VI, variegated, clump-forming grass with soft and densely hairy leaves; rare in the trade. *H. mollis* 'Variegata': see list 2.1.8.

5.7.4. Native and naturalised medicinal plants

Not all medicinal plants need a well-tended bed in order to flourish. Some of them (e.g. *Verbena officinalis*, *Malva sylvestris*, *M. neglecta*) can still be found as garden escapes in places where they were once cultivated. These naturalised plants also deserve our appreciation and protection. Those marked with an asterisk have become noxious weeds in some parts of North America.

*Mugwort	*Artemisia vulgaris*
*Black horehound	*Ballota nigra*
Good King Henry	*Chenopodium bonus-henricus*
Tansy	*Chrysanthemum vulgare*
*Chicory	*Cichorium intybus*
Mountain cranesbill	*Geranium pyrenaicum*
Motherwort	*Leonurus cardiaca*
Sweet cicely	*Myrrhis odorata*
Wild parsnip	*Pastinaca sativa*
Danewort, Dwarf elder	*Sambucus ebulus*
*Soapweed	*Saponaria officinalis*
Comfrey	*Symphytum officinale* and *S. asperum*

Tall (1.00–2.00), annual or short-lived, self-seeding species

Some mallows (e.g. *Malva mauritiana*), ornamental thistles (*Onopordon acanthium*, *Silybum marianum*) and the Himalayan touch-me-not (*Impatiens glandulifera*) will survive better on a piece of gravelly or stony wasteland than in a garden. Here they can regularly seed themselves without ever becoming troublesome.

The ruderal flora formerly associated with nitrate-rich wasteland in the neighbourhood of houses and farm buildings has almost disappeared from many rural areas. These specialised plant communities, often dominated by imposing burdocks and feathery, white-flowered umbellifers such as cow parsley and chervil, are a part of our heritage. They provide the habitat for a variety of wild creatures and are well worth encouraging by sowing seed in appropriate places.

6 Water's edge and marsh

Water and wetland areas exert a great attraction on a multitude of different creatures, including mankind. The planting of such areas may be designed to create structure and optical interest, but should also take account of more functional requirements, perhaps providing opportunities for the observation and feeding of various pond inhabitants. In an intensively used public park, ducks and other water-birds usually make it impossible to plant any but the most robust of perennials. In a garden, on the other hand, the various different types of water feature (see pp. 65 ff.) provide planting positions for an enormous range of beautiful and sometimes rare species. The choice of plants depends on the situation. The surroundings of an artificial pond may provide sites for moisture-loving perennials from a variety of garden habitats. Lush, broad-leaved species and moisture-loving grasses are particularly appropriate, often occuring naturally in the transitional vegetation between reedswamps and water-meadows or damp woodland.

It is remarkable how many native perennials are suitable for planting in a garden pond or stream, especially if these are natural rather than formal in design. The majority of water plants are vigorous colonizers which spread quickly and soon become a threat to weak-growing neighbours. If this uncontrolled development cannot be tolerated, then plants must be regularly cut out and removed, particularly where it is desired to maintain a clear expanse of water. Species that are not invasive have been listed separately. Many of them grow wild in marsh or moorland habitats rather than open water (see lists 6.3, 6.4.2 and 6.4.3).

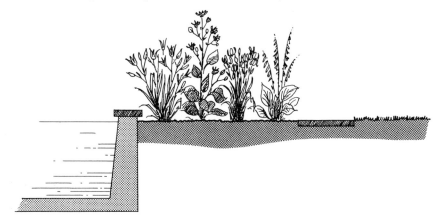

Water's edge and marsh: pond isolated from the surrounding soil.

6.1. Perennials for planting in the vicinity of artificial ponds without wet margins

The following are mostly tall, decorative perennials, suitable for planting on the rather dry margins of a concrete pond or other isolated water basin. Appropriate companions may be found in the lists to which these perennials are primarily assigned. Among the woody species, bamboos are particularly suitable for this sort of situation. The perennials from list 2.3.1, particularly the candelabra primulas, also have a strong affinity with water.

410

Plants for sun

Cortaderia selloana	List 3.6.2
Eupatorium spp.	Lists 3.5.4, 3.6.1, 5.3.5
Helianthus salicifolius and relatives	List 3.6.1
Hemerocallis spp. and cvs.	List 5.2.1
Iris spuria and relatives	List 5.3.5
Miscanthus spp.	List 3.6.1

Plants for bright shade and shade

Astilbe davidii and relatives	List 1.3.1
Hosta spp. and cvs.	List 1.1.3
Ligularia spp.	List 2.2.4
Peltiphyllum peltatum	List 1.3.1
Rodgersia spp.	List 1.3.1

6.2. Perennials for wet pond margins and shallow water

These plants mostly occur naturally in reedswamp and tall sedge communities on the shallow, nutrient-rich margins of lakes and ponds. The species from list 6.2.1 should only be used after careful consideration, as they are inclined to spread vigorously, suppressing any weaker neighbours and rapidly filling the whole of a small pond. Those from list 6.2.2 are not quite so invasive (though some may seed themselves prolifically), and therefore pose fewer problems for the maintenance of an open expanse of water and a species-rich planting.

6.2.1. Vigorous and invasive species for wet soil and shallow water

Tall, vigorous sedges, such as *Carex gracilis, C. riparia, C. elata* and *C. acutiformis* are available from specialised nurseries supplying plants for large-scale landscaping projects. Like the following species, they should only be used with caution in a small pond, perhaps planted in containers to restrict their spread.

Sweet flag *Acorus calamus* S & E Asia	0.60–1.00	V–VI, broad, swordlike, pointed, linear leaves; unspectacular, club-shaped inflorescences; strongly aromatic rhizomes. 'Variegatus', green and white leaves; less invasive.
Carex elata (*C. reticulosa*) 'Aurea'	030–1.00	IV–V, narrow, upright-growing leaves with yellow margins, appearing early in the year; clump-forming habit; thrives in marshy conditions or shallow water; rare in the trade.

Mare's-tail *Hippuris vulgaris* Eur., W Asia, N Am.	0.30	VII–VIII, dark green, linear leaves in whorls on unbranched shoots that grow up out of the water; insignificant, axillary inflorescences; spreads quickly by means of far-reaching rhizomes; best confined to a container in a small pond.
Common reed *Phragmites australis* (*P. communis*) Cosmopol.	1.00–4.00	VII–IX, leaf-bases with silvery-white tufts of hair; strongly spreading rhizomes; good for consolidating banks. 'Pseudodonax' (5.00–8.00 (up to 12.00)), rarely available in the trade. 'Striatopictus' (1.20–1.50), leaves striped yellowish-green; not so invasive.
Great spearwort *Ranunculus lingua* Eur., W Asia	0.70/1.00	VI–VII, large buttercup flowers; erect, grey-green, lingulate leaves. 'Grandiflora', large-flowered selection.
Great water dock *Rumex hydrolapathum* Eur., C & S Russ.	up to 2.00	VII–VIII, decorative plant with basal leaves up to 1 m long; reddish-green axillary spikes of flowers on powerful stems.
Bulrush *Scirpus lacustris* (*Schoenoplectus lacustris*) Eur., Asia	up to 2.50	VI–VII, stiff, glabrous, glossy, dark green, cylindrical stems with terminal clusters of brownish inflorescences; grows in up to 3 m of water. 'Albescens', whitish-green stems. *Scirpus tabernaemontani* (0.50–1.50), grey-green, cylindrical stems; compact heads of inflorescences; see list 6.2.2.
Bur-reed *Sparganium erectum* (*S. ramosum*) Eur., Asia, Med.	up to 2.00/0.50	VII–VIII, starry seed heads; insignificant flowers; long, upright leaves up to 3 cm across, triangular in section; may also grow with ribbon-like leaves in running water.
Reedmace, Cattail *Typha latifolia* Cosmopol.	up to 2.00	VI–VII, broad, blue-green leaves; blackish brown, club-like inflorescences. *T. angustifolia* (to 2.00), narrow, grass-green leaves; slender, rust-brown inflorescences. Further species: see list 6.2.2.

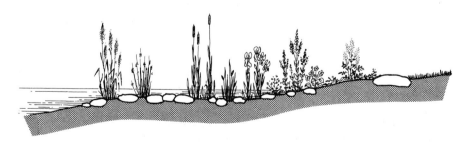

Water's edge and marsh: planting positions in shallow water and on the wet pond margin.

6.2.2. Non-invasive perennials for wet soil and shallow water

The following species have predominantly aerial leaves and flowers. They all flourish particularly well on the wet margins of a pond or in shallow water (up to 20 cm), though a few will also grow deeper. The plants spread strongly in suitable conditions, and in a small pond they may have to be divided and replanted after a few years.

Water plantain *Alisma plantago-aqua-* *tica* Eur., Asia, N & E Afr., N Am.	0.40/1.00 white	VII–VIII, flowers in large, graceful panicles; long-stemmed, spoon-like leaves. *A. gramineum* (0.80), long-stemmed, grass-like leaves. *A. lanceolatum* (0.60), leaves pointed at both ends. *A. subcordatum* (*A. parviflorum*) (0.60), almost round, acuminate leaves; small flowers; emerges late.
Flowering rush *Butomus umbellatus* Eur., Asia, N Afr.	0.50–1.00 pink	VII, narrow, rush-like leaves; flowers in terminal umbels on rigid stems; white- and red-flowered forms are also available.
Carex pseudocyperus Eur., Sib., Cauc., Jap., N Afr., N Am.	0.80	VI, stout, catkin-like inflorescences hanging on long, thin pedicels; broad, yellowish-green leaves on three-angled stems; for the water's edge.
Japanese water iris *Iris laevigata* Jap., Korea, China	0.80 blue	VII–VIII, narrow, erect standards; falls with a central yellow stripe; smooth leaves without a mid-rib; needs wet soil throughout the year; hardy, but not a good competitor; calcifuge. 'Alba', white. 'Albo Purpurea', white; red blotches on the falls. 'Colchesteri', marine-blue, segments white-edged. 'Monstrosa', deep blue with a white centre. 'Rose Queen', pink. 'Semperflorens', cobalt-blue. 'Snowdrift', double white flowers. 'Variegata', light blue; leaves striped green and white.
Yellow flag *Iris pseudacorus* Eur., W Sib., Cauc., Nr East, N Afr.	1.00/0.80 yellow	VI–VII, strong, broadly pointed, sword-like leaves; also grows in moist to dryish soil. 'Variegatus', young leaves striped yellowish. 'Bastardii', lemon yellow. 'Beuron', pale yellow. 'Golden Queen', 'Ilgengold', golden yellow.
Iris versicolor		List 3.5.2
Cut grass *Leersia oryzoides* N Am., S Am., Eur., Asia	0.50–1.00	VIII–X, rough, narrow, yellowish-green leaves; open, sinuous, branching panicles, which fail to emerge from the leaf-sheaths in f. *inclusa*; related to cultivated rice (*Oryza sativa*); somewhat tender; often annual.
Lysimachia thyrsiflora C Eur., Asia, N Am.	0.80 yellow	V–VI, opposite, lanceolate leaves arranged at right angles up the stiffly erect stems; flowers in squat axillary racemes; spreading roots; for the water's edge.
Arrow-head *Sagittaria sagittifolia* Eur., W Asia	0.60/0.60 white, with a reddish patch	VI–VII, ornamental leaves, shaped like an arrow-head; flowers in whorls of three on long, upright racemes; spreading roots. 'Flore Pleno', double flowers.

'Leucopetala', pure white.

S. graminea (0.30), N Am., narrow, grass-like leaves; tender.

S. latifolia (0.60), N Am., has broad and narrow leaves. Nearly 20 further North American species are sometimes grown. The walnut-sized tubers of all *Sagittaria* spp. are readily eaten by ducks.

Scirpus taber-naemontani 'Zebrinus' Eur., Asia	1.50	VI–VII, pretty, green, rush-like stems, banded whitish-yellow but often turning green with age; for shallow water; see list 6.2.1.
Dwarf reedmace *Typha minima* SE & C Eur., Cauc., W & C asia, N China	0.60	V–VI, short, thick, cylindrical to ovoid inflorescences, breaking up at the end of July; very narrow leaves; for water up to 20 cm. *T. gracilis* (0.60), VIII–IX, similar but flowers later; separate clusters of male and female flowers.
Typha shuttleworthii Alps, N It to Carp.	1.00	VI–VIII, similar to the above, but smaller and daintier; narrow leaves; greyish inflorescences, somewhat shorter and narrower than those of *T. augustifolia*. *T. laxmannii* (*T. stenophylla*) (1.60), leaves almost hemispherical in section; brown, ovoid inflorescences; separate clusters of male and female flowers.
Manchurian rice *Zizania latifolia* Manch.	1.00–1.50	VI–X, broad, swordlike, slightly overhanging leaves; attractive autumn colour.

6.2.3.   Tender species for damp or wet soil, and very shallow water

The following species benefit from a protective covering of leaves in winter. Some may overwinter better in a bright, frost-free cellar or glasshouse.

Acorus gramineus E Asia	0.20 yellowish-green	VI–VII, dark green, grassy foliage; for damp soil. 'Argenteostriatus', fan-like rosettes of white-variegated leaves; for the enthusiast. 'Pusillus' (0.10), fan-like rosettes of leaves. 'Variegatus', cream-variegated leaves.
Canna flaccida SE USA	0.40/1.80 sulphur-yellow	VII–IX, broad, long, blue-green leaves; rhizomes must be packed in fine sand and overwintered in frost-free conditions; for damp soil.
Galingale *Cyperus longus* C Eur, Med., Afr. to Ind.	1.30 rust-brown	VII–IX, clumps of gracefully overarching, glossy, dark green basal leaves; narrow stem-leaves in whorls; loose, brownish flower clusters; hardy, but benefits from protection in winter.
Swamp rose-mallow *Hibiscus moscheutos* SE USA	1.00–1.30 pink	VII–IX, very large, mallow-like flowers; serrate, ovate to ovate–lanceolate leaves, softly hairy beneath; thrives in warm, mild regions; for very damp soils that dry out in summer; needs a covering of leaves in winter. 'Chatelaine' (1.00), red-purple.

'Dixie Belle' (0.60), pinkish red.
'Southern Belle', various colours from red to white.

Cardinal flower *Lobelia cardinalis* N Am.	0.80 bright red	VII–IX, upright stems with flowers in long, one-sided racemes; green, pointed, elongate to ovate leaves; for damp soils; tender where wet winters follow cool, damp summers, but tolerates extreme cold in its native habitat.
Houttuynia cordata E Asia	0.30–0.90 white	VIII, small flowers in short, cylindrical spikes on branching stems; orange-scented leaves, reddish beneath, almost 10 cm long and broad; invasive runners and rhizomes; for the enthusiast. 'Chameleon' ('Variegata'), leaves variegated yellow, green, bronze and red. 'Flore Pleno', cone-shaped double flowers.
Mimulus ringens Mts of E & C N Am.	0.60–0.80 blue-violet	VI–VII, sturdy, branching plants with large flowers and serrate, elongate leaves; thrives in shallow water; intolerant of summer heat.
Arrow arum, Tuckahoe *Peltandra virginica* S USA	up to 1.00 green	V–VI, spherical, green seed heads; long-stemmed, arrow-shaped leaves; needs a covering of leaves in winter; hardy to zone 6B.
Pickerel weed *Pontederia cordata* N Am.	0.70/1.20 blue	VI–VIII, abundant spikes of flowers over glossy, green, long-stemmed, ovate–cordate leaves; exposed plants need a covering of leaves in winter. *P. lanceolata* (0.90), pale blue; long-stemmed, lanceolate leaves; young plants should not be set out under water.
Chinese lizard's tail, Chinese water dragon *Saururus chinensis* (*S. loureirii*) N China to Jap., Korea, Phil.	0.20/0.40 whitish- yellow	VII–VIII, flowers in erect, cylindrical racemes, which bend down as flowering progresses; broad, heart-shaped leaves with a long drawn-out tip; for very shallow water; needs a covering of leaves in winter. *S. cernuus*, American lizard's tail, (0.20/0.80), VII–VIII, creamy white; more vigorous than the foregoing; hardy when submerged.

6.3. Perennials for mostly sunny, wet or marshy sites (not only at the edge of a pond)

The following perennials grow wild not only at the edge of water but also in damp or wet, often marshy places, sometimes also in semi-shade. In gardens, these sorts of conditions are also enjoyed by various meadow plants (lists 3.5.1, 3.5.4 and 2.2.4).

Some of these species may also be effective used sparingly in an intensively maintained water garden, combined with the moisture-loving perennials for woodland edge conditions from list 2.3.1.

* = These species often do not combine well with the rest.

Asclepias incarnata		List 3.5.2
Marsh marigold *Caltha palustris* Eur., Asia, N Am.	0.30 golden-yellow	IV–V, glossy green, rounded, kidney-shaped leaves. 'Multiplex', double flowers. 'Alba' (to 0.20), III–IV, white; associates better with

potential neighbours such as *Primula rosea*.
Rare in the trade:
C. polypetala (0.40), III–IV, large, yellow, bowl-shaped flowers; glossy, dark green leaves; sprawling habit.
C. leptosepala (0.20), white flowers; sprawling habit.
C. tyermannii (0.20), IV–VI, pale yellow.

Chrysanthemum serotinum		List 3.5.4
Cotula coronopifolia Med.	0.15 yellow	VI–VIII, small, hemispherical heads of flowers; somewhat succulent, evenly incised, lanceolate leaves; short-lived; for rich, clayey, damp or wet soils in mild areas.
*Deschampsia cespitosa		List 1.1.4
Epipactis gigantea W USA, Mex.	0.60–0.90 greenish-yellow, with purple veins	VII–VIII, flowers in a loose raceme; very robust and undemanding; for damp or wet (but not marshy) soils.
Euphorbia palustris Eur., Sib., Altai	1.00 deep yellow	V–VI, forms broad clumps of willow-like, lanceolate leaves; good as an isolated specimen.
Gratiola officinalis Eur., N & W Asia	0.30 pale yellow and white	VI–VII, trumpet-shaped axillary flowers; lanceolate leaves; creeping rootstock; poisonous.
Glyceria maxima 'Variegata'		List 3.5.4
Iris pseudacorus		List 6.2.2
*Soft rush Juncus effusus Almost cosmopol.	0.70	VI–VIII, forms powerful clumps of glossy, grass-green, rounded, leafless stems; loose, brown inflorescence located on the upper third of the stem; a weed of pastureland; may look out of place on the water's edge. 'Spiralis', green, spirally twisted stems. *J. conglomeratus*, grey-green stems; congested inflorescences. *J. inflexus* (*J. glaucus*) (0.80), thin, hard, grooved, blue-green stems; forms evergreen clumps.
Juncus ensifolius W N Am.	0.25–0.40	Congested, dark brown to almost black inflorescences on leafy stems; clump-forming habit; thrives in shallow water; rare in the trade.
Summer snowflake *Leucojum aestivum* C & S Eur., SW Asia, Cauc.	0.40 white	V–VI, resembles a large snowdrop with a branching inflorescence; spreads well on a damp site; thrives at the water's edge or in shallow water. 'Gravetye Giant', robust and large flowered selection.
Leucojum vernum		List 2.4.2
Peppermint *Mentha × piperita*	0.60 pink	VIII–IX, upright, reddish, glabrous stems with slender, spike-like inflorescences; serrate, petiolate,

(*M. aquatica* × *M. spicata*)		elongate–lanceolate leaves; invasive rhizomes; various cultivars available for tea enthusiasts.
Monkey flower *Mimulus luteus* Chile	0.40 yellow	V–VIII, produces a long succession of large, colourful flowers; fresh green, opposite, ovate–cordate leaves; short-lived but seeds itself prolifically; many annual forms and hybrids, such as: *M.* × *tigrinus* 'Grandiflorus', red and yellow mottled. 'Orange Glut' (0.20), orange-red.
Water forget-me-not *Myosotis palustris* (*M. scorpioides*) Eur., Sib.	0.30 blue	V–X, long and free-flowering; decumbent, rooting stems with fresh green leaves; flowers again well if cut back early enough. 'Thüringen', selection valuable for cutting.
*Creeping buttercup *Ranunculus repens* 'Plenus' Eur., Asia, N Afr.	0.20 yellow	V, abundant double flowers; dark green leaves; spreads invasively by means of runners; to be used with caution.
*Wood club-rush *Scirpus sylvaticus* Eur., Cauc., Sib.	0.60	V–VI, spikelets in short-stemmed clusters; decorative, broad, grooved, lush green, overarching leaves; spreading rhizomes; very aggressive; to be used with caution.
Marsh sow-thistle *Sonchus palustris* Eur., Cauc.	2.00–2.50 yellow	VIII, attractive habit; stiff, upright stems with panicles of abundant small, composite flowers; lanceolate leaves with pointed auricles; for large-scale plantings; rare in the trade.
Thelypteris palustris		List 1.2.4

On the edge of a thicket

Bittersweet, Woody nightshade *Solanum dulcamara* Eur., Asia, N Afr.	1.50–2.00 violet	VI–VII, climbing woody species; small flowers; scarlet, ovoid fruits; poisonous.

Shade and semi-shade along a woodland stream

Carex pendula	List 1.1.4
Chrysosplenium alter-nifolium	List 4.5.3
Chrysosplenium oppo-sitifolium	List 4.5.3
Matteuccia stru-thiopteris	List 1.2.4

Sun and bright shade on a streamside

Ranunculus acon-itifolius	List 2.3.1

6.4.   Perennials for special conditions

6.4.1.   Sites that are wet in spring and early summer but dry in winter

Iris kaempferi **(0.80–1.00), VI–VII, pink, blue, violet.**

Japanese iris (*Iris kaempferi*) thrive in wet soil or even shallow water during spring and early summer, but cannot tolerate constant flooding, unlike the closely related *I. laevigata* (list 6.2.2), which needs damp or wet conditions even in winter. The plants flower prolifically in June and July, retaining their long, green leaves (with a dark mid-rib) until the autumn. Their special maintenance is discussed on page 66.

Many colour forms of *Iris kaempferi* have long been grown in Japanese gardens. The species differs from bearded iris in possessing large, flattened flowers with long-lasting and often richly patterned, horizontal falls which may also be wavy or ruffled. The standards are either weakly developed or spread out horizontally over the falls.

The plants thrive in any loamy garden soil that does not contain too much lime. They do not have thick rhizomes but a system of fine roots from a slender rootstock. Old specimens divide well, but nurseries mostly offer seedlings rather than clones. New selections are regularly imported from Japan, so the assortment is in a constant state of flux, and cultivars are sometimes offered under a variety of different names. The following cultivars are currently available in the European trade.

'Alba' white
'Aoigata', violet-red
'Benibotan', dark purple-pink
'Blaue Stunde', blue-lilac; double
'Emotion', lilac; double
'Hakubotan', pure white
'Innocence', white
'Kokuryuden'. purple-red
'Moonlight Waves', yellow

'Nagasaki', lilac pink
'Pink Frost', soft pink
'Taeheiraku', lavender
'Toryumon', pink and white
'Variegata', white-variegated leaves
'Windjammer', lilac, steel blue centre
'Yedo Kagami', violet; large flowers
'Higo', huge flowers in various colours

Breeders in the USA Pacific Northwest have produced many additional cultivars, but these grow less vigorously in inland regions.

6.4.2.   Variably damp or wet, predominantly moory conditions

By using peat and providing sufficient water (see p. 420), the keen gardener may grow a whole variety of rarely obtainable perennial species from wet, moory meadows and bogs, on sites that must in no way be connected with open water.

Most of the following species are available from specialist nurseries. The decimation of wild populations and removal of protected native plants should be absolute taboo for the true garden lover. See also lists 4.6.2 and 4.6.4.

Native European species

Yellow sedge *Carex flava* Eur., N Am.	0.30/0.50	VI–VIII, yellowish female spikelets; narrow, light green leaves. *C. flacca*, see list 3.2.2.
Spike-rush *Eleocharis palustris* Almost cosmopol.	up to 0.50	V–VIII, rounded, rush-like stems with a small brown inflorescence at the tip; very invasive rhizomes.

Marsh helleborine *Epipactis palustris* Eur., W Asia	0.30/0.50 white and reddish	VI–VIII, elongate–lanceolate leaves; rare in the trade.
Cotton grass *Eriophorum angusti-* *folium* Circumpol.	0.50	IV–V, insignificant flowers followed by drooping, silvery, cottony seed heads; narrow leaves; rough stems; invasive. *E. latifolium* (0.50), broad, flat leaves; rough stems; non-invasive; from base-rich moorland.
Spotted orchid *Dactylorhiza maculata* (*Orchis maculata*) Eur., Asia	0.20/0.50 pale pink	VI–VII, inflorescence pyramidal at first; bracts hardly as long as the flowers; leaves mostly spotted; flowers sometimes in the fourth year after seeding.
Dianthus superbus Eur., Sib., Jap.	0.40 pale lilac	VII–IX, large, finely cut flowers; forms a loose turf of fine, grass-green leaves; not very long-lived; rare in the trade.
Fritillaria meleagris		List 2.4.2. For wet but not stagnant, nutrient-rich, limy or lime-free soils.
Gentiana asclepiadea		List 4.6.1. For damp, basic soils.
Gentiana pneumonanthe Eur., W Asia, Cauc.	0.10/0.40 deep blue	VII–IX, erect stems with large, funnel-shaped flowers; for damp to wet, acid soils.
Gladiolus palustris C & E Eur., N Balk., N It.	0.50 purple-red	VI–VII, narrow, pointed leaves; 3–6 flowers per stem; ovoid corms; rare in the trade; easy to grow from fresh seed.
Iris sibirica		List 3.5.2. For base-rich soils.
Purple moor-grass *Molina caerulea* Eur. to W Sib., Asia Minor, Cauc., Med.	0.50/1.00	VIII–IX, long stems without nodes; bluish-green leaves which turn bright red-brown in autumn; also thrives on moist, humus-rich soils. 'Moorhexe', shorter, with long, stiff stems. 'Variegata', green and white leaf-blades. 'Strahlenquelle' (1.20), short tufts of foliage; stiff flowering stems. 'Winterfeuer', short; red-brown autumn colour.
Grass of Parnassus *Parnassia palustris* Circumpol.	0.20 white	VII–VIII, flowers on rigid stems over entire, heart-shaped basal leaves; rarely available in the trade.
Primula farinosa N Euras., Pyren., Alps, Carp., Mts of W, C & E Asia	0.02/0.15 pink	V–VI, small, very dainty flowers in loose umbels; leaves mealy beneath; rare in the trade. *P. frondosa*, similar but more vigorous; see list 4.5.1.
Trollius europaeus		Lists 3.5.1 & 4.6.4

Other species

Bog arum, Western skunk-cabbage *Lysichiton americanum* W, N Am.	1.00/0.60 yellow	IV–V, tropical-looking plant; inflorescences with large yellow spathes, followed by huge leaves; for rich soils and boggy conditions. *L. camtschatcensis*, V–VI, similar but with white spathes; needs a little protection in winter.
Onoclea sensibilis		List 12.2.4. Tolerates full sun when planted in shallow water.
Primula rosea		List 4.6.4

6.4.3.   Acidic, moory, damp or wet conditions

The following moorland species may be grown in small depressions on a rock garden, using a waterproof pond-liner and a relatively thin layer of peat. It may sometimes be possible to combine them with plants for slightly drier conditions (list 4.6.2) or with *Calluna vulgaris* and *Molinia caerulea* growing at the edge of the depression.

Sundew *Drosera rotundifolia* Circumpol.	0.02/0.10 white	VII, carnivorous plant with sticky, round leaves. *D. anglica*, upright, elongate, wedge-shaped leaves; for moderately acid soils.
Erica tetralix		List 4.6.2
Cotton grass *Eriophorum vaginatum* Circumpol.	up to 0.40 white	IV, clump-forming species with dull green, arching leaves; inflorescences with inflated sheaths on upright stems; cotton-wool-like seed heads appearing in June. Selection: 'Heidelicht'. *E. scheuchzeri* (0.30), shorter, and with spreading rhizomes; spherical, silvery-white seed heads.
White beak-rush *Rhynchospora alba* Eur., Sib.	up to 0.30 white	VI–VIII, dainty species with short rhizomes; white flowers clustered among the bracts; grows in wet flushes; rare in the trade.
Trichophorum alpinum (*Eriophorum alpinum*) Circumpol.	0.10–0.20	V, tiny spikes of flowers with silvery hairs; grows in wet flushes; for the enthusiast.
Trichophorum cespitosum (*Scirpus cespitosus*) Circumpol.	0.05–0.20	V–VI, hairless inflorescences; forms a turf in wet flushes; rare in the trade.

6.5.   Plants for water-filled depressions and shallow ponds

The following perennials, for slightly acid, peaty soils in ditches or at the water's edge, form a transition to the plants for open water. They may sometimes be combined with species from list 6.4.3.

Calla palustris Circumpol.	0.15/0.20 white	V–VI, dark green, heart-shaped leaves; arum flowers; spathes with snow white interior; bright red berries in September; thrives in very shallow water in the shade of alders; not for limy, nutrient-rich water.

Marsh cinquefoil *Potentilla palustris* (*Comarum palustre*) Circumpol.	0.40 brown–red	V–VI, typical cinquefoil leaves; erect inflorescences; for moderately acidic, wet, moory soils.
Bogbean *Menyanthes trifoliata* Circumpol.	0.15.15/0.30 whitish	V–VI, large, dark green, tripartite leaves; fringed and ciliate flowers; rhizomatous; grows in up to 50 cm water.
Nuphar pumila Needs at least 50 cm water.		List 7.1.2
Nymphaea candida Needs at least 1 m water.		List 7.1.1
Sparganium minimum Circumpol.	up to 0.30	VI–VIII, sprawling (or floating) leaves and stems; insignificant head of flowers; grows in shallow ponds; enthusiast's plant; rare in the trade.

Moist to damp soils at the edge of a depression:

Osmunda regalis   List 1.2.4
For sun and bright shade on acid, peaty, humus-rich, sandy soils; needs a lot of space; also thrives at the edge of flowing water.

7 Water

Aquatic perennials in a small garden pond often enjoy a precarious existence and therefore require some maintenance. Unlike the large ponds and lakes of a public park, a garden pond generally provides little space for expansion. The small area of open water must be regularly freed from invading marginal plants and vigorous aquatics to avoid its gradual conversion into marsh. Care should be taken that the areas of planted and open water remain in balanced proportion.

Submerged and floating perennials are characteristic for this garden habitat. Particularly in a new pond, these are often accompanied by troublesome algae, which multiply in any water exposed to warmth and light, and may sometimes indicate an excessive accumulation of nutrients (eutrophication). Difficulties may be caused by the dark green thread-like algae that appear periodically, turning light green or yellowish on the water surface. The easiest way to deal with them is simply to fish them out of the water, being careful not to disturb other plants. Excessive algal growth may be largely avoided by filling the pond with an uncultivated clay soil, rather than garden or farmland soil. Addition of peat and fallen leaves may also be effective, while some authorities recommend the use of water-fleas or species of *Chara* and *Nitella* (see list 7.3), though these only thrive in clean, well-oxygenated water. A little patience is required until the water in a new pond finally clears and the pH reaches its ideal value of 5.3 to 5.8.

7.1. Perennials with floating leaves for still water

7.1.1. Waterlilies (*Nymphaea* species and hybrids)

Waterlilies have attractive, floating leaves and large flowers that close at night. They are plants for still water, growing wild in ponds and the sheltered bays of larger lakes. Although they sometimes also occur in gently flowing water, the plants resent disturbance and do not tolerate the turbulence caused by a fountain. Still, clean water and sufficient space are essential requirements. Waterlilies thrive in a warm, sunny position with rich, silty soil at their roots. The European *Nymphaea alba* occurs in water up to 3 m deep but grows best in a depth of 1.00–1.50 m. Plants still flourish in only 40 cm but tend to grow up out of the water. Apart from a few exceptions (see p. 423), the hybrids require a depth of 0.40–0.80 m.

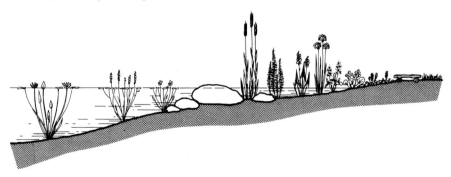

Water: shallow-water zone with transition to wet marginal zone.

Waterlily rhizomes are not very resistant to frost. Plants are safe in ponds that do not freeze right to the bottom, but in ponds that are emptied in winter, the rhizomes should be covered with 30 cm of fallen leaves. Yellow- and coppery-flowered waterlilies are more tender than their white-flowered relatives. The roots of waterlilies are very oxygen-hungry and should therefore be set in broad, shallow, well perforated containers if they cannot be planted directly into the pond substrate (see also p. 70). Plants that have ceased to flower abundantly should be taken up in spring and divided. Small divisions with healthy shoots grow on quickly in warm (never ice-cold), shallow water, even if they have few roots. Very thick, old rhizomes tend to rot easily and should therefore be treated with caution.

Garden hybrids are derived from the most part from the following hardy species, which, apart from *Nymphaea alba*, are seldom available in the trade.

Species

White waterlily *Nymphaea alba* Eur., Asia, N Afr.	to 3.00 (better 1.00– 1.50) white	V–VIII, fragrant, wide-open flowers; petals as long as or longer than the sepals; leathery, ovate leaves; for fertile, humus-rich, silty soil. *N.a.* var. *rubra*, red; occurs naturally (e.g. in Lake Fagertän, Sweden).
Nymphaea candida N, C & E Eur., Sib., N Spain	to 1.00 (2.00) white	VI–VIII, smaller, half-closed flowers; petals shorter than the sepals; for moory, silty soils; grows well in cold water; rare in the trade.
Nymphaea odorata E N Am., Mex.	to 0.40 white	VI–X, sweetly scented, starry flowers standing 6–10 cm over the water surface; rounded, glossy green leaves.
Nymphaea pygmaea (*N. tetragona*) NE Eur., N Asia, Jap., China, N Am.	to 0.15 white	VI–X, small, scented flowers; rounded leaves, red beneath.
Nymphaea tuberosa N Am	to 2.00 white	VI–VIII, massive flowers standing above the water surface; tuberous rhizomes; rounded, leathery leaves with wavy margins.

Selections and hybrids

20–40 cm depth of water

Dwarf varieties (0.10–0.30 cm) are marked with an asterisk. A good covering of leaves is necessary in winter.

White

*N. pygmaea 'Alba' (*N. tetragona* 'Alba'), the daintiest waterlily, with flowers only 2 cm across, produced until late in autumn; somewhat elongate leaves (5–10 cm); the only selection that comes well from seed; 10 cm is a good planting depth.

Pink

'Laydekeri Liliacea', lilac-pink; turning from carmine to almost pure pink as the flowers open and fade.
'Lusitania', pale pink; reddish leaves; similar to *N. tuberosa* 'Rosea'.
N. odorata 'W. B. Shaw', pale pink; scented; leaves almost completely circular.

*'Pink Opal', dark pink; very free-flowering.
'Princess Elizabeth', pale peach-pink; scented; similar to 'Irene'.
N. tuberosa 'Rosea', flesh coloured; olive-green to bronze sepals; scented.

Red

'Atropurpurea', very dark reddish flowers with darker spots.
'Ellisiana', fiery red; similar to 'Maurice Laydeker'.
'Froebellii', crimson; flowers reliably, even in cool weather.
'Mme Maurice Laydeker', wine-red; similar to the foregoing.
'Laydekeri Purpurata', wine-red; young leaves reddish, then with darker spots; 'Laydekeri Fulgens'
is similar.
'William Falkoner', ruby-red; double flowers.

Yellow

N. odorata 'Sulphurea', sulphur-yellow; leaves spotted brown.
*N. pygmaea 'Helvola', golden-yellow; suitable planting depth 10 cm; somewhat tender.

Coppery-orange

*'Aurora', yellowish-orange as the flowers open, then coppery-orange and finally red-orange.
*'Chrysantha', reddish-yellow flowers; leaves marbled brown.
*'Graciella', coppery-apricot to peach; small, spherical flowers.
*'Indiana', coppery-orange; spherical flowers.
'Paul Harriot', shades of yellow and coppery-red.

40–80 (–100) cm depth of water

(Cultivars suitable for deeper water are marked with an asterisk.)

White

N. alba; see p. 423.
*'Gladstoniana', very vigorous and large-flowered; only for large ponds; similar to N. tuberosa
'Poestlingberg'.
'Hermine', tulip-shaped flowers; early; very similar to 'Albatross'.
'Marliacea Albida', vigorous, popular cultivar.
N. odorata 'Maxima', almost spherical flowers; fragrant.
*N. tuberosa 'Richardsonii', lavish, scented, bowl-shaped flowers; similar to 'Maxima'.

Pink

*'Colossea', delicate flesh-pink, turning white; thick, blunt buds; long flowering season.
'Formosa', peach-pink.
'Marliacea Carnea', pale pinkish-white.
'Marliacea Rosea', similar to the foregoing; pink flowers; very vigorous; tolerates shade.
'Masaniello', deep rosy-red; scented, cup-shaped flowers.
'Rosennymphe', starry, flattened funnel-shaped flowers, fading with age. 'Wesernymphe' is an
improved selection with scented flowers.
'Rose Arey', salmon-pink; long, pointed petals.

Red

'Attraction', starry flowers; garnet-red petals with paler tips.
'Cardinal', large, dark red flowers, fading with age.
*'Charles de Meurville', very large, wine-red flowers; free-flowering.
'Conqueror', dark wine-red; outer petals paler.
'Escarboucle', scented, ruby-red flowers; vigorous but not invasive.
'Gloriosa', red flowers; vigorous.
'James Brydon', globular, cherry-red flowers; round leaves; very rewarding.
'Mrs. Richmond', carmine pink; similar to 'Rembrandt' and 'Gloriosa'; very vigorous.
'Newton', pink-red; pointed, starry flowers that stand well above the water.

Yellow

'Colonel J. Welch', canary-yellow, starry flowers, standing somewhat above the water.
*'Marliacea Chromatella', bright yellow flowers; somewhat tender.
'Moorei', yellow flowers with pale yellow stamens; dark green leaves; not invasive.
'Sunrise', pointed, starry, sulphur-yellow flowers that stand above the water and open in the early morning.

7.1.2. Further perennials with floating leaves for still, sunny conditions

The following perennials enjoy the same conditions as waterlilies and may sometimes be found growing wild with them. Most are rooted in mud at the bottom of the pond but a few float freely with their roots in water. All are most effective grown without competition.

Yellow waterlily *Nuphar lutea* Eur., Nr East, Sib.	yellow	VI–VIII, hemispherical flowers; oval–cordate leaves; for muddy, nutrient-rich ponds in 0.80–2.00 (4.00) m; also grows in bright shade and slowly flowing water.
Nuphar pumila N, C & E Eur., W Sib., Jap.	reddish-yellow	VII–VIII, smaller than the foregoing; for cool, moory, nutrient-poor water in semi-shade; 0.50–1.50 m deep. *N. japonica*, VI–IX, elongate–ovate leaves; large yellow flowers that stand well above the water.
Fringed waterlily *Nymphoides peltata* (*Limnanthemum nymphoides*) Eur., Sib., Jap., China	yellow	VII–VIII, small circular leaves; spreads quickly by means of long floating rhizomes with opposite leaves; for nutrient-rich ponds in 0.50–1.50 m.
Amphibious bistort *Polygonum amphibium* Circumpol.	pink	VII–IX, pretty spikes of flowers over floating, elongate–elliptic leaves; for depths of 0.30–1.00 m; spreads and may suppress its neighbours in a small pond.
Pondweed *Potamogeton natans* Circumpol.	whitish	VI–VIII, spike-like inflorescences over elongate–oval leaves; thrives in 0.50–1.50 m.
Water soldier, Water aloe *Stratiodes aloides* Eur., Cauc., W Sib.	white	V–VIII, submerged, free-swimming rosettes of spiny, sword-like leaves with a triangular cross-section; floats to the surface at flowering time (small flowers) but rests up to 2 m deep for the remainder of the year.
Water chestnut *Trapa natans* S & C Eur., C & S Asia	white	VI–VII, insignificant flowers; forms attractive floating rosettes that colour red in autumn; rhombic leaves with inflated petioles; edible, spiny fruits; annual, but

seeds itself well in water that is warm in summer (1.00–2.00 m).

Tender species

Water hawthorn, Cape pondweed *Aponogeton distachyos* S Afr.	0.15 white	VI–X, bifid inflorescences over floating, elongate, broad-linear leaves; grows best in 0.15–0.50 m; tender (zone 9); best planted in a container and overwintered in frost-free conditions.
Water hyacinth *Eichhornia crassipes* Trop. & subtrop. Am.	0.20 blue-violet	VI–IX, flowers in spikes surrounded by spoon-shaped, fleshy leaves with inflated petioles; only flowers in temperate conditions if its roots (to 40 cm) reach to the bottom; can sometimes be overwintered in a bright position indoors at 12–20 °C (on sphagnum moss).
Myriophyllum brasiliense		List 7.3
Nuphar advena USA, Mex., W Indies	yellow, with red anthers	VI–IX, leaves and flowers resemble those of *N. lutea*; vigorous; in shallow water (to 0.80 m) the plants develop attractive leaves that stand well above the water on thick, green stems; hardy to zone (5B) 6.
Golden club *Orontium aquaticum* USA	0.10 yellow	IV–VI; *Calla*-like spathes fall away after flowering, leaving long, yellow spadices; green *Convallaria*-like leaves that stand erect in very shallow water or float in slightly deeper water (to 0.30 m); hardy to zone (5B) 6.

7.1.3. Perennials for special conditions in still water

These delicate but hardy perennials may be grown by the enthusiast in a small pond with cool, clear, shallow, nutrient-poor water and a dark, moory substrate. They are difficult to combine with other aquatic perennials, particularly where space is limited.

Plants are normally only available from specialist nurseries, where native *Callitriche* species with small evergreen rosettes and insignificant flowers are also sometimes offered.

Water primrose, Water violet *Hottonia palustris* Eur., Asia Minor, S Sib.	delicate pink	V–VI, beautiful inflorescences standing up to 30 cm out of the water; comb-like, submerged leaves; sensitive to competition; thrives in lime-free water; for cool ponds in woodland or dappled shade.
Frog-bit *Hydrocharis morsus-ranae* Eur., W Sib., N Afr.	white	V–VIII, free-floating species; small, round, waterlily-like leaves and short stolons; very graceful but robust; also thrives in large, nutrient- and base-rich ponds; tolerates semi-shade.
Water buttercup *Ranunculus aquatilis* Eur., Asia, Am., Afr.	white	V–VIII, floating, 3–5-lobed, kidney-shaped leaves; for nutrient-rich but lime-free water in 0.30–1.50 m. *R. peltatus*, particularly large flowers.
Bladderwort *Utricularia vulgaris* Circumpol.	golden yellow	VI–VII, free-floating species; flowers up to 2 cm across in raceme-like inflorescences; hair-fine foliage with bladders that trap tiny insects; for lime-free, moory

ponds that are warm in summer; up to 0.50 m deep; rare in the trade.

7.1.4.   Small floating ferns and duckweed

These small, floating plants are spread by waterbirds and mostly appear without the agency of a gardener. Duckweeds (*Lemna* spp.) are sometimes offered for sale but cannot be recommended. Where the natural balance is disturbed these cover the water completely, blocking out the light for any submerged aquatics below. Other ferns and liverworts that grow in very shallow water at the water's edge are *Marsilea quadrifolia*, *Pilularia globulifera* and *Rizzia fluitans*.

Azolla caroliniana N & S Am.	Emerald green fern, up to 1 cm tall; turns red-brown in autumn; increases quickly in a warm position; often disappears entirely if not protected in winter. *A. filiculoides*, more vigorous.
Salvinia natans Eur., Asia to C Sib., Java, Alger.	Tender, warmth-loving, annual fern with opposite, oval pinnae, 1 cm long and hairy on the upper surface; forms plants 5–10 cm across. *S. rotundifolia*, S Am., smaller and somewhat hardier (zone 6); fertile fronds sink to the bottom in winter to produce new plantlets in spring.
Duckweed *Lemna gibba* Almost cosmopol.	IV–V, insignificant flowers; convex fronds; floats on the water surface. *L. minor*, small, rounded fronds. Both species are worth having but should not be allowed to over-proliferate.

7.2.   Perennials for springs, streams and ditches

The following may occasionally find a use in combination with perennials for damp conditions (list 3.5.4) and the species from list 6.2.2.

Mentha aquatica Eur., Med., W & N Asia	0.20–0.80 lilac-pink	VII–IX, terminal heads of flowers; serrate, ovate leaves; aromatic scent; particularly for still water. 'Crispa', ruffled leaves; medicinal plant. *M. longifolia*, Horsemint (0.80), elongate–ovate leaves with matted grey hairs beneath; tolerates water up to 10 cm deep.
Summer watercress *Nasturtium officinale* Eur., Asia	0.20–0.80 white	V–X, flowers in corymbose racemes; fleshy, fingery leaves that stay green until autumn; cultivated edible plant; spreads strongly.
Brooklime *Veronica beccabunga* Eur., Asia Minor, W Asia, Him.	0.30 blue	V–VIII, flowers in racemes over rounded ovate leaves; spreads quickly; old medicinal and salad plant.
Water speedwell, Brook pimpernel *Veronica anagallis-* *aquatica* Eurasia, W Am.	up to 0.30 pale violet	V–VIII, flowers in axillary racemes; weakly serrate, pointed leaves; rare in the trade. *V.a.* f. *anagalliformis*, inflorescence larger, bluish-lilac.

7.2.1.   Perennials for running water

Potamogeton species and the submerged forms of *Alisma*, *Hippuris*, *Sagittaria* etc. are not generally available in the trade.

Ranunculus aquatilis		List 7.1.3
Ranunculus fluitans C & S Eur.	white	VI–VII, floating, bowl-shaped flowers make an attractive sward at flowering time; floating leaves not always present. *R. circinatus, R. trichophyllus*, no floating leaves.

7.3.   Hardy submerged aquatics

Even in a small pond, the following plants can help to keep down excessive algae. They also oxygenate the water and provide cover for baby fish. Other plants worth mentioning are *Potamogeton* spp. (not available from nurseries), *Elodea canadensis* (dangerously invasive) and *Najas* spp. (annual).

Hornwort *Ceratophyllum demersum* Cosmopol.	Metre-long, branching, fragile stems with whorls of fine leaves; small fragments will form a new plant; insignificant, submerged flowers. *C. submersum*, similar but very rare.
Chara fragilis	Alga with delicate, greenish, fragile, lime-encrusted shoots, forming graceful foot-high 'meadows' on the pond floor.
Hottonia palustris	List 7.1.3
Ivy duckweed *Lemna trisulca* Almost cosmopol.	Pointed, lanceolate fronds up to 1 cm long, arranged at right angles to one another; plants drift freely under water, only surfacing in May and June to flower; should be tolerated to help keep the water clean.
Water milfoil *Myriophyllum spicatum* Eur., Asia, Afr., N Am.	VI–VIII, pink inflorescences standing above the water surface; pinnate leaves in whorls; similar to *M. verticillatum*. *M. brasiliense*, particularly beautiful but tender species; forms a feathery, emerald green carpet on the water surface; see p. 426. Additional hardy species include *M. alternifolium*, *M. exalbescens*, *M. heterophyllum*, *M. hippuroides*, *M. pinnatum*, *M. farwellii*, *M. humila* and *M. tenellum*. All may become too large for a small body of water.
Nitella flexilis Cosmopol.	Dainty alga with forking, whorled fronds; similar to *Chara fragilis* but more flexible; forms a tangled net; every fragment forms a new plant; for a bright position.

Source material

It is hardly possible to list sources for a collective body of experience that has been gathered over many years. However, the classification of herbaceous perennials according to their proper garden habitats could not be achieved from experience and observation alone. The starting point was in each case the natural growing conditions of the plant concerned. The lists below therefore consist primarily of sources that were necessary for the initial determination of the character and natural distribution of the plants dealt with.

For North American species: Britton and Brown: 'An Illustrated Flora of the Northern United States and Canada', 1970; Jepson, W. L.: 'Flowering Plants of California', 1966; Rydberg, P. A.: 'Flora of the Rocky Mountains and Adjacent Plains', 1964; Clark, L. J.: 'Wildflowers of British Columbia', 1973; Steyermark, J. A.: 'Flora of Missouri', 1977.

For East Asia: Ohwi, J.: 'Flora of Japan', 1965; Numata, E. M.: 'The Flora and Vegetation of Japan', 1974; along with numerous works dealing with plant sociology. Some information on natural habitats in SE Asia and China could also be gathered from the works of E. H. Wilson, F. Kingdon-Ward, G. Forrest and other plant collectors.

For Europe: the 'Flora Europaea' and Hegi, G.: 'Illustrierte Flora von Mittel-Europa' were of particular importance, along with G. Bonnier's French flora and the Swiss flora by H. E. Hess and E. Landolt. Further literature: Polunin, O. and Smythies, B. E.: 'Flowers of SW Europe', 1973; Fiori, A.: 'Flora Italiana', 1970; Rikli, M.: 'Das Pflanzenkleid der Mittelmeerländer', 1973; various publications from the Geobotanic Institute, Rübel, in Switzerland; Ursing, B.: 'Svenske Växter', 1961; Clapham, A. R., Tutin, T. G. and Warburg, E. F.: 'Flora of the British Isles', 1952; Fitter, R., Fitter, A. and Blamey, M.: 'The Wildflowers of Britain and Northern Europe'; Horvat, I., Glavac, V. and Ellenberg, H.: 'Die Vegetation Südosteuropas', 1974; Ungar, K.: 'Flora Siebenbürgens', 1925 and 'Die Alpenflora der S Karpaten', 1913; Römer, J.: 'Die Pflanzenwelt der Bürzenländer Berge', 1899; Rothmaler, W., Garke, A. and Oberdorfer, E.: 'Pflanzensoziologische Exkursionsflora', 1979, was particularly useful, along with the indispensable Ellenberg, H.: 'Vegetation Mitteleuropas mit den Alpen', 1978.

The following **gardening literature** was employed: Bailey, L. H.: 'The Standard Cyclopedia of Horticulture', 1953 and 'Manual of Cultivated Plants', 1954; the R.H.S. 'Dictionary of Gardening', 1956; 'Parey's Blumengärtnerei', 1958 was particularly useful, along with various old standard works such as Wehrhahn, H. R.: 'Die Gartenstauden', 1931; Silva Tarouka, E. and Schneider, C.: 'Unsere Freilandstauden', 1934; Wocke, E.: 'Die Kulturpraxis der Alpenpflanzen', 1940, and K. Foerster's important book 'Winterharte Blütenstauden und Sträucher der Neuzeit', 1924.

Particular attention was paid to some of the **more recent books on herbaceous perennials,** especially: Jelitto, L. and Schacht, W.: 'Die Freilandschmuckstauden', 1963; Jelitto, L., Schacht, W. and Feßler, A.: 'Die Freilandschmuckstauden', 1985; Seyffert, W.: 'Stauden', 1969 and 'Stauden für Natur- und Steingarten', 1970; Thomas, G. S.: 'Perennial Garden Plants', 1969; and in some respects: Bloom, A.: 'Hardy Perennials', *ca.* 1960; Boom, B. R. and Ruys, D.: 'Gekweekte kruidachtige Gewassen', 1950; Foerster, K.: 'Neuer Glanz des Gartenjahres', 1966; Krüssmann, G.: 'Winterharharte Gartenstauden', 1970; Seibold, H.: 'Gartenblumen, Mein Hobby', 1966; Meyer, K. H.: 'Gefährten des Gartenjahres', 1960.

In addition to a mass of British and American literature, the following **specialist works** are worth mentioning: Feldmaier, C.: 'Lilien', 1982; Feßler, A.: 'Gartenstauden', 1980; Foerster, K.: 'Einzung der Gräser und Farne' and 'Der Steingarten der sieben Jahreszeiten', 1962; Koehlein,

F.: 'Freilandsucculenten', 1984, 'Saxifragen', 1980, 'Primeln', 1984, 'Enziane und Glockenblumen', 1986, 'Iris', 1981; Maatsch, R.: 'Das Buch der Freilandfarne', 1980; Praeger, R. L.: 'An Account of the Genus Sedum', 1967; Schacht, W.: 'Blumenzwiebeln für Garten und Heim' and 'Der Steingarten', 1978; Synge, P.: 'Bulbs', 1961; Wachter, K.: 'Der Wassergarten', 1978; Wyman, D.: 'Groundcover Plants', 1970.

Valuable information was also provided by **journals** such as 'Gartenpraxis', the Austrian 'Gartenmagazin', 'Der Staudengarten' (journal of the Verein der Staudenfreunde), the journals of the Scottish Rock Garden and British Alpine Garden Society, 'The Garden' (R.H.S.) and the 'Gärtnerisch-Botanischen Briefe der Arbeitsgemeinschaft der Technischen Leiter der Botanischen Gärten'.

The **botanical names** and geographical distributions in this book are based on Zander 'Handwörterbuch der Pflanzennamen', 1984. Names that are well known to gardeners have occasionally been given preference to the currently scientifically valid name. In such cases, the modern name has been added in brackets. For practical reasons, the authorities for botanical names have been omitted.

Lastly, it is worth mentioning the species-rich **catalogues of German herbaceous nurseries.** Without these nurseries a practical classification of herbaceous perennials into their proper garden habitats would have been both senseless and impossible. Kayser und Seibert in Roßdorf/Darmstadt, H. Klose in Kassel-Lohfelden, Dr H. Simon in Marktheidenfeld and Gräfin Zeppelin in Laufen/Baden all have a particularly large assortment, while many other nurseries in the 'Bund Deutscher Staudenzüchter' also have their share of uncommon species.

Species Index

Key references are given in bold; asterisks refer to illustrations; † indicates species illustrated in the colour plates.

Acaena spp. 213
– *buchananii* **195, 217**
– *caesiiglauca* **217**
– *glaucophylla* **217**
– *microphylla* †, 4*, **195, 217**
– *pulchella* **217**
Acantholimon androsaceum ⸳ **273**
– *glumaceum* **273**
– *olivieri* **274**
– *venustum* 274
Acanthus balcanicus 244
– *caroli-alexandri* **218**
– *longifolius* **244**
– *mollis* 244
– *spinosus* **218**, 244
Achillea ageratifolia **274**, 301
– *aurea* 217
– *clavenae* **301**
– *clypeolata* **235**
– *conjuncta* 274
– *filipendulina* †, 94, **237**, 363
– × *jaborneggii* 301
– × *kellereri* **285**
– × *kolbiana* 301
– *lingulata* 301
– *millefolium* **199, 237**
– *moschata* 301
– *ptarmica* **377**
– *rupestris* **295**
– *serbica* 257, **295**
– *sibirica* **237**
– × *taygetea* **235**
– *tomentosa* 191
– *umbellata* **274**, 301
– × *wilczeckii* 301
Achnatherum calamagrostis 222, **239**
– *pekinense* **222**, 239
Acinos alpinus **295**

Aconitum spp. 334
– × *arendsii* **346**
– × *cammarum* 346
– *carmichaelii* **346**
– *fischeri* 346
– *henryi* 346
– *lamarckii* 114
– *lycoctonum* 114
– *napellus* **345**
– *paniculatum* **114**
– *pyrenaicum* **114**
– *septentrionale* **170**
– *variegatum* **114, 346**
– *volubile* **153**
– *vulparia* 114
– *wilsonii* **346**
Acorus calamus **411**
– *gramineus* **414**
Actaea alba **123**
– *pachypoda* **123**
– *rubra* 123
– *spicata* 120, **123**
Actinella scaposa **285**
Adenophora bulleyana 329
– *confusa* 329
– *farreri* 329
– *liliifolia* 229, **328**
– *potaninii* 329
– *tashiroi* 329
– *triphylla* 329
– *verticillata* **329**
Adenostyles alliariae **334**
– *alpina* 334
– *glabra* **334**
Adiantum pedatum **130, 328**
– *venustum* **328**
Adonis amurensis **329**
– *vernalis* **201**
Aegopodium podagraria 87, 92*, 149

Aetheopappus pulcherrimus 229
Aethionema grandiflorum †, **274**
– *oppositifolia* **274**
Agapanthus campanulatus **397**
– *praecox* **397**
– *umbellatus* 397
Ageratum houstonianum †, 353, 372, 376
– *Agropyron repens* 93*
Agrostis tenuis **200**
Ajuga pyramidalis **160**
– *reptans* 67, **152**, 160, 193, 199, 337
Alcea rosea 95, **392**
– *ficifolia* **392**
Alchemilla acutiloba 167
– *alpina erythropoda* **295**
– *hoppeana* **295**
– *mollis* 167
Alisma gramineum **413**
– *lanceolatum* **413**
– *parviflorum* **413**
– *plantago-aquatica* **413**
Allium spp. 358
– *albopilosum* 217
– *caeruleum* **315**
– *cernuum* **315**
– *christophii* **217**
– *cirrhosum* **315**
– *cyaneum* **315**
– *flavum* **315**
– *giganteum* **217**
– *jesdianum* 217
– *karataviense* **216**
– *moly* **315**
– *narcissiflorum* 315, **329**
– *oreophilum* **216**
– *ostrowskianum* 216

– *paradoxum* **154**
– *pulchellum* 315
– *rosenbachianum* **217**
– *roseum* **315**
– *schoenoprasum* 404
– *sphaerocephalon* **217, 229,**
 315
– *stipitatum* **217**
– *triquetrum* 154
– *tuberosum* **315**
– *ursinum* **122**
– *zebdanense* 154
Alopecurus pratensis 408
Alsine rosanii 276
Alstroemeria aurantiaca **397**
– *officinalis* **247,** 404
– *rosea* **392**
Alyssoides utriculata **285**
Alyssum arduinii **274**
– *argenteum* **218**
– *moellendorfianum* **295**
– *montanum* **295,** 310
– *repens* 274
– *saxatile* **257,** 274
– *serpyllifolium* **274**
– *spinosum* **277**
Armaracus dictamnus 285,
 289
– *scaber* 289
Amsonia tabernaemontana **247**
Amygdalus nana 212
Anacyclus depressus **285**
Anaphalis spp. 96
– *cinnamomea* **218**
– *margaritacea* 218, **221**
– *triplinervis* **218**
– *yedoensis* **218**
Anchusa spp. 74
– *azurea* 225
– *italica* 95, **225**
Androsace carnea brigantiaca
 301
– *laggeri* **301**
– *lactea* **301**
– *lanuginosa* **301**
– *primuloides* **295**
– *sarmentosa* †, **295**
– *sempervivoides* **295**
– *strigillosa* **301**
– *villosa* **301**
Andryala agardhi **285**
Anemone spp. 97

– *apennina* **123,** 127, 326
– *blanda* **124,** 127, 326
– *canadensis* 148, **154**
– *coronaria* **227**
– *cylindrica* 154
– × *fulgens* 227
– *hupehensis* †, 132, **342**
Japonica hybrids 74, 97, 132,
 342
– × *lesseri* 157
– *narcissiflora* **317**
– *nemorosa* †, **120,** 127, 154
– *pulsatilla* 312
– *ranunculoides* **120**
– *rivularis* **173**
– *sylvestris* **157,** 201
– *tomentosa* **343**
– *trifolia* **154**
– *vitifolia* 343
Anemonopsis macrophylla **137**
Anethum graveolens 406
Angelica archangelica 406
Antennaria aprica **310**
– *dioica* 9*, 160, **208, 310**
– *parviflora* **310**
– *plantaginifolia* **311**
– *tomentosa* 196, **311**
Anthemis spp. 74
– *biebersteiniana* **229**
– *marschalliana* 229
– *nobilis* **196, 221**
– *sancti-johannis* **393**
– *tinctoria* 95, **393**
Anthericum liliago †, **157,** 201
Anthriscus cerefolium 406
Anthoxanthum odoratum **201**
Anthyllis montana 199, **317**
– *vulneraria* **199**
Antirrhinum asarina 285
– *majus* 406
Aponogeton distachyos **426**
Aquilegia spp. 12*, 94, **163,**
 381
– *alpina* hort. 164
– *akitensis* **321**
– *atrata* 157, 163
– *bertolonii* **321**
– *caerulea* 163, **164**
– *canadensis* 163
– *chrysantha* **163**
– *discolor* **321**
– *ecalcarata* 324

– *einseleana* **321**
– *flabellata* **321**
– *glandulosa* **329**
– *longissima* **163**
– *pyrenaica* **321**
– *skinneri* 163, **226**
– *thalictrifolia* 321
– *vulgaris* †, **155,** 157, **163,** 164
Arabis albida 257
– *androsacea* **301**
– × *arendsii* 258
– *billardierii* 302
– *blepharophylla* **302**
– *caucasica* **257**
– *ferdinandicoburgi* **296**
– *procurrens* **193, 258**
– *scopoliana* 296
– × *suendermannii* 193, **296**
– *vochinensis* **296**
Aralia cachemirica **167**
– *californica* **167**
– *cordata* **167**
– *racemosa* **167**
Arctostaphylos nevadensis 329
– *uva-ursi* **329**
Arenaria grandiflora **274**
– *montana* **274**
– *purpurascens* **274**
– *rigida* **274**
– *tetraquetra* **285**
Argemone mexicana 362
Arisaema amurensis **138**
– *consanguineum* **138**
– *ringens* **137**
– *triphyllum* **138**
Aristolochia clematitis 404
Armeria alliacea **161**
– *alpina* **339**
– *cespitosa* 8*, **296**
– *elongata* **161**
– *juniperifolia* 296
– *latifolia* **258**
– *maritima* 161, **258,** 339
– × *suendermannii* **296**
Armoracia rusticana 403
Arnebia echioides **302**
– *pulchra* 302
Arnica montana **208**
– *longifolia* 208
Arrhenatherum bulbosum 408
Artemisia abrotanum **211,** 403
– *absinthium* 211, 403

– *albula* 221
– *austriaca* **221**
– *dracunculus* 405
– *lactiflora* †, 114, **170**
– *laxa* **285**
– *ludoviciana* 221
– *mutellina* 285
– *nitida* 296
– *pontica* **221**
– *purshiana* 221
– *schmidtiana* **296**
– *stelleriana* 218
– *vulgaris* 408
– *umbelliformis* 285
Arum italicum **124**
– *maculatum* †, 120, 124
Aruncus aethusifolius **133**, 326
– *americanus* **133**
– *dioicus* 114, 127, 133
– *sylvester* †, 114, 127, 132, **133**
Arundinaria auricoma **183**
– *fastuosa* **183**
– *graminea* **183**
– *japonica* **183**
– *nitida* 182
– *pumila* **183**, **195**
– *pygmaea* **183**, 195
– *variegata* 182
– *viridistriata* 183
Arundo donax 96, **255**
Asarina glutinosa **285**
– *procumbens* **285**
Asarum canadense **124**
– *caudatum* **124**
– *europaeum* †, **121**, 193
Asclepias cornuti 244
– *incarnata* **247**, 415
– *syriaca* **244**
– *tuberosa* **225**
Asparagus officinalis 153
– *pseudoscaber* **153**
– *tenuifolius* **218**
– *verticillatus* **153**
Asperula arcadiensis **285**
– *cynanchica* **311**
– *lilaciflora* 285
– *nitida* **285**
– *odorata* **121**
– *orientalis* 359
– *suberosa* 285
– *tinctoria* **158**
Asphodeline liburnica **218**

– *lutea* †, **218**, **229**
– *taurica* **218**
Asphodelus aestivus 225
– *albus* **225**
– *microcarpus* 225
Asplenium adiantum-nigrum **325**
– *platyneuron* 328
– *ruta-muraria* **325**
– *septentrionale* **326**
– *trichomanes* **326**
– *viride* **326**
Aster acris 237
– *ageratoides vesoensis* **168**
– × *alpellus* **258**
– *alpinus* †, 9*, 258, **265**
– *amellus* †, 74, 78, 97, **201**, 238, 258, **363**
– *andersonii* **196**, **296**
– *bellidiastrum* **321**
– *cordifolius* **369**
– *divaricatus* 168
– *dumosus* †, **367**
– *ericoides* **369**
– × *frikartii* †, **363**
– *incisus* 168
– *laevis* **240**, **369**
– *lateriflorus* **369**
– *linosyris* **201**, 229
– *macrophyllus* **168**
– *mongolicus* **235**
– *novae-angliae* 97, **368**
– *novi-belgii* 11*, 97, 367, **368**
– *ptarmicoides* 243
– *pyrenaeus* †, 363
– *schreberi* 168
– *sedifolius* **237**
– *sibiricus* 235
– *subcoeruleus* 238
– *tongolensis* **238**
– *vimineus* **369**
– *yunnanensis* 238
Astilbe spp. 97, 132
– × *arendsii* **343**
– *astilboides* **343**
– *chinensis* **114**, 124, 134, **152**, 267, 344
– × *crispa* **326**
– *davidii* **133**, 343, 411
– *glaberrima* 124, **326**
– *grandis* **134**
– *japonica* **134**, **343**

– *koreana* **134**
– *rivularis* **173**
– *simplicifolia* 133, **134**, 343
– *taquetii* **115**, 344
– *thunbergii* †, 134, **344**
Astilboides tabularis 132, **134**
Astragalus alopecuroides **218**
– *angustifolius* **285**
– *centralalpinus* 218
– *exscapus* **285**
Astrantia carniolica **334**
– *minor* **323**
– *major* **121**, 155
– *maxima* **155**
Athamanta cretensis 274
– *haynaldii* **274**
– *matthioli* 274
Athyrium alpestre 128
– *distentifolium* **128**, 334
– *filix-femina* **128**
– *goeringianum* 130
– *nipponicum* **130**
– *vidalii* **130**
Atriplex hortensis 406
Aubrieta hybrids 196, 257, **258**
– *tauricola* **196**, **258**
Avena candida 232
– *sempervirens* 232
Avenella flexuosa 144, **162**, **209**
Azolla caroliniana **427**
– *filiculoides* 427
Azorella trifurcata **193**
– *umbellata* 193

Ballota pseudodictamnus **225**
– *nigra* **225**, 408
Baptista australis **240**
Begonia evansiana 138
– *grandis* **138**
Belamcanda chinensis **397**
Bellidiastrum michelii 321
Bellis perennis 199
Berberis thunbergii **211**
Bergenia spp. 143, **176**, 329
– *acanthifolia* 177
– *ciliata* **177**
– *cordifolia* **176**
– *crassifolia* **177**
– *pacifica* **268**
– *purpurascens* 176, **268**
– × *schmidtii* **177**
– *stracheyi* 176, **177**

Betonica macrantha 169
– *nivea* 203
– *officinalis* 161
Blechnum penna-marina 130, **328**
– *spicant* **130**, 145
Bletilla striata **228**
Bocconia 245
Boltonia asteroides 240, **244, 247**
– *latisquama* 244, 253
Borago officinalis 406
Bouteloua curtipendula **222**
– *oligostachya* **222**
Boykinia aconitifolia **134**
– *tellimoides* 135
Brachypodium pinnatum 203
– *sylvaticum* **123**
Brimeura amethystina 320
Briza media 160, **201**, 203, **209,** 319
Brodiaea uniflora 293
Bromus erectus 203
Brunnera macrophylla 97, 148, **168**
Buglossoides purpurocaerulea 3*, 143, 149, 151*, 159
Bulbocodium vernum **319,** 331
Buphthalmum salicifolium **158**
Butomus umbellatus †, **413**

Calamagrostis × *acutiflora* †, **243**, 348
Calamintha alpina **295**
– *grandiflora* 331
– *nepeta* **296**
– *nepetoides* 296
Calandrinia umbellata **285**
Calceolaria biflora **323**
– *polyrrhiza* **323**
– *scabiosifolia* †
Calendula officinalis 406
Calla palustris **420**
Callianthemum anemonoides **302**
Callirhoë involucrata **218**
Callistephus sinensis 406
Callitriche spp. 426
Calluna 107
– *vulgaris* 95, 133, **160**, 204, **207,** 420
Calocephalus brownii †

Caltha leptosepala **416**
– *palustris* †, 337, **415**
– *polypetala* 416
– *tyermannii* **416**
Camassia cusickii **247**
– *esculenta* 247
– *leichtlinii* 247
– *quamash* **247**
Campanula alliariifolia **174**
– *barbata* **302**
– *carpatica* †, **258, 267,** 286
– *cochleariifolia* 286, **296**
– *collina* **317**
– *fenestrellata* **302**
– *garganica* 259, **302**
– *glomerata* **199, 238,** 363
– *grandis* †, **168**
– *grossekii* **218**
– *lactiflora* **170**
– *latifolia* †, **115,** 168
– *latiloba* 168
– *medium* 406
– *ochroleuca* **218**
– *persicifolia* **158,** 168, 201, 238
– *portenschlagiana* **259**
– *poscharskyana* 196, **259,** 329
– × *pulloides* 302
– *pulla* **302**
– *pusilla* 296
– *pyramidalis* 302
– *raddeana* **302**
– *raineri* **302**
– *rapunculoides* **174**
– *rotundifolia* 160, **208,** 317
– *sarmatica* **202**
– *tommasiniana* **302**
– *trachelium* **121**
– *turbinata* 258, **302**
– *versicolor* 286, **302**
– *waldsteiniana* **303**
– × *warleyensis* **286**
Canna flaccida **414**
Caragana jubata 211
Cardamine hirsuta 91
– *pentaphyllos* 124
– *pratensis* 199, **245,** 247
– *trifolia* **124,** 134
Cardiocrinum giganteum 53, **138**
Carduncellus mitissimus **286**
– *rhaponticoides* 286
Carduus nutans **234**

Carex acutiformis 411
– *alba* **123**
– *baldensis* **303,** 319
– *buchananii* **222**
– *comans* 222
– *digitata* **126**
– *elata* 118, **411**
– *firma* **303,** 319
– *flacca* **203,** 418
– *flava* **418**
– *gracilis* 411
– *grayi* 173, **247**
– *humilis* **203**
– *maxima* 119
– *montana* 158, **203,** 205
– *morrowii* **118,** 132
– *muskingumensis* 134, **173**
– *ornithopoda* **126**
– *pendula* **119,** 127, 417
– *plantaginea* **126**
– *pseudocyperus* **413**
– *reticulosa* 411
– *riparia* 411
– *sempervirens* **319**
– *sylvatica* 121, **126**
– *umbrosa* 203
Carlina acaulis **202**
– *acanthifolia* †, 229
Cassia marylandica **170**
Cassiope tetragona **335**
Catananche coerulea **229**
Cautleya gracilis **143,** 326
– *lutea* 143
Centaurea axillaris 229
– *bella* **229**
– *dealbata* **174**
– *glastifolia* 238
– *hypoleuca* 229
– *jacea* 199
– *macrocephala* **238**
– *montana* 94, **168**
– *nervosa* 158, **235**
– *pulcherrima* **229**
– *rhapontica* **239**
– *ruthenica* **158**
– *scabiosa* **199**
– *simplicaulis* 229
– *uniflora* 235
Centranthus ruber †, 95, **219,** 259
Cephalaria alpina 244
– *gigantea* 244

– *tatarica* **244**
Cerastium alpinum **303**
– *arvense* **296**
– *biebersteinii* **259**
– *columnae* 195, **259**
– *holosteoides* 199
– *tomentosum* **195, 259**
– *villosum* 303
Ceratophyllum demersum **428**
– *submersum* 428
Ceratostigma plumbaginoides 97, **195**, 219, **259**
Ceterach officinarum **286**, 325
Chaenorhinum crassifolium **286**
– *glareosum* 286
– *origanifolium* 286
– *villosum* 286
Chamaemelum nobile 221
Chamaenerion angustifolium 162
Chara fragilis **428**
Chelone barbatus 241
– *obliqua* **250**
Chenopodium bonus-henricus 408
– *purpurascens* 406
Chiastophyllum oppositifolium †, **267**
Chionodoxa spp. 271, 313
– *gigantea* **184**
– *luciliae* 143, **184**, 187
– *sardensis* **184**
– *tmolusii* **340**
× *Chionoscilla allenii* **187**
Chrysanthemum arcticum 97, **259**
– *balsamita* **235**, 403
– *cinerarifolium* 229
– *coccineum* 94, **393**
– *corymbosum* †, **158**
– *haradjanii* **286**
– × *hortorum* 74, 97
– *indicum* **353**
– *koreanum* **353**
– *leucanthemum* †, 76*, **199**, **394**
– *macrophyllum* **174**
– *majus* 235
– *maximum* 74, 76*, 95, **394**
– *millefoliatum* **229**
– *parthenium* **174**, 404

– *roseum* 393
– *rubellum* **353**
– *seriotinum* 250, 348, 416
– *tanacetum* 404
– *uliginosum* 250
– *vulgare* **174**, 408
– *zawadskyi* 260
Chrysogonum virginianum **240**
Chrysopogon gryllus **222**
– *nutans* †, **243**
Chrysopsis villosa **219**
Chrysosplenium alternifolium **327**, 417
– *oppositifolium* **194, 327, 337**, 417
Cicerbita alpina **334**
– *bourgaei* **155**
– *macrophylla* **155**
– *plumieri* **334**
Cichorium intybus 408
Cimicifuga spp. 17*, 97, 115, 132
– *acerina* **137**
– *cordifolia* **137**
– *dahurica* **137**
– *japonica* **137**
– *racemosa* †, **137**
– *ramosa* **137**
– *simplex* 97, **137**
Circaea intermedia 123, **326**
– *lutetiana* **122**, 326
Cirsium diacanthum **233**
– *eriophorum* **233**
– *rivulare* **245**, 247
Cistus laurifolius **225**
Cladanthus arabicus **362**
Claytonia sibirica 144
Clematis × *bonstedtii* **153, 168**
– × *durandii* **153**
– *heracleifolia* **153**
– *integrifolia* **153**
– × *jackmanii* 153
– × *jouiniana* **154**
– *recta* **158**
– *vitalba* 154
Codonopsis spp. 329
– *clematidea* **154**
– *convolvulacea* 154
– *mollis* 154
– *ovata* 154
– *vinciflora* 154
Colchicum 315, 331

– *agrippinum* **180**
– *autumnale* **179**
– *bornmuelleri* **180**
– *byzantinum* **180**
– hybrids **180**
– *neapolitanum* **180**
– *pannonicum* **179**
– *speciosum* **180**
Comarum palustre **421**
Convallaria majalis 14*, **121**, **153**
Convolvulus arvensis 93*
– *cantabrica* **286**
– *lineatus* **286**
– *nitidus* **286**
– *suendermannii* 286
Corbularia bulbocodium 320
Coreopsis grandiflora 95, 240, **395**
– *lanceolata* †, 95, 240, **395**
– *tripteris* 240, **250**, 394
– *verticillata* **240**, 395
Coriandrum sativum 406
Cornus canadensis 132, **145**
Coronilla cappadocica 311
– *coronata* 311
– *minima* 311
– *montana* 158, **311**
– *vaginalis* **311**
– *varia* **159**
Cortaderia selloana †, **255**, 411
Cortusa matthioli 138, **321**
Corydalis angustifolia **121**
– *bulbosa* 121
– *cava* 115, **121**, 187
– *cheilanthifolia* †, **321**
– *intermedia* **121**
– *lutea* **267**
– *nobilis* **155**
– *ochroleuca* **267**
– *ophiocarpa* 155
– *solida* 115, **121**
Corynephorus canescens 210
Cosmos sulphureus †, 348, 371
Cotoneaster dammeri **192, 195**
– *salicifolius* 192
Cotula coronopifolia **416**
– *dioica* **194**
– *potentillina* **194**
– *squalida* **194**
Crambe cordifolia **219**
Crassula milfordiae 225, **286**

Crepis aurea **317**
Crinum bulbispermum 398
– *moorei* 398
– × *powellii* **398**
Crocosmia × *crocosmiiflora* **398**
– *masonorum* **398**
Crocus albiflorus 186, **319**
– *ancyrensis* **314**
– *angustifolius* 314
– *asturicus* **316**
– *aureus* 314
– *balansae* **314**
– *banaticus* 315
– *biflorus* **313**
– *byzantinus* 187, **315**
– *chrysanthus* **271**, 314
– *etruscus* **313**
– *flavus* **314**
– *heuffelianus* 187, **313**, 319
– *imperati* **313**
– *iridoflorus* 315
– *karduchorum* **315**
– *kotschyanus* **315**
– *medius* **316**
– *neopolitanus* **187**, 272, **319**
– *pulchellus* **316**
– *sativus* **316**
– *sieberi* **313**
– *speciosus* 180, **315**
– *susianus* **314**
– *tommasinianus* 143, **186**, 272
– *vernus* **186**, 272, **319**
– *versicolor* **313**
– *zonatus* 315
Crucianella stylosa **262**
Cryptogramma crispa **326**
Currania dryopteris 128
– *robertianum* 128
Cyclamen spp. 331
– *abchasicum* 177
– *atkinsii* 177
– *coum* 143, **177**
– *europaeum* 177
– *hederifolium* 143, **177**
– *ibericum* 177
– *neapolitanum* **177**
– *orbiculatum* 177
– *purpurascens* 155, **177**
– *repandum* 177, **331**
– *vernale* 331
– *vernum* 177

Cymbalaria aequitriloba **323**
– *muralis* **267**
– *pallida* **323**
Cynara cardunculus **225**
– *humilis* 225
– *scolymus* **226**
Cynoglossum nervosum **219**
– *vulgare* 406
Cynosurus cristatus **201**
Cyperus longus **414**
Cypripedium acaule **140**
– *calceolus* **139**, **140**
– *macranthum* **140**
– *parviflorum* **140**
– *reginae* **140**
– *spectabile* 140
Cyrtomium fortunei **130**, 138
Cystopteris bulbifera **130**
– *fragilis* 130, **326**
– *montana* **328**
Cytisus austriacus **204**
– *decumbens* **195**, **211**
– *ratisbonensis* **204**
– *supinus* **204**

Daboecia cantabrica **335**
– × *scotica* 335
Dactylis glomerata 408
Dactylorhiza maculata **419**
Dahlia variabilis 405
Daphne blagayana 204, **211**
– *cneorum* **204**, 211
Deinanthe caerulea **138**
Delosperma aberdeenense 226
– *cooperi* †, **226**
– *sutherlandii* 226
Delphinium spp. 97
Belladonna hybrids †, **348**
– *brunonianum* 329
– *cashmerianum* **329**
– × *cultorum* †, **346**
– *elatum* 346
Elatum hybrids **347**
– *grandiflorum* **233**
– *nudicaule* **226**, 348
Pacific hybrids **347**
– × *ruysii* **348**
– *sulphureum* 233
– *tatsienense* **233**
– *zalil* **233**
Dennstaedtia punctilobula **127**

Dentaria enneaphyllos **124**
– *heptaphylla* **124**
– *pentaphyllos* **124**
Deschampsia cespitosa **119**, 170, 416
– *flexuosa* 162, **209**
Dianthus alpinus **303**
– *anatolicus* **286**
– *arenarius* **208**
– *atrorubens* 275
– × *avernensis* 286
– *banaticus* 275
– *barbatus* 406
– *caesius* 260
– *callizonus* 303
– *campestris* 275
– *carthusianorum* **202**
– *cruentus* **229**, 275
– *deltoides* **209**
– *erinaceus* **287**
– *freynii* 303
– *giganteus* 275
– *glacialis* 303
– *gratianopolitanus* †, 6*, 196, **260**, 286, **311**
– *grisebachii* **303**
– *knappi* **275**
– *monspessulanus* **275**
– *neglectus* **303**
– *noeanus* 275
– *pavonius* 303
– *petraeus* †, **275**
– *plumarius* †, **196**, **260**, **275**, 404
– *seguieri* **161**
– *spiculifolius* 275
– *subacaulis* **303**
– *suendermannii* **287**
– *superbus* **162**, **419**
– *sylvaticus* 161
– *sylvestris* **275**
Diascia cordata **226**
Dicentra eximia †, **164**, 268, 321
– *formosa* **164**, 321, 323
– *oregana* 164, **323**
– *spectabilis* †, 97, 111, 164, **348**
Dictamnus albus **158**, 404
– *caucasicus* **158**
– *fraxinella* 158
Dierama pendulum **226**

– *pulcherrimum* **226**
Digitalis ambigua 158
– *ferruginea* †, **115**
– *grandiflora* 115, **158**
– *lutea* **115,** 158
– × *mertonensis* **115**
– *purpurea* **115,** 162, 344
Diphylleia cymosa **138**
Dipsacus pilosus **234**
– *sativus* **234**
– *strigosus* 235
– *sylvestris* **234**
Dodecatheon spp. 329
– *jeffreyi* **140**
– *meadia* **140**
– *pauciflorum* 140
– *pulchellum* **140**
Doronicum spp. **165**
– *austriacum* **334**
– *caucasicum* 165
– *columnae* 165
– *orientale* **165**
– *pardalianches* **169**
– *plantagineum* 165
Dorycnium hirsutum **226**
Douglasia vitaliana **307**
Draba aizoides **296**
– *bruniifolia* **296**
– *bryoides* **303**
– *dedeana* **303**
– *haynaldii* **303**
– *olympica* 296
– *repens* 297
– *sibirica* **297**
– × *suendermannii* 303
Dracocephalum grandiflorum
  329
– *moldavica* 364
– *rupestre* 329
– *ruyschiana* **297**
– *sibiricum* 170
Drosera anglica **420**
– *rotundifolia* **420**
Dryas octopetala **196, 260**
– × *suendermannii* 260
Dryopteris abbreviata **130,** 328
– *affinis* **129,** 132
– *atrata* **129**
– *austriaca* 129
– *borreri* **129**
– *carthusiana* 129
– *cristata* **130**

– *dilatata* **129**
– *erythrosora* **130,** 132
– *filix-mas* **129,** 132, 143
– *goldiana* **129**
– *hirtipes* 129
– *linnaeana* 128
– *paleacea* 129
– *pseudo-mas* 129
– *rigida* 328
– *spinulosa* 129
– × *tavellii* 129
– *thelypteris* 128
– *villarii* **328**
– *wallichiana* **130**
Duchesnea indica 143, **150,** 193

Echinacea angustifolia 395
– *pallida* 395
– *paradoxa* 395
– *purpurea* 13*, **395**
Echinops spp. 363
– *banaticus* **238**
– *exaltatus* **244**
– *ritro* 238, **244**
– *sphaerocephalus* **244**
Echioides longiflorum 302
Echium vulgare **235**
Edraianthus dalmaticus **287**
– *dinaricus* 287
– *graminifolius* **287**
– *pumilio* **287**
– *tenuifolius* **287**
Eichhornia crassipes **426**
Eleocharis palustris **418**
Elodea canadensis 428
Elymus arenarius **221,** 243
– *canadensis* **221**
– *giganteus* 221
– *glaucus* 221
– *racemosus* 221
– *robustus* 221
– *sibiricus* **222**
Empetrum hermaphroditum
  335
– *nigrum* **335**
Eomecon chionanthum **138**
Ephedra distachya **211**
– *gerardiana* 211
– *major procera* 211
– *minuta* 211
Epilobium angustifolium **162**
– *fleischeri* **339**

– *dodonaei* **339**
Epimedium spp. 132
– *alpinum* 111, 143
– *diphyllum* **112**
– *grandiflorum* 111, 268, 326
– *macranthum* **111**
– *perralderianum* 112
– × *perralchicum* **112**
– *pinnatum* 111, 143
– *pubigerum* 111
– × *rubrum* 111
– × *versicolor* †, 111
– × *warleyense* 111
– × *youngianum* 112, 237
Epipactis gigantea 416
– *palustris* **419**
Eragrostis curvula **222**
Eranthis 143, 146
– *cilicica* **187,** 332
– *hyemalis* 145, **187,** 332
– × *tubergenii* **332**
Eremurus spp. 97, 215
– *altaicus* 216
– *bungei* 15*, **216,** 358
– × *elwesii* 216
– *himalaicus* 216
– × *isabellinus* 216
– *olgae* **216**
– *robustus* **216**
– *stenophyllus* 216
– *tauricus* 216
– *tubergenii* **216**
Erica arborea **179,** 206
– *carnea* 133, 204, 205
– *ciliaris* **206**
– *cinerea* **206**
– × *darleyensis* **206**
– *erigena* 179, **206**
– *herbacea* 95, 146, 158, **204,**
  205, 224
– *mediterranea* 206
– *purpurascens* 206
– *tetralix* 206, **335,** 420
– *vagans* **206**
– × *watsonii* 206
– × *williamsii* **206**
Erigeron spp. †, 97
– *aurantiacus* 266, 369
– hybrids **369**
– × *hybridus* 94
– *karvinskianus* **266**
– *macranthus* 369

– pulchellus **240**
– speciosus **240,** 369
Erinus alpinus **266**
Eriogonum allenii **287**
– racemosum **287**
– umbellatum **287**
Eriophorum alpinum 420
– angustifolium **419**
– latifolium **419**
– scheuchzeri **420**
– vaginatum **420**
Eriophyllum caespitosum 260
– lanatum 219, **260**
Eritrichum nanum 304
– rupestre **304**
– strictum 304
Erodium chamaedryoides 229
– cheilanthifolium **287**
– macradenum **287**
– manescavii **229**
Eruca sativa 406
Eryngium alpinum **230**
– amethystinum **230**
– aquaticum 247
– bourgatii **230**
– giganteum †, 230, **233**
– palmatum 230
– planum 12*, **230**
– tricuspidatum **230**
– variifolium 230
– yuccifolium **247**
– × zabelii †, 230
Erysimum × allionii 406
– arkansanum **266**
– helveticum 297
– kotschyanum 297
– pumilum **297**
Erythronium dens-canis **187,** 332
– revolutum **332**
– tuolumnense **332**
Eschscholzia californica 359, 362
Eucomis punctata **398**
Euonymus spp. 132
– fortunei 192
Eupatorium spp. 411
– ageratoides 251
– cannabinum **250,** 334
– coelestinum 251
– purpureum **253, 378**
– rugosum 251

Euphorbia amygdaloides **155**
– capitulata **219,** 275
– cyparissias **158**
– epithymoides 260
– griffithii **180**
– lathyris **233,** 406
– marginata 406
– myrsinites 6*, **219,** 260
– niciciana 260
– palustris **416**
– polychroma 219
– robbiae 143, 179, **329**

Festuca alpina **297**
– amethystina 204, **224**
– cinerea 224
– gigantea **123**
– glacialis **304**
– glauca **224,** 275
– mairei †, **232**
– ovina 160, **200, 210**
– pallens 275
– punctoria **222**
– rubra **200**
– rupicaprina 275
– rupicola **224**
– scoparia 192, **297,** 319
– sulcata 224
– tenuifolia 160, **201, 210**
– trachyphylla 210, **224**
– valesiaca **224**
Filipendula digitata **173**
– hexapetala **202**
– kamtschatica **253**
– palmata 173, **251**
– rubra †, **251**
– ulmaria **245,** 251
Foeniculum vulgare **230,** 406
Fragaria vesca **150**
Fritillaria acmopetala **332**
– imperialis †, **353,** 404
– meleagris **187,** 319, 332, 340, 419
– pallidiflora **332**
– persica **332**
– pontica **332**
– pyrenaica **319,** 332
– verticillata **333**

Gaillardia aristata 95, **395**
– grandiflora 395
– pulchella 395

Galanthus byzantinus **333**
– caucasicus **333**
– elwesii **184,** 333
– nivalis 145, 146, 184, **188**
– plicatus **333**
Galax aphylla **138**
– urceolata 138
Galega bicolor **168,** 174
Galeobdolon luteum 87, **112, 121,** 144, 149
Galium odoratum 121, 144
– verum 158
Galtonia candidans 362, **398,** 399
Gaultheria spp. 132
– procumbens **335**
– shallon **335**
Gaura lindheimeri **226**
Gazania spp. 211
Genista germanica **160**
– lydia **211**
– pilosa **160, 195,** 209
– sagittalis **160**
– tinctoria **160**
Gentiana acaulis †, 8*, **316**
– angulosa 318
– angustifolia **316**
– asclepiadea 138, 155, **334,** 419
– clusii **316**
– cruciata **202, 330**
– dinarica **316**
– farreri 133, **336**
– kochiana **316**
– lagodechiana **260**
– lawrencei 336
– lutea **248,** 334
– pneumonanthe **419**
– septemfida **260**
– sinoornata 133, **337**
– veitchiorum 336
– verna 201, **318**
Geranium argenteum **287**
– 'Biokovo' 150, **297**
– cinereum **276**
– dalmaticum **260,** 297
– endressii **150,** 192
– farreri 276
– grandiflorum †, 155
– macrorrhizum 149*, **150,** 192, 297
– maculatum **151**

– × *magnificum* †, **150***, **151,** 192

– *meeboldii* **155**, 260

– *nodosum* **155**

– *phaeum* **155**

– *platypetalum* 151

– *pratense* **246,** 247

– *psilostemon* 159, **246**

– *pyrenaicum* 408

– *rectum* 155

– *renardii* †, **151,** 176

– *robertianum* 91

– *sanguineum* †, **151,** 159, 176, **297**

– *sessiliflorum* **287**

– *stapfianum* **287**

– *subcaulescens* †, **276**

– *sylvaticum* **155**, 334

– *wallichianum* **151**

– *wlassovianum* **151**

Geum × *heldreichii* **165**

– *chiloense* (hybrids) **165**

– *coccineum* **165**, 173, 318

– *montanum* 165, **318**

– *rivale* **173, 246**

– *triflorum* **311**

Gillenia trifoliata 115, **124**

Gladiolus byzantinus 228

– *communis* **230**

– hybrids 405

– *illyricus* 248

– *imbricatus* **248**

– *italicus* **228**

– *palustris* 248, **419**

– *segetum* 228

Glaucium flavum **233**, 362

– *squamigerum* 233

Glechoma hederacea **152,** 199

Globularia cordifolia **297**

– *elongata* 202

– *nana* **287**

– *nudicaulis* 297

– *punctata* **202,** 297

– *pygmaea* 287

– *repens* 287

– *trichosantha* **297**

– *willkommii* 202

Glyceria maxima **252,** 408, 416

Glycyrrhiza glabra 403

Godetia grandiflora 375

Goniolimon tataricum 231

Gratiola officinalis 416

Gunnera manicata 254

– *tinctoria* **254**

Gymnocarpium dryopteris **128**

– *robertianum* **128**, 328

Gypsophila aretioides **287**

– *cerastioides* 287

– hybrids **261**

– × *monstrosa* 261

– *pacifica* **260**

– *paniculata* 219, 221, **261**

– *petraea* **288**

– *repens* **261**, 288

– × *suendermannii* **288**

– *tenuifolia* **288**

Haberlea rhodopensis **323**

Hacquetia epipactis **124**

Hakonochloa macra **119, 134**

Halimodendron halodendron 211

Hebe armstrongii **211**

– *pinguifolia* **211**

Hedera helix 132, 143, **192**

Helenium autumnale 370

– *bigelovii* **370**

– *hoopesii* **240**

– hybrids †, 76*, **370**

Helianthemum spp. 201, 297

– *alpestre* **304**

– *apenninum* 261, **311**

– *canum* **304**

– *chamaecistus* 312

– × *hybridum* 95, **261**

– *lunulatum* **304**

– *macedonicum* **288**

– *nummularium* 261, **312**

Helianthus annuus 406

– *atrorubens* †, 96, 371, **396**

– *decapetalus* **371**

– *microcephalus* †, **371**

– *multiflorus* **371**

– *rigidus* 11*, 14*, **371**

– *salicifolius* †, **253,** 371

– *sparsifolius* **396**

Helichrysum arenarium **209**

– *bracteatum* 406

– hybrids **219**

– *lanatum* 219

– *milfordiae* †, **288**

– *plicatum* 219

– *thianshanicum* **219**

Helictotrichon sempervirens 222, **232**

– *parlatorei* **232**

Heliopsis 94

– *helianthoides* 372

– *scabra* **372**

Heliosperma alpestre **297**

Helleborus spp. 144, 156, **178, 330**

– *abchasicus* 178

– *atrorubens* 178

– *corsicus* **179**

– *cyclophyllus* 178

– *dumetorum atrorubens* 178

– *foetidus* 121, **178**

– × *hybridus* 178

– *lividus* **179**

– *niger* **178**, 330

– *odorus* 178

– *olympicus* 178

– *orientalis* 178

– *purpurascens* 178

– *viridis* 178

Hemerocallis spp. †, 13*, 248, 411

– *aurantiaca* 173

– *citrina* **173**, 349

– *dumortieri* 174

– *flava* **173**, 378, 404

– *fulva* **169**, 349

– *graminifolia* 174

– hybrids 13*, 77*, **348, 349**

– *lilio-asphodelus* 173, 404

– *middendorffii* **173**

– *minor* **174**

– *multiflora* 349

– *thunbergii* 349

Hepatica acutiloba **124**

– *angulosa* **124**

– *nobilis* †, **121,** 124, 138

– *transsilvanica* **124**

– *triloba* 121

Heracleum laciniatum 253

– *lanatum* **253**

– *mantegazzianum* **253**

– *villosum* 253

Herniaria glabra **194**

– *latifolia* 194

– *pyrenaica* 194

– *serpyllifolia caucasica* 194

Hesperis matronalis 95, **168, 404**

Heuchera × *brizoides* **268**
– hybrids **268**
– *sanguinea* **269**
Heucherella tiarelloides **194,** 269
Hibiscus moscheutos 398, **414**
– *trionum* 364
Hieracium aurantiacum **160,** 162, 199
– *bombycinum* **298**
– *flagellare* 162
– *pilosella* 160, **209**
– × *rubrum* **162**
– *villosum* **276,** 298, 318
Hippocrepis comosa **202**
Hippuris vulgaris **412**
Holcus mollis **160,** 408
– *lanatus* 408
Horminum pyrenaicum **318**
Hosta spp. **115,** 132
– *albomarginata* **117**
– *crispula* **116**
– *decorata* **117**
– *elata* **116**
– *fluctuans* **117**
– *fortunei* **116**
– *lancifolia* **117**
– *longissima* **117**
– *minima* **118**
– *montana* **117**
– *nakayana* **118**
– *plantaginea* **116**
– *rupifraga* **117**
– *sieboldiana* **116**
– *sieboldii* **117**
– *tardiana* **118**
– *tardiflora* **118**
– *tokudama* **117**
– *undulata* **116, 118**
– *venusta* **118**
– *ventricosa* **116**
Hottonia 71
– *palustris* **426,** 428
Houstonia caerulea **337**
– *serpyllifolia* **337**
Houttuynia cordata **415**
Humulus lupulus **154**
Hutchinsia alpina 298
– *auerswaldii* **298**
Hyacinthus amethystinus **320**
– *azureus* 185
– *orientalis* 391

Hylomecon japonica **124**
Hydrocharis morsus-ranae **426**
Hypericum calycinum 95, 112, 144, **151,** 192
– *cerastoides* **276**
– *coris* **288**
– *olympicum* **276**
– *polyphyllum* †, **276**
– *rhodoppeum* **276**
Hyssopus officinalis **211,** 403
Hystrix patula **243,** 364

Iberis amara 406
– *candolleana* 262
– *sempervirens* †, **261**
– *saxatilis* 262, **276**
– *umbellata* 406
Impatiens balsamina 406
– *balfourii* 344
– *glandulifera* 408
Incarvillea compacta 330
– *delavayi* **330**
– *grandiflora* 330
– *mairei* **330**
Inula ensifolia **202**
– *glandulosa* 238
– *helenium* **238,** 404
– *hirta* **202**
– *hookeri* 238
– *hybrida* **235**
– *magnifica* **244**
– *orientalis* 238
– *royleana* 238
– *salicina* **202**
Ipheion uniflorum **293**
Iris anglica 333, 398
– Anglica hybrids **398**
– *aphylla* **230**
– *aurea* 219, 380
– *bakeriana* **292**
– Barbata Elatior 358, **359, 360**
– Barbata Media 358, **359**
– *brevicaulis* 248
– *bucharica* **288**
– *caespitosa* 219
– *cengialti* **230**
– *chrysographes* **248**
– × *chrysophor* 248
– *cristata* **339**
– *crocea* **219,** 380
– *danfordiae* **292**

– *delavayi* 248
– *ensata* **248**
– *foetidissima* 179, **339**
– *florentina* 359, 404
– *foliosa* **248**
– *forrestii* **248**
– *fulva* × *foliosa* **248**
– *germanica* †, 16*, 219, 231, **264, 359,** 404
– *gigantea* 380
– *gracilipes* **339**
– *graeberiana* **288**
– *graminea* 231, 404
– *halophila* 219
– Hispanica hybrids **398**
– *histrio* 292
– *histrioides* **292**
– Hollandica hybrids **398**
– *hoogiana* 288
– *humilis* 231
– *kaempferi* 66, **418**
– *kochii* **231**
– *koreana* **248**
– *korolkowii* 288
– *lacustris* **339**
– *laevigata* **413,** 418
– *monnieri* **380**
– × *monspur* 380
– *ochroleuca* **380**
– *orientalis* 380
– *pallida* 230, 358
– *pseudacorus* **248, 413,** 416
– *pumila* †, 201, **219,** 312, 359
– *reticulata* **292**
– *ruthenica* **219**
– *sanguinea* 248, **379**
– *setosa* 378
– *sibirica* †, **248,** 349, **378,** 419
– *sintenisii* **231**
– *spuria* 74, **379,** 411
– *stolonifera* 288
– *susiana* 288
– *tectorum* **339**
– *variegata* **231,** 358
– *verna* **339**
– *versicolor* **248,** 413
– *wilsonii* **248**
– *xiphioides* 333, **398**
– *xiphium* 333, **398**
Isopyrum thalictroides **124**
Ixiolirion tataricum **228**

Jasione laevis 209
– *montana* 209
– *perennis* **209**
Jeffersonia diphylla **138**
– *dubia* **138**
Jovibarba spp. **282, 284**
– *allionii* **284**
– *arenaria* **284**
– *hirta* 284
– *heuffelii* **284**
– *sobolifera* 8*, **284**
Juncus conglomeratus **416**
– *effusus* **416**
– *ensifolius* **416**
– *glaucus* 416
– *inflexus* **416**

Kalimeris incisa **168**
– *integrifolia* 169
Kirengeshoma palmata 134,
   138
Knautia macedonica **238**
Kniphofia spp. 74
– *galpinii* **399**
– *praecox* 400
– hybrids **399**
– *tuckii* **399**
– *uvaria* **400**
Koeleria glauca 210, **222**
– *gracilis* 203
– *pyramidata* 203

Lamiastrum galeobdolon 121
Lamium garganicum **156**
– *maculatum* **112,** 121, 149, 156
– *orvala* **156**
– *pyrenaicum* 156
Lasiagrostis calamagrostis 232
Lathyrus gmelinii 156
– *grandiflorus* **154**
– *latifolius* **154**
– *odoratus* 406
– *transsilvanicus* **156**
– *vernus* **122**
Lavandula angustifolia 5*, 95,
   212, 403
– *vera* 212
Lavatera cachemiriana 174
– *olbia* †, **392**
– *thuringiaca* **174,** 392
Leersia orycoides **413**
Lemna gibba **427**

– *minor* **427**
– *trisulca* 428
Leonurus cardiaca **175,** 408
Leontopodium alpinum **300**
– *calocephalum* **300**
– *himalayanum* 300
– *japonicum* 300
– × *lindavicum* 301
– *nivale* 300
– *palibianum* **300**
– *sibiricum* 300
– *souliei* **300**
– *stracheyi* **301**
Lepidium sativum 406
Leucojum aestivum 248, 349,
   416
– *autumnale* **293**
– *vernum* 145, **188,** 340,
   416
Leuzea rhapontica **239**
Levisticum officinale 403
Lewisia cotyledon **307**
– *heckneri* **307**
– *howellii* **307**
– hybrids †, **307**
– *nevadensis* **307**
Liatris cylindracea 240
– *elegans* 240
– *pycnostachya* **240**
– *scariosa* 241
– *spicata* †, **241**
Ligularia spp. 94, 251, 411
– *clivorum* 171
– *dentata* **170**
– × *hessei* 171
– *japonica* 171
– × *palmatiloba* **171**
– *przewalskii* 171
– *sachalinense* **171**
– *stenocephala* **171**
– *tangutica* 182
– *veitchiana* **171**
– *wilsoniana* **171**
Lilium amabile **364**
– × *aurelianense* 356
– *auratum* 78, **352**
– *bulbiferum* **159,** 231, 362,
   364, 404
– *canadense* 383
– *candidum* **363,** 404
– *chalcedonicum* 363
– *cernuum* 364

– *croceum* **231,** 364
– × *dalhansonii* **352**
– *dauricum* 362, **365**
– *davidii* †, **365**
– *giganteum* 138
– *hansonii* **351**
– *harrisianum* **383**
– *henryi* **356**
– × *hollandicum* **362,** 404
– *humboldtii* 383
– hybrids †, **357**
– *lancifolium* 79, **365,** 404
– × *maculatum* **362**
– *martagon* 79, 122, 132, 334,
   351
– *monadelphum* **365**
– *pardalinum* 79, **383**
– *pensylvanicum* 365
– *philadelphicum* **366**
– *pumilum* 79, 330, **365**
– *pyrenaicum* 330, **365**
– *regale* 15*, 97, **356**
– *speciosum* 78, 133, **352**
– *szovitsianum* 365
– *tenuifolium* 365
– × *testaceum* **363**
– *tigrinum* 79, **365**
– *tsingtauense* **365**
– *umbellatum* 362
Limnanthemum nymphoides
   425
Limonium gmelinii 231
– *latifolium* **231**
– *tataricum* **231**
– *vulgare* 231
Linaria aequitriloba 323
– *alpina* **304**
– *cymbalaria* **267**
– *genistifolia* **233**
– *pallida* **323**
– *purpurea* **266**
Linnaea 107
– *borealis* **145**
Linum altaicum 312
– *austriacum* 202
– *campanulatum* **312**
– *capitatum* **312**
– *dolomiticum* **298**
– *flavum* **231**
– *narbonense* 202
– *perenne* **202**
Lippia repens **195**

Liriope spp. 134, 326
– *graminifolia* **140**
– *minor* **141**
– *muscari* **141**
– *platyphylla* 141
– *spicata* **141**
Lithodora diffusa **288**
Lithospermum diffusum 288
– *purpurocaeruleum* 149, 176
Lobelia cardinalis **415**
– *fulgens* 251, **399**
– *siphilitica* 240, **251**
– × *vedrariensis* **251**
Lonas inodora 371
Lonicera spinosa 211
Lotus corniculatus **162, 199,**
318
Lunaria annua 122, 406
– *rediviva* **122**
Lupinus arboreus 163, 372
– hybrids 12*, 74, 94
– *perennis* 163, 372
– *polyphyllus* **163, 372**
Luzula albida 126
– *luzuloides* **126**
– *nivea* †, **126**
– *pilosa* **126,** 127, 144, 160
– *sylvatica* 112, **119,** 126, 127,
132, 144
Lychnis alpina **304**
– × *arkwrightii* 234
– *chalcedonia* 234, **239,** 363,
404
– *coronaria* 95, **233**
– *flos-jovis* **233**
– *fulgens* 234
– × *haageana* **234**
– *viscaria* 202, **234,** 318, 363
– × *walkeri* †, 233
Lysichiton americanum †, **420**
– *camtschatcensis* **420**
Lysimachia brachystachys **251**
– *clethroides* †, **251**
– *nemorum* 152
– *nummularia* 7*, 67, **152,** 194,
337
– *punctata* **170**
– *thyrsiflora* **413**
Lythrum salicaria †, **251**
– *virgatum* †, **249**

Macleaya spp. 97

– *cordata* **245**
– *microcarpa* **245**
– *yedoensis* 245
Maianthemum bifolium 107,
122, 127, **144**
– *canadense* **144**
Malva alcea **175,** 236, 392, 404
– *mauritiana* 392, 408
– *moschata* **175,** 392
– *neglecta* 408
– *silvestris* 392, 408
– *verticillata* 406
Mandragora officinarum **330**
Marrubium pseudodictamnus
225
– *supinum* †, **220**
– *vulgare* 220, 404
Matricaria caucasica **318**
– *oreades* 318
– *tschihatschewii* 318
Matteuccia orientalis **127**
– *pensylvanica* **127**
– *struthiopteris* **127,** 417
Marsilea quadrifolia 427
Matthiola incana 406
Mazus miquelli 337
– *pumilio* **337**
– *radicans* **338**
– *stolonifer* **337**
Meconopsis baileyi 141
– *betonicifolia* †, **141**
– *cambrica* **124,** 141, 168
– *grandis* **141**
– *napaulensis* 141
– *regia* 141
– × *sheldonii* 141
Medicago lupulina **159, 200**
Meehania urticifolia **135**
Melica altissima **175**
– *ciliata* **222**
– *nutans* **126**
– *transsilvanica* **222**
– *uniflora* **126**
Melilotus alba 159
– *officinalis* 159
Melissa officinalis 404
Melittis melissophyllum 122,
156
Mentha aquatica **427**
– × *citrata* **249**
– *crispa* 249
– *longifolia* **427**

– *odorata* **249**
– × *piperita* 249, 405, **416**
– *pulegium* **249,** 405
– *requienii* **195**
– × *rotundifolia* **249,** 405
– *spicata* **249,** 405, **417**
Menyanthes trifoliata **421**
Mercurialis perennis **122**
Mertensia echioides **304**
– *primuloides* 304
– *virginica* **125**
Mesembryanthemum othonna
226
Meum athamanticum **161,** 404
Micromeria croatica **276**
– *pygmaea* 276
Milium effusum **123,** 127
Mimulus cupreus **323**
– *luteus* **417**
– *ringens* **415**
– × *tigrinus* 417
Minuartia graminifolia **276**
– *imbricata* 276
– *juniperina* 276
– *laricifolia* **276**
– *rupestris* 276
– *stellata* 276
Miscanthus spp. **254,** 411
– *floridulus* †, **254**
– *japonicus* 254
– *purpurascens* **249**
– *sacchariflorus* **244**
– *sinensis* †, **249, 254**
Mitchella repens **335**
Mitella caulescens **125**
– *diphylla* 125
– *nuda* 125
– *ovalis* 125
Moehringia muscosa **321**
Molinia arundinacea †, 159,
250, 378
– *caerulea* 210, 239, 378, **419,**
420
Moltkia × *intermedia* 288
– *petraea* **288**
Monarda didyma **380**
– *fistulosa* **380**
– hybrids **380**
Montia sibirica **144**
Morina kokanica 220
– *longifolia* **220**
– *persica* 220

Muehlenbeckia axillaris **195,** **304**

Mulgedium alpinum 334

Muscari armeniacum **185**
– *aucheri* 314
– *azureum* **185**
– *botyroides* **185,** 404
– *comosum* 314
– *latifolium* 314
– *moschatum* **228**
– *muscarini* 228
– *neglectum* **185**
– *paradoxum* **314**
– *racemosum* **185**
– *tubergenianum* 185, **314**

Myosotis decora **304**
– *palustris* **417**
– *rehsteineri* **340**
– *scorpioides* 417
– *sylvatica* 406

Myriophyllum brasiliense 426, 428
– *spicatum* **428**
– *verticillatum* 428

Myrrhis odorata **175,** 408

Myrtus communis 404

Najas spp. 428

Narcissus spp. 189
– *asturiensis* **293**
– × *barrii* **189**
– *bulbocodium* **320**
– *canaliculatus* **293**
– *cyclamineus* 272, 320, **340**
– × *incomparabilis* **189**
– × *johnstonii* **190**
– *jonquilla* **190**
– *juncifolius* **293**
– × *medio-luteus* **190**
– *minimus* 293
– *minor* **293**
– *nanus* 293
– × *poetaz* 190
– *poeticus* **189**
– *pseudonarcissus* 145, **189,** **272**
– *rupicola* **293**
– × *tazetta* 190
– *triandrus* **190,** 272, **320**

Nardus stricta 161, **210**

Nasturtium officinale **427**

Nepeta spp. 74, 94
– *cataria* **175,** 404
– × *faassenii* †, **220,** 262
– *gigantea* 220
– *grandiflora* **175,** 236
– *macrantha* 170
– *mussinii* 220
– *nervosa* **236**
– *nuda* **175**
– *pannonica* 175
– *sibirica* 170

Nierembergia repens **338**

Nigella damascena 406

Nitella flexilis **428**

Nuphar advena **426**
– *japonica* **425**
– *lutea* **425**
– *pumila* 421, **425**

Nymphaea spp. **422,** 423
– *alba* †, **423**
– *candida* 421, **423**
– *odorata* **423,** 424
– *pygmaea* **423,** 424
– *tetragona* 423
– *tuberosa* **423,** 424

Nymphoides peltata 425

Ocimum basilicum 406

Oenothera fruticosa **241**
– *glabra* 241
– *glauca* 241
– *missouriensis* †, **220,** 221
– *speciosa* **241**
– *tetragona* **241**

Omphalodes cappadocica †, **330**
– *verna* 111, 125, **153,** 267, 330

Onobrychis viciifolia 159, **200**

Onoclea sensibilis **127,** 420

Onopordum acanthium **235,** 408
– *tauricum* 235

Onosma alborosea †, **289**
– *sieheana* 289
– *taurica* **289**

Ophiopogon japonicus **135,** 140, **323**

Opuntia spp. 213, **214**
– *compressa* **214**
– *engelmannii* 214
– *fragilis* **214**
– *humifusa* 214
– *phaeacantha* †, **214**
– *polyacantha* 214
– *rafinesquei* 214
– *rhodantha* **214**
– *utahensis* **214**

Orchis maculata 419

Origanum amanum **289**
– *laevigatum* **236**
– *pseudodictamnus* **289**
– *scabrum* **289**
– *vulgare* **159,** 404

Ornithogalum arabicum **228**
– *balansae* **228**
– *boucheanum* 185
– *latifolium* 228
– *narbonense* **228**
– *nutans* **185**
– *pyramidale* 228
– *pyrenaicum* **228**
– *thyrsoides* 228
– *umbellatum* †, **185**

Orobus luteus 156
– *transsilvanicus* 156
– *vernus* 122

Orontium aquaticum **426**

Orostachys spinosus **289**

Osmunda cinnamomea **130**
– *claytoniana* **130**
– *regalis* **129,** 421

Oxalis adenophylla **228**
– *acetosella* 122, 127, **144**
– *corniculata* 91

Pachysandra procumbens **112**
– *terminalis* 110, **112,** 132, 149, **192**

Paeonia anomala **180**
– *corallina* 180
– *delavayi* **181**
– *emodi* **181**
– hybrids **356**
– *japonica* **181**
– *lactiflora* †, 16*, **354**
– *lobata* 181
– *mascula* 180
– *mlokosewitschii* **181**
– *mollis* **181**
– *officinalis* **181,** 354, **355**
– *peregrina* **181,** 355
– *potaninii* **181**
– × *smouthii* **236**
– *tenuifolia* 180, 231, **236,** 363
– *trollioides* 181

– *veitchii* **181**
– *wittmanniana* **181**
Panicum bulbosum 232, **243**
– *clandestinum* **260**
– *maximum* 243
– *virgatum* †, **243**, 367, 375, 376
Papaver alpinum **304**
– *bracteatum* **361**
– *burseri* 304
– *kerneri* 304
– *monanthum* **266**
– *nudicaule* 95, **266**, 298, 305
– *orientale* **361**
– *pseudocanescens* 266
– *rhaeticum* **304**
– *sendtneri* 304
– *somniferum* 406
Paradisea liliastrum †, **231**
Pardanthus chinensis 397
Parnassia palustris 338, **419**
Paronychia kapela **298**
Patrinia gibbosa 135
– *triloba* **135**
Paxistima canbyi 179, **330**
Pelargonium endlicheranum **289**
Peltandra virginica **415**
Peltiphyllum peltatum †, 98, **135**, 411
Peltoboykinia tellimoides **135**
Pennisetum spp. 243
– *alopecuroides* 250
– *caudatum* †, 58
– *compressum* †, **232**, 375
– *flaccidum* 244
– *incomptum* **244**
– *japonicum* 173, 232, **250**, 375
– *orientale* **232**
– *rueppellii* 58
– *setaceum* 370
– *villosum* **58**
Penstemon azureus 396
– *barbatus* **241**, 396
– *caespitosus* **289**
– *campanulatus* **226**
– *cardwellii* **289**
– *cobaea* 396
– *confertus* **241**
– *cristatus* **226**
– *davidsonii* 277, **289**
– *digitalis* **241**

– *erianthera* 226
– *gentianoides* 396
– *hallii* **289**
– *hartwegii* 375, **396**
– *heterophyllus* **396**
– *hirsutus* **241**
– *humilis* **277**
– hybrids 369
– *laevigatus* 241
– *linarioides* 277, **289**
– *menziesii* **277**
– *ovatus* 241
– *pinifolius* 220, **277**
– *pubescens* 240
– *scouleri* **289**
Perovskia spp. **95**
– *abrotanoides* **212**
– *atriplicifolia* **212**
Petasites albus **144**
– *fragrans* **330**
– *hybridus* 253
– *japonicus* **253**
– *officinalis* 253
Petrocallis pyrenaica **289**
Petrocoptis lagascae **305**
– *glaucifolia* 305
– *pyrenaica* 305
Petrorhagia saxifraga 277
Petroselinum sativum 406
Peucedanum alsaticum **175**
– *cervaria* **159**
– *verticillare* **176**, 253
Phacelia tanacetifolia 159
Phalaris arundinacea **252**, 403, 408
Phleum bertolonii **201**
– *boehmeri* 204
– *phleoides* **204**
Phlomis herba-venti 220
– *samia* **220**, 236
– *tuberosa* 220
Phlox Arendsii hybrids 157, **242**
– *canadensis* 157
– *carolina* 242
– *divaricata* **157**
– *douglasii* 262, **298**
– Maculata hybrids **242**
– *ovata* **157**, 331
– Paniculata hybrids †, **373**
– *stolonifera* **157**, 331
– *subulata* 7*, 196, **262**, 298

Phragmites australis **412**
– *communis* 412
Phuopsis stylosa **262**
Phygelius capensis †, 226, **399**
Phyla nodiflora 195
Phyllitis scolopendrium **130**, 328
Phyllodoce coerulea **336**
Phyllostachys aureosulcata **182**
– *boryana* **183**
– *henonis* **183**
– *nevinii* 182
– *nigra boryana* 183
– *nigra henonis* 183
– *viridi-glaucescens* **183**
Physalis alkekengi **170**
– *bunyardii* 170
– *franchetii* 170
Physoplexis comosa 305
Physostegia virginiana **381**
Phyteuma betonicifolium **318**
– *charmelii* **318**
– *comosum* 305
– *michelii* 318
– *orbiculare* **202**, 318
– *scheuchzeri* **305**
Phytolacca acinosa **175**, 403
– *americana* **175**
Pimpinella anisum 406
– *saxifraga* **200**
Pilularia globulifera 427
Plagiorhegma dubia 138
Plantago media **200**
– *nivalis* **290**
Platycodon grandiflorus **236**, **331**
Pleione bulbocodioides 324
– *formosana* 324
– *hookeriana* **324**
– *humilis* **324**
– *limprichtii* 324
Poa alpina 319
– *caesia* **222**, 312
– *chaixii* **123**, 144
– *glauca* 222
– *pratensis* **200**
Podophyllum hexandrum **135**
– *japonicum* 136
Polemonium spp. 245
– *caeruleum* **246**, 247, **381**
– *carneum* 381

– *foliosissimum* 349, **381**
– × *jacobaea* 381
– *reptans* 169, 267, **381**
– × *richardsonii* **381**
Polygonatum commutatum **125**, 135
– *falcatum* **331**
– × *hybridum* †, **125**
– *latifolium* **125**
– *multiflorum* 13*, **122**, 125
– *odoratum* **159**
– *officinale* 159
– *roseum* 125
– *verticillatum* **125**
Polygonum affine †, 193, **269**
– *amphibium* **425**
– *amplexicaule* †, **251**
– *bistorta* **246**
– *campanulatum* †, **252**
– *capitatum* **269**
– *carneum* **249**
– *compactum* **152**
– *cuspidatum* **181**
– *filiforme* **135**
– *lichiangense* **252**
– *milletii* **249**
– *orientale* 373
– *polystachyum* **181**
– *sachalinense* **181**
– *sericeum* **246**
– *tenuicaule* **327**
– *vaccinifolium* **323**
– *weyrichii* †, **181**
Polypodium cambricum 128
– *interjectum* **128**
– *vulgare* **128**, 328
Polystichum spp. 132
– *acrostichoides* **131**
– *aculeatum* **131**
– × *bicknellii* 131
– *braunii* **131**
– *lobatum* 131
– *lonchitis* 131, **328**
– *polyblepharum* **131**
– *setiferum* **131**
Pontederia cordata †, **415**
– *lanceolata* 415
Portulaca grandiflora 211, 404
Potamogeton natans **425**
Potentilla alba **203**
– *ambigua* **305**
– *anglica* 317

– *arenaria* 203, 317
– *argyrophylla* **236**
– *atrosanguinea* **236**
– *aurea* 317
– *chrysocraspeda* †, **317**
– *cinerea* **203**
– *crantzii* 262, **317**
– *fragiformis* **236**
– × *hybrida* 236
– *megalantha* 236
– *nepalensis* **236**, 317
– *nevadensis* **305**
– *nitida* **277**
– *palustris* 421
– *recta* **162**, **236**
– *tabernaemontani* 162
– *ternata* 317
– × *tonguei* **317**
– *verna* 162, 317
Poterium obtusum 246
Pratia angulata **195**
Primula abchasica 156
– *acaulis* **156, 166**
– *alpicola* **142**
– *apennina* 325
– × *arctotis* 298, 325
– *aurantiaca* **172**
– *auricula* 166, **298,** 325
– *bauhini* 298
– *beesiana* **172**
– × *bullesiana* **172**
– *bulleyana* **172**
– *burmanica* **172**
– *calycina* 324
– *capitata* **142**
– *carniolica* 324
– *chionantha* **142**
– *chungensis* 172
– × *chunglenta* **172**
– *clusiana* 324
– *cortusoides* **135, 322**
– *denticulata* **166**
– *elatior* †, 107, 122, **156,** 159, **166**
– *farinosa* 322, 338, **419**
– *florindae* 142, **172**
– *frondosa* **322,** 338, 419
– *glaucescens* **324**
– *glutinosa* **325**
– × *helenae* 166
– *helodoxa* **172**
– *hirsuta* **325**

– *integrifolia* **325**
– *japonica* 132, **172**
– *juliae* 166, **269**
– *littoniana* 142
– *luteola* **172**
– *marginata* **298,** 324
– × *margotae* **166**
– *minima* **325**
– *oenensis* **325**
– *officinalis* 159
– *pedemontana* **325**
– × *polyantha* 8*, **166**
– *polyneura* **135**
– *prolifera* **172**
– × *pruhoniciana* **166**
– × *pubescens* 166, **167,** 325
– *pulverulenta* **173**
– *rosea* †, **338,** 340, 416, 420
– *saxatilis* **135, 322**
– *secundiflora* **142**
– *sieboldii* †, **167,** 172
– *sikkimensis* **142,** 172
– *spectabilis* **324**
– *tirolensis* **325**
– *veris* †, 156, **159,** 166, 199, 405
– *vialii* **142**
– *villosa* **325**
– *viscosa* **325**
– *vittata* **142**
– *vulgaris* **122, 156, 166**
– *vulgaris sibthorpii* 125, **156**
– *waltonii* **172**
– *warshenewskiana* **338**
– × *wockei* 298
– *wulfeniana* **324**
Prunella grandiflora 203, 269, **318**
– *vulgaris* 199
Prunus tenella **212**
Pseudosasa japonica 183
Pteridium aquilinum **128**
Pterocephalus parnassii **277**
– *perennis* 277
Ptilotrichum spinosum 277
Pulmonaria angustifolia 107, 122, **156**
– *officinalis* 113, **122**
– *rubra* 112, 122
– *saccharata* **112,** 122
– *visianii* 156
Pulsatilla grandis 203

– *halleri* 203
– *vernalis* **162**
– *vulgaris* **203, 312**
Puschkinia libanotica **185**

Ramonda myconi **323**
– *nathaliae* **323**
– × *regis-ferdinandii* **324**
Ranunculus aconitifolius **173**,
    334, 417
– *acris* **246**
– *amplexicaulis* **336**
– *aquatilis* **426**, 428
– *bulbosus* **203**
– *circinatus* 428
– *fluitans* **428**
– *gramineus* **318**
– *lingua* **412**
– *montanus* **319**
– *peltatus* 426
– *platanifolius* **173**
– *repens* **417**
– *trichophyllus* 428
Ranzania japonica **136**
Raoulia australis **305**
– *glabra* 305
– *hookeri* 305
– *lutescens* 305
– *subsericea* 305
Reineckea carnea **136**
Reseda lutea 406
Reynoutria japonica 152, 181
– *sachalinensis* 181
Rhazya orientalis **231**
Rheum palmatum **253**
– *rhabarbarum* 403
Rhodiola kirilowii **220**
– *rosea* 220, **305**
– *semenowii* 220
Rhododendron **132**, 140
Rhynchelytrum repens 57, 369
Rhynchospora alba **420**
Rizzia fluitans 427
Rodgersia spp. 97, 98, 132, 411
– *aesculifolia* **136**
– *pinnata* **136**
– *podophylla* †, **136**
– *purdomii* **136**
– *sambucifolia* **136**
– *tabularis* 134
Romneya coulteri **227**
Rorippa silvestris 92*

Rosa pimpinellifolia 204
– *spinosissima* **204**
Roscoea spp. **142**, 326
– *alpina* **324**
– *cautleoides* **142**
– *humeana* **143**
– *purpurea* **143**
Rosmarinus lavandulaceus 227
– *officinalis* **227**, 404
– *prostratus* 227
Rosularia chrysantha 290
– *pallida* **290**
Rubia tinctorum 405
Rubus arcticus **336**
– *calycinoides* **331**
– *chamaemorus* **336**
Rudbeckia deamii †, **375**
– *fulgida* 242, 375
– *hirta* **397**
– *laciniata* 242, **252, 375, 376**
– *maxima* **249**, 375
– *newmannii* 242
– *nitida* **375**
– *purpurea* 375, 395
– *speciosa* **242**, 375
– *subtomentosa* **376**
– *sullivantii* 242, **376**
– *triloba* **397**
Rumex acetosa 405
– *hydrolapathum* **412**
– *patientia* 403
Ruscus aculeatus **179**
– *hypoglossum* **179**
Ruta graveolens **231**, 403

Sagina subulata **194**
Sagittaria graminea **414**
– *latifolia* **414**
– *sagittifolia* **413**
Salvia amplexicaulis 239
– *argentea* **234**
– *azurea* **242**
– *farinacea* 377
– *glutinosa* **169**
– *haematodes* **234**
– *jurisicii* **232**
– *nemorosa* 94, **239**, 363
– *officinalis* **212**, 403
– *patens* 348
– *pratensis* **200**, 234, 239
– *sclarea* †, **234**, 406
Salvinia natans **427**

Sambucus ebulus 408
Sanguinaria canadensis **139**
Sanguisorba minor **200**
– *obtusa* **246**
– *officinalis* **246**, 247
– *sitchensis* 252
– *tenuifolia* **252**
Sanicula europaea **122**
Sansevieria sessiliflora 136
Santolina spp. 95
– *chamaecyparissus* 212
– × *lindavica* 212
– *pinnata* **212**
– *rosmarinifolia* **212**
– *tomentosa* 212
– *viridis* 212
Saponaria caespitosa 277, **290**
– *cypria* 262
– *haussknechtii* 262
– × *lempergii* †, **262**
– *ocymoides* **262**, 277
– *officinalis* **175**, 408
– × *olivana* **277**
– *pulvinaris* **277**
– *pumila* 277
Sasa palmata **183**
– *pumila* 183, 195
– *pygmaea* 183
– *tesselata* **183**
Satureja alpina 295
– *croatica* 276
– *grandiflora* **331**
– *hortensis* 298, 406
– *montana* **298**, 405
– *repandens* 299
– *subspicata* 299
Saururus chinensis **415**
– *cernuus* **415**
– *loureirii* 415
Saxifraga aizoides **340**
– *aizoon* 278
– *altissima* 279
– × *andrewsii* **322**
– × *anglica* **308**
– × *apiculata* **310**
– × *arco-valleyi* 308
– Arendsii hybrids **269**
– × *biasolettii* **309**
– × *borisii* 309
– × *boydii* 309
– × *burnatii* **279**
– *burseriana* 308, **309**

– *caespitosa* 8*, 270
– × *calabrica* **290**
– *callosa* **279**
– *callosa latoscana* 290
– *camposii* **278**
– *canaliculata* **278**
– *cartilaginea* **279**
– *catalaunica* **279**
– *cochlearis* **279**
– *cortusifolia* **139**, 322
– *cotyledon* 279, **299**
– *crustata* **279**
– *cuneata* **278**
– *cuneifolia* 145, **270**, 327
– *cymbalaria* **322**
– × *elisabethae* 309
– × *eudoxiana* **310**
– *ferdinandi-coburgii* **310**
– × *geum* **271**
– × *gloriana* 308
– *grisebachii* **308**
– *hirsuta* 271, 322
– × *hoerhammeri* 309
– *hostii* **279**
– *hypnoides* **270**
– × *irvingii* **308**
– *juniperifolia* **310**
– × *kellereri* 308, **309**
– *kingii* 270
– *kolenatiana* **279**
– *lilacina* **308**
– *lingulata* 279
– *longifolia* 279, **290**
– *marginata* 308, **309**
– *muscoides* **270**
– *oppositifolia* **308**
– *paniculata* †
– × *paulinae* 309
– × *polita* **327**
– × *pseudokotschyi* 309
– *rotundifolia* **322**
– *sancta* 309, **310**
– *sarmentosa* 322
– *sempervivum* **309**
– × *salmonica* 309
– *spathularis* 270, **327**
– *stolonifera* **322**
– *stribrnyi* **308**
– × *suendermannii* 309
– *thessalica* 309
– *trifurcata* 271, **278**
– *umbrosa* 270, 327

– × *urbium* †, 153, 194, **270**, 271, 327
– *valdensis* **290**
– *veitchiana* **322**
Scabiosa spp. 74
– *canescens* **312**
– *caucasica* 12*, 94, 239, **364**
– *graminifolia* 232, **299**
– *japonica* **299**
– *lucida* **299**
– *ochroleuca* **239**
– *suaveolens* 312
Schivereckia bornmuelleri **305**
– *doerfleri* **305**
– *podolica* **305**
Schoenoplectus lacustris **412**
Scilla amethystina 340
– *bifolia* 132, 145, 187, **188**
– *campanulata* 188
– *hispanica* **188**
– *mischtschenkoana* 314
– *non-scripta* **188**
– *nutans* 188
– *pratensis* **340**
– *siberica* 145
– *tubergeniana* 188, **314**
Scirpus cespitosus 420
– *lacustris* 412
– *sylvaticus* **417**
– *tabernaemontani* 412, 414
Scolopendrium vulgare 130
Scutellaria alpina 290, **305**
– *altissima* **113**, 122
– *amana* **299**
– *baicalensis* †, **331**
– *canescens* 239
– *incana* **239**, 363
– *macrantha* 331
– *orientalis* **299**
– *scordifolia* **299**
Sedum spp. 97, 192
– *acre* 161, **209, 281**
– *aizoon* **220**
– *alboroseum* **362**
– *album* †, 10*, **196, 281**
– *anacampseros* 220, **280**
– *anopetalum* 280
– *bellum* **290**
– *bithynicum* **281**
– *boloniense* 209
– *cauticolum* 237, **299**
– *cyaneum* 300

– *dasyphyllum* **281**
– *ellacombianum* **193**, 263, **271**
– *ewersii* 220, **280**
– *fabaria* 237, **299**
– *farinosum* 290
– *floriferum* **193**, 263
– *forsterianum* **280**
– *gracile* **281**
– *hispanicum* **281**
– *hybridum* 6*, **193**, 271
– *japonicum* 362
– *kamtschaticum* **193**, 263
– *krajinae* 281, **282**
– *lydium* 10*, **282**
– *maveanum* 281
– *macimowiczii* 220
– *maximum* **161**, 237
– *middendorffianum* **193**, 220, 263, **280**
– *mite* 209
– *nevii* **290**
– *nicaeense* 280
– *ochroleucum* **280**
– *oreganum* **290**
– *pachyclades* **290**
– *pilosum* **290**
– *pluricaule* **300**
– *populifolium* **221**
– *pulchellum* **340**
– *purpurascens* 237
– *reflexum* **280**, 404
– *roseum* 305
– *rupestre* 280
– *sarmentosum* **271**
– *sartorianum* 280
– *sediforme* **280**
– *semenowii* 220
– *sempervivoides* **291**
– *sexangulare* 161, 197, **209, 282**
– *sieboldii* **305**
– *spathulifolium* **291**
– *spectabile* 221, 237, 299, **362**
– *spurium* **193**, 263
– *stoloniferum* 263
– *stribrnyi* **280**
– *tatarinowii* **280**
– *telephium* †, 209, 221, **237**, 239
Selaginella douglasii **338**
– *helvetica* **338**
Semiaquilegia ecalcarata **324**

Semiarundinaria fastuosa 183
Sempervivella alba **306**
– *sedoides* 306
Sempervivum spp. **282**
– *arachnoideum* †, **282**
– *calcareum* 283
– *ciliosum* **284**
– × *fauconnetti* **283**
– hybrids †, 283
– *kosaninii* **284**
– *marmoreum* **283**
– *montanum* **284**
– *ossetiense* **284**
– *schlehanii* **283**
– × *schnittspahnii* **283**
– *soboliferum* †
– *stiriacum* **284**
– *tectorum* †, **282**, 295, 404
– × *thomayeri* **283**
Senecio abrotanifolius **300**
– *adonidifolius* **300**
– *bicolor* **227**
– *doria* **171**
– *fuchsii* **115**, 171
– *tanguticus* **182**
Sesleria albicans 223
– *argentea* 223
– *autumnalis* **223**, 240
– *caerulea* **223**
– *heufleriana* 223
– *nitida* 223
– *rigida* 223
– *uliginosa* 223
– *varia* **223**, 319
Shibataea kumasaca **182**
Shortia galacifolia **139**, **336**
– *uniflora* **336**
Sidalcea × *cultorum* 242, **393**
Sideritis glacialis **291**
Silene acaulis **306**
– *alpestris* **297**
– *armeria* **234**
– *maritima* **263**
– *saxifraga* **306**
– *schafta* **263**
Silybum marianum **235**, 408
Sinarundinaria murielae **182**
– *nitida* **182**
Sisyrinchium angustifolium **338**
– *bermudiana* 338
– *graminifolium* **338**

– *striatum* **399**
Smilacina racemosa **125**
– *stellata* **125**
Solanum dulcamara **417**
Soldanella alpina **338**
– *carpatica* **327**
– *montana* 145, **327**
– *villosa* **306**, 327
Soleirolia soleirolii **195**
Solidago brachystachys 242, **377**
– *caesia* **242**
– *canadensis* 161, **376**, **377**
– *cutleri* 242, 377
– *gigantea* 376
– *graminifolia* 242
– × *hybrida* †, **376**
– *rigida* **242**
– *virgaurea* **161**, 242
– × *Solidaster luteus* **243**
Sonchus palustris **417**
Sorghastrum nutans **243**
Sparaxis pulcherrima 226
Sparganium erectum **412**
– *minimum* **421**
– *ramosum* 412
Spartina michauxiana 250, **252**
– *pectinata* 252
Spiraea gigantea 253
Spodiopogon sibiricus **250**
Sporobolus heterolepis 222
Stachys byzantina 94, 196, 221, **263**
– *citrina* 277
– *densiflora* **306**
– *germanica* **176**
– *grandiflora* †, **169**
– *lanata* 263
– *lavandulifolia* †, **277**
– *monnieri* 306
– *nivea* **203**, 306
– *officinalis* **161**
– *recta* 203
– *spicata* 277
Statice latifolia 231
Sternbergia lutea **293**
Stipa spp. 201, 204, 232
– *barbata* **223**
– *calamagrostis* 232
– *capillata* **223**
– *extremiorientalis* 222
– *gigantea* **223**

– *grandis* 223
– *nudicostata* 223
– *pennata* †, **223**
– *papposa* 223
– *pulcherrima* 223
– *stenophylla* 223
– *tenacissima* 223
– *tirsa* 223
– *ucrainica* 223
– *viridula* **223**, 240
Stokesia laevis **306**
Stratiotes aloides 425
Streptopus amplexifolius **139**
– *roseus* **139**
Stylophorum diphyllum **139**
Symphyandra hofmannii **306**
Symphoricarpos 149
Symphytum asperum **176**, 408
– *cordatum* **125**
– *grandiflorum* †, **113**, 144, 149
– *peregrinum* **169**
– *rubrum* 139
Synthyris stellata **139**
– *reniformis* 139

Tagetes 406
– *patula* **371**
Tanacetum vulgare 174
– *haradjanii* 286
Tanakaea radicans **324**
Telekia speciosa 169
Tellima grandiflora **136**
Teucrium spp. 95
– *chamaedrys* 196, **212**, 277, 403
– *lucidrys* 212
– *marum* **291**
– *massiliense* 212
– *montanum* **312**
– *pyrenaicum* **300**
– *scorodonia* **161**
Thalictrum alpinum **306**
– *aquilegifolium* 94, **169**, 246, 247, 334
– *coreanum* **331**
– *dipterocarpum* **136**
– *flavum* 176
– *glaucum* **176**
– *kiusianum* **306**
– *rochebrunianum* 169
Thamnocalamus spathaceus 182

Thelypteris decursive-pinnata **131,** 328
– *limbosperma* **131,** 334
– *noveboracensis* 128
– *palustris* **128,** 417
– *phegopteris* **128**
– *thelypteroides* 128
Themeda triandra **227**
Thermopsis fabacea **221**
– *lanceolata* 221
– *lupinoides* 221
Thymus spp. 96
– *balcanus* 197, 264, **312**
– *ciliatus pubescens* **312**
– × *citriodorus* 4*, 196, 213, **263, 291,** 404
– *doerfleri* 197, **312**
– *lanuginosus* 312
– *marschallianus* 312
– *pannonicus* 312
– *procumbens* 312
– *pseudolanuginosus* 197, **312**
– *pulegioides* 209
– *rotundifolius* **264**
– *serpyllum* 161, 197, **209,** 264, 312
– *villosus* **291**
– *vulgaris* **227, 291,** 404
Tiarella spp. 132, 193, **267**
– *cordifolia* †, **113,** 149, 269
– *wherryi* 113
Tithonia speciosa **355,** 371
Tolmiea menziesii **139**
Tommasinia altissima **176**
Tovara virginiana 135
Townsendia exscapa **291**
– *wilcoxiana* 291
Trachelium rumelianum **306**
Tradescantia × *andersoniana* 94, **382**
Trapa natans **425**
Trichophorum alpinum **420**
– *cespitosum* **420**
Tricyrtis hirta 136
– *latifolia* **137**
– *macropoda* **136**
– *pilosa* **136**
Trientalis europaea 107, **145**
Trifolium pratense †, **200**
– *repens* 199, 264, **319**
Trigonella coerulea **406**
– *foenum-graecum* 406

Trillium chloropetalum 125
– *erectum* 125
– *grandiflorum* **125**
– *nivale* 125
– *sessile* 125
Trisetum flavescens **200**
Triteleia uniflora **293**
Trollius spp. 334, 337, 381
– *acaulis* **338**
– *asiaticus* **382**
– *chinensis* 246, 382, **383**
– × *cultorum* †, 77*, 173
– *europaeus* **246,** 319, 382, 419
– *laxus* 338
– *ledebourii* 383
– *patulus* **339**
– *pumilus* **338**
– *ranunculinus* 339
– *stenopetalus* 339
– *yunnanensis* **339**
Tropaeolum majus **406**
Tulipa (Garden tulips) †, 384
Tulipa acuminata **272**
– *batalinii* **294**
– *biflora* **294**
– *clusiana* **294**
– *chrysantha* **294**
– *dasystemon* 294
– *eichleri* 272
– *fosteriana* **272, 385**
– *greigii* **272, 385**
– *hageri* **294**
– *kaufmanniana* **273,** 294, **384** (garden t.)
– *kolpakowskiana* **294**
– *lanata* **273**
– *linifolia* **294**
– *marjolettii* **273**
– *montana* **294**
– *orphanidea* **294**
– *praecox* **273**
– *praestans* **273**
– *pulchella* **294**
– *sprengeri* **273**
– *stellata* **294**
– *sylvestris* 159, **185,** 221, 404
– *tarda* **294**
– *turkestanica* **294**
– *urumiensis* **294**
– *violacea* **294**
– *wilsoniana* **294**
– *whittalli* **294**

Tunica saxifraga **277**
Typha angustifolia **412,** 414
– *gracilis* **414**
– *latifolia* **412**
– *laxmannii* **414**
– *minima* **414**
– *shuttleworthii* **414**
– *stenophylla* **414**

Umbilicus spinosus 289
Uniola latifolia **250**
Utricularia vulgaris **426**
Uvularia grandiflora **125**
– *perfoliata* 126

Vaccinium 107
– *macrocarpon* **209**
– *vitis-idaea* **145**
Valeriana alliariifolia **252**
– *officinalis* 405
Vancouveria hexandra 126
Veratrum album **249,** 334
– *californicum* **169**
Verbascum bombyciferum **215,** 235
– *chaixii* 215
– *dumulosum* 291
– *lagurus* 215
– *longifolium* **215**
– *nigrum* 161, **215,** 237
– *olympicum* **215**
– *pannosum* 215
– *phoeniceum* **215**
– *speciosum* 215
– *spinosum* 291
– *thapsiforme* 214
– *thapsus* 214
– *wiedemannianum* **215**
Verbena bonariensis †, 355, 371, 380, **399**
– *hastata* **239**
– *officinalis* 408
– *peruviana* 211
– *rigida* 371, 372, 376, 380
Vernonia arkansana 252
– *crinita* **252**
– *noveboracensis* 252
Veronica allionii 144, 327
– *anagallis-aquatica* **427**
– *armena* 300
– *austriaca* 203, 264
– *beccabunga* 427

– *cinerea* 278
– *cuneifolia* 300
– *filiformis* †, 199
– *fruticans* **306**
– *gentianoides* 237, **264**
– *hendersonii* 239
– *incana* 9*, 232
– *longifolia* 239, **252**, 349
– *officinalis* 144, 327
– *poliifolia* **292**
– *prostrata* 264, 300, **313**
– *repens* 307
– *rupestris* (hort.) 313
– *saturejoides* **292**
– *saxatilis* 306
– *spicata* **203, 232, 264,** 313
– *surculosa* **278**
– *teucrium* **203, 264**
– *turilliana* **292**
– *virginica* **243,** 251, 252
Vinca spp. 110, 132
– *major* **113,** 405

– *minor* 110, **113,** 114, 122, 144, 149, 153, 169, 192, 405
Viola bertoloni **307**
– *cornuta* **266**
– × *floraiensis* **266**
– *jooi* **307**
– *labradorica* **327**
– *odorata* †, 156
– *palmata* **126**
– *papilionacea* **153**
– *rupestris* 162
– *sororia* 153
Viscaria alpina 304
– *vulgaris* 234, **318**
Vitaliana primuliflora 307

Waldsteinia geoides **114,** 143, 144, 169, 193
– *sibirica* 114
– *ternata* **114,** 144
– *trifolia* 114
Woodsia alpina 326

– *ilvensis* 326
– *obtusa* **326**
– *polystichoides* 326
Wulfenia amherstiana 322
– *baldaccii* **322**
– *carinthiaca* **319,** 322
– × *suendermannii* 322

Yucca filamentosa †, **213**
– *flaccida* **213**
– *glauca* **213**
– *gloriosa* 227
– × *karlsruhensis* **213**
– *recurvifolia* **227**

Zauschneria arizonica 227
– *californica* 227
Zigadenus elegans **249**
Zinnia 4, 406
Zizania latifolia **414**

Picture credits

Drawings
Adam Kutzner† with gratitude and respect, illustrations on pages 11, 12, 13, 16, 17, 75, 76, 77, 92 and 93;
Barbara Lang, Munich, illustrations on pages 3, 42, 56 and 57; all other illustrations by the authors.

Colour photographs
Martin Haberer, Raidwangen: plates 11 (top), 13 (bottom), 17 (bottom), 23 (bottom right), 27 (top).

Urs Walser, Weinheim: plates 3, 5 (top), 7 (top), 10 (bottom left), 11 (bottom), 12 (top), 13 (top), 14 (bottom right), 15 (top), 18 (top left), 19 (top), 20 (top right), 22 (bottom right), 24 (top right), 26 (top right), 29 (top), 31 (top and bottom left), 32 (bottom right).

Gretel Stölzle, Kempten: all other colour plates.